T0381099

THE GREATEST AND DEADLIEST HURRICANES TO IMPACT THE BAHAMAS

THE GREATEST AND DEADLIEST HURRICANES TO IMPACT THE BAHAMAS

The Stories behind the Great Storms

Wayne Neely

THE GREATEST AND DEADLIEST HURRICANES TO IMPACT THE BAHAMAS
THE STORIES BEHIND THE GREAT STORMS

iUniverse books may be ordered through booksellers or by contacting:

iUniverse
1663 Liberty Drive
Bloomington, IN 47403
www.iuniverse.com
1-800-Authors (1-800-288-4677)

Because of the dynamic nature of the Internet, any web addresses or links contained in this book may have changed since publication and may no longer be valid. The views expressed in this work are solely those of the author and do not necessarily reflect the views of the publisher, and the publisher hereby disclaims any responsibility for them.

Any people depicted in stock imagery provided by Getty Images are models, and such images are being used for illustrative purposes only.
Certain stock imagery © Getty Images.

ISBN: 978-1-5320-8923-7 (sc)
ISBN: 978-1-5320-8922-0 (e)

Library of Congress Control Number: 2019919740

Print information available on the last page.

iUniverse rev. date: 12/05/2019

CONTENTS

DEDICATION

This book is dedicated first and foremost to all the victims of these *Greatest and Deadliest Bahamian Hurricanes*. By telling of their stories of heroism and tragedy amid such adversity in this book; it is my hope and desire that their stories will forever be told in the annals of the Bahamian history. Furthermore, it is also my hope that these stories will live on for future generations of Bahamians to read about and to appreciate why these storms were regarded as, 'some of the greatest and deadliest hurricanes to impact The Bahamas.'

To my dad and mom Lofton and Francita Neely thanks for the great love and support you've showed me over the years. To my Uncle and Aunt Coleman and Dianna Andrews thanks for being there for me during my time of need...I will never forget what you did for me.

To the late Mr. William Holowesko, it was your great kindness and support for me by lending me personal copies of your books on hurricanes that got me started on this faithful and noble journey of documenting the great hurricanes of The Bahamas and the region. I will not forget you, nor the contributions you made in assisting me with writing these books...RIP.

To Mr. Les Brown, who at a conference held in The Bahamas, through his own unique way and method reminded me: 1) "Pass it on"; 2) "It is important how you use your down time"; 3) "Someone's opinion of you doesn't have to become a reality"; and 4) "In the time of adversity, expand!" To the late Dr. Myles Munroe, who always reminded me to: 1) "Die empty!" 2) "Pursue my purpose!" 3) "Purpose is when you know and understand what you were born to accomplish. Vision is when you see it in your mind and begin to imagine it!" and 4) "Maximize my potential." I listened to them, and this book is the result. Thank you, Mr. Les Brown and Dr. Myles Munroe, for your invaluable contributions to my life.

A) The secret of success is learning how to use pain and pleasure instead of having pain and pleasure use you. If you do that, you're in control of your life. If you don't, life controls you-Tony Robbins.

B) The secret of getting ahead is getting started-Mark Twain.

C) If there is no struggle, there is no progress-Frederick Douglass.

D) The ultimate measure of a man is not where he stands in moments of comfort and convenience, but where he stands at times of challenge and controversy-Dr. Martin Luther King, Jr.

FOREWORD

I am pleased to introduce the reader to Mr. Wayne Neely's latest book. "The Greatest and Deadliest Hurricanes to Impact The Bahamas – the stories behind the Great Storms of the Islands of The Bahamas". Mr. Neely is an accomplished meteorologist with the Bahamian Weather Service and is an acknowledged expert on hurricanes and The Bahamas. In this book Wayne provides a very detailed compilation of the meteorology, impact, and societal implications of the many storms that have crossed The Bahamas during the Nation's long history. While there are many documents that describe one or several of the important storms in our history, none have covered in one volume the entirety of hurricanes in The Bahamas. In doing so, Mr. Neely has provided a valuable service for those who wish to understand how hurricanes have shaped the history and economy of The Bahamas. Included in the book are easy to understand descriptions on the science behind hurricanes and of the changing understanding of the forecast challenges we who live along coasts threatened by these storms face.

As a collector of books written about hurricanes and society, I will treasure the addition of this new volume to my collection. I particularly enjoyed the added Bahamian history Wayne has included for context. I will enjoy referring to this book for interesting facts of storms from long ago. For people living in the Islands as well as other hurricane prone areas, "The Greatest and Deadliest Hurricanes to Impact The Bahamas – the stories behind the Great Storms of the Islands of The Bahamas" is a must read!

Bill Read
Director, U.S. National Hurricane Center 2008-2012

William (Bill) Read
Former Director of the U.S.A's National Hurricane Center in Miami, Florida
(Courtesy of the National Hurricane Center).

WILLIAM (BILL) READ

William L. Read has served the United States Navy and the National Weather Service during his career. His weather service career began in 1977, and he has worked in Sterling, Virginia, Fort Worth, Texas, San Antonio, Texas, Silver Spring, Maryland, Houston, Texas, and Miami, Florida over the years. Bill was appointed as the Deputy Director of the National Hurricane Center from August 2007 until he was selected for the position of Director on January 25, 2008.

Bill served in the U.S. Navy, where he served as an on-board meteorologist with the Hurricane Hunters. He began his weather service career in 1977 with the National Weather Service test and evaluation division in Sterling, Virginia. He served as a forecaster in the Fort Worth and San Antonio, Texas offices before becoming the severe thunderstorm and flash flood program leader at the National Weather Service headquarters in Silver Spring, Maryland. Read was appointed to direct the Houston/Galveston weather forecast office in 1992 and led it through the National Weather Service modernization and restructuring program of the mid-1990s. He was also part of the Hurricane Liaison Team at the National Hurricane Center in Miami when Hurricane Isabel came ashore on the Outer Banks of North Carolina in September 2003. Bill Read became the Director of the Tropical Prediction Center, which includes the National Hurricane Center and two other divisions, in Miami, Florida in January 2008 and served until June 4, 2012 when relieved by Richard Knabb. Read had previously served as the center's acting Deputy Director between August 2007 and January 2008.

Bill received the National Hurricane Conference Public Education Award in spring 2004 for hurricane preparedness efforts. Under his leadership, the Houston/Galveston forecast office conducted an annual Houston/Galveston Hurricane Workshop, which was considered the largest meeting of its kind in the United States.

"For the foreseeable future, policies that reduce disaster losses will be those that focus on increasing disaster preparedness. Linking rising disaster losses to climate change distorts the science and points us away from the policies that can be most effective in preparing for disasters."[1]

In 2005, when I first wrote a book of similar characteristic, I had every intention of not adding a second volume of that book. Over the last 14 years of increasing research materials, new and more accurate weather records and hurricane information available to me I felt compelled to add a more complete and accurate listing of the greatest hurricanes to affect The Bahamas. This is because increasing disaster threats not only reflect the devastating onset of events such as hurricanes, but also the changing demographic and socioeconomic characteristics of the North Atlantic coastal populations. A large, destructive, and violent hurricane, for instance, passing over the open ocean presents little danger. On the other hand, a relatively weak hurricane can pose significant risks to human life and can result in great economic losses in densely populated areas. While the intensity is important, of equal or greater importance is the presence of a population whose demographic or socioeconomic characteristics may place its members at greater risk of harm before, during, and after a hurricane disaster.

More than fifteen years ago, when I got the initial idea to write my first book about one of the greatest storms to affect The Bahamas called by the locals "The Great Bahamas Hurricane of 1929", or the "Great Andros Island Hurricane of 1929," one of the first and obvious places where I conducted research for my book was at the National Hurricane Center, the governing body for hurricanes of the North Atlantic basin, located in South Florida in the United States. About 90-95% of all the worldwide research

---

[1] Roger Pielke, Jr., *The Rightful Place of Science: Disasters & Climate Change*, (Arizona, Arizona State University's, Consortium for Science, Policy & Outcomes, 2014).

works on hurricanes or better yet tropical cyclones are conducted in the North Atlantic region even though it only accounts for 12% of the world's total of tropical cyclones. I got a lot of work done there and upon leaving one of the hurricane researchers suggested that I get a hold of several books by noted hurricane authors if I wanted to continue to write future books on hurricanes. He sarcastically wished me good luck as he wrote the names of the book titles and authors' names on a blank paper for me.

He commented that most of those books were out of print and if I did find any, the prices for these books would be very expensive. Sure, enough I searched everywhere including, all our libraries in The Bahamas, eBay and other online bookstores such as, www.amazon.com and www.barnesandnoble.com and found one of the books but at a crazy price out of range of my limited budget at the time. By the next day, it too was bought, and I was back at square-one. The names of the books among others were: 1) José Millas's, book published in 1968 called, *Hurricanes of The Caribbean and Adjacent Regions 1492-1800*. 2) Ivan Ray Tannehill's book published in 1950 called *Hurricanes-Their Nature and History-Particularly those of the West Indies and the Southern Coasts of the United States*. 3) Marjorie Stoneman Douglas's book published in 1958 called, *Hurricane*.

It is an amazing story of how I got my hands on some of these books. At the time, I had just started interviewing persons about their recollections about this deadly hurricane in 1929. One of the first persons I interviewed about his recollection of this hurricane was a man by the name of Mr. Andrew McKinney. After he was finished his recollections to me, he then recommended that I should interview a lawyer by the name of Mr. William Holowesko as he might be able to assist me. I asked myself how would an attorney be able to assist me with information on this or any other Bahamian hurricanes? I reluctantly took his advice and went to see Mr. Holowesko at his office in downtown Nassau called Bay Street, expecting nothing but a dead-end and wasted time. When I finally met him, and told him I was writing a book about, the Great Bahamas Hurricane of 1929 and someone recommended I speak to him. He then told me that he wasn't born in The Bahamas to experience this hurricane firsthand, but he said he heard his mother-in-law and others, frequently talking about this very devastating hurricane.

He told me that he has several books on hurricanes which he felt could help me. He then opened his metal bookcase and the first three books he removed from this bookcase and handed them to me made my heart skip a beat. To my surprise, there were those three books I searched desperately for locally and internationally but to no avail. In fact, his copy of *Hurricanes* by Marjorie Stoneman Douglas had the author's original signature in it further increasing its' value. I remembered staring at the books with no emotions on my face but deep inside I wanted to jump up and scream with joy. He then looked at my blank stare and asked me if these were useful books that I could use, and I immediately told him yes. Then he told me that I could use them but only in his office because he didn't know me, but he would put a desk and chair in the back of his office in the research area, to allow me to conduct my studies there while using these books.

After three or four consecutive days of me coming into his office to use these books, he came to my desk and asked me how my research work was coming along? I told him it was coming along just great and the books were of great help to my research. Surprisingly, he then told me that I could take the books home and simply bring them back when I was finished with them because he now trusted me. I thanked him and did just that and today all those books he loan to me formed the foundation of all my 13 books on hurricanes. It didn't end there; as the book project was coming to an end, he gave me a monetary contribution towards the publication of my next book. He then suggested I approach the local insurance companies to ask them for sponsorship in return I could feature their companies' names, address, and logos in my book as a form of advertisement to defray the cost of publishing my future books. Today, I still have many of these companies sponsoring my books each year and I owe this to Mr. William Holowesko.

Shortly, before he died, he summoned me to his office, and he went to his library and gave me stacks of books on Bahamian history and hurricanes in general. At the time, he was very frail and walked with the assistance of a cane. Clearly, he was gravely ill and didn't have much longer to live, he with his weak, feeble hands, hoarse voice and frail body shook my hand and hugged me and told me to make good use of the books he gave me. I promised him I would do just that and will make him proud of me one day thanks to the great sources of books I used from him. I then walked out of his office with stacks of books and tears in my eyes. That was the last time I ever saw him alive because he died shortly thereafter. This book is dedicated in memory of him.

In this book, the reader will learn about the "vulnerability" perspective in hurricane disasters, which is rapidly emerging as a dominant view in the North Atlantic, assumes that a real hurricane disaster occurs when it strikes an underprivileged population. Vulnerability is formally defined as "the characteristics of a person or group and their situation that influences their capacity to anticipate, cope with, resist, and recover from the impact of a natural hurricane hazard."[2] Implicit here is "differential vulnerability"; that is, different populations face different levels of risk and vulnerability. Consequently, policies aimed at addressing risk and vulnerability must also consider these differential impacts and outcomes of these storms disasters. Although the sources of vulnerability are multiple and quite diverse, some of the most important factors that affect vulnerability include population growth and distribution and social diversity, as this book will clearly show later.

This book is about devastating hurricanes and tropical storms and more specifically, how these great storms of The Bahamas impacted people and their lives. Furthermore, it depicts how they have changed the built and natural environments of The Bahamas over the last five hundred years. It is important to note that, it draws on the extraordinary expertise of dozens of historians, meteorologists, highly noted scholars, scientists, and institutions tracking hurricanes and understanding of, and relationship with, the climate system on planet Earth. This book was written for the general reader. It is intended to bring to life important and fascinating historical periods that were impacted by The Bahamas most devastating hurricanes. I must add that it is not an exhaustive history of these hurricanes. Indeed, many more pages would be required even to address adequately the tangled skein of these hurricanes impacting The Bahamas.

Contemporary weather forecasting has made it quite conceivable to monitor, track, and forecast the path of deadly hurricanes with ease, thanks in part to and with the help of advanced weather equipments and technology such as, satellites, radar, and 24-hour-a-day watch over the North Atlantic basin with the assistance of super-fast computers and dynamic computer weather models. Even with these advancements, these powerful storms have the strength to destroy homes, cities, and lives. As a result, there could be great devastation in the areas impacted by these storms.

Combining hurricane history, first-person accounts, and basic hurricane science, this book takes a closer look at the most terrifying and

---

[2] Ben Wisner et al., *At Risk: Natural Hazards, People's Vulnerability, and Disasters,* 2d ed. (London: Routledge, 2004).

devastating storms of The Bahamas. In addition, it also features the stories behind them and what made them so unique and memorable in the annals of The Bahamas' hurricane history. Witness nature's fury as some of the greatest and deadliest hurricanes to impact The Bahamas comes alive. Grab a chair, sit down and relax as I take you on a journey down memory lane through the archives of these deadly storms. Each of these hurricanes is like fingerprints on a hand: no two are alike but each one has a unique and compelling story to tell, as you will see later in this book.

Witness the rage of Hurricane Andrew, the great death tolls of the Great Bahamas Hurricanes of 1866 and 1899, which along with other deadly hurricanes greatly impacted the entire Bahamas. See the massive size and great clean-up costs associated with Hurricanes Dorian, Floyd or Matthew, the unbelievable deadly flood waters of Hurricanes Frances, Noel and Jeanne as they battered most of the eastern most islands. These islands, along the eastern-most coastal locations like Abaco, Eleuthera, Cat Island and Grand Bahama, experienced the brunt of these hurricanes. In this book you will visit many of the greatest and deadliest hurricanes of The Bahamas firsthand and see their destructive aftermaths. Spanning more than five centuries and drawing on extensive archival research in Europe, the Americas and the Caribbean, this book emphasizes the continuing role of race, societal inequality, and economic ideology in the shaping of our responses to hurricanes.

Hurricanes have played an amazing role in The Bahamas panorama. They have literally altered the lives and society of Bahamians great and small. At times they have even changed the course of our political, geographical, and economic history. Furthermore, they have even transformed the shape of our islands' coastlines, from Grand Bahama in the north to Inagua in the south. There have been hurricanes whose effects were felt on the shores of the Old World as well as the New. Hurricanes Matthew, Joaquin, Andrew, Floyd, Betsy, The Great Abaco Hurricane of 1932, The Great Bahamas Hurricane of 1929, The Great Nassau Hurricane of 1926 and others are mentioned in great details, partly because of the deadly, powerful and record-breaking features associated with them.

Today, it is fair to say that these hurricanes are now anchored in the archives of Bahamian weather history. Nonetheless, I must add that they are certainly not alone in significant deaths and massive devastation they created in the archipelago of The Bahamas. There have been many others before or after them, and they were certainly just as compelling, as this book will clearly show. This book will feature some of the strongest, most damaging and deadly hurricanes to ever affect The Bahamas. From the time of Christopher Columbus, the Spaniards and others traversing these waters in late 1490s and 1500s, the pirates of the 1600s and 1700s, the local Bahamian sponger men of the late 1800s to early 1900s, up to Hurricane Dorian in 2019, no stone will be left unturned to discover the effects of these mysterious but powerful hurricanes and the impact they had on the Bahamian society. This book does not include every single hurricane to significantly impact this country. However, it does provide an almost complete profile and history of some of the more notable or notorious Bahamian hurricanes.

Despite the numerous hurricanes that struck The Bahamas over the years and centuries, we still behave as if hurricanes disasters are outliers. Why else would we continue to build in flood prone areas or along the shorelines of The Bahamas in droves? The word 'disaster' in its simplistic form means 'a sudden calamitous event bringing great damage, loss, or destruction.' The word could have little meaning in the absence of humans; for example, it could only be used to describe the effects of a moving hurricane on the built environment. Without a human to judge whether that is a disaster or not, that concept remains in the world of academic discourse. Hurricanes, without a shadow of a doubt when they encounter man's ever-expanding society, are some of the greatest disasters the natural world can produce or throw at us on this volatile planet. Just the mention of its name makes humans quiver with fear, anxiety or fascination. Thankfully, hurricanes as large and powerful as they are, only become a significant issue or a great disaster when they encounter some populated town, city or country that humans have inhabited.

Scientists say that the Earth's climate is a non-linear system, and this is just another fancy way of saying, that the climatic changes on Earth are not all gradual but they can come suddenly in big jumps. The Earth's climate is like a giant heat engine that transports heat energy away from the equator towards the poles, and cold energy from the poles to the equator. The Earth has a simple but effective and fascinating way of achieving these dynamic mechanisms or processes. For example, to take the built-up cold air from the poles and transfer it to the hot equator is accomplished primarily by frontal systems, upper-level winds and oceanic currents. On the other hand, to remove warm air from the equator and transfer them to the poles, hurricanes, upper-level winds and oceanic currents are the primary sources for this cycle of heat transfer. Of all the various sources, hurricanes are some of the most efficient forms of heat transfer within the Earth's atmosphere. In the final analysis, none of these systems ever gets to completely accomplish their primary goals or mandates. For example, while taking heat from the equator to the poles, the hurricane eventually dies out in the tropical or temperate latitudes before making it to the poles. On the other hand, a cold front travelling from the poles to the equator becomes so modified that it eventually dies out before making it to the equator. The result of this heat and cold transfer of energy exchange is life on planet Earth as we know it to be today. In addition, it creates a climate, which we as humans can not only live with but thrives on a planet that supports all kinds of lifeforms due to these vital and dynamic mechanisms of heat and cold transfer within planet Earth.

When Hurricane Matthew in 2016 engulfed wide swaths of the coastal areas of The Bahamas, including North Andros, Nassau, Grand Bahama and other islands in the Northwest Bahamas, it became an instant symbol of a new age of extreme weather disaster fueled by the possibility of climate change. But is it, really? As one of the most dangerous kinds of extreme weather, hurricanes already pose a significant human threat to anyone living anywhere along the Atlantic, the Caribbean, The Bahamas, North and Central American and Gulf Coasts locales and other tropical cyclones troubled spots. If we face the prospect of routine superstorms amped up by the extra heat and moisture in the Earth's fickle atmosphere from global warming—or, in the case of Matthew, merging with other weather systems and turning into massive weather disasters—that's a truly apocalyptic threat.

But like many questions in science, this isn't a simple or straight forward case of cause and effect. Many scientists accept the broad premise that a hotter climate likely contributes to some increase in hurricane strength, that this process is already underway, and that it will intensify. There's also unambiguous evidence that sea-level rise, another product of climate change, will contribute to higher, more dangerous storm surges. Beyond that, though, the science of meteorology gets more speculative, as it's based on computer models tracking the complex dynamics of climate and weather and sometimes incomplete records of hurricane data. There's a lot of uncertainty built into hurricanes. Here's a look at what we know, and don't know, about global warming and hurricanes.

First, hurricanes act as the earth's filter system removing polluted and toxic air out of the atmosphere and without them the atmosphere over time will get more toxic and eventually not support life. Second, hurricanes, in a nutshell are giant heat engines. They play a critical role in the transfer of heat energy from the equator to the poles. They transfer latent heat energy from the oceans to the atmosphere, transforming some of it into mechanical energy in the process: the turbulence of hurricane-force winds and giant waves. If you introduce more heat into such a system, warming up the atmosphere and the oceans, it stands to reason that the venting will grow stronger. High sea surface temperatures lead to the evapouration of moisture, which provides fuel for the storm. Then it gives it up in the form as latent heat and that's what powers the storm. Together they provide for stronger storms.

Let's look at another storm as an example-Superstorm Sandy which devastated the Eastern Seaboard of the United States in 2012. Sea surface temperatures off the East Coast were about 3 degrees Celsius above average at the time Sandy approached and some speculated that perhaps 0.6°C of that, was attributable to global warming. With each degree rise in sea surface temperatures, the atmosphere holds 4% more moisture, which may have boosted rainfall by as much as 5% to 10% over what it would have been 40 years ago. Scientists have wrestled with this vexing question for decades, trying to understand the systematic relationships between the atmosphere, Earth's climate, the oceans, and hurricanes.

MIT climatologist Professor Kerry Emanuel (Ph.D.) first suggested a link between climate and hurricanes in a 1987 academic paper, which proposed a new method for measuring overall hurricane force. Normal measurements such as barometric pressure, maximum strength, sustained wind speeds, or size, are constantly changing, and thus do not convey much about the storm's overall performance. Instead, he came up with an absolute baseline called the "power dissipation," roughly equivalent to the total amount of energy a storm expends over its lifetime, which can last weeks. (In physics, "power" is a measurement of energy expended over time). Emanuel's analysis of past storm data demonstrates that this has fueled the cumulative violence of cyclones, far beyond what his initial theories predicted. Hurricanes Joaquin, Matthew, Irma and Dorian validated this point many times over in 2015, 2016, 2017, and 2019 respectively, when they struck and devastated The Bahamas.

AUTHOR'S NOTE

Over the last 28 years of my life as a professional Bahamian meteorologist, hurricanes and their impact on my country of The Bahamas and the region have led me to write thirteen books on hurricanes. These books have allowed me to procure some of the best meteorologists in the business to write the foreword for me, from Bryan Norcross (Ph.D.), Hurricane Specialist at the Weather Channel; the late Herbert Saffir, co-creator of the Saffir-Simpson Hurricane Wind Scale; Phil Klotzbach (Ph.D.), from Colorado State University; the late Professor William Gray, from Colorado State University. Steve Lyons (Ph.D.), former Hurricane Specialist at the Weather Channel and now meteorologist in charge of the San Angelo National Weather Service Office in Texas. Chris Landsea (Ph.D.), Science and Operations Officer at the National Hurricane Center; and Kerry Emanuel (Ph.D.), Professor of Meteorology at Massachusetts Institute of Technology (MIT). Michel Davison, lead Forecaster and Chief Coordinator of Administration at the US Weather Prediction Center, NCEP's (National Centers for Environmental Prediction) International Desks of the U.S. National Oceanographic Atmospheric Administration.

Every new book I write and publish on hurricanes, I feature a meteorologist or a person in the science field who has made a significant contribution to the science of meteorology to write the foreword for my new book. You might not know their names, but if I were to mention these individuals' contributions, I am sure most persons will immediately recognize them for their life's work. This book is no different with Mr. William Read. This was done not only to add credibility to these books but also to show the importance of hurricanes and their significant impact on the lives of people of all walks of life in The Bahamas, this region and worldwide.

INTRODUCTION

The weather may very well be mankind's most widely discussed topic. Its effects are all-pervasive, ranging from the trivial issue of whether we should wear a certain colour or style of clothing to work or whether we should take an umbrella to work to tragedies that unfold during extreme weather events such as hurricanes or floods. The weather dictates the kind of life we live, the way we build our homes, the way we dress and to what we eat. In conjunction with the geological forces at work on our planet, the weather has shaped the landforms around us, and the variety of life here on Earth reflects nature's myriad solutions to the range of meteorological conditions that have occurred throughout history. There is nothing like them in the atmosphere. Born in warm tropical waters, these spiraling hurricane masses require a complex combination of atmospheric processes to grow, mature, and then die.

Hurricanes are not the largest storm systems in our atmosphere or the most violent, but they combine these qualities as no other phenomenon does. In the North Atlantic basin, they are called hurricanes, a term that echoes colonial Spanish and Caribbean Indian words for evil spirits and big winds. These powerful storms have been a deadly problem for residents and sailors ever since the early days of colonization. Today, hurricanes damages cost billions of dollars, but fortunately, people injured or killed during tropical cyclones have been steadily declining. However, our risk from hurricanes is increasing. With population and development continuing to grow exponentially along coastal areas, greater numbers of people and property are vulnerable to the threat of hurricanes. Large numbers of tourists also favor coastal locations, adding significantly to the problems of emergency managers and local decision-makers during a hurricane threat. It is important to add that hurricanes can't be controlled, but our vulnerability can be reduced through preparedness and education.

The North Atlantic hurricane season is the period in the year when hurricanes usually form in the North Atlantic region. Tropical cyclones in the North Atlantic basin are called hurricanes, tropical storms, or tropical depressions. In addition, there have been several storms over the years that have not been fully tropical and are categorized as subtropical depressions and subtropical storms. Even though subtropical storms and subtropical depressions are not technically as strong as tropical cyclones, the damage can still be devastating. Worldwide, tropical cyclone activity peaks in late summer, generally late July to mid-September, when the difference between temperatures aloft and sea surface temperatures are at their greatest. However, each basin has its own seasonal and climatic tropical cyclonic patterns and can vary considerably from one year to the next, depending on the atmospheric and sea surface temperature conditions at the time.

The size of The Bahamas and its geographical and societal conditions makes it susceptible to influences associated with hurricanes. In fact, of the various types of hurricanes impacting the North Atlantic (Bahama Busters-type, Cape Verde-type, Gulf of Mexico-type and Southern or Western Caribbean-type) all make their presence felt here with most of these hurricanes passing through or near The Bahamas. In the North Atlantic there are four different types of hurricanes that influence us in some way or the other. The first is the Cape Verde type hurricane which as it namesake suggests, it originates off the African Coast in the vicinity of the Cape Verde Islands initially moving in a westerly direction and then in a west-northwest to a northwesterly track as it makes its way through the Caribbean. The Cape Verde Islands is an archipelago about 400 miles off the West African. One notable example of this would be Hurricane Dorian in 2019. This type of hurricane forms over the North Atlantic mainly during the early part of the season, June thru mid-September months when the easterly waves are most dominant features in the Caribbean region. At the beginning and the middle of the hurricane season, storms also tend to form near The Bahamas and this type has come to be known as 'Bahama Busters' according to world renowned late Professor William Gray from Colorado State University. An example of this type was Hurricane Katrina in 2005. This hurricane formed just east to The Bahamas from a TUTT Low and moved initially westward and then northwestward into the Gulf of Mexico and then over Louisiana.

Then there is the Gulf of Mexico type, which as its names suggest originates in the Gulf of Mexico and influences Latin America, and the Gulf Coast of the United States. With this type of hurricane, The Bahamas mainly only gets the outflow of this hurricane spiral rain bands. Finally, there is the southern or western Caribbean Sea type which forms during the early and late parts of the hurricane season and forms in the most notable location near the southern Caribbean Sea or the Gulf of Honduras mainly in May and June and mid-September thru late November. The formations of these cyclones are due in part to the seasonal movement of the Inter-Tropical Convergence Zone, also known as the equatorial trough. From its inception, this type of hurricane seems to take a northward movement, which normally takes a track over the island of Cuba and into The Bahamas, the severity of which is influenced by how long the cyclone remains over the mountainous terrain of Cuba. An example of this type of hurricane was Hurricane Michelle in 2001.

For this reason, many of the islands (notably Grand Bahama, Abaco and Andros) are in the top ten places to be hit or brushed by hurricanes passing through the North Atlantic. In fact, some other countries are only impacted by one or two of the different types of hurricanes impacting the region. Take, for instance, Barbados, which is basically only affected by the Cape Verde-type and the Southern Caribbean-type hurricanes. The Bahamas is in a unique position when it comes to the various types of hurricanes impacting the region, because it is affected by all four types of hurricanes, and only the state of Florida in the United States can equal this record.

Climatology serves to characterize the general properties of an average season and can be used as one of many other tools for making accurate forecasts. Most storms form in warm waters several hundred miles north of the equator near the Intertropical Convergence Zone (ITCZ) from tropical waves. A tropical wave, in the Atlantic Ocean, is a type of atmospheric trough, an elongated area of relatively low air pressure, oriented north to south, which moves from east to west across the tropics, causing areas of cloudiness and thunderstorms. The Coriolis effect is usually too weak to initiate enough rotation near the equator. The Coriolis effect is an inertial or apparent force which causes particles or objects in motion to be deflected towards the right of motion in the northern hemisphere. It is negligible near the equator because there is no turning of the surface of the Earth (in terms of rotation) underneath a horizontally and freely moving object's or particle's path as measured relative to the Earth's surface. The object path is straight, that is, there is no Coriolis effect. This is the reason why some countries like Venezuela and Trinidad and Tobago in the southern

Caribbean are rarely impacted by hurricanes due to their proximity to the equator.

Storms frequently form in the warm waters of the Gulf of Mexico, the Caribbean Sea, and the tropical North Atlantic Ocean as far east as the Cape Verde Islands, the origin of strong and long-lasting Cape Verde-type hurricanes. Systems may also strengthen over the Gulf Stream off the Eastern Seaboard of the United States, wherever water temperatures exceed 26.5°C (79.7°F), the minimum threshold for hurricanes to form. Meteorologists in the twenty-first century are still attempting to comprehend these powerful storms in greater detail and calculate the massive energy they release. Today, their power is sometimes expressed in a measure that did not exist in the distant past–atomic bombs. When a hurricane reaches its peak intensity, it may release energy equivalent to 500,000 Hiroshima-type atomic bombs, although that energy is distributed over a wide, expansive area and is not concentrated as it would be in an atomic bomb explosion.[3]

Although most storms are found within tropical latitudes, occasionally storms will form further north and east from disturbances other than tropical waves such as cold fronts and upper-level lows. These are known as baroclinically induced tropical cyclones. There is a strong correlation between the North Atlantic hurricane activity in the tropics and the presence of an El Niño or La Niña event in the Pacific Ocean. El Niño events increase the wind shear over the North Atlantic, producing a less-favorable environment for formation and decreasing tropical activity in the North Atlantic basin. On the other hand, La Niña causes an increase in activity due to a decrease in wind shear. In general, El Niño tends to decrease hurricane activity across the North Atlantic and vice-versa for La Niña across the North Atlantic.

El Niño causes strong upper-level winds that can prevent tropical cyclone development or tear apart a tropical system. El Niño is always a welcome sight in the North Atlantic, but stronger ones are always preferred. When it comes to La Niña the opposite applies. El Niño and La Niña have great impact on the world's weather. El Niño and La Niña are common meteorological terms that we hear frequently in the seasonal hurricane forecasts – and with good reason. El Niño is a naturally occurring

---

[3] Willie Drye, *For Sale-American Paradise-How Our Nation Was Sold an Impossible Dream in Florida* (USA, Rowman & Littlefield, 2016). Pg. 139.

phenomenon characterized by warmer than normal water in the eastern Pacific equatorial region. While El Niño occurs in the Pacific Ocean, it has widespread impact on the global climate and displaces the different weather patterns around the world in both negative and positive ways.

Climatologically, approximately 97 percent of tropical cyclones that form in the North Atlantic basin develop between June 1 and November 30 – dates which delimit the modern-day North Atlantic hurricane season. Though the beginning of the annual hurricane season has historically remained the same, the official end of the hurricane season has shifted from its initial date of October 31. Regardless, on average once every few years a tropical cyclone develops outside the limits of the season; in fact, today there have been 66 tropical cyclones impacting the North Atlantic basin in the off-season, with the most recent being Tropical Storm Arlene in 2017.

The first tropical cyclone of the 1938 North Atlantic hurricane season, which formed on January 3, became the earliest forming tropical storm and hurricane after reanalysis concluded on the storm in December 2012. Hurricane Able in 1951 was initially thought to be the earliest forming major hurricane – a tropical cyclone with winds exceeding 115 mph – however following post-storm HURDAT reanalysis it was determined that Able only reached Category 1 strength which made Hurricane Alma of 1966 the new record-holder; as it became a major hurricane on June 8. Though it developed within the bounds of the North Atlantic hurricane season, Hurricane Audrey in 1957 became the earliest developing Category 4 hurricane on record after it reached that intensity on June 27. However, reanalysis from 1956 to 1960 by NOAA downgraded Audrey to a Category 3, making Hurricane Dennis of 2005 the earliest Category 4 on record occurring on July 8, 2005. The earliest-forming Category 5 hurricane, Emily, reached its highest intensity on the Saffir–Simpson Hurricane Wind Scale on July 17, 2005.

Though the official end of the North Atlantic hurricane season occurs on November 30, the dates of October 31 and November 15 have also historically marked the official end date for the hurricane season. December, the only month of the year after the hurricane season, has featured the cyclogenesis of fourteen tropical cyclones. Tropical Storm Zeta in 2005 was the latest tropical cyclone to attain tropical storm intensity as it did so on December 30. However, the second Hurricane Alice in 1954 was the latest forming tropical cyclone to attain hurricane intensity. Both

Zeta and Alice were the only two storms to exist in two calendar years – the former from 1954 to 1955 and the latter from 2005 to 2006. No storms have been recorded to exceed Category 1 hurricane intensity in December. In 1999, Hurricane Lenny reached Category 4 intensity on November 17 as it took an unprecedented west to east track across the Caribbean; its intensity made it the latest developing Category 4 hurricane, though this was well within the bounds of the hurricane season. Hurricane Hattie (October 27-November 1, 1961) was initially thought to have been the latest forming Category 5 hurricane ever documented, though reanalysis indicated that a devastating hurricane in 1932 reached such an intensity later. Consequently, it made this hurricane the latest developing tropical cyclone to reach all four Saffir–Simpson Hurricane Wind Scale classifications past Category 1 intensity.[4]

June is the beginning of the hurricane season and is most closely related to the timing of increases in sea surface temperatures, convective instability, and other thermodynamic factors. Although June marks the beginning of the hurricane season, generally little activity occurs during the month with an average of 1 tropical cyclone every 2 years. Tropical systems usually form in the Gulf of Mexico or off the east coast of the United States. Since 1851, a total of 81 tropical storms and hurricanes formed in the month of June. During this period, two of these systems developed in the deep tropics east of the Lesser Antilles. Since 1870, three major hurricanes have formed during June, most notably Hurricane Audrey in 1957. Audrey attained intensity greater than that of any other North Atlantic tropical cyclone during the months of June or July until Hurricanes Dennis and Emily of 2005. The easternmost forming storm during June, Tropical Storm Ana in 1979, formed at 45°W.

Not much tropical activity occurs during the month of July, but on average most hurricane seasons see the formation of one tropical cyclone. From 1944 to 1996, the first tropical storm in half of these seasons occurred by July 11, and a second formed by August 8. Their formation usually occurs in the eastern Caribbean Sea around the Lesser Antilles, in the northern and eastern parts of the Gulf of Mexico, near the northern Bahamas (Bahama Buster-type hurricanes), and off the coast of The Carolinas and Virginia over the Gulf Stream. Storms travel westward

---

[4] "Tropical Cyclone Climatology." NOAA-National Hurricane Center. Retrieved: 12-12-2017.

through the Caribbean and then either move towards the north and curve near the eastern coast of the United States or stay on a north-westward track and enter the Gulf of Mexico. Since 1851, a total of 105 tropical storms have formed during the month of July. Since 1870, ten of these storms reached major hurricane intensity. Only Hurricane Emily of 2005, the strongest July tropical cyclone in the North Atlantic basin, attained Category 5 hurricane status during July, making it the earliest Category 5 hurricane on record. The easternmost forming storm and longest lived during the month of July, Hurricane Bertha in 2008, formed at 22.9°W and lasted 17 days.

In August, a decrease in wind shear from July to August contributes to a significant increase of tropical activity. An average of 2.8 North Atlantic tropical storms develops annually in August. On average, four named tropical storms, including one hurricane, occur by August 30, and the first intense hurricane develops by September 4. The peak of the hurricane season occurs on September 10 and corresponds with low wind shear and the warmest sea surface temperatures. The month of September sees an average of 3 storms a year. By September 24, the average North Atlantic season features 7 named tropical storms, including 4 hurricanes. In addition, two major hurricanes occur on average by September 28. Relatively few tropical cyclones make landfall at these intensities.

In October, the favorable conditions found during September begin to decay in October. The main reason for the decrease in activity is increasing wind shear, although sea surface temperatures are also cooler than in September. Activity falls markedly with 1.8 cyclones developing on average despite a climatological secondary peak around October 20. By October 21, the average season features 9 named storms with 5 hurricanes. A third major hurricane occurs after September 28, in half of all North Atlantic tropical cyclone seasons. In contrast to mid-season activity, the main focus of formation shifts westward to the Caribbean and Gulf of Mexico, reversing the eastward progression of June through August. By November, wind shear from westerlies increases substantially through November, generally preventing cyclone formation. On average, one tropical storm forms during every other November. On rare occasions, a major hurricane occurs. The few intense hurricanes in November includes, the Great Cuba Hurricane of 1932 in late October and early November 1932 (the strongest November hurricane on record peaking as a Category 5 hurricane), Hurricane Lenny in mid-November 1999, Hurricane Kate in late November 1985 which was the latest major hurricane formation on record until Hurricane Otto (a Category 3 storm) of the 2016 hurricane season. Hurricane Paloma was a very powerful Category 4 storm that made landfall in Cuba in early November 2008.

Although the hurricane season is defined as beginning on June 1 and ending on November 30, there have been several off-season storms. Since 1870, there have been 32 off-season cyclones, 18 of which occurred in May. In the same time span, nine storms formed in December, with two formed in April, and one each in January, February and March. For four years (1887, 1953, 2003 and 2007), tropical cyclones formed in the North Atlantic Ocean both during or before May and during December. In 1887, four storms occurred outside the season, the most in a single year. High vertical wind shear and low sea surface temperatures generally preclude tropical cyclone formation during the off-season. Tropical cyclones have formed in all months. Four tropical cyclones existed during the month of January and two of which formed during late December: the second Hurricane Alice in 1954/1955, and Tropical Storm Zeta in 2005/2006. The only two hurricanes to form in January are a Category 1 hurricane in the 1938 season, and Hurricane Alex in the 2016 season. A subtropical storm in January also began the 1978 North Atlantic hurricane season. No major hurricanes have occurred in the off-season.

On a worldwide scale, the month of May is the least active month, while September is the most active. In the Northern Atlantic basin, a distinct hurricane season occurs from June 1 to November 30, sharply peaking from late August through mid to late September; the season's climatological peak of activity occurs around September 10 each season. This is the norm, but in 1938, the North Atlantic hurricane season started as early as January 3 and more recently in 2017, it started as early as January 12 with a hurricane called Alex. Hurricane Alex was the first North Atlantic hurricane in January since Hurricane Alice in 1955, and the first to form in the month since 1938. The first tropical cyclone of the 2016 North Atlantic hurricane season, Alex originated as an extratropical cyclone near The Bahamas on January 7, 2016.[5]

---

[5] "Atlantic hurricane Best Track (HURDAT version 2)". (Hurricane Research Division (Database). Miami, FL: National Hurricane Center. April 11, 2017). Retrieved: 31-03-2018.

Tropical disturbances that reach tropical storm intensity are named from a pre-determined list. On average, 10.1 named storms occur each season, with an average of 5.9 becoming hurricanes and 2.5 becoming major hurricanes (Category 3 or greater). The most active season was 2005, during which 28 tropical cyclones formed, of which a record 15 became hurricanes. The least active season was 1914, with only one known tropical cyclone developing during that year. This, however, is considered suspect because of the lack of complete satellite coverage over the North Atlantic basin during this era. During the season, regular tropical weather outlooks are issued by the National Hurricane Center incoordination with the Weather Prediction Center and this occurs for systems which have not formed yet but could develop during the next three to seven days.

Hurricane author Poey (1855) considered hurricane historian Moreau de Jonnes's chronology of 1822 to be the first chronological list to attempt to document all the known hurricanes in the West Indies dating back to 1495. Southey (1827) produced an important list of hurricanes. He also appears to be the first person to use the newspaper collections of the Reverend Dr. Charles Burney, purchased by the British Museum in 1818. This collection is the core of the British Library-Newspaper Library Collection today. Subsequent lists lean towards relying heavily on pre-existing chronologies (Evans, 1848; Schomburgk, 1848; Johnston, 1855; Poey, 1855). By the time Poey produced his 1855 chronology, the scientific investigation of tropical cyclones had been underway for more than three decades. Sir William Reid (1838, 1849), William Redfield (1831, 1854), and Henry Piddington (1848) were the most important researchers publishing their results.

None of them produced a chronology as such, but Poey drew on their work to supplement his list. He spent time in New York with Redfield copying out all the notes on storms that Redfield possessed (Poey, 1855). The list of Poey is a famous document for students of tropical meteorology. Since 1855, dozens of authors have used his list to produce their own updated lists of hurricanes and tropical storms. Tannehill (1938) used Poey's list (and those made since Poey's time) in his updating of the North Atlantic basin hurricane history, omitting all storms in the months of December through May that were included in Poey's list. This was done because it was well-known by this time that tropical cyclones in these months are very rare and the number too great in the historical record to be accurate. Subsequent work by Jose Millas (1968) confirmed the dating errors from English sources prior to 1752 due to the late acceptance of the

Gregorian calendar in England, relative to that of France and Spain. He also made the first critical analysis of the sources used by Poey, rejecting some storms, and including new storms made by his own research. Ludlum (1963) constructed the best chronology of landfalling tropical cyclones in the United States; many of these storms can be associated with their counterparts in earlier history in the Caribbean region. These sources are carried into the North Atlantic hurricane database known as HURDAT (Landsea et al., 2004), and an assessment of their reliability based on new information was made. The National Hurricane Center (NHC) has the responsibility for issuing advisories and U.S. watches/warnings for tropical cyclones, which includes tropical depressions, tropical storms, and hurricanes, for the North Atlantic and east Pacific basins.

So, you might be wondering why the track forecasts are more accurate today than in the past. Well, the primary reason is the advancements in technology, specifically the improvements in the weather observing platforms (satellites and radars, for example) and the various modeling systems we use to make forecasts. The amount and quality of data available to the models so they can paint an initial picture of the atmosphere have increased dramatically in the last 20 to 30 years. Also, the resolution and physics in the models we use today are far superior to what forecasters had available in the 1990s or prior decades, in part due to the tremendous improvements in computational capabilities. In addition, the National Hurricane Center has found ways to even beat the individual dynamical models by using a balance of statistical approaches and experience.

Predicting the intensity of a tropical storm or hurricane is usually more challenging than forecasting its track. This is because the intensity of these weather systems is affected by factors that are both big and small. On the large scale, vertical wind shear (the change of wind speed and direction with height) and the amount of moisture in the atmosphere greatly affects the amount or organization of the thunderstorm activity that the tropical cyclone can produce. Ocean temperatures also affect the system's intensity, with temperatures below 80°F usually being too cool to sustain significant thunderstorm activity. However, smaller-scale features can also be at play. One of the more complex phenomena that affect a tropical cyclone's intensity is an eyewall replacement cycle. Initially, when two eyewalls, one inside the other, are present, the hurricane's wind field will begin to expand, and as the inner eyewall dies, the hurricane's peak winds start to weaken. However, if the second eyewall contracts, the hurricane can often re-intensify. Hurricane Irma in 2017, for example, had a double eyewall replacement cycle.

What is most striking about the historical hurricanes impacting The Bahamas one might ask? It is the one glaring fact that we tend to be incomprehensible about the dangers associated with hurricanes impacting The Bahamas. While we are praying and asking God for His Divine judgment to be spared or engaging in rescue and clean-up, it is patently clear that the modern Bahamas fares better in hurricanes than almost any other territory on the planet. That's important for us because three islands in The Bahamas (Grand Bahama, Abaco and Andros) are always in the top ten areas of the North Atlantic to be hit or brushed by a hurricane. Why was and will The Bahamas be continually be exposed to potential dangers from these historical storms one might ask? Part of the reason for country being actively hit by hurricanes comes directly from our very geography. We have a large and expansive area within our bounraries and over 700 islands and cays. We have no rivers to overflow and break their levees, and we have no mountains to create landslides or flash floods. In fact, the highest point in The Bahamas is Mount Alvernia (also known as Como Hill). It rises to 206 feet (63 meters) and is topped by a monastery called the Hermitage which is located on the Island of Cat Island. Therefore our geography will continue to make us vulnerable to the ravages of future hurricanes.

There are other common ways that people die in hurricanes and probing into our historical archives can tell us how they were killed. People are drowned in storm surges (as happened in Andros and New Providence in the powerful hurricanes of 1866, 1899, 1926, and 1929) and people are killed by falling debris when houses are torn apart, when roofs fly off. Since the 1930s, the number of houses that were torn apart in The Bahamas have been a whole lot fewer, and that is due to the nation's radio station ZNS coming on stream on May 26, 1936. It had an effective range that encompassed the entire island chain and provided adequate warnings well-ahead of time before the hurricane struck that island. Thankfully, it is fair to say that we have learned how to build for storms with our rigid building codes and this resulted in fewer fatalities.

One might wonder which islands and settlements around The Bahamas where the most intense hurricanes hit, how strong, deadly and impactful they were. What would happen if they were to hit today with the same intensity, and what would be the present-day costs when inflation is factored in? How many persons died in the Okeechobee Hurricane of 1928, the Great Andros Island Hurricane of 1929 or the Great Bahamas Hurricane of 1866? They are three of the deadliest hurricanes to affect The Bahamas. Meanwhile, the Great Abaco Hurricane of 1932, Hurricane Andrew of 1992, and Hurricane Dorian of 2019 were three of only 4 Category 5 hurricanes on record to impact The Bahamas. Furthermore, which islands were impacted by these hurricanes? Simply, read further on as this book will seek to provide comprehensive answers to these and many other thought-provoking questions. This book will provide a full and unbiased viewpoint of the most destructive, deadliest and strongest hurricanes ever faced by residents of The Bahamas over the last few centuries. This book will seek to examine these questions and come up with this list or gallery of mega-storms.

Today, it's hard for many younger Bahamians to imagine the possibility of experiencing more than 1 hurricane impacting The Bahamas in one season. Amazingly, one time ago in the 1920s and 1930s, having bumper years of more than one hurricane each year was the norm, as you will see later. What are the most notable circumstances behind these statistics? Many meteorologists and other scientists alike tend to blame it on the man-made event of 'climate change' rather than some naturally occurring event impacting these hurricanes. For example, every 100 years there seems to be one year that has a 'bumper' year of hurricanes. In the 2000s it was 2005, and in the 1900s it was 1933. Why that is the case or is it a naturally occurring cycle, no one seems to know the real answer or has a valid explanation for this occurrence. In most cases, this is due to our strategic location and our tough building codes which are considered one of the best hurricanes building codes in the region.

For many residents of The Bahamas, the big questions that seems to be on everyone's mind before and during hurricane season is: How active will the season be? Will it impact their island, and how severe will it be? Every storm is different, but one of the ways to answer these questions is to explore the hurricane history of The Bahamas. Here, you'll find diverse profiles of storms that this country will never forget. For many of the storms, I've gathered a vast amount of storm data from the USA's National Hurricane Center database reports, Bahamas House of Assembly Official Hurricane Reports, Family Islands Commissioner's Reports, personal recollections from a vast array of individuals who experienced some of the more recent storms, newspapers and magazine reports, individual islands climatological data reports, ships log reports, The Bahamas National Archives and various libraries' storm reports from around the country and the entire region and other ways to make this book as compelling, accurate, and reader-friendly as possible.

The narrative of this book and research work done is in some places are lengthy, in other places minimal. I've tried to provide only what appeared to be essential for furnishing context, and for connecting what I feel to be the most revelatory "sound bites" of long ago and extending all the way up to today's era. To add explanatory details without disruption of the narrative flow, footnotes have been supplied. However, I hasten to add that the value judgments have been left to the reader. You will, in the final analysis, I hope, find this an engaging story. This book has several main themes. Firstly, it begins with a general description of hurricanes, including an examination of historical data sets and a presentation of various hurricane statistics. Secondly, details on the origin, naming, track and meteorological history of some of the major hurricanes of The Bahamas are presented. Thirdly, this is followed by the Bahamian hurricane records most closely linked to people and society. Special focus is given to the major or more notable hurricanes, landfalling hurricanes and the analysis of cycles, trends, and return periods. Finally, the last theme is based on societal vulnerability to hurricanes, personal recollections of these hurricanes and the impact of the various hurricanes on each individual island. This book is my attempt to present the various historical hurricane records of The Bahamas going back as far as 1500 in a clear, precise, comprehensive, and original manner. The reader will decide if I have succeeded or not.

The North Atlantic basin hurricanes have been well documented and are perhaps the region where most of the research is conducted, even though the Pacific basin is the most active region where most tropical cyclones are formed. This table below shows the total and average number of tropical storms, and those which became hurricanes in the North Atlantic, by month, for the period 1851-2015:

The total and average number of tropical storms and hurricanes in the North Atlantic

Month	Tropical Storms		Hurricanes	
	Total	Average	Total	Average
JANUARY	2	*	1	*
FEBRUARY	1	*	0	*
MARCH	1	*	1	*
APRIL	1	*	0	*
MAY	21	0.1	4	*
JUNE	87	0.5	33	0.2
JULY	118	0.7	55	0.3
AUGUST	378	2.3	238	1.4
SEPTEMBER	571	3.5	395	2.4
OCTOBER	336	2.0	201	1.2
NOVEMBER	89	0.5	58	0.3
DECEMBER	17	0.1	6	*
YEAR	1619	9.9	991	6.0

The total and average number of tropical storms and hurricanes in the North Atlantic (* Less than 0.05). Excludes subtropical storms (Information Courtesy of the US National Hurricane Center).

List of some of the notable North Atlantic hurricane records

- The season in which the most tropical storms formed on record was the 2005 North Atlantic hurricane season (28). That season was also the one in which the most hurricanes formed on record (15).

- The 2005 North Atlantic hurricane season and 1961 North Atlantic hurricane season had the most major hurricanes on record (7). The 1950 North Atlantic hurricane season was once thought to have 8, but on HURDAT re-analysis, it showed that several storms were weaker than previously thought, and thus the record is now held by the 2005 season.

- The least active season on record since 1946 (when the database is considered more reliable) was the 1983 North Atlantic hurricane season, with four tropical storms, two hurricanes, and one major hurricane. Overall, the 1914 North Atlantic hurricane season remains the least active, with only one documented storm.

- The most intense hurricane (by barometric pressure) on record in the North Atlantic basin was Hurricane Wilma (2005) (882 millibars).

- The largest hurricane (in gale diameter) on record to form in the North Atlantic was Hurricane Sandy (2012) with a gale diameter of 1,100 miles.

- The longest-lasting hurricane was the San Ciriaco's Hurricane of 1899, which lasted for 27 days and 18 hours as a tropical cyclone.

- The longest-tracked hurricane was Hurricane Faith in 1966, which travelled for 6,850 miles as a tropical cyclone. Faith is also the northernmost moving tropical cyclone in the North Atlantic basin.

- The most tornadoes spawned by one hurricane were 127 by Hurricane Ivan (2004 season).

- The strongest landfalling hurricane was the Great Labour Day Hurricane of 1935 (892 hPa).

- The deadliest hurricane was the Great Hurricane of 1780 (22,000 fatalities).

- The deadliest hurricane to make landfall on the continental United States was the Great Galveston Hurricane in 1900 which may have killed up to 12,000 people.

- The most damaging hurricane was both Hurricane Katrina and Hurricane Harvey of the 2005 and 2017 seasons, respectively, both of which caused $125 billion in damages in their respective years.

However, when adjusted for inflation, Katrina is the costliest with $161 billion.

- The quickest forming hurricane was Hurricane Humberto in 2007. It was a minimal hurricane that formed and intensified faster than any other tropical cyclone on record before landfall. Developing on September 12, 2007, in the northwestern Gulf of Mexico, the cyclone rapidly strengthened and struck High Island, Texas, with sustained winds of about 90 mph early on September 13.[6]

---

[6] Eric S. Blake, Edward N. Rappaport, and Chris Landsea. NHC-The Deadliest, Costliest, and Most Intense United States Tropical Cyclones From 1851 to 2006 (and other frequently requested hurricane facts). Retrieved: 14-12-2017.

CHAPTER ONE

The History behind the word 'hurricane' and Other Tropical Cyclones' Names

" **T**he worst storms of all the world's seas are those of these islands and coasts," wrote Bartolomé de Las Casas in his log-book (1561), responding to his experiences with several hurricanes on the island of Hispaniola.[7] Christopher Columbus also feared these 'tempests' as he referred to them because of the great devastation they inflicted upon him and his crew in the Caribbean. He wrote, "On the island of Dominica, I wrote that up to here I had fair weather, what one would desire. The night I arrived there was a great tempest, one that followed me always...In all this time I did not enter any harbour, neither could I have done so, I was never without a tempest, rain, trombones (thunder) and continued lightning, that seemed the end of the world."[8] In a letter Columbus wrote to the King and Queen of Spain, he told them of his encounter with a hurricane. "Never have eyes seen the sea so high or so rough, and the foam seemed to burn in fire...One day and night it seemed that the sky burned in strong flames, because of the thunder, the flashes of lightning and thunderbolts that fell, that every moment I supposed we would all be burned, and the ship sunk, all broken in pieces, as the winds were so terrific. The thunder was so intense and so frightful that we

---

[7] Stuart, B. Swartz, <u>Sea of Storms-The History of Hurricanes in the Greater Caribbean from Columbus to Katrina,</u> (USA, Princeton University Press, 2015) pg. 1.
[8] José Millas, *Hurricanes of The Caribbean and Adjacent Regions 1492-1800,* (Edward Brothers Inc./Academy of the Arts and Sciences of the Americas Miami, Florida, 1968) pg. xvii.

thought in one ship that the others were firing cannons, asking for help because they were sinking."[9]

The forces of nature, such as deadly hurricanes, have shaped the lives of people from the earliest times. Indeed, the first 'meteorologists' were priests and shamans of ancient communities. Whatever lifestyles these ancient people followed, they all developed beliefs about the world around them. These beliefs helped them to explain how the world began, what happens in the future, or what happened after a person died. The world of spirits was very important. Those people, who became noted for their skills at interpreting signs in the world around them, became spiritual leaders in their communities.

All religions and different races of people recognized the power of the weather elements, and most scriptures contain tales about or prophecies foretelling great natural disasters sometimes visited upon a community because of the sins of its citizens. Ancient peoples often reacted to the weather in a fearful, superstitious manner. They believed that mythological gods controlled the weather elements, such as winds, rain and sun, which governed their existence. When weather conditions were favorable, there would be plenty of game to hunt, fish to catch, and bountiful harvests. But their livelihood was at the mercy of the wild weather, because fierce hurricanes could damage villages of flimsy huts, destroy crops and generate vast floodwaters that could sweep away livestock.

In times of hurricanes, food shortages and starvation were constant threats, as crops failed, and game animals became scarce when their food supplies dried up due to a hurricane. These ancient tribes, as you will see later, believed that their weather fortunes were inextricably linked with the moods and actions of their gods. For this reason, they spent a great deal of time and effort appeasing these mythological weather gods. Many of these ancient tribes tried to remain on favorable terms with their deities through a mixture of prayers, rituals, dances and sometimes even human sacrifices. In some cultures, such as the Aztecs of Central America, they would offer up human sacrifices to appease their rain-god, Tláloc. In addition, Quetzalcoatl, the all-powerful and mighty deity in the ancient Aztec society whose name means 'Precious Feathered Serpent', played a critical role; he was the creator of life and controlled devastating hurricanes. The Egyptians celebrated Ra, the sun god. Thor was the Norse

---

[9] Ibid, pg. xvii.

god of thunder and lightning, a god to please so that calm waters would grace their seafaring expeditions. The Greeks had many weather gods; however, it was Zeus who was the most powerful of them all.

The actual origin of the word 'hurricane' and other tropical cyclone names was based on the many religions, cultures, myths, and races of people. In modern cultures, 'myth' has come to mean a story or an idea that is not true. The word 'myth' comes directly from the Greek word 'mythos'(μύθος), whose many meanings include, 'word', 'saying', 'story', and 'fiction'. Today, the word 'myth' is used any and everywhere, and people now speak of myths about how to catch or cure the common cold. But the age-old myths about hurricanes in this book were an important part of these people's religions, cultures, and everyday lives. Often-times, they were both deeply spiritual and culturally entertaining and significant. For many of these ancient races, their mythology was their history, and there was often little, if any, distinction between the two.

Some myths were based on historical events, such as devastating hurricanes, or even wars, but myths often offer us a treasure trove of dramatic tales. The active beings in myths are generally gods and goddesses, heroes and heroines, or animals. Most myths are set in a timeless past before recorded and critical history began. A myth is a sacred narrative in the sense that it holds religious or spiritual significance for those who tell it, and it contributes to and expresses systems of thoughts and values. It is a traditional story, typically involving supernatural beings or forces or creatures, which embodies and provides an explanation, aetiology (origin myths), or justification for something such as the early history of a society, a religious belief or ritual, or a natural phenomenon.

The United Nations' sub-body, the World Meteorological Organization estimates that in an average year, about 80 of these tropical cyclones kill up to 15,000 people worldwide and cause an estimate of several billion dollars' worth of property damage alone. Hurricanes, typhoons and cyclones are all the same kind of violent storms originating over warm tropical ocean waters and are called by different names all over the world. From the Timor Sea to as far as northwestern Australia, they are called cyclones, or by the Australian colloquial term of 'Willy-Willies', from an old Aboriginal word (derived from whirlwind). In the Bay of Bengal and the Indian Ocean, they are simply called 'Cyclones' (an English name based on a Greek word meaning "coil", as in "coil of a snake", because the winds that spiral within them resemble the coils of a snake) and are not named even to this day.

They are called 'hurricanes' (derived from a Carib, Mayan or Taíno/Arawak Indian word) in the Gulf of Mexico, Central and North America, the Caribbean and Eastern North Pacific Oceans (east of the International Dateline). In the Indian Ocean, all the way to Mauritius and along the Arabian Coasts, they are known as 'Asifa-t'. In Mexico and Central America, hurricanes are also known as El Cordonazo, and in Haiti they are known as Taínos. While they are called Typhoons [originating from the Chinese word 'Ty-Fung' (going back to as far as the Song (960-1278) and Yuan (1260-1341) dynasties) translated to mean 'Big or Great Wind'], in the Western North Pacific and in the Philippines and the South China Sea (west of the International Dateline) they are known as 'Baguios' or 'Chubasco' (or simply a typhoon). The word Baguio was derived from the Philippine city of Baguio, which was inundated by a typhoon in July 1911, with over 46 inches of rain in a 24-hour period. Also, in the scientific literature of the 1600s, including the book *Geographia Naturalis,* by geographer Bernhardus Varenius, the term whirlwind was used, but this term never achieved regional or worldwide acceptance as a name for a hurricane.

In Japan, they are known as 'Repus', or by the more revered name of a typhoon. The word "taifū" (台風) in Japanese means typhoon; the first character meaning "pedestal" or "stand"; the second character meaning wind. The Japanese term for "divine wind" is kamikaze (神風). The kamikaze were two typhoons that were said to have saved Japan from two Mongol invasion fleets under Kublai Khan, who attacked Japan in 1274, and again in 1281. The latter is said to have been the largest attempted naval invasion in history, whose scale was only recently eclipsed in modern times by the D-Day invasion by the Allied forces into Normandy in 1944. This was the term that was given to the typhoon winds that came up and blew the Mongol invasion fleet off course and destroyed it as it was poised to attack Japan.

On October 29, 1274, the first invasion began. Some 40,000 men, including about 25,000 Mongolians, 8,000 Korean troops, and 7,000 Chinese seamen, set sail from Korea in about 900 ships to attack Japan. With fewer troops and inferior weapons, the Japanese were far outmatched and overwhelmed and were sure to be defeated. But at nightfall, just as they were attacking the Japanese coastal forces, the Korean sailors sensed an approaching typhoon and begged their reluctant Mongol commanders to put the invasion force back at sea, or else it would be trapped on the coast and its ships destroyed at anchor by this typhoon. The next morning, the Japanese were surprised and delighted to see the Mongol fleet struggling to regain the open ocean during a great typhoon. The ships, sadly, were no match for this great storm, and many foundered or were simply dashed to bits and pieces on the rocky coast. Nearly 13,000 men perished in this storm, mostly by drowning. This Mongol fleet had been decimated by a powerful typhoon as it was poised to attack Japan.

With the second storm, even as Kublai Khan was mounting his second Japanese offensive, he was waging a bitter war of conquest against southern China, whose people had resisted him for 40 years. But finally, in 1279, the last of the southern providences, Canton, fell to the Mongol forces, and China was united under one ruler for the first time in three hundred years. Buoyed by success, Kublai again tried to bully Japan into submission by sending his emissaries to the Japanese, asking them to surrender to his forces. But this time the Japanese executed his emissaries, enraging him even further and thereby paving the way for a second invasion. Knowing this was inevitable; the Japanese went to work building coastal fortifications, including a massive dike around Hakozaki Bay, which encompasses the site of the first invasion.

The second Mongol invasion of Japan assumed staggering proportions. One armada consisted of 40,000 Mongols, Koreans, and Chinese, who were to set sail from Korea, while a second, larger force of some 100,000 men were to set out from various ports in south China. The invasion plan called for the two armadas to join forces in the spring before the summer typhoon season, but unfortunately the southern force was late, delaying the invasion until late June 1281. The Japanese defenders held back the invading forces for six weeks until on the fifteenth and sixteenth of August, history then repeated itself when a gigantic typhoon decimated the Mongol fleet poised to attack Japan again.

As a direct result of these famous storms, the Japanese came to think of the typhoon as a 'divine wind' or 'kamikaze' sent by their gods to deliver their land from the evil invaders. Because they needed another intervention to drive away the Allied forces in WWII, they gave this name to their Japanese suicide pilots as nationalist propaganda. In the Japanese Shinto religion, many forces of nature are worshipped as gods, known as 'kami', and are represented as human figures. The Japanese god of thunder is often depicted as a strong man beating his drum. The Japanese called it kamikaze, and the Mongols never, ever returned to attack Japan again because of their personal experiences with these two great storms. In popular Japanese myths at the time, the god Raijin was the god who turned the storms against the Mongols. Other variations say that the god Fūjin or Ryūjin caused the destructive kamikaze. This use of *kamikaze* has come to be the common meaning of the word in English.[10]

Whatever name they are known by in different regions of the world, they refer to the same weather phenomena as a 'tropical cyclone'. They are all the same severe tropical storms that share the same fundamental characteristics, aside from the fact that they rotate clockwise in the southern hemisphere, and counterclockwise in the northern hemisphere. However, by World Meteorological Organization International Agreement, the term tropical cyclone is the general term given to all hurricane-type storms that originate over tropical waters. The term cyclone, used by meteorologists, refers to an area of low pressure in which winds move counterclockwise in the northern hemisphere around the low-pressure center and are usually associated with bad weather, heavy rainfall and strong wind speeds.

A tropical cyclone was the name first given to these intense circular storms by Englishman Captain Henry Piddington (1797-1848), who was keenly interested in storms affecting India and spent many years collecting information on ships caught in severe storms in the Indian Ocean. He would later become the president of the Marine Courts of Inquiry in Calcutta, India. He used the term tropical cyclone to refer to a tropical storm that blew the freighter 'Charles Heddles' in circles for nearly a week in Mauritius in February of 1845. In his book *'Sailor's Hornbook for the Laws of Storms in All Parts of the World,'* published in 1855, he called these storms cyclones, from the Greek word for coil of a snake. He called these storms tropical cyclones because it expressed sufficiently what he described as the 'tendency to move in a circular motion'.

The word cyclone is from the Greek word 'κύκλος', meaning 'circle' or Kyklos, meaning 'coils of the snake', describing the rotating movement of the storm. An Egyptian word 'Cykline', meaning to 'to spin', has also been cited as a possible origin. In Greek mythology, Typhoeus or Typhōn was the son of Tartarus and Gaia. He was a monster with many heads, a man's body, and a coiled snake's tail. The king of the gods and god of the sky and weather, Zeus, fought a great battle with Typhoeus and finally

---

[10] Kerry Emanuel, <u>*Divine Wind-The History and Science of Hurricanes*</u>, (New York, Oxford University Press, 2005). Pgs. 3-5.

buried him under Mount Etna. According to legend, he was the source of the powerful storm winds that caused widespread devastation, the loss of many lives and numerous shipwrecks. The Greek word 'typhōn', meaning 'whirlwind', comes from this legend, another possible source for the origin of the English word 'typhoon'. The term is most often used for cyclones occurring in the Western Pacific Ocean and Indian Ocean. In addition, the word is an alteration of the Arabic word, tūfān, meaning hurricane, and the Greek word typhōn, meaning violent storm and an Egyptian word 'Cykline', meaning to 'to spin'.

The history of the word 'typhoon' presents a perfect example of the long journey that many words made in coming to the English Language vocabulary. It travelled from Greece to Arabia to India and arose independently in China before assuming its current form in our language. The Greek word typhōn, used both as the name of the father of the winds and a common noun meaning 'whirlwind, typhoon', was borrowed into Arabic during the Middle Ages, when Arabic learning both preserved and expanded the classical heritage and passed it on to Europe and other parts of the world. In the Arabic version of the Greek word, it was passed into languages spoken in India, where Arabic-speaking Muslim invaders had settled in the eleventh century. Thus, the descendant of the Arabic word, passing into English through an Indian language and appearing in English in forms such as touffon and tūfān, originally referred specifically to a severe storm in India.

The modern form of typhoon was also influenced by a borrowing from the Cantonese variety of Chinese, namely the word 'Ty-Fung', and re-spelled to make it look more like Greek. 'Ty-Fung', meaning literally 'great wind', was coincidentally similar to the Arabic borrowing and is first recorded in English guise as tuffoon in 1699. The Cantonese tai-fung and the Mandarin ta-feng are derived from the word jufeng. It is also believed to have originated from the Chinese word 'jufeng', 'Ju' can mean either 'a wind coming from four directions' or 'scary'; 'feng' is the generic word for wind. Arguably, the first scientific description of a tropical cyclone and the first appearance of the word jufeng in the literature are contained in a Chinese book called *Nan Yue Zhi* (Book of the Southern Yue Region), written around A.D. 470. In that book, it is stated that "Many Jufeng occur around Xi'n County. Ju is a wind (or storm) that comes in all four directions. Another meaning for Jufeng is that it is a scary wind. It frequently occurs in the sixth and seventh month (of the Chinese lunar calendar; roughly

July and August of the Gregorian calendar). Before it comes, it is said that chickens and dogs are silent for three days. Major ones may last up to seven days, and minor ones last one or two days. These are called heifeng (meaning black storms/winds) in foreign countries."[11]

European travelers to China in the sixteenth century took note of a word sounding like typhoon being used to denote severe coastal windstorms. On the other hand, typhoon was used in European texts and literature around 1500, long before systematic contact with China was established. It is possible that the European use of this word was derived from Typhon, the draconian Earth demon of Greek Legend. The various forms of the word from these different countries coalesced and finally became typhoon, a spelling that officially first appeared in 1819 in Percy Bysshe Shelley's play 'Prometheus Unbound'. This play was concerned with the torments of the Greek mythological figure Prometheus and his suffering at the hands of Zeus. By the early eighteenth century, typhon and typhoon were in common use in European literature, as in the famous poem "Summer", by Scottish poet James Thomson (1700 - 1748):

> *"Beneath the radiant line that grits the globe,*
> *The circling Typhon, whirled from point to point.*
> *Exhausting all the rage of all the sky,*
> *And dire Ecnephia, reign."[12]*

In Yoruba mythology, Oya, the female warrior, was the goddess of fire, wind and thunder. When she became angry, she created tornadoes and hurricanes. Additionally, to ward off violent and tropical downpours, Yoruba priests in southwestern Nigeria held ceremonies around images of the thunder and lightning god Sango to protect them from the powerful winds of hurricanes. When these storms are over Senegal in West Africa, near the Cape Verde Islands, the Senegalese pray to the sea gods that give and take away life for protection from these storms. The elders of this nation chant supplications and toss a concoction of wine, grain, milk and water into the waves; priests cut a cow's neck and let it bleed into the surf,

---

[11] Kerry Emanuel, *Divine Wind-The History and Science of Hurricanes*, (New York, Oxford University Press, 2005). Pgs. 3-5.

[12] Kerry Emanuel, *Divine Wind-The History and Science of Hurricanes*, (New York, Oxford University Press, 2005). Pg. 21.

then throw its limbs into the water. They do all of this in hopes of appeasing the fickle, exacting sea and obtaining a quiet summer without storms.

In ancient Egyptian legend, Set was regarded as the god of storms. He was associated with natural calamities like hurricanes, thunderstorms, lightning, earthquakes and eclipses. In Iroquois mythology, Ga-oh was the wind giant whose house was guarded by several animals, each representing a specific type of wind. The Bear was the north wind, who brought winter hurricanes, and he was also capable of crushing the world with his storms or destroying it with his cold air. In Babylonian mythology, Marduk, the god of gods, defeated the bad-tempered dragon goddess Tiamat with the help of a hurricane. When the other gods learned about Tiamat's plans to destroy them, they turned to Marduk for help. Armed with a bow and an arrow, strong winds, and a powerful hurricane, Marduk captured Tiamat and let the hurricane winds fill her jaws and stomach. Then he shot an arrow into her belly and killed her and then became the lord of all the gods.

The Meso-American and Caribbean Indians worshipped many gods. They had similar religions based on the worship of mainly agricultural and natural elements gods, even though the gods' names and the symbols for them were a bit different. People asked their gods for good weather, lack of hurricanes, abundant crops and good health or for welfare. The main Inca god was the creator god Viracocha. His assistants were the gods of the Earth and the sea. As farming occupied such an important place in the region, the 'Earth mother' or 'Earth goddess' was particularly important. The Aztecs, Mayas, Taínos and other Indians adopted many gods from other civilizations. As with the Mayans, Aztecs and Taínos, each god related to some aspects of nature or natural forces, and in each of these religions, hurricanes or the fear of them and the respect for them played a vital part of their worship. The destructive power of storms like hurricanes inspires both fear and fascination, and it is no surprise that humans throughout time have tried to control these storms. Ancient tribes were known to make offerings to the weather gods to appease them. People in ancient times believed that these violent storms were brought on by angry weather gods. In some cultures, the word for hurricane means 'storm god', 'evil spirit', 'devil', or 'god of thunder and lightning'.

The word 'hurricane' comes to us via the early Spanish explorers of the New World, who were told by the Indians of this region of an evil god capable of inflicting strong winds and great destruction on their lives and possessions. The natives of the Caribbean and Central America had a healthy respect for hurricanes and an uncanny understanding of nature. In the legends of the Mayan civilizations of Central America and the Taínos of the Caribbean, these gods played an important role in their Creation. According to their beliefs and myths, the wicked gods Huracán, Hurrikán, Hunraken, and Jurakan annually victimized and savagely ravaged their homes, inflicting them with destructive winds, torrential rainfall and deadly floods. These natives were terrified whenever these gods made an appearance. They would beat drums, blew conch shells, shouted curses, engage in bizarre rituals and did everything possible to thwart these gods and drive them away. Sometimes they felt they were successful in frightening them off, and at other times their fury could not be withstood, and they suffered the consequences from an angry weather god. Some of these natives depicted these fearsome deities on primitive carvings as a hideous creature with swirling arms, ready to release his winds and claim its prey.

There are several theories about the origin of the word 'hurricane'; some people believe it originated from the Caribbean Taíno-Arawak speaking Indians. The Taínos were the indigenous inhabitants of The Bahamas, Greater Antilles, and some of the Lesser Antilles – especially in Guadeloupe, Dominica and Martinique. The Taínos ("Taíno" means "good" "people"), unlike the Caribs (who practiced regular raids on other groups), were peaceful seafaring people and distant relatives of the Arawak people of South America. The Taíno society was divided into two classes: Nitainos (nobles) and the Naborias (commoners). Both were governed by chiefs known as caciques, who were the maximum authority in a Yucayeque (village). The chiefs were advised by priest-healers known as Bohiques and the Nitaynos, which is how the elders and warriors were known.

It is believed that these Indians named their storm god 'Huracán', and over time it eventually evolved into the English word 'hurricane' that we are familiar with today. Others believed that it originated from the fierce group of cannibalistic Indians called the Caribs, but according to some historians this seems like the least likely source of this word. Native people throughout the Caribbean basin linked hurricanes to supernatural forces and had a word for these storms, which often had similar spellings, but they all signified death and destruction by some evil spirit, and the early European colonial explorers to the New World picked up the native names.

One early historian noted that the local Caribbean Indians, in preparation for these storms, often tied themselves to trees to keep from being blown away from the winds of these storms. According to one early seventeenth-century English account, Indians on St. Christopher viewed 'Hurry-Cano' as a "tempestuous spirit." These ancient Indians of this region personalized the hurricane, believing that it was bearing down on them as punishment by the gods for something they had done-or not done. In fact, the entire Mesoamerican religions recognized and respected the duality of forces so that the gods of wind could in their benevolent form bring rains for the crops. On the other hand, in their malevolent aspects were destroyers of homes and milipas, bearers of misery and death. These days, there is more science and less superstition to these powerful storms of nature called hurricanes. Yet we humanize hurricanes with familiar names, and the big ones become folkloric and iconic characters, their rampages woven into the histories of the Caribbean, North and Central American coastal towns and cities.

Another popular theory about the hurricane's origin is that it came from the Mayan Indians of Mexico, who had an ancient word for these storms, called 'Hurrikán' (or 'Huracán'). Hurrikán was the Mayan god of the storm. He was present at all three attempts to create humanity, in which he did most of the actual work of creating human beings under the direction of Kukulkán (known by the Aztec name Quetzalcoatl) and Tepeu. Unlike the other Creators, Hurrikán was not heavily personified by the Mayans and was generally considered to be more like the winds and the storms themselves. In the Mayan language, his name means "one-legged". The word hurricane is derived from Hurrikán's name. Hurrikán is like the Aztec god Tlaloc.

In Mayan mythology, 'Hurrikán' ("one legged") was a wind, storm and fire god and one of the creator deities who participated in all three attempts of creating humanity. 'Hurrikán' was the Mayan god of big wind, and his image was chiseled into the walls of the Mayan temples. He was one of the three most powerful forces in the pantheon of deities, along with Cabrakán (earthquakes) and Chirakán (volcanoes). He also caused the Great Flood after the first humans angered the gods. He supposedly lived in the windy mists above the floodwaters and repeated "Earth" until land came up from the seas. In appearance, he has one leg, the other being transformed into a serpent, a zoomorphic snout or long-nose, and a smoking object such as a cigar, torch holder or axe head, which pierces a mirror on his forehead.

The first human historical record of hurricanes can be found in the ancient Mayan hieroglyphics. A powerful and deadly hurricane struck the Northern Yucatán in 1464, wiping out most of the Mayan Indian population of that area. The Maya Temple of the God of the Wind, in Tulum, Mexico, used a web of holes to create a loud whistling sound that warned the population of an impending hurricane. Mexico's historical Maya civilisation created not only a written language and a binary mathematical system, but also a hurricane warning system that still works today. It is housed in the clifftop Templo Dios del Viento, or Temple of the God of the Wind, in Tulum, a Maya site that had its heyday in the years 1200 to 1450. The temple contained an intricate web of holes that caused an extremely loud whistling sound when early hurricane-force winds blew in from the Caribbean Sea towards Tulum.

According to Mayan mythology, the Mayan rain and wind god Chac sent rain for the crops. But he also sent hurricanes, which destroyed crops and flooded villages. The Mayans hoped that if they made offerings to Chac (including human sacrifices), the rains would continue to fall, but the hurricanes would cease. Every year, the Mayans threw a young woman into the sea as a sacrifice to appease the god Hurrikán, and a warrior was also sacrificed to lead the girl to Hurrikán's underwater kingdom. Also, one of the sacrifices in honour of this god was to drown children in wells. In some Maya regions, Chac, the god of rain and wind, was so important that the facades of their buildings were covered with the masks of Chac. In fact, at its peak it was one of the most densely populated and culturally dynamic societies in the world, but still they always built their homes far away from the hurricane-prone coast.

By customarily building their major settlements away from the hurricane-prone coastline, the Mayan Indians practiced a method of disaster mitigation that, if rigorously applied today, would reduce the potential for devastation along coastal areas. The only Mayan port city discovered to date is the small-to-medium sized city of Tulum, on the east coast of the Yucatán Peninsula, south of Cancun. Tulum remained occupied when the Spaniards first arrived in the sixteenth century, and its citizens were more prepared for the storms than for the Spaniards. As the many visitors to these ruins can see, the ceremonial buildings and grounds of the city were so skillfully constructed that many remain today and withstand many hurricanes.

The Indians of Guatemala called the god of stormy weather 'Hunrakán'. Of course, the Indians did not observe in what period of the year these hurricanes could strike their country; they believed that the devil or the evil spirits sent them whenever they pleased. Their gods were the uncontrollable forces of nature on which their lives were wholly dependent, the sun, the stars, the rains and the storms. On the islands of the Greater Antilles-Cuba, Jamaica, Hispaniola, and Puerto Rico, the Taíno people preferred to plant root crops like yucca, potato, malanga, and yautia because of their resistance to wind and to mitigate storm damage. It didn't take the Spanish and other European colonists to the Caribbean long to realize that the root crops preferred by the Taíno Indians were well adapted to a hurricane-prone environment, a lesson that was later learned by slaves and slave-owners throughout the region.

The Taínos were generally considered to be part of the Taíno-Arawak Indians, who travelled from the Orinoco-Amazon region of South America to Venezuela and then into the Caribbean Islands of The Bahamas, Dominican Republic, Haiti, Jamaica, Puerto Rico, and as far west as Cuba. Christopher Columbus called these inhabitants of the Western Hemisphere 'Indians' because he mistakenly thought he had reached the islands on the eastern side of the Indian Ocean. The word 'Taíno' comes directly from Christopher Columbus because they were the indigenous set of people, he encountered on his first voyage to the Caribbean, and they called themselves 'Taíno', meaning 'good' or 'noble', to differentiate themselves from their fierce enemies-the Carib Indians. This name applied to all the Island Taínos, including those in the Lesser Antilles. These so-called Indians were divided into innumerable small ethnic groups, each with its own combination of linguistic, cultural, and biological traits.

Locally, the Taínos referred to themselves by the name of their location. For example, those in Puerto Rico referred to themselves as Boricua or Borinquen, which means 'people from the island of the valiant noble lords' or La tierra del altivo Seor. Their island was called Borike'n, meaning 'great land of the valiant noble lord.' The Spaniards changed it to Puerto Rico. Those occurying Jamaica referred to their island as 'Yamaye', meaning 'the land of springs'. Those occupying The Bahamas called themselves 'Lucayo' or 'Lucayans', meaning 'small islands' or 'island people.' The name "Lucayan" is an Anglicization of the Spanish Lucayos, derived in turn from the Taíno Lukku-Cairi (which the people used for themselves), also translates to "people of the islands", (the Taíno word for "island", cairi, became cayo in Spanish and "cay" in English [spelled "key" in American English]). Although the Taínos are extinct as a separate and identifiable race or culture, they are alive in the region in their vocabulary, music, and beliefs.

The Taíno Indians believed in two supreme gods, one male and the other female. They also believed that man had a soul and that after death he would go to a paradise called 'Coyaba', where the natural weather elements such as droughts and hurricanes would be forgotten in an eternity of feasting and dancing. In the Taíno Indians culture, they believed in a female zemí (spirit) named Guabancex-meaning, the "Lady of the Winds" or also known as the "one whose fury destroys everything" and the god who controlled the power of the hurricanes, among other things-but when angered, she sent out her two assistants Guataubá (an assistant who produced hurricane winds) and Coatrisquie (who caused the accompanying floodwaters) to order all of the other zemís to lend her their winds, and with this great power she made the winds and the waters move and cast houses to the ground and uprooted trees.

According to Taíno mythology, the zemí of Guabancex was entrusted to the ruler of a mystical land, Aumatex. This granted Guabancex the title of "Cacique of the Wind", but it also imposed the responsibility of repeatedly appeasing the goddess throughout this god's long reign. Furthermore, due to the importance of the wind for travel between inter or intra-island and the need for good weather imperative for a successful crop, other caciques would offer her part of their food during the Chohoba ceremony. However, given Guabancex's volatile temper, these efforts often failed. When they did, she would leave her domain enraged and with the intent of bringing destruction to all in her path, unleashing the juracánes. She began by interrupting the balance established by Boinayel and Marohu, the deities of rain and drought. By rotating her arms in a spiral, Guabancex would pick the water of the ocean and land, placing it under the command of Coatrisquie who violently forced it back over the Taíno settlements destroying their bohios and crops.

She would threaten the other deities to have them join the chaos. She was always preceded by Guataubá, who heralded her eventual arrival with clouds, lightning and thunder. The easternmost of the Greater Antilles, Puerto Rico is often in the path of the North Atlantic tropical storms and hurricanes which tend to come ashore on the east coast. The Taíno believed that upon reaching the rainforest peak of El Yunque, the goddess and her cohorts would clash with their supreme deity, Yúcahu, who was believed to live there. Guabancex has an unspecified connection to Caorao, a deity that was also associated with storms and that was said to bring them forth by playing the cobo, a musical instrument made from a marine sea shell.

The word "juracán" merely represented the storms themselves, which according to Taíno mythology were spawned and controlled by the goddess Guabancex. The Taínos were aware of the spiraling wind pattern of hurricanes, a knowledge that they used when depicting the deity. Her zemí idol was said to depict a woman, but the most common depiction of Guabancex presents a furious face with her arms extended in a spiral ("~") pattern. Representations of Guabancex portrayed her head as the eye of the storm, with twisting arms symbolizing the swirling winds. The international symbol that we use today for hurricanes was derived from this zemí. The various likenesses of this god invariably consist of a head of an indeterminate gender with no torso, two distinctive arms spiraling out from its sides. Most of these images exhibit cyclonic (counterclockwise) spirals. The Cuban ethnologist Fernando Ortiz believes that they were inspired by the tropical hurricanes that have always plagued the Caribbean. If so, the Taínos discovered the cyclonic or vortical nature of hurricanes many hundreds of years before the descendants of European settlers did. How they may have made this deduction remains a mystery to this day.

The Indian origin of the international hurricane symbol

Representation of a female zemí (spirit) named Guabancex (image to the left)-the Lady of the Winds, who controlled hurricanes, among other things-but when angered, she sent out her two assistants Guataubá (an assistant who produced hurricane winds) and Coatrisquie (who caused the accompanying floodwaters) to order all the other zemís to lend her their winds, and with this great power she made the winds and the waters move and cast houses to the ground and uprooted trees. Today, the worldwide or international symbol used for hurricanes

(image to the right) was derived from this zemí or god (Courtesy of Wikipedia). Jpeg-scan page 4—1/4 page).

The spiral rain bands so well-known to us from satellites and radars were not officially 'discovered' until the meteorological radar was developed during World War II, and they are far too big to be discerned by eye from the ground. It is speculated that these ancient people surveyed the damage done by the hurricane and based on the direction by which the trees fell, concluded that the damage could only have been done by rotating winds. Or perhaps they witnessed tornadoes or waterspouts, which are much smaller phenomena whose rotation is clear, and came to believe that all destructive winds are rotary. They also believed that sickness or misfortunes such as devastating hurricanes were the works of malignant or highly displeased zemís, and good fortune was a sign that the zemís were pleased. To keep the zemís pleased, great public festivals were held to propitiate the tribal zemís, or simply in their honour. On these occasions, everyone would be well-dressed in elaborate outfits, and the cacique would lead a parade beating a wooden drum. Gifts of the finest cassava were offered to the zemís in hopes that the zemís would protect them against the four chief scourges of the Taínos' existence: fire, sickness, the Caribs, and most importantly devastating hurricanes.

The language of the Taínos was not a written one, and written works from them are very scarce. Some documentation of their lifestyles may be found in the writings of Spanish priests, such as Bartolomé de las Casas in Puerto Rico and the Dominican Republic during the early 16th century. In addition, Friar Ramon Pane arrived with Christopher Columbus in 1493. Columbus asked Pane to gather information about the Taíno religion. This myth was passed on to the friar by Guarionex, the chief of the Magua and Otoao regions on Hispaniola.[13] Some of the Taíno origin words were borrowed by the Spanish and subsequently found their way into the English Language and are modern day reminders of this once proud and vigorous race of people. These words include: avocado, potato, buccaneer, cay, manatee, maize, savanna, guava, barbacoa (barbecue), cacique (chief), jamaca (hammock), batata ("sweet potato"), Tabacú (tobacco), caniba (cannibal), canoa (canoe), Iguana (lizard), and huracán or huruká (hurricane).

---

[13] Osvaldo Garcia-Goyco, *Tales of the Gods: How the Caribbean Sea was born*, (Puerto Rico, Xlibris Corporation, 2016). Pg. 3.

Interestingly, two of the islands in The Bahamas, Inagua and Mayaguana, both derived their names from the Lucayan word 'Iguana.' Bimini (meaning "two small islands" in English), another island in The Bahamas, also got its name from these Indians; however, most of the other islands in The Bahamas and the rest of the Caribbean were also given Indian names, but they have been changed over the many years and centuries by various groups of people who settled or passed through The Bahamas or other Caribbean islands. For example, in The Bahamas the Lucayans called the island of Exuma-Yuma, San Salvador was called Guanahani, Long Island was called Samana, Cat Island was called Guanima, Abaco was called Lucayoneque, Eleuthera was called Cigateo, Rum Cay was called Manigua and Crooked Island was called Saomere. Christopher Columbus, when he came to The Bahamas and landed on Guanahani, renamed it San Salvador, Manigua, he renamed it Santa Maria de la Concepcion, Yuma, he renamed it Fernandina, Saomete, he renamed it Isabella, and the Ragged Island chain he renamed Islas de Arenas.[14] However, for the early Spanish explorers, the islands of The Bahamas were of no particular economic value, so therefore they established only temporary settlements, mainly to transport the peaceful Indians to be used as their slaves on the islands of Hispaniola and Cuba to mine the valuable deposits of gold and silver and to dive for pearls.

Jurakán is the phonetic name given by the Spanish settlers to the god of chaos and disorder that the Taíno Indians in Puerto Rico (and also the Carib and Arawak Indians elsewhere in the Caribbean) believed controlled the weather, particularly hurricanes. From this we derive the Spanish word huracán, and eventually the English word hurricane. As the spelling and pronunciation varied across various indigenous groups, there were many alternative names along the way. For example, many West Indian historians and indigenous Indians called them by the various names, including Juracán, furacan, furican, haurachan, herycano, hurachano, hurricano, and so on. The term makes an early appearance in William Shakespeare's King Lear (Act 3, Scene 2). Being the easternmost of the Greater Antilles, Puerto Rico is often in the path of many of the North Atlantic tropical storms and hurricanes that tend to come ashore on the east coast of the island. The Taínos believed that Juracán lived at the top of a rainforest peak called El

---

[14] Peter Barratt, *Bahamas Saga-The Epic Story of the Bahama Islands*, (USA, Author House Publishers, 2004). Pg. 51.

Yunque (literally, the anvil, but truly derived from the name of the Taíno god of order and creation, Yuquiyú), from where he stirred the winds and caused the waves to smash against the shore.

In the Taíno culture, it was said that when the hurricane was upon them, these people would shut themselves up in their leaky huts and shouted while banging drums and blew shell trumpets to keep the evil spirits of the hurricane from killing them or destroying their homes and crops. Boinayel and his twin brother Márohu were the gods of rain and fair weather, respectively. Guabancex was the non-nurturing aspect of the goddess Atabey who had control over natural disasters. Juracán is often identified as the god of storms but the word simply means hurricane in the Taíno language. Guabancex had two assistants: Guataubá, a messenger who created hurricane winds, and Coatrisquie who created floodwaters. According to Taíno legend, the goddess Atabei first created the Earth, the sky, and all the celestial bodies. The metaphor of the sacred waters was included because the Taínos attributed religious and mythical qualities to water. For example, the goddess Atabei was associated with water. She was also the goddess of water. Yocahú, the supreme deity, was also associated with water. Both deities are called Bagua, which is water, the source of life. This image of water as a sacred entity was central to their beliefs. They were at the mercy of water for their farming. Without rain, they would not be able to farm their conucos.

These Indians prayed to the twin gods of rain and fair weather so that they would be pleased and prayed to these gods to keep the evil hurricane away from their farms and homes. To continue her (Atabei) work, she bore two sons, Yucaju and Guacar. Yucaju created the sun and moon to give light and then made plants and animals to populate the Earth. Seeing the beautiful fruits of Yucaju's work, Guacar became jealous and began to tear up the Earth with powerful winds, renaming himself Jurakan, the god of destruction. Yucaju then created Locuo, a being that was an intermediate between a god and a man, to live in peaceful harmony with the world. Locuo, in turn, created the first man and woman, Guaguyona and Yaya. All three continued to suffer from the powerful winds and floods inflicted by the evil god Jurakán. It was said that the god Jurakán was perpetually angry and ruled the power of the hurricane. He became known as the god of strong winds, hence the name today of hurricane. He was feared and revered, and when the hurricanes blew, the Taínos thought they had displeased Jurakán. Jurakán would later become Huracán in Spanish and Hurricane in English.

The origin of the name "Bahamas" is unclear in the history of these islands in the West Indies. Some historians believe it may have been derived from the Spanish word 'baja mar', meaning lands of the 'shallow seas', or the Lucayan Indian word for the island of Grand Bahama, ba-ha-ma meaning 'large upper middle land.'[15] The seafaring Taíno people moved into the uninhabited southeastern Bahamas from the islands of Hispaniola and Cuba sometime around 1000-800 AD. These people came to be known as the Lucayans. According to various historians, there were estimated reports of well over 20,000 to 30,000+ Lucayans living in The Bahamas at the time of world-famous Italian explorer Christopher Columbus' arrival in 1492. Christopher Columbus' first landfall in the New World was on an island called San Salvador, which is generally accepted to be present-day San Salvador (also known as Watlings Island) in the southeastern Bahamas. The Lucayans called this island Guanahaní, but Columbus renamed it San Salvador (Spanish for "Holy Savior").[16]

Unfortunately, Columbus' discovery of this island of San Salvador is a very controversial and debatable topic among historians, scientists and lay people alike. Even to this day, some of them still suggest that Columbus made his landfall in some other island in The Bahamas, such as Rum Cay, Samana Cay, Cat Island, and some even suggested he landed as far south as the Turks and Caicos Islands. However, it remains a matter of great debate and mystery within the archeological and scientific community. Regrettably, that question may never be solved, as Columbus' original logbook has been lost for centuries, and the only evidence is in the edited abstracts made by Father Bartolomé de las Casas, a 16th-century Spanish historian, social reformer and Dominican friar. He became the first resident Bishop of Chiapas, and the first officially appointed "Protector of the Indians". His extensive writings, the most famous being *A Short Account of the Destruction of the Indies* and *Historia de Las Indias*, chronicle the first decades of colonization of the West Indies and focus particularly on the atrocities committed by the colonizers against the indigenous peoples,

---

[15] Ashley Saunders, *History of Bimini Volume 2*, (Bimini-Bahamas, New World Press, 2006). Pgs. 5-9.

[16] Ashley Saunders, *History of Bimini Volume 2*, (Bimini-Bahamas, New World Press, 2006). Pgs. 4-9.

some of them Lucayan Indians brought to Hispaniola from The Bahamas, which eventually resulted in the genocide of these Indians.

Arriving as one of the first European settlers in the Americas, he initially participated in, but eventually felt compelled to oppose, the atrocities committed against the Native Americans by the Spanish colonists. When he arrived on Hispaniola in 1508, Las Casas says, "There were 60,000 people living on this island, including the Indians; so, that from 1494 to 1508, over three million people had perished from war, slavery, and the mines. Who in future generations will believe this? I myself writing it as a knowledgeable eyewitness can hardly believe it...."[17] In 1515, he reformed his views, gave up his Indian slaves and encomienda, and advocated, before King Charles V, Holy Roman Emperor, on behalf of rights for the natives. In his early writings, he advocated the use of African slaves instead of Natives in the West-Indian colonies; consequently, criticisms have been leveled at him as being partly responsible for the beginning of the transatlantic slave trade. Later in life, he retracted those early views as he came to see all forms of slavery as equally wrong.

In The Bahamas, Columbus made first contact with the Lucayans and exchanged goods with them. The Lucayans-a word that meant 'meal-eaters' in their own language, from their dependence upon cassava flour made from the bitter manioc root as their staple starch food-were sub-Taínos of The Bahamas and believed that all their islands were once part of the mainland of America but had been cut off by the howling winds and waves of the hurricanes, and they referred to these storms as huruká. The Lucayans (The Bahamas being known then as the Lucayan Islands) were sub-Taínos who lived in The Bahamas at the time of Christopher Columbus' landfall on October 12, 1492. Sometime between 1000-800 A.D., the Taínos of Hispaniola, pressured by over-population and trading concerns, migrated into the southeastern islands of The Bahamas. The Taínos of Cuba moved into the northwestern Bahamas shortly afterwards. They are widely thought to be the first Amerindians encountered by the Spanish.

The Lucayan Indians had a form of self-government where the Cacique was the leader of the village who had many wives and was responsible for the governing of the village (such as, when to plant or harvest certain crops). These Indians lived by inter-island and intra-island trade. The main or stable foods in their diets were, yam, cassava (yucca), beans, maize, and

---

[17] http://www.historyisaweapon.com/defcon1/zinncol1.html. Retrieved: 14-02-2017.

pumpkins. Bread was made from cassava and a wine called kasira was made from fermented cassava juice. A ball game called batos was also played. The Lucayans were polytheists; their male god was called Yocahu and their female goddess, Atabeyra. Their lesser gods were called Zemis.

Early historical accounts describe them as a peaceful set of people, and they referred to themselves as 'Lucayos,' 'Lukku Kairi' or 'Lukku-Cairi', meaning 'small islands' or 'island people' because they referred to themselves by the name of their location. The name "Lucayan" is an English pronunciation of the "Spanish Lucayos", derived in turn from the Taíno word Lukku-Cairi. The Taíno word for "island" was "cairi" became cayo in Spanish and "cay" in English [spelled "key"(such as, the USA's Florida Keys) in American English]. The Lucayans spoke the Ciboney dialect of the Taíno language. This assumption was made from the only piece of speech that was recorded phonetically and has been passed down to us. Las Casas informs us that the Taíno Indians of the Greater Antilles and Lucayans were unable to understand one another, 'here'(in Hispaniola), he wrote "they do not call gold 'caona' as in the main part of the island, nor 'nozay' as on the islet of Guanahani (San Salvador) but tuob."[18] This brief hint of language difference tends to reinforce the theory that the Bahamian Islands were first settled by people coming from eastern Cuba of the sub-Taíno culture.

In 1508, the King of Spain gave the inhabitants of Hispaniola permission to conduct slave raids on the islands of The Bahamas. The result was that, from 1508 to 1520 the Lucayans were captured, enslaved and made to work in the gold mines of Hispaniola and the pearl fisheries of Margarita. Before Columbus arrived in The Bahamas, there were about 20,000 to 30,000+ Lucayans living there, but because of slavery, diseases such as smallpox and yellow fever (to which they had no immunity), and other hardships brought on by the arrival of the Europeans, by 1517 they were virtually non-existent. As a matter of fact, when Spanish Conquistador Ponce de Leon (the first European to discover Florida) visited those islands in 1513 in search of the magical 'Fountain of Youth,' he found no trace of these Lucayan Indians, except for one elderly Indian woman. These Indians of the Caribbean and Central America lived in one of the most hurricane prone areas of the Earth; thus, most of them built their temples, huts,

---

[18] Peter Barratt, *Bahamas Saga-The Epic Story of the Bahama Islands*, (USA, Author House, 2006). Pg. 51.

pyramids and houses well away from the hurricane prone coastline because of the great fear and respect that they had for hurricanes.

Many early colonists in the Caribbean took solace by displaying a Cord of Saint Francis of Assisi, a short length of rope with three knots with three turns apiece, in their boats, churches and homes as a protective talisman during the hurricane season. Various legends and lore soon developed regarding Saint Francis and his connection with nature, including tropical weather and hurricanes. According to tradition, if these residents untied the first knot of the cord, winds would pick up, but only moderately. Winds of 'half a gale' resulted from untying the second knot. If all three knots were untied, winds of hurricane strength were produced. Today, some descendants of African slaves in the West Indies still tie knots in the leaves of certain trees and hang them in their homes to ward off hurricanes.

Similar accounts also emerged from encounters with the Carib Indians. In old historical accounts, these Indians were referred to by various names, such as, 'Caribs,' 'Charaibes,' 'Charibees' and 'Caribbees', and they were a mysterious set of people who migrated from the Amazon jungles of South America.[19] They were a tribe of warlike and cannibalistic Indians who migrated northwards into the Caribbean in their canoes, overcoming and dominating an earlier race of peaceful people called the Taínos. While Columbus explored all parts of the West Indies, his successors colonized only those parts inhabited by the Taíno Indians, avoiding the Carib inhabited islands because they lacked gold, but most importantly because the Carib Indians were too difficult to subjugate. Ironically, the region became known as the Caribbean, named after these fierce Indians.

Their practice of eating their enemies so captured the imagination of the Europeans that the Caribbean Sea was also named after these Indians. The term the Caribbean Sea started with both the Carib Indians and Taínos Indians gods who saw the waters of the Caribbean Seas filled avast array of edible multi-coloured fish. The Spanish explorers picked up on the name and expanded it in our modern-day vocabulary based on the Carib Indians eating human flesh. The English word 'cannibal' is derived from the term 'Caniba', used by the Taínos and Carib Indians gods to refer to the Caribs eating the flesh of their enemies. Their raids were made over long distances in large canoes and had as one of their main objectives to take the Taíno

---

[19] Ashley Saunders, *History of Bimini Volume 2*, (Bimini-Bahamas, New World Press, 2006). Pg. 14.

women as their captives, wives and slaves. While on the other hand, the captured Taíno men were tortured and killed and then barbecued and eaten during an elaborate ceremony because it was believed that if they did this, they would obtain their enemies' personal power and control their spirits.

The French traveller Charles de Rochefort wrote that when these Caribs Indians heard the thunder clap, they would "make all the haste they can to their little houses and sit down on low stools about the fire, covering their faces and resting their heads on their hands and knees, and in that posture they fall a weeping and say...Maboya is very angry with them: and they say the same when there happens a Hurricane."[20] In fact, the early French comments about hurricanes often noted that the information about them had been acquired from the Carib Indians of the Caribbean. In the seventeenth-century works of Catholic Fathers Du Tertre and Labat and probably-Huguenot Rochefort, the hurricanes appeared as a feature of life in the islands and a sign of God's power and justice, but all of these authors also expressed a curiosity about the specific nature and natural causes of the storms. Labat, for instance, stated that the calm before the storm, the cloud formations, the erratic movement of birds, and the rising sea-level as signs of a storm's approach, and noted from his personal experience on Guadeloupe the damage that a hurricane could cause.[21]

The Caribs were terrified of spilling freshwater into the sea because they believed that it aroused the anger of hurricanes. They had no small stone gods but believed in good and powerful bad spirits called 'Maboya', which caused all the misfortunes of their lives. They even wore carved amulets and employed medicine men to drive the evil Maboya away. When a great and powerful storm began to rise out of the sea, the Caribs blew frantically into the air to chase it away and chewed manioc bread and spat it into the wind for the same purpose. When that was no use, they gave way to panic and crouched in their communal houses, moaning with their arms held over their heads. They felt that they were reasonably safe there because they fortified their houses with corner posts dug deep into the ground. They also believed that beyond the Maboya were great spirits, the male sun and the female moon. They believed that the spirits of the stars controlled the weather. They also believed in a bird named Savacou, which

---

[20] Matthew Mulcahy, *Hurricanes and Society in the British Greater Caribbean, 1624-1783*, (Baltimore, The John Hopkins University Press, 2006). Pg. 35.

[21] Labat, *Nouveau voyage aux Isles de l'Amerique*, pgs. 165-66.

was sent out by the angry Maboya to call up the hurricane, and after this task was finished, this bird would then be transformed into a star.

The power and danger of hurricanes was no less important to the Caribs. They also recognized the destructive nature of hurricanes and believed the evil spirits or Maboya caused them. They, like every other Indian group, feared hurricanes but recognized their seasonal nature and integrated them into the rhythm of their year, and especially into their cycle of vengeance and war against their archenemies, the Taínos. Each year when the constellation of Ursa Minor, also known as the 'Little Dipper,' appeared in the Caribbean sky following the summer solstice, it signaled to the Caribs the approach of their raiding season. They called this constellation, "the canoe of the heron," and its reoccurrence each year around the middle of June signaled the opening of the hurricane season when, following the stormy months of July, August, and early September (the peak of the present-day hurricane season), their own canoes were launched. The Carib raids against the Taínos for women, food, and captives, and later against the Europeans, were carried out principally from late September to December after the passage of the peak of the hurricane season. These patterns continued for almost a century after the Europeans arrival in the Caribbean. Caribs raids against Puerto Rico lasted until the early seventeenth century despite Spanish counterattacks against the Caribs' home islands of Dominica and Guadeloupe.

Noted English historian John Oldmixon of the late 1600s and early 1700s, reported that the Carib Indians excelled in forecasting hurricanes. Writing about a hurricane that occurred in 1740 on the island of St. Christopher he said: "Hurricanes are still frequent here, and it was some time since the custom of both the English and French inhabitants in this and the other Charibbees-Islands, to send about the month of June, to the native Charibbees of Dominica and St. Vincent, to know whether there would be any hurricanes that year; and about 10 or 12 Days before the hurricane came they constantly sent them word, and it was rarely failed."[22]

According to Carib Indians, 'Signs or Prognosticks,' a hurricane comes "on the day of the full change, or quarters of the moon. If it will come on the full moon, you being in the change, then observe these signs. That day you will see the skies very turbulent, the sun redder than at other times, a great calm, and the hills clear of clouds or fogs over them, which in the high

---

[22] *The Writings of English Historian John Oldmixon-The British Empire in America*, 2nd ed. (London, Cambridge University Press. 1741). Retrieved: 12-10-2015.

lands are seldom so. In the hollows of the Earth or wells, there will be great noise, as if you were in a great storm; the stars at night will look very big with Burs about them, the north-west sky smelling stronger than at other times, as it usually does in violent storms; and sometimes that day for an hour or two, the winds blow very hard westerly, out of its usual course. On the full moon, you have the same signs, but a great Bur about the moon, and many about the moon, and many about the sun. The like signs must be taken notice of on the quarter-days of the moon."[23]

In fact, several elderly Carib Indians of the Caribbean stated that hurricanes had become more frequent in the recent years following the arrival of the Europeans to the Caribbean, which they viewed as punishment for their interactions with them. As early as the 1630s, English colonists reported that Carib Indians knew when storms would strike by the number of rings that appeared around the moon: three rings meant the storm would arrive in three days, two rings meant two days and one ring meant the storm would arrive in one day. Of course, the connection between such signs and the onset of hurricanes was indeed a very unreliable way to predict the onset of hurricanes. The Carib Indians, while raiding islands in the Caribbean, would kill off the Taíno men and take the Taíno women as wives and mothers to their children. When the Europeans came to the Caribbean, they surprisingly found that many Carib women spoke the Taíno language because of the large number of female Taíno captives among them. So, it is speculated that a word like 'hurricane' was passed into the Carib speech and this was how these fierce people learned about the terror of these savage storms. Native Indians of the West Indies often engaged in ritual purifications and sacrifices and offered songs and dances to help ward off hurricanes.

Some European observers sought to record the signs the Indians used. The Spanish Augustinian Father Iñigo Abbad y Lasierra, in his 1788 account of Puerto Rico, noted that the Indians had read certain signs as a premonition of a hurricane's approach, such as a red sun at sunrise and sunset, a strong odor from the sea, the sudden change of the wind from east to west. However, not every European observer was convinced of the Indians' abilities at prediction. Father Jean Baptiste du Tertre, a Jesuit priest

---

[23] *An Early Colonial Historian: John Oldmixon and the British Empire in America-Journal of American Studies Vol.3 (August 1973),* (London, Cambridge University Press, 1741). Pgs. 113-123.

who wrote from experience in the French islands in the mid-seventeenth century, noted that many settlers believed that the Indians could predict the arrival of hurricanes. They speculated that since the storms came in the same period each year, it was natural for them to conclude that sometimes their predictions were correct, even though they had no special knowledge or ability to truly predict these storms.

By the mid-seventeenth century, the reading of the 'natural signs' was no longer a skill exclusively reserved to the indigenous Indians population of the islands or to the mariners. It had become a region wide knowledge, a necessary skill practiced by all. Generally, as time progressed, colonist observations and mariners' experiences were joined with the clues learned from the indigenous peoples and developed into a kind of local wisdom on each island of the signs to look for in the arrival of a hurricane. Indians had observed the behavior of certain birds and fish, and the colonists learned from them. Father Jean-Baptiste Labat, a French Dominican, in his description of the French islands in the seventeenth century, noted that on approach of a hurricane, the birds instinctually exhibited certain uneasiness and flew away from the coast for shelter inland or to another location in the Caribbean until the storm had passed. Furthermore, other signs and behavior were also observed with the crickets, cicadas, toads and frogs, as they all disappeared before the passage of a hurricane.

An Aztec myth tells that when the gods created the world, it was dark and cold. The youngest of the gods sacrificed himself to create a sun. But it was like him, weak, dim and feeble. Only when more powerful gods offered themselves did the sun blaze into life and shine brightly on them. However, there was one disadvantage, and that was that these gods needed constant fuel, human lives, and the Aztecs obliged. They offered tens of thousands of humans' sacrifices a year just to make sure that the sun rose each morning and to prevent natural disasters such as devastating hurricanes from destroying their communities and villages. Tlaloc was an important deity in Aztec religion, a god of rain, fertility, and water. He was a beneficent god who gave life and sustenance, but he was also feared for his ability to send hurricanes, hail, thunder and lightning and for being the lord of the powerful element of water. In Aztec iconography, he is usually depicted with goggle eyes and fangs. He was associated with caves, springs and mountains. He is known for having demanded child sacrifices.

Tezcatlipoca the Aztec god had a Smoking Mirror. He was the god of the nocturnal sky, god of the ancestral memory, god of time and the

Lord of the North, the embodiment of change through conflict. Together with his eternal opposite Quetzalcoatl, he created the world. Tezcatlipoca ([teskatɬi'po:ka]) was a central deity in Aztec mythology. He was associated with many concepts. Some of these are the night sky, the night winds, hurricanes, the north, the earth, obsidian, enmity, discord, rulership, divination, temptation, sorcery, beauty, war and strife. Tezcatlipoca ("smoking mirror") represents conflict and change in Aztec mythology. As his name suggests, he is often portrayed with a smoking obsidian mirror at the back of his head and with another replacing one of his feet. Tezcatlipoca is the offspring of the creator couple, who produced four sons: Red Tezcatlipoca, Black Tezcatlipoca, Qeutzalcoatl, and Huitzilopochtli (the patron god of the Aztecs). It is the black Tezcatlipoca that most Aztec myths refer to. He is sometimes the adversary of the god Quetzalcoatl and sometimes the ally. Originally the personification of the air, the source both breath of life and of the hurricane, Tezcatlipoca possessed all the attributes of a god who presided over these phenomena. Tezcatlipoca naturally advanced so speedily in popularity and public honour that it was little wonder that within a comparatively short space of time he came to be regarded as a god of fate, nature and fortune, and as inseparably connected with the national destinies.

The Aztec god Tezcatlipoca (meaning 'Lord of the Hurricane') was believed to have special powers over the hurricane winds, as did the Palenque god Tahil (Obsidian Mirror) and the Quiché Maya sky god Huracán. The Aztec god Tezcatlipoca was feared for his capricious nature, and the Aztecs called him Yaotl (meaning 'Adversary'). Tonatiuh was the Aztec Sun god, and the Aztecs saw the sun as a divinity that controlled the weather, including hurricanes and consequently, all human life forms. The Aztecs of Mexico built vast temples to the sun god Tonatiuh and made bloody sacrifices of both human and animal to persuade him to shine brightly on them and not send any destructive hurricanes their way and to allow for prosperity of their crops. When they built these temples, they were constructed in accordance with the Earth's alignment with the sun, but most importantly they were always constructed with hurricanes in mind and away from the hurricane-prone coastline. The other gods were worshipped for some special purpose, but the worship of Tezcatlipoca was regarded as compulsory, and to some extent as a safeguard against the destruction of the universe, devastating hurricanes, a calamity the Nahua

(The Nahuas are a group of indigenous people of Mexico and El Salvador) had been led to believe might occur through his agency.

The Aztec people considered Tonatiuh the leader of Tollán, their heaven. He was also known as the fifth sun because the Aztecs believed that he was the sun that took over when the fourth sun was expelled from the sky. Mesoamerican creation narratives proposed that before the current world age began, there were several previous creations. The Aztecs' account of the five suns or world ages revealed that in each of the five creations, the Earth's inhabitants found a more satisfactory staple food than eaten by their predecessors. In the era of the first sun, which was governed by Black Tezcatlipoca, the world was inhabited by a race of giants who lived on acorns. The second sun, whose presiding god was a serpent god called Quetzatzalcóatl, was believed to be the creator of life and in control of the vital rain-bearing winds, and he saw the emergence of a race of primitive humans who lived on the seeds of the mesquite tree.

After the third age, which was ruled by Tláloc, in which people lived on plants that grew on water, such as the water lily, people returned to a diet of wild seeds in the fourth age of Chalchiúhtlicue. It was only in the fifth and current age, an age subject to the sun god Tonatiuh that the people of Mesoamerica learned how to plant and harvest maize. According to their cosmology, each sun was a god with its own cosmic era. The Aztecs believed they were still in Tonatiuh's era, and according to their creation mythology, this god demanded human sacrifices as a tribute, and without it he would refuse to move through the sky, hold back on the rainfall for their crops and would send destructive hurricanes their way. It is said that some 20,000 people were sacrificed each year to Tonatiuh and other gods, though this number, however, is thought to be highly inflated either by the Aztecs, who wanted to inspire fear in their enemies, or the Spaniards, who wanted to speak ill of the Aztecs. The Aztecs were fascinated by the sun, so they worshiped and carefully observed it and had a solar calendar second only in accuracy to the Mayans.

It was Captain Fernando de Oviedo who gave these storms their modern name when he wrote, "So when the devil wishes to terrify them, he promises them the 'Huracan,' which means tempest."[24] The Portuguese word for them is Huracao, which is believed to have originated from the

---

[24] http://hrsbstaff.ednet.ns.ca/primetl/school/juan/hurricanesheets.html. Retrieved: 16-5-2015.

original Taíno word Huracán. The Native American Indians had a word for these powerful storms, which they called 'Hurucane', meaning 'evil spirit of the wind.'

When a hurricane approached the Florida coast, the medicine men of the North American Indians worked frantic incantations to drive the evil hurricane away. There's a folklore that the Seminole Indians can mystically sense a storm or hurricane well ahead of time by watching the sawgrass bloom. These Indians of Florida were the first to flee from a storm, citing the blooming of the Florida Everglades sawgrass. They believed that only 'an atmospheric condition' such as a major hurricane would cause the pollen to bloom on the sawgrass several days before a hurricane's arrival, giving the native Indians an advanced warning of the impending storm. Black educator Mary McLeod Bethune repeated a story that these Indians were seen leaving several days before the storm, saying, "Follow Indian, Indian no fool, going to dry land, big water coming." One must wonder if the Seminoles, like other Indians of the region, had a 'sixth sense' when it came to hurricanes.

Many other sub-culture Indians had similar words for these powerful storms, which they all feared and respected greatly. The Quiche people of southern Guatemala believed in the god Huraken, for their god of thunder and lightning. For example, the Galibi Indians of Dutch and French Guiana called these hurricanes Yuracan and Hyroacan, or simply the devil. Other Guiana Indians called them Yarukka, and other similar Indian names were Hyrorokan, Aracan, Urican, Huiranvucan, Yurakon, Yuruk or Yoroko. As hurricanes were becoming more frequent in the Caribbean, many of the colonists and natives of this region had various words and spellings, all sounding phonetically similar for these powerful storms. The English called them 'Hurricanes', 'Haurachana', 'Uracan', 'Herocano', 'Harrycane', 'Tempest', and 'Hyrracano.' The Spanish called them 'Huracán'and 'Furicane', and the Portuguese called them 'Huracao', and 'Furicane.' The French had for a long time adapted the Indian word called 'Ouragan', and the Dutch referred to them as 'Orkan.' The Italians called them 'Uragano', the Polish, 'Huraghan', the Hungian, 'Orká', and the Turkish, 'Hurrikan'. These various spellings were used until the word 'hurricane' was finally settled on in the English Language. Among the Caribbean, Central and North American peoples, the word 'hurricane' seems to have always been associated with evil spirits, destruction, and violence.

After his First Voyage to the New World, Columbus returned to Isabella in Hispaniola with seventeen ships, and Columbus's settlers built houses, storerooms, a Roman Catholic church, and a large house for Columbus. He brought more than a thousand men, including sailors, soldiers, carpenters, stonemasons, and other workers. Priests and nobles came as well. The Spaniards brought pigs, horses, wheat, sugarcane, and guns. Rats and microbes came with them as well. The settlement took up more than two hectares. At the time, some estimated the Taíno Indian population in Hispaniola to be as high as one million persons. They lived on fish and staples such as pineapple, which they introduced to the Spaniards. The food that they provided was important to the Spaniards. Describing these Indians, Columbus said that there were no finer people in the world. In March 1494, Columbus' men began to search, with Taíno Indians, in the mountains of Hispaniola for gold, and small amounts were found. In June 1495, a large storm that the Taíno Indians called a hurican hit the island. The Indians retreated to the mountains, while the Spaniards remained in the colony. Several ships were sunk, including the flagship, the *'Marie-Galante.'*

Christopher Columbus, on his first voyage, managed to avoid encountering any hurricanes, but it wasn't until some of his later voyages that he encountered several hurricanes that disrupted these voyages to the New World. Based on his first voyage before encountering any hurricanes, Columbus concluded that the weather in the New World was benign: "In all the Indies, I have always found May-like weather," he commented. Although sailing through hurricane-prone waters during the most dangerous months, he did not have any serious hurricane encounters on his early voyage. However, on his final voyages, Christopher Columbus himself weathered at least three of these dangerous storms. The town of La Isabella was struck by two of the earliest North Atlantic hurricanes observed by Europeans in 1494 and 1495. Columbus provided the earliest account of a hurricane in a letter written to Queen Isabella in 1494. In this letter, he wrote, "The tempest arose and worried me so that I knew not where to turn; Eyes never behold the seas so high, angry and covered by foam. We were forced to keep out in this bloody ocean, seething like a pot of hot fire. Never did the sky look more terrible; for one whole day and night it blazed like a furnace. The flashes came with such fury and frightfulness that we all thought the ships would be blasted. All this time the water never ceased to fall from the sky…The people were so worn out, that they longed for death to end their terrible suffering."[25]

The extensive shallow banks and coral reefs near most Caribbean islands present hazards to navigation that were immediately appreciated by the Spanish explorers. These dangers were compounded by violent tropical storms and hurricanes that appeared without enough warning and by the unseaworthy character of vessels that had spent months cruising in shipworm-infested waters. Despite the explorers' exercising what must have seemed like due caution, there is an extensive list of shipwrecks. Columbus himself lost nine ships: *Santa María*, which was wrecked near Haiti on Christmas Eve on his first voyage; *Niña* and three other vessels at La Isabella in 1495; and the entire fleet of his fourth voyage-*Vizcaina* and *Gallega* off the coast of Central America in 1503, and *Capitana* and *Santiago* in Puerto Santa Gloria, Jamaica, 1504. However, as early as June of 1494, the small town of Isabella, founded by Columbus on Hispaniola, became the first European settlement destroyed by a hurricane. The Spaniards who accompanied Columbus on his four voyages to the New World took back to Europe with them a new concept of what a severe storm could be, and naturally, a new word of Indian origin. It seems that the Indian word was pronounced 'Furacán' or 'Furacánes' during the early years of discovery and colonization of America. Peter Martyr, one of the earliest historians of the New World, said that they were called by the natives 'Furacanes,' although the plural is obviously Spanish. The Rev. P. du Tertre, (1667) in his great work during the middle of the seventeenth century, wrote first 'ouragan', and later 'houragan.'

After 1474, some changes in the Spanish language were made. For instance, words beginning with 'h' were pronounced using the 'f consonant.' The kingdoms of Aragon and Castile were united in 1474, before the discovery of America, and after that time some changes in the Spanish language were made. One of them involved words beginning with the letter 'h.' In Aragon; they pronounced such words as 'f'. As Menéndez Pidal said, "Aragon was the land of the 'f', but the old Castilian lost the sound or pronunciation," so that Spanish Scholar Nebrija (Nebrija wrote a grammar of the Castilian language and is credited as the first published grammar of any Romance language) wrote, instead of the lost 'f', an aspirated 'h.' Menéndez wrote concerning the pronunciation of the word

---

[25] http://www.fascinatingearth.com/node/311. Retrieved: 10-11-2009.

'hurricane' and its language used by Fernando Colón, son of Christopher Columbus, "Vacillation between 'f' and 'h' is very marked predominance of the 'h.' And so, the 'h' became in Spanish a silent letter, as it still is today."

Father Bartolomé de las Casas, referring to one of these storms, wrote: "At this time the four vessels brought by Juan Aguado were destroyed in the port (of Isabella) by a great tempest, called by the Indians in their language 'Furacán.' Now we call them hurricanes, something that almost all of us have experienced at sea or on land..." Las Casas, outraged by the brutal treatment of the Indians on Hispaniola, declared that the wrath of the hurricane that struck Hispaniola was the judgment of God on the city and the men who had committed such sins against humanity. All other European languages coined a word for the tropical cyclone, based on the Spanish 'Huracán.' Gonzalo Fernandez de Oviedo (Oviedo y Valdes, 1851, Book VI, Ch. III) is more explicit in his writings concerning the origin of the word 'hurricane.' He says: "Hurricane, in the language of this island, properly means an excessively severe storm or tempest; because, in fact, it is only a very great wind and a very great and excessive rainfall, both together or either these two things by themselves." Oviedo further noted that the winds of the 'Huracán' were so "fierce that they toppled houses and uproot many large trees."[26]

Even in the English language, the word 'hurricane' evolved through several variations. For example, William Shakespeare mentioned it in his play 'King Lear', where he wrote "Blow, winds, and crack your cheeks! Rage! Blow! You catracts and hurricanes, spout till you have drench'd out steeples, drown'd the cocks!" Girolamo Benzoni, in 1565 in his Book History of the New World, mentioned his encounter with a hurricane in Hispaniola, which at the time he referred to as 'Furacanum.' "In those days, a wondrous and terrible disaster occurred in this country. At sunrise, such a horrible, strong wind began that the inhabitants of the island thought they had never seen or heard anything like it before. The raging storm wind (which the Spaniards called Furacanum) came with great violence, as if it wanted to split heaven and Earth apart from one another, and hurl everything to the ground.

---

[26] Jose Millas, *Hurricanes of The Caribbean and Adjacent Regions 1492-1800*, (Edward Brothers Inc/Academy of Arts and Sciences of the Americas Miami, Florida, 1968). Pg. xi.

The people were so despairing because of their great fear that they run here and there, as if they were senseless and mad, and did not know what they did…The strong and frightful wind threw some entire houses and capitals including the people from the capital, tore them apart in the air and threw them down to the ground in pieces. This awful weather did such noticeable damage in such a short time that not three ships stood secure in the sea Harbour or came through the storm undamaged. For the anchors, even if they were yet strong, were broken apart through the strong force of the winds and all the masts, despite they are being new, were crumpled. The ships were blown around by the wind, so that all the people in them were drowned. For the most part the Indians had crawled away and hidden themselves in holes to escape such disaster."[27]

As stated earlier, Christopher Columbus did not learn on his first voyage, the voyage of discovery, of the existence of such terrible 'tempests' or 'storms.' He had the exceptional good fortune of not being struck by any of them during this voyage. The Indians, while enjoying pleasant weather, had no reason to speak about these storms to a group of strangers who spoke a language that they could not understand. Naturally, Columbus did not say one word about these awful storms in his much-celebrated letter *"The letter of Columbus on the Discovery of America."* However, on his second voyage things were quite different.

After arriving on November 3, 1493, at an island in the Lesser Antilles that he named Dominica, Columbus sailed northward and later westward, to Isabella Hispaniola, the first city in the New World, at the end of January 1494. Then in June of that year, 1494, Isabella was struck by a hurricane, the first time that European men had seen such a terrible storm. A "violent hurricane" struck Hispaniola near Isabella from southwest. It was the first hurricane in the North Atlantic basin observed and reported by Europeans. This storm occurred during Christopher Columbus's second voyage to Hispaniola. A Spanish fleet arrived to Saona on the day before September's eclipse on September 14 and the storm occurred shortly thereafter. Surely, for the first time they heard the Taíno Indians, very much excited, extending their arms raised upward into the air and shouting, "Furacán! Furacán!" when the storm commenced. We can indeed say that it was that moment in history when the word 'hurricane' suddenly appeared to the Europeans. Columbus was not at that time in Isabella because he was sailing near

---

[27] G. Benzon, *History of the New World Vol. 21*, (Hakluyt Society, 1837)

the Isle of Pines, Cuba. So, his companions of the ships *Marigalante* and *Gallega* were the first white men to hear these words, which were of Indian origin and about a phenomenon of the New World. Knowledge of 'Furacanes,' both the word and the terrifying storms it described, remained limited to Spanish speakers until 1555, when Richard Eden translated Columbus' ship report and other Spanish accounts of the New World, making it the first time it appeared in the English vocabulary.

As the hurricane passed on June 30, 1502, heavy rains and wind caused much of Columbus' fleet to break anchor and all but the boat he captained were pulled out to sea. Despite these events, however, all Columbus' ships survived and sustained only moderate damage. Orvando's fleet, on the other hand, did not fare as well. Shortly after his ships departed Hispanolia, the hurricane arrived. Twenty-five of de Orvando's ships sank, 4 turned back to Hispaniola, and only 1 ship made it to Spain. Approximately 500 of Orvando's men lost their lives during the hurricane.

Columbus was banned from Hispaniola after his Third Voyage to the island in 1498. In 1492, Columbus had been given orders to expand a Spanish colony in Hispaniola. During his first voyage to the island nation, he marked the Spanish colony by building a fort the western side of the island. In 1493, during his second voyage, Columbus arrived in Hispaniola only to find the colony in ruins. Columbus then rebuilt and refortified the settlement. In 1498, the explorer returned to Hispaniola only to find the colony again in chaos. As Columbus tried to reorganize the colony, Francisco de Bobadilla, a knight of Calatrava, Spain's oldest chivalric order, arrived in Hispaniola. At this time, the colonists of Hispaniola had grown tired of Columbus and de Bobadilla recognized this. They contacted the King and Queen of Spain and they had Columbus brought back to Spain in chains, banning the explorer from going back to Hispaniola.

The only ship of de Orvando's to make it through the hurricane and reach Spain was the *Aguja*. Interestingly, this ship was only carrying Columbus's gold. The King and Queen of Spain allowed Columbus, in a post arrest settlement, to appoint an accountant to tally his gold during his final voyage. Columbus chose Alonso Sanchez de Carvajal who was an accountant as well as a sea captain. Orvando had thought that the *Aguja* was the most pitiful and fragile ship in the fleet, so he assigned Carvajal and the gold of Columbus to it. This plan backfired on de Orvando, as already noted, the *Aguja* was the only ship of de Orvando's fleet to survive the hurricane.

In October of 1495, probably in the second half of the month, another hurricane struck Isabella, which was much stronger than the first. It finally gave Columbus, who was there at the time, the opportunity of knowing what a hurricane was and of its destructive abilities. It also gave him the opportunity of hearing the Indians shouting the same word with fear and anxiety on their faces, on the account of these terrible storms of the tropics, which they believed were caused by evil spirits. Christopher Columbus would later declare that "nothing but the service of God and the extension of the monarchy would induce him to expose himself to such danger from these storms ever again."[28] The *Niña* was the only vessel that was the smallest, oldest and the most fragile at the time, but amazingly it withstood that hurricane. The other two ships of Columbus, *The San Juan* and *The Cordera* were in the harbour and were lost or badly damaged by this hurricane. Columbus gave orders to have one repaired and another ship known as *India* constructed out of the wreck of the ones that had been destroyed, making it the first ship to be built in the Caribbean by Europeans.

In 1502, a rapidly moving hurricane with a small diameter probably came from vicinity of Grenada, moving northwesterly through the Mona Passage. On the fourth of the voyages of Christopher Columbus, he predicted the storm and took refuge in a natural harbour on the Dominican Republic. Meanwhile, his rivals refused to heed his warning and sent a convoy of 31 treasure ships toward Spain. According to Bartolomé de las Casas, "twenty ships perished with the storm, without any man, small or great, escaping, and neither dead nor alive could be found." Those drowned included Francisco de Bobadilla and Francisco Roldán. It was the first great maritime disaster in the New World. The only ship that reached Spain held money and belongings of Christopher Columbus, who survived the storm with Rodrigo de Bastidas. The center likely crossed Hispaniola about 40 miles east of the city of Santo Domingo, which it "smashed flat." The death toll likely exceeded 500.[29]

During Columbus' term as Viceroy and Governor of the Indies, he had been accused of governing tyrannically, and ironically was called 'the tyrant of the Caribbean.' By this time in the Caribbean, Columbus

---

[28] Ivan Ray Tannehill, *Hurricanes-Their Nature and History*, (USA, Princeton University Press, 1950). Pg. 141.

[29] Patrick Hughes, *"Hurricanes Haunt Our History"*, (1987, Weatherwise, 40 (3):) Pgs. 134–140, doi:10.1080/00431672.1987.9933354.

was physically and mentally exhausted by being on the seas for such a long time had taken its toll on his body, as it was plagued with arthritis and his eyes by ophthalmia. In October 1499, he sent two ships to Spain, asking the Cortes Generales of Castile to appoint a royal commissioner to help him govern. The Cortes appointed Francisco de Bobadilla, a member of the Order of Calatrava; however, they gaved him more power than Columbus had bargained for and Bobadilla's authority stretched far beyond what Columbus had requested. Bobadilla was given complete control as governor from 1500 until he was killed in a hurricane in 1502.

Arriving in Santo Domingo while Columbus was away, Bobadilla immediately received vast amount of serious legitimate complaints about all three Columbus brothers: Christopher, Bartolomé, and Diego. Upon his arrival in the colony of Santo Domingo on Hispaniola in August 1500, de Bobadilla upheld accusations of mismanagement made against Columbus, and had Columbus sent back to Spain in chains. As a member of the Order of Calatrava, in 1499, de Bobadilla was appointed to succeed Christopher Columbus as the second Governor of the Indies, Spain's new territories in America, by King Ferdinand and Queen Isabella. He died on July 11, 1502 during a hurricane that wrecked 20 vessels of the 31-ship convoy, including the flagship, *El Dorado*, in the Mona Passage returning to Spain. Among the surviving ships was the *Aguja*, the weakest ship of the convoy and which carried the gold Columbus was owed—spurring accusations that Columbus magically invoked the storm out of vengeance.

The testimonies of 23 people who had seen or heard about the cruel treatment dished out by Columbus and his brothers—had originally been lost for centuries but were rediscovered in 2005 in the Spanish National Archives in Valladolid. It contained a very vivid account of Columbus's seven-year reign as the first Governor of the West Indies. Consuelo Varela, a Spanish historian, stated that, even those who loved, respected and admired him (Columbus) had to admit the atrocities that had taken place under his reign. As a result of these testimonies and without being allowed a word in his own defense, Columbus upon his return, had manacles placed on his wrists and chains placed on his ankles and were cast into prison to await return to Spain. At the time of his arrest, he was 49 years old. Bobadilla also pardoned Francisco Roldán, who had revolted against the rule of Columbus's brother Bartholomew Columbus. During his short term as governor, he canceled mining taxes in a successful attempt to stimulate gold production. But this action may have offended the Spanish Crown and possibly lead to his recall to Spain. In 1502, he was replaced as Governor of the West Indies by Nicolás de Ovando y Cáceres.

Columbus had observed that the Governor was preparing a large fleet of ships to set sail for Spain, carrying large quantities of gold and slaves, and warned him to delay the trip until the hurricane had passed. Refusing both the request and the advice, Orvando read Columbus' note out loud to the crew and residents, who roared with laughter at Columbus' advice. Unfortunately, the laughter was very short-lived, and Orvando's ships left port only to their own demise when 21 of the 30 ships were lost in a hurricane between Hispaniola and Puerto Rico. An additional four of them were badly damaged, but fortunately they could return to port, where they, too, eventually sunk. Only one ship, the *Aguja*, made it to Spain, and that one, no doubt to Orvando's intense distress, was carrying what little remained of Columbus' own gold.

Meanwhile, Columbus, anticipating strong winds from the north from this hurricane, positioned his fleet in a harbour on the south side of Hispaniola. On June 13, the storm hit with ferocious northeast winds. Even with the protection of the mountainous terrain to the windward side, the fleet struggled. In Columbus' own words, "The storm was so terrible and on that night the ships were parted from me. Each one of them was reduced to an extremity, expecting nothing save death; each one of them was certain the others were lost."[30] The anchors held only on Columbus' ship; the others were dragged out to sea, where their crews fought for their lives. Nevertheless, the fleet survived with only minimal damage. Almost 18 months later, Columbus returned to Santo Domingo, only to discover that it had been largely destroyed by the hurricane.

When the Europeans first attempted to create settlements in the Caribbean and the Americas, they quickly learned about these storms. As time passed and these settlers learned more about their new homeland, they experienced these storms on such a regular basis that they became accustomed to them. Eventually, they began calling them equinoctial storms, as the storms would normally hit in the weeks around the period of the fall equinox, which in the northern hemisphere occurs in late September.

---

[30] National Geographic Magazine, *A Columbus Casebook-A Supplement to "Where Columbus Found the New World."* November 1986.

By the 1590s, about a hundred ships a year were sailing from Havana for Seville, most of them leaving in July and August before the height of the hurricane season. The storms usually came in the late summer just as the harvest of sugar and several other crops had ended. Thus, there was always a danger of substantial losses after a year of investment and labour. The felling of maize fields was always a risk. Root crops like yucca and potatoes had better resistance to the wind and water, but too much moisture rotted them in the ground as well. Not only were current crops, but the seeds for the next years were also vulnerable.

In 1546, the judge Alonso López de Cerrato wrote from Santo Domingo that the island had never been so prosperous when it was struck by three hurricanes which decimated the island which left no trees, sugarcane, maize, yucca, or shacks (bohíos) standing. Similar conditions occurred in Cuba, when a powerful hurricane in 1692 struck western Cuba and destroyed all the seed and plantings of plantains, yucca, and maize on which they had to rely on to feed themselves. The problems with these storms were more exacerbated on the smaller islands of the Caribbean when a hurricane struck them, because real starvation would set in, especially when an overconcentration on export or cash crops had already placed foodstuffs in short supply, even under normal circumstances. Portable water sources were often fouled by brackish water from the storm, and food became a major problem. In the first days after a hurricane, there were plantains, guanabana, and other edible fruits that had fallen to the ground, but these soon were consumed or rotted, and then hunger would set in.

English explorers and privateers soon contributed their own accounts of encounters with these storms. In 1513, Juan Ponce de León completed the first recorded cruise along the Florida coast and came ashore near present-day St. Augustine to claim Florida for Spain. Famous for his unsuccessful search for the magical 'Fountain of Youth,' he might have discovered Florida earlier had it not been for the ravages of hurricanes. In August of 1508, he was struck by two hurricanes within two weeks. The first drove his ship onto the rocks near the Port of Yuna, Hispaniola, and the second left his ship aground on the southwest coast of Puerto Rico.

Soon after Hernando Cortés found treasures of gold and silver in the newly discovered lands of the West, expeditions to retrieve the riches of the New World for Spain began in earnest. In 1525, Cortés lost the first ship he sent to Mexico in a severe hurricane, along with its crew of over seventy persons. Famous English explorer Sir John Hawkins wrote his own encounters with these storms. Sir John Hawkins wrote that he left Cartagena in late July 1568 "Hoping to have escaped the time of their stormes...which they call Furicanos."[31] Hawkins did not leave soon enough, and he and his ships were bashed by an "extreme storme", as he referred to it, lasting several days.

Failure to leave Havana on time was, as one commander put it in 1630, was to "tempt God," by placing the treasure-laden fleets at risk to losses from these hurricanes. However, the very regularity and predictability of these weather systems also made the fleets vulnerable to corsairs (sometimes referred to as 'buccaneers') and foreign rivals, who would simply just lay in wait off the Florida Keys or The Bahamas in the natural deep-water channels, knowing and strategically waiting until the silver-laden fleet would appear and simply attack them at this vulnerable time. Losses to corsairs or rivals were usually of individual ships, whereas the destruction caused by hurricanes at sea were more generalized, but together these maritime risks sometimes produced disastrous results not only for ships and men, but for Spanish policy as well. In 1624 three more galleons were lost, along with over a million pesos belonging to private individuals and about another half million belonging to the Royal Treasury. The New Spain fleet left Veracruz too late in 1631 and was caught by a hurricane, losing its flagship and all its silver off Campeche. In addition, the Dutch captured a whole fleet off Matanzas, Cuba, in 1628. With these disruptions of trade and the flow of silver to the royal treasury, it was difficult for Spain to finance its domestic commitments, its foreign policy, imperial responsibilities.[32]

English Explorer Sir Francis Drake encountered several major hurricanes while sailing the dangerous seas of the Americas and the Atlantic Ocean, and in most cases, these encounters changed the course of West Indian and American history. Francis Drake nicknamed "my pirate" by Queen Elizabeth I, was among the so-called "Sea Dog" privateers licensed by the English government to attack Spanish shipping. Drake sailed on his most famous voyage from 1577 to 1580, becoming the first English captain to circumnavigate the globe. On that same trip, he lost four

---

[31] Matthew Mulcahy, *Hurricanes and Society in the British Greater Caribbean, 1624-1783*, (Baltimore, The John Hopkins University Press, 2006). Pgs. 14-15.

[32] Stuart Schwartz, *Sea of Storms-A History of Hurricanes in the Greater Caribbean from Columbus to Katrina*, (New Jersey, Princeton University Press, 2015). Pgs. 36-39.

of his five boats, executed a subordinate for allegedly plotting a mutiny, raided various Spanish ports and captured a Spanish vessel loaded with treasure. A delighted Queen Elizabeth immediately knighted him upon his return. Eight years later, Drake helped defeat the Spanish Armada. Sir Francis Drake, who travelled the seas of the globe in quest of glory and valuable loot, nearly lost his ships in the fleet on the Outer Banks of Carolina.

One of his most famous encounters was with a major hurricane that occurred while he was anchored near the ill-fated Roanoke colony in present day North Carolina in June of 1586. His ships were anchored just off the banks while he checked on the progress of Sir Walter Raleigh's colonists on Roanoke Island. The hurricane lasted for three days, scattering Drake's fleet and nearly destroying many of his ships. There was no greater thorn in the side of the Spaniards than Francis Drake. His exploits were legendary, making him a hero to the English but a simple pirate to the Spaniards, and for good reasons because he often robbed them of their valuable treasures. To the Spanish, he was known as El Draque, "the Dragon"; "Draque" is the Spanish pronunciation of "Drake." As a talented sea captain and navigator, he attacked their fleets and took their ships and treasures. He raided their settlements in America and played a major role in the defeat of the greatest fleet ever assembled, the "Spanish Armada."

No other English seaman brought home more wealth or had a bigger impact on English history than Drake. At the age of 28, he was trapped in a Mexican port by Spanish war ships. He had gone there for repairs after an encounter with one of his first major hurricanes at sea. Drake escaped, but some of the sailors left behind were so badly treated by the Spanish that he swore revenge. He returned to the area in 1572 with two ships and 73 men. Over the next fifteen months, he raided Spanish towns and their all-important silver train across the Isthmus from Panama. Other English accounts reported ships damaged or lost in storms characterized by extreme wind and rain, some of which were hurricanes. The English (including Drake and Hawkins) had a great respect for hurricanes, to such an extent that as the hurricane season was understood to be approaching, more and more pirates went home or laid up their ships in some sheltered harbour until the last hurricane had passed and was replaced by the cool air of old man winter.

Probably those that first discovered the period of the year in which hurricanes developed were Spanish priests, officers of the navy or army, or civilians that had lived for a long time in the Caribbean. After living a considerable time in the Caribbean, like 60-100 years, Spanish officials and settlers were by the time no strangers to the natural disasters of the New World. They had already experienced many hurricanes, and in some ways their explanations of these hurricanes were consistently providential, and even so they were considered normal within divine purpose. But despite their acceptance of God's will as a primary cause for these hurricanes, there were always a practical and a political aspect to their perceptions and to their responses as well.

By the end of the sixteenth century, they should have already known the approximate period that these hurricanes occurred. The Roman Catholic Church knew early on that the hurricane season extended at least from August to October because the hierarchy ordered that all the churches in the Caribbean say a special prayer to protect them from these deadly hurricanes. The prayer that had to be said was: 'Ad repellendas tempestates,' translated to mean 'for the repelling of the hurricanes or tempests.' It was also ordered that the prayer should be said in Puerto Rico during August and September and in Cuba in September and October. This indicates that it was known that hurricanes were more frequent in those islands during the months mentioned. Even to this day, many of the Roman Catholic Churches in the Caribbean during the late spring to early summer months continue with this tradition of praying to God to protect them during the upcoming hurricane season. Eventually, West Indian colonists, through first-hand experiences with these storms, gradually learned that hurricanes struck the Caribbean within a well-defined season. Initially, those early colonists believed that hurricanes could strike at any time of the year, but by the middle of the seventeenth century most of them recognized that there was a distinct hurricane season. This was because the hurricanes simply occurred too frequently within a defined period for them to remain strange and unusual in their eyes. Numerous letters and reports written by colonists specifically discussed the period between July and October as the 'time of hurricanes.'

One case in point, by the 1660s the dangers of the storms were known well enough that advertisements in Europe to attract colonists to Suriname highlighted the fact that this colony was more fertile than other lands in this region, and moreover free of the dangers of hurricanes (which they called 'Orcanen') which are all too common in other parts of the North Atlantic. The Dutch had originally believed that Curaçao was also free from hurricanes as well, but that hope was dashed when a very destructive hurricane in October of 1681 proved their theory wrong and decimated the island.[33]

The geography of hurricanes challenged the concept of these storms as 'national judgments or divine favor' by which God spoke to a specific group of people or country. Individual storms routinely struck various islands colonized by different European powers. For example, in 1707 a hurricane devastated the English Leeward Islands, the Dutch Islands of Saba and St. Eustatius, and the French Island of Guadeloupe. In 1674, a Dutch attack on the French Islands was thwarted by a hurricane, which also caused significant damage in the English Leeward Islands and in Barbados. Guadeloupe, Martinique, and nearby Antigua were located on the same or nearby geographical boundary (16-17°N) that made them vulnerable to the Cape Verde-type storms, which forms in the far eastern Atlantic and traverse the wide and expansive Atlantic Ocean and then increase in energy and destructive abilities as they move westward into the eastern most Caribbean countries of the Lesser and Greater Antilles.

The French islands were hit by a destructive hurricane in 1635, the first year of their settlement, Guadeloupe averaged a hurricane strike every ten years or so in the seventeenth century. Along with Martinique and St. Christopher, it was devastated again in August 1666, at which time an English fleet attacking the island under the command of Lord Willoughby was caught and lost. Between 1699 and 1720, four heavy storms struck the island, and it then suffered other intense periods between 1738 and 1742 (four strikes) and 1765 and 1767 (three strikes). Martinique also was often hit, suffering from the ravages of hurricanes in 1680 and 1695, with great loss of life and damage to shipping in its harbour, and then was periodically visited by storms in the eighteenth century.

The presence of hurricanes made colonists question their ability to transform the hostile environment of the Caribbean and by extension their ability to establish successful and stable societies here. But hurricanes raised other questions as well: What caused them? What forces gave rise to such powerful and dangerous storms? For some-probably a significant majority during the first several decades of the seventeenth century-they believed

---

[33] Stuart Schwartz, *Sea of Storms-A History of Hurricanes in the Greater Caribbean from Columbus to Katrina*, (New Jersey, Princeton University Press, 2015). Pg. 52.

that these storms came directly from the hands of God. They interpreted hurricanes as 'wondrous events' or 'divine judgments' for human sins. Others linked hurricanes to various natural processes, including shifting wind patterns. The explosion of various natural processes, including shifting wind patterns, the explosion of various chemicals in the atmosphere, and the celestial movement of the planets and stars.

Gradually, the colonists and their governors learned from their first-hand experiences with these storms and therefore adapted to them. First, they learned to avoid shipping during the hurricane season to prevent losses. Second, they insured their ships and cargoes against the loss inflicted on them by hurricanes. Third, they would often spread the cargo among several ships to mitigate the losses by having several vessels instead of just one ship. Fourth, they encouraged their slaves to plant root crops, which were less susceptible to losses from a hurricane. Finally, they would avoid the purchase of new slaves until after the hurricane season had passed.

CHAPTER TWO

The Naming of Hurricanes

North Atlantic Tropical Cyclone Names

2019	2020	2021	2022	2023	2024
Andrea	Arthur	Ana	Alex	Arlene	Alberto
Barry	Bertha	Bill	Bonnie	Bret	Beryl
Chantal	Cristobal	Claudette	Colin	Cindy	Chris
Dorian	Dolly	Danny	Danielle	Don	Debby
Erin	Edouard	Elsa	Earl	Emily	Ernesto
Fernand	Fay	Fred	Fiona	Franklin	Francine
Gabrielle	Gonzalo	Grace	Gaston	Gert	Gordon
Humberto	Hanna	Henri	Hermine	Harold	Helene
Imelda	Isaias	Ida	Ian	Idalia	Isaac
Jerry	Josephine	Julian	Julia	Jose	Joyce
Karen	Kyle	Kate	Karl	Katia	Kirk
Lorenzo	Laura	Larry	Lisa	Lee	Leslie
Melissa	Marco	Mindy	Martin	Margot	Milton
Nestor	Nana	Nicholas	Nicole	Nigel	Nadine
Olga	Omar	Odette	Owen	Ophelia	Oscar
Pablo	Paulette	Peter	Paula	Philippe	Patty
Rebekah	Rene	Rose	Richard	Rina	Rafael
Sebastien	Sally	Sam	Shary	Sean	Sara
Tanya	Teddy	Teresa	Tobias	Tammy	Tony
Van	Vicky	Victor	Virginie	Vince	Valerie
Wendy	Wilfred	Wanda	Walter	Whitney	William

North Atlantic Tropical Cyclone Names Jpeg-scan page 6—3/4 page (Information Courtesy of NOAA-National Hurricane Center).

For as long as people have been tracking and reporting hurricanes, also known as tropical cyclones, they've been struggling to find ways to identify them. Until well into the 20th century, newspapers and forecasters in the Caribbean and the Americas devised names for storms that referenced their time, geographic location or intensity or some other distinguishing factor. It's a funny thing, this naming of storms. We don't name tornadoes, blizzards, or frontal systems. It would seem silly, but we do name our hurricanes. On the opposite corners of our stormy planet, meteorologists name their cyclones, too (although with sometimes more meaningful or symbolic names).

Hurricanes are the only weather disasters that have been given their own iconic names, such as Hurricanes Sandy, Matthew, Irma, Joaquin, Andrew, Katrina, Camille or Mitch. No two hurricanes are the same, but like people, they share similar characteristics; yet, still, they have their own unique stories to tell. The naming of storms or hurricanes has undergone various stages of development and transformation. Initially, the word 'Hurricane' accompanied by the year of occurrence was used. For example, 'the Great Hurricane of 1780', which killed over 22,000 persons in Martinique, Barbados, and St. Eustatius. Another example was 'the Great Storm of 1703', whose incredible damage of the British Isles was expertly detailed by Robinson Crusoe's author, Daniel Defoe. The naming scheme was later substituted by a numbering system (e.g. Hurricane #1, #2, #3 of 1833 etc...); however, this became too cumbersome and confusing, especially when disseminating information about two or more storms within the same geographical area or location.

For the major hurricanes of this region, they were often named after the country or city they devastated. This was especially true for severe hurricanes, which made their landing somewhere in the Caribbean or the Americas. Three notable examples were: first, 'the Great Dominican Republic Hurricane of 1930', which killed over 8,000 persons in the Dominican Republic. The 1930 Dominican Republic Hurricane, also known as 'Hurricane San Zenon', is the fifth deadliest North Atlantic hurricane on record. The second of only two known tropical cyclones in the very quiet 1930 North Atlantic hurricane season, the hurricane was first observed on August 29 to the east of the Lesser Antilles. The cyclone was a small but intense Category 4 hurricane.

Next was 'the Pointe-à-Pitre Hurricane of 1776', which devastated the country of Guadeloupe and killed over 6,000 persons and devastated its largest city and economic capital of Pointe-à-Pitre. The 1776 Pointe-à-Pitre hurricane was at one point the deadliest North Atlantic on record. Although its intensity and the complete track is unknown, it is known that the storm struck Guadeloupe on September 6, 1776, near Pointe-à-Pitre, which is currently the largest city on the island. At least 6,000 fatalities occurred on Guadeloupe, which was a higher death toll than any other known hurricane before it to hit that country. The storm struck a large convoy of French and Dutch merchant ships, sinking or running around 60% of the vessels. The ships were transporting goods to Europe.

Finally, 'the Great Nassau Hurricane of 1926', which devastated the city of Nassau in The Bahamas during the 1926 North Atlantic hurricane season. The Great Nassau Hurricane of 1926, also known as 'The Bahamas-Florida Hurricane of July 1926' and 'Hurricane San Liborio,' was a destructive Category 4 hurricane that affected The Bahamas at peak intensity. Although it weakened considerably before its Florida landfall, it was reported as one of the most severe storms to affect Nassau in The Bahamas in several years until the Great Lake Okeechobee Hurricane of 1928, which occurred just two years later. Approximately 258 to 268 persons died in this storm in The Bahamas.

In some cases, they were even named after the holiday on which they occurred, for example, the 'Great Labour Day Hurricane of 1935.' This hurricane in 1935 was the strongest tropical cyclone during the 1935 North Atlantic hurricane season. This compact and intense hurricane caused extensive damage in The Bahamas and the upper Florida Keys. To this day, this hurricane is the strongest and most intense hurricane on record to ever have struck the United States in terms of barometric pressure. As a matter of fact, it is one of the strongest recorded hurricane landfalls worldwide. It was the only hurricane known to have made landfall in the United States with a minimum central pressure below 900 millibars; only two others have struck the United States with winds of Category 5 strength on the Saffir-Simpson Scale. It remains the third-strongest North Atlantic hurricane on record, and it was only surpassed by Hurricane Gilbert (888 millibars) in 1988 and Hurricane Wilma (882 millibars) in 2005. In total, at least 408 people were killed by this hurricane.

In some cases, they were named after the ship which experienced that storm. Three notable examples were: 'Antje's Hurricane of 1842', the 'Racer's Storm of 1837' and the 'Sea Venture Hurricane of 1609.' In 1842, a North Atlantic hurricane that ripped off the mast of a boat named *Antje* became known as Antje's Hurricane. A westward-moving hurricane, nicknamed Antje's Hurricane after a schooner of the same name that was dismasted by the storm. The cyclone moved across the Florida Keys on September 4. It continued westward across the Gulf of Mexico, hitting between Matamoros and Tampico, Mexico. Its unusual westward movement, also seen by a hurricane in 1932 and Hurricane Anita in 1977, was due to a strong high-pressure system to its north.

The 1837 Racer's Storm was a very powerful and destructive hurricane in the 19th century, causing 105 deaths and heavy damage to many cities on its 2,000+ mile path. The Racer's Storm was the 10th known tropical storm in the 1837 North Atlantic hurricane season. The Racer's Storm was named after the British warship *HMS Racer*, Racer's Hurricane was a destructive tropical cyclone that had severe effects on northeastern Mexico and the Gulf Coast of the United States in early October 1837. It takes its name from the Royal Navy ship called *Racer*, which sustained some damage when it encountered the hurricane in the northwestern Caribbean Sea. The storm first affected Jamaica with flooding rainfall and strong winds on September 26 and 27, before entering the Gulf of Mexico by October 1. As the hurricane approached northern Tamaulipas and southern Texas, it slowed to a crawl and turned sharply eastward. The storm battered the Gulf Coast from Texas to the Florida Panhandle between October 3 and 7, and after crossing the Southeastern United States, it emerged into the Atlantic shipping lanes off the Carolinas. For most of the storm's duration, the strongest winds and heaviest rains were confined to the northern side of its track.

Another example was the 'Sea Venture Hurricane of 1609.' On July 28th of 1609, a fleet of seven tall ships, with two pinnaces in tow carrying 150 settlers and supplies from Plymouth, England, to Virginia to relieve the starving Jamestown colonists, was struck by a hurricane while en route there. They had been sent by the Virginia Company of London to fortify the Jamestown settlement. Sir George Somers' mission was to resupply the six hundred or so pioneers who a year before had settled in the infant British colonial settlement of King James' Town, situated in one of the estuaries south of the Potomac River.

The ship *Sea Venture* was grounded at Bermuda, which for some time was called Somers Island after the ship's captain, Admiral Sir George Somers. After being struck by this hurricane, the *Sea Venture* sprung a leak and everyone on board worked frantically to save this ship and their lives by trying to pump the water out of the hull of the ship. They tried to stem the flow of water coming into the ship by stuffing salt beef and anything else they could find to fit into the leaks of the ship. After this proved futile, most of the crew simply gave up hope, falling asleep where they could, exhausted and aching from their relentless but futile efforts. But just as they were about to give up and face the grim reality that they would be lost to the unforgiving Atlantic Ocean, they spotted the island of Bermuda. Somers skillfully navigated the floundering *Sea Venture* onto a reef about half a mile to the leeward side of Bermuda. They used the ship's longboat to ferry the crew and passengers ashore.

The passengers of the shipwrecked *Sea Venture* became Bermuda's first inhabitants, and their stories helped inspire William Shakespeare's writing of his final play 'The Tempest', making it perhaps the most famous hurricane in early American history. "And another storm brewing," William Shakespeare wrote in 'The Tempest.' "I hear it sing in the wind." Most of those venturing to the New World had no knowledge of the word or the actual storm. The lead ship, the three-hundred-ton *Sea Venture*, was the largest in the fleet and carried Sir Thomas Gates, the newly appointed governor of the colony, and Sir Georges Somers, Admiral of the Virginia Company.[34]

It is interesting to note that Shakespeare did not name his play 'The Hurricane.' He did know the word "hurricano" because it appears in two earlier plays, King Lear and Troilus and Cressida. Maybe he recognized that such a title would be confusing and unfamiliar to most of his audience, so he chose a more familiar word 'The Tempest', instead. Though the island was uninhabited, Spaniards had visited Bermuda earlier and set ashore wild pigs. The shipwrecked passengers fed on those wild pigs, fish, berries and other plentiful game on the island. Although they yearned to stay on that island paradise, they managed to make two vessels *'Patience'* and *'Deliverance'* out of what was left of the *Sea Venture*, and ten months later they set sail for Jamestown. However, some persons remained on the island and became the first colonists of that island, including Admiral Sir George Somers, who initially left with the other Jamestown passengers but eventually returned and died on that island. To this day, Bermuda still celebrates 'Somers' Day' as a public holiday.

---

[34] http://www.william-shakespeare.info/shakespeare-play-the-tempest.html. Retrieved: 13-06-2014.

In some instances, hurricanes were named after important persons within this region; one such storm was the 'Willoughby Gale of 1666.' The word 'gale' during these colonial times was often interchanged with the word 'hurricane', but they often meant the same thing-a hurricane and not the official term we now use today for the definition of a 'meteorological gale.' This storm was named after the British Governor of Barbados, Lord Francis Willoughby, who lost his life aboard the flagship *Hope* along with over 2,000 of his troops in his fleet in this hurricane. He was appointed Governor of Barbados by Charles II in May of 1650 and attempted to negotiate the strained politics of that island, which also experienced a division between the Royalists and Parliamentarians. His last act on behalf of the English Crown came in July 1666, when having learned of the recent French seizure of St. Kitts; he formed a relief force of two Royal Navy Frigates, twelve other large vessels (including commandeered merchant ships), a fire ship, and a ketch, bearing over 2,000 men.

Lord Willoughby had planned to proceed north to Nevis, Montserrat, and Antigua to gather further reinforcements before descending on the French. Leaving Barbados on July 28th, his fleet waited for the French just off the coast of Martinique and Guadeloupe, where he sent a frigate to assault the harbour and ended up capturing two French merchant vessels on August 4th. This success could not be exploited, however, as that night most of his force was destroyed by a strong hurricane, including the flagship *Hope*, from which Willoughby drowned during the storm. This hurricane occurred in 1666 and was a very intense storm which struck the islands of St. Kitts, Guadeloupe, and Martinique. The fleet was caught by surprise by this hurricane after leaving Barbados en route to St. Kitts and Nevis to aid the colonists there to help battle against the French attacks. After the storm, only two vessels from this fleet were ever heard from again, and the French captured some of these survivors. All the vessels and boats on the coast of Guadeloupe were dashed to pieces. For a period in the late seventeenth century, some colonists referred to especially powerful and deadly hurricanes as "Willoughby Gales."

Personal names were also used elsewhere in this region, for example, 'Saxby's Gale' which occurred in Canada in 1869 and was named after a naval officer who was thought to have predicted it. The Saxby Gale was the name given to a tropical cyclone that struck eastern Canada's Bay of Fundy region on the night of October 4–5, 1869. The storm was named for Lieutenant Stephen Martin Saxby, a naval instructor and amateur astronomer who, based on his astronomical studies, had predicted extremely high tides in the North Atlantic Ocean on October 5, 1869, which would produce storm surges in the event of a storm. The hurricane caused extensive destruction to port facilities and communities along the Bay of Fundy coast in both New Brunswick and Nova Scotia, as well as Maine, particularly Calais, St. Andrews, St. George, St. John, Moncton, Sackville, Amherst, Windsor, and Truro. Much of the devastation was attributed to a 2-meter storm surge created by the storm, which coincided with a perigean spring tide; the Bay of Fundy has one of the highest tidal ranges in the world. The Saxby Gale storm surge produced a water level that gave Burntcoat Head, Nova Scotia, the honour of having the highest tidal range ever recorded. It is also thought to have formed the long gravel beach that connects Partridge Island, Nova Scotia, to the mainland.

The storm (which pre-dated the practice of naming hurricanes) was given the name 'Saxby' in honour of Lieutenant Stephen Martin Saxby, Royal Navy, who was a naval instructor and amateur astronomer. Lt. Saxby had written a letter of warning, published December 25, 1868, in London's 'The Standard' newspaper, in which he notes the astronomical forces predicted for October 5, 1869, which would produce extremely high tides in the North Atlantic Ocean during the height of hurricane season. Lt. Saxby followed this warning with a reminder published on September 16, 1869, to 'The Standard', in which he also warns of a major 'atmospheric disturbance' that would coincide with the high-water level at an undetermined location. Many newspapers took up Saxby's warning in the coming days.

In a monthly weather column published October 1, 1869, in Halifax's 'The Evening Express,' amateur meteorologist Frederick Allison relayed Lt. Saxby's warning for a devastating storm the following week. Despite the warning, many readers throughout the United Kingdom, Canada, Newfoundland, and the United States dismissed Saxby since there were frequent gales and hurricanes during the month of October. The fact that the high tides occurred throughout the North Atlantic basin was unremarkable and astronomically predictable, except for their coinciding with the hurricane that struck the Gulf of Maine and Bay of Fundy to produce the devastating storm surge. Lt. Saxby's predictions were considered quite lunatic at the time. Some believed that his predictions were founded upon astrology, which was not the case.

Another example was 'the Daniel Defoe Hurricane of 1703', which occurred in November of 1703 and moved from the Atlantic across to southern England. It was made famous by an obscure political pamphleteer, Daniel Defoe. It was six years before he wrote the world-famous book 'Robinson Crusoe.' At the time the hurricane struck, he needed money, so the storm gave him the idea of collecting eyewitness accounts or personal recollections of the storm and publishing them in a pamphlet. He printed and sold this pamphlet under the very strange and exceptionally long title of 'The storm or collection of the Most Remarkable Casualties and Disasters which happened in the late Dreadful Tempest both by Sea and Land.' In total, around 8,000 sailors lost their lives, untold numbers perished in the floods on shore, and 14,000 homes, 400 windmills, and 16,000 sheep were destroyed. Some of the windmills burned down because they turned so fast in the fierce winds that friction generated enough heat to set them on fire. The damage in London alone was estimated to have cost £2 million (at 18th-century prices).

An additional example was 'the Benjamin Franklin Hurricane of October 1743,' which affected the Northeastern United States and New England, brought gusty winds and rainy conditions as far as Philadelphia, and produced extensive flooding in Boston. This was the first hurricane to be measured accurately by scientific instruments. John Winthrop, a professor of natural philosophy at Harvard College, measured the pressure and tides during the storm passage. This storm wasn't particularly powerful, but it was memorable because it garnered the interest of future patriot and one of the founders of the United States, Benjamin Franklin, who believed the storm, was coming in from Boston. He was wrong because it was going to Boston. From this information, he surmised that the storm was travelling in a clockwise manner from the southwest to northeast. Putting two and two together, Franklin concluded that the low-pressure system was causing the storm to move in this manner.

One aspect of the Earth's general circulation is that storms are not stationary; they move, and in somewhat predictable ways. Until the mid-eighteenth century, it had been generally assumed that storms were born, played out, and died in a single location and that they did not move across the Earth's surface. Benjamin Franklin had planned to study a lunar eclipse one evening in September 1743, but the remnants of this hurricane ruined his evening. This was a big disappointment to him because he had been looking forward to the lunar eclipse that this storm had obscured. His curiosity aroused, Franklin gathered additional details about the storm by reading the Boston newspapers and learned that the storm had moved up the Atlantic seaboard and against the surface winds. He learned that this hurricane struck Boston a day later, sending flood tides sweeping over the docks, destroying boats, and submerging waterfront streets. In the succeeding months, he collected additional reports from travelers and newspapers from Georgia to Nova Scotia and satisfied himself that at least in this part of the world, storms tend to take a northeasterly path up the Atlantic Coast. Thus, science took the first step toward a basic understanding of hurricanes and their movements.

Benjamin Franklin is also popularly known for his off-the-wall weather experiment years later, where during a thunderstorm, in 1752, he carried out a dangerous experiment to demonstrate that a thunderstorm generates electricity. He flew a kite, with metal objects attached to its string, high in the sky into a thunderstorm cloud (cumulonimbus). The metal items produced sparks, proving that electricity had passed along the wet string. After discovering that bolts of lightning were in fact electricity, with this knowledge Franklin developed the lightning rod to allow the lightning bolt to travel along the rod and safely into the ground. This discovery by Franklin is still used even to this day all over the world. A year later, after Benjamin Franklin's famous kite flight, Swedish physicist G.W. Richmann conducted a similar experiment following Franklin's instructions to the letter, and as fate would have it, he was struck by lightning, which killed him instantly. Sailing home from France on September 5, 1789, after his great years as a U.S. Ambassador, Benjamin Franklin experienced a storm that may have been the same storm that devastated Dominica. He was eighty years old and suffering from "the Stone" but was busy observing the temperatures of the sea water, which would eventually lead to his discovery of the Gulf Stream.

Finally, there was the 'Alexander Hamilton Hurricane of 1772,' which he experienced growing up as a boy living in the Caribbean on the island of St. Kitts in the Leeward Islands. It sent Hamilton directly to America's shores, figuratively speaking, and altered the US and world history. It barreled through the Leeward Islands of St. Thomas, Puerto Rico and St. Croix on August 31, 1772, described in a local paper as, "the most dreadful hurricane known in the memory of man . . . the whole frame of nature seemed unhinged and tottering to its fall . . . terrifying even the just, for who could stand undisturbed amid the ruins of a falling world." This was an extremely powerful and deadly hurricane.

He later in life became the confidential aide to George Washington, and his greatness rests on his Federalist influence on the American Constitution as much as on his financial genius as the first United States Secretary of the Treasury. Today he is featured on the United States $10 bill, and he is one of two non-presidents featured on currently issued United States bills. The other is Benjamin Franklin, who is found on the United States $100 bill. A westward-moving hurricane hit Puerto Rico on August 28. It continued through the Caribbean, hitting Hispaniola on August 30, and later Jamaica. It moved northwestward through the Gulf of Mexico and hit just west of Mobile, Alabama, on September 4th. Many ships were destroyed in the Mobile area, and its death toll was very severe. In Pensacola, it destroyed most of the wharves. The most devastation occurred near Mobile and the Pasca Oocola River. All shipping at the Mouth of the Mississippi was driven into the marshes; this included the ship 'El Principe de Orange', from which only 6 persons survived.

This storm was famously described by Alexander Hamilton, who was living on the island of St. Croix at the time and wrote a letter about it to his father in St. Kitts. He was a 17-year-old and working as a clerk. When the hurricane passed, he wrote a letter to his father, a "melodramatic description" of the storm, which he managed to publish in the Royal Danish American Gazette on Oct. 3, 1772, attracting the attention of the island's elite. The letter was so dramatic and moving that it was published in newspapers locally on the island and first in New York, and then in other states, and the locals on St. Kitts raised enough money to have him brought to America to receive a formal education to make good use of his intellectual abilities. This was because this letter created such a sensation that some planters of St. Kitts, amid the hurricane devastation, took up a collection to send him to America for better schooling because they saw in him great potential. By 1774, he was a student at King's College, now Columbia University, in New York. On St. Kitts, the damage was considerable, and once again many houses were flattened, and there were several fatalities and many more injuries. Total damage from this storm alone was estimated at £500,000 on St. Kitts. The second storm struck just three days later, causing even more significant damage to the few remaining houses on this island already battered and weakened by the previous storm in 1772.

Several claimants have been put forth as the originators of the modern tropical cyclone 'naming' system. However, it was forecaster Clement Lindley Wragge, an Australian meteorologist who in 1887 began giving women's names, names from history and mythology and male names, especially names of politicians who offended him, to these storms before the end of the 19th century. He was a colourful and controversial meteorologist in charge of the Brisbane, Australia's Government weather office. He initially named the storms after mythological figures but later named them after politicians he didn't like. For example, Wragge named some of these storms using biblical names, such as Ram, Raken, Talmon, and Uphaz, or the ancient names of Xerxes and Hannibal. Wragge even nicknamed one storm Eline; a name that he thought was reminiscent of "dusty maidens with liquid eyes and bewitching manners." Most ingeniously, he gained a measure of personal revenge by naming some of the nastiest storms with politicians' names, such as Drake, Barton, and Deakin. By properly naming a hurricane, he could publicly describe a politician (perhaps a politician who was not too generous with the weather bureau appropriations) as "causing great distress" or "wandering aimlessly about the Pacific." By naming these storms after these hated politicians, he could get a degree of revenge on them without suffering any repercussions from them. During his last days in office, he fought with the Australian government over the right to issue national forecasts, and he lost and was fired in 1902.

For a while, hurricanes in the West Indies were often named after the Saint's Day on which the hurricane occurred. As Christianity took hold in the West Indies, the naming system of storms here in the Caribbean was based on the Catholic tradition of naming these storms with the 'Saint' of the day (e.g. San Ciprian on September 26th). This system for naming them was haphazard and not really a system at all. Powerful hurricanes hitting especially the Spanish speaking islands of the Caribbean got Catholic Saints' names. According to Historian Alejandro Tapia, the first hurricane to be named with the Saint of the day was the 'Hurricane of San Bartolomé', which devastated Puerto Rico and the Dominican Republic on August 24th and 25th of 1568. The earlier tropical cyclones were simply designated by historians years later after their passages.

One example of a great storm named after a Saint of the day was 'Hurricane Saint Felipe I', which struck Puerto Rico on September 13, 1876. Another example was 'Hurricane Saint Felipe II', which occurred, strangely enough, on the very same date 52 years later September 13, 1928.

Another hurricane, which was named the 'Hurricane of Saint Elena', struck Puerto Rico on August 18, 1851, and caused massive casualties. Then there was the 'Hurricane of Santa Ana' (in English, Saint Anne), which struck Puerto Rico and Guadeloupe on July 26, 1825, the date of the feast in honour of the Mother of the Blessed Virgin, which killed over 1,300 persons. In addition, there was the 'Hurricane of Saint Ciriaco', which killed 3,369 persons in Puerto Rico on August 8, 1899, (feast day of Saint Cyriacus) and remains one of the longest duration tropical storms (28 days) to hit the Caribbean or anywhere in the world.

The tradition of naming storms after the Saint of the day officially ended with Hurricane Betsy in 1956, which is still remembered as the 'Hurricane of Santa Clara.' However, years later with the passage of Hurricane Donna in 1960, the storm was recognized as the 'Hurricane of San Lorenzo.' Then, only the major hurricanes were given names, so most storms, especially the minor storms before 1950 in the North Atlantic, never received any kind of special designation. Therefore, The Bahamas hurricane in 1929 was never named but was simply referred to as 'the Great Bahamas Hurricane of 1929.' The word 'Great' simply meant that the hurricane was a powerful storm and that it had sustained winds of 136 mph or greater and a minimum central pressure of 28.00 inches or less.

Later, latitude-longitude positions were used. At first, they listed these storms by the latitude and longitude positions where they were first reported. This was cumbersome, slow, open to errors and confusion. For example, a name like 'Hurricane 12.8°N latitude and 54.7°W longitude' was very difficult to remember, and it would be easy to confuse this storm with another that was seen two months later but almost at the same location. In addition, this posed another significant problem in the 1940s, when meteorologists began airborne studies of tropical cyclones and ships and aircrafts communicated mainly in Morse code. This was fine for the letters of the alphabet, but it was awkward at dealing with numbers because it was slow and caused confusion among its users.

In this region, these early storms were often referred to as gales, severe gales, equinoctial storms, or line storms. The latter two names referred to the time of the year and the location from which these storms were born (referring to the Equatorial line). Gauging the strength and fury of a seventeenth or eighteenth-century storm was quite a difficult task because at the time these colonists had no means of measuring the wind speeds of a hurricane. Contemporaries recognized a hierarchy of winds ranging from 'a stark calm' to 'a small Gale' to 'a Top-Sail Gale' to 'a fret of wind' and 'a Tempest.' These terms were later replaced by the word 'hurricane', but such terms offered little help in interpreting the power of hurricanes or differentiating lesser strength tropical storms from hurricanes.

Experience has shown that using distinctive names in communications is quicker and less subject to error than the cumbersome latitude-longitude identification methods. The idea was that the names should be short, familiar to users, easy to remember and that their use would facilitate communications with millions of people of different ethnic races threatened by the storm. This was because a hurricane can last for a week or more and there can be more than one storm at a given time, so weather forecasters started naming these storms so that there would be absolutely no confusion when talking about an individual storm. Names are easier to use and facilitate better communications among individuals and meteorologists with language barriers within the same geographical region, such as within the Caribbean, Central America, and North America.

The first U.S. named hurricane (unofficially named) was Hurricane George, which was the fifth storm in 1947 season. George had top winds of 155 mph as it came ashore around mid-day on September 17th, between Pompano Beach and Delray Beach. The second hurricane unofficially named was Hurricane Bess (named for the outspoken First Lady of the USA, Bess Truman, in 1949). The third storm was nicknamed by the news media 'Hurricane Harry', after the then president of the United States Harry Truman. United States Navy and Air Force meteorologists working in the Pacific Ocean began naming tropical cyclones during World War II when they often had to track multiple storms. They gave each storm a distinctive name to distinguish the cyclones more quickly than listing their positions when issuing warnings.

Towards the end of World War II, two separate United States fleets in the Pacific lacking enough weather information about these storms were twice badly damaged when they sailed directly into them, resulting in massive causalities. Three ships were sunk, twenty-one were badly damaged, 146 planes were blown overboard, and 763 men were lost. One of the results that came out of these tragedies was the fact that all U.S. Army and Navy planes were then ordered to start tracking and studying these deadly storms to prevent similar disasters like those ones from occurring again. During World War II, this naming practice became widespread in weather map discussions among forecasters, especially Air Force and Navy meteorologists, who plotted the movements of these storms over the wide expanses of the Pacific Ocean.

Using the convention of applying 'she' to inanimate objects such as vehicles, these military meteorologists, beginning in 1945 in the Northwest Pacific, started naming these storms after their wives and girlfriends. However, this practice didn't last too long, for whatever reason, but my guess is that those women rejected or took offense to be named after something that was responsible for so much damage and destruction. Another theory was that this practice was started by a radio operator who sang, "Every little breeze seems to whisper Louise" when issuing a hurricane warning. From that point on, that hurricane and future hurricanes were referred to as 'Louise' and the use of female names for hurricanes became standard practice.

An early example of the use of a woman's name for a storm was in the bestselling pocketbook novel Storm, by George R. Stewart, published by Random House in 1941, which has since been made into a major motion picture by Walt Disney, further promoting the idea of naming storms. It involved a young meteorologist working in the San Francisco Weather Bureau Office tracking a storm, which he called 'Maria,' from its birth as a disturbance in the North Pacific to its death over North America many days later. The focus of the book is a storm named Maria but pronounced 'Ma-Rye-Ah.' Yes, the song in the famous Broadway show 'Paint Your Wagon' named "They Call the Wind Maria" was inspired by this fictional storm. He gave it a name because he said that he could easily say 'Hurricane Maria' rather than 'the low-pressure center which at 6 pm yesterday was located at latitude seventy-four degrees east and longitude forty-three degrees north', which he considered too long and cumbersome. As Stewart detailed in his novel, "Not since at any price would the Junior Meteorologist have revealed to the Chief that he was bestowing names-and girls' names-upon those great moving low-pressure areas." He unofficially gave the storms in his book women names such as Lucy, Katherine, and Ruth, after some girls he knew, because he said that they each had a unique personality. It is not known whether George Stewart was indeed the inspiration for the trend toward naming hurricanes, which came along later in the decade, but it seems likely.[35]

By 1947, tropical cyclones developing in the North Atlantic were named by the United States Army Air Force in private communications

---

[35] George Stewart, <u>Storm</u>, (USA, University of Nebraska Press., 1941).

between weather centers and aircraft using the phonetic alphabet. This practice continued until September 1950, when the names started to be used publicly after three hurricanes (Baker, Dog, and Easy) had occurred simultaneously and caused confusion within the media and the public. Over the next 2 years, the public use of the phonetic alphabet to name systems continued before at the 1953 Interdepartmental Hurricane Conference it was decided to start using a new list of female names during that season, as a second phonetic alphabet had been developed. During the active but mild 1953 North Atlantic hurricane season, the names were readily used in the press, with few objections recorded; thus, the same names were reused during the next year, with only one change: Gilda for Gail. Over the next 6 years, a new list of names was developed ahead of each season, before in 1960 forecasters developed four alphabetical sets and repeated them every four years. These new sets followed the example of the typhoon names and excluded names beginning with the letters Q, U, X, Y, and Z, and keeping them confined to female names only.

In 1950, military alphabet names (e.g. Able, Baker, Charley, Dog, Easy, Fox etc.) were adopted by the World Meteorological Organization (WMO), and the first named Atlantic hurricane was Able in 1950. The Joint Army/Navy (JAN) phonetic Alphabet was developed in 1941 and was used by all branches of the United States military until the promulgation of the NATO phonetic alphabet in 1956, which replaced it. Before the JAN phonetic alphabet, each branch of the armed forces used its own phonetic alphabet, leading to difficulties in inter-branch communications. This naming method was not very popular and caused a lot of confusion because officials soon realized that this naming convention would cause more problems in the history books if more than one powerful Hurricane Able made landfall and caused extensive damage and death to warrant retirement. This was because hurricanes that have a severe impact on the lives or the economy of a country or region are remembered for generations after the devastation they caused, and some go into weather history, so distinguishing one storm name from another is essential for the history books.

The modern naming convention came about in response to the need for unambiguous radio communications with ships and aircraft. As air and sea transportation started to increase and meteorological observations improved in number and quality, several typhoons, hurricanes or cyclones might have to be tracked at any given time. To help in their identification, in 1953 the systematic use of only regular women names were used in alphabetical order, and this lasted until 1978. 1953's Alice was the first real human-named storm. At the time, they named them after women because these meteorologists reasoned that people might pay more attention to a storm if they envisioned it as a tangible entity, a character, rather than just a bundle of wind. But the use of only women names eventually was rejected as sexist, and forecasters finally went with both male and female names. Beginning in 1960, four semi-permanent sets of names were established, to be recycled after four years. This list was expanded to ten sets in 1971, but before making it through the list even once these sets were replaced by the now familiar 6 sets of men and women names.

This naming practice started in the Eastern Pacific in 1959, and in 1960 for the remainder of the North Pacific. It is interesting to note that in the Northwest Pacific basin, the names, by and large, are not personal names. While there are a few men and women names, the majority of the Northwest Pacific tropical cyclone names generally reflect Pacific culture, and the names consist of flowers, animals, birds, trees, or even foods, while some are just descriptive adjectives. In addition, the names are not allotted in alphabetical order but are arranged by the contributing nation, with the countries being alphabetized. For example, the Cambodians have contributed Naki (a flower), Krovanh (a tree) and Damrey (an elephant). China has submitted names such as Yutu (a mythological rabbit), Longwang (the dragon king and god of rain in Chinese mythology), and Dainmu (the mother of lightning and the goddess in charge of thunder). Micronesian typhoon names include Sinlaku (a legendary Kosrae goddess) and Ewiniar (the Chuuk Storm-god). Hurricanes in the central Pacific have name lists for only four years and use Hawaiian names.

There were some exceptional hurricanes which became both a hurricane and a typhoon during its lifespan. Hurricane Genevieve also referred to as Typhoon Genevieve, a notable example was the fourth-most intense tropical cyclone of the North Pacific Ocean basin in 2014. A long-lasting system, Genevieve was the first one to track across all three northern Pacific basins since Hurricane Jimena in 2003. Genevieve developed from a tropical wave into the eighth tropical storm of the 2014 Pacific hurricane season well east-southeast of Hawaii on July 25. However, increased vertical wind shear caused it to weaken into a tropical depression by the following day and degenerate into a remnant low on July 28. Late on July 29, the system degenerated into a tropical depression, but it weakened into a remnant low again on July 31, owing to vertical wind shear and dry air. The remnants redeveloped into a tropical depression and briefly became a tropical storm south of Hawaii on August 2, yet it weakened back into a tropical depression soon afterward.

Late on August 5, Genevieve re-intensified into a tropical storm and intensified into a Category 1 hurricane on the next day when undergoing rapid deepening because of favorable environmental conditions. Early on August 7, Genevieve strengthened into a Category 4 hurricane, shortly before it crossed the International Date Line and was reclassified as a typhoon, also becoming the thirteenth named storm of the 2014 Pacific typhoon season. Late on the same day, Genevieve reached maximum intensity, when it was located west-southwest of Wake Island. The typhoon crossed 30°N at noon on August 10 and weakened to a severe tropical storm soon afterward, because of unfavorable sea surface temperatures and expanding subsidence. Genevieve weakened into a tropical storm on August 11 and a tropical depression the following day, as its deep convection diminished.

In the North Atlantic basin in 1979, gender equality finally reached the naming process of hurricanes when thousands of sexism complaints written to the WMO and feminists' groups in the USA and worldwide urged the WMO to add men's names; hence, both men and women names were used alternately, and this practice is still in use today. That year would also herald the practice of drawing up a list of names in advance of the hurricane season, and today an alphabetical list of 21 names is used. Hurricane Bob was the first North Atlantic storm named after a man in the 1979 hurricane season; however, it was not retired (it would eventually be retired in the 1991 hurricane season). Hurricane David was the second storm named after a man, and it was the first male storm to be retired in the North Atlantic Region. This was due to the great death toll and substantial damage it inflicted to the countries of Dominica, the Dominican Republic, and The Bahamas during the last week of August and the first week of September in 1979.

Since 1979, the naming list now includes names from non-English speaking countries within this region, such as Dutch, French and Spanish names, which also have a large presence here in the Caribbean. This is done to reflect the diversity of the different ethnic languages of the various countries in this region, so the names of Spanish, French, Dutch, and English persons are used in the naming process. The names of storms are now selected by a select committee from member countries of the World Meteorological Organization that falls within that region of the world, and we here in the Caribbean come under Region IV for classification purposes. This committee meets once a year after the hurricane season has passed and before the beginning of the new hurricane season to decide on which names to be retired and to replace those names with a new set of names when and where necessary. As of Otto of 2016, 82 tropical cyclones have had their names retired in the North Atlantic basin.

The practice of giving different names to storms in different hurricane basins has also led to a few rare circumstances of name-changing storms. For example, in October of 1988, after Atlantic Hurricane Joan devastated Central America, it proceeded to move into the Pacific and became Pacific tropical storm, Miriam. Hurricane Joan was a powerful hurricane that caused death and destruction in over a dozen countries in the Caribbean and Central America. Another example was Hurricane Hattie, which was a powerful Category 5 hurricane that pounded Central America on Halloween during the 1961 North Atlantic hurricane season. It caused $370 million in damages and killed around 275 persons. Hattie is the only hurricane on record to have earned three names (Hattie, Simone, Inga) while crossing into different basins twice. Hattie swept across the Caribbean and came ashore in the town of Belize City, British Honduras (now called Belize), on October 31st. It was a strong Category 4 hurricane at landfall, having weakened from a Category 5 hurricane just offshore. After making landfall, its remnants crossed over into the Pacific and attained tropical storm status again under the name Simone. In a remarkable turn of events, after Simone itself made landfall, its remnants crossed back over to the Gulf of Mexico, where the storm became Tropical Storm Inga before dissipating. However, it is debatable whether Inga in fact formed from the remnants of Simone at all.

It is interesting to note here that the letters Q, U, X, Y, and Z are not included in the hurricane list because of the scarcity of names beginning with those letters. However, in other regions of the world, some of these letters are used; for example, only "Q" and "U" are omitted in the Northeastern Pacific basin. When a storm causes tremendous damage and death, the name is taken out of circulation and retired for reasons of sensitivity. It is then replaced with a name of the same letter and of the same gender, and if possible, the same language as the name being retired (e.g. neither Hurricane Irene in 2011 nor Hurricane Katrina in 2005 will ever be used again). The list includes one tropical storm, Allison of 2001, which caused billions in damage from its heavy rains.

The name used the most, at least with the same spelling, is Arlene (seven times), while Frances and Florence have been used seven and six times, respectively. However, considering different spellings of the same name, Debbie/Debby has been used seven times, and Anna/Ana has been used eight times. The first name to be called into use five times was Edith, but that name hasn't been used since 1971. After the 1996 season, Lilly has the distinction of being the first 'L' name to be used three times, while Marco is the first 'M' name to be used more than once. The name Kendra was assigned to a system in the 1966 hurricane season, but in the post-season analysis it was decided it had not been a bona fide tropical storm. This storm marked the birth of reclassification of storms in the post-hurricane season (Hurricane Andrew was a storm that was reclassified from a Category 4 hurricane to a Category 5 hurricane in the off-season ten years later).

In only five years (2005, 1995, 2010, 2011,2012) have names beginning with the letter 'O' and beyond been used, but there have been several other years in which more than 14 storms have been tracked, such as 1887-19 storms, 1933-21 storms, 1936-16 storms, 1969-18 storms, 1995-19 storms, 2005-28 storms, 2010-19 storms, 2011-19 storms, and 2012-19 storms. The 2010 Atlantic hurricane season has been extremely active, being the most active season since 2005. It must be noted that 2010, 2011 and 2012 seasons tie the record with the 1995 North Atlantic hurricane season and the 1887 North Atlantic hurricane season for the third most named storms (19). Furthermore, 2010 also ties the record with the 1969 North Atlantic hurricane season and 1887 for the second most hurricanes (12). The 2012 North Atlantic hurricane season was the third most active season, tied with 1887, 1995, 2010, and 2011. It was an above average season in which 19 tropical cyclones formed. All nineteen depressions attained tropical storm status, and ten of these became hurricanes. Two hurricanes further intensified into major hurricanes. The first three of these years were well before the naming of storms began, but 1969 requires an explanation. This was early in the era of complete satellite coverage, and forecasters were still studying the evolution of non-tropical systems (sub-tropical) into warm-core, tropical-type storms. Several systems that year were not named as tropical because they began at higher latitudes and were initially cold-cored.

Formal classification of subtropical (hybrid type) cyclones and public advisories on them began in 1972, and a few years later a review was made of various types of satellite images from the late 60s and early 70s, and several of these systems were included as tropical storms. In fact, two of the storms added in 1969 were hurricanes, so 1969 now stands as having 12 hurricanes. Today, subtropical storms are named using the same list as tropical storms and hurricanes. This makes sense because subtropical cyclones often take on tropical characteristics. Imagine how confusing it would be if the system got a new name just because it underwent internal changes. There is no subtropical classification equivalent to a hurricane. The assumption is that once a storm got that strong, it would have acquired tropical characteristics and therefore be called a hurricane, or it would have merged with an extratropical system in the North Atlantic and lost its name altogether. For example, on October 24, 1979, a subtropical storm briefly reached hurricane strength as it neared Newfoundland, Canada. It quickly combined with another low-pressure system, but it was never named.

Whenever a hurricane has had a major impact, any country affected by the storm can request that the name of the hurricane be 'retired' by agreement of the World Meteorological Organization (WMO). Prior to 1969, officially, retiring a storm name meant that it could not be reused for at least ten years to facilitate historic references, legal actions, insurance claim activities, and so on and to avoid public confusion with another storm of the same name. But today, these storms are retired indefinitely, and if that happens, it is replaced with a storm's name with the same gender because the retired storm often becomes a household name in the regions or countries it affected. The practice of retiring significant names was started in 1955 by the United States Weather Bureau, after hurricanes Carol, Edna, and Hazel struck the Northeastern United States and caused a significant amount of damage in the previous year. In 1977, the United States National Oceanic and Atmospheric Administration passed control of the naming lists to the WMO Region IV Hurricane Committee, who decided that they would retire names at their annual session when required.

The deadliest storm to have its name retired was Hurricane Mitch, which caused over 10,000 fatalities when it struck Central America during October 1998 (only one storm, 2008's Hurricane Paloma, caused no deaths at all), while the costliest storm was Hurricane Harvey, which caused over $125 billion in damage when it struck the U.S. Gulf Coast in August 2017. Since the formal start of naming during the 1947 North Atlantic hurricane season, an average of one storm name has been retired each season, though many seasons (most recently 2009) have had no storm names retired. The most recent tropical cyclone to have its name retired was Hurricane Joaquin, which caused severe flooding in The Bahamas in 2015.

When that list of names is exhausted, the Greek Alphabet (Alpha, Beta, Gamma, Delta, Epsilon, Zeta, Eta, Theta, Iota, Kappa and Lambda) is used. It must be noted that so far, this list has only been used once in either the Pacific or the North Atlantic basins, which was in the North Atlantic hurricane season of 2005. It is important to note here that there were a few subtropical storms that used the Greek Alphabet in the 1970s, but they were not truly tropical in nature. There was Subtropical Storm Alpha of 1972, which was a pre-season storm that made landfall in Georgia, and then there was Subtropical Storm Alfa in 1973, which briefly threatened Cape Cod but stayed out to sea. The 22nd named storm of a year when the naming list is exhausted would be Tropical Storm Alpha. Additional storms, if needed, would be named Beta, Gamma, Delta, and so on.

Several extremely rare weather events occurred in the 2005 North Atlantic hurricane season. First was the fact that Tropical Storm Alpha formed, which was a moderately strong tropical storm that made landfall in the Dominican Republic killing nine persons and then over Haiti, killing 17 persons before being absorbed by Hurricane Wilma's large circulation. This was notable because it was the first tropical storm to be named with the Greek Alphabet in the North Atlantic basin after the list of hurricane names was exhausted. Second, at the time it was thought that Alpha was the twenty-second storm of the season, and so was the storm which broke the 1933 season's record for most storms in a single season. However, in the post-season analysis it was revealed that there was also a previously unnoticed subtropical storm, on October 4, which made Alpha the twenty-third storm of the season.

Finally, the WMO Region IV Hurricane Committee (the governing body for hurricanes of the North Atlantic) after the 2005 North Atlantic season faced a serious dilemma, like that of the early 1950s with the naming of a storm after the military alphabet. Alpha caused significant damage and deaths over Haiti and the Dominican Republic that warranted this storm name to be retired, but just like the early 1950s, they realized that this storm would cause confusion in the record books if the primary list is once again exhausted and another tropical storm or hurricane named Alpha forms. So, this committee decided to retire the name 'Alpha of 2005' rather than just the Greek Alphabet 'Alpha' so that should this situation occur again, the name 'Alpha' can be reused again.

A majority of the costliest North Atlantic hurricanes in recorded history have peaked as major hurricanes. However, weaker tropical cyclones can still cause widespread damage. Both tropical storms Allison in 2001 and Matthew in 2010 have caused over a billion dollars in damage; the former of which accounted for a higher damage total. Due to their excessive damage, the names of tropical cyclones accruing over $1 billion in damage are often retired by the World Meteorological Organization. However, this is not always the case. Hurricane Juan in 1985 was the first hurricane to cause over a billion dollars in damage and not be retired; its name was retired on a later usage in 2003 that did not cause over a billion in damage. Since Juan, five tropical cyclones that caused over a billion in damage were not retired, the most recent of which being Hurricane Isaac in 2012.

The first hurricane to cause over $1 billion in damage was Hurricane Betsy in 1965, which caused much of its damage in southeastern Louisiana. Four years later, Hurricane Camille slightly exceeded Betsy's damage total after affecting similar regions, becoming the second tropical cyclone to cause as much damage. After the 1960s, each decade saw an increase in tropical cyclones causing at least a billion in damage over the last, due to increasing urban development and population located on or near the vulnerable hurricane-prone coastlines. In the 1970s, four hurricanes caused over a billion dollars in damage; the costliest of which was Hurricane Frederic, which caused $2.3 billion in damage, particularly in the Southeastern United States. The following decade featured seven hurricanes causing more than of a billion dollars in damage. In the 1990s, nine tropical cyclones accrued more than a billion dollars in damage. Hurricane Andrew in 1992 greatly exceeded the damage figure of any preceding tropical cyclone after causing $26.5 billion in damage, mostly in South Florida. Seventeen tropical cyclones in the 2000s caused more than a billion in damage. Both the 2004 and 2005 seasons had 5 billion dollars in damage individually, the most of any season on record. Hurricane Ivan caused at least a billion dollars in damage in three separate countries. Thus, far in the 2010s six tropical cyclones have amounted to over $1 billion in damage.

If a storm forms in the off-season, it will take the next name on the list based on the current calendar date. For example, if a tropical cyclone formed on December 29th, it would take the name from the previous season's list of names. If a storm formed in February, it would be named from the subsequent season's list of names. Theoretically, a hurricane or tropical storm of any strength can have its name retired; retirement is based entirely on the level of damage and deaths caused by a storm. However, up until 1972 (Hurricane Agnes), there was no Category 1 hurricane that had its name retired, and no named tropical storm had its name retired until 2001 (Tropical Storm Allison). Allison is one of only three tropical storms (Matthew in 2010 and Erika in 2015 were the other two) to have their names retired without ever having reached hurricane strength. This is at least partially since weaker storms tend to cause less damage, and the few weak storms that have had their names retired caused most of their destruction through heavy rainfall rather than winds.

While no requests for retirement have ever been turned down, some storms such as Hurricane Gordon in 1994 caused a great deal of death and destruction but it was still not retired, as the main country affected-Haiti-did not request retirement. Hurricane Gordon in 1994 killed 1,122 persons in Haiti, and 23 deaths in other nations. Damage in the United States was estimated at $400 million, and damages in Haiti and Cuba were severe. Despite the tremendous damage caused, the name 'Gordon' was not retired and was reused in both the 2000 and 2006 North Atlantic hurricane seasons. Since 1950, 77 storms have had their names retired. Of these, two (Carol and Edna) were reused after the storm for which they were retired but were later retroactively retired, and two others (Hilda and Janet) were included on later lists of storm names but were not reused before being retroactively retired. Before 1979, when the first permanent six-year storm names list began, some storm names were simply not used anymore. For example, in 1966, 'Fern' was substituted for 'Frieda,' and no reason was cited.

In the North Atlantic basin, in most cases, a tropical cyclone retains its name throughout its life. However, a tropical cyclone may be renamed in several situations. First, when a storm crosses from the Atlantic into the Pacific, or vice versa, before 2001 it was the policy of National Hurricane Center (NHC) to rename a tropical storm that crossed from the Atlantic into the Pacific or vice versa. Examples included Hurricane Cesar-Douglas in 1996 and Hurricane Joan-Miriam in 1988. In 2001, when Iris moved across Central America, NHC mentioned that Iris would retain its name if it regenerated in the Pacific. However, the Pacific tropical depression developed from the remnants of Iris was called Fifteen-E instead. The depression later became Tropical Storm Manuel. NHC explained that Iris had dissipated as a tropical cyclone prior to entering the eastern North Pacific basin; the new depression was properly named Fifteen-E, rather than Iris. In 2003, when Larry was about to move across Mexico, NHC attempted to provide greater clarity: "Should Larry remain a tropical cyclone during its passage over Mexico into the Pacific, it would retain its name. However, a new name would be given if the surface circulation dissipates and then regenerates in the Pacific." Up to now, it is extremely rare for a tropical cyclone to retain its name during the passage from the Atlantic to the Pacific, or vice versa.

Second, storms are renamed in situations where there are uncertainties of the continuation of storms. When the remnants of a tropical cyclone redevelop, the redeveloping system will be treated as a new tropical cyclone if there are uncertainties of the continuation, even though the original system may contribute to the forming of the new system. One example is the remnants of Tropical Depression #10 reforming into Tropical Depression #12 from the 2005 season, which went on to become the powerful and deadly Hurricane Katrina. Another example was a storm that had the most names, as stated earlier; in 1961, there was one tropical storm that had three lives and three names. Tropical Storm Hattie developed off the Caribbean Coast of Nicaragua on October 28, 1961 and drifted north and west before crossing Central America at Guatemala. It re-emerged into the Pacific Ocean on November 1st and was re-christened, Simone. Two days later, it recurved back towards the coastline of Central America and crossed over into the Atlantic via Mexico, re-emerging into the Gulf of Mexico as Inga.

CHAPTER THREE

How Bahamians Tracked and Monitored Hurricanes in the late 1800s and early 1900s

During the late 1800s up until the mid-1930s (the era before satellite and radars), there were several ways in which residents knew that a storm was approaching The Bahamas. Many of these methods were often weather folklores or simple deductions of the weather based on past knowledge or experiences with them. Unfortunately, the warning system back then was not as effective or efficient as the warning system nowadays. Typically, coastal residents may have had less than a day or even just a few hours to prepare or evacuate their homes from an approaching hurricane. For this reason and because of more substandard housing, the damages sustained, and the death toll back then were much higher than that of today.

Watching the sea-level rise or the storm surge before the onset of the hurricane.

Before the onset of an approaching storm, the sea-level often rose significantly above normal positions. Many persons on land would measure the time between the waves hitting the shoreline either with a stopwatch or mentally and that gave them an indicator of how far away the storm was located. By watching this rise in the sea-level and swells approaching the shoreline, the locals could tell whether there was an approaching storm. Today, this rise in the sea-level just before the onset of the storm and during the storm is referred to as the storm surge. Just before the onset of an approaching hurricane, the sea would give these residents a small window of opportunity to prepare for a hurricane or to evacuate to a hurricane shelter.

Watching the clouds and other weather elements

The weather lore that follows has been derived from several sources, including older Bahamian fishermen and older persons within the Bahamian community. The sayings are very old and have been passed on from generation to generation. One of the first signs of an approaching hurricane is the clouds. These clouds often appeared in stages. First are the high-level cirrus-form clouds, which is then changed to altostratus or nimbostratus clouds, then to stratus-form clouds, and finally to cumulus and cumulonimbus clouds. These residents, especially on the Family Islands, might not have known the types of clouds or names of the clouds. They knew the process by which these storm clouds appeared during a storm's arrival, and they used that as an indicator to prepare for an approaching storm. They also had the clouds in combination with the winds and the rainfall, which over time became stronger and heavier as the hurricane approached the islands.

According to other Bahamian fishermen, atmospheric pressure also helped them determine the weather. They said that knowing from which direction the wind was blowing helped them to locate where the highs and lows were relative to their position. For example, if they stood with their backs to the wind, a high-pressure cell will probably be to their right. If their right was west, then they predicted fair or improving weather because weather systems usually move from west to east. Furthermore, the ways in which the wind direction changed also helped them to predict the weather. If the wind was out of the south, then it changes to the southwest, then west, then northwest, it is changing in a clockwise direction and they deduced that the wind was veering. If it changes in a clockwise direction, such as first blowing out of the west then southwest, then south, then southeast, the wind was said to be backing. Sometimes a backing wind is a sign of an approaching storm front, they speculated. The speed of the wind was also an indicator of the changing weather. A strong wind usually means a big differential in air pressure over a small space. This meant that a low-pressure system was approaching, and it would likely be intense.

Many of the sayings of weather folklore made use of the correlation between these weather indicators and the effects they may have on observable phenomena. For example, as the humidity becomes higher, human hair becomes longer. It follows, then, that if your hair seems to curl up at the end and seems more unmanageable, it could be a sign of the rain. They also said another good sign of high humidity is salt. Salt tends to become sticky and clog the holes in the saltshaker if the humidity is high.

Placing hurricane signal flags on the forts and lighthouses in Nassau and on the various Family Island lighthouses

All British Imperial Lighthouse Service light stations were issued a set of signal flags. These flags were kept ready once there was an approaching storm or hurricane to warn incoming or outgoing ships and residents of an approaching hurricane. For centuries before the invention of the radio, sharing of information between ships from shore to shore and from sea to shore posed communications problems. The only way for mariners to pass a message from one ship to another or from ship to land was by visual signals. For many years preceding the invention of the telegraph (and during its invention), some type of semaphore signaling from high places, towers or forts was used to send messages between distant points. To this day, we still signal ships at sea with flags flown from shore-based towers and from other ships displaying storm warning flags.

On Hog Island (now called Paradise Island), there was a lighthouse located there and to the right of this lighthouse would be a flag and a flagpole displaying the Union Jack of Britain. If there was a known hurricane travelling near to or was scheduled to pass over The Bahamas, that flag would be removed and replaced with a specialty hurricane flag. This flag consisted of a red flag with a black square in the middle or a gale flag (two red triangle flags indicated gale warnings with winds from 34 to 47 knots) just before the onset of the hurricane or gale. The flag would be removed only after the hurricane or gale conditions had passed.

There were also hurricane flags placed on Forts Charlotte and Fincastle to warn residents of an impending storm. Similar events would also take place on Family Island Lighthouses if they had knowledge of an approaching hurricane. This signal flag also gave residents on Nassau and the Family Islands a small grace period to prepare for a storm. Currently, with satellite communications and instant weather information, these flags are rarely used. There is a famous watercolour painting by the world-famous artist Winslow Homer showing pastel-coloured houses with the trees and hurricane signal flag and flagpole swaying in the winds near the lighthouse on Paradise Island during this hurricane in 1899. This painting is now on display in the Metropolitan Museum of Art in New York.

The Parameter or Barometer Shell

A top and bottom view of an unpainted or non-dyed "Barometer" Shell (Image courtesy of Wayne Neely).

One of the ways residents on some Family Islands tried to forecast the weather was by using a local shell called the 'parameter' or 'barometer shell.' The shell got its name from the barometer instrument used for measuring atmospheric pressure. The content of the shell would be allowed to dry out, and then it was painted in a blue dye called 'Iniqua Blue.' According to some residents, they swore that this method of weather forecasting was indeed very accurate and quite reliable. Muriel Rolle, a resident of The Bluff, South Andros stated that "as a young girl, my father Didamus Dames taught me and my sister how to forecast the weather using this shell by looking at the changes in the colour of the dye of this shell. He would hang it at the back door and when he went out to sea he would take this shell with him", she recalled. "Many times he would ask me to remind him to take this trusty weather indicator with him out to sea on his boat", she noted.

My grandfather Jerry Gibson, said everyone in South Andros had and used this shell frequently to forecast the weather because that was all they had because there were no weather offices, radios or televisions to give them a more accurate reading. The shell would be hanged up in most of the homes at the time, and if it was going to rain the shell turned speckled white. For heavy rain, the dots would turn significantly bigger and the colour of the blue ink would turn a deeper shade of blue. If the rain was light, the dots would become much smaller in size, and if it was calm or fair weather, the shell turned ashy white. As you can guess, this was an unreliable method to forecast the weather, as compared with the modern methods and instruments of today. Today, meteorologists still use an instrument called a barometer to measure air pressure.

Watching the birds and other animals

According to some residents, especially on the Family Islands, they would watch the birds, especially the seabirds preparing for an approaching storm. They said that if there was a storm approaching the island, the seabirds would instinctively fly back in droves to the mainland from the various cays for shelter from the storm. Numerous Family Island residents said that these birds had a 'sixth sense' when it came to a hurricane because they would not return seaward until the hurricane had passed over that island. Others said that the caged and farm animals like the chickens, pigs, and goats would start behaving differently just before the onset of a hurricane by trying to get out of their cages or simply making much louder noises than usual. This, of course, was a very unreliable method as compared to the methods of today and perhaps was one of the main reasons why the death toll was so high on many of the Family Islands.

Birds and hurricanes have always co-existed in an annual life-and-death struggle. Survival has never come easy for birds, be they migratory land birds, shorebirds or birds that spend most of their time over the open waters. During the periods from 1866 to 1899, mid to late 1920s and early 1930s were especially treacherous, especially for migratory land birds such as, thrushes, warblers, flycatchers and sparrows and seabirds such as, white crown pigeons, seagulls, frigate birds. The frigate bird was also called the 'Hurricane Bird' by the residents because of its uncanny nature to show up just beyond the onset of a hurricane. The residents noticed this irregular migration pattern of these sea birds and deduced that a hurricane was approaching their island.

The effects of these hurricanes on their migration patterns were watched closely by native residents and the fishermen at sea. Watching these birds were critical to their survival because by observing their movements, it provided a small window of opportunity for them to prepare for an impending storm and in the end, these birds no doubt saved many lives in the process both on land and at sea. This forced hurricane migration occurs because these birds face a dual threat and one threat is the loss of food resources, like insects or fruiting fall flowers and berries that have been stripped of vegetation. The other is the possibility of birds being carried off course by the storm. While a hurricane is at sea, some ocean-dwelling birds will seek shelter in the eye and just keep flying inside the eye until the storm passes over the coast where they will take refuge on land. This phenomenon is why birders flock to areas struck by hurricanes. The storms afford them the opportunity to spot other species of birds in places where they are not supposed to be. As a result, they can be carried 100 miles or more off their intended course.

Before giant waves slammed into the Bahamian coastline in the 1800s and 1900s, many Bahamian residents said that wild and domestic animals seemed to know what was about to happen and fled to higher ground for safety. According to several eyewitness accounts, they said that the following events happened just before the onset of a hurricane. First, wild and domestic animals such as hogs, chickens, goats, sheep, and other animals screamed and ran to higher ground or away from the coastal areas. Second, dogs and cats would refuse to go outdoors or leave the yard. Egrets, wild pigeons, seagulls, frigate or hurricane birds, flamingos, and other seabirds would abandon their low-lying breeding areas near or on the coast and would proceed to move to higher ground.

The belief that wild and domestic animals possess a sixth sense and that they knew in advance when a hurricane would strike has been around for centuries. Wildlife experts believe that animals' more acute hearing and other senses might enable them to hear or feel the Earth's pressure changes, tipping them off to an approaching hurricane long before humans realize what's going on. In most cases, after the passage of a hurricane over that island, many of these residents reported that relatively few animals had been reportedly found dead, reviving speculation that those animals can somehow sense an impending storm. On the beach, some Bahamians were washed away by the storm surge, but some of these residents reported seeing very few if any animals washed ashore in the storm. In 1929, the Bahamian coast was home to a variety of animals, including crabs, iguanas, lizards, shorebirds, seagulls, flamingos, and other land animals. Quite a number of these residents reported that they did not see any animal carcasses, nor did they know of any, other than one or two fish caught up on the shore in the wake of the storm. Along the shore, many persons perished from the storm surge; however, many Family Islanders reported that most of the goats, sheep, cattle, and dogs were found unharmed after the storm passage.

Flamingos, White Crown Pigeons and other birds that breed during the summer months on many of the Bahamian Islands, including, Andros, Abaco, Eleuthera, Exuma, Inagua, and quite a few other islands as well, flew to higher and safer grounds ahead of time and away from the hurricane-prone coastal areas. Many of these residents said that they, too, watched this movement and prepared for the impending storm. South Andros native the late Mr. Daniel Rahming recalled watching the White Crown Pigeons and other seabirds frantically flying away just before the onset of the Great Bahamian Hurricanes of 1926 and 1929. Also, the late Mr. Illford Forbes, who lived on the coast in the settlement of High Rock, South Andros said his two dogs would not go for their daily walk before the hurricane in 1926 struck. "They are usually excited to go on this outing," he said, "But on this day of the hurricane, they refused to go for their walk and most probably saved my and their lives." Alan Rabinowitz, Director for science and exploration at the Bronx Zoo-based Wildlife Conservation Society in New York, says animals can sense impending danger by detecting subtle or abrupt shifts in the environment. He noted that, earthquakes bring vibrational changes in the atmosphere, but some animals have acute senses of hearing, touch, and smell that allow them to determine something in there. He concluded by saying that humans did have this sixth sense, but they lost this ability when it was no longer needed or used.

Radio, Telegraph, and Telephone

News about an impending storm was broadcast over the radio, back then radio was considered a luxury item out of the reach of the masses. The much-needed radio service provided by ZNS never really began to operate as a broadcast medium until May 26, 1936. The telegraph was also another method of hurricane warning that came in handy for the Family Island residents.

During the time of rapid change in the telegraph industry, the telephone was patented by Alexander Graham Bell in 1876. Although the telephone was originally expected to replace the telegraph completely, this turned out not to be the case: both industries thrived side by side for many decades.

On some of the major islands, there was a local telegraph station, and this station provided a valuable link between the islands and New Providence, and indeed the rest of the world. The phone was also available but not to the masses, and at the time it was considered a luxury item that only the rich in the society could afford. Eventually, with ZNS coming on stream on May 26, 1936, it provided a valuable tool as a hurricane warning service. At the time, officials in The Bahamas Government were concerned that residents on the Family Islands were not getting timely weather reports and hurricane warnings. The result of this was that many lives were lost in the process to these storms. One of ZNS Bahamas' first mandates was to provide a hurricane warning service to the major Family Islands around The Bahamas. Because of this important mandate, many lives were saved.

Newspaper

Often news about an impending storm would be featured in the local newspapers of the Nassau Guardian, the Nassau Tribune and The Bahamas Gazette. Many times, if some other island in the Caribbean experienced this storm and it was headed in the general direction of The Bahamas, it was given prominent front-page coverage in these newspapers.

Barometer

The instrument used to measure atmospheric pressure is called a barometer. The change in the pressure and how fast it is changing are more indicative of the weather than the pressure itself. Pressure differences are caused by the uneven heating of the Earth's surface. Rapidly falling pressure or low-pressure areas almost always means an approaching storm system. Rapidly rising pressure or high-pressure areas almost always means clearing and cooler weather ahead. High-pressure areas are produced by heavy, sinking air. They are characterized by pleasant weather and little or no precipitation. An area of high pressure is sometimes called a high-pressure cell, or simply a 'high.' Low-pressure cells are usually called 'lows.' As air rises, it cools, and cooler air can hold less moisture. So, if the rising air reaches an altitude where it is too cool to hold the amount of moisture it had on the ground, that moisture condenses out as clouds and precipitation. Thus, low-pressure areas produce cloudy and rainy weather.

The barometer in days gone by was the Bahamian residents' version of the radio and television of today. Many residential homes had as a staple in their homes a local barometer to warn them about impending hurricanes. However, these barometers gradually faded out of these homes once radios and televisions were introduced to the masses as a hurricane warning system. Most of the fishing boats going out on sponging and fishing trips at sea often had a barometer on their boats, especially during the hurricane months of June through November, when the hurricanes were known to strike. Whenever there was a steep drop in atmospheric pressure, that would be the first sign of an approaching storm. They would immediately then make their way back to the mainland. Some of the fishermen would move their boats onto the land or into the mangrove swamps, where they would be protected from the storm.

The local Family Island Commissioner had a barometer stationed at his residence or in his office. If the barometer showed any indication that a storm was approaching that island by a steep drop in pressure, he would then go about informing the residents to start making the necessary preparations for the storm. In addition, those private residents who had a household barometer often took it upon themselves to warn other residents who didn't have a barometer of an approaching storm. That would mean battening down their houses and staying indoors or moving to the nearest hurricane shelter, which at the time was comprised mostly of churches and schools on the various islands.

Although Evangelista Torricelli, a student of Galileo, invented the mercury barometer in 1643, it was the discovery of the Aneroid Barometer in 1843 by Lucien Vidie that brought the barometer into common usage. This barometer was used in The Bahamas as early as 1854, but it came into widespread use during the late 1800s and early 1900s. Sponging was the number one industry in The Bahamas during this hurricane. With the falling pressure of this barometer of this era, it was virtually impossible to predict a storm's track, timing, velocity, or the falling pressure difference between a normal afternoon thunderstorm and a hurricane, both of which would cause a steep drop in atmospheric pressure.

The following rules for the use of the barometer were explained by an unnamed observer, an inhabitant of Harbour Island, Eleuthera: -

1) In the hurricane months, if the barometer falls with a N or NE wind, it should awake attention, and if it falls below 29.90 inches, it is almost certainly a gale approaching, even though it might be perhaps 100 miles away.

2) During the approach, the barometer falls from noon until morning and then rises to noon again; every day falling lower than the previous day.

3) From sunrise to noon, any rise of fewer than 0.05 inches is unimportant, but the smallest fall during that period certainly indicates bad weather.

4) On the contrary, from noon to morning its fall is not conclusive of bad weather, but its rise certainly indicates improved weather.

5) Though the weather is ever so threatening at sunset, the rise of 0.05 inches or upward assures you that there will be no gale before morning.

6) Though the weather is ever so fair in the morning, the fall of 0.05 inches before noon, betokens a gale before night (provided it's already below 29.90 inches).

A normal barometer reading in The Bahamas is 30.00 inches. An area of depression that is generally attended by winds varying from moderate to hurricane force causes a fall in the barometer at a rate varying with the rapidity and strength of the approaching storm. As the storm recedes and the depression fills the barometer and rises to normal, the distance away from the center can only be estimated.

Fall of Barometer per hour from distance in miles from the storm center:

0.02 to 0.06 ins. 250 to 150 miles.
0.06 to 0.08 ins. 150 to 100 miles.
0.08 to 0.12 ins. 100 to 80 miles.
0.12 to 0.15 ins. 80 to 50 miles.

The following may serve as a light guide, but too much reliance should not be placed on it. In these latitudes storms travel at varying rates of progression, ranging from 5 to 20 mph, generally decreasing as the storm track turns northward and recurves, increasing again as it reaches the North Atlantic. The storm area is usually small, the region of violent winds seldom extending more than 150 miles from the center. The barometer falls rapidly as one progresses from the circumference toward the center. There are two periods of high barometer readings each day, one occurring about 10 am, the other at 10 pm and two corresponding periods of low barometer reading at 4 am and 4 pm.[36]

These rules and guidelines were strictly adhered to by most of the residents and fishermen on the various Family Islands to give them an indicator of an approaching weather system. These rules or laws governing the barometer usage remained in place until May 26, 1936, when ZNS Radio Bahamas began broadcasting as a hurricane warning station.

Word of mouth

This was a very effective form of a warning system for the residents on the various Family Islands. If there was a steep drop in pressure indicated on the barometer, a usual rise in the sea-level, or if a resident read in the newspaper or by other means found out that there was a hurricane travelling, that person would take it upon himself to go around and warn residents that they needed to take the necessary precautions before the storm passed near to or over the island. This also meant that once the word was received in Nassau and on the Family Islands, this resident would proceed to warn other residents on the respective islands about an approaching storm.

---

[36] J & A, Lawlor, *The Harbour Island Story*, (Oxford, Macmillan Publishers Ltd., 2008). Pg. 206.

CHAPTER FOUR

The Major Bahamian Hurricanes from 1494 – 1600

The Vicente Yáñez Pinzón Hurricane or the Crooked Island Hurricane of 1500: –In the year 1500, there was a major hurricane to hit during the latter part of June or early July near Crooked Island in the SE Bahamas. Vicente Yáñez Pinzón lost two caravels (ships) with their crews near the island of Crooked Island in The Bahamas; his other two vessels sustained damage but escaped to Hispaniola for repairs. This is the first hurricane known in The Bahamas and probably Florida as well. This case was first mentioned by Moreau de Jonnes in 1822 and other historians later. According to another historian, Justin Winsor in 1891 wrote: "Vincente Pinzón (Commander of the ship *Niña* during Columbus' First Voyage to the New World) had just returned from discovering Brazil, crossed the Gulf of Paria, continued sailing into the Caribbean Sea and the Gulf of Mexico, until he found himself in The Bahamas Islands, and there he lost two of his caravels and two others severely damaged, on account of being shattered against some rocks in the vicinity of Crooked Island."[37]

Spanish navigator Vicente Yáñez Pinzón (1463-1514) captained the ship *Niña* during Italian explorer Christopher Columbus's First Voyage to the New World in 1492. Furthermore, he went on to participate in the exploration of Brazil, becoming that nation's first governor. When 15th-century Genoese-born explorer Christopher Columbus embarked upon the voyage that would change the course of world history, he travelled with a crew of what he considered foreigners. Funded by the king of Spain

---

[37] José Millas, *Hurricanes of The Caribbean and Adjacent Regions 1492-1800*, (Miami, Edward Brothers Inc./Academy of the Arts and Sciences of the Americas, Florida, 1968). Pgs. 36-37.

rather than Italy, he headed what was primarily a Spanish expedition. From the controls of the flagship *Santa Maria*, Columbus benefited from the navigational skills of the brothers Pinzón in captaining the two remaining ships in his small squadron. Martín Alonso Pinzón, who was destined to become a thorn in Columbus's side during the voyage, oversaw the *Pinta* while the less volatile Vicente Yáñez Pinzón captained the *Niña*. While Martín died, dishonoured, shortly after his return from the New World, Vicente went on to distinguish himself as an exceptional explorer in his own right in subsequent years and is credited with the discovery of the Brazilian mainland and being the first European to sail up the mouth of the Amazon River.

The squadron sailed to the Caribbean and arrived without incident within four weeks. Reaching the coast of Brazil and landing at Cabo Santa Maria de la Consolacion, near what is now Pernambuco, on January 26, 1500, Pinzón and his crew followed the Brazilian coast northward, eventually reaching the mouth of the Orinoco river in what would eventually become Venezuela. During this part of his voyage, he became the first European to enter the Amazon, which he mistook for the Ganges River of India due to the inaccuracy of his map. Encountering groups of native Arawaks, Pinzón accomplished what his late brother had wished to do on Columbus's First Voyage: he acquired a great quantity of gold, as well as emeralds and pearls, through trades. By July, with his four ships fully laden, Pinzón and his men decided to turn northward and begin their return trip to Spain. During a stop off the coast of Haiti, he encountered Columbus, now on his Third Voyage, whose efforts to colonize the area were proving problematic due to the animosity developing between the Taíno Indians and the European intruders.

In late July of 1500 Pinzón's good luck finally ran out, as the *Pinta* was lost, caught in a hurricane while anchored near Crooked Island in The Bahamas and near the Turks and Caicos Islands. She sank, fully loaded with gold and jewels, along with another ship, the *Frailia*. Suffering the loss of many men and now with only two somewhat battered ships remaining, Pinzón managed to barely make it back to Palos, in Spain arriving there in October. Two years later, during a subsequent voyage, he tried to salvage the cargo of the two vessels lost on this expedition, but no record remains regarding the success or failure of this attempt. Instead, he reported of success in trade, as he anchored in the Gulf of Paria and traded with the native tribes for gold and other valuables. Turning southeast toward the

South American continent, Pinzón made the return trip to Spain via Santo Domingo where in July of 1504 he encountered a distraught Columbus, now on what would be the Italian's explorer's fourth and final voyage.

In September of 1500 Columbus went back to Palos in Spain after suffering the loss of two of his ships. The following words about Vicente Pinzón are in Justin Winsor's book (1891, pg. 377): "Vicente Pinzón touched at Espanola (Hispaniola) in the latter part of June 1500. Proceeding thence to the Lucayan Islands, two of his caravels were swallowed up in a gale, and the other two were disabled. The remaining ships crossed to Espanola to refit, whence sailing once more reached Palos in September 1500." From Peter Martyr, another historian we have: "When in the month of July, they were overtaken by such a sudden and violent storm that, of the four caravels composing the squadron, two were engulfed before their eyes. The third was torn from its anchorage and disappeared; the fourth held good but was so shattered that its hull almost burst wide open. The crew of this fourth ship, in despair of saving it, landed. The tempest ceased; the caravel which had been driven off by the fury of the elements returned with eighty of the crew, while the other ship, which held to her anchorage, was saved. It was with these ships that, after being tossed by the waves and losing many of their friends, they returned to Spain, landing at their native town of Palos, where their wives and children awaited them."

Washington Irving, another historian, wrote: "He (Pinzon) reached the island of Hispaniola about June 23 from whence he sailed for The Bahamas. Here, in July, while at anchor, there came such a tremendous hurricane that two of the caravels were swallowed up with all their crews in sight of their terrified companions; a third parted her cables and was driven out to sea, while the fourth was so furiously beaten by the tempest that the crew threw themselves into the boats and made for shore...They again made sail for Spain and came to anchor in the river before Palos, about the end of September."[38]

Vicente Yáñez Pinzón was a Spanish navigator, explorer, and conquistador, the youngest of the Pinzón brothers. Along with his older brother Martín Alonso Pinzón who captained the *Pinta*, sailed with Christopher Columbus on the First Voyage to the New World in 1492,

---

[38] José Millas, *Hurricanes of The Caribbean and Adjacent Regions 1492-1800*, (Edward Brothers Inc./Academy of the Arts and Sciences of the Americas Miami, Florida, 1968). Pgs. 36-37.

as captain of the *Niña*. While the ships were near Crooked Island in The Bahamas in 1500, a hurricane struck, causing two ships to sink. The other two returned to Spain. In March 1980, treasure hunters Mr. Olin Frick and Mr. John Gasque located what they believed to be the wreck of the *Frailia*, the second ship that sank. Later they returned and removed two cannonballs, which turned out to be made of solid lead. This dated the wreck before 1550, after which iron and lead together were used in the manufacture of cannonballs.

These two treasure hunters claimed to have found the *Pinta*, one of three ships Christopher Columbus sailed to the New World in 1492. They hoped to raise the vessel from its grave on a tropical reef and bring the remains to the United States for display. Olin Frick and John Gasque, president, and vice-president, respectively, of Caribbean Ventures, Inc., first located the shipwreck in 1977 in 30 feet of water near The Bahamas on the West Caicos Bank, about 125 miles off the northern coast of Haiti. Based on the archeological opinions and 15th-century historical records, they felt sure that the sunken wreck was that of the *Pinta*, believed to have gone down in a hurricane in July 1500 while on another New World expedition. The following year, Gasque returned to the site and discovered another shipwreck which reportedly fits the description of the *Pinta's* sister ship *Frailia* which also went down in the same hurricane.[39]

The Hurricane of 1550: –The two-hundred-ton Spanish carrack (nao in Spanish) *Visitación* left Havana with treasure for Spain but was lost during a hurricane just off the Florida Keys and The Bahamas.

The Hurricane of 1551: –A Spanish galleon *Hernando de Escalante Fontaneda*, owned by the viceroy of Mexico, Don Luis de Velasco, sailing in the *Nueva España Flota*, commanded by Captain-General Sancho de Viedma, separated from the convoy during a hurricane and was wrecked on the 'Silver Shoals', then sank in deeper water. Divers could recover only 150,000 pesos of the treasure it carried. Hernando de Escalante Fontaneda survived a shipwreck, and the *Calusa* rescued the crew and passengers. They then sacrificed all the other castaways but enslaved him; he escaped after 17 years in captivity and reported the tale.

The Hurricane of 1554: –In February of 1552, the preparation by the Spanish rulers began to prepare a fleet of ships to be dispatched to the New World and on November 4, 1552, fifty-four ships left Spain under the

---

[39] https://www.upi.com. Retrieved: 21-06-2015.

command of Captain-General Bartolemé Carrano. These ships included the three that were to be eventually wrecked on Padre Island. Of the 54 ships, 16 were bound for Vera Cruz, but only six of the 16 were scheduled to make the round trip back to Spain. The vessel carried a cargo of slaves, manufactured goods, hardware (nails, knives), textiles, wine, and even a harpsichord. However, sometime in February 1553 or as late as March 1553, 14 of the 16 ships bound for Vera Crus arrived. Due to a powerful hurricane, which wrecked the port in September 1552, only two of the six boats were scheduled to return in 1553, which got unloaded and reloaded to return to Spain with three other vessels. Then in the spring of 1553, the other four had to wait until 1554 for the next scheduled fleet. For their protection, ships could only travel in designated fleets. On April 9, 1554, four ships were organized as a fleet and left Vera Cruz bound for Spain, via Havana, Cuba loaded with returning conquistadors, Dona Catalina de Ribera, wife of Juan Ponce de Leon (murdered in 1552), and a combined cargo of about £96,000 of precious metals or approximately 2 million pesos ($9.2 million at today's rate of exchange). The ships included:

1) *San Andrés* - Master Francisco de Huertos
2) *San Esteban* - Master Franciso del Huerto
3) *Espírutu Santo* - Master Damián Martín
4) *Santa Maria de Yciar* - Master Alonso Ojos and Captain and pilot, Miguel de Jáuregi, the ship's owner.

The *Santa Maria de Yciar* - ship of 220 tons that had 20 officers and seven ship's boys. It was armed with ten pieces of heavy artillery, 22 versos, and had 5000 numbers of hardtack, 2 barrels of meat, 50 barrels of water, olive oil, beans and vinegar, 22,000 pounds of cochineal, 1226 cow hides, 13 barrels of sugar, and about 27,500 pounds of silver/gold. The three ships carried a combined total of 87,000 pounds of precious metal (if all silver, approximately $6.6 million with silver at $4.75 an ounce). Approximately, 35,801 pounds were salvaged, leaving some 51,330 pounds unaccounted for after the expedition. The Spanish recovered about 40% of the precious metal. Of course, most of the remaining cargo was pretty much a total loss. For example, on the *Santa Maria Yciar,* only about 41% of the silver/gold were recovered, and of approximately 15,000 pounds of treasure, only 6,225 pounds were recovered.

This hurricane passed near the extreme eastern end of the Old Bahama Channel (between Cuba and the SE Bahamas). About the year 1554, two vessels carrying a load of silver were sailing and encountered a storm in the Bahama Channel. The ships were wrecked, but all on board were saved and taken ashore, also the money. They placed the silver in a corral that they made of stone, with a wall separating the two halves, and in each part, the treasury section of one ship was deposited. Those that found room boarded in a frigate that they made with the remains of the two vessels, but they were wrecked sailing towards Cuba, all being drowned except two persons, a sailor, and a Negro woman. The only island near Hispaniola where the ships were lost is Great Inagua, but it is very small, and not near the Old Bahama Channel. Near Hispaniola could be taken as in the direction of Hispaniola. Perhaps the entire region between Cay Lobos and the Ragged Island chain can be considered as the possible place of the disaster. Salvors were sent from Cuba, but they were not able to locate the island where the survivors and silver were marooned.[40]

The Don Tristan de Luna y Arellano Hurricane of 1559: –During the night of September 19, 1559, a massive hurricane entered Pensacola Bay and devastated the colonial fleet of Don Tristán de Luna y Arellano at anchor near the recently established settlement of Santa María de Ochuse. Seven ships were lost because of the storm, including six that were grounded and sank, and one that was pushed a short distance inland and deposited on land within a grove of trees. There were seven ships lost that day, three of which have now been discovered and investigated by the faculty, staff, and students of the University of West Florida maritime archaeology program.

The Spanish conquistador Don Tristan de Luna y Arellano was sent to conquer Florida in 1559. On August 15, 1559, he landed near present-day Pensacola, establishing the first European settlement in the continental United States. Just weeks later, on the evening of September 19, 1559, a hurricane, which lasted for 24 hours, decimated the settlement and destroyed de Luna's fleet. Those who survived tried to re-establish the settlement, but due to famine and attacks, their attempts failed. The site was abandoned in 1561. After de Luna's colony was destroyed, it was concluded that Florida was too dangerous to colonize, and the Spanish

---

[40] Robert F. Marx, *Shipwrecks in the Americas*, (New York, Dover Publications Inc. 1987). Pg. 314.

did not attempt to settle on the U.S. Gulf Coast again until 1693, 134 years later. In 1992, the Florida Bureau of Archaeological Research discovered the remains of a Spanish sailing ship, a galleon, off Emanuel Point during a survey of Pensacola Bay. It is thought that this may be one of Tristan de Luna's sunken ships. Thousands of artifacts and field specimens have been recovered, and a substantial portion of the ship's hull architecture was recorded.

The Don Tristan de Luna y Arellano Hurricane of 1559 wrecked a Spanish expedition fleet and the first documented hurricane to strike Florida. A Spanish fleet sent to recapture Florida sailed into a hurricane. Most of the fleet was sunk, but one ship survived and founded a colony near Pensacola, Florida. This storm destroyed 7 of the 13 ships anchored in what is now called Pensacola Bay, the fleet of Spaniard Don Tristán de Luna y Arreland, who had been appointed to the task by the viceroy of New Spain, Luis de Velasco. This storm also impacted The Bahamas (Image courtesy of Wikipedia).

.This failed, and the project was abandoned within two years of de Luna's initial landing at Pensacola Bay. When news of the devastation finally arrived in Veracruz on October 5, the de Luna expedition was instantly transformed from a bold colonial venture into a rescue operation, and all subsequent ship traffic between Veracruz and Pensacola focused on sending food and other supplies to the hapless colonists. The colonists ultimately became so hungry that they moved inland to the nearest large Indian town along the Alabama River, and were eventually forced to send a detachment of soldiers hundreds of miles upriver to the edge of the Appalachian summit in northwest Georgia, trading whatever they owned in exchange for corn and other food supplies. The Spanish would not return to the area until 1698 when they re-established a settlement that persists today as the American city of Pensacola. There is no written record of tropical cyclone activity in this area again until the early 18th century: though other storms came before, it was in 1559 that Spanish explorers recorded the first hurricane in Florida, 'The Great Tempest', as it was called back then, and nature had gotten the better part of the small colony.

In 1992, the Florida Bureau of Archaeological Research discovered the remains of a Spanish sailing ship, a galleon, off Emanuel Point during a survey of Pensacola Bay. They are known as the Emanuel Point shipwrecks. It is thought that this may be one of Tristan de Luna's sunken ships. Thousands of artifacts and field specimens were recovered, and a substantial portion of the ship's hull architecture was recorded. In addition, this powerful and deadly hurricane also struck The Bahamas on September 19, 1559. This hurricane was first spotted just off the coasts of The Bahamas and Florida, where it sunk several ships and killed a significant number of sailors. Pensacola history notes this hurricane sinking five ships, with a Spanish galleon, grounding a caravel, and killing nearly 500 of 1,500 colonists and crewmen at Punta de Santa Maria across from Santa Rosa Island. Approximately, 15 years after the first ship was found, another was discovered, helping archaeologists unlock secrets to Florida's Spanish past. The colony at the site of present-day Pensacola was abandoned in 1561, and no trace of it has been found on land. The first de Luna ship was found in 1992 in the same area, near what de Luna founded as Florida's initial European settlement.

A view of 18th century sailing ships in Pensacola Bay. The settlement of Pensacola, Florida vanished for more than a century after the Don Tristan de Luna y Arellano Hurricane of 1559 (Courtesy of Wikipedia).

The Hurricane of 1563: –This hurricane of this era was recorded in 1563, and again the Bahama Channel was the setting. There was the loss of the ship *Urca of Tristan de Salvatierra* with thirty-five persons drowning during a storm in an undetermined month of the year. There was another hurricane which also sunk several other Spanish ships in the treasure fleet bound for Spain. It is an unprecedented Florida tale of fathers and sons spanning the better part of 500 years. Not only does the story stretch the length of the Spanish treasure route, it incorporates lost history, sunken treasure, the establishment of St. Augustine (the oldest continually occupied European city in North America), Hernando de Escalante Fontaneda, Pedro Menendez de Aviles, and the son he lost as the result of a 1563 hurricane.

Pedro Menendez's son, Juan Menendez, grew up to be a marine and military expert who achieved the rank of general before the age of 30. Like his father, Captain General Juan Menendez was tasked with protecting Spain's treasure fleets and placed in charge of the 1563 New Spain fleet's *Capitana*, and *La Concepcion*. The 500-ton warship led the fleet as it sailed away from the New World to deliver its gold and silver to Spain while the *Almiranta Santa Catalina*, a ship of war just like the *Capitana*, guarded the rear of the convoy. The treasure fleet is thought to have been carrying more than 17,000 pounds of gold home to Spain with the clear majority being carried by the *Capitana, Almiranta*, and a third ship, *El Angel Bueno*.

A reported slave ship, in addition to as much as 5,000 pounds of gold, the *El Angel Bueno* is thought to have been carrying ivory and Incan artifacts. As a matter of comparison, when the Spanish treasure ship *Nuestra Senora de Atocha* sank off the Marquesas in the Florida Keys during a 1622 hurricane, the ship had less than 1,000 pounds of gold on its manifest.

In 1563, the commander of the fleet, Captain General Juan Menendez, decided to ignore wise advice from his father regarding safe sailing practices. According to Barbara Purdy's book 'West of the Papal Lines,' the elder Menendez told his son, "In the whole month of July you can come out of the Bahama Channel, but do not sail after the first of August because of the great hurricanes."[41]

Unfortunately, the 1563 New Spain fleet encountered severe weather conditions in the lower Caribbean causing the convoy to arrive at Havana Harbour later than expected. To make matters worse, by the time the last two Honduran merchant ships scheduled to join the convoy arrived in Havana, July had turned to August. It was September 7 when Menendez led 12 ships bound for Spain out of Havana Harbour. Hurricane conditions quickly engulfed the fleet. Along with the *Angel Bueno, La Concepcion* was reported lost September 10. Eleven ships in the convoy survived the storm's ravages.

The location of the two ships lost in the storm has never been determined. Early searches for the *Angel Bueno*, as well as the *Concepcion*, were concentrated near Bermuda after 35 crew members from the *Angel Bueno*, swept away by the currents of the Gulf Stream, were rescued in a long boat six days later at 32.1°N latitude.

Because it is thought the shipwreck survivors had been considered mutineers, after their rescue they lied about where their ship had gone down. The disappearance of the *Angel Bueno* and *Concepcion* has been considered one of the great mysteries of the Spanish treasure fleet era. While the story of the 1563 treasure fleet is still unraveling today, the mystery began to reveal itself in the late 1950s to early 1960s when several of the ships' cannon were found in the Bahama Channel near the Florida Keys by treasure hunters, however, the mother lode of the treasures from these ships were never recovered even to this day.

---

[41] http://treasureworks.com/forums/32-shipwreck-hunting/14391-1563-wrecks-of-the-angel-bueno-and-la-concepcion-been-found. Retrieved: 28-12-2016.

The Hurricane of 1564: –The Spanish Galleon *Santa Clara*, weighing approximately 300 tons, Captain Juan Diaz Bozino, sailing in the *Tierra Firme Armada* of Captain-General Estevan de las Alas, ran aground on October 6 on the El Mime Shoal but fortunately, all its people, goal, and silver were saved by other ships in the fleet or convoy. On sixteenth-century charts, this shoal was situated several miles north of Memory Rock on the Little Bahama Bank and later, the shoal was called 'Mimbres' by the Spaniards.

The San Mateo Hurricane of 1565: –A powerful hurricane in 1565 destroyed the French fleet near Florida. The French had an outpost at Fort Carolina (near modern-day Jacksonville, Florida), lost their bid to control the Atlantic coast of North America when a storm destroyed their fleet, allowing the Spanish at St. Augustine to capture Fort Carolina, Florida. In September 1565, France and Spain were both trying to seize sole possession of Florida to oust the other from having a presence in the New World. The French were based in Fort Caroline, near present-day Jacksonville, and were led by the naval officer and navigator, Jean Ribault. Admiral Pedro Menéndez de Avilés led the Spanish, located at the newly established city of St. Augustine, some 40 miles from Fort Caroline. Jean Ribault (1520 – October 12, 1565) was a French naval officer, navigator, and a colonizer of what would become the southeastern United States. He was a major figure in the French attempts to colonize Florida. A Huguenot and officer under Admiral Gaspard de Coligny, Ribault led an expedition to the New World in 1562 that founded the outpost of Charlesfort on Parris Island in present-day South Carolina. Two years later, he took over command of the French colony of Fort Caroline in what is now Jacksonville, Florida. He and many of his followers were killed by Spanish soldiers near St. Augustine.

On September 20, Ribault and his troops set south by sea to attack the Spanish settlement at St. Augustine. Ribault's top aide, René de Laudonnière, warned the French leader not to do so as he believed a powerful storm could be at sea and a Spanish attack on Fort Caroline might also occur. Ribault did not heed these helpful warnings. As a result, the hurricane did make landfall across the area on September 22, destroying the French fleet. A few hundred crewmen working the five ships survived and were tossed ashore somewhere between present-day Matanzas Inlet and Cape Canaveral, Florida. Interestingly, while Ribault was at sea trying to get to St. Augustine, de Avilés and his troops were marching north towards Fort Caroline. The Spanish fleet killed most of the remaining Frenchmen at the unguarded fort and later destroyed Ribault and the remainder of his battalion when the two groups finally crossed paths some place near Matanzas Inlet, which is about 14 miles south of St. Augustine. This defeat, accomplished in part with the help of the hurricane, eliminated French control in Florida.

The Spanish founded St. Augustine about a month before the hurricane. The establishment greatly strengthened the Spanish influence in the New World, as this permanent settlement became a critical outpost that served to protect Spain's control of the Americas. This outpost was especially important for their Spanish treasure fleets which often travelled through the Florida Straits and the Bahamian waters taking their valuable treasures back to Spain. The Spanish refer to this hurricane as "San Mateo" as it occurred one day after the feast day for the patron Saint, Matthew.

The Hurricane of 1567: –An unidentified ship of Captain Gonzalo de Peñalosa was wrecked on Cayo Romano in the Little Bahama Bank.

The Hurricane of 1568: –This hurricane led to a British conflict against the Spanish over Central America. Sir John Hawkins was a notable British shipbuilder, naval administrator, commander, navigator, and merchant. As a navigator, he went on three overseas voyages to the Caribbean, based largely on the slave trade. His third voyage in 1568 proved to be quite troublesome. In early September 1568, as Hawkins was crossing the Gulf of Mexico, his fleet was blown off course by a hurricane. The fleet spotted the port of San Juan de Ulua, near present day Vera Cruz, Mexico, and landed there on September 16, 1568. This was a Spanish-controlled territory, but the lost, British sailors were able to form an initial truce with the Spanish upon their landing. Unfortunately, this truce did not last for long. A fierce battle ensued that month as the Spanish launched a surprise attack on the English. Many men lost their lives and all but two British ships were sunk. Sir Hawkins commanded one of the surviving ships, Francis Drake the other.

After his experiences with the hurricane and resultant battle with the Spanish, Hawkins went on to greatly strengthen the British Navy. He became chair of the English Naval Board and enacted beneficial financial reforms. He also redesigned the British Galleon, a ship that would help the British defeat the Spanish Armada in 1588. Many of these battles occurred in or near The Bahamas and in the Old Bahama Channel. After commanding the second of the remaining British ships, Francis Drake was knighted (Sir Francis Drake), and vowed revenge against Spain. Drake sailed to the West Indies several times looking to attack the Spanish. In 1572, he and his men were able to raid 20 tons of gold and silver from the Spanish settlements in Panama. Taking back as much as they could, Drake returned to England very rich and his exploits made him a hero in British legend in the annals of British history. Craving more adventure, he set off to circumnavigate the world, gaining another historical achievement for England.

The Hurricane of 1569: –A storm passed in the Old Bahama Channel in the month of September of this year.[42]

The Hurricane of 1586: –A Spanish treasure fleet of 61 ships under Juan Tello de Guzmán gathered together from all parts of the Caribbean at Havana and then left for Spain. During a storm in Old Bahama Channel, most of the ships caught in this hurricane were lost including:

- The 120-ton ship of the line (*navío* in Spanish) *San Francisco* under Juan Alonso from Puerto Rico.
- The 120-ton *navío Nuestra Señora de la Concepción* under Simón Rixo (or Rizo) from Puerto Rico,
- The 120-ton carrack (*nao* in Spanish) under captaincy of Martín de Irigoyen from Mexico, and
- Five or six other vessels.

Surviving ships included the 120-ton *Navío San Sebastián* under Diego Hernández from Puerto Rico.

The Hurricane of 1589: –An English squadron (naval) awaited the return of Spanish treasure-laden ships from the Caribbean. Philip II of Spain, King of Iberian Union, consequently ordered that the Spanish Navy (Armada in Spanish) under Captain General Alváro Flores de Quiñones, Tierra Firma fleet, and Spanish treasure fleet (Flota de Nueva España in Spanish) from Vera Cruz all meet in Havana and travelled together in a large convoy to Spain. The convoy of 75 to 100 ships left Havana on 9 September and entered Old Bahama Channel; a hurricane quickly struck. Even before the hurricane, the 350-ton merchant carrack (nao in Spanish) *Santa Catalina* under ownership of Fernando Ome and captaincy

---

[42] García-Herrera, Ricardo; Gimeno, Luis; Ribera, Pedro; Hernández, Emiliano (2005), "New records of Atlantic hurricanes from Spanish documentary sources", Journal of Geophysical Research. Retrieved: 17-02-2017.

of *Domingo Ianez Ome*, coming from Mexico with cargo, sank in 30 fathoms (180 feet or 55 meters) of water "in about 30 degrees of latitude." The 400-ton nao *Jesús María* under ownership of Domingo Sauli and captaincy of *Francisco Salvago*, coming from Mexico, also sank in similar circumstances. A third merchant *nao* also sank with these two. In the hurricane at the month of Old Bahama Channel, the *Almiranta* of Flota de Nueva España developed a bad leak and fired a cannon for assistance and sank quickly with her great treasure lost in very deep water.

In addition, Gonzalo Méndez de Canço, later governor of Florida, reports that Martín Pérez de Olazábal commanded a fleet; during a storm, one of his ships was wrecked at Cape Canaveral. San Agustín (now St. Augustine, Florida) assisted four battered and dismasted ships carrying more than 450 persons; one ship entered the port and departed for Spain. The frigate of the presidio at San Agustín also discovered and rescued forty members of the crew of the ship lost on Cape Canaveral. This 'hurricane' event may continue or be mixed up with another storm of this season. If the "Old Bahama Channel" in the other entries for this year refers instead the northern extension of the "Straits of Florida," then this and the preceding listing may originate in different recollections of the same storm event.

The Hurricane of 1595: –There was a loss of seventeen Spanish treasure bearing ships off the coast of Abaco in 1595 with no indication of the time of year. To lose that many ships would imply a storm of great fury (or extremely poor seamanship) but no indication of the time of the year.

The Hurricane of 1599: –This hurricane struck sometime in the latter part of June or the first few days of July near the island of Great Inagua in The Bahamas. Captain Hernando Del Castillo, Andrés de Samaniego and perhaps a third person were sailing to Havana, where an English pirate robbed them and took them to his vessel. Afterwards, driven by a storm, they arrived at the island of Inagua, where the ship was lost, but he and two other Spaniards were saved by another passing ship. Later, while leaving, they went searching for water on this cay, and while they were leaving, they discovered an enormous treasure of silver bars, plates of gold, and pieces of ordnance in the water. They speculated that it must have been part of the cargo of the fleet of ships that were also lost there by this same hurricane. They took special note and position of the nearby islands and cays so that they can remember the location of the treasure when they return to salvage it. Eventually, they took two tenders, salvaging what they could and took it to the Royal Officers of Cuba (or Hispaniola as some documents showed) and after deducting their expenses, they were left with the remaining portion.[43]

---

[43] José Millas, <u>Hurricanes *of The Caribbean and Adjacent Regions 1492-1800*,</u> (Edward Brothers Inc/Academy of the Arts and Sciences of the Americas Miami, Florida, 1968). Pgs. 91-92.

CHAPTER FIVE

The Major Bahamian Hurricanes from 1600 – 1800

The Sea Venture Hurricane of 1609: – From its start, the Virginia colony suffered from unrealistic expectations, political infighting, violence between Indians and settlers, and deprivation. Within weeks of being deposited on Jamestown Island by Captain Christopher Newport, the first settlers realized that the promises made by the Virginia Company of London—that the settlement would be safe, prosperous, and bounteous—had been greatly exaggerated. While the colonists futilely searched the forests for gold and the "other sea" (and a quick passage to the Far East), their leaders quarreled and alienated the powerful leader Powhatan (Wahunsonacock). Colonist George Percy quickly decided "There were never any Englishmen left in a foreign country in such misery as we were in this new discovered Virginia." Half the colonists who arrived in April 1607 were dead by October, and fewer than forty survived the winter. Newport made two supply trips to Virginia, in January and October 1608, both times bringing home more bad news: John Smith, a brash commoner, had assumed authority over a quarreling, ineffective colonial Council, the colonists refused to take orders, the Powhatan Indians struck at will, and famine and illness raged.[44]

By January 1609, with Newport back from the second supply trip, Sir Thomas Smythe, treasurer and de facto head of the Virginia Company of London, understood that his enterprise at Jamestown was failing in every conceivable way. The response of Smythe and the principal investors in the Virginia Company was not, however, resignation and evacuation, although

---

[44] http://www.encyclopediavirginia.org/Sea_Venture#start_entry. Retrieved: 29-01-2017

they considered it. Rather, they undertook a wholesale reorganization of their company and its colony and commenced an unprecedented public relations campaign to entice "adventurers"—their word for people who would wager either their money or their lives on Virginia.

Then on June 2, 1609, the Virginia Company of London sent across the Atlantic Ocean the largest fleet England had ever amassed in the West: nine ships, 600 passengers, and livestock and provisions to last a year. The audacious effort was born out of desperation to save Jamestown, and with it the whole idea of an English, Protestant presence in the Americas. Newport, the most experienced mariner of his age, was hired to captain the flagship *Sea Venture*. He carried the admiral of the fleet, George Somers; the new governor, Sir Thomas Gates; and significant passengers and crew members. Unlike the earlier crossings, which had transported too many gentlemen, this fleet carried skilled workers: shipwrights, carpenters, fishermen, masons, and farmers capable of building and sustaining a self-sufficient community.

Under Newport's experienced leadership, the fleet made good time. On July 24, the voyagers were within seven days of landfall when they were hit by a hurricane. As the rest of the fleet was scattered by this storm, one of the ships was lost in The Bahamas, but the *Sea Venture* bore the brunt of the storm and was soon separated from the other ships. As thirty-foot waves and violent winds rocked the ship, it sprung a leak so severe that, as one passenger put it, "we almost drowned within whilst we sat looking when to perish from above." For three days, the passengers and crew fought the rising water, but they were fighting a losing battle. In fact, to stop the water from flowing into the ship, they stuffed salt beef, clothing and anything else they could find to stem the leaks of the ship. On the fourth morning, the exhausted men and women gave up, and "commending our sinful souls to God, committed the ship to the mercy of the gale."[45]

In the late evening of June 2, 1609, the Virginia Company of London sent an impressive fleet of nine ships launched out of Plymouth Sound carrying 600 passengers and supplies to secure the Jamestown settlement in Virginia. The fleet was the largest England had ever sent across the Atlantic. It was an audacious effort born out of the desperate desire to save the dying colony huddled around Jamestown. The largest of the

[45] http://www.encyclopediavirginia.org/Sea_Venture#start_entry. Retrieved: 29-01-2017.

ships, the *Sea Venture*, carried both the governor of the new colony, Sir Thomas Gates, the admiral of the Virginia Company, Sir George Somers and captain Christopher Newport. Three of England's "most worthy, honoured gentlemen." Captain Christopher Newport was the nation's most experienced mariner, while Admiral George Somers, was a veteran of campaigns in Ireland, the Netherlands, and the Caribbean. Of the 150 passengers and crew on the *Sea Venture*, it included an assortment of soldiers, grocers, fishmongers, clothworkers, tailors, farmers, families, an Anglican minister and the newly appointed leaders of the colony.[46]

As the fleet drew near the Azores, a storm separated the ships. All the other ships but the *Sea Venture* made it to Jamestown, and it was presumed lost. The ship was not lost but endured a treacherous journey. As the *Sea Venture* continued to sail west, it had the misfortune of being struck by yet another hurricane on July 25. The deputy governor of Virginia, William Strachey, describes the event: "For four-and-twenty hours the storm in a restless tumult had blown so exceedingly as we could not apprehend in our imaginations any possibility of greater violence...the waters like whole rivers did flood the air...winds and seas were as mad as fury and rage could make them."[47]

The crew worked frantically during the hurricane and tirelessly pumped water out of the ship for three days following. The damage was so great, however, that water levels would not decrease. The ship had become "shaken, torn, and leaked." They did any and everything to stop the leak including stuffing salt beef into the leaking cracks. The crew and passengers were exhausted and discouraged. On July 28, just as the ship was about to sink, it came upon a rocky coast. It was the islands of the Bermudas, or "Island of Devils," as declared by Juan Bermudez, the Spanish explorer who had come upon the island in 1511 but refused to colonize it. Mariners often avoided the infamous area, as it was a place of "gusts, storms, and foul weather" that some believed was inhabited by evil spirits. The true source of Bermuda's infamy lay in the coral reefs that surrounded the island. It was these reefs, not devils, which were responsible for numerous shipwrecks along the atolls island's shores. Admiral Somers

---

[46] Lorri Glover and Daniel Blake Smith, *The Shipwreck That Saved Jamestown-The Sea Venture Castaways and The Fate of America*, (New York, Henry Holt and Company). Retrieved: 15-11-2016.

[47] http://www.hurricanescience.org. Retrieved:25-03-2017.

deliberately ran the *Sea Venture* aground onto one of these coral reefs to save those onboard. The boat "fell in between two rocks", and remarkably, all the people on the boat were saved.

The wreckage of the *Sea Venture* on the reefs of Bermuda inadvertently marked the island's settlement by the British. The settlers and crew found the land to be quite fruitful and would spend nine months on the island. As the men enjoyed bountiful food sources and adequate shelter, they built two new ships, *Deliverance* and *Patience*, to continue the journey to Jamestown. Although these ships did eventually set-sail for the Virginia colony on May 10, 1610, some passengers stayed behind. Even Admiral Somers eventually returned to the island and remained there till his death. William Strachey's account of the storm quickly circulated amongst his friends, one of which was William Shakespeare. The wreck of the *Sea Venture* off the coast of Bermuda is thought to have been the inspiration behind the playwright's "The Tempest" (even though the play took place in the Mediterranean).

For ten months, the castaways remained on Bermuda, while their countrymen in Virginia and England assumed them dead. As stated before, they built two small boats, which they named *Patience* and *Deliverance*, and sailed to Virginia, arriving on May 24, 1610. Word of their odyssey fascinated English men and women, who saw in the story providential design: surely, many concluded, God had saved the *Sea Venture* voyagers. The tale also attracted London's leading playwright: The *Sea Venture* contributed to the inspiration behind William Shakespeare's last major play, 'The Tempest.' Most importantly for the still-floundering Virginia colony, the amazing story encouraged the English to stick with their American enterprise and even expand their colonial presence in North America.

The saga of the *Sea Venture* swept London, far more importantly, many seventeenth-century Londoners believed that nothing, but the divine intervention of God could explain the events surrounding the *Sea Venture*. Protestant ministers, already committed to challenging the Catholic-Spanish domination of the Americas, and Virginia Company promoters, desperate for profits, eagerly spread the word. God, they claimed, had acted to save English America. As one minister put it, the events "could proceed from none other but the singular providence of God." As a result of this hurricane and the consequences that ensued, encouraged the English not to give up the American colony, which prior to 1609 they wanted to do.

The Somers Island (Bermuda) Company, named for George Somers, operated as a subsidiary of the Virginia Company from 1612 until 1615. During those years, the company sent about 600 colonists to Bermuda and consistently turned a profit. Bermudians enjoyed lower mortality rates and longer life expectancy than their countrymen in both Virginia and England. By 1625, nine forts secured the island from Spanish encroachments, ministers led services at six churches, and 2,500 residents were governed in part by an elective assembly. From the loss of the *Sea Venture* and the founding of Bermuda, England gained an invaluable entry into the Spanish-dominated Caribbean and the profits and hoped to continue pursuing its colonial ambitions.

One of the settlers to leave Bermuda after the shipwreck was John Rolfe. In Bermuda, he and first wife welcomed a baby girl, who unfortunately died on the island. Shortly after arriving at the Jamestown settlement, Rolfe then lost his wife. Within a few years, he would meet and then marry the famous Indian princess, Pocahontas. In 1615, the Somers Isles Company was formed to operate the English colony of Somers Isles, also known as Bermuda, as a commercial venture. Today, Bermuda is still a British Overseas Territory and acts as a popular tourism resort destination.

The Atocha Hurricane of 1622: –This storm was reported having traversed the Old Bahama Channel on September 15, 1622. This storm approaching from the east seemingly caught the Spanish Fleet (which was destroyed) by surprise as it came through the Old Bahama Channel. On September 6, 1622, at least six ships of the Spanish Terra Firma Fleet were wrecked by this hurricane taking the lives of 550 persons. Perhaps the most famous of these ships was the *Atocha* which Mel Fisher discovered back in 1985. The *Atocha* was driven by a severe hurricane onto the coral reefs near the Dry Tortugas, about 35 miles west of Key West. With her hull, severely damaged, the vessel quickly sank, drowning everyone on board except for three sailors and two slaves.

Nuestra Señora de Atocha ("Our Lady of Atocha") was the most famous of a fleet of Spanish ships that sank in 1622 off the Florida Keys in the Old Bahama Channel. They carried copper, silver, gold, tobacco, gems, jewels and indigo from Spanish ports at Cartagena and Porto Bello in New Granada (modern-day countries of Colombia and Panama, respectively) and Havana bound for Spain. The ship was named for the parish of 'Atocha' in Madrid. An unfortunate series of difficulties kept the *Atocha* in Veracruz before she could rendezvous in Havana with the vessels of the Tierra Firme

(Mainland) Fleet. The treasure arriving by mule to Panama City was so immense that during the summer of 1622, it took two months to record and load the precious cargo on the *Atocha*. After still more delays in Havana, what was ultimately a 28-ship convoy did not manage to depart for Spain until September 4th, 1622, six weeks behind schedule.

Spanish expansion in the New World was rapid, and by the late 1500s Mexico City, Lima and Potosi had populations that exceeded the largest cities in Spain. It would be another half a century or more before the chief cities of colonial North America-Boston, Philadelphia, and New York were to be founded. Colonists were granted vast tracts of land to grow tobacco, coffee, and other products for export to the European mainland. More important to the throne, however, was the region's significant amount of mineral wealth of silver and gold, which were vital to Spain's continued growth and expansion in the New World. Trade with the colonies followed a well-established system. Beginning in 1561 and continuing until 1748, two fleets a year were sent to the New World. The ships brought supplies to the colonists and were then filled with silver, gold, and agricultural products for the return voyage back to Spain. Spain needed these treasures to pay off loans and to continue to be the dorminant European superpower to maintain reign in the region over other European countries battling for control of the New World.

The two fleets sailed from Cadiz, Spain, early in the year, following the approximate route that Columbus had taken years before. Upon arrival in the Caribbean, the two fleets split up; the Nueva España Fleet continued onto Veracruz, Mexico and the Tierra Firme Fleet went onto Portobello in Panama. Here, the ships were unloaded, and the cargo of silver and gold brought aboard. For the return trip, the divided fleets reassembled in Havana then rode the Gulf Stream and the Old Bahama Channel north along the coast of Florida before turning east when at the same latitude as Spain. The treasure fleets faced many obstacles the two most significant of which were first, pirates and second, weather, but more specifically the dreaded hurricanes of the region. It was well-known that the hurricane season began in late July, so, for this reason, the operation was timed for an earlier departure. For protection against pirates, each fleet was well-equipped with two heavily armed guard galleons. The lead ship was known as the *Capitaña*. The other galleon, called the *Almiranta*, was to bring up the rear. A recently constructed 110-foot galleon, the *Nuestra Señora de Atocha*, was designated the Almiranta of the Tierra Firme Fleet.

The fleet departed Spain on March 23, 1622, and after a brief stop at the Caribbean Island of Dominica, the *Atocha* and the Tierra Firme Fleet continued to the Colombian port city of Cartagena, arriving in Portobello on May 24th. Treasure from Lima and Potosi was still arriving by mule train from Panama City, a port on the Pacific side of the Isthmus. It would take nearly two months to record and load the *Atocha's* cargo in preparation for departure. Finally, on July 22, the Tierra Firme Fleet set sail for Havana, via Cartagena, to meet the fleet returning from Veracruz. In Cartagena, the *Atocha* received an additional cargo load of treasure, much of it gold and rare first-year production silver from the recently established mints there and at Santa Fe de Bogata. It was late August, well into the hurricane season, before the fleet arrived in Havana.

As a military escort, the *Atocha* carried an entire company of 82 infantrymen to defend the vessel from attack and possible enemy boarding. For this reason, she was the ship of choice for wealthy passengers and carried an extraordinarily large percentage of the fleet's treasure. Unfortunately, firepower could not save her from the forces of nature. On Sunday, September 4th, with the weather near perfect, the decision was made to set sail for Spain. The twenty-eight ships of the combined fleet raised anchor and in a single file set a course due north towards the Florida Keys and the strong Gulf Stream current. The *Atocha*, sitting low from its heavy cargo, took up its assigned position in the rear. By evening, the wind started to pick up out of the northeast, growing stronger through the night. At daybreak, the seas were mountainous, and for safety, most everyone was below deck seasick or in prayer. Throughout the next day, the wind shifted to the south, driving most of the fleet past the Dry Tortugas and into the relatively safe waters of the Gulf of Mexico.

The *Atocha, Santa Margarita, Nuestra Señora del Rosario* and two smaller vessels all at the tail end of the convoy received the full impact of the storm and were not so fortunate. With their sails and rigging reduced to shreds, and masts and tillers battered or broken, the ships drifted helplessly toward the reefs. All five ships were lost, the *Atocha* being lifted high on a wave and smashed violently onto a coral reef. She sunk instantly, pulled to the bottom by her heavy cargo of treasure and cannon. The next day, a small merchant ship making its way through the debris rescued five *Atocha* survivors still clinging to the ship's mizzenmast. They were all that was left of 265 passengers and crew.

Salvage attempts began immediately. The *Atocha* was found in 55 feet of water with the top of its mast in plain view. Divers, limited to holding their breath, attempted recovery but were unable to break into the hatches. They marked the site and continued searching for the other wrecks. The *Rosario* was found in shallow waters and was relatively easy to salvage, but the other vessels could not be located. While the salvagers were, in Havana obtaining the proper equipment to retrieve the *Atocha's* treasure, a second hurricane ravaged the area, tearing the upper hull structure and masts from the ship. When they returned, the wreck was nowhere to be found, and salvage attempts over the next ten years proved futile. However, the *Santa Margarita* was discovered in 1626 and much of her cargo salvaged over the next few years. But time and events slowly erased memories of the *Atocha*. Copies of the ship's register and written events of the times eventually found their way into the Archives of the Indies in Seville, Spain. These documents, like the treasure itself, were to lay in obscurity, waiting for the right set of circumstances centuries later. Treasure hunter Mel Fisher discovered the *Santa Margarita* in 1980 and the *Atocha* on July 20, 1985, her hull lying in 55 feet of water, exactly as recorded by the first salvagers in 1622.

The *Santa Margarita* was a Spanish ship that sank in a hurricane in the Florida Keys about 40 miles west of the island of Key West in 1622. The story of the *Santa Margarita* begins in 1622. The namesake of the patron saint of homeless people, midwives, and reformed prostitutes, *Santa Margarita*, was a Spanish galleon of 600 tons, armed with twenty-five cannons. One of a fleet of 28 ships, she was voyaging to Spain with an enormous cargo of plundered New World wealth of treasures. In registered wealth, the *Santa Margarita* carried 166,574 silver "pieces of eight" treasure coins, more than 550 ingots of silver weighing some 10,000 pounds, and over 9,000 ounces of gold in the form of bars, discs, and bits. Additionally, there was contraband — a fortune in "unregistered" treasure having been smuggled on board to avoid paying a 20 percent tax to the Spanish king. The *Santa Margarita* also carried riches in the form of copper, silverware, indigo, and personal possessions of officers, passengers, and crew, including medical tools, navigational instruments, gold coins, and precious jewelry of almost unimaginable opulence.

Spain and her creditors awaited the arrival of the fleet anxiously; as its return would refresh the royal coffers, repay loans, and lessen the financial pressures that plagued the kingdom. When news of the fleet arrived, it wasn't good. After departing the island of Cuba on September 4, the fleet was overtaken by a rapidly developing hurricane. Within days, the *Santa Margarita*, along with five other ships in the fleet, were wrecked near the Marquesas Keys in the Florida Straits. Drowned were 550 passengers and crew, 142 from the *Santa Margarita*. Lost was a king's ransom in treasure, a serious setback for Spain, whose supremacy in the world was upheld by the wealth of the Indies. Margarita in Greek means pearl, and the first attempt to find and salvage the *Santa Margarita* and other fleet casualties were undertaken almost immediately by the Spanish mariner Captain Gaspar de Vargas, who, knowing of their skills, sent for pearl divers — from the island of Margarita — to aid in the search. Today, Mel Fisher's Maritime Heritage Museum in Key West in Florida displays salvaged artifacts salvaged from the wreckage of these two ships the *Atocha* and the *Santa Margarita*.[48]

The Hurricane of 1623: –Another hurricane moved through the same region as the one in 1622 and again caught the Spanish fleet at sea. Two ships were lost along with 150 members of their crew. The Tierra Firma Fleet or New Spain Armada under the General Antonio de Oquendo departed Havana on 26 April. The 480-ton Spanish galleon *Espíritu Santo el Mayor* under the captaincy of Antonio de Soto carried 1 million Spanish pesos. At the mouth of the Old Bahama Channel, a hurricane-generated massive waves that tossed the ships like corks. The *Espíritu Santo el Mayor* "opened and sank" in the hurricane so quickly that the other vessels rescued only 50 of the 300 persons aboard her; the additional 250, including her captain, drowned, and Spain lost all her supply of treasures. The 600-ton admiral galleon *Santísima Trinidad* under the captaincy of Ysidro de Cepeda sank slowly enough that other vessels of the fleet saved all persons aboard her, and several patches even recovered 1 million Spanish pesos of treasure. This tragedy occurred either on the high seas off West Palm Beach, Florida, the Old Bahama Channel or in nearshore waters of the Ais people on Treasure Coast of Florida sometime in September but this date can't be confirmed. The Ais, or Ays Indians were a tribe of Native Americans who inhabited the Atlantic Coast of Florida. They ranged from present-day Cape Canaveral to the St. Lucie Inlet, in the present-day counties of Brevard, Indian River, St. Lucie and northernmost Martin.

---

[48] https://www.revolvy.com/main/index/Atlantic hurricanes. Retrieved: 12-11-2016.

The Hurricane of 1630: –The Bahama Channel was once again the scene of a hurricane as two galleons under D. Antonio de Oteiza were lost during their journey to carry reinforcements to Florida, but this time all lives were saved.

The La Conception Hurricane of 1641: –This hurricane struck Cuba in September, and it was very likely that it moved through the SE Bahamas before hitting the Cuban coast. This course projection was based on the progression of wind patterns observed as the storm moved past Cuba. This hurricane was noted because of the loss of La Concepcion in this storm.[49] On September 28, 1641, the Spanish treasure fleet set sail for Europe from Havana. It was their second attempt for the season. Only ten days before: the fleet had sailed and encountered a storm and had to return to port for repairs.

The 680-ton Spanish galleon *Nuestro Señora de Ia Pura y Limpia Concepcion* flew the flag of Vice Admiral Juan Luis de Villavicencio. The *La Concepcion*, this leaking galleon with too small a rudder and overly high freeboard, was loaded to the gunwales with the treasures of the New World and the Orient. She carried tons of silver from the rich mines of Mexico and Potosi. Also, aboard were large quantities of gold and jewels, silks, spices, porcelain, and jade. Treasures from the Orient, which had been sent on the Manila galleons to Acapulco then transshipped overland to Veracruz and loaded aboard the fleet. In addition to the government cargo, the *La Concepcion* and other ships also carried a significant amount of personal treasure of Diego de Pacheco, Viceroy of New Spain, and payments being remitted by major merchants of all the New World colonies.

On the second voyage, the fleet once again encountered severe storms; the hurricane season was in full swing. The fleet was scattered in a hurricane during her voyage through the Old Bahama Channel en-route to Spain, and the *La Concepcion* was severely damaged. She drifted damaged for many days without masts or rudder, the pumps going full-time. On November 2, 1641, the hull and keel of the *La Concepcion* ran aground amidst the Silver Shoals coral reefs north of Hispaniola, present-day Haiti, and the Dominican Republic. Between the storm and the shipwreck, itself, starvation, exposure, and sharks killed over three hundred of those aboard the *La Concepcion*, and the others had no idea where they were located. Eventually, some reached Santo Domingo in makeshift rafts and boats

---

[49] https://www.facebook.com/notes/shipwreckhunter/the-loss-of-la-conception-in-1641. Retrieved: 24-03-2017.

constructed from the wreck but were unable to say exactly where the ship had sunk. Bad weather initially prevented salvage operations for several months, and when the weather finally moderated, the sandbar had been washed away, and the rescuers could not locate the wreck site.

Late in 1686 William Phips sailed for the island of Hispaniola with two ships and their crews, provisions and diving equipment, and in January of 1687, Phips' men found the wreck site. Phips and his men worked from February to April 1687 salvaging silver, jewels and some gold from the wreck. Some sources say the crew worked with the experienced Indian divers in the shallow waters. Other sources mentioned a diving bell. The diving bell was designed by Edmund Halley in 1691 and was used to provide divers with an additional supply of oxygen while underwater, allowing them to remain submerged much longer to collect the sunken treasure, yesterday's version of an oxygen tank.

Phips recovered 30 tons of silver worth over £200,000 which was a vast sum of money. Most of this went to the noble sponsors of the expedition when Phips returned to England. The new English King, James II, had not invested in the expedition but claimed a Royal share of the proceeds anyway. King James II must have been pleased by the contribution William Phips made to the Royal Treasury. The King knighted Phips and made him the Provost Marshal General or Sheriff of New England. Phips' share, about £12,000, made him a very wealthy man. Phips knew that he had recovered only a small fraction of the treasure which the *Concepción* had carried, so he returned to the wreck later to find it crawling with other adventurers, none of whom had much success. Eventually, the location of the *La Concepción* was forgotten, but over the years, the legend of the unclaimed sunken treasures grew. The reefs where the ship went down came to be known as, the "Silver Shoals," as occasionally, a piece of eight scattered from a chest would glint in the sun. In November 1978, the *La Concepcion* was found again by treasure hunter Burt Webber. Other members of the team were Jim Nace, Jack Haskins, Don Summer, Duke Long, Johnnie Berrier, John Harrier, Bob Coffey, and Henry Taylor.

Jim Nace found a coin, and by the end of the day, they'd found 128 pieces of eight, and some porcelain from the late Ming period. Although the treasure salvagers did find treasure scattered among the bottom about 60,000 silver cobs, most of the treasure had already been salvaged by William Phips. The coins were mainly 4 and eight reales, but there were some rare Potosi' and Colombians cobs from the Cartagena mint. It took

Webber's team eleven months to salvage all they could find at the site. Weber's crew retrieved an estimated thirteen million dollars' worth of treasure. Even to this day, the site is still worked with some success of finding buried treasure. After everything was divided between the Dominican government and the treasure salvagers, the government took its portion and placed it on the second floor of the Dominican Republic National Museum. A selection of this treasure toured a dozen US cities, where over 1.5 million people saw it. A CBS documentary, "The Lost Treasure of the Concepcion," was also broadcast on TV.

The story of Sir William Phips's recovery of the treasure from this ship in 1687 is well-known, but for some unknown reason, a myth has persisted stating that he did not recover all the treasure from this wreck. The fact is that he recovered almost twice the amount that the ship's registers reported she carried, and other salvors worked on the wreck both before and after Phips arrived on the scene, so there is little likelihood that there is much more left. Still, almost every year during the past two decades, there have been major expeditions after this wreck, including one in the summer of 1968, by world-famous explorer and scientist the late Jacques Cousteau who failed to locate the wreckage.

The Hurricane of 1644: –This hurricane severely impacted, western Cuba, The Bahamas, Straits of Florida (the Florida Keys). According to a later history of Franciscan priest-historian Diego López de Cogolludo, an English pirate armada of 13 hulk (medieval ship type) (urcas in Spanish) carrying 1500 men under the squadron Jacob Jackson (possibly William Jackson (pirate)) encountered this storm. In September, the fleet captured two Franciscan priests, Antonio Vazquez, and Andres Navarro, from a village in Mexico; the vessel also held eight other Spanish prisoners. Three ships stranded on the Arcas Reef in the Old Bahama Channel, and ten continued for Havana. Before leaving the Old Bahama Channel in The Bahamas, they suffered a violent southeasterly hurricane during which nine of the ten ships sank. During a lull in the storm (perhaps the eye), the sole surviving vessel deposited the ten Spaniards ashore, allegedly in Florida but probably in Cuba. The hurricane resumed from the opposite direction, and the ship sank also. Despite great hardships, the Franciscans eventually arrived in Havana to tell the amazing tale of surviving with great odds and demanding challenges that they had to overcome.

The Hurricane of 1657: –Within the Tierra Firme Fleet from Veracruz, the 650-ton ship *Nuestra Señora de las Maravillas* with Captain-General

Margues de Monte-negro collided with another Spanish vessel during the night. The whole fleet found itself in shallow waters and veered seaward and sunk in 30 to 35 feet of waters within The Bahamas and near the Straits of Florida with a loss of about 5 million pesos of silver. Of the more than seven hundred persons on this ship, only fifty-six were saved. The Spaniards began several marine salvage operations for the next three years aimed to recover this silver. This storm sunk two small marine salvage vessels with a considerable amount of recovered treasure of over 1,500,000 pesos of the 5 million pesos on the ship's manifest. This ship and its treasure were loss just off the south side of Gorda Cay in The Bahamas (now Disney's Castaway Cay). The survivors recovered and buried the treasure on the island until some Spanish ships came to their rescue and removed most of the treasure the following year. However, shifting sands, soon completely covered the wreck, so they had to abandon future salvage operations.

In modern times, many treasure hunters have searched for this wreck, but most of them in the Florida Keys-where other experts have placed the site of the wreck-until author and shipwreck expert Robert Marx discovered documents in Spain and learned its exact location, and even with this newly found evidence so far, no one has still not located it.

The Hurricane of 1692: –The final storm of this era presumed to have struck The Bahamas occurred on October 24, 1692. This storm caused significant damage in Cuba and based on its movement as it left that island and perhaps moved over The Bahamas and then over Florida.

The Hurricane of 1696: –A hurricane of unknown strength impacted South Florida and due to its proximately to South Florida and the NW Bahamas as well. The death toll in this storm is not known, but it impacted these areas sometime in late September or early October. Jonathan Dickinson, a Quaker merchant, and several of his travelling companions aboard the barque *Reformation* fell victim to the high seas whipped up by the storm. Tossed and battered by persistent wind and waves, the *Reformation* wrecked on a sandbar near what is today known as Jupiter Inlet.

The Hurricane of 1713: –This was the first hurricane reported to have impacted The Bahamas in the eighteenth century and is connected to a hurricane which devastated Charleston, South Carolina during the first week of September. Catesby reported visiting Eleuthera after this storm where he observed a boat stuck up in a tree some ten or twelve feet above ground and attributes this unique circumstance to the impact of the September storm.

The Hurricane of 1714: –The Spanish galleon *San Juan Evangelista*, part of the Armada de Barlovento, sailing from Veracruz to Puerto Rico and Santo Domingo with 300,000 pesos in treasure to pay the royal officials and military at both islands, was struck by a storm in the Bahama Channel and wrecked at 27 degrees latitude in 30 feet of water near Grand Bahama Island. Salvors recovered all the treasure and the ship's cannon.

The General D. Juan de Ubilla Hurricane of 1715: –This hurricane occurred in the early morning hours of July 31st near The Bahamas and the Straits of Florida. A hurricane struck the fleet (flota in Spanish) of General D. Juan de Ubilla in the Bahama Channel. Ten ships were lost, and with them, the General and one thousand persons. The 1715 Treasure Fleet was a Spanish treasure fleet returning from the New World to Spain. At two in the morning on Wednesday, July 31, 1715, seven days after departing from Havana, Cuba, eleven of the twelve ships of this fleet were lost in this hurricane. Because the fleet was carrying a large shipment of silver, it is also known as the 1715 Plate Fleet (Plata being the Spanish word for silver). Some artifacts and even coins still wash up on Florida beaches from time to time. Around 1,000 sailors perished while a small number survived on lifeboats. Many ships, including pirates, took part in the initial salvage. Initially a privateer, Henry Jennings was first accused of piracy for attacking such salvage ships and claiming their salvages.

In 1700 Charles II of Spain died, leaving no children or any apparent heirs. In his will, he nominated the grandson of Louis XIV of France to succeed him as Philip V. The English, Dutch, and Austrians looked upon this extension of Bourbon power as a highly dangerous threat to their countries. As a result, they joined forces to wage a destructive and costly war against Spain and France – the War of Spanish Succession – which continued until 1713. Although France lost, in the peace treaty the major European powers did agree to accept Philip V if the crowns of France and Spain were never joined.

During the war fought between the Dutch and English, they focused a great deal of their efforts and attention on disrupting communications between Spain and her American colonies. This deprived her of the prized treasures of the New World which she so badly needed to meet the mounting costs of war. In 1702, a combined Anglo-Dutch fleet destroyed a fleet of returning Spanish treasure ships and their French warship escorts in Vigo

Bay off the coast of Spain. Following this disaster, the Spaniards suspended the annual sailings of their treasure fleets to the Indies and made only three other attempts to bring back treasure to the mother country; two of these attempts failed. The English destroyed one fleet off Cartagena in 1708, and a storm wrecked another off the north coast of Cuba in 1711. In fact, so little treasure had reached Spain during the war that the Spanish Crown was on the verge of bankruptcy. As the war ended, Phillip V ordered that "as much treasure as possible must be brought back from the Indies without any regard for the costs or the dangers involved." He was so anxious for the safe arrival of the returning treasure ships that he expended the last monies and jewels in his coffers for masses to be said in churches throughout his realm.

At sunrise on July 24, 1715, a fleet consisting of twelve ships set sail from Havana Harbour for the long voyage back to Spain. It was composed of the five ships of the New Spain Flota (fleet), commanded by Captain-General Don Juan Esteban de Ubilla; six ships of the Squadron of Tierra Firme, commanded by Captain-General Don Antonio de Echeverz y Zubiza; and a French ship, the *Grifon*, under the command of Captain Antonio Daire.

Echeverz's squadron had sailed from Spain directly to Cartagena, Columbia, carrying assorted merchandise for sale at Cartagena, Porto Bello in Panama, and Havana. Upon arriving in Cartagena, Echeverz sent word to the viceroy of Peru to deliver, as usual, the treasure of Peru and Chile to Panama City; from there mules generally transported it overland to Porto Bello where a fair was held. The treasure would then be loaded aboard the ships of the Squadron of Tierra Firme and carried back to Spain. Echeverz also notified the governor of New Granada in Bogata to send his stored-up treasure, and the governor of the island of Margarita to send pearls. Because an English fleet under the command of Admiral Wager had destroyed the last Tierra Firme Squadron near Cartagena in 1708, the viceroy of Peru did not comply with Echeverz's request; instead, he had his treasure transported overland to Buenos Aires, thence by ship to Spain.

For some unknown reason, both the viceroy of New Grenada and the governor of Margarita Island also ignored the Captain-Generals orders. So, instead of the large amount of treasure he expected from South America, Echeverz received so little it was hardly worth the effort. The only treasure he netted was from the Governor of Cartagena, his royal officials, and some private individuals. Three of his ships, the *Capitana*, *Almiranta*, and *Nuestra Senora de Concepcion* carried both treasure and the usual cargo from the colonies which would be sold in Europe. The ship *El Ciervo* only carried 96 tons of brazilwood. On Echeverz's other two ships no known cargo or treasure was loaded in Cartagena or Porto Bello, but as with all other ships in this squadron, it is believed they took on a large shipment of tobacco in Havana.

Ubilla's flota consisted of eight ships when it sailed from Spain to Veracruz, but four were lost during a severe storm while in port, and when he sailed for Havana, he had only four ships. In Havana, he added a small frigate to his flota. Like the ships in Echeverz's squadron, Ubilla's *Capitana, Almiranta*, and *Refuerzo* carried both treasure and normal cargo. His patache, a much smaller vessel than the other three, had no royal treasure on board but did carry 44,000 pesos of silver specie in twelve chests and some loose sacks of leather. The ship's general cargo included a type of incense. Documents do not show or include whether the small frigate Ubilla bought in Havana shipped any cargo or treasure, but it is unlikely she carried valuables. The total of the registered treasure carried on four ships of Ubilla's flota – excluding the silverware, jewelry, and a small number of gold coins – was 6,388,020 pesos.

After the convoy left Havana, it made its way up the Bahama Channel. During the night of July 30, it was struck by a fierce hurricane that wrecked all the ships upon the coast of Florida, with the single exception of the *Grifon* which miraculously escaped. Over a thousand persons lost their lives, including Ubilla and his principal officers. About 1,500 persons reached shore by swimming or floating on pieces of wreckage, but some of them perished from exposure, thirst, and hunger before aid could reach them from Havana and St. Augustine.

Salvage efforts on the wrecks began immediately, and by the end of December, the officials in charge of the operation reported they had already recovered all the King's treasure and the major part of that belonging to private individuals, totaling 5,200,000 pesos. The following spring, they recovered an additional small amount, so that by July the Spaniards called a halt to their salvage efforts. When the Spaniards stopped their salvage work, a total of 1,244,900 pesos of registered treasure remained. Add an estimated 19% contraband, and it is believed that only 2,200,000 pesos remained unaccounted for. Using a conservative estimate of the sale price of $250 per coin, over $550 million of treasure remains to be recovered. Gold, which in terms of weight was sixteen times more valuable than silver, was the most common item smuggled back to Spain, and since there were almost no gold coins registered aboard the ships, those recovered in recent years from the wrecks must have been contraband. This is substantiated by the fact that most of the gold disks recovered lacked the required markings of registered gold bars. It is more than likely that a substantial amount was being smuggled in this convoy. No further mention of the wrecks was recorded until around the beginning of the nineteenth century when a surveyor reported discovering several hundred gold and silver coins on the beach near the Ft. Pierce inlet. Then once again the flota ships slipped into obscurity until recent times.[50]

List of the Deadliest Hurricanes of the North Atlantic from 1500-1825[51]

Name:	Dates Active:	Areas Affected:	Deaths:
Nicaragua	1605	Central America	1,300
Straits of Florida	**1622**	**Bahamas and Florida**	**1,090**
Cuba and Florida	1644	Cuba and Florida	1,500
Caribbean	1666	Caribbean	2,000
Barbados	1694	Barbados	1,000+
Bahamas	**1715**	**Bahamas**	**1,000-2,500**
Martinique	1767	Greater and Lesser Antilles	1,600
Havana	1768	Cuba	43-1,000
Newfoundland	1775 August 29-September 9	North Carolina, Virginia, Newfoundland	4,000-4,163
Pointe-à-Pitre Bay	1776	Guadeloupe, Lesser Antilles	6,000
Great Hurricane/San Calixto	1780 October 9-20	Barbados, St. Lucia, Martinique, St. Eustatius	22,000
Gulf of Mexico	1780	Mexico and US Gulf Coast	2,000
Savanna-la-Mar Hurricane	1780	Jamaica and Cuba	42-1,090
Florida	1781	Florida	2,000+
Central Atlantic	1782	Central Atlantic	3,000+
'Cuba' Hurricane	1791	Cuba	3,000
Martinique	1813	Martinique, Leeward Islands	3,000
Caribbean	1824	Caribbean	372-1,300+

List of the Deadliest Hurricanes of the North Atlantic from 1500-1825 (Image courtesy of NOAA-NHC).

---

[50] http://www.1715treasurefleet.com. Retrieved: 15-01-2017.
[51] The Deadliest Hurricanes of the North Atlantic from 1500-1825 (Information Courtesy of HURDAT, NOAA-NHC and Wikipedia). Retrieved: 15-10-2016.

The Hurricane of 1720: –In 1720, the Spanish fleet again met with disaster as two frigates of the Armada de Barlovento was lost in a storm in the Bahama Channel (Millas, 1968). The crew was saved, but Millas speculates that to do so would have required they be shipwrecked on one of the islands of The Bahamas, as attempts to rescue them during the storm would have been impossible.

The Woodes Rogers Hurricane of 1729: –Seven years after his first trip to The Bahamas as the first Royal Governor, Woodes Rogers returned to The Bahamas to take up his role as the Royal Governor for a second time and was faced with the aftermath of another hurricane. He had left England at the end of May 1729 and arrived in Nassau on August 25. This hurricane reportedly did significant damage to the city of Nassau, during the first week of August 1729. This provides the first report of substantial storm damage at one of the settlements in The Bahamas, although there presumably would have been several such incidents by this point in the colony's history. Its occurrence dates it three weeks before the arrival of the first Royal Governor of The Bahamas, Woodes Rogers in the colony.

Upon his arrival in the colony on August 25, 1729, he reported that this storm was very violent and that it had blown down the greatest part of the houses on the island, with many of these houses destroyed by the recent hurricane. The hurricane destroyed the timber guard room and two rooms built by Rogers. Furthermore, the magazine, prison and cook room built under the ramparts were so severely damaged that they were rendered unusable. He further stated that the Royal Assembly had not been able to sit and conduct the business of the colony because of the extensive damage was done by this hurricane. This storm has not been previously carried in any of the chronologies of hurricane activity in the North Atlantic.

The Hurricane of 1733: –When a Spanish Fleet tried to cross the Bahama Channel on July 15, 1733, they met their demise by a severe storm. This storm moved through the SE Bahamas before moving into the Bahama Channel where it caused the sinking of sixteen of the twenty vessels that comprised the fleet.

The Hurricane of 1752: –Sixteen ships were lost in a hurricane just off the north shore of Havana and struck The Bahamas on September 23 and Cuba on September 26.

The Hurricane of 1775: –During a hurricane on November 2, at least eleven merchantmen and several English warships were lost in the Windward Passage near the Turks and Caicos Islands.

The Savanna-la-Mar Hurricane of 1780: —Early in October, this hurricane sunk the British transport ship *Monarch*, killing several hundred Spanish prisoners and the ship's entire crew. The hurricane began to move northwest towards Jamaica, where it destroyed the port of Savanna-la-Mar on October 3. Many of the town's residents gathered at the coast to spectate, and a massive 20-foot surge engulfed the onlookers, docked ships, and many of the town's buildings. In the nearby port village of Lucea, 400 people and all but two structures perished, with 360 people also killed in the nearby town of Montego Bay. It would go on to sink the British frigate *Phoenix* (killing 200 of its crew) and ships-of-the-line *Victor, Barbadoes*, and *Scarborough* and crippled many others. It continued its direction, and hit Cuba on October 4, followed by a pass over The Bahamas. Overall, it is speculated by some estimates, that this storm caused 3,000 deaths.

Folklore places the devastation of this western town in Jamaica as the work of the runaway slave known as Plato the Wizard, from beyond the grave. Just before his 1780 execution, the renowned obeahman pronounced a curse on Jamaica - predicting that his death would be avenged by a terrible storm set to befall the island before the end of that same year. It is said that Plato and his band of other runaways kept the parish of Westmoreland in a state of perpetual alarm from his stronghold in the Moreland Mountains. Plato warned that whoever dared lay a finger on him would suffer spiritual torments. It is not surprising that no slave would set traps for Plato even though the reward for his capture was great.

Plato, was an example of the type of spirit slavery could not hold, but he did have one weakness, and that was drinking pure Jamaican rum, and it was proved to be his downfall. During a time when his usual supplies were curtailed because of a massive hunt on for his arrest, he arranged with a watchman he knew well, to go out and get him some rum. The watchman decided to use the rum as bait. It was easier than he expected. Soon after he handed Plato the rum, he fell into a drunken stupor and right into the watchman's trap. Plato was captured, tried and immediately sentenced to death. In response, he coolly cursed any and everything in sight as a dreadful power is said to have descended on him. Plato terrified the jailor who tied him to the stake by announcing that he had cast an obeah spell on him, and he did not have long to live. Soon after Plato's death, the jailor fell ill and died. Before the year was over, Plato's other curse came true - the island was hit by what was described as the most terrible hurricane that ever-spread death and destruction even in West Indian Seas. The region where Plato the Wizard had roamed free and died in betrayal was hardest hit.[52]

The Great Hurricane of 1780: –The Great Hurricane of 1780, also known as 'Huracán San Calixto,' the Great Hurricane of the Lesser and Greater Antilles, and the 1780 disaster, is the deadliest North Atlantic hurricane on record. Approximately 22,000 people died throughout the Lesser Antilles when the storm passed through these islands from October 10–16. The exact details on the hurricane's track and strength are unknown because the official North Atlantic hurricane database only goes back to 1851. The hurricane struck Barbados with winds possibly exceeding 200 mph based on empirical evidence, before moving past Martinique, Saint Lucia, and Saint Eustatius; thousands of deaths were reported on these islands.

Coming during the American Revolution, the storm caused heavy losses to British, Dutch, Spanish, and French fleets contesting for control of the area. The American Revolution (1775-83) is also known as the American Revolutionary War and the U.S. War of Independence. The conflict arose from growing tensions between residents of Great Britain's 13 North American colonies and the colonial government, which represented the British Crown. Skirmishes between British troops and colonial militiamen in Lexington and Concord in April 1775 kicked off the armed conflict, and by the following summer, the rebels were waging a full-scale war for their independence. France entered the American Revolution on the side of the colonists in 1778, turning what had essentially been a civil war into an international conflict. After the French assistance helped the Continental Army to force the British to surrender at Yorktown, Virginia, in 1781, the Americans had effectively won their independence, though fighting would not formally end until 1783.

The hurricane later passed near Puerto Rico and over the eastern portion of Hispaniola. There, it caused substantial damage near the coastlines. It ultimately turned to the northeast and was last observed on October 20 southeast of Atlantic Canada. The death toll from the Great Hurricane alone exceeds that of many entire decades of North Atlantic hurricanes. Estimates are significantly higher than for Hurricane Mitch in 1998, the second-deadliest North Atlantic storm, for which figures are likely more

---

[52] http://old.jamaica-gleaner.com/pages/history/story008.html. Retrieved: 12-12-2014.

accurate of about 12,000 persons killed and over with over 11,000 left missing by the end of 1998 in Central America from this hurricane. The Great Hurricane of 1780 was part of the disastrous 1780 North Atlantic hurricane season, with two other deadly storms occurring in October. While this hurricane didn't pose a direct threat to The Bahamas, the storm likely generated quite a few large northerly to northeasterly ocean swells along the eastern shores of The Bahamas during its' short lifespan, creating high surf conditions and dangerous rip currents along the northern and eastern coasts of The Bahamas.

The Hurricane of 1785: –Great damage occurred on Harbour Island and the Eleuthera mainland and damage occurred mainly to crops, buildings, and vessels, including two sloops belonging to Captain Higgs. Three ships were lost at New Providence Island: English transport ship *Hope Sherrer* was lost during a hurricane in September. Also, a ship of unknown registry, *Sally-Captain Croskill*, was wrecked at Nassau on October 24; and the American ship *Rodney*, with the ship's Captain Jenkins, while sailing from Florida to Jamaica sprung a leak and sunk on the Samphire Reefs near Nassau.

The Hurricane of 1789: –Lord Dunmore reported that the Anglican Church in Eleuthera was destroyed in this hurricane.

The Hurricane of 1796: –This hurricane occurred in the afternoon of October 3 and into the early morning hours of the October 4. It struck The Bahamas and caused significant interruptions to shipping and widespread damage throughout the country. The sloop *Rainbow* was lost in this storm, and at Harbour Island in Eleuthera, five boats were lost, and many houses were blown down by a very 'severe storm' as acting Governor Robert Hunt described it. This hurricane came from the western Caribbean Sea, and it recurved and moved from the southern part of the Isle of Pines to the northern coast of Cuba, near Havana: then it moved northeastward heading for The Bahamas on the afternoon of October 3.

The Hurricane of 1797: –This hurricane affected The Bahamas and South Carolina between October 15–19. Significant damage and losses occurred to shipping, where several ships were reported lost during this hurricane.

CHAPTER SIX

The Major Bahamian
Hurricanes from 1800 – 1900

The **Lowestoffe Hurricane of 1800:** –The British ship *HMS Lowestoffe* and eight homeward bound merchant ships, with cargoes of colonial produce, were shipwrecked in August on the island of Inagua. The loss was estimated at £600,000, exclusive of personal property. A loss of nine ships was undoubtedly a significant sea disaster, and the hurricane devastation was severe. The center of the storm crossed over the island of Inagua, moving west-northwest or northwest; it must have struck other islands of The Bahamas. The *HMS Lowestoffe* was a 32-gun fifth-rate frigate of the Royal Navy. Built during the latter part of the Seven Years' War, she went on to see action in the American War of Independence and the French Revolutionary War and often served in the Caribbean. The *Lowestoffe* has become famous as the ship in which a young Horatio Nelson served shortly after passing his lieutenant's examination.

Lowestoffe set-sailed from Kingston, Jamaica on July 22, 1801, and encountered a convoy five days later at Port Antonio. The escorts consisted of the ships *Lowestoffe*, *Acasta*, the sloop *Bonetta,* and the schooners *Musquito* (or *Muskito*), and *Sting*. While *Lowestoffe* was sailing through the waters of the Turks and Caicos Islands with the passage through these islands late on August 10, Pamplin realized that the strong currents known to run through the channel had reversed direction and *Lowestoffe* was running into shallow waters. He attempted to avoid grounding, but to no avail, and the *Lowestoffe* ran broadside onto Little Inagua ("Heneaga") Island. The two islands of Great and Little Inagua in early Bahamian history were generally called Heneauga or Heneaga.

The crew threw stores and equipment overboard to lighten the ship, and boats came from other ships in the convoy to try to pull her off.

The attempts to refloat her failed and her crew abandoned her by mid-afternoon. The only casualties were five men who drowned when their boat capsized in the surf. The change in currents also caused the wreck of five merchantmen (a ship used in commerce). In the late afternoon of August 11, *Acasta* left *Bonetta* and three of her boats to help the wrecked vessels and then took command of the convoy. The subsequent court-martial at Port Royal on September 3, ruled that a sudden change in the current after dark had caused the loss. The British marine investigation board impaneled after the devastation, acknowledged that the ship's captain Pamplin had sailed in a judicious manner and exonerated him and his officers from blame both for the loss of *Lowestoffe* and the vessels in convoy. In April 1803, the officers and crew of *Lowestoffe* and *Bonetta* received payment for the salvage of the specie that *Lowestoffe* was carrying.[53] On August 27 and August 28, another hurricane struck Exuma in The Bahamas with some damages reported.

The Hurricane of 1801: –A major hurricane struck Nassau, on July 22, and 120 ships of various descriptions and sizes were reportedly destroyed in this hurricane, where the most of them were wrecked onshore. Only a slave ship named *George* was identified. The system moved westward into the Gulf of Mexico shortly after that.

The 1804 Antigua/Charleston Hurricane: –This was the most severe hurricane in Georgia since 1752, causing over 500 deaths and at least $1.6 million (1804 USD) in damage throughout the southeastern United States. Originating near Antigua on September 3, it initially drifted west-northwestward, soon nearing Puerto Rico. Throughout its existence in the Caribbean Sea, the hurricane damaged, destroyed, and capsized numerous ships, and at Saint Kitt's, it was the worst since 1772. By September 4, the storm arrived in The Bahamas and turned northward before approaching the coast of northern Florida on September 6. The hurricane eventually came ashore along the coastline of Georgia and South Carolina while producing mostly southeasterly winds.

A 'severe gale' was noted in New England later that month, on September 11 and 12, although it was likely not the same system as that

---

[53] J. J. Colledge, Ben Warlow, (2006) [1969]. *Ships of the Royal Navy: The Complete Record of all Fighting Ships of the Royal Navy* (Rev. ed.). London: Chatham Publishing. ISBN 978-1-86176-281-8. OCLC 67375475. Retrieved: 17-06-2015.

which had passed through the Caribbean and the southeastern United States earlier that month. This major hurricane struck The Bahamas during the first week of September in 1804. The storm was felt throughout The Bahamas from September 5-7, but the greatest damage was focused in the south where most of the vessels at Inagua and Turks and Caicos were driven ashore. The following month a ship reported a hurricane at sea to the east of The Bahamas on October 12. Then on September 14, the shipping at Andros and Crooked Island were affected by a 'severe gale.' Another 'strong gale' on October 29, caused the wreckage of numerous ships at Abaco.

The Great Coastal Hurricane of 1806/The Great Hurricanes of 1806: –The Great Coastal Hurricane of 1806 was a severe and damaging storm along the East Coast of the United States which produced upwards of 36 inches of rainfall in parts of Massachusetts. This hurricane was first observed east of the Lesser Antilles on August 17. Shortly after that, the hurricane then entered The Bahamas sometime on August 19, and intense winds persisted until August 21, when approximately 150 miles east of the Bahamian island of Eleuthera, it made a beeline for the United States. Steering currents brought the storm northward, and it approached Charleston, South Carolina on August 22, where a generally easterly flow preceded the storm indicated its passage far east of the city. The disturbance continued to drift northward and made landfall at the mouth of the Cape Fear River in North Carolina on August 22.

The storm soon moved out to sea as a Category 2-equivalent hurricane on the Saffir–Simpson Hurricane Wind Scale, persisting off New England before dissipating south of Nova Scotia on August 25, as a markedly weaker storm. Several French and British military ships were damaged out at sea. In the Carolinas, salt, sugar, rice, and lumber industries suffered considerably, and several individuals were killed — wharves and vessels endured moderate damage, with many ships wrecked on North Carolina's Barrier Islands. Most of the deaths caused by the hurricane occurred aboard the boat *Rose-in-Bloom* offshore of Barnegat Inlet, New Jersey, with 21 of the ship's 48 passengers killed and $171,000 (1806 USD) in damage to its cargo. Upon arriving in New England, reports indicated extreme rainfall; however, no deaths were reported; in all, the hurricane killed more than 24 individuals along the entirety of its track. Deaths are totaled as follows: 21 were killed aboard the *Rose-in-Bloom*, one died in a wall collapse at Wilmington, North Carolina, one drowned at a nearby plantation, and one died out at sea, off the Core Banks. Although several slaves were killed, no exact number is known or has been estimated.

In April of 1806, Governor Cameron reported that The Bahamas was in a state of tranquility, the garrison, and community in good health. Unfortunately, that statement was short-lived, and he had to rescind those words because by September both he and more than half of the 99th Regiment were sick, and The Bahamas faced four hurricanes within a few weeks from August 30-The Great Coastal Hurricane to October 5. While recovering from a fever at Royal Island with his family, the Governor found himself in great danger. As the storm of September 14 raged and the roof of the house they were staying in blew off. During the peak of the storm, he with great difficulty moved his family to the cellar of the house, which was full of water. Eighteen people died, the two dwelling houses belonging to Benjamin Barnett were blown down, and his Negro houses received considerable damage. The Government schooner *Nassau* was washed ashore at Royal Island being severely damaged, the stern post and keel were destroyed.

In that same hurricane, 34 free people of colour from the settlement of Bogue in Eleuthera were drowned, and not a house was left standing. The home of Benjamin Claxton at the plantation of George Butler was blown down. Claxton was crushed, and Mrs. Claxton was severely bruised. The bodies of 20 people were found about a mile from their place of residence. Seventeen people who escaped the fury of the storm were on the peak of a hill, surrounded by water and without provisions or freshwater. During these storms, on Harbour Island, a total of 160 houses were damaged, of which 121 were destroyed. The church and the barracks containing 60 men (a detachment of the 99th Regiment) were blown down, a soldier was killed, and another one was taken to the hospital. Subscriptions opened in Nassau for the relief of the impoverished, and the money was given to James Dunshee and William R. Edgecombe, representatives for the Harbour Island District.

Names of the free-coloured persons who died during the hurricane in the settlement of Bogue in Eleuthera[54]

Resident:	Family members who also perished:
Rebecca Benson	1 daughter
Elizabeth Carmichael	McBeth
Benjamin Claxton	-
Moses Easton	-
Mary Feston	-
Hannah Frances	2 children
Jane Johnson	2 children
Willet Kemp	-
W. Martin	2 children
Hannah	-
William Middleton	1 daughter
Mrs. Middleton	-
William Rivers	2 children
Nancy Smith	2 children
Lucinda Wilson	3 children
Rose Wilson	1 daughter

Names of the free-coloured persons who died in the settlement of Bogue in Eleuthera (Courtesy of Jim and Anne Lawlor).

At Exuma, the hurricane of August 30/31 continued for five hours and blew down all cotton machines on Exuma and its Cays, and on September 13/14 the storm from the north and northwest lasted for 14 hours and caused extensive damage. The church and nearly all the houses in the Harbour were blown down. At Little Exuma, not a house was left standing. The loss of the cotton, corn and salt crops were immense. Similar damage was reported in Crooked Island, Acklins, and Long Island. Cameron reported that the colony faced severe problems of no food and few boats to trade with after the passage of the hurricane. The food shortage was so severe that Cameron asked permission to import pork, salt beef, and butter for a limited period, and England granted this request for the subsequent six months.

Shortly after the first hurricane which struck The Bahamas, another storm struck The Bahamas within a space of a week and a half, which was by far more devastating than its predecessor. This destructive hurricane hit The Bahamas on August 30, 1806, where the storm was reported to

---

[54] Jim and Anne Lawlor, *The Harbour Island Story*, Oxford, Macmillan Caribbean Limited, 2008. Pg. 206.

last over twelve hours in duration. Twenty-one ships were destroyed in Nassau Harbour while five other vessels were reportedly lost elsewhere in The Bahamas, including the 18 guns' English warship *HMS Wolfe, Brandy Wine* en-route from New York to Jamaica, and American ship *Rattlesnake*. There was also a report of the loss of cotton machines at Exuma and Little Exuma. Most of the damages from this storm appeared in the Central Bahamas. At Harbour Island, two-thirds of the houses (160 houses) were demolished, and the remaining forty-six homes all suffered some degree of damage. Harbour Island also experienced the loss of all its crops in the storm. At Spanish Wells, only four houses were left standing. All the homes in the Harbour area at Exuma were destroyed, and all the houses at little Exuma were reported to have suffered some degree of damage. The southern and middle districts of Long Island suffered similar fates. All the homes at Crooked Island were either unroofed or destroyed, and sixteen people were reportedly drowned.

An American merchantman *Polly*, with Captain Bigby, encountered a hurricane sailing from Jamaica to Wilmington, on September 13; English ship *Speedwell*, with ship Captain Fairbotham, English ship *Mentor*, with Captain Bellow, carrying cotton and stores salvaged from the wreck of the *Speedwell*. During this hurricane, 34 free coloured persons from the settlement of Bogue in Eleuthera were drowned, and not a house was left standing. The home of Benjamin Claxton at the plantation of George Butler was blown down. Claxton was crushed and Mrs. Claxton severely bruised. The bodies of 20 people were found about a mile from their place of residence. The church and the barracks containing 60 men (a detachment of the 99th Regiment) were blown away, a soldier killed, and another one taken to the hospital. At Exuma, all the cotton machines were destroyed, and nearly all the houses were blown down, and at Little Exuma, all the homes were destroyed. The hurricane impact lasted for over 14 hours. Similar damage was reported at Crooked Island, Acklins and Long Island. The shortage of food was so severe that Governor Cameron asked Great Britain permission to import pork, salt beef and butter for a limited period and Britain granted this request for the ensuing six months.

Houses destroyed at Harbour Island by the 1806 Hurricane

House Owner	Houses Destroyed	Comments	Houses Destroyed	Houses Destroyed	Comments
Benjamin Albury	1	-	Joseph Harris	2	-
Jemmy Albury	1	-	Jeremiah Higgs	2	-
Joseph Albury	1	-	Mrs. Higgs	4	-
Joseph Albury	1	-	Benjamin Holmes	1	-
Joseph Albury	1	-	James Ingram	1	Free Black
Sally Albury	1	-	Polly Johnson	1	-
Widow Albury	1	-	Samuel Johnson	1	-
William Albury	1	-	Thomas Johnson	1	-
William Albury	1	-	Samuel Kemp	1	-
William Brady	1	-	William Kerr	1	-
Caesar Brown	1	Free Black	Martha Petty	1	-
Widow Cash	1	-	Joseph Pierce	5	-
Ephraim Cleare	1	-	Martha Pierce	1	-
Joseph Cleare	1	Broken arm	Thomas Pierce	1	-
Reuben Cleare	1	-	Thomas Pinder	1	-
Widow Cleare	1	-	Benjamin Roberts	1	-
Widow Coleman	1	-	George Roberts	1	-
John Collins	1	-	James Roberts	1	-
Dim Cox	1	Free Man	Joseph Roberts	4	-
Benjamin Curry	1	-	Joseph Roberts	2	-
Benjamin Curry Jr	2	-	Joseph Roberts	1	=

Joseph Curry	4	-	Joseph Roberts	1	-
Joseph Curry	1	-	Joseph Roberts	1	-
Pierson Curry	1	-	Joseph Roberts	1	-
Widow Curry	1	-	Joseph Roberts	1	-
Joseph Evans	1	Part down	Joseph Roberts	1	-
Christopher Fisher	7	-	Joseph Roberts Jr	1	-
Sarah George	1	Free Woman	Joseph Roberts Sen	1	-
Benjamin Sweeting	1	-	Lawrence Roberts	1	-
Joseph Sweeting	1	-	Mott Roberts	1	Free Black
Thomas Sweeting	2	-	William Roberts	1	-
Thomas Sweeting	1	-	Benjamin Russell	2	-
William Sweeting	1	-	Joseph Russell	1	-
William Sweeting	1	-	Joseph Russell	1	`
Mrs. Tedder	1	-	Widow Russell	1	-
Mrs. Tedder	1	-	Widow Russell	1	-
Widow Tedder	1	-	Benjamin Saunders	1	-
Dick Thomson	1	-	Benjamin Saunders	1	-
John Thomson	1	-	Joseph Saunders	1	-
Nathaniel Thomson	1	-	Joseph K Saunders	1	-
Sarah Thomson	1	-	Nathaniel Saunders	1	-
Mrs. Weatherford	1	-	Widow Saunders	1	-
Joseph Wood	1	-	William	1	-

			Saunders		
Joseph Young	1	-	William Saunders	1	-
Adam	1	Free Black	William Saunders	1	-
Rachel	1	Black Woman	William Saunders	1	-
Tom	1	Yellow	Alexander Sawyer	1	-
Benjamin Sweeting	1	-	Edmund Sawyer	1	-
William Sawyer	1	-	Joseph Sawyer	1	-

Houses destroyed at Harbour Island by the 1806 Hurricane (Courtesy of Jim and Anne Lawlor).

The Hurricane of 1813: – On July 22, this hurricane struck Barbados, killing 18. It then continued moving through the Antilles, affecting Puerto Rico on the July 22, causing more damage and deaths along its path. A major hurricane, probably this same storm, struck The Bahamas on July 26 and hurricane conditions started to be experienced shortly before noon and ended at midnight with the eye passing over Nassau between 5-6 pm. Thirty persons lost their lives and significant damage to many homes and shipping. During the hurricane, the new chapel, which was only recently built, had a woman who sheltered in the building was crushed to death at the western side of the church and a man named Josiah Young was severely injured but sadly, died a few days from his injuries. All the 40 vessels in Nassau Harbour were wrecked, sunk or cast ashore including the English ship *Dart* which was sailing from Jamaica to Nassau. Another English ship *Conck*, sailing from Nassau to Jamaica, was wrecked on Eleuthera, and there were three deaths reported at Spanish Wells and a schooner *Dart* was also destroyed at Current Island. A vessel *Hesperus* was caught in the hurricane and all person were onboard drowned. Approximately, one-third of the houses on islands of the NW Bahamas were either severely damaged or destroyed as were most of the public buildings and there was extensive damage to crops. The storm caused very little damage elsewhere in The Bahamas. After leaving The Bahamas, it recurved west of Bermuda by July 29.[55]

---

[55] The Nassau Tribune, June 28th, 1987, pg. 1, *More on Storms and Nassau Histiory.* Retrieved: 22-12-2016.

The Hurricane of 1814: –During October 4 and 5, 1814 a hurricane struck the SE Bahamas and Turks and Caicos Islands. In Nassau, the stormy weather lasted for about four days and caused damage to the crops and some of the small ships in the harbour. The plantations on Crooked Island and the Turks and Caicos Islands experienced severe damage, and their situation was as severe as they were still attempting to recover from the hurricanes of the previous year.

The Hurricanes of 1815: –Storm activity in 1815 proved somewhat more destructive than the previous year. The ship *Comet* of London was sunk at sea during a storm on August 9th, and the crew of the *Comet* was rescued by *The America* of Portland only to have that ship destroyed as well during a hurricane at the end of August. Luckily, the crews were all rescued by a long boat and made a safe landing at Watling's Island. The storm was first felt at Turks and Caicos on August 29th and 30th where eight vessels were lost. Eleuthera was the scene of some of the most significant destruction where several ships were driven ashore. A seized American schooner was sunk in the harbour at Harbour Island. Harbour Island had several houses which were either damaged or destroyed and at Spanish Wells, the settlement was flooded by a brutal combination of torrential rainfall and a massive storm surge.

The third hurricane of 1815 often called 'The Great Gale of 1815', impacted the region on September 20. The Great September Gale of 1815 was the first major hurricane to affect New England in 180 years. At least 38 fatalities were a result of the Great September Gale. The hurricane also caused the destruction of some 500 homes and 35 ships in Narragansett, Rhode Island, as an 11 feet storm surge funneled up Narragansett Bay. Salt spray and salt deposition were noted in many areas after the hurricane. Historical reports recount the rain "tasting like salt," the grapes in the vineyards "tasting like salt," the houses had all turned white, and the leaves on the trees appeared "lightly frosted."

The hurricane first struck the Turks and Caicos Islands near The Bahamas on September 20 and then The Bahamas, with a strength estimated to have been equivalent to a Category 4 hurricane. This storm was particularly damaging to Turks Island where half of the houses were destroyed, and the salt ponds were inundated, and seven vessels were lost accounting for 22 deaths. One ship was run aground on the reef at Cat Island. Two additional storms came through the region in October, and while both storms caused the loss of ships, neither was reported as being of hurricane strength.

Early in the 19th century, scientists established the concept of hurricanes as cyclones spinning in a counterclockwise direction. Based on this hurricane in 1815, a Harvard professor concluded in an 1819 article that "it appears to have been a moving vortex and not the rushing forward of a great body of the atmosphere." Several years later, William C. Redfield published an account in the American Journal of Science identifying a hurricane as a progressive whirlwind. Redfield made the observation after studying trees and other objects scattered by a storm. John Farrar (July 1, 1779 – May 8, 1853) was an avid early American storm chaser, an exceptional scholar, Hollis professor of Mathematics and Natural Philosophy at Harvard University, and maintained weather records between 1807-1817.

He first coined this concept of hurricanes moving as a cyclonic system and not the rushing forward as a great body of the atmosphere, after observing the Great September Gale of 1815 in the United States and first presented this 'theory' at Harvard University in 1819. Farrar remained Professor of Mathematics and Natural Philosophy at Harvard University between 1807 and 1836. During this time, he introduced modern mathematics into the curriculum. He was also a regular contributor to the scientific journals. He also observed the veering of hurricane winds, and the variable timing of their impacts on the cities of Boston and New York. The storm then journeyed north through the Atlantic, eventually striking Long Island on September 23, at 7 am. The gale descended upon southern New England with the force of what now would be designated as a Category 3 hurricane.[56]

The Hurricane of 1818: –A hurricane on October 12-14, affected both Jamaica and the islands of the NW and Central Bahamas. This hurricane affected The Bahamas on October 14, which caused the destruction of sixteen ships in Nassau Harbour. There is no mention of damage to structures at Nassau, nor is there any indication of the storm's impact elsewhere in The Bahamas.

The Hurricanes of 1819: –Three storms hit The Bahamas in 1819. A storm on September 18, caused some damage to shipping, but no damage on the land. A more intense storm occurred on September 22-25. This

---

[56] https://www.chicagotribune.com. Retrieved: 29-4-2018.

storm was particularly damaging at Caicos Island, where the corn and cotton crops were destroyed, and several ships were demasted or driven ashore. The third storm of the year hit on October 13 and brought about the destruction of several ships at Abaco, Egg Island, and Lee Stocking Island. This hurricane is recorded to have struck Cuba and then moved northward into The Bahamas.

The Hurricane of 1822: –On September 26 and 27, a particularly damaging hurricane hit Cherokee Sound in Abaco damaging the plantations to such an extent that they petitioned the House of Assembly for assistance. Shipping was also severely affected during this storm at Nassau, Abaco, and Exuma. This hurricane then moved north-northwest from The Bahamas on September 25, to hit Charleston, South Carolina on September 27. It claimed the lives of hundreds of slaves who found themselves trapped in the low-lying Santee Delta, miles from higher ground and with no shelter. It caused 300 (or more deaths) but managed to break a drought in the Richmond area.

The Hurricane of 1824: –In 1824 a particularly damaging storm hit the islands on September 13 and 14. The Central Bahamas suffered the most significant damage from this storm. At Nassau, the church, barracks, jail and 103 houses were destroyed. The northern end of Long Island was devastated where housing stock and provisions were destroyed. At Rock Sound, Eleuthera only 16 of the 80 houses were left standing, and three-quarters of the homes were destroyed at Harbour Island. Also, several unidentified ships were wrecked at Rum Cay. At the Current, on the west end of Eleuthera, twenty houses were destroyed along with all the crops in the fields, and the hurricane went on to demolish homes on Abaco as it exited the region.

The Hurricane of 1830: –This hurricane was first spotted in the Leeward Islands on August 11, it then moved into the Caribbean Sea in the middle of August. It then moved into The Bahamas between August 11-14, as it went up the entire length of the Archipelago chain. As it then exited The Bahamas, it then moved west-northwestward and approached the coast of Florida. It came close to present-day Daytona Beach on August 15, but recurved northeastward before landfall, although the land was not spared from effects. It made landfall near Cape Fear on the 16th and went out to sea that night, eventually well to the north of Bermuda just offshore the Canadian Maritimes.

In The Bahamas, this hurricane broke a three-month drought but caused massive crop damage in the process. The damage was the greatest in the NW Bahamas, but the Central and the SE Bahamas also reported significant losses. The storm damaged houses and crops at Watling's Island and caused the loss of one ship and its entire crew. At San Salvador, the wind blew down houses and barns, but there was no loss of life. Eleuthera reported several vessels destroyed, and at Cupid's Cay all the houses were blown down and of the animals were drowned. At Harbour Island, all the shipping vessels in the Harbour were destroyed, forty homes were destroyed, and another sixty-three houses suffered varying degrees of damage. At Grand Bahama, many houses were destroyed. There were no reports of damage at Nassau because of this storm.

The Hurricane of 1832: –A hurricane moved through The Bahamas around June 5, causing 52 deaths. At Bermuda, the storm began from the northeast of Bermuda at 8 pm on June 6, with the center likely passing quite close to the island as the wind shifted to southwest at 10:30 pm. The storm lasted until 3 am on June 7. Two schooners were damaged during the system.

The Six Hurricanes of 1837: –In 1837 five separate hurricanes blew across The Bahamas, and a sixth hurricane may have grazed the northern islands. On July 30, the hurricane that hit Barbados on July 26, moved into the SE Bahamas. At Nassau, the storm lasted a full twenty-four hours and caused five vessels to be sunk in the harbour, numerous fruit and ornamental trees were destroyed, fences were blown down, and a few frail houses were destroyed. Five ships were wrecked at Andros and another in the Berry Islands. Two vessels were lost at Grand Bahama and a third at Gun Cay, while at Conception Island one vessel was lost. On August 4, the season's second hurricane swept into the region. It struck at Turk's Island on August 3, causing the loss of one ship with twenty fatalities. This storm caused very little damage except several vessels were driven ashore cutting wood on the island of Andros.

As the hurricane moved through The Bahamas, it left a trail of death and wrecked ships in its wake. Eight deaths and fourteen wrecked ships were reported at Harbour Island and New Providence. One vessel sank at Grand Bahama with the loss of thirteen lives, and another vessel was lost at Great Guana Cay. Allen's Harbour reported the loss of one ship with four fatalities, one ship was lost at Beak's Cay, three ships were run aground in Bimini, and two schooners were lost at Castle Rock.

The Calypso Hurricane of 1837: –A tropical system was observed east of the West Indies on August 13. It moved through the islands and passed The Bahamas on August 16. While recurving, it hit the North Carolina coast on August 18. It slowly moved over land, causing 48 hours of strong winds, and moved back offshore into the Atlantic on August 20, bypassing southern New England by August 22. This was the third storm of the 1837 hurricane season, and it hit Nassau on August 16, producing heavy winds and rains. There was little damage at Nassau, but three ships later pulled into the harbour for repairs having lost their mast in the storm. At Grand Bahama, the storm produced lowland flooding, and at San Salvador, several houses were blown down with an accompanying loss of crops and livestock. Homes and crops were destroyed at Long Island, and many livestock were drowned. At Rum Cay, almost all the houses were destroyed as was the wharf and the salt buildings and one ship was run aground in the harbour.

The fourth storm of the season was of lesser intensity. Nassau reported stormy weather for September 12-15. Two ships were reported lost at Gun Cay, one at East Cays and a fourth ship lost its sails in the storm. The fifth storm of the season was reported at hurricane strength in Nassau on October 25, with the loss of nineteen ships in Nassau Harbour. A captured slave ship with five hundred aboard was wrecked at Governor's Harbour with many fatalities, and three additional ships were lost at Stirrup Cay. The sixth and final storm of the season produced heavy winds and rains at Nassau but little in the way of damage across the Archipelago. Only one ship was lost in the storm at Green Turtle Cay in Abaco.

In an interesting story, the newly built passenger steamboat *SS Home* was en-route from New York City to Charleston, South Carolina, when she encountered powerful northeasterly winds on October 8. As the storm worsened that night, the 220 feet craft began to leak due to a broken boiler feed pipe. The next morning, as the *Home* took on more water than the pumps could handle, the captain steered her aground 22 miles north of Cape Hatteras. The vessel got underway again shortly after that, to reach the relative shelter of the cape's leeward side and the beach there. At this point, all the passengers and crewmen were ordered to assist in bailing out the water pouring into the hold, but despite their best efforts, the engine rooms were inundated, and the *Home* was forced to continue under sail.

On the night of October 9–10, the vessel grounded out 300 feet from the shore, just south of Cape Hatteras. The largely submerged *Home* rapidly broke up amid the hurricane's pounding surf, and of the 130 people aboard the steamboat, only about 40 made it to shore alive, 20 out of 90 passengers and 20 crew members, including the captain. A lifeboat carrying between 10 and 15 passengers capsized shortly after being launched, leading to their deaths, and the two other lifeboats were destroyed before they could be used. Two men used the only two life preservers aboard the *Home* to safely reach the beach. Following this disaster, the US Congress passed a law mandating that all commercial vessels must always carry enough life preservers for all passengers.

The Hurricane of 1844: –On October 5, 1844, a storm caused great destruction on the island of Cuba and then it moved into The Bahamas, where one resident reported that "We experienced a severe hurricane on the banks on the night of October 5, and the loss of lives and property has been greater than in any previous gale for some years."[57] The Nassau Guardian in its inaugural issue in print form, reported on the danger faced by men encountering this hurricane aboard a ship called *Rio*, "The gale continues, and the joy of our deliverance from the peril of yesterday, was somewhat clouded towards evening…having only 8 hands, including the mates; the ship lying in a gale, a heavy sea running and the decks filled with freight."[58] It also reported that a very heavy gale occurred at about midnight with the winds coming from the SW with a large quantity of rainfall occurring during the hurricane and the barometer fell to 29.27 millibars.

The Hurricane of 1848: –The next report of a hurricane landfall in The Bahamas was in late August 1848. This storm was first noted as being off the island of Guadeloupe in the Caribbean. From there it passed through the Virgin Islands before traversing the entire length of The Bahamas Archipelago. The hurricane then recurved through the North Atlantic shipping lanes towards Europe between August 19 and September 2. This storm was one of the earliest tropical cyclones to have a track created.

The Hurricane of 1852: –The first tropical cyclone of the year, also known as the 'Great Mobile Hurricane of 1852', was first observed on August 19 about 140 miles just north of Puerto Rico. It moved on a west-northwest track before passing through the islands of The Bahamas as it attained hurricane status on August 20. After paralleling the northern

---

[57] William Redfield, *On three several hurricanes of the Atlantic, and their relations to the northers of Mexico and Central America, with notices of other storms* New Haven: B.L. Hamlen, 1846 USA. Pgs. 343-344.

[58] The Nassau Guardian, Saturday, November 23, 1844, Volume 1. Retrieved: 21-10-2016.

coast of Cuba, the storm passed between the Dry Tortugas and Key West, Florida on August 22, and it is estimated that the hurricane attained peak winds of 115 mph two days later. The storm slowed down in forward speed on August 25 before turning northward, and early on August 26 it made landfall near Pascagoula, Mississippi at peak strength, and the hurricane rapidly weakened to tropical storm status as it accelerated east-northeastward. On August 28, it emerged into the North Atlantic Ocean from South Carolina, and after turning to the northeast, it was last observed on August 30 about 130 miles southeast of Cape Cod.

The Hurricane of 1853: –The ship *Edward* reported a hurricane about 50 miles north of Grand Bahama on October 19. Several other ships encountered the storm between October 19 and October 20. It moved north-northwestward slowly and gradually strengthened. On October 20, the storm reached maximum sustained winds of 105 mph, making it a Category 2 hurricane on the modern day Saffir-Simpson Hurricane Wind Scale. Additionally, ships reported a minimum barometric pressure of 996 millibars. After weakening back to a Category 1 hurricane on October 21, the storm veered east-northeastward, avoiding a landfall in the southeastern United States. It was last noted on October 22, while centered about 80 miles east-southeast of Charleston, South Carolina.

Several churches, including, Zion Baptist, St. Andrews Presbyterian, St. Agnes and several others took up special offerings during regular church hours to assist the stricken residents of the Out Islands devastated by this hurricane. The French brig *l'Ocean's* cargo and ship were destroyed at Memory Rock located on the western tip of Grand Bahama, but thankfully the entire crew was rescued by the sloop *Avenger*.[59] A boat with eight men who went to salvage a Spanish wreck near Rum Cay was lost in the storm with all persons onboard perishing. A sloop *Butterfly* of Nassau was driven out to sea with seven persons on board, and after drifting from Monday night until Wednesday morning, she sank about a mile from the north shore of San Salvador. Except for one man, her entire crew were able to swim ashore on portions of the wreck and the cargo. The name of the person who perished was Joseph MacNeil. His body was washed ashore several days later. An American barque *The Antelope*, with a cargo of 6,000 bushels of salt onboard, was driven out to sea with all the crew onboard perishing. A

---

[59] The Nassau Guardian, *Colonial Summary* December 17, 1853, pg. 1. Retrieved: 12-12-2011.

Spanish steamer *General Armera* was driven ashore and destroyed near South Bay, Watling's Island. Slaves were loading bushels of salt onto a ship named *Cooper*, and three of them escaped into the bushes on Watling's Island, but they were later caught and detained by their master. The ship *Fly* was lost near the north end of Long Island and destroyed, with three persons onboard drowning during the hurricane.

The house belonging to Mr. S.B. Dorsett collapsed on top of him, his wife and their infant child during the storm. They found safety between two beams with severe wounds and just a few scratches and had to be rescued by others after the hurricane had abated. The public-school house near Christ Church Gardens was destroyed. All the year's supply of salt consisting of over one hundred thousand bushels on the various islands were destroyed. All the corn, peas, potato and other crops on the different islands were destroyed. The entire island of Exuma was devastated in this hurricane, where most of the crops, homes, businesses, and boats were destroyed, and residents faced starvation for months after the hurricane. At Long Island, the government schooner *Union* captained by John Ramsey was destroyed at the south end of the island. The schooner *Teazer* and two other boats belonging to Mr. A.W.G. Taylor were destroyed. An unnamed sponging schooner was lost at sea during a sponging trip, and 3 of the six crew members drowned. An American barque and three brigs (one from Nova Scotia, Canada) lying off Matthew Town were driven ashore and destroyed. Three other boats in Matthew Town, Inagua were also destroyed, and they were, *Justina, Julia, Adeona*, and the sloop *Splendid*.[60]

The Hurricane of 1854: –This storm occurred on October 10 and the schooner *J.H. Johnson* capsized causing the death of Dr. George Walter Hall. A British barque *Young Queen* ran ashore on Crooked Island and sunk with a load of copper ore. About 300 persons worked on this wreck to retrieve this cargo.

The Hurricane of 1856: –A hurricane formed north of Hispaniola on August 25. It moved westward, passing over the island of Inagua before striking the north coast of Cuba as a Category 2 hurricane on August 27. The cyclone weakened to Category 1 strength as it crossed the island, close to Matanzas, but regained first Category 2 and then Category 3 strength as it moved north through the Gulf of Mexico. The cyclone made landfall

---

[60] The Nassau Guardian, *Colonial Summary & The Hurricane*. December 7, 1853, pg. 1. Retrieved: 12-12-2011.

near Panama City, Florida, on August 31 as a Category 2 hurricane. After that, it then quickly weakened to a tropical storm while moving northward through Georgia and South Carolina. The storm entered the Atlantic from the state of Virginia on next day and dissipated on September 3. The hurricane destroyed thirty houses on Inagua, and four people died there. Several vessels were run ashore on the Cuban coast.

The two Hurricanes of 1871: –A severe hurricane impacted Abaco causing the death of 23 persons and the schooner *Corine* was destroyed. A Category 1 hurricane was spotted northeast of The Bahamas on August 14. Hurricane #3 continued a westward track, eventually becoming a major hurricane east of Abaco. The hurricane maintained its intensity up until landfall in east-central Florida on August 16 with winds of 120 mph.

Another hurricane, Hurricane Santa Juana of 1871, a Category 3 storm lasted from August 17 to August 30 with a peak intensity of 115 mph and a pressure of 962 millibars (hPa). On August 17, a tropical storm developed west of Cape Verde. The system progressed on a west-northwest track and steadily intensified, becoming a major hurricane east of the Lesser Antilles. On August 21, at peak intensity with winds of up to 120 mph, the hurricane passed over Antigua, St. Eustatius, Saint Kitts, and St. Thomas. Continuing to track to the northeast, it moved 30 miles northeast of Fajardo. The hurricane then weakened to a Category 2 hurricane, maintaining this strength while making further landfalls in The Bahamas and Florida, respectively. The storm weakened over Florida before entering the Gulf of Mexico and making a final landfall on the Florida Panhandle as a tropical storm. The storm then moved north and east over land, weakening into a tropical depression before strengthening back into a tropical storm after re-emerging off South Carolina into the Atlantic. The storm was last sighted east of Cape Cod.

The Pensacola Hurricane of 1882: –A tropical storm was first seen to the north of the Mona Passage on September 2. It moved to the west-northwest through the islands of the Central and SE Bahamas, reaching winds of 100 mph before hitting Cuba. It crossed the island and turned north in the Gulf of Mexico. The hurricane peaked at 125 mph before hitting near Pensacola, Florida on September 10. It accelerated over the southeastern United States, crossing central Georgia, the western area of South Carolina and entered North Carolina on September 11. Continuing northward the storm moved offshore at Chesapeake Bay and after reaching the Atlantic Ocean, became extratropical near Nova Scotia. At Pensacola, the hurricane damaged crops, shipping and buildings. In Louisiana, half of the rice crop in Plaquemines Parish was destroyed by flooding. Flooding also occurred at Quarantine, Louisiana. It caused a landslide, and property damage throughout North Carolina but no deaths were reported.

In The Bahamas, damage was extensive in the islands of the Central and SE Bahamas. Two lives were lost aboard the schooner *Cicero* captained by Mr. William Clarke. This schooner was en-route from Nassau to Long Cay and anchored at Newfound Harbour, Long Island to ride out the storm there, but she was stranded at her moorings and lost her rudder. The crew and the passengers left the schooner in boats, and the one containing teacher, Mr. George T. Knowles, mates B. Hanna, Barnard Rolle, a boy, and the cook was capsized after leaving the schooner. Mr. Knowles sunk and drowned immediately because he wore some heavy clothes apart from his watch and money. The last words he uttered were "O Lord help me!" The mate Barnard Hanna also drowned. All the others reached Sandy Cay (below Newfound Harbour) with the greatest difficulty but safely. Stranded without clothes and with scarcely any provisions, they waited to be rescued by a boat from Nassau. Mr. Knowles was a schoolteacher in charge of the Public School at Long Cay for some years and had just recently been promoted to the school teacher at Harbour Island. The schooner called *Perseverance* encountered the storm at Rum Cay with the crew of six on board, but the sixth man Mr. Paul Johnson drowned and his last words before sinking were "Oh save me!"[61]

The Bahamas-North Carolina Hurricane of 1883: –This major hurricane moved through the Lesser Antilles on September 4. It crossed Hispaniola, weakening to a minimal hurricane. It re-strengthened as it passed The Bahamas and struck North Carolina as a Category 2 hurricane on the 11th. It dissipated over Virginia on September 13. On September 4-5, this hurricane crossed over The Bahamas, and it was reported that over 106 persons lost their lives along with the tremendous amount of property and boats damaged. At Inagua, the lowest reported barometric pressure reading was 29.60 (inches), and just a few boats and houses were damaged.

Approximately, 90 mph winds were experienced on Exuma when it passed just west of this island from a southerly direction. On Eleuthera, 15 houses and all the trees were destroyed. In New Providence, many of the homes and businesses were destroyed in this hurricane, and two of the

---

[61] The Nassau Guardian, *The Hurricane*. September 13 & 4, 1882, pg. 1. Retrieved: 12-12-2011.

wooden wharves at the Board of Trade yard were destroyed, and two persons died from drowning. The Baltimore schooner *Mary Jane and Elizabeth* was sunk alongside Mr. Sands' Wharf. The Nova Scotia brig *Peeress's* was cut away from its' mooring and destroyed. The lighthouse-keeper and his assistant had to rescue the crew of a small sloop but unfortunately two persons drowned. The schooner *General Whitfield* sunk at the Wharf #2 along with the other schooners *Enchantress, Lady Hennessy, Chance, Resolute* and others were also sunk. The lowest barometer reading in New Providence was 28.86 (inches) which occurred at 1:45 pm on September 8, during the passage of the hurricane.[62]

The 9-masted schooner *Melisa Track-Trask Master* with a shipment of ice was driven ashore during the hurricane at Norman's Cay in Exuma and was supposed to get a cargo of salt to take back to New York. The schooner *Victor* on her way from Norman's Cay to Jamaica was lost in the vicinity of the schooner *Melisa Track-Trask Master* and Mr. Chas Weech, and a lady who arrived there from Belize and three men, on their way to Jamaica in the *Victor* were all drowned. The sloop *Liberty* was torn apart and destroyed in the same vicinity of the *Victor*, but fortunately, the crew members were all saved. The *Monteagle* was reported lost with all persons onboard perishing.

The Rev. Jeremiah S.J. Higgs and Mrs. Higgs, while on their way to The Bight, Cat Island and San Salvador on the mail schooner *Carleton* encountered the hurricane on the NE coast of Eleuthera on September 8. Their ship was wrecked there, and Mr. and Mrs. Higgs were washed overboard and drowned. The schooner *Pride* was lost at Ship Channel Cay, but fortunately, the crew members were all saved. At Green Turtle Cay, Abaco, many of the buildings were destroyed. On the mainland of Abaco, all the pineapples, oranges, grapefruits, sapodillas, mangoes, bananas and sugarcane crops (over £4,000 worth) were destroyed along with most of the houses on the island. At Ragged Island, there were 20,000 bushels of salt in storage which was lost and another 26,000 in the salt pans destroyed. The schooner *Minnie* was driven ashore at Moore's Island, Abaco but the crew was saved, however, the cargo of sponges onboard was lost. Nine houses were destroyed, and four were severely damaged along with one Baptist Church at Little Abaco.

The schooner *Bonnregard*, belonging to Messers. Brown & Musgrove, chartered to carry wood to Cay Lobos, was sunk at sea by a waterspout

---

[62] The Nassau Guardian, *Destructive Cyclone*. September 8, 1883, pg. 1. Retrieved: 12-12-2011.

during the storm in four fathoms of water, between Grassy Cay and Grassy Creek in South Andros but fortunately, the crew were all saved. The Bahamas Government dispatched the schooner *Wanderer*, after the hurricane to travel to the Ship Channel Cay and other outlying cays within the Exuma range to rescue any stranded persons or ships lost in this hurricane. A Coroner's Inquest was held after the hurricane on the body of Elijah Knowles, a seaman on board the schooner *Violin*, owned by Mr. William Smith, of North End, Long Island. It capsized during the hurricane, and the crew had to swim to the mainland, but Mr. Knowles never made it ashore and drowned in his attempt to get there. His body was recovered and taken to the New Providence Asylum, and the Coroner found that Mr. Knowles did in fact drowned.[63]

Damage and loss to Shipping in Nassau Harbour during The Bahamas-North Carolina Hurricane of 1883[64]

Boat Name:	Damage:	Boat Type:	Boat Name:	Damage:	Boat Type:
Western	**District**		**Market**	**Wharf**	
Prosper	Damaged on the rocks	Sloop	*Emily Hope*	Total Loss	Schooner
Navy Yard			*Hester Ann*	Total Loss	Schooner
Perseverance	Badly damaged	Schooner	*Eager*	Damaged	Schooner
Traffic	Badly damaged	Schooner	*Cornacopia*	Total Loss	Schooner
Barrack	**Wharf**		*Isabel*	Damaged	Sloop
Royal Exclusive	Total Loss	Sloop	*Shamrock*	Total Loss	Sloop
William H. Curry	Total Loss	3-Masted Schooner	*Village Bella*	Damaged	Sloop
Eliza White	Unknown	American Barque	*Nimble*	Total Loss	Sloop
Prudent	Total Loss	Schooner	*Mary Ellen*	Total Loss	Sloop
Phantom	Total Loss	Sloop	**Sands**	**Wharf**	
Mary Beatrice	Badly damaged	Schooner	*Mary Jean*	Sunk	Schooner
Kate	Badly damaged	Schooner	*Elizabeth*	Damaged	Schooner
Vendue	**Wharf**		**Adderley**	**Slip**	
Eva	Sunk	Sloop	*Fearless*	Badly Damaged	Schooner
Sun	Sunk	Sloop	*Flash*	Damaged	Schooner
Sarah Cargill	Slightly damaged	Sloop	*Belle of the Ball*	Total Loss	Schooner

---

[63] The Nassau Guardian, *The Hurricane*. September 12, 1883, pg. 1. Retrieved: 12-12-2011.
[64] The Nassau Guardian, *The Hurricane*. September 12, 1883, pg. 1. Retrieved: 12-12-2011.

#2 Wharf			Non-Such	Total Loss	Schooner
Resolute	Total Loss	Schooner	Bennie	Total Loss	Sloop
Enchantress	Total Loss	Schooner	Choir	Damaged	Schooner
Chance	Total Loss	Schooner	Shannon	Damaged	Sloop
General Whitfield	Total Loss	Schooner	John Byron	Total Loss	Sloop
Lady Hennessy	Sunk at Board of Trade's Wharf	Schooner	Triton	Slightly Damaged	Sloop
Trial	Sunk at J.S. Johnson's Wharf	Schooner	Island Queen	Total Loss	Sloop
Speedwell	Stranded at E. Dupuch's Wharf	Schooner	Anna	Total Loss	Sloop
Eastern	**District**		Leo	Total Loss	Sloop
Ida E. Hilton	Damaged	Schooner	Sarah Ann	Slightly Damaged	Sloop
Margaret Ann	Damaged	Schooner	Pickle at Folly	Slightly Damaged	Schooner
Magnet	Damaged	Schooner	Minnie	Slightly Damaged	Schooner
Charlotte	Damaged	Schooner	Union at Hermitage	Badly Damaged	Sloop
Rival	Damaged	Schooner	Rescue	Total Loss	Schooner
Vivid	Damaged	Schooner	Belle	Total Loss	Schooner
Astarte	Damaged	Schooner	Frolic	Damaged	Schooner
Silver Lake	Damaged	Schooner	Eva	Damaged	Schooner
Sirina	Damaged	Schooner	Ida	Damaged	Schooner
Spica	Damaged	Schooner	Neva	Total Loss	Schooner
Violin	Badly Damaged	Schooner	Mand	Missing	Schooner

Damage and loss to Shipping in Nassau Harbour during The Bahamas-North Carolina Hurricane of 1883. (Courtesy of The Nassau Guardian). (Jpeg-scan Picture page 21—3 pages).

The Hurricane of 1884: – The last known tropical cyclone of the season was first observed in the Caribbean Sea by the steamship *Cienfuegos* on October 7, while located about 120 miles south-southeast of Kingston, Jamaica. That day, the storm dropped heavy rainfall on the island, resulting in at least eight fatalities. Moving north northeastward, the system strengthened into a Category 1 hurricane on October 8. Early the next day, the hurricane made landfall in Cuba near modern-day Guantánamo Bay with winds of 80 mph. While crossing the island, the system weakened to a tropical storm on October 9. In Oriente Province, "some heavy damage" and several injuries were reported. Around midday on October 9, the storm emerged into the Atlantic Ocean near Frank País, Cuba.

Continuing northward, the system became a Category 1 hurricane again on October 11. In the Bahamas, considerable damage was inflicted upon crops and fruit plantations. Several shipping vessels were also lost. A three-masted 650 ton, -iron schooner from Philadelphia, *Jonathon Knight*, bound for New Orleans with a cargo of coal, ran ashore on a reef near Palmetto Point, Eleuthera, on Wednesday night, October 15. All persons except for two, Thomas Severt (2nd Mate) and Anders Peterson (Seaman) were drowned, and none of the cargo was saved. The American Bark *Send* was severely damaged, and one of the crew George Williams was lost overboard. The schooner *San Blas* from Baltimore was lost with the captain and crew reported missing after the hurricane. The brigantine *Emma L. Hall*, which was carrying 12,000 bushels of salt, suffered severe damage. A man named Colley was drowned in a pond at Acklins. At Grand Turk Island, the hurricane was considered the worst storm in 25 years. After moving north of The Bahamas, the storm strengthened into a Category 2 hurricane on October 14 and peaked with sustained winds of 105 mph. Shortly after that, the hurricane curved north northeastward and weakened to a Category 1 hurricane on the next day. Further weakening occurred, and the system fell to tropical storm intensity by October 17. The storm was last noted about 450 miles southeast of Bermuda.

The Sea Island Hurricane of 1893: –On August 27, a major hurricane which came to be known as the Sea Islands Hurricane struck the United States near Savannah, Georgia. It was one of three deadly hurricanes during the 1893 North Atlantic hurricane season; the storm killed an estimated 1,000–2,000 people, mostly from the storm surge. On August 15, a tropical storm formed east of the Cape Verde Islands. It likely passed directly through the islands on the 16th, leaving their vicinity during the evening of the 17th. It became a hurricane on the 19th while crossing the Atlantic between the Cape Verde Islands and the Lesser Antilles.

The hurricane continued to strengthen, attaining Category 3 status on August 22 while located just northeast of the Lesser Antilles. By the evening of the 25th, the storm was approaching the SE Bahamas. During the approach, it began to deviate slightly from its westerly track and moved more on a west-northwest track. It is believed that the first effects of the storm were beginning to be felt in the Sea Islands area, with the winds steadily increasing during the night of the 25th. Some of the inhabitants anticipated the storm and left the islands as quickly as possible. The conditions soon rapidly deteriorated on the island, and the hurricane passed over the island sometime on the 26th. By then, the storm was turning more and more towards the north. It moved parallel to the coast for about one hundred miles before making landfall.

One of nature's true wonders, the Glass Window Bridge will undoubtedly leave you breathless as you drink in the magnificent panoramic view. It is one of the few places on Earth where you can compare the vibrant blue waters of the Atlantic Ocean on one side of the road and the calm turquoise-green waters of the Exuma Sound (Caribbean Sea) on the other side, separated by a strip of rock just 30 feet wide. The Bridge is about two miles east of Upper Bogue and joins Gregory Town and Lower Bogue at the narrowest point on the island. The land here is high on both sides, falling away abruptly to nearly sea-level, almost dividing the island in two. A bridge on its topside connects the northern and southern points of Eleuthera by a paved road.

Mother Nature has carved and shaped some distinctive and unique features into the limestone rock formations on various islands of The Bahamas. One of the more notable ones is located at Ridley's Head near Spanish Wells on North Eleuthera. At a certain angle and from some distance this outcrop bears the distinct resemblance to a man's head. Another attractive design, which is not common, is a large hole right through the rock. Such a hole can be seen today at the south end of the island of Abaco. Years ago, another similar feature also existed on the island of Eleuthera, about four miles from Harbour Island, which was then known as the 'Harbour Island Hinterland.' The residents of Abaco gave their hole in the rock the distinctive name of 'Hole-In-The-Wall.' The residents of Harbour Island, showing greater imagination, called theirs the 'Glass Window.' Well into the nineteenth century, these distinctive rock formations were both distinctive maritime signposts. Today, Hole-In-The-Wall is still there, but the Glass Window is not there anymore and is replaced by a bridge known as the 'Glass Window Bridge.' There were two versions on why it is no longer there. The first was that the structure collapsed naturally and the second was that this hurricane destroyed it in 1893. While this natural 'bridge' stood, it was considered a thrilling adventure to walk its 60 feet length and look straight down to 90 feet below, where the deep waters of the Atlantic met the shallow waters of the Caribbean Sea. The daring walk was not performed by men alone, but also by ladies with nerves of steel, as one nineteenth-century writer states:

"To lie down on the top of this arch, which was only about three feet wide in the center, and looked over its outer edge down upon the seething, foaming cauldron below, afforded a picture of wild beauty and rugged grandeur not easily matched and never to be forgotten."[65]

In the United States, landfall occurred near Savannah, Georgia, on August 27. Reports from the time say that wind during landfall was around 120 mph, making it a Category 3 storm on the Saffir-Simpson Hurricane Wind Scale. The barometric pressure in Savannah was measured at 960 millibars (28 inches). However, modern estimates put the pressure around 954 millibars (28.2 inches) at landfall, and possibly as low as 931 millibars (27.5 inches) out at sea. A tremendous storm surge of 16 feet, completely submerged many of the Sea Islands. This meant that the hurricane was most likely stronger than a Category 3 storm on the Saffir–Simpson Hurricane Wind Scale. Researchers believe the hurricane was of equal intensity to the 1900 Galveston Hurricane. The hurricane passed north over South Carolina on August 28 and moved parallel up the U.S. East Seaboard before becoming extratropical over Atlantic Canada.

The hurricane's storm surge caused a significant amount of destruction to the Sea Islands and the peninsulas that line the Georgia and South Carolina coastlines. Some 2,000 people are said to have drowned during the event. Nearly every building on the Sea Islands was damaged beyond repair leaving 30,000 people homeless. It took over a month for the American Red Cross to arrive at the disaster areas, possibly due to ongoing efforts in response to another hurricane that had hit South Carolina in June. Relief efforts were further hampered by another Category 3 hurricane, which struck just north, near Charleston, South Carolina, on 13 October. After a significant 10-month relief campaign, housing and food resources had been restored to the Sea Islands. Damages from the hurricane totaled at least $1 million (1893 USD [$27.1 million 2019 USD]).

At the time, the 1893 Atlantic hurricane season was the most destructive in U.S. history with two storms killing 2,000 people each. The 1893 hurricane season is also one of only two seasons (the other in 1998), where four hurricanes existed concurrently on the same day in the Atlantic basin. The hurricane reduced Beaufort, South Carolina to rubble. The phosphate industry that had thrived in the city since the 1870s was practically wiped out. Rice cultivation also ceased, as the fields became filled with saltwater. Economic turmoil plagued Beaufort for nearly half a

---

[65] The Nassau Guardian, *The Hurricane*. September 12, 1883, pg. 1. Retrieved: 12-11-2011.

century after the hurricane. The destructive Hurricane Hugo in 1989 would follow a similar track as the Sea Islands Hurricane almost a century later. Damage reports from the 1893 hurricane are also very like the damage sustained from Hurricane Floyd in 1999.

This is also the hurricane that made famous United States Life-Saving Service Keeper Dunbar Davis. Davis is known for his numerous rescues at sea but is most famous for his daring rescue during this hurricane. Davis, who was the Keeper of the Oak Island Station, gathered his few crewmen and set off. Braving the storm and the treacherous waters of the Graveyard of the Atlantic, he and his crew rescued all crewmembers aboard the four ships: *Three Sisters, Kate Giffor, Wustrow,* and *Enchantress.* This seaman's final resting place is the Old Morse Cemetery in a quiet corner of Southport. There, a row of simple granite tombstones marks the births and deaths of most of the Davis family. Standing the tallest, however, is that of Dunbar Davis. Numerous books tell of the many rescues Davis had over his career. There is even a song about his famous rescue called "The Long Day of Dunbar Davis" by the band Scearce & Ketner.

CHAPTER SEVEN

The Great Bahamas Hurricane of 1866 (or the Great Nassau Hurricane of 1866)

Highlights of this hurricane

- This storm remains one of the greatest and deadliest hurricanes to impact The Bahamas.

- Over 387 persons died in this storm in The Bahamas, and it devastated the entire Bahamas and impacted the economy of The Bahamas for years to follow.

- This storm occurred just after the blockade running era and during the wrecking and salvaging era. Many boats were out at sea on wrecking and salvaging trips and were caught at sea during the storm and many persons perished onboard these ships.

- The American boat *Eagle* sunk near Cat Island and San Salvador and it was reported that well over 100 dead bodies floated ashore on these two islands.

- A French boat was wrecked at Great Stirrup Cay. It capsized and destroyed with all persons onboard perishing. A large center-board schooner was wrecked on Crossing Rock, Abaco. All hands onboard drowned.

- A large vessel called *Race*, her port and nation unknown, loaded with lumber, sunk at Berry Island; all persons onboard drowned.

The 1866 North Atlantic hurricane season was originally one of only four Atlantic hurricane seasons in which every known tropical cyclone attained hurricane status, along with 1852, 1858, and 1884. Initially, there were three known storms during the season, but a HURDAT re-analysis confirmed the increased activity. There were also two other systems that were included as tropical cyclones at one time, although both were considered to have been other storms already in the database. All tropical activity occurred between the middle of July and the end of October. There may have been additional unconfirmed tropical cyclones during the season.

Every storm but the fourth hurricane affected land during the season. The first hurricane hit Matagorda, Texas in July, the only one of the seasons to hit the United States as a hurricane. A month later a hurricane made two landfalls in Mexico. The third hurricane of the season formed near Bermuda and was last observed along the southern coast of Newfoundland. A few weeks later another storm executed a similar track, although it struck Newfoundland as a hurricane and caused damage. The most notable storm of the season was the Great Bahamas Hurricane of 1866 (also called the 'Great Nassau Hurricane of 1866'), which killed at least 387 people in The Bahamas. It attained winds of 140 mph, which is a Category 4 on the modern-day Saffir-Simpson Hurricane Wind Scale.

Meteorological History of the Great Bahamas Hurricane of 1866

Known as the Great Nassau Hurricane of 1866, the sixth hurricane of the season was also the longest-lasting storm. The brig Jarien encountered the hurricane on September 24 to the west-southwest of the Cape Verde Islands. The track is unknown for the following five days until another ship reported a hurricane about 20 miles north of Anegada in the British Virgin Islands. The hurricane affected the Leeward Islands, washing several vessels ashore and destroying a pier in St. Thomas. On September 30 through the following day, the cyclone moved through the Turks and Caicos Islands, becoming what was considered one of the deadliest hurricanes that impacted the Turks and Caicos Islands in the last 500 years. About 75% of the population was left homeless and moneyless.

After affecting the Turks and Caicos Islands, the hurricane passed through The Bahamas. The eye crossed over Nassau, where a barometric pressure of 938 millibars (27.70 inches) was reported. Based on this observation, the hurricane was estimated to have had sustained winds of 140 mph. The hurricane struck without warning in The Bahamas, either washing ashore or sinking every ship but one in Nassau Harbour. In addition, strong winds downed trees and destroyed roofs. Every building in Nassau was damaged or destroyed. After moving through the islands, the hurricane curved northeastward, affecting dozens of other ships and wrecking four. On October 4, it passed north of Bermuda, where it produced Force 11 winds on the Beaufort Scale. The hurricane was last observed on October 5 to the southeast of Atlantic Canada. Along its path through the Turks and Caicos, The Bahamas, and the western Atlantic, the hurricane killed at least 387 people alone in The Bahamas, making it among the top 5 deadliest Bahamian hurricanes on record.

Damages sustained in The Bahamas during the Great Bahamas Hurricane of 1866

RUINS OF THE TRINITY WESLEYAN CHAPEL.

The Illustrated view of the damaged ruins of the Trinity Wesleyan Methodist Church after the 1866 Hurricane taken from photographs by Mr. W. Davenport. This building was built for the Wesleyan Methodists, at a cost of nearly £8000, one-fourth of which

was contributed by a grant from the local Bahamas Government. It was opened for public worship in April 1865. (Courtesy of Jonathon Ramsey, Balmain Antiques). Jpeg-scan Picture page 14—1/2 page)

In 1861 the official population of the city of Nassau was estimated to be approximately 11,503 persons, and of that total, about 3,713 persons lived in the suburbs of Grants Town, Bain Town, and Delancy Town. By 1866, the unofficial population was estimated to be somewhere near 12,000 to 13,000 persons. In the Nassau Harbour, every vessel and boat, with one single exception, was driven ashore or severely damaged and wrecked. The southern shore was strewn with wrecked ships, and in some places, they were piled on top of one another. The road along the coast to the east of the island was blocked up with colonial vessels stacked on top of one another making the road impassable. The saltwater in the capital city of Nassau went two miles inland, destroying many boats and homes along the shores of the island. Graves were torn up and destroyed and flooded resulting in many dead bodies floating about the town. Hundreds of persons were left wounded and destitute as they huddled together among the ruins. One house was left completely buried in the sand filled with humans all were reported to be found dead under the sand, some mothers were found clinging to their infant children in their arms.

The Nassau Tribune reporter gave a vivid account of this storm and reported that "The sky presented a calm, beautiful and tranquil appearance, the town was a mass of destruction as if done by destroying angel, who retired after executing his disastrous work. We skipped from ruin to ruin with careful steps, lest we shall fall into the depth beneath. Passing along, we heard a pitiful groan beneath the ruins of a house, among the debris... The following day, I walked about the town, to view the desolation. No traces of the churches were to be seen, not even finding the spot on which they were initially located. Dead bodies were brought from all directions from the ruins of houses that only a few days ago were the happy and quiet homes of families. One man was discovered with his head severed from the body by the windowsill of the house. Another was found crushed beneath the debris. I attended the burial service that afternoon with over eight corpses were being buried. In a few moments, thirty bodies were also brought to be buried. I visited several houses where there lay the wounded and dying men, women and children, piercing groans and lamentations were heard everywhere. I tried to administer words of comfort to all I met.'[66]

One ocean steamer was found miles away from its mooring and another *The General Clinch* the last of the blockade runners remaining in the Nassau Harbour was smashed into countless pieces against the public wharf, after having crushed and inflicted a similar fate upon a colonial schooner. Proximity to the U.S. continued to provide an opportunity for illegal shipping activity. During the American Civil War (1861 to 1865), The Bahamas prospered as a center of Confederate blockade running. During the Prohibition era, these islands served as a base for American rumrunners. Nassau was a place of no particular importance before the war. Its inhabitants lived chiefly by fishing, sponging, and wrecking. But with the demands of the blockade, it suddenly became a commercial emporium. The Nassau Harbour was always crowded with ships during this era. Its wharves were covered with cotton-bales awaiting transportation to Europe, and with merchandise ready to be shipped for the blockaded country. Confederate agents were established here and took charge of the interests of their government relating to the contraband trade. Money was quickly earned and was freely spent, and the war, at least while it lasted, enriched the community.

The number of foreign vessels in the harbour at the time was small, but of the colonial vessels and boats, the number was great. Of the crafts in the harbour, 92 were destroyed, 97 were severely damaged, and 43 were only slightly damaged. With these vessels, a greater part of the population depended on them for their income and survival. As stated earlier, The Bahamas in 1866 relied heavily on sponging, fishing, and wrecking and salvaging for their livelihood and with these industries, they depended heavily on these vessels for daily survival. After the hurricane, many of the streets of New Providence were filled with debris of fallen trees, destroyed houses and roofs that were torn off entirely from the buildings, sometimes in whole and at other times in pieces and many trees were uprooted and their branches were torn off. No building escaped severe damage and some, such as John S. George's brand-new warehouse, was destroyed.

At Fort Charlotte, the Artillery Barracks were unroofed-the Western Esplanade wall was destroyed, and the terrace washed away. The two

---

[66] The Nassau Tribune, Tuesday, October 02nd, 1866, pg. 1, *The 1866 Hurricane.* Retrieved: 22-12-2006.

beacons, one on the terrace and the other on the top of the hill, used as leading landmarks for entering the Nassau Harbour, were blown down. The sea had broken through the Western Esplanade and shore barrier and washed hundreds of tons of sand and wreckage onto the main road, which further on was washed away in several places so that it was rendered impassable. Communications with the west of the island were halted for carts and carriages for a considerable time because the roads remain impassable because they were cluttered with downed trees and debris. Between the fort and Fleming Square, many of the houses were severely damaged, blown down or destroyed and the road was rendered impassable. In some cases, wooden houses were displaced and found several hundred feet away from where they were initially located.

In the Navy and Ordnance yards, which adjoined one another, and the piers were washed away, and the wooden stores, bathing-houses, boatsheds and parts of the surrounding walls were blown down. The eastern wing of the Police Barracks was unroofed, and part of the officers' quarters was unroofed, and the other sides escaped with only slight damage. The Military Hospital, just repaired and improved, was unroofed, and some parts of its walls were blown down. One portion of the Commandant's Quarters was blown down, and the remainder unroofed and badly damaged. The other officer's detached quarters and Mess House were unroofed and flooded. The Government House and all the public buildings were badly damaged, and the entire upper story was rendered uninhabitable. The Governor and his family were relocated to a private resident's house until the repair could be done to the building itself. The main public building, accommodating the courthouse and council member quarters was unroofed and severely damaged. The dome of the prison was partly stripped, and the main building of the New Providence Asylum was partly unroofed.

Trinity Church, which had been finished just a few months before the hurricane at considerable expense, was blown down and Bethel Baptist Church was also blown down but was rebuilt by the congregation and aided by a grant of £200 by the Legislature. The Church at St. Anne's and Dunmore Chapel, to the east were destroyed. The Cathedral, St. Mathew's Church, the Missionary Hall, St. Andrew's Presbyterian Church and Ebenezer Church were all severely damaged. The Girls Western School, the principal school house on the Woodcock property and Mr. Watkins School-House Chapel were among those that were blown down. The theatre was also unroofed and severely damaged. The extensive buildings at the

Quarantine Station on Athol Island, which was only recently completed a few months before the hurricane, were all blown down. On Bay Street, many stores were destroyed, and many others suffered tremendous damage to both the buildings and the supplies within them. In the Downtown area, a total of 27 shops or warehouses were destroyed, 46 were severely damaged, and 19 were unroofed. Almost all the street lamps were destroyed or severely damaged. The lantern at Hog Island (now Paradise Island) was broken, and most of the lamps and reflectors were either destroyed or severely damaged.

After the hurricane, there was a reported rise in the price of building materials and carpenters were said to be in high demand often being hired weeks in advance to help with relief and rebuilding efforts. It was estimated the repair work for all public buildings was near £18,900 pounds. Most of the schools were so severely damaged or destroyed that there was no school for a considerable time after the hurricane. When they finally got the schools opened 17 of them had to be transferred to other buildings to accommodate the children. The available vessels that were left undamaged after the storm were dispatched to some of the islands and cays to rescue persons who were left there stranded from the storm. On the first trip, 29 men, the crew of six vessels were picked up on some of the cays stranded, naked and starving because of the storm. Members of The Bahamas Legislative Council and the House of Assembly met and held an Extraordinary Session of the Legislature on November 6, to assess the damages from the storm and to provide a government response and to assist the people affected by the storm.

One of the measures they enacted was appointing a 'Central Relief Committee' which comprised of members of the two houses of the legislature, leading public officers, the Receiver General, and the Police Commissioner. Their jobs were, first, to report back to the House of Assembly on the damages incurred because of the hurricane, second, to help with the distribution of relief aid and finally, to render assistance to the entire population of The Bahamas when and where possible. The Bishop of Nassau sent to England one of his clergy, the Rev. R. Saunders, to ask for assistance in rebuilding the churches and schools. Relief Aid was made available from Cuba consisting of corn and cottonseeds, which were distributed to many of the residents of Nassau and the various Family Islands to replace the ones that were lost because of the hurricane. Loans of a considerable amount were made available by the government of England to help the residents to return their lives to some degree of normalcy.

The reports of the summary of damages to the city of Nassau were as follows: -

	Eastern District	Grants Town	Western District	Total
Houses Destroyed	231	269	112	612
Houses Damaged	287	277	49	613
Warehouses Destroyed	3	14	-	17
Warehouses Damaged	5	13	-	18
Shops Destroyed	9	1	3	13
Shops Damaged	17	4	-	21
Out Buildings Destroyed	319	228	85	632
Out Buildings Damaged	48	77	5	130
Churches and Chapels Destroyed	3	2	-	5
Churches and Chapels Damaged	1	1	-	2
Schoolhouses Destroyed	4	1	1	6
Schoolhouses Damaged	-	2	-	2
Theatre Destroyed	-	1	-	1
Persons Rendered Homeless	487	339	208	1034

Governor Rawson's report of the summary of damages to the city of Nassau after the Great Bahamas Hurricane of 1866. (Courtesy of The Bahamas Department of Archives Jpeg-scan Picture page 15—1 page)[67]

Sir Rawson William Rawson KCMG-CB (8 September 1812 – 20 November 1899) was a British government official and statistician. During this hurricane, Governor Rawson (1864-1868) was the Governor of The Bahamas. After the passage of this hurricane, he wrote a very detailed account on the impact of the hurricane on the various islands of The Bahamas. "I have had two objects in preparing and printing the present Report. First, to put on record the history of that calamitous visitation

---

[67] *The Official Report of Governor Rawson on the impact of the Great Bahamas Hurricane of 1866 on the various islands of The Bahamas.* Governor's Dispatches Files-CO23 (The Bahamas Department of Archives, Nassau, Bahamas.

which swept the greater part of The Bahamas Islands, and inflicted so much injury on the City of Nassau, in October 1866. Secondly, to make public, in the most useful form, the data which I was able to obtain as to the track and rate of progress of the hurricane. I doubt whether any opportunity has ever been offered, or rather taken, of collecting similar data from so many detached points. This is confirmed by the interest which Mr. John H. Redfield, the son of the eminent American Meteorologist, W.C. Redfield, and himself no mean proficient in the same science, has taken in working out the results of the observations collected on this storm.

As my motto is SUUM CUIQUE, I desire to record that I am much indebted to Captain Stuart, the Deputy Inspector of Lighthouses, for his assistance in collating and arranging the Abstract of the Observations received. The description of the city of Nassau is a further contribution, which I offer to the people of The Bahamas, towards a correct knowledge of the islands and their capital city."

Rawson W. Rawson.

Report on the Great Bahamas Hurricane of October 1866

Forming an Appendix to the Report of Governor Rawson, C.B., upon the Blue Book for the Year 1866.[68]

---

[68] *The Official Report of Governor Rawson on the impact of the Great Bahamas Hurricane of 1866 on the various islands of The Bahamas.* Governor's Dispatches Files-CO23 (The Bahamas Department of Archives), Nassau, Bahamas.

The various types of damages reported to ships after the Great Bahamas Hurricane of 1866

Ship's Name:	Type of Vessel:	Owner:	Type of Damage:
Adeline	Smack	WM Pritchard	Severely Damaged
Comet	Schooner	R. Stirrup	Severely Damaged
Industry	Sloop	W.A. Hall	Totally Destroyed
Surprise	Sloop	W.A. Hall	Totally Destroyed
Whym	Sloop	W.A. Hall	Totally Destroyed
White Squall	Sloop	Alexander Elden	Severely Damaged
Flying Cloud	Sloop	WM Elden	Slightly Damaged
Sarah	Sloop	WM. H. Bethel	Severely Damaged
Ernest	Sloop	James Fernandez	Totally Destroyed
Lady Slipper	Sloop	Joseph Fernandez	Badly Damaged
Lady Bannerman	Sloop	Mathew Hall	Badly Damaged
Firefly	Sloop	James Fernandez	Badly Damaged
Lelia	Smack	Thomas Finlay	Slightly Damaged
Willow	Smack	Christopher Brown	Slightly Damaged
Pilot Boat	-------	-----	Slightly Damaged
Union	Smack	WM. Moxey	Slightly Damaged
Dolphin	Smack	WM. Moxey	Slightly Damaged
Charles	Schooner	W.D. Albury	Badly Damaged
Ark	Sloop	Christopher Brown	Slightly Damaged
Defiance	Smack	WM Moxey	Very Badly Damaged
Handith	Sloop	Joseph C. Stirrup	Very Badly Damaged
Kate	Schooner	George Preston	Slightly Damaged
Ellen	Sloop	John Neely	Totally Destroyed
Surprise	Sloop	Salv. Green	Totally Destroyed
Star of the East	Schooner	Dennis Evans	Slightly Damaged
Trent	Sloop	Ben Bethel	Slightly Damaged
Lion	Smack	John Moran	Totally Destroyed
Margaret	Sloop	James Farrington	Totally Destroyed
Elizabeth	Sloop	James Neely	Totally Destroyed
William	Sloop	Joseph W. Pinder	Slightly Damaged
Mary	Sloop	-----	Slightly Damaged
Maria	Sloop	P. Sands	Slightly Damaged
Squirrel	Sloop	John W. Thompson	Slightly Damaged
Rose of Sharon	Sloop	WM. Moxey	Slightly Damaged
John	Sloop	Benj. Thompson	Slightly Damaged
Edwin	Sloop	John Russell	Slightly Damaged
Proceed	Sloop	John Evans	Severely Damaged
Jeff Davis	Sloop	John T. Thompson	Severely Damaged
Ella	Sloop	John A. Simms	Severely Damaged

Lily	Schooner	Charles Thompson	Slightly Damaged
Confidence	Schooner	Robert Sturrup	Slightly Damaged
Pinta	Sloop	Joseph W. Pinder	Severely Damaged
Lauretta	Smack	Joseph Moxey	Badly Damaged
Yellow Tail	Smack	WM. Thompson	Slightly Damaged
Henrietta	Smack	Alexander Hart	Totally Destroyed
Nassau	Boat	John W. Thompson	Totally Destroyed
James Powers	Boat	John T. Thompson	Totally Destroyed
Susan Drew	Smack	John Pearce, Jr.	Totally Destroyed
Smoothing Iron	Smack	John Pearce, Sr.	Totally Destroyed
Fancy	Sloop	J. Wells	Badly Damaged
Arrow	Sloop	Ben Bethel	Badly Damaged
John W. Pinder	Sloop	J.W. Pinder	Badly/Dismasted
Confederate	Sloop	Henry Pinder	Totally Destroyed
Sparrow	Schooner	Thomas Pinder	Totally Destroyed
Lucy	Sloop	Clement Pinder	Severely Damaged
Louisa	Sloop	B.V. Hall	Severely Damaged
Elector	Schooner	John Pinder	Severely Damaged
Independent	Schooner	C. Pinder	Slightly Damaged
Fairplay	Schooner	John W. Pinder	Slightly Damaged
Cecelia	Sloop	James Price	Badly Damaged
Guide	Sloop	Theo Sturrup	Badly Damaged
G.L. Blond	Sloop	John Swain	Badly Damaged
Wanting	Sloop	WM. Swain	Badly Damaged
Fish Hawk	Sloop	Joseph B. Kemp	Badly Damaged
Diana	Sloop	Robert Pearce	Totally Destroyed
Emulous	Sloop	Robert Pearce	Badly Damaged
May Flower	Sloop	Robert Pearce	Slightly Damaged
Julia	Smack	WM. Pearce	Slightly Damaged
Dis Ting	Sloop	John Swain	Slightly Damaged
Triumph	Schooner	Theo Stirrup	Slightly Damaged
Arabella	Sloop	Thomas Kemp	Severely Damaged
Star	Sloop	Coffee Thrift	Totally Destroyed
Mary Hooper	Sloop	Symonette	Severely Damaged
Unknown	Schooner	Unknown	Totally Destroyed
Unknown	4 Smacks	Unknown	Badly Damaged
Isabella	Schooner	Benjamin V. Hall	Severely Damaged
Maria	Sloop(Sponger)	Thomas Brown	Severely Damaged
Grace	Smack	Edward Brown	Totally Destroyed
Unknown	Smack	Unknown	Totally Destroyed
Unknown	Smack	Sweeting	Totally Destroyed
Ocean Monarch	Schooner	W.S. Whitehead	Severely Damaged

Hattie	Schooner	W.E. Ambrister	Severely Damaged
Valiant	Sloop	January Rolle	Severely Damaged
United Force	Schooner	Catto	Totally Destroyed
Trial	Schooner	H. C. Lightbourn	Totally Destroyed
Priscilla	Schooner	Benjamin V. Hall	Severely Damaged
Unknown	Schooner	Unknown	Totally Destroyed
Unknown	Sloop	Unknown	Totally Destroyed
None	Smack	Charles Minns	Severely Damaged
Lion	Schooner	Hepburn and Deal	Totally Destroyed
Unknown	Sloop	J. Demeritt	Totally Destroyed
Ellen	Sloop	Byron Bode	Slightly Damaged
Zebra	Schooner	P. Coakley	Severely Damaged
New Year	Sloop	Henry McBride	Slightly Damaged
Express	Sloop	Boyd	Severely Damaged
Eureka	Sloop	WM. Simmons	Slightly Damaged
Hornet	Sloop	Cargill	Severely Damaged
Unknown	Sloop	Unknown	Totally Destroyed
Blooming Youth	Sloop	Evans	Split Open
Trial	Sloop	S. Sweeting	Foundered
Newton	Sloop	G. Renouard & Co.	Slightly Damaged
Olivia	Schooner	G. Renouard & Co.	Severely Damaged
Unknown	Sloop	Eppes Sargent	Severely Damaged
Mary Jane	Sloop	John Demeritt	Severely Damaged
Pearl	Schooner	John Demeritt	Slightly Damaged
Telfair	Schooner	WM. Eneas	Severely Damaged
Water Boat	Sloop	H.C. Lightbourn	Severely Damaged
No Name	2 Boats	H.C. Lightbourn	Severely Damaged
Little Emily	Sloop	H.C. Lightbourn	Severely Damaged
Arabella	Sloop	R.G. Sawyer	Totally Destroyed
Lauretta	Schooner	----	Severely Damaged
Golden Eagle	Schooner	J. Saunders	Severely Damaged
Charley	Sloop-Boat	C.J. Marshall	Slightly Damaged
Dat Ting	Sloop-Boat	B.L. Burnside	Totally Destroyed
Alice Flora	Schooner	Knowles, Sands	Severely Damaged
Reform	Schooner	H.E. Johnson	Slightly Damaged
John G.	Brigantine	Sawyer & Menendez	Slightly Damaged
Jane	Sloop	B.V. Hall	Totally Damaged
No Name	3 Boats	Saunders & Son	Totally Destroyed
No Name	2 Lighters	----	Foundered
Mary	Schooner	J.W. Pinder	Dismasted
Tweed	Schooner	Fanning & Hasgill	Severely Damaged
Unknown	17 Boats	Unknown	Totally Destroyed

Unknown	8 Boats	Unknown	Severely Damaged
Unknown	2 Boats	W.S. Whitehead	Totally Destroyed
Unknown	1 Boat	Culmer	Totally Destroyed
None	2 Lighters	Sawyer & Menendez	Severely Damaged
None	1 Lighter	H. Adderley	Severely Damaged
None	1 Iron Lighter	George Preston	Severely Damaged
None	1 Boat	John S. Howell	Severely Damaged
None	1 Boat	McKinney	Severely Damaged
Unknown	Sloop	R. Simons	Severely Damaged
Unknown	Sloop	C. Cooper	Severely Damaged
Unknown	Sloop	A. Williams	Severely Damaged
Unknown	Sloop	G Stuart	Severely Damaged
Relief	Steamer	John S. Howell	Severely Damaged
Teviot	Schooner	Unknown	Totally Destroyed
Sylvia	Schooner	Barlow & Armbrister	Totally Destroyed
No Name	2 Boats	M. Lowe	Totally Destroyed
Unknown	Smack	Unknown	Slightly Damaged
No Name	3 Boats	J.C. Rahming & Co.	Totally Destroyed
No Name	9 Boats	Unknown	Severely Damaged
No Name	1 Boat	H.M. Customs	Totally Destroyed
No Name	1 Gig	H.M. Customs	Slightly Damaged
Nimble	H.M.S. Ship	----	Slightly Damaged
None	1 Boat	Commissariat	Totally Destroyed
None	2 Boats	Garrison	Severely Damaged
Evelina	Schooner & Boats	Squires Brothers	Totally Destroyed
Union	Schooner & Boats	Rich	Slightly Damaged
Nelia Covert	Schooner	M. Lowe	Totally Destroyed
Oreto	Schooner	H. Thurston	Severely Damaged
Lily	Schooner	----	Totally Destroyed
W. Fletcher	Sloop	W.D. Albury	Totally Destroyed
Charles	Schooner	W.D. Albury	Severely Damaged
Sunbeam	Schooner	W.D. Albury	Severely Damaged
Evelina	Sloop	H. Bannister	Totally Destroyed
Madeline	Schooner	Deveaux	Slightly Damaged
Resolute	Sloop	Alexander Pratt	Slightly Damaged
Telfair	Sloop	Pearce	Slightly Damaged
Miriam	Schooner	H. Thurston	Severely Damaged
Home	Sloop	B.R. Shariff	Severely damaged
General Clinch	Steamship	Unknown Agent	Totally Destroyed-- This ship had just

			entered the Court of Vice-Admiralty
No Name	1 Boat	R.W.H. Weech & Co. Schooner Union	Totally Destroyed
Number of Vessels Totally Destroyed:	93		
Number of vessels Severely Damaged:	97		
Number of Vessels Slightly Damaged:	41		
Total:	231		

The various types of damages reported to ships after the Great Bahamas Hurricane of 1866-The Official Report of Governor Rawson on the impact of the Great Bahamas Hurricane of 1866 on the various islands of The Bahamas. Governor's Dispatches Files-CO23 (Courtesy of The Bahamas Department of Archives, Nassau, Bahamas).

Foreign Vessels Destroyed in The Bahamas during the Great Bahamas Hurricane of 1866:

Of the foreign vessels, thirty were cast ashore, lost or severely damaged. Of the latter number, the most significant portions were brought into Nassau, as well as the cargoes saved from several boats which were stranded. The following two tables show the nature of the several disasters and the district in which they occurred.

Type of Vessel:	Nature of Damage:	Total:
Vessels ashore	Total Loss.	15
Vessels ashore	Got off and towed to Nassau.	1
Vessels ashore	Repaired and proceeded on voyage.	1
Vessel	Dismasted at sea.	4
Vessel	Dismasted and towed into Nassau.	1
Vessel	Damaged at sea.	2
Vessel	Totally destroyed at anchor and condemned.	2
Vessel	Abandoned.	1
Total:		**30**

Foreign vessels destroyed in The Bahamas during the Great Bahamas Hurricane of 1866-The entire crew of three of the above vessels died in the boats during the hurricane, number unknown, and four seamen in another vessel drowned. (The Official Report of Governor Rawson on the impact of the Great Bahamas Hurricane of 1866 on the various islands of The Bahamas). Governor's Dispatches Files-CO23 (Courtesy of The Bahamas Department of Archives, Nassau, Bahamas).

Islands where the wrecks and the number of the wrecks occurred because of the hurricane:

Island:	Number of wrecks:
Abaco	7
Harbour Island	1
Eleuthera	4
New Providence	1
Andros	3
Great Stirrup's Cay	1
Grand Bahama	1
San Salvador	1
Fortune Island	1
Mayaguana	1
Inagua	2
Bimini	1
Sheep Cay Shoal, Grand Bahama Bank	1
Dismasted at sea	5
Total:	30

Islands where the wrecks and number of the wrecks occurred because of the hurricane. (The Official Report of Governor Rawson on the impact of the Great Bahamas Hurricane of 1866 on the various islands of The Bahamas. Governor's Dispatches Files-CO23 (Courtesy of The Bahamas Department of Archives, Nassau, Bahamas).

Damages sustained to houses and businesses in the city of Nassau

Name:	Damage:
	Bay Street:
J.R. Hall	Warehouse and Stable destroyed.
C.W. Weech	One House and two warehouses damaged.
Thomas Williams	Roof of house partly blown off.
H.R. Saunders	House damaged, and the roofs of three Warehouses partly blown off.
J.J. Boyd	Warehouse and Out-buildings destroyed.
Sawyer & Mendez	Warehouse destroyed.
H. Gomez	Roof of house blown off.
G. Renouard	Roof of house blown off.
G. Renouard	House damaged.
W. Farrington	Roof of store blown off.
Sawyer & Menendez	Part of roof blown off.
Sawyer & Menendez	Roof and upper story of store destroyed.
Sawyer & Menendez	Roof blown off house.
G.D. Harris	Roof of Store blown off.
G.D. Harris	Roof and upper story of store destroyed.
G.D. Harris	Store damaged.
G.D. Harris	Store destroyed.
G.D. Harris	House damaged.
H. Adderley	Roof of store Damaged.
J.H. Rahming	Tin roof of store blown off.
Kemp & Albury	House damaged, and Coach-house destroyed.
H. Adderley	Roof of house damaged.
H. Adderley	House damaged and Out-buildings and Stables destroyed.
Mrs. G. Adderley	House Damaged.
Mrs. M.C. Johnson	Roof of house damaged and Piazza blown away.
Mrs. Goodman	Roof of house damaged and Piazza blown away.
W.J. Weech	Roof and piazza damaged.
H. Adderley	Roof of house destroyed
Mrs. Wall	Piazza and Gate damaged.
Squiers Brothers	Roof of store damaged.
R.W.H. Weech	Roof and upper story of store blown down.
R.W.H. Weech	Roof and upper story of store blown down.
J.S. George	House damaged.
J.S. George	Roofs and upper stories of two large stores destroyed.
Mrs. G. Adderley	Store destroyed.
W.J. Weech	Roof blown off store.
W. Albury & Sons	Roof and upper story of store blown down.

Alexander Johnson	Warehouse damaged.
J.C. Rahming	Warehouse destroyed and Stable damaged.
Mrs. Advenson	House destroyed.
Mrs. Smith	House destroyed.
R.E. Rigby	House destroyed.
	Dowdeswell Street:
Mrs. Easton	House destroyed.
A. Wallace	One house destroyed.
A. Wallace	One house destroyed.
E. Royley	One house destroyed.
E. Royley	One house destroyed.
Mrs. Knowles	One house destroyed.
R. Sumner	One house destroyed.
	Shirley Street:
W. Higgs	House destroyed.
Mrs. Sweeting	House destroyed.
A. Punchbar	House destroyed.
A. Wallace	House destroyed.
Mrs. Hill	House damaged.
Ebenezer Chapel	Damaged and three classrooms destroyed.
J.J. Corlett	School house destroyed.
C. Burnside	House significantly damaged.
Zion Chapel	Significantly damaged.
Mrs. Mathews	House damaged.
T.B. Tynes	House destroyed.
B.L. Burnside	Roof of house damaged.
Bishop of Nassau	House damaged, kitchen and a small Bedroom destroyed.
N. Webb	House Damaged.
	Duke Street:
A. Johnson	House destroyed.
Missionary Hall	Damaged.
	East Hill Street:
H.R. Saunders	Part of roof blown off house; Carriage-house damaged.
S.O. Johnson	House destroyed.
S.O. Johnson	House very badly damaged.
F. Duncombe	Stable blown down.
E.C. Moseley	Piazza and Pantry blown down, and servants room

	destroyed.
E.C. Moseley	Iron roof of house blown off.
West Hill Street:	
T.C. Harvey	Roof partly blown off house.
J.A. Brook	House damaged.
J.H. Webb	House damaged, and out-buildings destroyed.
Judge Doyle	Piazza.
Woodcock Trustees	House damaged.
Dillet Street:	
Bethel Chapel	Destroyed.
Bain's Town:	
Woodcock Schools	One destroyed and two damaged.
East Street:	
Dr. Kirkwood	House and Outbuildings damaged.
Judge Doyle	Roof and upper story of house blown down.
Judge Doyle	Roof of Piazza blown off.
Mrs. Butler	House damaged.
Mrs. Farrington	House damaged.
A. Bain	House destroyed.
Parliament Street:	
G.C. Anderson	Gates damaged.
J. Pinder	Outbuildings destroyed.
A. Johnson	Roof of house partly blown off.
Charlotte Street:	
G.W.G. Robins	Piazza damaged and out-houses blown down.
G.D.Harris	Iron roof of Warehouse blown off.
Theatre	Destroyed.
Fredrick Street:	
W. Maura	Roof of house partly blown off.
A.T. Holmes	Out-buildings damaged.
Wesleyan Chapel	Destroyed, and outbuildings damaged.
Mrs. Butler	House damaged.
W.H. Curry	Upper story of new building blown down.
Market Street:	

A.T. Holmes	Roof blown off warehouse.
R. Sweeting	Roof of house blown off and store damaged.
T.K. Moore	Piazza damaged.
M. Menendez	Roof of house damaged.
E.B.A. Taylor	House and outbuildings destroyed.
	George Street:
A. Johnson	Roof, Piazza and Gates damaged.
H. Adderley	Roof of House damaged.
A. Johnson	Piazza damaged.
B. Bode	Roof of house damaged.
	Cumberland Street:
W.E. Armbrister	House partly damaged, and Out-buildings destroyed.
G.P. Wood	House damaged and Coach-house destroyed.
T.K. Moore	Roof of Coach-house blown off.
B. Bode	House and out-buildings damaged.
	Queen Street:
J. Roker	House destroyed.
Mrs. Jones	House destroyed.
E.A.J. Bethel	Roof of house blown off and Outbuildings destroyed.
J. Roker	House destroyed.
W. Sweeting	House damaged.
	West Street:
Baptist Mission	Five Out-buildings destroyed.
H.J. McCartney	House damaged.
H.J. McCartney	House damaged.
	Nassau Street:
Mrs. G. Adderley	Roof and Piazza partly blown away.
	King Street:
T.K. Moore	New Buildings partly destroyed.
Mrs. Farrington	House destroyed.
	Marlborough Street:
G. Preston	Roof of house damaged and Kitchen destroyed.

Damages sustained to houses and businesses in the city of Nassau. The Official Report of Governor Rawson on the impact of the Great Bahamas Hurricane of 1866 on the various islands of The Bahamas. Governor's Dispatches Files-CO23 (Courtesy of The Bahamas Department of Archives, Nassau, Bahamas).

Damages sustained on the major islands of The Bahamas during the Great Bahamas Hurricane of 1866

Inagua

The storm first made its impact in The Bahamas on the island of Inagua on September 30. The first sign of an approaching storm was felt sometime around 11 am EDT, and the storm reached its' peak intensity sometime around 9 pm to midnight. The damage to the island was said to be minimal except for three lost fishing vessels and two others which were slightly damaged. Fortunately, the lifeblood of Inagua-the salt ponds were not severely damaged or disrupted.

Mayaguana

The center of the hurricane passed over the island sometime just before midnight on the September 30. At Betsy Bay, the main settlement, on the northwestern shore, ten out of the thirteen houses were destroyed.

Long Cay

The canal of the salt pond suffered significant damage. Between 50,000 to 60,000 bushels of salt or about one-third of the year's crop, were destroyed. Houses to the leeward side of the salt heaps had salt showered on them like hail, and all the tanks were filled with salt or saltwater. Here is the list of the damages sustained to Long Cay: -

Destroyed

1 church (Episcopal)
1 Chapel (native Baptist)
28 dwelling houses
4 fishing vessels
12 boats

Damaged, Unroofed or Otherwise Affected by the Hurricane

6 vessels
5 boats
1 Jailhouse
39 dwelling houses

Crooked and Acklins Islands

About 75% of the dwelling homes were destroyed, and the population of this island was left in a deplorable state without food or shelter after the hurricane. In many areas, the sea overflowed the fields, destroying all the vegetation, while the high lands devastated by the strength of the wind and the torrential rainfall. At Crooked Island, two native Baptist churches were destroyed, and at Acklins there were three churches destroyed. After the hurricane, the residents survived of subsistence farming and the profitable wrecking and salvage industries.

Ragged Island

From this island, it was reported that the public-school house was blown down, but none of the private dwellings were significantly impacted. However, about 50,000 bushels of salt were lost by the rise of the tide and floodwaters. One schooner was driven ashore, and ten boats and vessels were destroyed. The farming grounds were flooded and contaminated with saltwater from the storm surge making them unusable.

Long Island

The entire island of Long Island was said to be devastated, and almost every building on the island was destroyed. Ten days after the storm, the residents were said to be suffering severely from starvation and only surviving of the limited local crabs and fish. During the hurricane, 62 residents had to seek shelter in the prison, and 23 residents had to seek refuge in the police station because the hurricane destroyed their private residence. The cotton plantations were destroyed or otherwise devastated.

The damages to Long Island were as follows: -

3 churches (Episcopal)
2 churches (Baptist)
1 schoolhouse
5 stores
230 dwelling houses
5 schooners
2 sloops
16 boats

Rum Cay

On this island, it was said to be devastated by this hurricane. All the crops were destroyed, and starvation was reported to be widespread, and most of the residents were left homeless for quite a while after the hurricane. The population of Rum Cay was mainly employed in raking salt and about 130,000 bushels, the greater part of an unusually large crop, was destroyed by this hurricane.

1 church (Episcopal) destroyed
2 chapels (Baptist) destroyed
2 chapels (Baptist) severely damaged
1 police station and prison, unroofed
1 schoolhouse destroyed
3 canals of salt pond destroyed
2 stores destroyed
2 wharves destroyed
22 dwellings destroyed
18 dwellings, severely damaged

The Illustrated view of the Wreckage at Nassau Harbour after the 1866 Hurricane… This illustration shows the effects of the hurricane at Nassau Harbour, from photographs by Mr. W. Davenport where it shows the sea wall or as it was called then The Public Abutment, broken and bestrewed with fragments of the wreck of *The General Clinch*-The last of the Blockade Runners ships in Nassau Harbour and other vessels driven against it (Courtesy of Mr. Jonathon Ramsey, Balmain Antiques).

Exuma

This island suffered significant damages, and this hurricane destroyed all the boats and means of transportation. Fortunately, the residents survived of cotton and corn crops, which were to some extent left not too severely damaged by the storm. When Governor Rawson first arrived on Exuma, the local 'Justice of the Peace' first informed him that relief supplies were not needed nor wanted. However, about 200 residents who had come to the ship to procure the supplies and distribute them found this quite unacceptable. After hearing this news, they immediately threatened to lynch the local Justice of the Peace and tear down his office and home if he did not make haste and distribute those hurricane supplies.

The damages sustained to the island of Exuma were as follows: -

2 chapels (Episcopal) damaged
4 chapels (Baptist) destroyed

1 chapel (Baptist) damaged
2 lock-up houses unroofed
1 public school unroofed
2 salt stores destroyed
112 dwelling houses destroyed
97 out-houses destroyed
8 vessels (Exuma) destroyed
5 vessels (Nassau) destroyed
12 boats (Exuma) destroyed

San Salvador

On this island, there was an old schoolhouse which was blown down, and several dwelling houses were damaged, and a schooner was lost on the coast with all persons onboard perishing. On this island, two Episcopal churches and several private dwellings were destroyed. Also, seven Baptist churches were also destroyed and three others severely damaged. They survived of a wreck on the western shore of the island and some local crops (corn, peas, and potatoes) in the fields that were left unaffected by the hurricane.

Eleuthera

The damages sustained to the island of Eleuthera were as follows: -

19 churches and chapels destroyed
2 Episcopal churches destroyed
13 Wesleyan churches destroyed
4 Baptist churches destroyed
2 schoolhouses
240 dwellings destroyed
56 dwellings significantly damaged
831 persons left homeless
8 vessels and boats destroyed
16 vessels and boats badly damaged

In terms of farming, about half of the pineapple crop was destroyed. Unemployment was said to be widespread, and the people were almost near starvation and had to rely on the government for its survival after the storm. In the early nineteenth century, Rock Sound was visited by Methodist Missionaries who built a large house (Manse) on the Sound in the center of the settlement; this was to be the focus for their teachings and mentoring for the inhabitants of South Eleuthera. The settlements of Spanish Wells, The Current, Governor's Harbour and other parts of Eleuthera were nearly swept away. In this hurricane, it went on record as the forerunner of today's hurricane shelters when it housed many Rock Sound families whose homes were subsequently destroyed in the storm.

The old American brig *Baltic* with captain John Maddocks of New York was en-route from New York to a port in Galveston with a general cargo. It was struck by this hurricane near Eleuthera and floundered, sunk and wrecked on a reef there with a part of her cargo. The officers and crew of this ship were as follows: John Maddocks, Francis R. Maddocks and Robert C. Wooster, mates, and Gilbert Sinclair, W.M. Boyd, John Morrison, Manfred A. Dyer, and John S. Ferris, seamen. The brig *Baltic* was an American general merchant ship, a wooden two-masted vessel brigantine rig. Her weight was 281 tons, and she was built in Camden, Maine in 1854. Her owner was William H. Hooper of Camden, Maine. On September 17, 1866, she was headed for the number one port in the United States at the time, Galveston, Texas. While en-route from Europe and New York with a large shipment of porcelain, English, Scottish, French and German China, medical and pharmaceutical supplies and food items and had to pass through The Bahamas to get to Galveston. Many persons drowned, and Bahamian wreckers recovered part of her cargo after the storm. The remainder of the cargo was only just recently recovered from Bahamian waters by Bahamian and American salvagers in 1995 perfectly preserved under a protective layer of sand, and thus her wooden hull remained intact, and her valuable cargo was untouched for well over 100 years. Bahamian treasure hunter and archaeological salvage expert, Nicholas Maillis, president of the Long Island-based Maillis Marine, made the initial discovery back in 1995.

Harbour Island was given this name because some of the earliest colonists wrote that because of the 'goodness of the harbour' and the name stuck with the local population. The northern shore of Eleuthera crowded with high cliffs or bluffs, and even in fair weather, the waves of the ocean beat down continually along these cliffs. During this hurricane, which was so devastating and powerful, it caused the waves to lash forcefully against that part of the cliff known as the "Narrow Crossing." Today, it is referred to as the 'Glass Window' or 'Glass Window Bridge.' Which is west of the 'Cow and Bull,' and causes jets streams or columns of water to be propelled or blown upwards into the air like dense columns of smoke. These sprays are often thrown upwards to heights of over 200 feet above the cliffs, and when the upward force of the water is expended, they are dispersed into spray like sparks from a fire, glittering in the rays of the sun like burnished silver. In the settlement of Harbour Island, the damages sustained were as follows: -

1 church (Episcopal) destroyed
1 police station and prison partially destroyed
2 schoolhouses destroyed
26 dwellings destroyed
21 dwellings significantly damaged
4 schooners lost
12 schooners considerably damaged
2 sloops badly damaged

Abaco

The destruction on this island was said to be widespread and very devastating, the schoolhouse was blown down, many houses were destroyed and many others severely damaged. Green Turtle Cay, Hope Town, and Marsh Harbour were in ruins after the hurricane. There was said to be no less than ten wrecked ships located at Ship Channel Cays. One native Baptist church and two Wesleyan Churches were destroyed. Regarding farming, the fields were destroyed, and the saltwater contaminated the soil and rendered it unusable for quite some time after the hurricane. Many of the islanders had to rely on the relief aid brought in from Nassau for survival. Also, most of them survived from the wrecking and salvaging industry on the southern shore of the island.

Andros

In the settlement of Red Bays, two churches were destroyed, and most of the homes were washed away by the storm. Many persons lost their lives when the storm surge came in and washed away many of the houses with the inhabitants still inside. At Fresh Creek, the church, the schoolhouse and several of the dwelling homes were blown down or severely damaged. At Calabash Bay, Staniard Creek, Bowen Sound, and Man-of-War Sound, several churches and many dwelling homes were destroyed or severely damaged.

The Berry Islands

The population of Berry Islands was very low and sparsely scattered throughout the island in small numbers. Their dwelling homes suffered significant damage, and the church and the schoolhouse were destroyed.

Bimini

There were several deaths and severe injuries inflicted to persons on this island both onshore and at sea. The population of North Bimini at the time was 210 persons. There were two churches blown down from the hurricane along with several dwelling homes. However, like the people in Abaco, they survived of the wrecking and salvaging industry after the hurricane. An endemic of the cholera disease caused by persons drinking contaminated water swept through this small island community with rapid pace and left behind many deaths on this island. There are no exact figures available for the total number of deaths on this island, but the count is believed to have been extremely high. All the victims of this disease were buried in a pit dug by the inhabitants just south of the public cemetery in Alice Town.[69]

Grand Bahama

Grand Bahama at the time was considered one of the poorest islands in this group of islands. They had very little cotton crop and very little agriculture to rely on. Most of the dwelling homes and churches on this island were destroyed and the little crops which they had were wiped out from this hurricane as the hurricane passed directly over this island.

---

[69] Ashley Saunders, *History of Bimini Vol. 2*, New World Press, Bimini, 2006. Pg. 159.

Turks and Caicos Islands

On this island some 800 homes were destroyed, and 3,000 persons were rendered homeless and penniless. The natives were left only with the clothes on their backs because the hurricane destroyed everything else, including all the food, clothing and living accommodations. Approximately 1,200,000 Bushels of salt were destroyed, and 18 vessels were wrecked and destroyed. There were 20 persons (15 from Grand Turk and 5 from Salt Cay) who drowned in this storm and in total at least 63 persons died as a direct result of this hurricane. This does not include those that were lost at sea and those who sustained significant injuries such as, broken bones and severe internal injuries and would have likely died from those injuries.

After the hurricane

After the hurricane, there was a reported steep rise in the price of building materials. Carpenters were said to be in such a great demand that they often had to be hired weeks in advance to help with relief work and rebuilding efforts of the many homes and businesses destroyed. It was estimated that the repair work for all the public buildings was near £18,900. Most of the schools, both in Nassau and on the Out Islands were so badly damaged or simply destroyed, that they were rendered unusable. As a result, there was no school for a few weeks after the passage of the hurricane. When they finally got the schools re-opened, 17 of them had to be transferred to other buildings to accommodate the children. The available vessels that were left undamaged after the storm were dispatched to some of the islands and cays to rescue persons who were left stranded from the storm. On the first trip, 29 men and the crew members of six vessels were picked up on several of the cays stranded, naked and starving because of the storm.

CHAPTER EIGHT

The Great Bahamas Hurricane of 1899 impact on the islands of The Bahamas (or The Great San Ciriaco Hurricane of 1899)

One of the most remarkable storms to ever hit the Caribbean was the Great Bahamas Hurricane of 1899 (officially known in the record books as the 'Great San Ciriaco Hurricane of 1899'), which cut a swath of destruction from the West Indies to the coast of France in the late summer of 1899. This powerful and very destructive hurricane, with maximum sustained winds of about 150 mph, was responsible for many deaths and much destruction during its lifetime. This storm has the distinction of being the eleventh most deadly storm in the annals of the North Atlantic hurricanes. The 1899 North Atlantic hurricane season lasted through the summer and the first half of fall in 1899. The season was an average one, with nine tropical storms, of which 5 became hurricanes, and only two became major hurricanes. The most notable storm was Hurricane San Ciriaco (or the Great Puerto Rico Hurricane of 1899), or locally known as the Great Andros Island Hurricane of 1899 or the Great Bahamas Hurricane of 1899 in The Bahamas, which caused more than 3,800 fatalities. Hurricane San Ciriaco also lasted almost a month. The hurricane was tied with Hurricane Ginger for the longest lasting hurricane on record in the North Atlantic.

Hurricane Ginger was the second-longest-lasting North Atlantic hurricane on record. The eighth tropical cyclone and fifth hurricane of the 1971 North Atlantic hurricane season, Ginger spent 27.25 days as a tropical cyclone, lasting from September 6 to October 3. The storm formed northeast of The Bahamas, and for the first nine days of its duration, it generally tracked eastward or northeastward while gradually strengthening to peak winds of 110 mph. This storm was significant for another reason, and that was, while over the western Atlantic Ocean, Ginger became the last target of Project Stormfury, which sought to weaken hurricanes by depositing silver iodide crystals into their rainbands.

The 1899 San Ciriaco Hurricane, was the eleventh deadliest hurricane in the North Atlantic basin. It was an incredibly intense and long-lived North Atlantic Cape Verde-type hurricane which crossed the island of Puerto Rico over the two days August 8 to August 9, 1899, causing $20 million (1899 USD or $585 million 2018 USD) of dollars in damage.[70] Many deaths occurred as a result, due to flooding and the hardest hit was the coastal city of Ponce, where five hundred people were killed. This deadly hurricane then crossed over the Turks and Caicos and then over The Bahamas where it killed well over 270 people on the island of Andros and 64 people on the island of Exuma.[71]

The cyclone kept tropical storm strength or higher for 28 days, which makes it the longest duration North Atlantic hurricane on record and the second-longest anywhere in the world. Hurricane John (also known as Typhoon John, international designation: 9420, Joint Typhoon Warning Center (JTWC) designation: 10E) formed during the 1994 Pacific hurricane season and became both the longest-lasting and the farthest-travelling tropical cyclone ever observed. John formed during the strong El Niño of 1991 to 1994 and peaked as a Category 5 hurricane on the Saffir-Simpson Hurricane Wind Scale, the highest categorization for hurricanes. Throughout its existence, it followed a 7,165 miles path from the eastern Pacific to the western Pacific and back to the central Pacific, lasting 31 days in total. Because it existed in both the eastern and western Pacific, John was one of a small number of rare tropical cyclones to be designated as both a hurricane and a typhoon during its existence. Despite lasting for a full month and breaking a few records, John was a non-issue storm and barely affected land at all, bringing only minimal effects to the Hawaiian Islands and a United States Military base on Johnson Atoll.

---

[70] https://westegg.com/inflation/infl.cgi. Retrieved: 08-12-2016.
[71] Wayne Neely, *The Great Bahamian Hurricanes of 1899 and 1932: The Story of Two of the Greatest and Deadliest Hurricanes to Impact The Bahamas*, (Bloomington, iUniverse Publishing Inc., 2012). Pgs. 132-34.

Meteorological History of the Great Bahamas Hurricane of 1899 (The Great San Ciriaco Hurricane of 1899)

This Great Bahamas Hurricane of 1899 formed somewhere near the Cape Verde Islands, but the exact origin of this hurricane is still unknown because of the lack of satellite data to determine its origin. However, it was first observed on August 3, to the west-southwest of the Cape Verde Islands. That day, a British steamship *Grangense* reported tropical storm force winds and a barometric pressure of 995 millibars as it passed directly through it just 1,880 miles east of Guadeloupe. At noon that day, located at latitude 11°51' north and longitude 35°51' west, Captain Spedding noted in his logbook that the weather began to change for the worse: "Clouds increased, and by 4 pm the wind was blowing out of the north-northwest, with Beaufort Wind Scale force being increased to fresh gale, accompanied by heavy rain." An hour later, the ship's barometer reached its lowest reading of 29.38 (inches) as the winds calmed and the rain ended temporarily, but it returned with even greater force after the lull. The storm was over by 10 pm, and the sky began to clear for good. Captain Spedding continued his voyage, observing that in his many years of travel between Europe and the Amazon, this was the farthest east he had ever encountered such a storm. For a few days, its exact path was unknown due to lack of observations, although it is estimated that the storm continued to move on a west-northwestward track and it became a hurricane on August 5.[72]

On August 7, after stations in the Lesser Antilles reported a change in wind from the northeast to the northwest, the United States Weather Bureau posted warnings and ordered hurricane signal flags to be flown at Roseau in Dominica, Basseterre in St. Kitts, San Juan in Puerto Rico and Santo Domingo in the Dominican Republic. Information on the hurricane was also sent to other locations throughout the Caribbean including The Bahamas. Estimates of storm-related fatalities range from 3,400 to 3,700, with millions of dollars in crop damage in Puerto Rico. The Bahamas reported millions of dollars in damage to the sponging industry and over well over 334 deaths, many of them sponge fishermen from the islands of Andros and Exuma.

---

[72] Wayne Neely, *The Great Bahamian Hurricanes of 1899 and 1932: The Story of Two of the Greatest and Deadliest Hurricanes to Impact The Bahamas*, (Bloomington, iUniverse Publishing Inc., 2012). Pg. 134.

North Carolina had considerable tobacco and corn damage from the longevity of the strong winds and torrential rain. Overall, the island of Puerto Rico was swamped by 28 days of heavy rain, contributing to the overall disaster. As it approached the northern Lesser Antilles, passing directly over the islands of Guadeloupe and Montserrat, the hurricane began to be tracked continuously by ship and land observations. It was during this time that, it quickly intensified into a powerful storm, and a station on Montserrat reported a pressure of 930 millibars. The latter of these two islands said that "All the churches, estates, and villages, were destroyed, and nearly 100 persons drowned," a correspondent for the New York Times observed. "In addition, many were injured and rendered homeless, and terrible distress exists amongst the sufferers."[73] This suggested sustained winds of 150 mph, making it a strong Category 4 hurricane of the Saffir-Simpson Hurricane Wind Scale. Thankfully, this was the strongest intensity of the hurricane.

Late on August 7, the hurricane moved through the northern Lesser Antilles, passing directly over the island of Guadeloupe and a short distance to the south of St. Kitts; in the latter island, a station reported winds of 120 mph. On the island of Guadeloupe, the hurricane made landfall near Point-à-Pitre at approximately 11:00 am and lasted until about 4:30 pm. The damage was extensive and widespread along the coast as well as in the interior of the island. A correspondent noted, "Many houses had their roofs blown off and were flooded, and some of them were demolished, but no fatalities were reported. Twenty-three flatboats and fishing boats were sunk in the harbour, in addition two schooners, two small steamboats, and a steamship named *Hirondale*, were wrecked at other places. *The Aleyou* had her stern damaged. The French cruiser *Cecille*, which was in the harbour, did not suffer at all." Antigua endured severe damage, but there was no report of life lost. On Nevis, the destruction was general, and at least twenty-one people were known to have died because of the hurricane. With its continuing west-northwest track, the hurricane skirted just south of the Virgin Islands. The island that suffered most in this group was St. Croix. One eyewitness noted: "Nearly every estate has been wrecked, the

---

[73] http://www.aoml.noaa.gov/hrd/Landsea/Partagas/1898-1900/1899_1.pdf. Retrieved: 16-07-2017.

large buildings in the towns have been unroofed, the stock has been killed, and a minimum of eleven deaths have occurred among the labourers."[74]

It then continued a west-northwestward track, and the hurricane weakened slightly before making landfall on August 8 along the southeastern coast of Puerto Rico. This island was trying to recover from the turmoil following the end of the Spanish-American War, and many communities were ill-prepared to cope with a natural disaster of this magnitude. The city of Guayama recorded a pressure of 940 millibars, suggesting a landfall intensity of 140 mph. On August 8, the feast day of Saint Ciriaco, it crossed the island of Puerto Rico in an east-southeast to west-northwest direction, causing maximum sustained wind speeds between 110 and 140 mph. The most devastating effect of San Ciriaco on the island of Puerto Rico was the destruction of the farmlands, especially in the mountains where the coffee plantations were located. San Ciriaco aggravated the social and economic situation of Puerto Rico at the time and had severe repercussions in the years that followed. After it passed Puerto Rico, it grazed the northern section of the Dominican Republic as a Category 3 hurricane but passed north enough not to cause significant damage. It then passed through The Bahamas, retaining its strength as it moved slowly northward.

Captain Lobb, The Bahamas Inspector of the Lighthouses, made the following observations from the log of the Imperial Lighthouse Ship Richmond who experienced this hurricane living in The Bahamas and at a lighthouse station: "On August 11th at 8am, wind NE, force 6 (equal to 31 miles an hour) barometer 30.00 inches; no shift of wind, but increasing in force until 10pm. ENE, barometer 29.58 inches, midnight barometer 29.46 inches; 1 am August 12th, wind ESE barometer 29.33 inches; 3 am the lowest barometer 29.32 inches; the force of the wind, 11 to 12 (equal to 75 to 90 mph) full force of a hurricane. Wind ESE until 6 am shifted to the SE and at 2 pm began to decrease, barometer 29.68 inches; wind SE by S; midnight wind S and barometer 29.83 inches."

After slowly drifting northeastward, the hurricane then made a northwestward track, hitting the Outer Banks of North Carolina near Diamond City as a Category 3 storm of 140 mph on August 17. As it then passed over the Outer Banks of North Carolina, entire islands were flooded,

---

[74] Wayne Neely, *The Great Bahamian Hurricanes of 1899 and 1932: The Story of Two of the Greatest and Deadliest Hurricanes to Impact The Bahamas*, (Bloomington, iUniverse Publishing Inc., 2012). Pg. 135. Retrieved: 16-07-2017.

and fishing villages were destroyed. Some communities never recovered and were forced to relocate further inland. It drifted northeast over the state, re-emerging into the Atlantic on the 19th. Ships were damaged and destroyed all along the Atlantic seaboard from Florida to Massachusetts. Severe damage also occurred at Diamond City and Shackleford Banks, where nearly every house was swept away. Several farm animals drowned. The tides unearthed caskets, damaging them and left bones scattered throughout the towns. After the storm, residents began abandoning the area and re-settled in other cities, most of them located elsewhere in the Outer Banks. On Ocracoke Island, the island was covered with 4 to 5 feet of water. A total of 33 homes were destroyed, and nearly every other suffered damage.

Additionally, two churches were demolished. Several cows, horses, and sheep drowned. Among the ships that wrecked was the Barkentine *Priscilla*. Rasmus Midgett, a United States Life-Saving Service member, single-handedly rescued ten people from the *Priscilla*. On October 18, Midgett was awarded the Lifesaving Medal by Secretary of the Treasury Lyman J. Gage. Heavy rains and strong winds as far inland as Raleigh resulted in "great damage" to crops. There were at least 20 fatalities in North Carolina.

For several weeks after the storm, ships came into ports all along the East Coast with reports of encounters with this powerful tempest. Some survivors of ill-fated vessels who were lucky to be alive told stories of the difficult time of trying to stay alive on the high seas. Others told accounts of how they had to abandon ships that had lost their rigging and their crew and were floating aimlessly on the high seas. It continued eastward, where it became extratropical on August 22. The extratropical cyclone then took a southeast track where, on August 26, it became a tropical storm again. Like most of the rest of its lifetime, it drifted, first to the northwest then to the east. It strengthened as it moved eastward, and on September 3, as it was moving through the Azores, it again became a Category 1 hurricane. The intensification didn't last long, and the hurricane became extratropical for the final time on September 4. It dissipated that day while racing across the northeastern Atlantic.

One of the most tragic episodes of the hurricane was the ordeal of the men aboard the Norwegian barque *Drot*, which encountered the storm well out in the Atlantic between Cape Hatteras and Florida. The crew bravely fought the howling winds and raging seas, but eventually, nature prevailed.

A gigantic wave hit the ship, washing the captain and seven of his crewmen overboard. Despite their best efforts, the boat was thrashed to pieces by the waves. At that point, the men finally decided to save themselves before the ship was lost. A raft was pieced together from planks ripped from the *Drot's* deck, upon which the mate and the seven remaining seamen took to the sea. In the rough seas and raging storm, their makeshift raft broke into two pieces. On one part rode the mate and one of the men. Being overcome with fear, the mate jumped overboard and committed suicide. The remaining man did not give up so quickly and continued riding out the storm. His confidence paid off, as he was picked up off the Carolina coast by the *Titania,* a German steamship, and subsequently landed in Philadelphia.

The six men on the other portion of the raft had their hell to deal with as one man lost his mind and jumped into the raging seas where he drowned. As time passed and the storm continued unabated, two of his companions followed his example, taking their own lives by plunging into the sea. The three remaining men were Maurice Anderson, Goodmund Thomason and a German whose name was not recorded. They drifted on the storm-tossed waters of the Atlantic, without water to quench their thirsts, or food to prevent starvation. Realizing that they would die of thirst or hunger, the three men agreed to draw lots-the loser would be killed and consumed by the other two. The German lost the wager and was immediately killed by Thomason and Anderson, who quenched their thirst by drinking the blood from his veins.

This gruesome act of murder and cannibalism was too much for Anderson's conscience to deal with. The thought of the brutal deed wreaked havoc on his mind, and he soon went insane. In the fit of madness, he attacked Thomason, biting huge chunks of flesh from his chest and face before he could be subdued. On August 31, after two weeks of terror on the high seas, the raft containing the pitiful men was picked up by the British steamer *Woodruff* drifting 250 miles off the South Carolina coast. They were taken into port at Charleston, where they were given to local authorities. Word of their story soon leaked out, and press reports noted: "Anderson is a raving maniac, and his companion is shockingly mutilated from bites of the crazed man." Both men were hospitalized and then turned over to the Norwegian Consul in Charleston, who took them back to Norway to answer for their crimes. Wrecked ships littered the coastline of the Atlantic Seaboard from Florida in the south to New England in the north. In North Carolina alone on the US East Coast, over fifty ships were wrecked along the coast between Cape Fear and Currituck. These wrecks were distributed on the beaches facing the ocean, as well as in the sounds where the smaller vessels that plied these local waters fared severely from the effects of the storm.

After making landfall near Cape Lookout, the slow-moving storm made a sharp right turn and passed back out to sea off the vicinity of Ocracoke. After leaving the Outer Banks, the San Ciriaco Hurricane continued to be a menacing storm for mariners in the Atlantic. The long-lived storm was tracked by the U.S. Weather Bureau across the Atlantic, past the Azores and on to France. A report in October 1900 edition of the Monthly Weather Review noted: "On September 9, it was center of the coast of Provence, France, gales prevailed in this region until September 12, on which date the storm had joined with an area of low barometer covering southeastern Europe."

In all, this remarkable and deadly storm existed for about thirty-six days, making it the longest-lived tropical cyclone ever observed in the North Atlantic basin. Along a dangerous stretch of coast of the Caribbean and the Eastern Seaboard renowned for its turbulent weather, few storms have ever equaled the San Ciriaco Hurricane. Hurricane San Ciriaco set many records on its path. Killing nearly 3,500 people in Puerto Rico, it was the deadliest hurricane to hit the island and the strongest at the time, until 30 years later when the island was hit by the Hurricane San Felipe Segundo, a Category 5 hurricane, in 1928. It also killed over 334 persons in The Bahamas, the deadliest hurricane since the Great Bahamas Hurricane of 1866. The next storm to have that significant amount of death toll in The Bahamas was the Great Nassau Hurricane of 1926. It was also the tenth deadliest North Atlantic Hurricane ever recorded.

With an Accumulated Cyclone Energy (ACE) of 73.57, it has the highest ACE of any North Atlantic hurricane in history. In 2004, Hurricane Ivan became the second North Atlantic hurricane to surpass an ACE value of 70 but did not exceed the San Ciriaco Hurricane. ACE is a measure used by the National Oceanic and Atmospheric Administration (NOAA) to express the activity of individual tropical cyclones and entire tropical cyclone seasons, particularly the North Atlantic hurricane season. It uses an approximation of the energy used by a tropical system over its lifetime and is calculated every six hours. The ACE of a season is the sum of the ACEs for each storm and considers the number, strength, and duration of all the tropical storms in the season. The highest ever ACE estimated for a single storm in the Atlantic is 73.6, for Hurricane San Ciriaco in 1899. This single storm had an ACE higher than many whole Atlantic storm seasons. Other Atlantic storms with high ACEs include Hurricane Ivan in 2004, with an ACE of 70.4, Hurricane Donna in 1960, with an ACE of 64.6, Hurricane Isabel in 2003 with an ACE of 63.28, and the Great Charleston Hurricane of 1893 with an ACE of 63.5. San Ciriaco is also the longest lasting North Atlantic hurricane in recorded history, lasting for 28 days (31 including subtropical time).

Damages sustained on the major islands of The Bahamas during the Great Bahamas Hurricane of 1899 (The Great San Ciriaco Hurricane of 1899)

This is a famous watercolour painting called '*After the 1899 Hurricane,*' painted by world-renowned water colour artist **Winslow Homer** in 1899 while he was in The Bahamas. The scene shows a man lying on a sandy beach in The Bahamas surrounded by rough seas and pieces of his dinghy boat destroyed by the Great Bahamas Hurricane of 1899. Winslow Homer is considered one of the foremost painters in the 19th century America and a pre-eminent figure in American Art. (Courtesy of Jonathan Ramsey-Balmian Antiques).

Nassau

The members of the House of Assembly voted to support a measure authorizing expenditure to provide hurricane relief throughout the islands of The Bahamas. Several vessels were dispatched by the authority of the Colonial Secretary Mr. Joseph Chamberlain to send relief supplies and to render assistance to the respective Out Islands. The schooner *E.B.A. Taylor* was dispatched to the Exuma Cays and Long Island. The *Attic* was dispatched to the Berry Islands, Williams Cay, and Bimini. The sloop *Eastern Star* was sent to Behring Point and Cargill Creek. The *Albertine Adoue* was sent to Abaco, the schooner *Glynn* for Eleuthera and *Sappho* for the island of Andros. In all the cases, the boat captains were expected to take relief supplies to the respective islands and to make a complete report of the damages sustained and report it back to the Colonial Secretary Mr. Joseph Chamberlain and the Legislature. Collections were taken by many of the churches in Nassau, to send to needy residents throughout The Bahamas left devastated by the storm.

When morning arrived, the daylight revealed the severity of the damages that had occurred from this powerful storm during the night. Among the first severe losses observed was the destruction of a new building recently erected by Mr. G.B. Adderley to the west of the sponge exchange, which was completely leveled to the ground. It had been constructed of a wooden frame and enclosed with corrugated iron. Its proximity to the waterside left it exposed, and the building was blown over from the foundation. The covering of the J.S. Johnson Company's Wharf fell in, and a portion of the wharf to the east was carried away. Numerous sheds in front of the stores on Bay Street and other streets were blown down and business signs removed.

Several house properties in the city of Nassau sustained comparatively little damage as compared to the suburbs. In the suburbs, most of the humble dwellings of the poor sustained considerable damage. Small houses throughout the suburbs were devastated, and many homes and outhouses were blown down. The effects of the storm did not in the least shake the British Colonial Hotel. Within the hotel, however, the temporary cloth frames that were set in the windows allowed rainwater to access the building, which inflicted damage to the new plastering. The building otherwise was left intact. The walls of the building during erection at the Hotel Royal Victoria was severely damaged. The boundary walls and fences of most houses and businesses were blown down in every direction both in the city and outskirts. At the casino on Hog Island, the roof of the dancing pavilion was blown away.

The prison roof was damaged at one corner, and a long length of the boundary wall was blown down. The wind anemometers at Government House and the Verandah Wharf were damaged but were repaired shortly after the storm. Several fences and walls were blown down in the Government House grounds, and a few slates were blown off the roof. A piece of fence at the Eastern Burial Ground was blown down. The gate and signal hut at Fort Fincastle were slightly damaged. At Hog Island, some shingles on the keeper's dwelling were blown off. At the Quarantine Station at Athol Island, the wharf was entirely blown away and displaced about ½ mile to the west by the Sea Gardens. The hospital kitchen roof was partially blown off. The hospital (main) leaders were blown away, and the walls cracked. The hospital (convalescent) leaders around the building were blown away. One of the strange turn of events after the storm was the loss of a steamboat *Minnie* at Hog Island but was refloated just before the hurricane. It was then anchored in Nassau Harbour, but during the hurricane, it was blown out of the harbour. Eventually, the engine was found near Silver Cay, a piece of board with her name on it was located in the Berry Islands, and the remainder of the hull with the propeller still attached at Water Cay, Grand Bahama.

In St. Mary's Church, the recently erected chapel was severely damaged by water, and all the books and other miscellaneous items were destroyed or damaged. The clock in the tower of St. Matthew's Church stopped working when water from the storm affected its machinery, and the windows of the church sustained minor damage. The southern district was in some portions flooded when the flood waters reached the floors of several dwelling houses. The flood waters on the main roads were reported to have been at least two feet deep in some places. One of the most devastating losses to many people in the 'Over-the-Hill' areas was the loss of fruit-bearing trees and vegetables.

After the storm, it was said that many of the residential properties across the island were covered with young fruits and vegetables. The beautiful foliage around the library grounds was destroyed, and the trees on the avenues and in private and government grounds were blown down. It was made to appear that it made the city and country look desolated. There was a fire which broke out at the Colonial Hotel after the hurricane, but thankfully it was quickly extinguished by a group of workmen using buckets of water. During the hurricane between 1 am to 2 am, a house the property of Mrs. Adelaide Burns blew down and almost crushed her to death, but Mr. Erskine Mason rescued her. When he heard her screams, he immediately came and moved the house off her chest with the assistance of another man. She was taken to the hospital for treatment of her injuries.

The following damages were sustained to several multi-family homes around Nassau, on Shirley Street-3 multi-family homes destroyed, Mackey Street-2, Kemp Road-2, Fowler Street-1, Christie Street-1, Armstrong Street-2, Dowdeswell Street-1, Delancy Town-12, Grant's Town-12 and Bain Town-8. The homes destroyed were all built of wood and were already very frail and dilapidated. After the storm, many of the homes in Adelaide were blown down, and many of the residents (twelve families in all) were forced to live in the church. At Gambier, there was a church and part of a house blown down. A house belonging to Mr. Henry Mostyn at Orange Hill near Gambier was destroyed, and three persons on the inside were severely hurt. The orchard of Mr. David Patton in Bain Town and that of Mr. Robert Forcecr in Grant's Town, suffered severely because many trees were uprooted, and thousands of fruits were lost.

Shipping in Nassau also suffered severely. Many lives were lost, and many people were reported missing. Many schooners and sailboats were seen lining the southern shore of Hog Island (now called 'Paradise Island'-a tourism mecca for The Bahamas), some of which had been anchored off "Burnside's" and getting ashore on the soft bottom sustained no damage. A few sloops were damaged on the Hog Island side of the harbour and several boats sunk at their moorings. A sloop was driven against the rocks near the lighthouse, the schooner *Thrasher* drifted as far as the Bar, and her masts were cut away when she held on. The crew of this vessel remained on board, and the ship *Richmond* captain by Mr. S.A. Dillet had to rescue the nine-member crew. The steamboats *Minnie* and *Non-Pareil* owned by Mr. Ernest were blown away never to be seen again. The old tug *Nassau* was blown away from its anchorage in Nassau Harbour and destroyed. It was reported that the settlement of Gambier was devastated, and the local Baptist Church was blown down. The sisal factory at Old Fort was destroyed, and all the other sisal plantations were also destroyed.

As the schooner *Rapid*, drifted down the harbour it encountered the J.S. Johnson Company's Factory Wharf when the crew took the opportunity of getting ashore. One of the crew Robert Edden, who was the first to leave the vessel, but he was injured by a beam when he fell into the water. The rest of the crew managed to extricate him, but his injury was so severe that he had to be taken to the New Providence Asylum for treatment but eventually succumbed to his injuries. The schooner *Waterloo* owned by the Estate of W.R. Pyfrom was driven out of the Nassau Harbour, and four of her crew went missing and were never found. They were Alfred Evans of Nicholl's Town, Andros, Alex Smith, Jason Rahming of Long Island, and Herbert Gibson of Grand Bahama. Captain Dillon of the ship *Cocoa* while using a searchlight from his ship reported seeing many dead bodies floating past his boat in Nassau Harbour. The schooner *Southern Queen* and sloop *Guide* were blown out to sea from the south end of New Providence with 18 men onboard. The schooner *Waterloo* sunk on the western end of New Providence.[75]

After this storm and the massive death toll incurred, the British Government, decided to put into law a 'Hurricane Warning Act' to establish special hurricane signal flags which would be prominently displayed from the signal staffs on Forts Charlotte and Fincastle. Before this hurricane, signal flags were hoisted at the various forts but only randomly based on the location and strength of the storm. The new regulation required that signals be raised when the barometric pressure reading fell below a certain point. In addition to this, it was required that there should be some means by which mariners should become acquainted with any information that was acquired by means of the telegraph to decrease the loss of life and property both at sea and land. Because of this hurricane, all British Imperial Lighthouse Service light stations were issued a set of signal flags. They were kept ready once there was an approaching storm to warn incoming or outgoing ships and residents of the impending hurricane. For centuries before the introduction of radios, sharing of information between ships, from shore to shore and from sea to shore posed communications problems. The only way for mariners to pass a message from one ship to another or from ship to land was by visual signals. For many years preceding the invention of the telegraph (and during its invention), some types of semaphore signaling from high places, towers or forts were used to send messages between distant points.

To this day, we still signal ships at sea with flags flown from shore-based towers and other ships displaying storm warning flags. On Hog

---

[75] The Bahamas Governor's Dispatches (CO23), (*The Hurricane*, August 21, 1899). Retrieved: 11-10-1899.

Island (now called Paradise Island), there was a lighthouse and to the right of this lighthouse was a flagpole which displayed the Union Jack of Great Britain. If there was a hurricane travelling near The Bahamas, that flag would be removed and be replaced with a specialty hurricane flag. This flag consisted of a red coloured flag with a black square in the middle. Similarly, if any gale conditions were being experienced, the gale flag would be used (two red triangle flags indicated gale warnings with winds between 34 to 47 knots). These flags were only taken down after the dangers associated with the hurricane or the gale conditions had dissipated. Similar events would also take place on the Family Island lighthouses if they knew an approaching hurricane. These signal flags also gave residents on Nassau and the Family Islands a small grace period to prepare for a storm. In this day of satellite communications, radios, televisions, computers and instant information everywhere, these flags are rarely used.

The barometer was used in The Bahamas as early as 1854 to predict the weather but came into widespread use after this storm. Sponging was the number one industry in The Bahamas during this hurricane. Most if not all Bahamian fishermen going out at sea on fishing or sponging trips would take with them a barometer. If they noticed a steep drop in the atmospheric pressure indicated on the gauge, they would immediately turn the boat around and head back to shore because it meant that a hurricane or some other form of severe weather was approaching that part of The Bahamas.

Inagua

Three vessels were lost, and the schooner *Vivid* was stranded at Lantern Head, and the boats that were hauled up on the bay were severely damaged. A Turks Island schooner was lost at Little Inagua, and a Crooked Island craft was damaged on the south side of Inagua. The rain fell on this island from 3 pm on September 10th to 2 am on September 11th, and the lowest barometer reading was 28.28 inches with a southerly wind.

Long Cay

The canal of the salt pond was severely damaged. Between 50,000 to 60,000 bushels of salt or about one-third of the year's crop, were destroyed. The damages sustained to the homes on this island were slight.

Cat Island

Very light damage was reported on this island. The schooner *Leader* en-route to Nassau rescued a small child just east of the island. Captain Burns attention was attracted by the loud cries of a boy on the shore. He immediately stopped the vessel and sent a boat on shore in the direction from which the voice was heard. A boy named David Mackey of Cat Island was discovered to be on the island, totally naked and was there for several days. He was one of the crews of the schooner *Choir* who with four others had clung to the booby hatch of the schooner when it capsized. All but Mackey were washed off the hatch, Captain Russell, Elijah Whymns, and two others were reported missing and presumed dead.

Ragged Island

From this island, it was reported that the public-school house was blown down, but none of the private dwellings were severely impacted.

Long Island

Deadman's Cay did not report any losses of life or damage to buildings, but the plantain and banana plantations were destroyed.

Rum Cay

The hurricane occurred on September 10 at noon and did not decrease until 5 pm on the following day, but very little damage was done to the properties on this island. About 10 bushels of salt that were not beached were lost. This was mainly due to the sea breaking in over the Eastern Canal and washing away the salt out of the salt pans. The schooners *Signal* and *Professor* which were in the harbour were beached. The sloop *Annie D* which runs the mail service between Rum Cay and Watling's Island was blown ashore and considerably damaged. The *Signal* was not damaged, so it was re-launched on September 17. The keel of the *Professor* was broken, but it was quickly repaired.

Exuma

This island suffered tremendously, as all the boats and means of transportation were destroyed in this hurricane. Many of the plantations on this island were destroyed by salt and rainwater, the storm surge at some settlements rose several feet above the land. The following boats were reported missing: *Choir, Phoebe, Solent* (with the entire crew onboard perishing), *Savage* (crew reported to be lost), Sloop *Experience* (3 of the crew saved), and the *Terror* was badly damaged. However, the schooner *Phoebe* would later be found out to be sunk between Norman's Cay and Ship Channel Cays. The *Sea Breeze* sunk, and the Schooners *Emma, Charlotte*, and *Minerva* were dismasted. The schooners *Emmeline, Choir,* and *Phoebe* were blown out to sea from Pigeon Cay, Exuma with all persons onboard perishing. The schooner *Lizzie Wall* and sloop *Lillian* were lost at Exuma. The mail schooner *Hattie Darling* was wrecked at Pipe Creek, Exuma. The sloops *Linnet* and *Syren* went out on the Sunday and Monday shortly after the storm and rescued many persons from different Cays. Several dead bodies were discovered on the shore and were immediately buried. It was reported that 46 lives were lost from the vessels near Exuma and many native Exuma women were left widows with no means of support. Of the many lives lost, many children were among the dead, including a few children as young as eight years of age.

Mr. E.H. McKinney went to Exuma, mainly to Highbourne Cay, Gray's, Black Point and along the shore as far as George Town, shortly after the hurricane to take relief supplies, and to determine the needs of the people of Exuma. He then reported this information to the Central Government in Nassau. False keels of three vessels and other small pieces of wrecks were found destroyed on the rocks located at Highbourne Cay. At Shroud's Cay, two houses were blown down, and one small kitchen was destroyed. The schooner *Savage* was destroyed at Hall's Pond with Captain Ernest Rolle being the sole survivor, as he was forced to swim on a spar from Compass Cay to Belle Island, which is about 4 miles in distance. The sloop *Linnet* rescued him and took him to Black Point. Captain Rolle received several cuts which were in the process of healing at the time of the rescue. The schooner *Annie* was also lost at this cay.

At Compass Cay, which was not inhabited at the time, the sloop *Terror* was blown up on the rocks and was destroyed, while the sailboat and a schooner went ashore. At Staniel Cay, Gray's Settlement-forty-five people lived here, and several of their houses and outbuildings were destroyed, and those that remained received slight to moderate damage. The Baptist Chapel was also destroyed. In many instances, the roofs of buildings located on or near the coast were blown out to sea. At Barraterre, the roof of the Baptist Chapel and a few small buildings were destroyed. At Rolleville, the roof of the Baptist Chapel was destroyed, and several small boats were lost.

Corn seeds were freely distributed to all the needy residents of Exuma after the storm. The number of vessels lost or damaged along the Exuma Range of Cays: Lost-11 and damaged-9. In addition to the above, about 25 small boats were lost or damaged. The number of buildings destroyed in the storm numbered 97 and 131 were damaged, and these do not include 14 kitchens and barns and houses reported to have been destroyed at Stuart's Manor and Alexandria. As far can be ascertained, the number of lives lost from Exuma and its Cays amounted to over 64 persons, and several persons were left widows with no means of support when their husbands died. Of the number of lives lost in Exuma, several were young children from eight years of age.

San Salvador

On this island, two Episcopal Churches and several private dwellings were destroyed. Other than that, very little damage was reported to the homes on this island.

Eleuthera

The sloop *Lilly* was destroyed at the Current Island, but all her crew and cargo were saved. The schooner *Ghost* was lost at East End, and Captain Bethel and one other person were reported missing. During the storm, Mr. Albury lost his smack *Wm. Elder*, which was forced out of the Nassau Harbour and wrecked on North Cay. His smack *Royal* lost a mast in the same port and was otherwise undamaged. The boat *Harrison* of Bluff was reported missing. The *Siren* was wrecked on the east end of Eleuthera.

Abaco

Damages sustained on this island was said to be widespread and quite devastating. At Hole-In-The-Wall, the lowest barometric reading of the barometer during the peak of the storm was 29.21 inches. The smack *Dazzle*, owned by Henry Albury of Cherokee Sound, was lost on the September 12 during the hurricane, while located at Crab Cay in the Berry Islands with three of her crew drowned.

Andros

In the settlement of Red Bays, two churches were destroyed, and most of the homes were washed away by the storm. The center of the hurricane passed over Red Bays as the wind there was reported to have been from the NE with a period of calm and then it blew from the SW. One house was left standing in this settlement after this storm. In Red Bays, many sponging vessels were blown ashore, and the causalities were said to be astronomical. At Nicholl's Town, there were only seven houses left standing in this settlement, and an Episcopal Church at Staniard Creek was blown down. Several houses at Coakley Town were blown down and several vessels sunk and stranded. Several schooners *Forest Belle, Alert, Vigilant, Eager, Lealy Lees* (Thos Evans, master, and Robert Murphy, mate drowned); Sloops *Complete, Snowbird, Nonsuch* (all the crew but one was missing) *Douglass, Stinging Bee, and Challenge* were all lost near Andros. Many schooners were driven ashore and were either severely damaged or destroyed in the storm. Among them were *Traffic* (six men missing), *Admired, Alicia, Victoria, Equal, Naomi, May Queen, Beaureguard, Experience, Eunice, Hattie Don, Seahorse, Rosebud*, and others, about 30 in all. In addition to the many persons who succumbed to the storm at sea, the following persons were drowned at Lowe Sound and Red Bays-Simon Demerritt, Mary Brown, Christopher Miller, Gladys McQueen, George Miller, and David Miller.

In the northern part of Andros, many of the settlements were devastated, and many losses of lives occurred, and the agricultural products were wiped out. About 114 persons lost their lives in this location on land, and many houses were blown down, and it mostly occurred to that part of Andros lying north of the Northern Bight. The Resident Justice went to Nicholl's Town and surrounding settlements and provided hurricane aid to all persons in need, particularly the widows and those who lost their main support. All the crops including, oranges, grapefruit and coconuts were destroyed, and the fields of corn, peas and potatoes, and other plants were also destroyed, and it was speculated that it would take many months for them to recover. Mr. E.H. McKinney was dispatched to Andros by the Government at the request of the Hurricane Relief Committee for assisting the Resident Justice, also to help people in starting to repair the damage done to their houses. Also, to direct and supervise the Government's rebuilding efforts with regards to all public works.

The Central Relief Committee dispatched two expeditions to Andros with 50 barrels of relief aid under the care of Mr. K. G. Malcolm. His instructions were to proceed as rapidly as possible to Staniard Creek and to make a connection with Mr. Forsyth, the Resident Justice at that place. Failing to find Mr. Forsyth there he was told to find out his whereabouts and join him and place himself under the jurisdiction of the acting Resident Justice. At Mangrove Cay, the roof of the resident Justice's Office was very much damaged. The Government flagstaff was blown down and smashed, and the jail yard wall was broken in several places. All the settlements between Nicholl's Town and Fresh Creek suffered significant damage both on land and at sea. But the most significant damages sustained were at Nicholl's Town and Mastic Point. Three Government buildings were severely damaged, the jail roof was blown down, part of the schoolhouse was lifted, and the teacher's residence was destroyed. The number of houses blown down at Nicholl's Town was 58. There were about 23 schooners which were lost in the Pine Barrens at Red Bays. Of the 104 homes in Staniard Creek, 48 were damaged, and 42 were destroyed. The Rev. F.W. Gostick, Superintendent of the Wesley Missions, Mr. K.G. Malone, Mr. E.Y. V Sutton went to North Andros shortly after the hurricane to take relief supplies, determine the needs of the people of North Andros and then report back this information to the Central Government in Nassau.

The Berry Islands

The Episcopal Church at Bullock's Harbour was blown down. The schooner *Lena Gray* belonging to Mr. Thomas Sweeting was lost. The Ven. Archdeacon Churton, who in company with the Rev. S. Floyd was on a visit to the Berry Islands and Bimini in the schooner *Leander*. Not having returned before the hurricane, the Rev. Audley J. Browne left in search of them in the schooner *Ready*. Fortunately, they were found safe on the Berry Islands and were towed back to Nassau. Another boat captain Robert Ranger was lost in the Berry Islands. There were at least twelve boats driven ashore and wrecked on the coast of the Berry Islands in this storm.

Bimini

Damage to the island was widespread and quite devastating. In one settlement, two houses were destroyed, five homes were blown off their pins and carried some distance away. Twelve houses were severely damaged or destroyed. Clement Pinder's house had his gable ends blown down and the kitchen destroyed. Thomas Kemp's new home was blown off its pins. Adriana Saunders house was blown down and severely damaged and his tenant Joseph W. Saunders furniture and clothing were severely damaged by the sea water. Mrs. Jesse Roberts's kitchen was destroyed. The government office north gable end was blown in, and many of the books, forms, papers were destroyed or damaged. Joseph H. Kelly's kitchen was severely damaged. All of Edward Wilkinson outbuildings were destroyed, and his residence and kitchen were badly damaged. John Charles Kelly's house was blown away and the roof badly damaged. George Bethel's house was blown down, and his kitchen was destroyed. St. Mary's Methodist Church belfry was blown away and the church severely damaged. The Mission House was severely damaged, and the kitchen destroyed. The steeple of the Wesleyan Church was blown away, and the building sustained significant damage. Sarah Cash house was blown off its pins.

Mr. James Symonette's kitchen was destroyed and the house badly damaged. Mr. W.J. Saunders, furniture and clothing were damaged, and John Wright's house sustained some damage. Mr. George S. Sherry's kitchen and other outbuildings were damaged, Mr. W.A. Butler's house was destroyed, and Mr. Prince Alfred Rolle's house was blown down. Mr. Henry Rolle Jr.'s new house was blown 10 feet from its pins. Mr. James Pinder's roof was severely damaged, and Mr. Daniel Smith's home was severely damaged, and the kitchen destroyed. Rev. James A. Hanna, who was a Baptist minister, had his house severely damaged and his outbuildings destroyed. Mr. Alex Pinder's house was destroyed and his roof partially damaged, and Mr. Alex Deveaux's home was damaged and the outbuildings destroyed. Mrs. Elinor Forbe's kitchen was blown away, and the house was blown off its pins. One vessel, The Glide was washed ashore but not severely damaged. The soil was unusable because it was contaminated with saltwater.

This hurricane commenced on Friday morning, and the barometer fell from 30.20 inches at 8:06 am on August 13 and continued to fall. Every family on Bimini received significant losses especially those on the high ridge. Many of those residents lost everything including their furniture, bedding, and clothing. All the crops were also lost, so many residents starved for many days until outside help arrived to bring much-needed hurricane relief aid. The lowest barometer reading at the peak of the storm was 28.00 inches at which time the winds were blowing from the SW to W.

Grand Bahama

There was considerable damage reported on this island, as most of the homes and all the crops were lost. At Eight Mile Rock, there were 22 houses blown down along with a church and a chapel. At West End, there were six houses which were blown down. At Rhode Rock, one schooner was lost. At Holmes Rock, one house was blown down. At Brandy Point, 11 homes were blown down. At Barnett's Point, 17 houses were blown down and others damaged. At Free Town, four houses were blown down and many others severely damaged, and at Water Key, four homes were blown down. Not only the crops of peas, sugarcane and a variety of fruits were lost, but many of the farmers were rendered homeless. No less than sixty-two houses from Smith Point East, to Settlement Point West, were destroyed and among them were St. Stephen's Church and its Mission House. St. John's Baptist Chapel was severely damaged, and the roof blew off. All the streets and bridges were wiped away. Eight Mile Rock school room and West End Church were only slightly damaged. Smith's Point, Russell Town, and Grant's Town residents suffered greatly when an ESE wind destroyed their homes. At Smith's Point, six homes were destroyed, four houses at Russell's Town were destroyed, and five at Grant's Town were destroyed. Mr. Joseph E. Adderley, the Resident Justice reported that the entire island looked as if it had been ravaged by fire.

CHAPTER NINE

Damages Sustained to Shipping after the Great Bahamas Hurricane of 1899

I n 1899, most Bahamian men were engaged or gainfully employed in the sea sponging industry in The Bahamas. To collect the sponges, these men would go out at sea to selected areas of The Bahamas by boat, where the water was clear and sponges were widespread and easy to harvest from the sea floor. One of the more popular areas was 'the Mud' on the western coast of Andros. Because of this, many of the boats that were lost occurred in this general area of the Mud. The Great Bahamas Hurricane of 1899 was such a deadly hurricane that hundreds of homes were left without fathers and many Bahamian women throughout the country became instant widows.

This storm impacted the sponge industry for many years because of the significant number of ships lost during the storm. The ships were very costly, and it took quite a while and a tremendous amount of money to replace them. Most of the information obtained in this chapter came from the Nassau Guardian, The Tribune, Family Island Commissioner's Reports, House of Assembly Reports, the Governor's Dispatches (CO-23), Shipping Reports to the Governor of The Bahamas by Mr. Nigel B. Burnside who at the time was the Acting Registrar of Shipping and other sources. In total, the loss to ship owners amounted to well over £15707 (1899 UKP). The different lists below are by no means complete because of the significant number of ships lost, and persons who drowned in this storm are too numerous to mention. Therefore, I am including excerpts from the various reports.

Lost to Shipping

Ship's Name:	Type of Vessel:	Owner:	Type of Damage/Comments:
Mary	Schooner	J.S. Johnson	Destroyed Boat Captain Mr. Forbes drowned.
Neptune	Schooner	Unknown	Blown over the Bar.
Post Boy	Smack	Unknown	Destroyed.
Minnie	Yacht	Mr. Ernest Bethel from Saratoga, Florida	Destroyed.
Non Pareil	Yacht	Mr. Ernest Bethel from Saratoga, Florida	Destroyed.
R.J.C.	Schooner	Unknown	Slightly Damaged and lost rudder.
Clarita	Sloop	Owner from Exuma	Destroyed when it sunk between Silver Cay and North Cay and captain and crew missing and presumed dead.
Wonderful	Sloop	Unknown	Slightly Damaged.
Sprite	Sloop	Unknown	Lost spar and badly damaged.
Glide	Schooner	Unknown	Damaged at Sliver Cay.
Trent	Schooner	Unknown	Capsized east of Nassau.
Sparkle	Schooner	Unknown	Badly Damaged.
Challenge	Schooner	Unknown	Damaged.
Ralph	Schooner	Unknown	Dismasted.
Frolic	Schooner	Unknown	Dismasted.
Priscilla Maud	Schooner	Unknown	Sunk.
Royal	Smack	Unknown	Sunk.
Sun	Schooner	Unknown	Damaged.
Thrasher	Schooner	Unknown	Dismasted.
Invincible	Schooner	Unknown	Came ashore on Hog Island but sustained only slight damage and was refloated.
Julia Howard	Schooner	Unknown	Slightly Damaged.
Greyhound	Schooner	Unknown	Slightly Damaged.
Gem	Schooner	Unknown	Mainmast blown away.
Old Sal	Smack	Unknown	Very badly damaged.
Daisy	Schooner	Unknown	Damaged.
WM Elder	Smack	Unknown	Washed up on North Cay and was destroyed and

			one crew member lost.
Income	Sloop	Unknown	Sunk and damaged.
Muriel	Pilot Boat	Unknown	Sunk.
Monstrat Viam	Pilot Boat	Unknown	Sunk at Bar.
Ghost	Yacht	Unknown	Sunk but was refloated.
Idler	Yacht	Unknown	Sunk.
Southern Queen	Schooner	Unknown	Sunk on Southern Side of New Providence.
Guide	Sloop	Unknown	Sunk on Southern Side of New Providence.
Elder	Smack	Unknown	Drifted out to sea but the crew saved.
Lena Gray	Schooner	Unknown	Lost at Berry Islands.
Lizzie Wall	Schooner	Unknown	Lost at Exuma.
Lillian	Sloop	Unknown	Lost at Exuma.
Hattie Darling	Schooner	Government Mailboat	Lost at Pipe Creek, Exuma.
Experience	Schooner	Thomas Russell	Lost at Andros.
Hero	Schooner	Rev. D. Wilshere	Lost in the creek at the East end of Nassau.
Gold River	Schooner	James Wemyss	Badly Damaged and lost at Staniard Creek, Andros.
Gypsy Queen	Schooner	John Brown	Badly damaged and lost at Exuma.
Hattie Don	Schooner	G.B. Adderley	Badly damaged and lost at Red Bays.
Handsome	Sloop	H.C. Albury	Badly Damaged.
Handsome	Sloop	J.P. Nixon	Badly damaged at Farmers Cay, Exuma.
I-See All	Sloop	Manuel La Fleur	Lost at Conch Sound.
Lady Lees	Schooner	G.B. Adderley	Came ashore and badly damaged and 5 persons died.
Prudence	Schooner	W.P. Sands	Badly damaged.
Phoebe	Schooner	G.B. Adderley	15 persons died in Pigeon Cay, Exuma.
Queen of Clippers	Schooner	W.H. Deveaux	Lost at Port Howe, San Salvador.
Remembrance	Sloop	Estate, W.R. Pyfrom	Damaged at Red Bays.
Sea Horse	Schooner	O.F. Pritchad	Came ashore and 8 persons died on this boat.
Soud	Sloop	R.N. Musgrove	Lost at Staniard Creek and 2 persons died on this

			boat.
Southern Queen	Schooner	P. Bullard	Lost at Nassau and 11 persons died on this boat.
Savage	Schooner	G.B. Adderley	Came ashore and 12 persons died on this boat.
Try Me	Sloop	L.E. Forsyth	Slightly damaged.
Waterloo	Schooner	Estate, W.R. Pyfrom	Totally lost with 4 persons on this boat.
Dolphin	Schooner	Estate, W.R. Pyfrom	Lost at Conch Sound when it sunk.
Height	Schooner	John Edgecombe	Slightly damaged.
Income	Schooner	Edward Wilchombe	Dismasted at Grand Bahama.
Linnet	Sloop	W.H. Curry & Sons	Lost at Exuma.
Let Her Be	Sloop	Cupid Brown	Badly damaged at Moore's Island, Abaco.
Magic Light	Schooner	J. Pinder	Lost at Red Bays with 3 persons on board.

Lost to Shipping.

The list below shows the names of the persons, who perished in the Great Bahamas Hurricane of 1899 on the 11th and 12th August 1899.

Deaths occurring on the sponging vessels and the names of the persons and vessels lost during the Great Bahamas Hurricane of 1899

Ship's Name:	Type of Vessel:	Number of Persons who Perished:	Names of the persons who Perished:
Solent	Schooner	9	Wm Nixon Fred K Smith Thos Sands T. Dawkin Jos Miller Samuel Miller Robert Wilson Hezekiah Tynes Daniel Miller
Catherine Ella	Sloop	1	Fred McKenzie
Ghost	Schooner	4	Daniel Bethel Luke Humes Two other names not known
Traffic	Schooner	6	Albert Kemp Esau Miller James Miller W. Black Horatio Summons Israel Aunett
Annie	Schooner	6	Hamilton Forbes George Mackey Thomas Sweeting Alexander Franks Samuel Adderley Simeon Thurston
Lilla	Sloop	2	T. Roach James Burke Roach
Sea Horse	Schooner	8	Captain Glinton, his son and six others drowned.
Claretta	Sloop	Unknown	Names unknown.
Terror	Sloop	8	Granville Wilson Nathaniel Humes Percival Wilson Naaman Sumner Daniel Knowles Thos Adderley Joshua Rolle Michael Knowles
Empress	Schooner	3	Robert Russell Nathaniel Bode

			Michael Rolle
Remembrance	Sloop	8	Matthias Woodside Solomon Woodside Cubit Woodside Jack Colebrook John White James Nottage Wm Flower Joe Ormond Woodside
Savage	Schooner	12	James Clarke Alfred Edin Jeremiah Pattern James Rolle Tobias Rolle Theophilus Rolle Gabriel McPhee Buddie McPhee Mitchell Rolle 3 others unnamed
Magic Light	Schooner	3	James Moxey Daniel Kemp Newton Jones
Eager	Schooner	1	Charles Martin
Snow Bird	Sloop	4	Charles Saunders John Bennett Robert George Miller Joseph Johnson
Magnolia	Sloop	1	Unknown
Complete	Sloop	11	Edward Johnson Sylvester Mackey Ramon Dorsett Uriah Bain Alfred Davis James Davis Wm. Johnson W. Pratt Benjamin Johnson Henry Evans
Soud	Sloop	2	Jeremiah Storr W. Rogers
Waterloo	Schooner	4	Alfred Evans Alexander Smith James Rahming

				Herbert Gibson
Uno	Schooner	3		James Ball
				Virginius Gordon
				Horatio Rolle
Sea Horse	Schooner	8		W. Glinton
				Horatio Lightbourn
				George Thompson
				Joshua Thompson
				Henry Edgecombe
				Samuel Glinton
				W. McBride
				Hezekiah Pinder
Julia	Schooner	8		Jeremiah Ferguson
				W. Adderley
				Wilfred Sands
				Melville Moxey
				Theodore Bain
				Alex Williams
				Thos Johnson
				Henry Douglas
Unknown	Schooner	6		Joseph Rolle
				Castilio Butler
				John Fox
				James Coakley
				Smith
				Coakley Johnson
Challenge	Sloop	9		Joseph Hamilton
				Jas Taylor
				Joseph Williams
				Frederick Deveaux
				Herbert Edgecombe
				Achilles Rolle
				Joseph Johnson
				Robert Bennett
				1 Unknown
Western Queen	Sloop	10		Joseph Eulin
				Jacob McKey
				Joseph Bootle
				Joseph Western
				George Eulin,
				Daniel Taylor
				Thos Minnis
				Zodoc Armbrister

			George Weech Andrew Francis
Southern Queen	Schooner	11	Jas Adderley Norman Adderley Alex Bain Joseph Finn Arthur Pratt Felix Gibson J.F. Miller Sylvanus Hepburn Jas Rolle Jonathan Reckley Simeon Rolle
Guide	Sloop	7	Nathl. Wright H. Wallace Alphia Wallace Richard Thompson Simon Simons Adolphus Adderley Anthony McKinney
Dazzle	Schooner	3	Menin Albury Harthy Pinder Daniel Pinder
Mary	Schooner	4	Robert Forbes Tim Higgs Hezekiah Stubbs Joseph Rolle
Douglass	Sloop	7	Prince Woodside Tim Marshall W.H. Mackey Nathaniel Marshal Arthur Oliver Smith Sirus Butler W. Marshall
Will O' The Wisp	Schooner	6	Caiaphas McKenzie Wilson Rolle Leslie Rolle Henry Humes Isaac Curtis Nathl. Taylor
Equal	Schooner	1	W. Bain
Bowkin	Schooner	6	George Bain Ezekiel Nesbit

			Richard Farrington
			Three names unknown
Stinging Bee	Sloop	12	Benjamin Oliver
			11 names unknown
Alert	Schooner	10	Sidney Delancy
			Alix Lightbourn
			Hezekiah Reckley
			John Moxey
			Alex Miller
			Sam Bowe
			Alfred Ferguson
			Jonathan Williams
			Thos Gould
			Neptune Storr
Proceed	Schooner	8	Wm Rolle
			Stephen Romer
			Daniel Forbes
			Nathan Forbes
			Samuel Rolle
			John Rolle
			Andrew Forbes
			P. Rolle
Choir	Schooner	6	Chas Russell
			Absalom Dorsett
			W. Haley
			Elijah Humes
			Jos Miller
			Alfred Frances
Jane	Schooner	1	J.T. Mckey Jr.
Experience	Sloop	6	Hezekiah Farrington
			Alfred Brown
			Theo Munroe
			Jos Sims
			Jos Allen Winder
			Herman Boyd
Nonsuch	Sloop	12	Jas Rattray
			Ruben Sweeting
			Jas Mackey
			Jeremiah Strachan
			W. Rodgers
			Bruce Boyd
			Jas Bowleg
			Isaac Evans

203

			Wilfred McKenzie
			Three names unknown
Phoebe	Schooner	15	Isaac Bethel
			Liberty Sturrup
			Thaddeus Bethel
			Isaac (Sardens) Hart
			William Sturrup Jr.
			Enoch Bethel
			Chas Clark
			Mark Marshall
			Jas Wallace
			Michael Bethel Jr.
			Five names unknown
Lady Shea	Schooner	5	Robert (John) Murphy
			Daniel (Pompey) Whyley
			Abraham Rolle
			Edward Dean
			Thos Evans
Florence	Schooner	1	Israel McQueen
Alpine	Schooner	2	Samuel Demerritt
			Christopher Brown

Deaths occurring on the sponging vessels and the names of the persons and vessels lost during the Great Bahamas Hurricane of 1899 (Courtesy of The Nassau Guardian).

The Colonial Secretary Mr. J.S. Churchill on the November 15 published the list of names of the persons who died in this storm from the island of Andros. This list was provided to him by Mr. Lennox Elgin Forsyth, the Resident Justice for the entire island of Andros but was stationed at Mangrove Cay, Andros.

Below are some of the names of the men and boys who drowned at Red Bays:

Dan Russell	Wm Glinton & Son	John Bunch	Robert Murphy
Charles Saunders	Sydney Delancy	Charles Martin	Thomas Evans
Abraham Rolle	James Ball	Thaddeus Johnson	William Dorsett
Uriah Bain	Henry Evans	Solomon Woodside	William Fowler
Bartheus Woodside	James Nottage	John Colebrooke	Jonathan White
Cubit Woodside	Levi Marshal	Cyrus Butler	Charles O' Brien
James Anderson	James Moxie	Darrell Kemp	

Names of men and boys who drowned at Red Bays during the Great Bahamas Hurricane of 1899. (Courtesy of The Nassau Guardian).

Below are the names of the persons who drowned at Andros during the Great Bahamas Hurricane of 1899:

Name:	Where They Drowned:	Name:	Where They Drowned:
Ambrister, Zadoc	Joulter Cays	Bain, Bartholomew	Joulter Cays
Bain, Joseph	Red Bays	Bain, Daniel	Joulter Cays
Bain, Uriah	Red Bays	Bennett, John	Red Bays
Bennett, Robert	Joulter Cays	Bode, Nathaniel	Red Bays
Bootle, Joseph	Joulter Cays	Boyd, Bruce	Joulter Cays
Bowleg, Jos-Alex	Joulter Cays	Bunch, John	Unknown
Bain, George	Joulter Cays	Colebrooke, John	William Cays
Davis, James	Red Bays	Davis, Alfred	Red Bays
Duncombe	Unknown	Deveaux, Fred	Joulter Cays
Dorset, Ramon	Red Bays	Duncombe, Claudius	Joulter Cays
Evans, Henry	Red Bays	Evans, Thomas	Red Bays
Edgecombe, Henry	Red Bays	Edgecombe, Sylvanus	Joulter Cays
Edgecombe, Herbert	Joulter Cays	Forbes, Hamilton	Fresh Creek
Franks, Alexander	Fresh Creek	Fowler, William	Williams Cay
Ferguson, Esau	Unknown	Francis, Andrew	Joulter Cays
Farrington, Richard	Joulter Cays	Glinton, Samuel	Red Bays
Glinton, William	Red Bays	Gordon, Virginia	Red Bays
Hepburn, George	Joulter Cays	Hanna, Theophilus	Joulter Cays
Hamilton, Joseph	Joulter Cays	Johnson, James	Red Bays
Johnson, Joseph	Red Bays	Johnson, Joseph	Joulter Cays
Johnson, Edward	Red Bays	Johnson	Unknown
Lightbourn, Horatio	Red Bays	Mockey, G	Fresh Creek
Miller, Robert Geo	Red Bays	Mackey, Henry	Red Bays
Mickey, James	Joulter Cays	McKenzie, Wilfred	Joulter Cays
McQueen, Israel	Unknown	McKay, Jacob	Joulter Cays
McBride, William	Red Bays	Moxey, James	Unknown
Martin, Charles	Joulter Cays	Thomas, Minuis	Joulter Cays
Miller, Solomon	William Cays	Murphy Robi	Red Bays
Nottage, James	William Cays	Nesbitt, Nicholas	Joulter Cays
Oliver, Samuel	Fresh Creek	Oliver, Samuel	Joulter Cays
Oliver, Benjamin	Joulter Cays	Oliver, Cornelius	Joulter Cays
Pinder, Hezekiah	Red Bays	Rolle, Horatio	Red Bays
Rolle, Michael	Red Bays	Russell, Robert	Red Bays
Rattray, Joseph	Joulter Cays	Rolle, Archillus	Joulter Cays
Rolle, Graham	Red Bays	Rogers, William	Joulter Cays
Simmons, Edgar	Unknown	Saunders Charles	Unknown

Simmons, Horatio	Unknown	Simms, Theophilus	Joulter Cays
Sweeting, Reuben	Joulter Cays	Sweeting, Thomas	Fresh Creek
Saunders, Charles	Red Bays	Strachan, Jeremiah	Joulter Cayss
Thurston, Simeon	Fresh Creek	James, Taylor	Joulter Cays
Thompson, George	Red Bays	Thompson, Joshua	Red Bays
Ulin, Joseph	Joulter Cays	Ulin, George	Joulter Cays
Wemyss, Henry	Red Bays	Williams	Joulter Cays
Woodside, Mathis	Williams Cay	Woodside, Jno. Sol	Williams Cay
Williams, Joseph	Joulter Cays	Woodside, Cubit	Williams Cay
White, John	Williams Cay	Wylly, John	Williams Cay
Daniel, Wylly	Red Bays	Wylly, John	Joulter Cays

The names of the persons who drowned at Andros during the Great Bahamas Hurricane of 1899. (Courtesy of The Nassau Guardian).

In addition to the above names, there were 4 persons who drowned whose names are unknown. The list of persons who drowned by the storm surge overflowing the land in the hurricane were, Mary Brown, Simon Demeritt, Samuel Demeritt, Gladis McQueen, David Miller, George Miller, and Christopher Miller.

CHAPTER TEN

The Major Bahamian Hurricanes from 1900-1919

The Four Hurricanes of 1908: –The 1908 North Atlantic hurricane season ran from June 1 to November 30 in 1908. These dates conventionally demarcate the year in which most tropical cyclones form in the North Atlantic basin. However, this season got off to a very early start, with a Category 2 hurricane forming on March 6, making it the third earliest hurricane on record to form in the North Atlantic basin after Hurricane #1 in 1938 and Hurricane Alex in 2016, and the only known North Atlantic tropical cyclone on record to exist in March. Another hurricane formed and survived during the last week of May and became the earliest hurricane to hit the U.S. in recorded history. Cape Hatteras was affected by two hurricanes and one tropical storm this year. Overall, this season was near average with ten tropical storms forming.

Hurricane #2 of 1908: –This hurricane lasted from May 24 to May 31 and had a peak wind intensity of 75 mph (Category 2 hurricane on the Saffir-Simpson Hurricane Wind Scale) and the lowest recorded barometric pressure of 989 millibars (hPa). This hurricane destroyed or significantly damaged the churches of the ten Anglican parishes of Long Island and brought priest architect John C. Hawes to The Bahamas to assist with the rebuilding efforts.

A tropical depression developed on May 24 at 8 am EDT about 50 miles southwest of Cockburn Town, Crooked Island and Turks, and Caicos Islands. Moving northwestward, the depression struck and devastated the Turks and Caicos Islands. Around 2 am EDT on May 26, the depression intensified into a tropical storm. By late on May 27, the storm curved northeastward. The cyclone strengthened into a hurricane by 2 am EDT the following day. It made landfall west of Cape Hatteras, North Carolina, with winds of 75 mph around 5 pm EDT on May 29. A barometric pressure reading of 989 millibars (29.20 inches) was observed at Cape Hatteras, the lowest in relation to the storm. A few hours later, the storm re-emerged into the Atlantic Ocean. Early on May 30, the hurricane weakened to a tropical storm. Accelerating northeastward, the storm struck eastern Long Island, New York, with winds of 40 mph late on May 30, just before making landfall near Noank, Connecticut, at the same intensity around 7 pm EDT. The storm became extratropical over southern Maine early on May 31. The remnants continued northeastward until dissipating over the northern portion of the state several hours later.

This hurricane hit the US in May, causing minor effects. It was one of only three May hurricanes during the 20th century in the North Atlantic basin; the others were Able in 1951 and Alma in 1970. It marked the earliest date for the season's second hurricane to form in any North Atlantic season on record, and it was the earliest hurricane to hit the U.S. in recorded history.

Hurricane #3 of 1908: –This hurricane lasted from July 24 to August 2 and had a peak wind intensity of 80 mph (Category 1 hurricane on the Saffir-Simpson Hurricane Wind Scale) and the lowest recorded barometric pressure of 985 millibars (hPa). This storm formed north of The Bahamas on July 24. The storm then made a loop north of The Bahamas and became a hurricane shortly after that. The storm grazed North Carolina and moved into the Atlantic. The storm dissipated on August 3.

Hurricane #6 of 1908: –This hurricane lasted from September 7 to September 18 and had a peak wind intensity of 120 mph (Category 3 hurricane on the Saffir-Simpson Hurricane Wind Scale) and the lowest recorded barometric pressure reading of 985 millibars (hPa). The sixth and strongest storm of the season was a Category 3 in mid-September that moved across the Central Bahamas and turned out to sea. On the islands of Turks and Caicos, they experienced sustained winds of over 100 mph and several deaths reported. The vessel *Sarrimner* ran ashore on Nassau and was destroyed near the Government Wharf. Long Island particularly, Clarence Town and at Deadman's Cay were the two settlements of the greatest devastation. The 4,000 residents were left in a dangerous state and near starvation because all the houses and crops were destroyed in this hurricane. Some residents had to live in caves for a while after the passage of the storm.

Large almond trees were uprooted and blown down on the Eastern Parade after the Hurricane #6 of 1908 (Courtesy of Bob Davies/Old Bahamas).

The land was saturated from saltwater intrusion so nothing new could be planted in the soil until the salt was removed from the soil. Furthermore, all the freshwater wells were contaminated with saltwater making them undrinkable. In Long Island, approximately 20 persons died in this hurricane from drowning and fallen houses crushing the occupants of the homes. At Clarence Town, only six houses were left standing and a man Mr. John Turnquest died and ten persons died at Deadman's Cay and one of them was Mr. Solomon Knowles who died from drowning. Two persons were killed at South End. The body of the wife of David Mane was discovered under the wreckage of their house with her neck, back and legs broken. She was later found, still holding her four months old baby's hand and thankfully the baby was still alive, unhurt but crying loudly when they rescued her. After the hurricane, the government dispatched some seedlings of corn, tomatoes, onions, pigeon peas, cassava and potato cuttings to the islands most devastated by the hurricane in the Central and SE Bahamas to replace the ones lost in the storm. The schooner *Hattie H. Roberts* was hired by the government to take relief supplies to the residents of Rum Cay, Conception Island and Clarence Town, Long Island. The schooner *Emma* was also hired to take relief supplies to Watlings Island and the schooners *Invincible* and *Signal* went to Deadman's Cay and Simms's, Long Island, and The Bight, Cat Island.

All the homes on Long Island except for five houses at Clarence Town were destroyed. The Commissioner's residence and office, the jail and schoolhouse were all destroyed. This island reported sustained winds of over 100 mph. The main thoroughfare was blocked up with fallen trees and buildings, and the streets were all severely flooded. There were 57 houses destroyed at Burnt Ground. A portion of the roof of Virginius Ritchie was blown 300 yards away from her home. At the settlement of The Bight 27 houses were destroyed, and at North End, 100 houses were destroyed, and two persons killed. At Miller's settlement, two persons were killed, and ten reported missing. All the schooners on this island were destroyed and the schooner *Sarah Douglass* while en-route from Rum Cay to Long Island encountered the hurricane at sea and Captain William Armbrister was washed overboard and drowned. At Ragged Island 9 houses were destroyed, two boats damaged, and the sisal fields and several thousand bushels of salt were destroyed.[76]

Large storm surges batter the Western Esplanade with the Nassau Harbour Lighthouse (This is billed as the oldest and best-known lighthouse in The Bahamas

[76] The Nassau Guardian, *Colonial Summary & The Hurricane*. September 23, 1908, pg. 1. Retrieved: 12-12-2011.

and the oldest surviving lighthouse in the West Indies. It is located at the western tip of Paradise Island, marking the northwest entrance to New Providence and the Port of Nassau. It was built in 1817, when the island was known by its previous name, Hog Island) and a ship is seen in the background during the Hurricane of 1908 (Courtesy of Bob Davies/Old Bahamas).

At Williamstown, Exuma 18 houses were destroyed. At Inagua, Long Cay and Rum Cay only 20 and 30 homes were destroyed respectively. At Rum Cay, just nine houses were left standing, and most of the coffins were washed out of the cemetery onto the main road during the hurricane. At Watlings Island, the lowest pressure reading was 28.30 inches at 4 pm on Sunday and the sustained winds of approximately 100 mph. On this island, about 90% of the houses were destroyed. In the settlements of United Estates and Reckley Hill, 2 out of a total of 38 homes were left standing, and two Baptist churches were also destroyed. In the settlement of Cockburn Town, only nine houses were left standing out of a total of 40 homes and a church was also destroyed. In the settlement of Fortune Hill, no houses were left standing out of a total of 18 houses and a Baptist church was also destroyed. In the settlement of Victoria Hill, all ten houses were blown down and destroyed. At Inagua, the lowest reported pressure reading during the storm was 28.90 inches, and in the settlement of Matthew Town, 19 buildings were either damaged or destroyed.[77]

Hurricane #8 of 1908: –This hurricane lasted from September 21 to October 7 and had a peak wind intensity of 110 mph (Category 2 hurricane on the Saffir-Simpson Hurricane Wind Scale) and the lowest recorded barometric pressure of 971 millibars (hPa). The eighth storm was a Category 2 hurricane in late September, and early October that crossed the Lesser Antilles moved over Hispaniola and eastern Cuba and passed over The Bahamas before turning northeast. It then made a loop and became extratropical on October 7. It caused extensive damage to the Greater Antilles.

Most of the fruit-bearing trees (approximately 75%) in Nassau were destroyed during the hurricane. Most of the Spanish Wells (Eleuthera) homes and fishing vessels were destroyed during this hurricane. During the passage of this storm, 17.64 inches of rainfall fell in New Providence. In the eastern section of New Providence and Grants Town, these settlements

---

[77] The Nassau Guardian, *Colonial Summary & The Hurricane*. September 26, 1908, pg. 1. Retrieved: 12-12-2011.

reported severe flooding in low-lying areas. All the fruit-bearing trees on Eleuthera were destroyed, and most of the homes on Spanish Wells were also destroyed and the ship *Hattie Darling* was blown ashore and severely damaged. At Gregory Town, a boat with an unknown name sunk and three of the crew members drowned. The ship *Hesleyside* was wrecked near Cherokee Sound, Abaco. Most of the oranges and grapefruits were destroyed in Abaco. The schooner *Sirocco* sunk near Abaco and 6 of the crew drowned. In Bimini, the storm didn't claim any lives, but extensive damage was done to the sisal plants and farm crops on South Bimini.

Ninety persons drowned on the steamship *The San Juan* when it sunk near Matthew Town, Inagua in the hurricane. Several sponging schooners were destroyed in this storm, including, the sloops, *Fury, Maude, Sea Bird* (lost its mast) and *Cora Lie*. Several schooners were also destroyed. The 22-ton schooner *Mary Bell* came ashore on the rocks near Fort Charlotte and was destroyed. The schooner *Increase* lost its mast during the hurricane, and the schooner *Sway* and *Pride* were lost at sea during the storm. Several schooners also reported being severely damaged during the hurricane, including, *Mary-Jane*, and *Drifter*. In Grant's Town several houses were blown down and destroyed, and the water was reported to be knee-deep in some places. The telephone and electrical lines in New Providence were destroyed in this storm. Between 2 am to 10 am on Thursday, the lowest atmospheric pressure reading was 28.68 inches and the sustained winds recorded were between 60 to 80 mph.[78]

The Great Florida Keys Hurricane of 1919: –The 1919 North Atlantic hurricane season was among the least most active hurricane seasons in the North Atlantic on record, featuring only five tropical cyclones. Of those five tropical cyclones, two of them intensified into hurricanes, with one strengthening into a major hurricane (Category 3 or higher on the Saffir–Simpson Hurricane Wind Scale). Two tropical depressions developed in June, both of which caused negligible damage. A tropical storm in July brought minor damage to Pensacola, Florida, but devastated a fleet of ships. Another two tropical depressions formed in August, the first of which brought rainfall to the Lesser Antilles.

The most intense tropical cyclone of the season was the Great Florida Keys Hurricane of 1919. At least, 94 persons from The Bahamas were

---

[78] The Nassau Guardian, *Colonial Summary & The Second Hurricane*. October 3, 1908, pg. 1. Retrieved: 12-12-2011.

killed in the hurricane after their ships sunk or capsized in The Bahamas. Strong winds left about $2 million (USD) in damage in Key West. After crossing the Gulf of Mexico, the severe impact was reported in Texas, especially the Corpus Christi area. Overall, the hurricane caused 828 fatalities and $22 million in damage, $20 million of which was inflicted in Texas alone. Three other tropical cyclones developed in September, including two tropical storms and one tropical depression, all of which left a negligible impact on the land. The final tropical system of the season also did not affect land and became extratropical on November 15.

A tropical wave developed into a tropical depression on September 2, while located near Guadeloupe. Early on September 3, the system became a tropical storm. It oscillated slightly in intensity during the next few days, while brushing Puerto Rico and north coast of Hispaniola. By September 5, the storm headed northward toward the SE Bahamas. The system crossed Mayaguana and began curving northwestward. Early on September 7, the storm strengthened into a Category 1 hurricane on the modern-day Saffir–Simpson Hurricane Wind Scale, while curving just north of due west. After intensifying into a Category 2 hurricane later that day, the hurricane struck Long Island and Exuma. Around 8 am on September 8, the storm strengthened into a Category 3 hurricane, shortly before hitting Andros. Roland Bowleg, a boy, got his leg broken and had to be taken to the hospital for treatment.

After the hurricane, the motorboat *Vim* along with Mr. Kenneth Butler and Constable Frank D. Kelly were dispatched to Andros to determine the extent of the damage on this island and to take hurricane relief supplies to the persons impacted by the hurricane. There were 15 persons confirmed dead, and 40 declared missing. Most of the causalities on this island occurred at sea. At Mangrove Cay, 60 houses were blown down. All the crops on this island were destroyed, including the sisal crop. In the vicinity of the Mud in Andros, several boats were destroyed like the *Surpass*, while others were driven ashore and badly damaged like the sloops *Waverly, Hand of Hope* and *Complete* and some of them even lost their spars. Throughout the island of Andros, the potatoes, peas, corn trees, beans, and cassava crops were all destroyed. In the settlement of Fresh Creek, Andros, the schooner *Band* was blown upside down, and one boy was drowned while he was in the boat. The schooners *AMR* and *Early Bird* were driven ashore and severely damaged.

At Mangrove Cay, 62 houses were blown down. Also, 3 Baptist churches and 1 Church of England were severely damaged. The sloop *Water Pearl* from Mangrove Cay with 11 persons onboard was drowned. The sloop *Andros* from Long Bay Cays was destroyed with eight persons perishing onboard. The bodies of 6 of the persons onboard were later recovered and given proper burials. At South Andros, the schooner *Resource* was wrecked at Long Bay Cays. Several other sloops including, *Sea Horse, Gull, Lona, Morning Cloud,* and *Rose Bell* were all damaged to some degree or the other. The yacht *Emily* was severely damaged. The sloop *Steady* had two of its crew drowned.

Cat Island and Watlings Island were reportedly completely devastated, and in the settlement of Devil's Point, about 30 houses were blown down, and one of the churches had its' roof blown off. The mail boat schooner *Doris* was smashed to pieces on the rocks at Cat Island.[79]

In New Providence, many of the boats were blown out of Nassau Harbour, and most of the fruit-bearing trees throughout the island were destroyed. The telephone and electrical systems were mostly destroyed or severely damaged, especially on Dowdeswell Street and East Shirly Street. Strong winds lashed The Bahamas, destroying buildings on Eleuthera and demolishing houses on San Salvador Island. While passing through The Bahamas on September 8, the Ward Line steamer *Corydon* struck land in the Bahama Channel and later sank during the storm. The ship was not found until September 11, at which time it was discovered that 27 people on board had drowned while nine others managed to survive after swimming to shore. On these islands, strong winds produced by the hurricane destroyed numerous homes and sank several schooners, leaving many homeless.

After leaving The Bahamas, the hurricane strengthened into a Category 4 hurricane early the following day. It intensified further over the Straits of Florida and peaked with maximum sustained winds of 150 mph, and a minimum barometric pressure of 927 millibars (27.4 inHg) at 2 am on September 10. Hours later, the system made landfall in Dry Tortugas, Florida. The storm weakened while crossing the Gulf of Mexico and fell to Category 3 intensity around 8 am on September 12. However, early the following day, it re-strengthened into a Category 4 hurricane. While

---

[79] The Nassau Guardian, *The Hurricane*. September 20, 1919, pg. 1. Retrieved: 17-12-2011.

approaching Texas, the system began to weaken again, deteriorating to a Category 3 hurricane on September 14. Later that day, it made landfall in Kennedy County with winds of 115 mph. The storm weakened while moving inland and dissipated near El Paso on September 16.

CHAPTER ELEVEN

The Great Nassau, Miami and Havana–Bermuda Hurricanes of 1926

The 1926 North Atlantic hurricane season featured the highest number of major hurricanes at the time. At least eleven tropical cyclones developed during the season, all of which intensified into a tropical storm and eight further strengthened into hurricanes. Six hurricanes deepened into a major hurricane, which is Category 3 or higher on the modern-day Saffir–Simpson Hurricane Wind Scale. The first system, the Great Nassau Hurricane, developed near the Lesser Antilles on July 22. Moving west-northwest for much of its duration, the storm struck or brushed several islands of the Lesser and Greater Antilles. However, The Bahamas later received greater impact. At least 573+ deaths and $7.85 million (1926 USD $109 million USD 2018) in damage was attributed to this hurricane. The next cyclone primarily effected mariners in and around the Maritimes of Canada, with boating accidents and drowning's resulting in between 55 and 58 fatalities. In late August, the third hurricane brought widespread impact to the Gulf Coast of the United States, especially Louisiana. Crops and buildings suffered $6 million (1926 USD) in damage and there were 25 people killed. The next three storms left relatively little to no damage on land.[80]

The 1926 North Atlantic hurricane season was an average but very eventful one. The first storm of the season was a Category 2 hurricane that

---

[80] *Atlantic Basin Comparison of Original and Revised HURDAT. Hurricane Research Division; Atlantic Oceanographic and Meteorological Laboratory (Report). Miami, Florida: National Oceanic and Atmospheric Administration. February 2014. Retrieved: 08-05-2016.*

made landfall over The Bahamas and then continued onto make a direct hit near Melbourne, Florida. The next was a Category 3 storm that grazed Bermuda and struck Nova Scotia as an extra tropical cyclone. The third struck Louisiana as a Category 2 storm. Another Category 3 storm made a loop around the Azores. It struck Miami dead on as a Category 4 hurricane. The storm surge tore through the city, wiping away homes and businesses. Over 200 people were killed in Florida alone and several dozen more were killed when the hurricane skimmed the Gulf Coasts of the Florida Panhandle, Alabama, and Mississippi. 'The Great Miami Hurricane' as it was known (also called 'The Big Blow') was one of only three hurricanes to ever come so close to perfect storm status.

It hit Fort Lauderdale, Dania, Hollywood, Hallandale and Miami. The death toll range was estimated to be from 325 to perhaps as many as 800 persons but the official Red Cross total was 373 persons who perished in this storm. No storm in previous history had done as much property damage to the state of Florida. It ranks as one of the costliest and deadliest hurricanes in US history, causing over $100 million in damage in 1926 dollars. If adjusted for 2019 inflation and increased population density, the Great Miami Hurricane would dwarf Hurricane Andrew in cost with a bill of over $140 billion. For all intents and purposes, we will be dealing with both the Great Miami Hurricane which was hurricane #4 of 1926 and Hurricane #1 of 1926 or the Great Nassau Hurricane of 1926. However, the one that inflicted the most damage here was hurricane #1 of 1926 and we will be concentrating on this hurricane, but it is important to add here that both hurricanes did indeed hit The Bahamas but the hurricane that was responsible for most of the damages sustained in The Bahamas was hurricane #1 of 1926.

The Great Nassau Hurricane of 1926

The Great Nassau Hurricane of 1926, known as the San Liborio Hurricane in Puerto Rico, was a destructive Category 4 hurricane that affected The Bahamas at peak intensity. Although it weakened considerably before its Florida landfall, it was one of the most severe storms to affect the Bahamian capital Nassau and the island of New Providence in several years until the Great Okeechobee Hurricane, which occurred just two years later. The storm also delivered flooding rains and loss of crops to the southeastern United States and Florida. On its path, the storm killed more than 287 people in Puerto Rico, the Dominican Republic, The Bahamas, and Florida. In The Bahamas, the storm caused over 258-268 deaths, but the exact total varies from 106 to 400+, however, according to the 1928 House of Assembly Reports, the unofficial total was 258.[81] Combined with two later storms in September and October, it is estimated that the entire hurricane season killed more than 550+ persons in The Bahamas.[82] This was because many persons, mainly boys (from 14 years old-school ended at age 14 in 1926) and men were actively involved in the sea sponging trade. As a result, many sponging boats involved in the trade were lost at sea in the hurricane and were simply counted as 'missing' and therefore the crew were not included in the official hurricane death totals, so the exact official death toll can never be determined due to this and other mitigating factors.

The Pelicaus Sponge Warehouse in the background-destroyed in the Great 1926 Nassau Hurricane and workers in the foreground gathering the natural sea sponges after the hurricane had scattered them throughout the sponge warehouse yard in Nassau, Bahamas (Courtesy of Charles. J.Whelbell Collection-The Department of Archives).

---

[81] *"400 Persons Missing in the Bahama Storm"*. New York Times. August 2, 1926. pg. 3. Retrieved: 12-12-2004.

[82] Family Island Commissioners' Reports for individual Islands, *Votes of The House of Assembly & House ofAssembly Reports*, 04-05-1929 to 10-10-1935. Retrieved:12-12-2004.

Meteorological History of the Great Nassau Hurricane of 1926

The first storm of the season formed early on July 22 about 200 miles east of the island of Barbados and gradually strengthened into a hurricane a day later. At 8pm EDT on July 24, the hurricane made landfall at Cabo Rojo, Puerto Rico, with winds of 105 mph. Weakening as it crossed Puerto Rico, the cyclone quickly regained strength on July 25 as it moved through The Bahamas; rapidly reaching maximum sustained winds of 130 mph, it attained the equivalence of Category 4 intensity—one of only four North Atlantic hurricanes to have done so in or before the month of July. After peaking at 140 mph with an estimated central pressure of 938 millibars (27.70 inches), based on several ships observations, the cyclone struck the island of New Providence, the seat of the Bahamian capital Nassau, on the morning of July 26, with sustained winds of 135 mph. Weakening thereafter, the storm moved northwestward, paralleling the east coast of Florida, but came ashore near New Smyrna Beach early on July 28 with winds of 105 mph. Thereafter, the cyclone quickly diminished in intensity, becoming a tropical depression on July 29, as it curved west-northwestward over Georgia; three days later, it became an extratropical cyclone and dissipated over Ontario, Canada, on August 2.[83]

Prior to the record-breaking 2005 North Atlantic hurricane season, this was the strongest hurricane ever recorded in July until Hurricane Dennis of 2005, a strong Category 4 hurricane with top sustained winds of 150 mph and a minimum central pressure of 930 millibars (27.46 inches), surpassed the intensity of the Great Nassau Hurricane of 1926. It is important to note here that Hurricane Audrey was also more intense and occurred even earlier in the season in June.

---

[83] https://en.wikipedia.org/wiki/1926_Nassau_hurricane. Retrieved: 20-10-2016.

Some of the Wettest Bahamian Hurricanes on Record

Rank	Rainfall in mm	Rainfall in inches	Storm Name	Island/Location	Year
1	747.5	29.43	Noel	Long Island	2007
2	436.6	17.19	Flora	Duncan Town	1963
3	390.1	15.36	Inez	Nassau International Airport	1966
4	337.1	13.27	Fox	Nassau International Airport	1952
5	321.1	12.64	Michelle	Nassau International Airport	2001
6	309.4	12.18	Erin	Church Grove, Crooked Island	1995
7	260.0	9.88	Fay	Freeport	2008
8	236.7	9.32	Floyd	Little Harbour, Abaco	1999
9	216.4	8.52	Cleo	West End, Grand Bahamas	1964

Some of the wettest Bahamian hurricanes on record (Courtesy of Wayne Neely).

Men repairing damaged electrical wires in the foreground and the home of Mr. Uriah Saunders and his wife Rebecca Roberts Saunders on the left and Trinity Methodist Church on the right on Fredrick Street both badly damaged in the background during the Great Nassau Hurricane of 1926 (Courtesy of Charles. J. Whelbell Collection-The Department of Archives).

The Great Miami Hurricane (The Big Blow Hurricane) of 1926

At the time, the 1926 storm was described by the U.S. Weather Bureau in Miami as "probably the most destructive hurricane ever to strike the United States." It hit Fort Lauderdale, Dania, Hollywood, Hallandale and Miami. The death toll is estimated to be from 325 to perhaps as many as 800. No storm in previous history had done as much property damage. It was not a good year for South Florida. A wild real-estate boom had collapsed. Millionaires at the end of 1925 had become poor folks by the middle of 1926. Solid citizens skipped monthly payments and tax bills and lost their homes. Businesses failed in great numbers. The sun still shined brightly, but its rays bounced off the bleaching skeletons of unfinished buildings. Where had the good times of the Roaring '20s gone? Sadly,

Floridians and new residents to Florida thought that things couldn't get worse, but unfortunately, then they did, on September 18, 1926.

From out of the Caribbean a storm, described by the U.S. Weather Bureau in Miami as "probably the most destructive hurricane ever to strike the United States," hit Fort Lauderdale, Dania, Hollywood, Hallandale and, most viciously of all, Miami. In the storm's eerie darkness, winds as high as 150 mph, resulting in the deaths of between 325 and 650 people. More than 800 others were never accounted for when the count was taken. Property damage was the worst in U.S. history, at that time. Striking some 25 years before hurricanes were named, the 1926 storm became known in South Florida simply as The Great Miami Hurricane or The Big Blow, a ghoulish honour it held until Andrew struck on August 24, 1992. Born near the Cape Verde Islands off Africa on September 6, 1926, the storm moved across the North Atlantic and into the Caribbean. It was reported off St. Kitts on September 14. Two days later it had moved into The Bahamas, and by September 17, it had taken aim at South Florida.

The grim reality however, there was no sense of alarm. Most of the 200,000+ people living in the storm's projected path were new to Florida, lured here by the easy money of the land boom. Having never seen a hurricane, they had little knowledge of a storm's destructive force. It would cost many of them their lives. In the early 1920s, Miami, Florida was the fastest growing city in the United States. The boom that put the city of Miami on the map so rapidly would quickly turn to bust during September of 1926. The Great Miami Hurricane also impacted the Florida Panhandle. It struck Pensacola, Florida with hurricane conditions for 20 hours on September 20, before making its final landfall near Mobile, Alabama later that day. Almost every boat, wharf, pier or warehouse situated on Pensacola Bay were destroyed. The city of Miami began experiencing the Great Depression because of the hurricane and that was 3 years earlier than the rest of the country.

By September 1926, the population of Dade County and the young City of Miami had blossomed to well over 100,000 (more than doubling from the census figure of 42,753 in 1920) and construction was everywhere. Smaller nearby settlements of Lemon City, Coconut Grove, and Little River were absorbed as Miami swelled with new residents; optimistic, speculative, and woefully under-educated about hurricanes. New buildings were constantly starting on Miami Beach, which had been built across Biscayne Bay on a series of barrier islands, bulldozed from their mangrove beginnings. The

US Government, including, the Department of Agriculture and the Weather Bureau recognized that Miami would soon be an important American city with tremendous growth and economic potential. In 1900, the cooperative weather station originally started in 1895 in Lemon City (about 5 miles north near NE 2nd Avenue and 61st Street) was moved to Miami. In June 1911, a first order Weather Bureau Office was established in downtown Miami, headed by Richard Gray.[84]

Meteorological History of the Great Miami Hurricane of 1926

The Great Miami Hurricane of 1926 was of classic Cape Verde origin, first known to the Weather Bureau from ship reports in the central tropical Atlantic on September 11. It passed north of the Leeward Islands and Puerto Rico on the 14th, 15th, and 16th, avoiding normal channels of Caribbean information. In those days before satellite pictures, radars and reconnaissance aircrafts, the hurricane remained somewhat of a mystery, with only a few ship reports to tell of its existence. Back then, storm warnings were centralized in Washington, D.C., and disseminated to field offices like Miami. However, as late as the morning of September 17, less than 24 hours before the Category 4 storm's effects would begin in South Florida, no warnings had been issued. At noon, the Miami Weather Bureau Office was authorized to post storm warnings (one step below hurricane, or winds of 48 to 55 knots). It was only as the barometer began a rapid fall, around 11pm the night of September 17, that Gray hoisted hurricane warnings.

Many of the exact hurricane-force conditions experienced in Miami were estimated because the hurricane passed directly over the Miami Weather Bureau offices and the weather instruments responsible for collecting data were destroyed. On September 11, ships notified the U.S. Weather Bureau that a hurricane existed about 1000 miles east of the Leeward Islands. This hurricane lasted from September 11 to September 22 and had a peak wind intensity of 150 mph (making it a Category 4 hurricane on the Saffir-Simpson Hurricane Wind Scale) and the lowest recorded barometric pressure of 930 millibars (hPa).

---

[84] https://www.weather.gov/mfl/miami_hurricane. Retrieved: 17-07-2016.

By 8am EDT on September 11—just twelve hours after the formation of the preceding cyclone—a new tropical storm formed in the North Atlantic about 1,100 miles just east of the island of Martinique in the Leeward Islands, although it probably originated earlier and was undetected due to lack of satellite coverage technology; operationally, the storm was not tracked until September 14. Steadily moving north of due west, the storm quickly became a hurricane the next day, and over the next three days, while bypassing the Greater Antilles to the north, it continued to intensify to a major hurricane, with maximum sustained winds of at least 111 mph, yet few ships were near the eye with which to determine its path. On the afternoon of September 16, the cyclone peaked at 150 mph, near the upper threshold of the modern-day classification of Category 4, and shortly thereafter passed just 10 miles north of the island of Grand Turk, striking Mayaguana at peak intensity early the next day.[85]

Continuing over the Central Bahamas and Andros Island on September 17–18, the cyclone, with winds of 145 mph, then struck South Florida near Perrine, 15 miles south of Downtown Miami, shortly before 8am EDT on September 18, with its large eye passing over the Miami metropolitan area. Swiftly crossing southernmost Florida, the potent hurricane weakened slightly before entering the Gulf of Mexico near Punta Rassa in the afternoon, and its path gradually curved northwest on September 19. Late on September 20, its path slowed drastically and curved west, making landfall near Perdido Beach, Alabama, with winds of 115 mph and a measured pressure of 954.9 millibars (28.20 inches) in the calm eye. Quickly weakening thereafter, the cyclone paralleled the coasts of Alabama and Mississippi, dissipating more than two days later over Louisiana.

Throughout The Bahamas, reports of damage were relatively scarce despite the intensity with which the storm struck the region. However, numerous structures were destroyed. The storm was attributed to 372 deaths in the Southeastern United States, 114 of which took place in Miami and at least 150 at Moore Haven, where a storm surge estimated as high as 15 feet overtopped portions of a levee on Lake Okeechobee. Many people in Miami, migrant workers predominantly from The Bahamas and to a lesser extent from the greater Caribbean who knew little of hurricanes, perished after examining damage during the passage of the eye, unaware that the back end of the storm was approaching. Flimsy structures built

---

[85] https://en.wikipedia.org/wiki/1926_Miami_hurricane. Retrieved: 26-10-2015.

to house migrant workers during the Florida land boom of the 1920s were completely leveled. The hurricane partially contributed to the end of the land boom, which was in decline by early 1926. In terms of monetary losses, damage from the hurricane was estimated to be as high as $125 million (1926 USD, $190.3 billion 2018 USD).

Up to 4,725 structures throughout southern Florida were destroyed and 8,100 damaged, leaving at least 38,000 people displaced. A storm surge of 14 feet occurred south of Miami and winds on Miami Beach were recorded at 130 mph before the anemometer blew away. The lowest pressure was estimated at 930 millibars (27.46 inches), the seventh most intense in a storm to strike the United States. The storm also produced significant damage, rainfall up to 16.2 inches, and a storm surge up to 14.2 feet in the Florida Panhandle. The entire state of Florida lost 35% of its grapefruit and orange crops combined, including nearly 100% losses in the Miami area.

In all, the storm caused at least 478 deaths along its path accounting for the revised toll in the United States since 2003. The storm's slow movement caused it to produce substantial effects to coastal regions between Mobile and Pensacola; these areas experienced heavy damage from wind, rain, and storm surge. Wind records at Pensacola indicate that the city encountered sustained winds of hurricane force for more than 20 hours, including winds above 100 mph for five hours. The storm tide destroyed nearly all waterfront structures on Pensacola Bay and peaked at 14 feet near Bagdad, Florida. Rainfall maximized at Bay Minette, Alabama, where 18.5 inches (470 mm) fell.

Damages sustained on the major islands of The Bahamas during the Great Nassau Hurricane, The Great Miami Hurricane and the Havana-Bermuda Hurricane of 1926:

- The Family Island Commissioner of Abaco, Mr. Roberts, during the Nassau Hurricane of 1926 got caught in the storm at Marsh Harbour, Abaco and had to remain up in a tree clinging to its branches for his dear life, for the entire duration of the storm.

- In the Nassau Hurricane of 1926, approximately 258-268 persons comprising mostly of sponge fishermen lost their lives at sea in

The Bahamas with the most occurring on the various Family Islands.

- A Long Island man with his young bride, a child and a crew of three from the sloop *'Celeste'* were reported drowned near Farmer's Cay in Exuma.

- In the Great Miami Hurricane of 1926, well over 25 persons died in Exuma alone.

- In the Great Nassau Hurricane of 1926, on the island of Cat Island, well over 74 persons died in the Bight District alone.

- The crew and passengers of the mail boat *'The Brontes'* which on its regular trip from Nassau to San Salvador was caught in the Great Nassau Hurricane of 1926 and the 30 persons (passengers and crew) were lost in this storm.

- Over 90% of the houses in Exuma were destroyed and over 97% of the houses on Acklins (over 427 houses were destroyed) and Long Island 500 houses were destroyed and most of the houses on most of the Family Islands by the end of the 1926 North Atlantic hurricane season were wiped out by these three hurricanes.

- For over 6 months to a year after these hurricanes, the average household in Abaco consisted of well over 30 to 50 persons before they could rebuild their own homes.

- On Eleuthera, the seven passengers and crew of the schooner *'Imperial'* were lost between Rock Sound and Green Castle, among them were, Mr. William McCartney of Tarpum Bay a leading tomato farmer and Eleuthera's leading businessman.

- On Cat Island, *'The Mountain King'* another mail boat which was used to take passengers to and from Cat Island to Nassau, was caught in the first storm-The Great Nassau Hurricane of 1926. Sadly, it was caught out at sea in the storm near Little San Salvador (now Disney's Half Moon Cay) and was lost with 26 persons (14 women, 7 men and 5 children) onboard.

- Unfortunately, only one-person Napoleon Rolle-a crew member survived this fateful journey when he swam to Bird Cay during the storm. He advised and managed to convince the *Mountain King's* captain Elliston Bain not to ride out the storm on one of the cays in the Exumas as the ship's captain initially wanted to do but try to 'outrun' the storm to their destination of Cat Island. In a rare twist of fate-Napoleon Rolle was the lone survivor.

- There is a compelling story of the former Governor General of The Bahamas, the late Sir Clifford Darling's experience with the Great Nassau Hurricane of 1926 when his home in Acklins was destroyed by the hurricane forcing his family into the elements of the hurricane and losing 4 uncles in this storm.

- The first two hurricanes were so devastating that the Governor of these Bahamian Islands made an urgent appeal to the King of England George V to request a British Warship to assist him in travelling to the various islands to take much needed hurricane relief supplies to them. His wish was granted when the king dispatched a ship called the '*HMS Valerian*' to The Bahamas and unfortunately after the task was finished, it got caught in the third hurricane (Hurricane #10) and 88 of the 115 men died when this ship sunk near Bermuda.

Costliest U.S. North Atlantic Hurricanes 1900–2010

(Total estimated property damage, adjusted for wealth normalization)

Rank:	Hurricane:	Season:	Cost (2018 USD):
1	Harvey	2017	$198.63 billion
2	**"Great Miami"**	**1926**	**$190.3 billion**
3	Katrina	2005	$130.9 billion
4	"Great Galveston"	1900	$120.4 billion
5	"Galveston"	1915	$82.3 billion
6	Andrew	1992	$67.5 billion
7	"Great New England"	1938	$47.5 billion
8	"Cuba-Florida"	1944	$46.9 billion
9	"Great Okeechobee"	1928	$40.6 billion
10	Ike	2008	$34.1 billion
11	Donna	1960	$32.4 billion

Wayne Neely

Costliest All-Time North Atlantic Hurricanes

Name:	Damage (Billions USD):	Season:	Storm classification at peak intensity:	Areas affected:
Harvey	$198.63	2017	Category 4	• Windward Islands • Suriname • Guyana • Nicaragua • Honduras • Belize • Cayman Islands • Yucatán Peninsula • Southern and Eastern United States (especially Texas and Louisiana)
Katrina	$130.9	2005	Category 5 hurricane	• The Bahamas • United States Gulf Coast
Sandy	$75.0	2012	Category 3 hurricane	• The Caribbean • The Bahamas • United States East Coast • Eastern Canada
Ike	$37.5	2008	Category 4 hurricane	• Greater Antilles • Texas • Louisiana • Midwestern United States
Wilma	$29.4	2005	Category 5 hurricane	• Greater Antilles • Central America • The Bahamas • Florida
Andrew	$26.5	1992	Category 5 hurricane	• The Bahamas • Florida • United States Gulf Coast
Ivan	$23.3	2004	Category 5 hurricane	• The Caribbean • Venezuela • United States Gulf Coast
Irene	$16.6	2011	Category 3 hurricane	• The Caribbean • The Bahamas

				• United States East Coast • Eastern Canada
Charley	$16.3	2004	Category 4 hurricane	• Jamaica • Cayman Islands • Cuba • Florida • The Carolinas
Matthew	$15.09	2016	Category 5 hurricane	• Columbia • Venezuela • The Bahamas • The Caribbean • United States East Coast
Rita	$12.0	2005	Category 5 hurricane	• Cuba • United States Gulf Coast
Hugo	$10.0	1989	Category 5 hurricane	• The Caribbean • United States East Coast

Costliest All-Time North Atlantic Hurricanes (Chart courtesy of NOAA-NHC, wikipedia).

Although no fatalities were reported, the hurricane wrought extensive property damage to Grand Turk Island. Rain gauges recorded 10 inches (254 mm) of rain during the storm, and high surf left knee-deep sand drifts on the island. The ocean covered the land up to 0.75 miles inland, and winds unroofed buildings at the weather station. Reportedly, the winds even ripped spines from prickly pear cacti. Nearly all lighters at port were lost. The storm left 4,000 people homeless on three of the islands in the Turks and Caicos. Due to hampered communications, the extent of damage in The Bahamas was initially unclear. In The Bahamas, the storm flattened hundreds of structures and killed many of the Family Islands residents, mostly on Bimini, where seven people died and the greatest property damage occurred.

According to the American Red Cross, the storm caused 372 fatalities, including 114 from the city of Miami, but these totals apparently do not include deaths outside the United States. Prior to 2003, the National Weather Service had long accepted 243 as the number of deaths, but historical research indicated that this total was far too low. The NWS then updated its totals to reflect the new findings. Even the estimates for the United States are uncertain and vary, since there were many people, especially transients and coloured migrants in South Florida, listed as "missing". About 43,000 people were left homeless, mostly in the Miami area. The hurricane weakened as it moved inland over Louisiana and nearly every pier, warehouse, and vessel on Pensacola were destroyed. The Great Miami Hurricane of 1926 ended the economic boom in South Florida and would be a $90 million disaster had it occurred in recent times. It had not been a good year for South Florida because a wild real-estate boom had collapsed and millionaires at the end of 1925 had become poor folks by the middle of 1926. Most of the 200,000-people living in the storm's projected path were new to Florida, lured there by the easy money of the Florida land boom. Having never seen a hurricane, they had little knowledge of a storm's destructive force and it ended up costing many of them their lives.

The hurricane also leveled many structures on Andros, including churches and large buildings, and downed trees and other homes on New Providence. On parts of Andros, the storm snapped or felled almost all the coconut palms, and in the Exuma district a large storm surge ruined many crops. The storm also destroyed 60% of the homes on the north island of Bimini, left water up to 7 feet (2.1 meters) deep in some areas, and was widely considered the worst storm on record in Bimini to date. Some sources say 25 people died on Bimini, but these may have been indirect deaths, as many people reportedly perished after drinking contaminated well water.

Winds were reported to be nearly 150 mph as the hurricane passed over The Turks and Caicos Islands on the 16th and it moved in The Bahamas on the 17th. Little in the way of meteorological information about this impending storm was available to the Weather Bureau in Miami. As a result, hurricane warnings were not issued until midnight on September 18th, which gave the booming population of South Florida little notice of the impending disaster. The Category 4-hurricane center moved directly over Miami Beach and Downtown Miami during the morning hours of the 18th. This hurricane produced the highest sustained winds ever recorded in the United States at the time, and barometric pressure fell to 26.61 inches as the eye moved over Miami. A storm surge of nearly 15 feet was reported in Coconut Grove. Many causalities resulted as people ventured outdoors during the half hour lull in the storm as the eye passed overhead. Most residents, having not experienced the passing of a hurricane, believed that the storm had passed during the lull because the last major hurricane had hit Florida in 1910 when the population was indeed much smaller than in 1926. They were suddenly trapped and exposed to the eastern half of the hurricane shortly thereafter. Most of the causalities succumbed after the lull.

During the hurricane's second half, winds reached a terrifying 128 mph, and floodwaters drowned people who didn't reach shelter in time. The storm left major damages to the State of Florida and it was said that every building in the downtown district of Miami was badly damaged or destroyed. At the time, Miami's hurricane was considered the country's greatest natural disaster since the San Francisco earthquake and fire of 1906. Today, this Category 4 storm ranks among 20th Century worst U.S. hurricanes and as the 12th strongest and the 12th deadliest. The town of Moore Haven on the south side of Lake Okeechobee was completely flooded by the lake surge from the hurricane. Hundreds of people in Moore Haven alone were killed by this surge, which left behind floodwaters in the town for weeks after the storm. The hurricane continued northwestward across the Gulf Mexico and approached Pensacola on September 20th. The storm became near stationary just to the south of Pensacola later that day and grazed the central Gulf Coast with 24 hours of heavy rainfall, hurricane force winds, and storm surge.

The destroyed warehouse (showing barrels of rum for shipment into the United States) of James Alvin Haugh in Nassau, Bahamas after the Great Nassau Hurricane of 1926 (Courtesy of Charles.J. Whelbell Collection, the Department of Archives, Nassau, Bahamas).

The University of Miami (UM), located in Coral Gables, had been founded in 1925 and opened its doors for the first time just days after the hurricane passed. The university's athletic teams were nicknamed the Hurricanes in memory of this catastrophe. The school's mascot is Sebastian, an ibis. The ibis is a small white bird that can be seen around South Florida, including on the UM campus. An ibis was selected to represent the Hurricanes because of folklore in which it is typically the last bird to leave before a hurricane strikes and the first to return once it's gone.

Several events, including the sinking of a ship in the Miami Harbour and an embargo by the Florida East Coast Railroad before the storm, weakened the Florida land boom of the 1920s in South Florida. However, the storm is considered the final blow to end the boom locally. Thousands of newcomers to Florida left the state and cleared their bank accounts, leaving many banks to the brink of bankruptcy. As a result, the Great Depression of 1929 did not make a great impact to Florida unlike the rest of the country. Many planned developments, which had fallen into deadlock due to insufficient resources, were abandoned due to the economic effects of the hurricane. In Boca Raton, for instance, one planned community by Addison Mizner, called Villa Rica, was destroyed by the hurricane and never rebuilt. South Florida did not achieve full economic recovery until the 1940s.

On October 21, with the eye of the storm still 700 miles from Bermuda, weather forecasts from the United States called for the hurricane to strike the island on the following morning with gale force. The Arabis-class sloop *HMS Valerian*, based at the HMD Bermuda, was returning from providing hurricane relief in The Bahamas and was overtaken by the storm shortly before she could make harbour. Unable to enter through Bermuda's reef line, she fought the storm for more than five hours before she lost the battle and sunk with the loss of 88 men. The British merchant ship *Eastway* was also sunk near Bermuda. When the center of the storm passed over Bermuda, winds increased to 114 mph at Prospect Camp, whereupon the Army took down its anemometer to protect it. The Royal Naval Dockyard was being hammered and never took its anemometer down. It measured 138 mph at 9am EDT, before the wind destroyed it.

Late in the summer of 1926, these two hurricanes brought great damage to the British colony of The Bahamas. The Governor of The Bahamas, Sir Harry Cordeaux sent an urgent appeal to the King of England-George V, requesting his assistance in providing a British warship to take him and a few government representatives to the various islands which were greatly devastated by these two hurricanes. In addition, to take much needed hurricane relief supplies such as, building materials, freshwater, food and clothing to the starving residents. As the naval headquarters for the British West Indies, the HMS Dockyard at Ireland Island dispatched a sloop, a minor vessel from its fleet to render what aid it could to The Bahamas. A duty which, today, would fall on the West Indies Guard Ship, a frigate that the Navy rotates through deployments to protect British West Indian Waters, and that with the HMD Dockyard long closed, only have stops in Bermuda on its way to and from its deployment. The ship sent to the aid of The Bahamas was the *HMS Valerian*. An Arabis-type of the Flower Class built during the Great War, she was under the command of Commander W.A. Usher, with a full complement of 115 men.

On the October 18, having rendered what assistance it could, it then left Nassau to return to her base in Bermuda. Due to a shortage of coal in The Bahamas, the boat began the voyage with little more than what it needed to complete the 1,100-mile journey. This left the boat relatively light in the water with a detrimental effect on its stability. A day after she began her voyage, the *HMS Valerian* received reports from the US weather service that a tropical storm was forming to the south of Puerto Rico. This storm initially moved north and seemed to be no threat to the ship, but unfortunately, it soon began curving to the northeast to follow the *HMS Valerian* home. Since the weather reports indicated that the "eye" would pass some 300 miles north of the island, Commander Usher never really gave it much thought. Besides, no major hurricane had hit Bermuda in October for well over 100 years - a dangerous precedent on which to rely on because it meant that Bermuda was well overdue for a major hurricane to hit this island. Despite the late date, the storm quickly grew far more powerful than the weather forecasters had predicted. The *HMS Valerian*, unaware of the true strength or speed of the storm still raced for home, not wanting to be caught at sea in precarious condition and lacking the coal to fight the weather for long if she were to ever to encounter this storm at sea. She very nearly made it.

By 8am on the morning of October 28, she radioed the Bermuda Dockyard to say that she was situated about eight miles from Gibbs Hill Lighthouse, to the southwest of Bermuda. At that time, Commander Usher would report, there was no sign of the approach of a large storm inhibiting the ship from making safely into port at Bermuda. Even though the wind howled about them and waves came with tremendous force over on her deck, still he anticipated no difficulty making Timlin's Narrows-the channel, located a handful of miles to the east of Bermuda, which provided the sole access through the isles' enclosing reefs. Commander Usher anticipated no difficulty in entering the Narrows, having done so many times before under similar conditions. Inside the reefs, the vessel would be protected from the worst the sea had to offer. But this was not to be because; this would be his last report from this ship.

Only when the few survivors were plucked from the waters near Bermuda and only by the following day would the extent of this tragedy be known, because the *HMS Valerian* was finally succumbing to the powerful winds and rough seas of the storm. At 10:00am the following day, 19 men were picked from the waters surrounding Bermuda by the cruiser *HMS Capetown* which rode the storm out safely at sea. The *HMS Capetown* had begun a search for the *HMS Valerian* the previous day but had been called away by the SOS of the steamer the *Eastway*, which also reported being in a desperate plight with her bunkers awash. While the *HMS Valerian* went down less than five miles from the safety of the Royal Naval Base in Bermuda, another ship, the *Eastway* sunk near Bermuda in the same storm, taking 22 crew members with her. The dead from the *HMS Valerian* numbered 4 officers, and 84 men. A commemorative plaque for those who lost their lives first hung in the Dockyard RN Chapel in Bermuda but was moved and is now held at Commissioner's House at the Bermuda Maritime Museum. This storm would become one of the most powerful hurricanes in Bermuda's history.

A survivor of the *HMS Valerian*, one of only 19, would recall the events of that day on the front page of The Royal Gazette and Colonist Daily. But the events surrounding the loss of the *Eastway*, and the rescue were never published-until much later. As a survivor would later testify before a court martial he said: "Indeed, at that time, I felt assured of reaching harbour in safety as there was no immediate indication of a violent storm, also there was a complete absence of swells that sometimes denotes the approach of a storm."[86] However, this was no ordinary storm and a half-hour later the weather changed so drastically that Commander Usher himself realized he

---

[86] Wayne Neely, *The Great Bahamian Hurricanes of 1926: The Story of Three of the Greatest Hurricanes to Ever Affect The Bahamas*, (Bloomington, Ind. USA, iUniverse Publishing 2009). Pg. 160.

could no longer proceed through the Narrows. He turned the ship around and headed straight into the storm. Gale force winds were lashing the ship at more than 100 mph with blinding rainfall and flying spray obliterating everything from view.

By noon the center of the storm was reached, and the clearing came, but with it mountainous seas that seemed to approach the ship from all sides, shooting the vessel onto a crest and dragging it down into the trough until it seemed she would snap in two. Once the center of the storm had passed over, the winds picked up from the northwest and again tossed the ship from crest to trough as if it were no more than a bath toy. At 1pm a series of squalls struck the ship on the port side with such force that it was thrown on its' beam ends and heeled 70 degrees over to starboard in a stomach-churning movement. It was at this moment that the mainmast and wireless equipment were carried away in the storm and preventing the possibility of sending out another SOS to Bermuda or any other passing ships. Above the howling winds, Commander Usher heard the engines stop and word reached him that the *HMS Valerian* had run aground. Before he could catch his breath, the enormous vessel keeled over about 60 degrees and started going down fast. Word spread "all hands-on deck" and with only enough time to cut away one raft, the crew had less than one minute to abandon ship before the ocean claimed the *HMS Valerian*.

Hanging onto the bridge, Commander Usher was swept away by waves, bumped his head and finally came up alongside a raft to which he and 28 of his men clung. In his account before the court later, Commander Usher recalled the events that followed: "Unfortunately, the bottom of the raft got kicked out and this entailed much greater effort in holding on. The experience of clinging to this raft for 21 hours, with only a problematical chance of being picked up was indeed trying enough for the hardest. Luckily, the water was warm, but the northwest wind felt bitterly cold to those parts which were exposed. Sunset came and as it grew dark, we looked for Gibbs Hill Light, or some other light, as we had no idea of our position, but nothing was seen, not even the glare.

The 12 hours of night, with waves breaking over us, was an experience never to be forgotten and many gave up during that time. They got slowly exhausted and filled up with water and then slipped away. The raft was slowly losing its buoyancy and as everyone wanted, as far as possible, to sit on the edge, it capsized about every 20 minutes, which was exhausting; we all swallowed water in the process and the effort of climbing back again.

Twelve held out until the end, when *HMS Capetown* was most thankfully sighted at about 10am the following day." By the time the *HMS Capetown* picked up the survivors, the buoyancy of the raft was such that it would not have supported anyone for another hour. The *Capetown*, which had ridden the storm out safely at sea, had begun a search for the *HMS Valerian* the previous day, but had been called away by the SOS of the steamer, the *SS Eastway*, which was about 70 miles south of Bermuda and in serious trouble.[87]

During a formal investigation in the United Kingdom in April of the following year, it was revealed that the *Eastway* was overloaded by 141-tons when she left Virginia. This decision cost the crew their lives, and the registered manager, Watkin James Williams, was found "blame-worthy" and culpable, and ordered to pay £1,000 towards the costs of the inquiry. On the other hand, a court-martial on the survivors of *HMS Valerian* was conducted, but later this court acquitted all the survivors of the *HMS Valerian* of all blame. They examined 15 or 16 witnesses, including ten of those who were saved from the shipwreck, others being technical witnesses. While it was described as a court-martial, it was really an inquiry. A court-martial was held because it was, pursuant to the practice of the British Naval Laws in such cases, to inquire into the cause of the wreck, loss and destruction of the *HMS Valerian*.

The Great Havana–Bermuda Hurricane of 1926

On October 14, a tropical depression developed in the southern Caribbean Sea about 350 miles north-northwest of Colón, Panama. Strengthening into a minimal tropical storm the next day, it gradually curved to the north-northwest over the next four days, becoming a hurricane on October 18. It then quickly intensified to a major hurricane early on October 19 as it turned northward toward western Cuba. Shortly before striking the Isla de la Juventud south of Nueva Gerona, it attained maximum sustained winds of 145 mph on October 20. The cyclone then continued strengthening, peaking at 150 mph before making landfall on the Cuban mainland south of Güira de Melena. The center passed just 10

---

[87] http://www.geocities.ws/gpvillain/news3novpg1.html. Retrieved: 14-11-2009. The Royal Gazette, November 03, 1926. Pg.1. *Wind and Weather Swept Valerian to Doom-Court Martial Acquit Survivors of Negligence*. Retrieved: 15-11-2009.

miles east of the capital Havana before entering the Straits of Florida about 80 miles south of Key West, Florida.

The cyclone then weakened and turned to the northeast on October 21, passing within 20 miles of the Florida Keys while remaining east of Florida. Nearly two days later, about 48 hours after turning east-northeast, the cyclone passed over Bermuda late on October 22 with sustained winds up to 120 mph; Hamilton, Bermuda, recorded calm winds and 963.4 mb (28.45 inches) in the eye, along with sustained winds up to 102 mph with gusts to 138 mph afterward. Three days thereafter, on October 25 the storm executed a clockwise, semicircular loop to the south-southwest, and a day later it lost hurricane intensity. Gradually curving to the west, the cyclone dissipated early on October 28, though it was once believed to have been an extratropical cyclone as early as October 23.

The hurricane inflicted devastation along its path, causing at least 709 deaths in Cuba and Bermuda. Upon striking Cuba, the hurricane caused catastrophic damage and as many as 600 deaths. Several small towns in the storm's path were destroyed and damage estimates exceeded $100 million (1928 USD). In the upper Florida Keys and on Key Biscayne, minimal hurricane conditions occurred, causing minor damage in South Florida. In Bermuda, 40% of the structures were damaged and two homes destroyed, but otherwise damage was light in the harbour. While weather forecasters knew of the storm's approach on Bermuda, it covered the thousand miles from The Bahamas to Bermuda so rapidly it apparently struck with few warning signs aside from heavy swells.

CHAPTER TWELVE

The Impacts of the three Hurricanes of 1926 on the Various Islands throughout The Bahamas

E ach hurricane was responsible for, taking many lives, wrecking thousands of houses, sinking and destroying numerous fishing vessels on many of the Family Islands to such an extent that many of these islands devastated by these storms took years to recover. Financially, the loss was significant because it was estimated that well over £1,000,000 was needed to bring The Bahamas back to some form of normalcy after the first hurricane and twice that amount for the second hurricane. Besides, these 'native' houses as they were called throughout the Family Islands were sub-standard houses. They were comprised of just galvanized tin, a straw or wooden roof and the walls were made of dry limestone rocks, sometimes coral and built without the benefit of any cement. As a result, they were no match for the ferocity of winds in these storms, so they were often the first things to be destroyed in the storm.

Under these desperate and dire circumstances, the government was faced with the tremendous problem of feeding, clothing and sheltering a large proportion of the population throughout the hurricane-ravaged islands for many months and even years to follow. Furthermore, the government had to spend record sums of money in relief and reconstruction work. On most of the islands, most of the houses, farms and other infrastructures such as roads were destroyed in the first hurricane. After the first hurricane, many homeowners rushed to rebuild their homes, boats, and replant their farms devastated by the Great Nassau Hurricane of 1926. This would prove to be an unwise decision because the second storm came along and destroyed them again putting them into far greater debt than they had been by the first hurricane. By the time the third hurricane had struck, there wasn't much for it to destroy. This was merely because the other two storms had done so much damage and displacing most of the residents and destroying most of the infrastructure, homes, farms, and ships on each of the islands. Most residents simply waited until the end of the hurricane season to re-start any rebuilding efforts because of the fear of being hit by another major hurricane.

Abaco

After the first hurricane, all the piers and seawalls were destroyed, and those houses within reach of the docks were just washed away. A significant portion of the damage throughout the island was inflicted on the fruit-bearing trees such as pears, mangoes, sapodillas, grapefruits, and oranges. For example, in settlement of Marsh Harbour-no trees were left standing. At Hopetown, there was widespread devastation because most of the houses were destroyed. It was estimated that in settlement of Marsh Harbour alone, they suffered a loss of well over £2,000. Also, in this settlement, the schoolhouse and many of the dwelling homes were blown down, and two Wesleyan Churches and one native Baptist Church were destroyed. The three-mast schooner, owned by Messer's Jas. P. Sands Co. of Nassau, parted one of the anchors; refuge was found at the point near Marsh Harbour, but the motor tender and small boat were broken up. Most of the three-mast schooners near Marsh Harbour were destroyed. Three fishing smacks, *Forward, Venture*, and *Iona* from Cherokee Sound were destroyed, and five of the crew members drowned in the waters off Nicholl's Town, Andros. The three-mast schooner *Beecham* contracted to transport lumber from Norma's Castle to Cuba, was wrecked on the west side of Great Abaco Island.

Throughout most of the settlements in Abaco, flood waters were said to be well over four and a half feet deep. Many trees were uprooted, and several of them fell across the main roads which made them impassable for many days. Many of the homes, toilets, and kitchens were either severely damaged or destroyed by the storm. In the settlement of Cherokee Sound, seven men lost their lives beside the ones lost at sea. In Marsh Harbour, there was one loss of life, which was a 5-year-old boy who lost his life when he came out of his home and saw a large hole filled with water in the schoolyard, and probably thinking the water was not deep, through childish ignorance plunged into it, unknown to anyone. He was missed at home, and a search discovered him dead at the bottom of the hole. A great deal of effort was done by the public-school teacher and others to resuscitate him but to no avail.

After the Hurricane #10 of October 21 and 22, the Governor visited Abaco by seaplane and by boat and found that the island was completely devastated by this hurricane and it didn't help the situation that two other previous storms had also devastated the island. He found out that in every settlement the wharves and seawall were destroyed, and those houses which were within reach of the waves were washed away. On this island, there were hundreds of homes which were destroyed leaving thousands homeless by this storm. After the storm, there were very few houses which remained standing, and for weeks and months, it was said that those few remaining houses which were not destroyed supported each on average of 30 to 40 persons in them until their homes were repaired or rebuilt. Hundreds of chickens, many cats, dogs, and hogs were also killed in the storm, many decayed and the stench of these dead animals could be smelled for many miles for many days and even weeks after the storm had passed. Also, thousands of fish were carried inland for many miles by the storm surge, and they also added to the unbearable stench in this settlement.

Much of the fishing and shipping transport vessels including several large schooners were destroyed. At Guana Cay, a few houses were destroyed, but the damage was relatively light compared to that of the other settlements. One large motorboat was swept away never to be seen again, while another was simply destroyed and the only road in this settlement was washed away. At Green Turtle Cay, the Government Dock and the main road were washed away, and many homes were destroyed. At Man-O-War, considerable damage was sustained in this settlement especially to the fruit trees such as, oranges and grapefruits which were wiped out and one house was destroyed, and ten others were blown off their foundations. This settlement shipped annually to Nassau citrus fruits to the value of £2,000, and this hurricane wiped out their primary source of income-citrus for years to come. The Commissioner of Abaco would later declare in his hurricane report that in this settlement, "There is absolutely nothing left. What had once been a pretty little town covered with fruit trees and nice homes is today nothing but wilderness and a swamp."

At Marsh Harbour, the destruction was almost complete, and no other settlement suffered more damage than this settlement because all but two houses which stood on high ground were destroyed. The storm surge at Marsh Harbour rose to about twenty feet above the high-water level, many of the homes could not endure the battering waves and were carried inland for distances of nearly a mile. Three persons Mrs. Dells Weatherford, Lydia Bethell, and an infant child Eleanor Van Ryn, daughter of August Van Ryn, drowned in this settlement. Most persons said that had the worst part of the storm had occurred in the night rather than during the daylight hours, the casualties would have been significantly higher. At Hopetown, there was widespread devastation because many houses were destroyed when the storm surge swept over the settlement. In this settlement, sixty houses were partly damaged, and one-third of the houses were destroyed, and the roof of the lighthouse keeper's home was blown-off. During the storm, this island had sustained winds of over 150 miles per hour. The estimated damage to government and private properties were about £2,000. The water rose as high as 8 feet in this settlement, and the sea rushed in as far as the Methodist Mission House a quarter of a mile inland from the seafront. A building was carried 1,000 feet and deposited upside down in the front of the cemetery.

The streets were blocked in several places, and many houses floated onto the roads from their original sites. Only two boats remained untouched after the storm in this settlement and Dr. Dolly's yacht, well known in Nassau, received considerable damage. The two wireless towers and the Government Dock were destroyed. The public-school house was blown down, and it would end up costing the Government £200 to repair it. The three-masted schooner Abaco dragged her moorings and was blown up on the land in a place where ordinarily the tide would never come. Another fishing boat *Abaco-Bahamas*, which sailed from Hope Town to Marsh Harbour during the storm was similarly blown up on the rocks and was destroyed.

At Marsh Harbour, the experiences of the Acting Commissioner Mr. Roberts and his wife, both over sixty years of age, were unusual but not exceptional. The winds during the first part of the storm had been blowing off the land and caused very little damage. During the calm, which fell soon after daylight, while the center of the storm was passing, the acting Commissioner left his house to secure his boat *The Vigilant* which was lying in the creek about 400 yards away and having succeeded in doing this he started to return home if the hurricane had passed. Most persons at the time didn't fully understand the anatomy of a hurricane especially the fundamentals of the eye feature of the storm. Before he could reach his house, however, the wind began to blow once again more furiously than before but from the opposite direction.

Mr. Roberts crept for safety behind a sapodilla tree, up which he was forced to climb as the sea swept over the land and the water rose higher and higher; finally, he took refuge among the top branches where he clung onto the branches for dear life for several hours. It was not until late in the afternoon, after some of the flood waters had subsided that his cries for help were heard and the aid of a tall ladder rescued him from his dangerous and undignified position. In the meantime, Mrs. Roberts, who had remained at home, was driven upstairs by the rising water. The house (a wooden one) was soon swept off its' foundations and carried inland, gradually sinking, while Mrs. Roberts made a vain attempt to get through the attic window onto the roof. Her danger was seen by people in another house who were also floating away and a young Spanish Wells woman by the name of Marion Higgs, with great gallantry, swam from one home to the other and succeeded in pulling Mrs. Roberts onto the roof of the house where both remained until the storm subsided.

Most of the inhabitants of Marsh Harbour lost everything they owned-houses, boats and fruit orchards were all destroyed, while many people who had before the storm been comparatively well-to-do owned nothing afterward and rendered penniless with only the clothes on their backs. The most beautiful building in Abaco containing the public library, post office, and courthouse, a new building of over forty feet long was blown 1000 feet away into a swamp from its original site and destroyed. The cemeteries in Marsh Harbour and other settlements were destroyed, and the coffins and bodies were washed out of the graves. The large 9-bedroom house of the wireless operator was carried about half a mile inland. Mr. Goodwin Roberts's large home was moved three-quarters of a mile away, and he lost his child during the storm. Mrs. Lydia Bethell drowned in the storm, but her body was never found until three days later in a swamp a quarter of a mile away from where she went missing. Abaco shipbuilder Mr. John Lowe's house was destroyed along with all his tools.

At Guana Cay, the damage was moderate, and all the sugar cane crop and the sugar mills were destroyed. A few houses were destroyed and the others badly damaged in this settlement, and quite a few of them were blown off their pillars. The Bahamas Cuba Lumber Mill at Norman's Castle was only partially damaged, and the total damage to this mill and surrounding houses were estimated at £10,000. At Cherokee Sound, the waves from the east met those from the west. It rose about six feet high, and considerable damage was done. A few houses were destroyed, and a significant number were partially destroyed and blown off their pillars. The Methodist Church which stood near the street was destroyed, and the Government Dock was partially destroyed. Most of the persons living on Abaco were fishermen or farmers, so the loss of their only means of livelihood devastated this island, leaving many penniless for months or even years to follow. After this storm, the generosity of many persons throughout The Bahamas and outside the country eased the hardship of the inhabitants of Abaco by donating funds, building materials, food and clothing to the hurricane-stricken residents to supplement the relief given by the central Government. Besides, to persuade the inhabitants to rebuild their houses in a safer position, a grant of land on higher ground was offered to the residents to rebuild on.

Andros

During the first hurricane, the Commissioner's Office at Staniard Creek was blown down. All the bridges were destroyed, and most of the dwelling homes in most of the settlements were also destroyed. Part of the Methodist Church roof was blown off; the roof of the Social Union Society Hall was blown off. The Good Samaritan Lodge Hall and other buildings were also destroyed. The sisal crop of well over £1,500 was wiped out. About 95% of the coconut trees estimated to be in the hundreds were blown down. Throughout most of the settlements, the standing water was said to be well over five feet deep. About 89 houses, many of them stone buildings were destroyed at Mastic Point.

One eyewitness Percy Wemyss said that the settlement of Staniard Creek was devastated and that if anyone who saw this settlement a few days before the storm had hit as compared with a few days after the storm, they would not have been able to recognize it as the same settlement. In Staniard Creek, it was estimated that more than 25 houses and several churches were destroyed. In Nicholl's Town, 27 homes were destroyed and many others severely damaged and rendered uninhabitable. At Lowe Sound, only ten buildings were left standing, and three of them were severely damaged. At Conch Sound, just nine buildings were left standing, and the rest were blown down or washed away. The roof of the Commissioner's Office was blown off, and the prison's roof was severely damaged. The teacher's residence at Nicholl's Town was completely blown down, and nearly all the furniture inside were destroyed. After the storm passed over the settlement of Nicholl's Town, 97 homeless persons had to seek shelter in the public schoolroom. Nearly all the streets were blocked with portions of shattered houses, walls, boats, fallen coconut trees and all sorts of rubbish and miscellaneous items. Damage to government property alone was estimated at well over £10,000.

At Fresh Creek, the bridge connecting the eastern and western ridges was blown down. During the hurricane, a surge of water from the beach came ashore and met the floodwaters from the creek on the east ridge with that of the west ridge. There were 48 buildings destroyed and 35 severely damaged and 500 coconut trees blown down. The schooner *Imperial* was found wrecked off the settlement of Red Bays on the western shore of Andros. The crew of 7 persons was lost with the vessel, and several other ships near North Andros with many persons onboard were reported missing and never found. At Red Bays, the sea washed up to the houses and swept them away taking several lives in the process. Most of the sponges in the kraals which were kept on the west coast of Andros were swept out to sea. The surge was so destructive that those boats lying on the outside of the creek, except for the Bishop's Yacht *Lavonia,* were unable to make the harbour, but she forced her way into the creek with great difficulty. The sponging schooners *Mary B, Sea Breeze* and *Anne* the latter two owned by W.J. Amaly, a sponge merchant, were destroyed with five of the crew members perishing. At least three men drowned in the storm from Fresh Creek.

In the settlement of Long Bay Cays, South Andros, several vessels were destroyed while others were sunk or stranded. Also, in this settlement of Long Bay Cays, the main road located along the seashore was washed away for many miles, and where the road remained, it was blocked with debris, fallen trees and shrubs, together with heaps of seaweed and other marine growth making it impassable in many places. The large drainage canal which was constructed in 1925 for draining about two miles of the coastal swamp was wrecked, the sea making a clear breach over it, tearing away the sea ridge to a width of 30 or 40 feet, and filling the canal with hundreds of tons of sand. It was estimated that it would cost well over £50 to put the drainage canal back in operation and £150 to repair the damaged road.

After the second hurricane, the conditions throughout Andros was said to be in a deplorable state. In Nicholl's Town, only one boat was available to bring the Commissioner's Report to Nassau as the district was almost totally wrecked. The hurricane was accompanied by very consistent torrential rainfall beginning at 5:30 pm on the 17th and lasting for over twelve hours. More than thirty individuals lost their lives and hundreds more rendered homeless after this hurricane. Every settlement had suffered severely, and towards the northern end of the island only a small percentage of the houses in each settlement remained standing and even the ones that remained standing were also severely damaged. The damage to homes at Nicholl's Town, Conch Sound, and Lowe Sound were as follows: 39 destroyed and 60 severely damaged. At Nicholl's Town, one gable end from the Commissioner's Office roof was blown away (the top was blown off in the first hurricane), the schoolroom walls were cracked in several places, and the roads were blocked in several areas. The Baptist Church at Nicholl's Town was severely damaged, and the one at Conch Sound was destroyed. At Mastic Point, the roof of the Commissioner's Office was blown down, the teacher's residence was destroyed, and the schoolroom was slightly damaged. Also, there were 60 houses destroyed and 99 homes severely damaged in this settlement. The Methodist, Baptist and Episcopal Churches at Mastic Point were all destroyed.

The public graveyards at Fresh Creek and Calabash Bay were washed away, and the coffins with dead bodies had to be reburied in new burial grounds. In the settlement of Little Harbour, Mangrove Cay there were 70 houses destroyed and many others severely damaged. One child was crushed to death by a falling house, and several other persons were injured. Nearly all the boats in Mangrove Cay were destroyed or severely damaged, and six men were reportedly drowned in their sponging vessels. The entire landmass, except the hills at Mangrove Cay, was covered in water for days and most of the coconut trees were snapped off and blown down by the wind. At Victoria Point, there were 68 dwelling houses and 3 Baptist Churches which were destroyed. In South Andros, very few homes remained standing, and the public schoolhouse and teacher's residency was blown away. Many fishing and sponging vessels were destroyed or severely damaged including, *The Repeat* which was sunk at Pure Gold but fortunately it would later be repaired. *The Repeat* would eventually be destroyed in the Great Bahamas Hurricane of 1929. In South Andros, there was a fishing vessel with six of the seven crew members perishing in the storm. One child was also killed when a house fell on top of him.

Many of the persons who received building materials to aid them to replace their homes damaged by the Great Nassau Hurricane of 26th July had only begun to rebuild, and the Great Miami Hurricane of 1926 struck The Bahamas leaving them further in a state of devastation than before because this hurricane swept away their materials. The people in many of the settlements throughout the island were living in the open and sleeping at night either in damaged churches or on the ground in the ruins of their homes. Most of the sponging vessels which the people depended on for their livelihood were mostly destroyed during the hurricanes. Much needed relief supplies were dispatched from Nassau, the following day after the storm. The inhabitants didn't suffer from food but from the difficulty of obtaining freshwater, because most of the wells were contaminated by saltwater due to the abnormally high storm surge.

At the time of the hurricane, the Commissioner for the entire island of Andros was Mr. Elgin Forsyth whose tenure lasted from 1922 to 1946, gave a very detailed report to the Governor. He was responsible for distributing the food, clothing and building materials to the residents after each of these hurricanes. Mr. Forsyth, a resident of Mangrove Cay was born August 28, 1877, at Rum Cay and he moved with the family to Wood Cay, Andros in 1880, however, in 1886, the family migrated to Florida. His family moved back to Nassau when he was 14 years old, where his father, L.E. Forsyth, worked as a land surveyor. However, his father will be remembered for overseeing the 20,000-acre Chamberlain Sisal Plantation near Mastic Point Andros. In 1892 his father gave up surveying and became a Resident Justice for the Andros district. Elgin's three main duties as a Commissioner were first, to take care of the sponge fishermen and their needs (there were several thousand men during this time engaged in the sponging trade). Secondly, he had to report on the impact of hurricanes on the island of Andros to the Governor in Nassau. Third, to make a comprehensive report on the conditions in Andros after a major hurricane disaster had passed.

San Salvador

During the first storm, slight damage was reported to this island as compared to the other southern islands. There were a few blown down trees throughout the island. There were two Episcopal and more than seven

Baptists Churches destroyed. *The Brontes*, a mail schooner of 42 tons and built in 1921, had set sail from Nassau on Friday for its regular trip to San Salvador and Rum Cay. Including the crew, there were 30 persons on board, among them were Rum Cay's Commissioner Mr. T.A. Greenslade's wife, four other members of his family, and the wife and children of H.A. Varence, the schoolmaster at Roker's Point, Exuma. At the time of *The Brontes* departure, the hurricane was quite some distance away-only approaching Hispaniola. The captain of *The Brontes*, W.P. Styles, was a much-admired figure in the maritime life of the colony. Renowned for his reliability as a mailboat captain and exceptional skill as a sailor, he was in the words of Sir Etienne Dupuch, a "very, very valuable mariner." *The Brontes*, then, was a ship that had many lives because a year before the hurricane, it had sunk between Graham's Harbour and Riding Rocks (Cockburn Town), San Salvador, taking its then captain, a man named Burrows, to his watery grave.

By the time *The Brontes* got to south Eleuthera near Powell's Point, they had started to experience some deteriorating weather conditions of the storm. So, they decided to wait out the storm at Powell's Point, but the weather conditions deteriorated so fast that they decided to outrun the storm-a move that they would soon live to regret. The problem, however, was not one of direction but of timing. As fate would have it, Styles had waited too late; as a result, he was not able to outrun the storm but rather the direction of movement of his ship took them directly into the heart of the storm. A pastor at Wemyss Bight, just south of Powell's Point, would later report that he saw *The Brontes* 'scudding past the settlement, apparently steering for the Exuma Cays.' Two hours later the weather had deteriorated so badly that he 'didn't think the Captain would be able to see to go through the Cays.' At some point on that Sunday night, *The Brontes*, probably after broaching, would be smashed to pieces somewhere in the vicinity of Highbourne Cay in the Exuma Cays, hurling its 30 passengers and crew into the unforgiving and dangerous waters of The Bahamas.

Sadly, there would be no survivors. Pieces of the wreckage would later turn up at Beacon Cay in the Exumas. A few days later, a search party from Cat Island would make a gruesome discovery at Highbourne Cay (Norman's Cay according to another account). Two women, one of them the wife of Commissioner Greenslade, lay dead on the beach. Describing the scene in gratuitously morbid detail, Arthur's Town Commissioner Duncombe noted that the bodies were "swollen, one having her head bound up in the usual manner for keeping out the draught and the other having sand all through her hair; the former was more swollen than the latter, and her face was bursting open, the skin mostly peeled off." Fearing contagion, the search party buried the bodies right away. Another body or two would turn up in the ensuing days, but for the rest of *The Brontes'* passengers, captain and crew would forever be lost to the merciless waters of the Atlantic.[88]

Exuma

On Exuma, there were many stories of persons sailing to and from different Family Islands who were caught in the storm but were forced to stop on the Exuma mainland or one of its cays to escape the strong winds and torrential rainfall. Some were lucky and were rescued while others were not so fortunate because they would later be found dead on some of the deserted cays in the Exuma chain of islands, most likely from starvation or the overexposure to the weather elements. The schooner *Ladysmith* (Captain Solomon Smith) on its route from Exuma to Nassau, rescued 27 survivors of the schooners *Graceful* and *Columbia* who were picked up at Highbourne Cay in the Exumas. The vessel *Graceful* left Nassau at six o'clock on Saturday morning just before the storm for Watlings Island with ten persons onboard. The storm struck her just off Highbourne Cay, and the captain anchored offshore there to escape the strong winds and torrential rainfall. Soon the boat began to drag her anchors so dangerously that the captain decided to put the crew ashore. They saved a small number of provisions, but sadly, they were ruined by water. They took shelter under a piece of torn sail and remained in this precarious situation for three days until they were rescued.

The *Invincible*, a small schooner was lost in the storm, but fortunately, the five persons on board were able to swim ashore. The boat was a total wreck, and the sheep, sisal, and fruits onboard were all lost, as well as about £60 in cash. The *Sarah Jane* was lost with six persons onboard perishing. Another sloop, name unknown, was reported sunk near Cat Island with twenty persons onboard perishing. The sloop *Doris* and its captain Gustave Rolle rescued 22 persons on Brigantine Cay and brought them to Nassau.

---

[88] Wendall Jones, *Hurricane a Force of Nature*. (Nassau, Jones Communications Ltd. Bahamas, 2005). Pgs. 29-35.

Also, two other sloops were wrecked on Brigantine Cay, the *Ella Jane* of Rolleville and the *C.E.M.I* from Ragged Island. The sloop *Sidney* on its way from Long Island was caught in the storm and was wrecked just offshore forcing the occupants to swim ashore. An unknown sloop from Acklins sunk in the storm with one person drowning as he tried to make it ashore to one of the Exuma Cays during the storm.

At George Town, the Anglican Church was left standing with little damage, but the Rectory was swept away. Approximately, about 90% of all the houses were destroyed on the island itself. Also, there were 4 Baptist and 2 Episcopal churches destroyed at George Town alone. On the island, about 500 houses were destroyed, while another 300 were partially destroyed and well over 1,000 persons were rendered homeless. In fact, at Georgetown alone, more than half of the houses were destroyed forcing many of the residents to take refuge in the schoolhouse, jail and in any of the other buildings left standing. They were forced to remain in these few remaining structures for weeks after the storm. The bridge over the canal at Farmer's Cay was swept away along with many of the roads. Sheep and cattle lay dead everywhere, and all the unharvested crops and every fruit tree on the island were destroyed. The two vessels employed temporarily to convey mails and several other ships which were anchored in the harbour were severely damaged when they sunk during the storm. After the storm, there were no vessels which remain unaffected or undamaged to take the news of the devastation in Exuma to Nassau.

The churches at Williamstown and The Forest were destroyed, and a great deal of damage was inflicted to the church at Hart's. On the island itself, there were six to seven Baptist Churches which were destroyed. Among the more notable church structures to be destroyed in this hurricane was St. Andrews Anglican Church at Georgetown. It was located above a hill overlooking the most picturesque harbour in The Bahamas. The church rectory had also been wrecked, adding Father Devard, an English Priest, to the list of homeless persons. He would later move into the Commissioner's Residency which together with the schoolhouse, library, jail and administrative office, would soon be overflowing with others of the homeless for a long time after the hurricane. Many hundreds of others, however, would be left with nowhere to live except under the open skies or amidst the remains of their destroyed homes. The Commissioner's Residency provided safe refuge to so many and had itself suffered severe damage, losing its porch and four of its out-buildings one of which had been intended for use as a wireless station.

At the peak of the storm, the Commissioner of the island George Clarke went outside during the storm to catch the French doors which had become separated from the porch frame by the strong gusty winds. In doing so, he slipped and fell and was tossed against the Poinciana tree, hitting his side. Soon it would become swollen and infected. Little could Clarke have known it then but that injury, soon to be exacerbated by his tireless exertions and the horrific nightmares for Exuma that still lay ahead, would eventually send him to an early grave. George H. Clarke, who was only 52 years old at the time, had less than three months to live after the storm. Well over ten vessels in George Town alone were destroyed during the storm, and the entire corn crop and other field crops of the whole island were destroyed in the storm. Survivors reported shipwrecked persons from Acklins, and other islands were stranded and starving on many of the Exuma Cays and were said to be in terrible condition. Most of the deaths in Exuma occurred from the turtling crew of *The Ready*, a schooner belonging to George Smith, who himself would be included among the dead.

During the second hurricane, many houses were destroyed in various settlements throughout the island, and in some locations, no buildings were left standing, and the sisal fields were also severely damaged. Several fishing vessels including the sloop *Invoice* and several houses were destroyed at Staniel Cay leaving over 40 persons homeless. In the settlement of Black Point, there were more than 300 individuals rendered homeless, 23 houses, one church, and one shop were destroyed leaving only three homes standing, and people had to find refuge under the damaged roofs of their homes for weeks after the storm. Five sloops were destroyed, while many more were severely damaged. The storm surge rose several feet high and came inland and destroyed all the field crops at Farmer's Cay. It had an average population of over 250 persons before the hurricane but during the storm, only 70 persons were located here because most of the men and boys were pre-occupied at Andros and Eleuthera on sponging trips. There were 16 houses and 1 Baptist Church destroyed and nine badly damaged. At George Town, very few buildings remained standing, and the Commissioner's Office and residence were severely damaged. St Andrew's Church was severely damaged along with the main roads and recreation grounds. Some buildings at William's Town and Little Exuma were destroyed.

At Bimini, the new Anglican Church lost its roof, and several houses were destroyed. The public-school room and the Methodist Church were destroyed. Most of the crops were wiped out by the hurricane. The Episcopal Church roof was blown off. The wireless station and the lighthouse at Bailey Town north Bimini were destroyed. Following the storm, the Imperial Lighthouse Service decided not to rebuild the lighthouse at the original location, but instead, it erected a new tower at North Rock, which is about 2 miles north of Cayce Point. Six vessels were wrecked at Gun Cay, and two sank at Bimini. The *U.S.S. Bay Spring*, with Captain Thomas James and a crew of 25 Navy men brought much needed 1000 tons of food, water, and building materials courtesy of the United States Government's Bureau of Navigation to the residents of Bimini after this storm.

On September 17 at 4:00 p.m., the radio operator at North Bimini received a telegram from Nassau that read, "Storm coming, prepare quickly." News of this impending storm passed quickly by word of mouth throughout the settlements of Alice Town, Bailey Town and Porgy Bay for what would be called the worst hurricane in Bimini's history to date. After the second hurricane, it was estimated that sixty percent of the houses on the island were destroyed and the hotel was also severely damaged, and all communications were cut off. Most of the wooden houses in low-lying areas floated off their ground pins and floundered like ships. Many persons abandoned their homes in the low-lying areas and ran to seek shelter in houses on higher ground. The school teachers' residence was destroyed and the public-school building severely damaged, forcing the suspension of classes for many months. Mt. Zion Baptist Church, Wesley Methodist Church, Our Lady's and St. Stephen's Anglican Churches were all severely damaged, and most of their church records were destroyed.

There were approximately twenty-five deaths and six persons severely injured. All the vessels in the harbour with one exception were destroyed and all the provisions lost. The ship *The William H. Albury* and *Monarch*, chartered by Messer's, Finley and Kemp were destroyed, and their much-needed provisions were lost. Mr. Kemp, who was on the schooner *William H. Albury*, took refuge at Cat Cay which lies opposite Gun Cay and was taken in at one of Mr. Strong's houses. Mr. Bruce and Bertie Bethell, who were on the three-masted schooner *Purceller* which had been partially wrecked in the July hurricane, had to abandon their boat and make for the shores of Cat Cay. While there they spent a terrible night clinging onto the rocks and hanging onto the bushes to save themselves. Unfortunately, the

Purceller was destroyed in this storm. During this storm, *The Finisterre* was sent to Bimini Harbour for safety but was lost with most of her cargo. The schooner *Laura Louise* as well as the mail schooner *Defence* sunk and were smashed to pieces and the vessel *The Tryon* was blown out of the harbour. Mr. Bethell's warehouse and dwelling house were destroyed. Mr. Saunders, who with his family lived there, was found alive, but sadly, his wife, sister, and daughter were all found dead in the wreckage.

Bishop Randal Saunders, whose boat was the only one that survived the hurricane, just because it sank instead of being wrecked or washed away, played a significant role following this hurricane. He was able to repair his boat very quickly after the storm and sailed it to Miami, Florida to gather much-needed emergency supplies of food, water, and clothing to relieve the hurricane-stricken inhabitants on this island. Then for nearly three months, he substituted his boat for mail, passengers and freight services between Nassau and Bimini, because the original mail boat was destroyed in the hurricane.

All the farms on the south side of Bimini were destroyed. Saltwater from the storm surge contaminated the freshwater wells. It was estimated that as much as six to seven feet of water flooded the streets in some areas of North Bimini. As the days went by, drinking water became a problem increasingly as the island residents became thirstier and more impatient for relief supplies to come from Nassau and the United States. As a result, many persons ended up drinking the contaminated salty water from the brackish wells and were stricken with typhoid fever, and sixteen of them died from the disease. Eventually, they obtained safe drinking water from South Bimini, and this freshwater well was attributed with saving the lives of many of the inhabitants of Bimini. The well was called 'Brother Peter's Well' named after an early settler to South Bimini called Peter Russell. Mr. Russell, an ex-slave, carved the well with only a hammer and chisel into the solid limestone rock. He used this well to irrigate his field crops and sugarcane, located adjacent to the well. After this hurricane, they hired Bradford Saunders and Henry Hanna to construct a historical stone monument around the well in early October of 1926. The vessel *S.S. West Ekonk* supplied the starving residents with a limited amount of emergency supplies. Approximately, 4,000 gallons of distilled water and necessary medical supplies, foodstuff and clothing were furnished by the local doctor, Dr. Little, and the United States Navy and Coast Guard.

After the third hurricane, approximately seven persons were killed, and most of the remaining houses which survived the previous two hurricanes were destroyed, and the entire island was said to be devastated by this storm. Great suffering occurred because the storm surge from the hurricane contaminated the freshwater wells with saltwater. Some vessels from Nassau were dispatched to the island with an abundant supply of clean water, food, clothing, and building materials.

As soon as the residents of Bimini were able to begin to recover from the three hurricanes, a major rebuilding program was launched, particularly in the area of housing and public works. It started in October 1926 after the second hurricane and continued into the following year. The Bahamas Government carried out repairs on the courthouse, Commissioner's Office, jail, and quarters for the Radio Operator and three concrete water tanks which were heavily damaged by these hurricanes. Eight houses destroyed in this storm were built at the expense of The Bahamas Government for the destitute widows who lost their husbands in this storm.

The Berry Islands

There were significant damages reported in the Berry Islands where there were only a few houses which were left standing, and not a single boat escaped destruction. Food, clothing, water, and building supplies were dispatched to this island by the Central Government in Nassau, the American Red Cross and the British Embassy in Washington to alleviate starvation. In the second hurricane, at Bullock's Harbour, the farms were destroyed, the sisal crop was ruined, all the houses left standing from the previous storm were blown away, and many of the inhabitants were in great distress. There was not a single morsel of food on the island for sale for quite some time after the storm.

Nassau

After the Great Miami Hurricane of 1926, His Excellency, Sir Harry Cordeaux the Governor of The Bahamas toured the hurricane-ravaged areas of The Bahamas on the British warship, *HMS Valerian*. After rendering assistance to The Bahamas Government after the hurricanes of July and September 1926, it was lost near Bermuda. A Special Committee was appointed by the Governor to oversee hurricane relief in the islands, to raise funds for the people affected by the hurricane and to gather information as to the extent of the damage of the storm on the domestic and economic life of the Colony. The Hurricane Relief Committee consisted of the Hon. G.H. Gamblin, Mr. W.C.B Johnson, and His Lordship the Bishop, Rev. W.H. Richards and Mr. W.H.H. Maura. This Committee reported widespread damage throughout Nassau with significant damage to many of the houses and businesses and many fallen trees across the major thoroughfares of Nassau. The number of buildings destroyed in Nassau was well over 4,300 buildings. The number of persons left destitute, with no shelter but that afforded them by neighbours, was well into the thousands in Nassau and neighbouring districts alone. The damage done to buildings in Nassau and suburbs was roughly £82,762. The cost to government property alone in Nassau was well over £150,000. The damage to shipping was severe and far exceeded well over £250,000.

Significant damages were reported to many of the churches in Nassau such as St. Matthew's, St. Ann's, Salem, St. Mark's, Zion Baptist and Trinity Church. Immediately after the storm, the Trustees and Finance Committee of Trinity Church got together and arranged for the immediate repair of the roof and the building (unfortunately, it was again severely damaged in the second storm). Almost the entire roof of Salem Baptist Church was blown off. The pastor of Salem Baptist Church at the time was Rev. D. Wilshere who estimated that it would cost well over £3,000 to rebuild the church. Zion Baptist Church and its Mission House were destroyed and would end up costing over £500 to repair it. St. Ann's Church on the top of Fox Hill was unroofed and the building severely damaged and would end up costing well over £2,000 to repair it. St. Matthew's Church had some broken windows and part of the eastern wall torn down. Wesley Chapel, Grant's Town had the roof completely blown off and the church and its interior badly damaged. St. John's Church had the roof completely torn away, and the eastern and western walls were blown down, it was later repaired at the cost of over £7,000. St. Mark's Church needed over £7,000 to repair the roof and the building and Gambier Church, was almost destroyed also required a similar amount to fix.

Adelaide Village in the southwest district of Nassau was almost destroyed as all of the dwelling homes with one exception and the churches in this settlement were all destroyed. Food, clothing and building supplies were supplied to them to ease their hardships. Until help arrived, 38 of the residents were forced to live off a few green mangoes fallen off the trees during the storm. It was reported that only one habitable house was left standing and many persons were forced to live in this house and under the fallen roofs of their homes. At the Eastern Parade on East Bay Street was blocked entirely by fallen trees and access to Shirley Street was blocked off by fallen trees. The Fort Montagu Hotel suffered significant damage because the roof was practically stripped of its red Spanish tiles and the front part of the roof was torn off, and many of the glass panes and windows were blown out and the interior badly damaged by flood waters. The Fort Montagu Hotel stood in several feet of water for days after the storm, and all of the trees on the property were blown down and would end up costing over £1,000 to fix and repair the damages. The damage to the New Colonial Hotel was well over £500. Significant damage was reported to the Royal Victoria Hotel and Gardens and would cost over £4,000 to fix and repair the damages.

There was widespread devastation in the settlements of Fox Hill and Grant's Town because most of the dwelling homes were destroyed resulting in many of these residents becoming homeless. The trees and wreckage of many of the houses littered the streets for days after the storm. To make matters worse, there was flood waters of four feet and higher in depth on many of the roads, preventing any movement by Nassauvians after the storm. The following buildings suffered significant damages, St. Matthews Church, 'Miramar' home of Mr. G. K.K. Brace. 'Breezy Ridge' home of Capt. Corbett, R.N., Outbuildings on Knowles Dairy Farm, Mr. R.W.D. Albury's house on West Bay Street, Mr. Sumner's house and Dr. Hess's house in Cable Beach which had his roof completely blown off and his house destroyed. The Keepers dwelling on the Eastern Lighthouse was blown away. The roof of the Hon. P.W. Ambrister and the Verandah on East Bay were blown off. Mr. Theo. M. Knowles' new house opposite St. Anne's Rectory had his roof completely blown off, and the garage was turned upside down during the hurricane. The Bahama Islands Import and Export Company's liquor warehouses (better known as Murphy's Buildings) on the north side of Bay Street were completely wrecked. Two of Mr. C.E. Bethell's warehouses on the south side of Bay Street had their roofs entirely blown off. The roof was partially lifted off the Girls' Eastern School, leaving only four walls.

Mr. Cedric Farrington's new house on East Shirley Street, opposite the Fort Montagu Hotel, was demolished; the family who lived in a bungalow in the rear had to take refuge in a Ford Sedan during the storm. Mr. R.T.

Symonette ship house and home on Paradise Island were destroyed costing well over £2,500 to repair. Mr. T.G. Johnson's Restaurant on the Waterloo Slope property near the hotel was destroyed. Great havoc occurred at Salt Cay but the bungalows there were not damaged. The New Piccadilly Restaurant was severely damaged, and its stock almost ruined entirely. The Star also owned by Capt. Isaac had its stock destroyed. Capt. Isaacs had to leave the building (residence upstairs) and take refuge with Ned Isaacs, and his estimated loss was about £500. The roof of the West Indian Oil Company roof was blown off. Emma Whylley's roof and house were torn down leaving five people destitute and would end up costing £80 to fix. Miss A. Armbrister house and outbuilding were destroyed costing £200 to fix. Mr. R.H. Curry roof, porch, and outbuildings were destroyed costing £800 to repair. Alfred Maycock house was destroyed costing £150 to repair. Tiliacos, Christofilis, and Christodoulakis sponge warehouses were destroyed costing £300, £250 and £700 to repair respectively.

Commissioner Thompson's house and kitchen were severely damaged. Jane Davis and Eliza Saunders houses in Grant's Town were destroyed and the occupants left destitute, and it would end up costing £30 and £150 to repair respectively. The home of the Hon. W.K. Moore on West Hill Street was severely damaged. 'Ocean View,' home of Mr. R.M. Lightbourn, was badly damaged along with his verandah and part of his roof. Dr. Hess home on Nassau Street had his roof completely blown off and destroyed. Mr. Jas. H. Rhodes and Co, large sponge rooms on West Bay Street split in two and was destroyed and the car belonging to Mr. Mike Nicholas (who was in Greece on vacation at the time) was destroyed when the building collapsed on it. Mrs. John Bosfield home on Delancy Street was destroyed. The sponge room on Curry's Wharf was destroyed and the sponge warehouse owned by Mr. P.C. Smith was destroyed, but the sponges inside were saved. The home of Mr. Alfred Holmes reported significant roof and other damages. 'The Farm's' eastern and northern verandahs were blown away, and the sisters inside were forced to seek refuge in St. Agnes rectory during the storm. The storerooms of Mr. C.E. Bethell were blown away. Mr. Thaddeus Johnson restaurant was destroyed and would end up costing £500 to repair.

Mr. W.E.G. Pritchard building was destroyed costing £400 to repair. Mr. and Mrs. Kingsbury Moore had a fearful experience in their home adjacent to their dairy farm near Chapman's Estate. The roof was torn off, and they sought shelter in the various outbuildings during the storm but slowly but surely all the accommodations where they sought refuge were eventually blown down forcing them back into the raging winds and torrential rainfall of the storm. Their cattle stampeded in the sheds, which they had to break open to release the frightened animals. Eventually, Mr. and Mrs. Moore found refuge in a garage at Westward Villas. The Workshop-Board of Trade was damaged beyond repair, and many windows were blown away, and the sashes were smashed in the main building, and a very valuable dinghy was destroyed. A portion of the roofs of Mr. Wheatley's Turtle's and Mr. Edwin Mosley's homes were all destroyed. All the bathhouses and bathing piers from Ramsay's to the Parade were washed away. The home of Mr. W.E. Fountain was severely damaged. Charles. E. Bethell warehouse roof was blown off and would cost over £800 to fix. Mr. G. Maillis had two of his outbuildings destroyed at the cost of over £300.

When the storm was raging on Sunday night, and part of Monday, a large iron safe and other valuable goods were stolen from Mr. Geo Farrington's Liquor Store on Market Street. Fortunately, the culprits were caught in the act by Mr. William Armbrister during the peak of the storm trying to lift the heavy safe across the street. The two men, Leonard Tucker, and Lawrence Pennyman were caught, arrested and charged in connection with this theft. They were eventually tried in the Supreme Court and were found guilty, and both men were sentenced to three years imprisonment. The electrical and telephone wires in the eastern and western suburbs were destroyed, and it was estimated that it would take over a month before they can be repaired. The acting Chief Justice Mr. H.F. Cox postponed the session of the Supreme Court for over a week until the standing water in the Supreme Court building could be removed.

The *Columbia, Mathoke* and *Home Comfort* were sunk and destroyed in the Nassau Harbour and of the forty-nine boats in the Nassau Harbour Channel; forty-two were blown out of the channel and destroyed. *The Old Vim* and several other ships were destroyed and smashed against the rocks over on Hog Island (Paradise Island). The *Eula M* skipper and owner Capt. Robert Archer came into the Nassau Harbour on Sunday afternoon with lumber for the Bahamas Cuban Company from Norman's Castle, Abaco; she could not make safe anchorage and was abandoned near the bar. She was smashed to pieces on the rocks below Fort Charlotte during the storm. The sloop *Handy* owned by Mr. Rolly Cleare, of Fresh Creek, Andros, left on Friday morning for Nassau. Running into bad weather, he sailed to the south side of Nassau and anchored near Adelaide. Two of the crew,

Milton Thompson and Daniel Solomon, were sent ashore for provisions. When they returned to the south side where the sloop was located, they discovered that the sloop was gone with Milton Ambrister and his wife Ann, who they left onboard. Parts of the missing vessel and some clothing would later show up on the Adelaide Beach, but the two persons onboard were never heard from again.

A seaplane was sent from Miami by the Associated Press and the Miami Daily News to Nassau to cover the aftermath of the storm. Somehow the plane got lost and ran out of gas on his reconnaissance mission and was forced to land on Billy Island, near Andros but fortunately, another seaplane in the vicinity provided them with some gas for them to resume their flight. This other plane had come to search for the staff and crew of the yacht *Seminole*, which was hired to take the team of the American Museum of Natural History in New York to Nassau and Andros for research work. According to the pilot, the reason why the plane missed her original course was that the islands were unrecognizable by air because they were all flooded making them appear as if they were merely dotted with lakes with only a few landmasses sticking above the flood waters. They were still uncertain of their bearings until they sighted the familiar sponging vessel *Resolute* just West of Morgan's Bluff, Andros.

Grand Bahama

Most of the boats on this island were destroyed and the remaining ones were severely damaged. Most of the damage done on this island was to the dwelling homes and the field crops. A Baptist church was also blown down and destroyed. The Police Dock was swept away, and the Ambrister, Crawford and Maury docks were all destroyed. The schooner *Dauntless* was lost with at least nine persons onboard perishing. The bridge at Hawks Bill Creek was destroyed. This island had sustained winds of well over 120 miles per hour during the hurricane. On this island, two doctors were dispatched by the American Red Cross to assist the residents after the storm. Some residents objected to these doctors being sent to Grand Bahama because they felt they were being sent with ulterior motives in mind, so a few persons pelted them with stones and others just refused to be seen by them.

Long Cay

Between 400 to 500 buildings including dwelling houses, churches, kitchen, barns, and shops were destroyed in the first hurricane. The remaining 12 homes left standing after the first hurricane were all destroyed in the second hurricane.

Ragged Island

The public-school house was blown down, and as much as 50,000 bushels of salt were washed away by the storm surge.

Rum Cay

Most residents on Rum Cay never received any warnings that a massive storm of such great intensity was heading directly towards this island. As a result, they never made any preparations for this storm, and that would be a mistake they would soon live to regret. All the salt ponds were completely flooded, and all of the 130,000 bushels of salt accumulated from the previous months were destroyed. The damage to the salt pond was estimated at £1,000 and conditions were so rough on this island that one resident even offered to fix the salt pond for half of the estimated price if he along with his labourers could be paid in flour and corn seeds-the offer was refused. This storm was devastating for the island because most persons on this island were employed in raking of the salt for local consumption and export. The island's entire field crops were destroyed. There was widespread devastation throughout the island as one church (Episcopal) destroyed, two chapels (Baptists) destroyed and two severely damaged, one police office and prison were unroofed, one schoolhouse destroyed, two wharves destroyed, 22 dwellings destroyed and 18 severely damaged and twelve kitchens were destroyed and eight kitchens badly damaged. Approximately 317 coconut trees fell, 27 sheep and 417 chickens drowned.

St. John Baptist Church collapsed and destroyed (its roof flying off and penetrating a woman's house on the other side of the road), and one person was reportedly drowned. After the Great Miami Hurricane of 1926 on September 17, the Governor left Nassau on the *HMS Valerian* on the morning of October 8 and returned to Nassau on the morning of the October 16. Between those dates, he visited San Salvador (Watlings

Island), Rum Cay, Fortune Island (Long Cay), Inagua, Mayaguana, Long Island, Exuma, and Cat Island. The Governor attempted to visit Acklins by a local boat from Long Cay but was, unfortunately, he was hindered by a series of accidents and had to abandon his attempts. On all the islands he visited, except Inagua and San Salvador, he reported that the damage done by the Great Miami Hurricane of September 17, was very much more significant than that done by the first hurricane. At Rum Cay, the salt pond, which provided a means of livelihood for the greater part of the population, was severely damaged and was only restored at great expense after the hurricane.

Cat Island

Cat Island was the island of the highest fatalities of the Great Nassau Hurricane of 1926. The Commissioner of the island Nathaniel Dorsett would claim in his annual report for 1926 that '74 persons were all drowned from the Bight District alone.' At Arthur's Town, nine houses were destroyed and twelve badly damaged. At Devil's Point, 27 houses were blown down including two churches and one Society Hall. Several boats from Cat Island were lost at sea, and sadly they were never heard from again. The sloop *Surprise* was wrecked at Alligator Bay near Roker's, but all persons on board were saved. The sloop *Saucy Sea Bird* of Mason's Bay, Acklins was wrecked at the Bight, but fortunately, the crew of five were all saved.

The Rev. James Smith of Port Howe, Cat Island built the vessel *The Mountain King* which was used as a freight and passenger vessel between Cat Island and New Providence. This vessel was caught by the Nassau Hurricane of 1926 between Bird Cay and Little San Salvador (later Disney's Half Moon Cay) on the return trip to Cat Island, Captain Elliston Bain wanted to put the vessel into the shallow waters and let the passengers wait out the hurricane on either of the two named cays. The mate, Napoleon Rolle of Devil's Point, Cat Island who was also a captain, strongly disagreed stating that the vessel could outrun the approaching storm and would arrive at home well ahead of the storm. Unfortunately, somehow, he managed to convince Captain Bain to continue the journey to Cat Island against his better judgment. Captain Bain was said to have stated that if they continued the trip as planned, by the next day, "They would all surely die!"

Some 25 miles from Orange Creek and Arthur's Town, Cat Island, *The Mountain King* sunk in the rough seas and raging winds of the hurricane and all 26 souls (fourteen women, seven men, and five children) on board with one noted exception was lost. The mate Napoleon Rolle was as fate would have it, was the sole survivor on this boat when he swam to Bird Cay during the storm. There he would be taken care of by the five shipwrecked crew of another Cat Island, vessel *Hero*. While searching the island in the aftermath of the storm, they came across a rickety 20 feet boat and used it to make their way back to Cat Island, landing at Orange Creek with the 'miracle boy' onboard in early August. Napoleon was said to for the rest of his life regretted not listening to Captain Bain's advice. Many persons in this community became overnight paupers, widows, and orphans due to this incident. The bodies of Sally Davis and Claudius Simmons were two of the few bodies ever found from *The Mountain King*, and they were eventually buried in a special burial service.

During the second hurricane, many houses were destroyed in various settlements throughout the island and in some settlements no buildings were left standing. The precious and productive sisal fields were severely damaged. The Commissioner's Office at The Bight was severely damaged, several schoolhouses were blown down, and all schools were closed as the buildings were found to be unsafe for occupancy. At the Bight, at least one life was lost, and two boats loaded with supplies were lost.

Long Island

Many houses were destroyed, all the public roads were blocked, and the bridge was severely damaged. There were four churches (2 Baptist and 2 Episcopal), one schoolhouse, five stores, 230 dwelling houses, five schooners, two sloops and 16 boats which were destroyed from this hurricane. Most of the damage from the storm occurred on the southern end of the island where very few houses were left standing. During the storm, 62 persons found shelter in the jailhouse and 23 in the police officer's residence, and they had to remain living there for a few weeks after the storm because their homes were destroyed in the hurricane. On one of the most flourishing estates at the North End, all the buildings were blown down except one kitchen which was left standing, and 47 persons had to take refuge there for several weeks because their houses were destroyed. One man, Sidney Burrows, was drowned on the southern shore of the island. The cotton fields, which were destroyed or severely damaged by the first hurricane was replanted immediately afterwards, but sadly they were again destroyed in the second hurricane.

Several vessels including the sloops *Lilla* and *Speedwell* and a few other smaller boats were also lost. Eight ships of various sizes that were away on voyages; six were lost and two severely damaged. The fishing vessels *Albertine* and *Iona* from Clarence Town were washed ashore during the first hurricane. Four men and three women were lost on these boats. The sloops *Rose Bell*, *Serene* and *Sacramore*, were sunk and driven ashore at Deadman's Cay, and the *Eclipse* and two Acklins vessels were lost, but fortunately, no lives were lost. A Long Island man with his young bride, a child and a crew of nine from the sloop *Celeste* were reported drowned near Farmer's Cay in Exuma. Three young boys aboard the vessel, however, would have better luck by hanging onto a piece of wreckage, they made it safely ashore. The light stations at North End and Simms were blown away during the storm. A bridge at Simms forming part of the road was severely damaged from the storm surge. Many of the Clarence Town public buildings suffered some damage, and most of the private properties throughout the island sustained significant losses.

During the second hurricane, many houses were destroyed in various settlements throughout the island and some settlements, no buildings were left standing, and the sisal fields were wiped away. Approximately, twenty-five persons throughout the island died during this hurricane and hundreds more rendered homeless. In the settlement of Simms, only 1 building was left standing and water flowed inland for about two to three miles and in some places the fields were submerged and many sheep, goats, chickens, turkey buzzards and cattle drowned. Many sections of the main road were destroyed or washed away. The Methodist, Anglican and Baptists Churches at Simms were all destroyed. The mail schooner *Columbia* was washed ashore along the beach. In the settlement of Clarence Town 42 houses were destroyed, at Victoria Village, 21 houses were destroyed, at Scrub Hill, at Gaythorn's 129 houses were destroyed, in the Southern District-31 houses, two schools, one church, and one chapel were destroyed. The Commissioner's residence and kitchen, the teacher's resident and jail were severely damaged. The wharf at Clarence Town was washed away, and the light at the harbour was destroyed. One of the radio towers was blown down and shattered to pieces. In the settlement of Dunmore South End, only one house was left standing after the storm. All the fields were wiped away and to make matters worse, all the foodstuffs in the various stores and homes were destroyed.

After the third hurricane, over eleven persons were killed and just about every house which survived the first and second hurricanes were destroyed.

Acklins

In the Nassau Hurricane of 1926, well over 427 houses were destroyed, and many persons from different settlements throughout the island drowned from the storm surge. Most of the island residents were left homeless and starving after this hurricane. In Snug Corner all but one of the 92 houses in the settlement were flattened, at Hard Hill, some 90 houses were blown down, and at Spring Point 53 houses were destroyed including the church and schoolhouse. In the settlement of Thompson's three houses were destroyed. In the settlement of Anderson's 19 homes were destroyed and in Pine Field and Jew Fish settlements 22 and nine respectively were destroyed. In the settlement of Relief, 17 houses were destroyed, and six persons drowned. In the settlements of Chester's and Pastell's 22 and 13 homes were destroyed respectively. In the settlement of Delectable Bay, 43 buildings were destroyed, and a building collapsed and crushed the female occupant to death. In the settlements of Pompey Bay, Aston Cay, and Binnacle Hill, 48, 26 and 26 houses were respectively destroyed. Many losses also occurred at sea when Moses Hanna and his two crew members comprising of two young boys were lost at sea.

According to Sir Clifford Darling, the former Governor General of The Bahamas recalled that this was the most powerful and frightening hurricane he had ever experienced. During the storm, he recalled how nine families in the settlement of Chester's, including his own, were trapped in their homes between the waterfront in the north and the overflowing waters of a tidal creek in the south. As the houses started to collapse from the battering waves and storm surge, a significant amount of water rising within these houses during the hurricane put the occupant lives in grave danger. A quick decision was made to flee to the hilltop some 60 to 80 feet above the beach. Young Sir Clifford, who was only four years old at the time, was placed in a canvas sack along with his sister with just their heads sticking out, slung over his brother's back.

In total, 45 persons in all assembled themselves into a human chain, and together they made that fateful journey to the safety of the hilltop and rode out the rest of the storm on top of that hill. When the storm abated, and they went back home, they were surprised to find that the wind blew the roof off their house. His brother turned the roof right-side up and took a hand saw and cut a hole in that roof resting a few yards away from the damaged house and they lived in the cramped-up confines of that roof for a few weeks after the storm, until his father returned home from working on the farms in Florida to repair the damaged house. Unfortunately, four of his uncles were on a fishing vessel and were on the way back from working on a wreck at San Salvador to Acklins, but they were all lost at sea during the storm.

After the second hurricane, there was widespread devastation, and much more lives were lost in this storm than in the first hurricane. At Acklins many of the settlements were destroyed, and well over 52 lives were lost. Over 300 buildings and virtually all the local vessels were destroyed on this island. At Ashton Cay to Delectable Bay 25 houses were destroyed, Spring Point 6 homes were destroyed, the Church of England and the schoolhouse were also destroyed. At Mason's Bay 71 houses and shops were destroyed, and 10 persons died, at Chester's 50 homes were destroyed, at Pastel 20 houses were destroyed and at Lovely Bay 30 houses and one schoolhouse were destroyed. Seven persons drowned at Lovely Bay, eight at Brown's, Ashton Cay 5, Thompson Creek 3, and 19 returning from wrecks at San Salvador. After the hurricane, many persons suffered from severe cases of diarrhea due to drinking contaminated groundwater and quite a few of them died from drinking this contaminated water. Foodstuff from Nassau was dispatched within 48 hours after the hurricane to relieve the starving population on Acklins.

Crooked Island

After the first hurricane, this island suffered widespread devastation. The Broon settlement lost 4 houses, True Blue 10 houses, Bullock's Hill 12 houses, Thompson's 7 homes, Major's Cay 30 houses, including the walls of the new schoolhouse, MacKay's 9 houses, Colonel Hill 63 houses, Moss Town, Fair Field and Richmond 39 houses respectively and Church Grove 20 houses and one church. After the second hurricane, many of the settlements were destroyed and many lives lost. At Colonel Hill, there were

30 houses and shops destroyed. The Government office at Church Grove was destroyed, and only three homes in this settlement were left standing. At Clearfield 15 buildings were destroyed. In total, some 200 buildings and virtually all the local vessels were destroyed on this island. Foodstuff from Nassau was dispatched within 48 hours after the hurricane to relieve the starving population on Crooked Island.

Mayaguana

On this island, some lives were lost, and the people were in great distress and starving with very little food and all their freshwater wells were contaminated by sea water from the hurricane surge. A 34-year-old man, Daniel Brown, drowned when he tried to secure his boat into a safe harbour. The Governor on his visit to this island after the second hurricane supplied the residents with food, clothing and a medical doctor and he speculated that it would be some time before a sufficient supply of freshwater could be restored to the island. Island-wide devastation from Pirate's Well to Betsy's Bay was reported.

The Abaco sloop *Magdalene D* captained by Herbert Archer but owned by Mr. W.J. Amaly, a sponge merchant and the mailboat *None Such* owned by Fred Black were destroyed. Archer had also been on his way to San Salvador with a 6-man crew to take Bahamas Customs Officer, Joseph Sands, to the *S.S. Kembala*, a 9000-ton British steamer, bound from Norfolk to New Zealand, which had struck a reef and taken in 14 feet of water. As for Captain Archer and the sloop of the *Magdalene D*, the vessel would founder in the Exuma Cays, drowning five of its crew members in the process. As for Archer, mate George Hudson and Customs Officer Sands, they would be 'dashed on the rocks' of an uninhabited cay. Sands would sustain several gashes on his head, and Archer would be injured as well.

For three days they remained on that deserted cay and starving. As their desperation was growing, the three men decided to swim to a nearby cay. Much weakened by his injuries, however, Sands lost contact with Archer and Hudson during the crossing and by the time night fell he was nowhere to be seen, nor would he ever be seen again. Reaching another cay and discovering that it was no more helpful to their precarious plight than the one they had just abandoned, Archer and Hudson built a raft from floating debris and set out once again. They would be adrift for another eight hours before being spotted by a search party and taken to Nassau to recover from their ordeal. Weeks after, Archer would still be suffering from the ill-effects of exposure and complaining of 'severe pain in his feet.' These afflictions notwithstanding, he could well have counted himself the luckiest man on Earth.

Eleuthera

During the first hurricane, the damages reported were slight as compared to the other islands; several houses were destroyed, and many coconuts and other fruit-bearing trees were blown down throughout the island. There were 14 churches and two schoolhouses which were destroyed on this island. There were 240 dwelling houses destroyed, 56 severely damaged and 831 persons rendered homeless. There were eight fishing vessels and boats destroyed and another 16 severely damaged. Most of the farm crops throughout the island were destroyed except for the pineapple crop which only sustained 50% crop damage. Most roads were destroyed and rendered impassible, and the major causeways were all washed away. In some of the settlements, more houses were destroyed than were left standing. Throughout all the settlements, there was standing water between two to four feet in depth, but fortunately, it drained away quickly in most places.

On Harbour Island, the damage consisted of, 1 Episcopal Church destroyed, one police office and prison were partially destroyed, two schoolhouses destroyed, 26 dwelling homes destroyed and 21 dwelling homes severely damaged, four schooners lost, 12 vessels badly damaged. At Spanish Wells and the Current, one Episcopal Church and 4 Wesleyan Chapels were destroyed in each settlement. Four women and five men drowned in the settlement of James Cistern. A child of three drowned in a water hole in the schoolyard who went there to play without realizing the depth. Two persons got injured when an old house collapsed on them. The fishing schooner *Imperial* was lost at Rock Sound with 7 people onboard. The schooner *Imperial* left Tarpum Bay for Rock Sound for safe harbour, but as it reached Sound Point and anchored, it later parted moorings and went adrift and was never heard from again taking those seven lives with the vessel. William McCartney of Tarpum Bay who was one of the leading merchants and tomato exporters of Eleuthera, together with his son, Charles, and a crew of five had set out at noon on Sunday to take McCartney's schooner, *Imperial* to safe harbour but got only as far as Rock Sound due to the deteriorating weather conditions. It would prove to be a fatal decision because three days later, a search party was assembled and would find bits and pieces of the *Imperial* scattered between Rock Sound and Green Castle. McCartney, his son, and the entire crew had all perished.

A fishing vessel owned by Inspector Albury was destroyed. Another schooner with fourteen or fifteen females and an unknown number of children onboard, as well as the crew, dragged her anchors, and was driven out to sea and was never heard from again. The sloop *Lily G* arrived at the settlement of Deep Creek just before the storm but parted her moorings and was never heard from again. Nine houses fell, six at Green Castle, two at Wemyss' Bight and one at Tarpum Bay. At Spanish Wells, a newly built boat was lost during the hurricane, and a search party was dispatched to find and salvage her from on the Great Bahama Bank. The light at Powell's Point was destroyed. Several small houses at Governor's Harbour and up shore were blown down and destroyed.

Mr. W.T. Cleare, the Commissioner for Governor's Harbour, reported that four women and five men left that Sunday morning for Nassau and was never heard from again. Two persons got injured when an old house collapsed. A body was spotted floating in the waters on the western side of the island on the night of the hurricane, but by the time lanterns, a boat and a search team could be assembled, it had disappeared never to be seen again. The ship *Molly O* was travelling through the Northwest Channel on her way to Gun Cay also saw a body afloat on the water. The vessel *Isles of June* was dispatched from Nassau to Governor's Harbour by the Governor a few days after the storm had passed with 500 bags of flour and much-needed hurricane relief supplies.

After the hurricane (the third hurricane) of October 21 and 22, there were significant damages reported, and practically every pier was destroyed, and all the roads and causeways near the sea were swept away. It was said that water was up to six feet deep and up to the windowsills in many of the settlements. The vessel *Endion* was severely damaged at Harbour Island. The Eastern Cemetery was washed away, causing the coffins to be floated away like little boats to over 1,000 feet from the cemetery. The damage to Government property at Governor's Harbour alone was estimated at £10,000. In the outlying settlements of Palmetto Point and Tarpum Bay, the piers were destroyed, and the one at Rock Sound was partially destroyed. The main road and bridge leading to Tarpum Bay for a length of about ½ mile were submerged underwater to a depth of over 18 feet in the storm surge. Twelve homes on Cupid Cay were washed away, and the prison and engine room were used as temporary shelters for the homeless. The causeway on the mainland was washed away. The water in Colebrookville was deep enough to carry small boats. The sea came in so rapidly that some people, including the wireless operators, had to flee for their lives in a depth of water of over four feet. A large proportion of the tomato fields were washed away, and the farmers had to sow fresh seeds setting them back 4 to 6 weeks. At James's Cistern, some portions of the main street were washed away, and a few homes were blown away and destroyed.

The work of The Bahamas Government after these three hurricanes in 1926 to stabilize the economy of The Bahamas

After the hurricanes, the Governor of The Bahamas, Sir Harry Edward Spiller Cordeaux explained the British Government's plans for reconstruction relayed through the Family Island Commissioners, the people, and to settle any doubtful questions as to the amount of relief to be given in exceptional cases. At every settlement, His Majesty's King George V message of sympathy was received with gratitude and loyalty. Immediately after the second hurricane, the Governor dispatched relief boats filled with a small number of relief supplies and freshwater to each island. Two ships were sent to Andros, one to Bimini and the Berry Islands, and *The Halcyon* left for Exuma, Long Island, and Long Cay. *The Graceful* was sent to Rum Cay and San Salvador. Also, the Governor travelled to each island after each hurricane on the British Naval ship *HMS Valerian* to find out the extent of the damages which occurred on each island and to assure the residents that the government will meet their needs. After his tour throughout the Family Islands, he was satisfied that the preliminary reports of the widespread devastation and damages done in these islands were not exaggerated and that he promised them that he would do everything in his power to assist them to the best of the government's ability.

On the Governor's return to Nassau after the first and second hurricanes, he immediately summoned a meeting of the Executive Council to consider what measures should be taken to deal with the situation at hand. The first emergency measures taken were to supply the people with food, clothing, seeds and a small number of building materials. This council approved of the following actions: -

- Notices were posted up in all the Family Islands warning the residents not to proceed to Nassau, where work was scarce, and housing accommodations were difficult to obtain and assuring them of the government's assistance if they remained in their respective settlements in the various islands.

- To compensate for the loss of vessels, the government arranged for at least two sloops to be built in each district by local builders at the public's expense, these vessels when completed were sold at cost price to local persons who were required to pay for them in easy installments.

- Loans on easy terms were made available to persons whose vessels were damaged in the hurricane and who were prepared to repair them immediately.

- Instead of confining relief works to the construction of roads and other public utilities, the Family Island Commissioners were directed to employ people in the construction of kilns and the burning of lime (the lime was given away to those who were ready to rebuild their homes) and to employ others to clear and prepare the fields for planting.

- To leave the people time to rebuild and repair their own homes damaged during the hurricanes, relief work was given on three days a week schedule only, except in individual cases.

- Seeds for planting were distributed freely in all districts.

- Wooden homes of a standard size were constructed for distribution throughout the islands; the lumber was cut to given dimensions by the Bahamas Cuban Lumber Company at their mills at Abaco, and it was a simple matter for the homes to be erected without employing skilled labour.

- The Deputy Civil Engineer was instructed to proceed on tour through those islands which were affected by the hurricanes to advise the Commissioners on the reconstruction of roads, wharves, and public buildings, and, if desired, to encourage the people on the need for a speedy rebuilding of their homes and churches.

- Competent and practical spongers were sent at The Bahamas Government's expense to the sponging grounds to report on the condition of the sponge beds (which, they feared, was severely impacted by the hurricane) and this was done to prevent vessels from making useless trips to the sponging grounds.

- To assist the owners of fishing and sponging vessels, a grant of £13,000 was loaned by the British Government in sums of £100 each in respect to any boat lost or severely damaged in these storms and the loan was required to be paid off after five years to help stimulate the local Nassau and Family Island economies.

Family Island Commissioners were instructed by the Governor Sir Harry Edward Spiller Cordeaux to begin work on the damaged and destroyed roads and government buildings to generate employment within the various communities throughout the islands. The clearing and preparing of the fields at the public expense was an unusual step, but the Governor considered it to be justified in this peculiar set of circumstances that existed after these hurricanes. The Great Nassau Hurricane of 1926 destroyed a growing number of crops in most of the islands. A second crop was immediately planted and was doing well when it too was destroyed by the Great Miami Hurricane of 1926 on September 17. The small farmers who made up the bulk of the population were so disadvantaged by this second disaster that they were abandoning their fields and seeking employment elsewhere. If matters were left to adjust themselves naturally, the Governor doubted whether any crops would be replanted for another year. This would result in the population being dependent on imported food, which, would besides increasing the cost of living, add significantly to the already difficult problem of transportation.

In addition to The Bahamas Government schemes for relief and reconstruction, private organizations assisted the people by the distribution of food, clothing, and water. In the meantime, private donations were received by the Hurricane Relief Committee, a semi-official body appointed by the Governor Sir Harry Cordeaux after the first hurricane. This body gave financial aid to persons in need after careful inquiry into each case. The contribution of £1,000 from Crown Funds, approval of which was conveyed to the Governor by the King of England via a telegram on the October 4, was gratefully accepted by the Hurricane Relief Committee and was much appreciated by the public.

CHAPTER THIRTEEN

The Great Okeechobee Hurricane of 1928's Impact on the Islands of The Bahamas and Florida

"On the sixteenth day of September, in the year of nineteen twenty-eight, God started riding early, and He rode very late. He rode out on the ocean, chained the lightning to His wheel, stepped on the land at West Palm Beach, and the wicked hearts did yield. In the storm, oh, in the storm, Lord, somebody got drowned. Got drowned, Lord, in the storm!"[89]

This storm was one of the greatest and deadliest hurricanes to impact the region even to this day. This storm was called the 'Great Okeechobee Hurricane of 1928' because it occurred during an era when meteorologists had not started the process of giving tropical storms and hurricanes assigned names. That process of naming storms never began until 1950 where they named storms after the military alphabet (e.g., Able, Baker, Charley, etc...) and then in 1953 they exclusively named storms after women. This however ended in the 1978 North Atlantic hurricane season. Shortly after that, they added men names to the list after vigorous complaints were registered by angry women from around the region to the World Meteorological Organization and the United States Government about the unfairness of this naming process to exclude men names from this list. As a result, in the 1979 North Atlantic hurricane season, these governing bodies finally gave in to their request and started naming hurricanes alternately between men and women.

---

[89] Elliot Kleinberg, *Black Cloud-The Deadly Hurricane of 1928*, (New York, Carroll & Graf Publishers 2003). Pg. 95.

During this era of not giving assigned names to storms, some major storms or very destructive and deadly storms were often named after the city or country they devastated followed by the year of occurrence. This hurricane was given the name the 'Great Okeechobee Hurricane of 1928' because it devastated the region around Lake Okeechobee in Florida. The term 'Great' was a standard term used in this era to classify storms of significant intensity. This meant it had sustained winds of 136 mph or higher. Today, it would be equivalent to a Category 4 hurricane on the Saffir-Simpson Hurricane Wind Scale. This term is no longer used after the introduction of the Saffir-Simpson Hurricane Wind Scale in the early 1970s.

In life, black migrant workers helped turn a South Florida swamp into a booming tropical mecca and one of the major agricultural areas of the United States. In death, they were pitched into an open trench and left to be ignored for three-quarters of a century, neglected and nearly forgotten for this time. To make it even worse, a sewer treatment plant and a slaughterhouse were built adjacent to the site, and a road was built over a section of the mass grave in Florida. You might ask yourself, why were these storm victims 'forgotten' in the archives of Bahamian and American history? First and foremost, this storm occurred during the 'Jim Crow Era' in the United States, a time when racial segregation was not only rampant in The Bahamas but in the United States as well and it was considered the norm to discriminate against the black population in these two countries. Blacks were often considered 'second class' citizens not only in The Bahamas but the United States as well. This played a vital role in the clean-up efforts in the United States because most of these storm victims were black migrant workers from The Bahamas.

Reasons for Bahamians migrating to Florida in the early 1900s:

- Bahamian migrant workers contributed to the higher proportion of farm workers in Florida and other southern states in the early to mid-1900s. Today that is mostly accomplished by persons from Central America, notably Mexicans and other members of the Hispanic race.

- To find employment working on the vegetable and citrus farms as migrant farm workers in Florida around the Okeechobee region.

- Working on the construction of the railroads and in the local hotels and other South Florida industries.

- Lack of sustainable employment opportunities in The Bahamas, especially on the Family Islands.

- Failure of major industries in The Bahamas, such as cotton, wrecking and salvaging, turtle exports, pineapples, tomatoes, sisal, salt, and sponging.

The Impact of the Great Okeechobee Hurricane of 1928 on the Islands of The Bahamas:

- In The Bahamas, significant damage occurred to shipping in the Nassau Harbour, and many schooners, such as *Carkum* and *Capt Charley*, and some other mailboats, were destroyed by the hurricane. Some of the mailboats that were destroyed were, San Salvador's mailboat *Guanahani* and the Andros Island's mailboat, *The William Carlos*. The Mayaguana's mailboat *Non-Such* sank in the Nassau Harbour, opposite Malcolm's Park.

- In The Bahamas, the western portion of Trinity Wesleyan Methodist Church roof was torn away. The roof of St. Mary's Church on Virginia Street, and Wesley Church in Grant's Town also suffered some damage. The northern half of the Higgs' sponge shed near the sponge exchange was blown away. The roof was blown away from the Munson Steamship Line building on Bay Street during the storm.

- On Cat Island, significant damage was reported as many roads, bridges and homes were destroyed. In Arthur's Town, the Public Wharf, the doctor's residence, churches, and about 100 homes were destroyed. In the Bight alone, about 60 houses were severely damaged or destroyed. Many roads were either washed away or rendered impassible after the storm.

- On the island of Eleuthera, the storm destroyed 128 homes, and an additional 154 were severely damaged. At Harbour Island alone, it was reported that about 95 houses, including a few churches such as the Church of England, were severely damaged or destroyed.

- The island of Bimini reportedly sustained winds of 140 mph during the peak of the storm. Significant damage was reported to several buildings, and nearly every home on the island was damaged or destroyed.

Damages reported in the State of Florida after the Great Okeechobee Hurricane of 1928:

(1) Damage at Cromer Block (2) Damage at Delray Motor Co-Ford Agency (3) Damage at Delray Laundry (4) Damage at Casa Del Rey Hotel (Images courtesy of NOAA-NHC).

- Early on September 17, the storm made landfall near West Palm Beach, Florida with winds more than 145 mph making it a Category 4 hurricane on the Saffir-Simpson Hurricane Wind Scale. In the city, more than 1,711 homes were destroyed. Elsewhere in the county, the impact was severest around Lake Okeechobee.

- The storm surge caused water to pour out of the southern edge of the lake, flooding hundreds of square miles as high as 20 feet above the ground.

- Numerous houses and buildings were swept away in the cities of Belle Glade, Canal Point, Chosen, Pahokee, and South Bay.

- After this storm, the Herbert Hoover Dike was built around the lake to prevent future devastations like this one from occurring from a hurricane ever again in the USA.

The hurricane passed over the eastern shore of Lake Okeechobee in South Florida, causing terrible flooding in the towns of Pahokee, Canal Point, Chosen, Belle Glade, and South Bay, killing many of these black migrant workers in the process. The cleanup efforts in the state of Florida after the hurricane was assigned to the blacks and the degrading and often challenging task of retrieving the dead bodies from the lake, swamps, and anywhere else they were found. The job was a difficult one because many of the corpses were rapidly decomposing and, in some cases, the workers had to use fishing hooks and lines to extract the bodies from the lake and swamps. These black workers were simply given strong whiskey with no pay to help them carry out this difficult task. The dead black storm victims were basically gathered up with little or no documentation and buried in mass graves or simply burned wherever they were found. The white storm victims, on the other hand, were also collected and were placed in a holding area for twelve to twenty-four hours. They had the advantage of having their families pay their last respects to them. Furthermore, they were given proper burials in marked graves in the local 'whites only' Woodlawn Cemetery, and in many instances, their names were-documented in an official registry.

The chances are good that you have never heard of the Great Lake Okeechobee Hurricane of 1928, or if you have, it has long been forgotten in distant memory. Numerous books and papers have been written on the Great Galveston Hurricane of 1900, Hurricane Katrina, Hurricane Andrew, and many other notable storms. Even the *Titanic's* sinking has been portrayed on film. Sadly, the Okeechobee's storm, the second largest USA's peace-time calamity in terms of loss of lives, have been neglected. Now, for possibly the first time, you may learn about all aspects of this storm and from a meteorological perspective of what it was like to experience such a cataclysm.

One word adequately describes this hurricane, and that is 'hell.' This storm became a raging inferno of rolling, swirling waters, of shrieking, demonic winds, lashing rain, and darkness, black and absolute. There were no atheists that night on the shores of Okeechobee, because, for those still living, came the second phase of hell. The period of absolute desolation and despair came next. That was followed by persons searching in the flooded woods and marshes, in elder clumps and saw grass for the horrible remains of family members, friends, and neighbours. Then came the dark process of loading them into trucks by unending scores. Then began the final process of burning them in heaps of dozens when they could no longer transport them, and this was due in part to their advanced stage of decomposition. It is hard to know which hell was worse. Those who have experienced this storm firsthand have endeavored to erase the recollections from their memories.

Its extensive exposed coastline, uniquely flat land, shallow coastal waters, and the massive Lake Okeechobee make it perfect for growing fruits and vegetables but prone to hurricane surge. Much of its existing land was originally a swamp. Perhaps that's the way we should have left it—pristine, remote, full of wildlife, and very susceptible to hurricanes. Today, it is fair to say that it is too late for that now, with the significant developments taking place in the state of Florida over the recent years. Most of the land in Florida is within sixty miles of the ocean, making it and everything built on it extremely vulnerable to the ravages of hurricanes and the accompanying storm surge. Florida's exploding population is a significant concern for hurricane planners. Consider this, every day 600 people move into the state of Florida alone, and 220,000 per year move into the coastal areas of Florida, and sadly, most of these new Florida residents have little or no hurricane experience. Nearly all the state's residents live in or near coastal zones, which exacerbates the hurricane threat. Gusting winds coming from the ocean don't get much of a chance to slow down over Florida's flat, smooth, swampy landscape before impacting residents and their property. Florida's coastline is the most densely populated area of the state.

Unfortunately, hurricane waves have pounded every portion of Florida's coast. Florida's hurricanes have long been a significant factor in the overall vitality of the state. At times, storms have changed the course of Florida's growth, development, and history. The first changes likely occurred when Florida's indigenous peoples learned how to adapt their living conditions to the threat of hurricanes. Many of Florida's economic woes have been associated with big storms. In modern times, Florida's agricultural and tourism industries have sometimes faltered with the passage of major hurricanes. In 1992, Hurricane Andrew ravaged South Florida, temporarily crippled the state's home insurance industry by inflicting over $26.5 (1992 USD) billion in damages, causing many insurers to pull out of the state of Florida.

This storm occurred in 1928 when racism was not only deeply entrenched-it was the norm, and that played a significant role in the impact of the storm. To put it quite frankly, blacks were second-class citizens in their own country, and it was even worse for the foreign migrant workers. In the heart of the black community, and among some of the oldest neighbourhoods in the city of West Palm Beach, at the intersection of Tamarind Avenue and 25th Street, sits a large 1-1/2-acre lot containing the remains of some 674 unidentified men, women, and children; victims of the Great Okeechobee Hurricane. At the Port Mayaca Cemetery in Martin County, another stone marker was placed over a mass grave of about 1,600 victims. Near the Belle Glade Public Library in downtown Belle Glade, a beautiful memorial stands as a remembrance of the deadly storm and its devastation. They were farmers and migrant farm labourers of western Palm Beach County. Mostly blacks from The Bahamas, they were segregated even in death and were interred without coffins, as coffins were reserved for whites only.

In Florida, although the hurricane destroyed everything in its path with impartiality, the death toll was by far highest in the poor areas in the low-lying grounds right around Lake Okeechobee. Black workers did most of the cleanup, and the few caskets available for burials were mostly used for the bodies of whites; other bodies were either burned or buried in mass graves. Burials were segregated, and the only mass grave site to receive a memorial contained only white bodies.

About 35 miles to the east, in West Palm Beach, is Tamarind Avenue. At the corner of Tamarind and 25th Street is a field enclosed by a chain-link fence. For three-fourths of a century, no marker noted the fact that over seven hundred people lay entombed under the street. Treated as second-class citizens in life, they became genuinely invisible in death when racial tensions forced them not to get a proper burial. They are the faceless dead of the Great Okeechobee Hurricane of 1928. The inequity has caused ongoing racial friction that still exists. The effects of the hurricane on black migrant workers are dramatized in Zora Neale Hurston's world-famous bestselling novel 'Their Eyes Were Watching God.'

Some 80 years later, community leaders such as, Robert and Dorothy Hazard and others came together and worked to have the site beautified and registered as a National Historic Landmark, ensuring the site and the dignity of those who died in Florida's most deadly hurricane is preserved. In total, the hurricane killed over 4,118 people and caused around $100 million (over $1.46 billion 2018 US dollars) in damages throughout its path. This hurricane was the deadliest weather disaster in The Bahamas history and the second deadliest hurricane in US history. It occurred before hurricanes, and tropical storms were named, and so they in some circumstances were named instead by the country, city or area they hit and caused the greatest devastation.

As the winds howled in the Glades on September 16, 1928, black migrant workers huddled, wept and prayed, and while they stared into the darkness, "their eyes were watching God," Zora Neale Hurston wrote. One of Florida's bestselling authors, Zora Neale Hurston described the mass burial in her 1937 classic novel 'Their Eyes Were Watching God':- "Don't let me ketch none uh Y'all dumpin' white folks, and don't be wastin' no boxes on coloured," a guard in the book says. "They's too hard tuh git ahold of right now." In this book, Hurston also describes how a character in the book, Tea Cake, and other black workers laboured to bury the hurricane dead in two giant pits. White supervisors made sure the labourers checked each of the swollen, discoloured bodies as carefully as possible to make sure whites went in the correct hole and blacks in the other.[90]

Zora Neale Hurston (January 7, 1891 – January 28, 1960) was an American folklorist, anthropologist, and author. Of Hurston's four novels and more than 50 published short stories, plays, and essays, she is best known for her 1937 book Their Eyes Were Watching God. In addition to new editions of her work being published after a revival of interest in her

[90] Zora Neale Hurston, *Their Eyes Were Watching God*, (New York, Harper Perennial Publishers, 1937). Pg. 205.

in 1975, her manuscript Every Tongue Got to Confess (2001), a collection of folktales gathered in the 1920s, was published posthumously after being discovered in the Smithsonian Archives.

Hurston wasn't at Lake Okeechobee, or even in Florida when the winds and surge took the lives of so many black men, women, and children. Much of her narrative of that night was based on her experience with a powerful hurricane in The Bahamas called, the 'Great Bahamas Hurricane of 1929' or the 'Great Andros Island Hurricane of 1929.' This storm lasted over The Bahamas for three consecutive days and resulted in the deaths of 142 persons and destroyed hundreds of homes. Many of the people she spoke with were also described in this work. But she immortalized the hurricane just as she captured the lives and humanity of mid-twentieth-century black Americans. This book was made into a movie starring Halle Berry, who starred as the main character, Janie. It was a made-for-TV movie, which aired for the first time on March 6, 2005, and was produced and developed by Quincy Jones and Oprah Winfrey. The TV movie was watched by an estimated 24.6 million viewers, further entrenching the novel in the public consciousness and the American literary canon. Zora Neale Hurston encountered this hurricane in The Bahamas while she researched this book.

From New Orleans, she travelled to South Florida and on to The Bahamas. Her stay in The Bahamas was devoted mostly to the collection of native folk songs and learning about the Jumping Dance. Hurston called on the memory a few years later to develop and duplicate the terror in her Everglades hurricane in this her most famous book, which was based on the Great Okeechobee Hurricane, which struck Florida in 1928 and caused severe flooding. She repeated her trips to The Bahamas during the latter part of the 1920s and early 1930s. Today, this book is widely regarded as a literary masterpiece.

During her life, Huston had limited success in the literary world. She died in obscurity, but there has been a resurgence of interest in her writing after her death in 1960, and she has finally taken her place among America's most influential black writers. She was staying in The Bahamas when a powerful hurricane struck these islands. Inspired partly by that experience and partly by the end of a romantic relationship, she later wrote, 'Their Eyes Were Watching God' in Haiti. In her autobiography, Dust Tracks on the Road, she said Their Eyes Were Watching God "was dammed up in me." She wrote it in seven weeks. It was published in 1937. The story takes some liberties. For example, it described winds of an unrealistic 200 mph, and it perpetuates the legend of the Seminoles fleeing the storm before everyone else because they saw the sawgrass blooming. Otherwise, Hurston does give an accurate account of the storm's slow, but steady assault and its deadly aftermath.

Their Eyes Were Watching God did not draw significant attention to the legacy of the Great Okeechobee Hurricane. Perhaps this is because it came out nearly a decade later, after the Great Labour Day Hurricane of 1935 and others had created all-new stories of horror, or on the other hand, perhaps because, as with many news events, people move on to the next one. And probably because, while the storm was the mechanism that formed the climax of the book, it was the characters, not the weather, that people remembered

Coffins being transported to West Palm Beach, Florida for Mass Burial in Woodlawn City Cemetery (Courtesy of Florida State Archives).

Early on the evening of September 16, a powerful Category 4 storm, with sustained winds of more than 140 mph, roared ashore both in The Bahamas and in South Florida. Storm surge or better yet, lake surge of 12 to 25 feet inundated the whole of Lake Okeechobee region, as well as other portions of the nearby Florida coast, according to a National Hurricane Center (NHC) historical accounts. These tides were primarily responsible for 'at least 2,500' deaths (with an estimate of that total comprised of about 1,400 Bahamian migrant workers killed in the Okeechobee region) attributed to the storm.

The lack of weather forecasting and detection technology, such as weather satellites, high-speed supercomputer modelling systems, and radar now used to track hurricanes, meant that there wasn't as much warning for the Okeechobee residents as there would be for those in hurricane-prone areas now. However, warnings were issued by what was then known as the Weather Bureau. The real problem, according to a NOAA analysis: "Many didn't heed the warnings, preferring instead to continue their daily lives as if there was not an approaching Category 4 hurricane of gigantic proportions." It didn't help either that the weather Bureau advised the residents of Florida that the hurricane would not pose a threat to them, but would more than likely it turn northeastwards harmlessly into the Atlantic Ocean.

The Greatest and Deadliest Bahamian Hurricanes on Record

Year	Hurricane	Category	Deaths
1500	The Vicente Yáñez Pinzón Hurricane or the Crooked Island Hurricane of 1500	Unknown	2 ships lost with entire crew
1559	The Don Tristan de Luna y Arellano Hurricane of 1559	Unknown	7 of 13 ships lost with entire crew of at least 1,2340 persons
1563	The Hurricane of 1563	Unknown	35 persons
1589	The Hurricane of 1589	Unknown	410 persons
1609	The Sea Venture Hurricane of 1609	Unknown	32 persons
1622	The Atocha Hurricane of 1622	Unknown	~1090 persons
1623	The Hurricane of 1623	Unknown	~400 persons
1657	The Hurricane of 1657	Unknown	~644 persons
1715	The Hurricane of 1715	Unknown	1,000 persons
1800	The Lowestoffe Hurricane of 1800	Unknown	5 persons
1806	The Great Coastal Hurricane of 1806	Unknown	207 persons
1813	The Hurricane of 1813	Unknown	3 persons
1832	The Hurricane of 1832	Unknown	52 persons
1837	The Hurricane of 1837	Unknown	45 persons
1853	The Hurricane of 1853	Unknown	12 persons
1856	The Hurricane of 1856	Unknown	4 persons
1866	The Great Bahamas Hurricane of 1866	4	387 persons
1871	The Hurricane of 1871	3	23 persons
1883	The Bahamas-North Carolina Hurricane of 1883	2	109 persons
1899	The Great San Ciriaco Hurricane of 1899	4	~334 persons
1908	Hurricanes #6 & #8 of 1908	3	134 persons
1918	The Great Florida Keys Hurricane of 1918	4	'At least-95 persons'
1926	The Great Nassau Hurricane of 1926	4	~258-268 persons
1926	The Great Miami Hurricane of 1926	4	~123 persons
1928	**The Great Okeechobee Hurricane of 1928**	4	**~4,118 persons in total but ~1,400 persons of Bahamian origins**
1929	The Great Bahamas of 1929	4	142 persons
1932	The Great Abaco Hurricane of 1932	5	18 persons
1933	The Great Bahamian Hurricanes of 1933	5	20 persons
1941	The 1941 Florida Hurricane	3	4 persons
1942	Tropical Storm #10 of 1942	Tropical Storm	10 persons
1945	The Great Homestead Hurricane of	4	2 persons

	1945		
1965	Hurricane Betsy	5	1 person
1992	Hurricane Andrew	5	3 persons
1999	Hurricane Floyd	5	2 persons
2004	Hurricane Frances	4	1 person
2005	Hurricane Wilma	5	1 person
2007	Hurricane Noel	1	1 person
2012	Hurricane Sandy	3	2 persons
2015	Hurricane Joaquin	4	No deaths
2016	Hurricane Matthew	5	No deaths
2017	Hurricane Irma	5	No deaths

The Greatest and Deadliest Bahamian Hurricanes on Record (Courtesy of NOAA-NHC, HURDAT, Wikipedia, Bahamas House of Assembly Hurricane Reports, Family Island Commissioner's Hurricane Reports (CO23), Bahamas National Archives Birth/Death Records...)...(~ means 'approximate totals' where exact totals are not known).

Meteorological History of the Great Okeechobee Hurricane of 1928

On September 6, ships reported a tropical depression developing just off the west coast of Africa near Dakar, Senegal. The next day, a ship reported winds of 60 mph or tropical storm status; on this basis, the Atlantic hurricane reanalysis project estimated that the system attained tropical storm status late on September 6. However, lack of observations for several days prevented the system from being classified in real time as it generally moved westward across the Atlantic Ocean. On September 10, the *S.S. Commack* first observed the storm about 900 miles to the east of Guadeloupe, which at the time was the most easterly report of a tropical cyclone ever received through ship's radio. Later that day, two other vessels confirmed the intensity of the storm, and the Hurricane Research Division estimated it strengthened into a hurricane at 2 pm EDT on September 10.

As the storm neared the Lesser Antilles, it continued to intensify. Between 1:30 pm EDT and 2:30 pm EDT on September 12, the hurricane's eye moved over Guadeloupe with a barometric pressure of 940 millibars (28.00 inches), suggesting maximum sustained winds of 140 mph, or Category 4 on the Saffir–Simpson Hurricane Wind Scale. While continuing a west-northwest track, the hurricane passed about 10 miles south of Saint Croix before approaching Puerto Rico. On September 13, the 15 miles eye crossed Puerto Rico in eight hours from the southeast to the northwest, moving ashore near Guayama and exiting between Aguadilla and Isabela. A ship near the southern coast reported a pressure of 931 millibars (27.5 inches), and the cup anemometer at San Juan reported sustained winds of 160 mph before it was destroyed by the hurricane's strong winds. As the wind station was 30 miles north of the storm's center, winds near the landfall point were unofficially estimated as high as 200 mph. On this basis, the hurricane is believed to have landfall in Puerto Rico as a Category 5 hurricane on the Saffir-Simpson Hurricane Wind Scale, although there was uncertainty in the peak intensity, due to the large size and slow movement.

After emerging from Puerto Rico, the hurricane had weakened to winds of about 140 mph, based on a pressure reading of 941 millibars (27.8 inches) at Isabela. The storm brushed the northern coast of Hispaniola while moving west-northwestward, gradually restrengthening. On September 15, it passed within 35 miles of Grand Turk, by which time the winds increased to 155 mph. The storm continued through The Bahamas as a strong Category 4 hurricane, passing near Nassau at 5 am EDT on September 16. Initially, Richard Gray of the U.S. Weather Bureau was optimistic that the storm would spare the South Florida region. However, at 8 pm EDT on September 17, the massive hurricane made landfall in southeastern Florida near West Palm Beach with estimated winds of 145 mph. This was based on a pressure reading of 929 millibars (27.4 inches) in the city, which at the time was the lowest central pressure reading in the United States. This record broke the previous record of 935 millibars (27.6 inches) set during the 1926 Great Miami hurricane, and peak gusts were estimated near 160 mph at Canal Point.

The hurricane quickly weakened as it progressed inland and moved over Lake Okeechobee, although the large size allowed it to maintain hurricane status for several more days. Late on September 17, the hurricane recurved to the northeast and passed near Jacksonville early the next day with winds of 75 mph. At 3 am EDT on September 18, the storm once again reached open waters. Later that day, the hurricane restrengthened slightly over open waters, making a second United States landfall near Edisto Island, South Carolina at 3 pm EDT with winds of 85 mph. Accelerating northeastward, the system quickly weakened into a tropical storm over North Carolina. On September 19, the storm evolved into an extratropical cyclone, although it restrengthened slightly to hurricane status. The hurricane turned to the north-northwest, moving quickly through the eastern United States. On

September 21, the former hurricane dissipated over Ontario, having merged with another disturbance.

The San Felipe II-Great Okeechobee Hurricane as it is commonly called was a classic 'Cape Verde-type' hurricane that was first detected over the tropical Atlantic. It was remembered as the San Felipe II Hurricane because the eye of the cyclone made landfall on the Christian feast day of Saint Phillip; the Latin American custom, since the Spanish colonial era began in 1492, was to name these storms upon their arrival after Catholic religious feast days. It was called "Segundo" (Spanish for "the Second") because of the eerie similarity in devastation with another hurricane which made landfall in Puerto Rico on that very same day 52 years earlier. This hurricane caused heavy casualties and massive destruction along its path from the Leeward Islands to Florida.

The worst tragedy occurred at inland Lake Okeechobee in Florida, where the hurricane caused Lake Surge of up to 9 to 15 feet that inundated the surrounding areas. The hurricane tracked across Lake Okeechobee's northern shore, causing the shallow waters to reach heights of more than 15 feet. The surge was forced southward, causing terrible flooding in the lowlands at the lake's south end, a region farmed primarily by migrant workers, most of them comprised of Bahamian migrant workers. To prevent future similar disasters, dikes were built around the lake by the U.S. Corps of Engineers.

After the hurricane, the Florida State Legislature formed the "Okeechobee Flood Control District." The organization was authorized to cooperate with the U.S. Army Corps of Engineers in actions to prevent this disaster from happening again. U.S. President Herbert Hoover visited the area personally and afterward; the Corps designed a new plan incorporating construction channels, gates, and levees. Approximately, 2,500 persons died in Florida, mainly due to Lake Surge but the unofficial count was much higher because more bodies and skeletons were discovered in later years. Of this total, about 75% were blacks, many of which were working on the railroads and as farm workers who were ill-served by the rudimentary emergency management of those segregated times. An additional 312 people died in Puerto Rico, and 18 more were reported dead in The Bahamas. Damage to property was estimated at $50,000,000 in Puerto Rico and $25,000,000 in Florida.

In 1928, the death toll in the United States was subdivided into two categories, whites and Negroes or coloured. The fact that racial distinction was made in classifying the death toll was very significant for those living in The Bahamas. The non-white population suffered considerably more than the white population in most areas. In 1928 in southern Florida, it can be speculated that the more affluent white population of South Florida in 1928 may have been more at risk from hurricanes than the non-white population. This is because these persons lived in more expensive homes on or near the water, thus being more susceptible to the storm surge. On the other hand, whites were more at risk because of automobile ownership, because many fatalities occurred as residents of Miami Beach tried to drive back to the mainland during the lull in the eye of the hurricane, many victims were swept into the bay and drowned as the wind and seas returned on the opposite side of the eye. However, such speculation must be balanced by the known fact that non-whites of that era often lived in substandard housing, which would be very susceptible to hurricane-force winds.

The extent of The Bahamian influx to Florida's new tourist town was revealed in the United States census reports. Miami had only a few hundred people when it was incorporated as a city in 1896. By 1900, the population had increased to 1,681, including a sizable number of black immigrants from The Bahamas. Over the next twenty years, the Bahamian influx helped to swell the population. By 1920, when Miami's population stood at 29,571, the foreign-born made up one-quarter of the total population. More than sixty-five percent of Miami's foreign-born residents were blacks from the West Indies. Black Islanders, almost all from The Bahamas, totaled 4,815. They comprised fifty-two percent of all Miami's blacks and 16.3 percent of the city's entire population. By 1920, Miami had a larger population of black immigrants than any other city in the United States.

The story of how Miami became a destination for black immigrants from The Bahamas begins early in Florida history. Bahamian Blacks had been familiar with Florida's lower east coast, and particularly the Florida Keys, long before the building up of the Miami area. In the early nineteenth century, when Florida was isolated and undeveloped, South Florida was commonly frequented by Bahamian fishermen, wreckers, and seamen, as well as traders who dealt with Seminole Indians. Many black Bahamians first arrived in the islands from Florida as slaves of the 3,200 British Loyalist who fled after the American Revolution. Still later, in the early nineteenth century, numbers of Seminole blacks from Florida settled on Andros Island. But a reverse migration had also begun to take place by the mid-nineteenth century.

Unlike the rest of the British West Indies, plantation agriculture was never successful or profitable in The Bahamas. Only about two percent of the total Bahamian land area of about 4,000 square miles was considered suitable for crops. Most nineteenth-century Bahamians earned a livelihood from the sea or subsistence agriculture. By the 1830s, black and white Bahamians were beginning to migrate to the Florida Keys, especially Key West, where they worked in fishing, wreckage and salvaging, sponging, and turtling industries. Facing little economic prospects at home, free Bahamian blacks found better employment opportunities in Key West. By 1892, 8,000 of the 25,000 people in Key West were Bahamians and sponging were their mainstay.

Most Key West blacks can trace their ancestry to Bahamian origins. By the late nineteenth century, the second stream of Bahamian blacks had begun arriving on Florida's lower east coast for seasonal work in the region's emerging agricultural industry. As a result, after 1890 these newcomers from The Bahamas served as an early migrant labour force in Florida agriculture. The scrubby pine and oolitic limestone topography of South Florida were like that of The Bahamas Islands. The Bahamians 'knew how to plant' on the Florida land, and they brought in 'their own commonly used trees, vegetables, and fruits.' Thus, they demonstrated to Native American planters the rich agricultural potential of what seemed at first a bleak and forbidding land. In Florida, the Bahamian newcomers found jobs in a variety of occupations and activities. The Bahamians were noted for their masonry skills. They were adept at building with oolitic limestone common to The Bahamas and South Florida. Thus, Bahamian blacks who came to Miami after its founding in 1896, found work in the burgeoning construction industry. As Flagler pushed his railroad south into the Keys, some clearing, and grading work was assigned to Bahamians.

The Bahamians also worked in local lumber yards and gravel pits, as stevedores on the docks, in the rail yards and terminals in the city, and more generally, as day labourers in whatever jobs could be found in Florida's growing economy. Most of the Bahamian newcomers were men, but the emergence of Miami as a tourist resort provided unique job opportunities for Bahamian women, primarily as maids, cooks, and laundry and service workers in the city's new hotels and restaurants. Also, Bahamians worked as domestic servants and caretakers for wealthy whites with permanent or winter residences in Miami. However, most of The Bahamian workers worked extensively in the citrus groves and vegetable fields. The census at the time suggested that these workers were mostly young, single Bahamian men living in boarding houses. The boom years of the 1920s brought tremendous population growth and urban development to South Florida from The Bahamas.

The Lake Okeechobee region in Florida in the late 1920s was a new and sparsely populated frontier. Only within ten years or so had the Everglades region near Lake Okeechobee had been drained to expose the fertile black muck soil for agriculture. Many Bahamian blacks and other non-white persons had come to or were brought to the Lake Okeechobee region to live and provide field labour. The lake itself, a large but very shallow lake on average less than 15 feet deep, was partially surrounded by a levee from 5 to 9 feet above the ground. The hurricane moved ashore in Palm Beach County on the evening of 16 September 1928, only two years after the Great Miami Hurricane of 1926 devastated Miami. Damages from this hurricane were estimated around $25 million, which, normalized for population, wealth, and inflation, would be around $16 billion today. It passed over the eastern shore of Lake Okeechobee, causing terrible flooding in the towns of Pahokee, Canal Point, Chosen, Belle Glade, and South Bay.

It was estimated that many of the storm victims lost in the flood waters and probably three-quarters or more were non-white field workers, and of that total, three-quarters were determined to be Bahamian farm and railway workers. This total is significant because this would make the Great Okeechobee Hurricane of 1928 the deadliest hurricane to impact The Bahamas indirectly with such a massive death toll. The exact number of those who perished in the Great Okeechobee Hurricane can never be determined. The Miami Daily News on September 25 gave a death toll of 2300 persons who died in the storm, the Red Cross gave a total of 1810 persons, and many other newspapers gave sums ranging from 1800 to 2350 persons. However, the official National Weather Service death toll was 1,836 persons. Then in 2003, on the 75th anniversary of the hurricane, this total was revised to 'at least 2,500 persons', making the Great Okeechobee Hurricane the second-deadliest natural disaster in United States history a record that still stands to this day.

The exact number of those who perished in the hurricane can never be determined because 75% of those blacks who died were Bahamian migrant workers and it was complicated by the fact that most of them were known, even to their friends, only by a nickname. Another reason the number cannot be determined because many persons were carried away by the flood waters far into the sawgrass wastes. Furthermore, after the storm, a considerable amount of time and effort was made in returning this state to some degree of normalcy and recover financially in the aftermath of the hurricane. The reasoning behind this lack of apathy to these victims was because officials were not focused on trying to obtain an 'official' death toll and recording the names of the black victims. As a result, many bodies and skeletons were simply buried without any documentation in makeshift mass graves because they were too many to count, too decomposed to identify, and rotting so quickly that they had to be burned and buried in mass graves. This process was done to prevent the spreading of disease and contamination from the dead bodies. As a result, many of the black bodies didn't even get a decent funeral, whereas, the white bodies did, and the black victims were buried without trying to find the names or contacts of the black bodies. Also, many bodies and skeletons were also discovered years later thereby increasing the death toll even more.

Damages sustained on the major islands of The Bahamas during the Great Okeechobee Hurricane of 1928

Nassau

After the storm, 10-year-old Hilda May Sturrup died when she ventured outside and fell into an open trench filled with water and drowned. The death toll in The Bahamas from this hurricane was reported to be 18 persons. Many persons were severely injured and had to be taken to the hospital for treatment. Significant damage occurred to the shipping sector in the Nassau Harbour and many schooners such as *Carkum,* and *Capt Charley.* Some mail boats were wrecked and destroyed by the hurricane's strong winds and storm surge. Some of the mail boats that were destroyed were, the San Salvador's *Guanahani,* and the Andros Island mailboat, *The William Carlos* and Mayaguana's mailboat *Non-Such* sank in the Nassau Harbour opposite Malcolm's Park. A small harbour dredger sank in the Nassau Harbour and turned over. The five-masted schooner *Abaco* was blown out of the Harbour and sunk east of Athol Island. Several small boats sank opposite Malcolm's Park and over at Hog Island (now Paradise Island).

The heaviest sufferers in property damage were the churches. St Agnes in Grant's Town was completely unroofed and otherwise destroyed. St

John's Baptist Church on Meeting Street and the Mission House were destroyed after only being recently rebuilt after the 1926 hurricanes. The western portion of Trinity Wesleyan Methodist Church roof was torn away. The interior of the church was severely damaged when a flying missile smashed into the window of the west of the church causing the full force of the wind to rush into the building and tore away the roof. The Rev and Mrs. W.H. Richards and their daughter barely escaped death and had to take up refuge on the back verandah for some hours in the hurricane. This was because escaping from the building was nearly an impossible task because they were blocked in from both the back and front exits of the church by massive debris. Unfortunately, this was quite a devastating blow for them because the roof had only recently been repaired after the Great Nassau Hurricane of 1926.

This church was designed in England by Mr. Pockock, and Mr. Walsh of the Royal Engineers Department and Mr. H.J. McCartney was the builder. The architecture is gothic, and its' roof being very sharp, and it was destroyed both in the 1866 and 1926 hurricanes. After being destroyed in the Great Bahamas Hurricane of 1866, it was rebuilt in 1868 or thereabouts, in rebuilding, the height of the roof was reduced by 10 feet. The original building and the rebuilding together cost the legislature and £300 granted £14,000 and £250 by the conference and special collection in England. The roof of St. Mary's Church, Virginia Street and Wesley Church in Grant's Town also suffered significant damage. Wesley Church in Grant's Town was completed in the year 1868, to replace a small wooden building which was destroyed along with many others by the hurricane which struck The Bahamas in 1866.

The roof and front verandah of Mr. R.B. Shepherd's home on West Hill Street were badly wrecked by a small porch, which flew in the air over from Mr. R.H. Curry's House on the opposite side of the street and smashed into it. The home of the Hon. Dr. G.H. Johnson who was away with his family in New York was also blown away. The roof of Dr. Fisher's house was blown away. The roof of Lucayan Garage on West Bay Street was swept away. Mr. J.E. Williamson, a movie studio executive, had several of his movie studio equipment badly damaged or destroyed by the storm. The roof of the Aurora Hall on East Hill and Charlotte Streets was blown away and the building collapsed. Mr. P.A Huyler's Black Smith Shop and Mr. C.E. Bethell's Wharf were destroyed, and Mr. P.C. Smith's sponge house was destroyed. Mrs. D. Sweeting's storeroom on Deveaux Street was destroyed. Mr. Morrison's sponge shed on Bay Street collapsed, and all his sponges were lost. Another sponge shed owned by Mr. C.E. Bethell was also destroyed, and the sponges in the shed were washed away by the storm.

The northern end of Mr. Chas L. Lofthouses' home on George Street was blown away. The southern roof of 'Blair' East Bay Street owned by Mr. R.H. Curry was blown over in Capt. Charley's yard. The roof of 'The Hermitage' was also destroyed. Government Hill was flooded to such an extent that the ballroom looked like a swimming pool. A part of the roof of the warehouse of the Home Furniture Company was blown away, and some of the furniture was damaged by water. Mr. Barton's tailor shop on Blue Hill Road collapsed. The two Government liquor bonded warehouses on the Southern Recreation Grounds, and the one at the rear of Mr. Edward Saunders's Store on Bay Street, were unroofed and Mr. R.T. liquor warehouse on Bay Street was also unroofed. The windows, doors and the furniture of the Fort Montague Hotel were severely damaged. The roof of the Royal Victoria Hotel was severely damaged, and the furniture significantly damaged most beyond repairs, while the British Colonial Hotel also suffered some damage. The gardens of all these hotels were damaged almost beyond recognition, and the building where the plants were stored at the British Colonial Hotel was blown onto the street.

Mr. J.L. Lightbourn's home on the top of Blue Hill Road was severely damaged. A portion of the south-western section of the prison wall was blown down. The front verandah of Mr. Victor Saunders' home on Shirley Street was blown away. The roof of Dr. Albury's home on George Street was badly damaged. The home of Mr. Jonah Cox on Cunningham Lane was almost destroyed. Several sheds on the Knowles Dairy Farm were destroyed, and the roof of the house was also damaged. Mr. H.S. Black and his family were forced to leave their home on Village Road during the hurricane because it was badly damaged, and the furniture destroyed. The bandstand on Rawson Square was demolished. The home of Mr. Thomas Murray was destroyed. Part of the roof was blown off the Church Hall, formally St. Hilda's High School.

The Upper Piazza of the building overhead Mr. W.M. Hilton Store was blown away. The upper back verandah of the Law Courts Building was blown away, and the building was flooded. Dr. Higgs building, east of the Botanical Station on East Bay Street, the upper verandah was blown away. The back porch, home of Mr. Rill Albury on West Bay Street, was blown away. Captain Allen Johnson's Garage and servant's quarters at the rear of Fort Charlotte was destroyed. The small house at the south of Mr. W.E. Fountain's old home on West Street, occupied by Mr. Jack Fountain, collapsed on a Buick car.

The northern half of the Higgs' sponge shed near the sponge exchange was blown away. The roof was blown away from the Munson Steamship Line building during the storm. The roof of the West India Oil Company on West Street was blown away. Mrs. Louis' O'Neil's house in Mason's Addition was blown away. Several buildings in Rainbow Village and Chippingham were severely damaged. In Fox Hill, many houses were damaged, but most of the damages occurred was to fruit-bearing trees. Some damage occurred to the buildings in the Grove Development, West Bay Street, but nothing of a significant nature. The southern district of the island was devastated, some homes were destroyed, while many more were badly damaged. No property owner on the island of Nassau has escaped entirely without suffering some loss.

This storm wasn't a very deadly hurricane in The Bahamas, but it became a notable hurricane when it brought to Nassau, Prince George, the youngest son of King George V and Queen Mary. He was serving with the British Royal Navy, and his ship was attached to the Bermuda and West Indies Station and was sent to aid a hurricane-prone colony. The excitement was great, as His Royal Highness was the first member of a British Royal Family to visit The Bahamas in almost seventy years, when Queen Victoria's youngest son, Prince Albert, spent a short time in Nassau. He, too, came in a ship of the Royal Navy. During this time, the new dock built off Rawson Square was given the name of the Prince George Wharf.[91]

Cat Island

Significant structural damage was reported to many of the roads, bridges, and homes. In Arthur's Town, the public wharf, the doctor's residence, churches, and about one hundred homes were destroyed. In The Bight, about sixty houses were severely damaged or destroyed. Many roads were either washed away or rendered impassible after the storm.

---

[91] Ronald Lightbourn & Valeria Moss, *Reminiscing, Memories of Old Nassau,* (Nassau, Media Publishing Ltd., 2001.) Pgs. 46-51.

Eleuthera

At Harbour Island, about ninety-five houses including, a few churches were severely damaged or destroyed. The government buildings were severely damaged but not destroyed. Fortunately, no lives were lost during the hurricane.

Exuma

The hurricane passed over the island with only slight damage reported.

Long Cay

No damage reported.

San Salvador

No lives were lost during the passage of the hurricane. Severe damages occurred to the properties in the district but not bad as initially expected. Four buildings were destroyed including two Baptist churches and many other buildings received slight damages. The sisal plantations and food crops were severely damaged.

Long Island

No major damage reported.

Rum Cay

There were sustained winds of 80 mph reported but fortunately, no lives were lost. Minor damages were reported to some houses, and most of the food crops were destroyed.

Bimini

Sustained winds of 140 mph were reported with significant damage to most of the buildings on the island.

Grand Bahama

The schooner *Nellie B. Nora* was driven ashore by the hurricane, and the bow split off from the rest of the boat. Three other ships were destroyed while; many other vessels were severely damaged. Docks belonging to Maury, Crawford, Ambrister, Bruce-Roberts, Claridge, and the Government Docks were all swept away. The dock belonging to DeGregory was the only one left standing. The roads were completely washed out, destroyed and rendered impassable. Most of the houses were either destroyed or severely damaged.

CHAPTER FOURTEEN

The Great Bahamas Hurricane of 1929 or the Great Andros Island Hurricane of 1929's Impact on the Islands of The Bahamas

Workers salvaging used timber amid the rubbles from ships destroyed in Nassau Harbour after the Great Bahamas Hurricane of 1929 (Courtesy of The Charles Whelbell Collection-Bahamas Department of Archives, Nassau, Bahamas).

A powerful hurricane can be terrifying. The darkened skies, the strong howling winds, and torrential rainfall can be traumatic. This hurricane in 1929 was particularly devastating to residents of The Bahamas. The sad reality is that when you talk about The Bahamas, you must speak of catastrophic storms, and when you speak about devastating hurricanes, you must talk about this hurricane in 1929 and its' impact on The Bahamas. The Great Bahamas Hurricane of 1929 (also known as the Great Andros Island Hurricane of 1929) was the second hurricane and the only major hurricane during the very inactive 1929 North Atlantic hurricane season. The storm was the only hurricane to cause any significant damage, resulting in $676,000 (1929 USD, $10.1 million 2019 USD) in damage. Only a year after the 1928 Okeechobee Hurricane, the hurricane caused only three deaths in southern Florida, a low number due to well-executed warnings. The hurricane was much more severe in The Bahamas, where damage was near extreme due to the hurricane stalling over the area for an extended period of 3 consecutive days.

The highlights of this massive storm:

- This storm killed 142 persons, and well over 5,000 persons were left homeless in New Providence (the population of New Providence in 1929 was approximately 13,000 persons). On this island, 456 houses were destroyed, and 640 were severely damaged. About 73% of all the homes and businesses in Nassau were destroyed in the hurricane.

- This storm lasted for three consecutive days in The Bahamas.

- Approximately 95% of all the churches in Nassau and all the churches in Andros were destroyed. About 77% of the Government's Annual Budgets in 1930 and 1931 were devoted to the rebuilding efforts from this hurricane.

- Approximately 70% of all the sponge vessels throughout The Bahamas were destroyed in this storm (the sponging industry was the number one industry of The Bahamas at the time).

- This storm was one of the main reasons why the government of The Bahamas switched from sponging to tourism as the number one industry of The Bahamas. It must be noted, however, that the primary reason for the decline of this industry was the sponge disease which decimated the sponge beds in 1938. This hurricane destroyed almost all the sponge warehouses, and 336 sponge vessels and twice that amount were severely damaged.

- This hurricane was the main reason why the first Bahamas building codes laws were implemented shortly after this storm. This was because of the significant damage and destruction that occurred to the buildings in New Providence and Andros. The Bahamas Government realized that these flimsy homes that were being constructed during that era were no match for the powerful storms in the late 1920s and early 1930s so, they implemented building codes to help mitigate the losses caused by these devastating hurricanes.

- The song "Run Come See Jerusalem" by Blind Blake was based on the destruction caused by this storm. Three boats bound for Andros, *The Ethel, Myrtle,* and *Pretoria,* were caught in the strong winds and rough seas of the storm. The *Pretoria* sunk, and 35 lives were lost when it sunk at the entrance of Fresh Creek Harbour Channel. Unfortunately, only three lives were saved from this ship, and they were Yorick Newton of Blanket Sound, Victor Spence of Small Hope Bay and Henley Brown of Blanket Sound. These 'lucky three,' as they were referred to at the time, swam ashore after the *Pretoria* capsized.

- This and other significant hurricanes of this era in the 1920s (3 in 1926, 1 in 1928, and 1 in 1929) and early 1930s (1 in 1932 and 4 in 1933) were the main reasons why the first Bahamas radio station ZNS 1540 am was introduced to the masses. This radio station was to be exclusively used as a hurricane warning station. Many residents throughout the Family Islands (especially the widows of Cat Island who lost their husbands and to a lesser extent their children to hurricanes led the charge). As a result, they bitterly complained and petitioned the then Bahamian Governors-Sir Charles William James Orr (1927-1932) and Sir Bede Edmund Clifford (1932-1934) and the King of England George V. They believed that if a radio station with a band width wide enough to encompass the entire Bahamas, it could prevent or reduce the significant number of deaths that were occurring in these hurricanes due to lack of warnings or knowledge of an impending storm. Because of their prolonged, determined, and vigorous complaints to these Bahamian Governors and King George V, on May 26, 1936, ZNS 1540 am radio station was built and went into operation. After the introduction of this radio station, the death toll significantly dropped, especially on the Family Islands. ZNS 1540 am radio station coverage encompassed the entire Bahamas from Grand Bahama in the north to Inagua in the south.

- Most Bahamians have heard or sang the song "Run Come See Jerusalem" at some point in time of their lives without even realizing the lyrics of this song were referring to or speaking about this devastating hurricane in 1929. This song was written about the impact of the Great Bahamas Hurricane of 1929, and today this song is known the world over thanks to a man by the name of Blind Blake.

Run, Come See Jerusalem
By *Alphonso 'Blind Blake' Higgs*

It was in nineteen hundred and twenty-nine,
Run come see, run come see,
I remember that day very well
It was in nineteen hundred and twenty-nine
Run come see, Jerusalem.
That day they were talkin' 'bout a storm on the islands
Run come see, run come see,
My God, it was a beautiful mornin'
Run come see, Jerusalem.

That day there were three ships leavin' out the harbour
Run come see, run come see,
It was the Ethel, the Myrtle and the Pretoria,
Run come see, Jerusalem.

These ships were bound for a neighbouring island
Run come see, run come see,
With mothers and children on board

Run come see, Jerusalem.

Now when the Pretoria was out on the ocean,
Run come see, run come see,
Rocking from side to side
Yes, the Pretoria was out on the ocean,
Run come see, Jerusalem.

My God, when the first wave hit the Pretoria
Run come see, run come see,
The mothers grabbin hold unto the children
When the first wave hit the Pretoria
Run come see, Jerusalem.

My God, there were thirty-three souls in the water
Run come see, run come see,
They were swimming and praying to the good Lord
There were thirty-three souls in the water
Run come see, Jerusalem.

My God, now George Brown he was the captain
Run come see, run come see,
He shouted my children now come pray
He said, "Come now, witness your judgment"
Run come see, Jerusalem.

It was in nineteen hundred and twenty-nine,
Run come see, run come see,
I remember that day very well
It was in nineteen hundred and twenty-nine
Run come see, Jerusalem.

Blind Blake (center) and his band The Royal Victoria Hotel 'Calypso' Orchestra seen here with two of his band mates (two not pictured) in this picture posing in the front the Silk Cotton Tree in The Royal Victoria Hotel Gardens at The Royal Victoria Hotel. (Image courtesy of Bob Davies/www.oldbahamas.com).

In 1951 a man by the name of Mr. Blake Alphonso Higgs better known by his stage name of 'Blind Blake' and his band the 'Royal Victoria Hotel "Calypso" Orchestra' consisting of Blind Blake, Dudley Butler, Chatfield Ward, Freddie Lewis and George Wilson recorded that song in 1951 on a vinyl record LP called 'A Group of Bahamian Songs.' This record was a hit record for years to follow because of popular songs like, 'Yes, Yes, Yes,' 'Pretty Boy,' 'Jones! Oh Jones', 'Watermelon Spoiling on the Vine' and the most popular and most recognized of them all was 'Run come see Jerusalem.' Most persons who now sing this song don't know that this song was based entirely on the destruction caused by the Great Bahamas Hurricane of 1929.

Today, it is one of the most recognized and recorded folk songs in The Bahamas. Today, this song has appeared in many movies, stage shows, plays, and television shows yet we seem to have lost the original message of the song that Blind Blake so vividly wrote and sang about in this hurricane. The ships *The Ethel, Myrtle* and *Pretoria* like many other ships at the time were real sailing boats that were sunk in this hurricane as they tried to sail from Nassau to Andros. The *Pretoria*, which was a 43-foot schooner built by Mr. Jeremiah Duncan Lowe Sr. of Marsh Harbour, sank at the entrance of Fresh Creek Harbour Channel.

Meteorological History of the Great Bahamas Hurricane of 1929

The second storm of the season originated from a tropical wave that developed near the Cape Verde Islands on September 11. The wave became a tropical depression at 8 pm EDT on September 19, while located about 300 miles north-northeast of Anegada in the British Virgin Islands. The depression drifted just north of due west while strengthening slowly, becoming a tropical storm early on September 22 and a hurricane at 8 pm at 22.0°N and 65.9°W, the second tropical storm of the 1929 hurricane season formed just to the North of Puerto Rico. Later that day, the storm curved northwestward. Around noon on September 23, it intensified into a hurricane. A blocking action to the north from a strong high-pressure system forced the hurricane to change course and to turn dramatically towards the southwest. While turning southwestward on the following day, the hurricane began to undergo rapid deepening. Late on September 25, the system peaked with maximum sustained winds of 155 mph, an estimate based on the pressure-wind relationship, with a minimum barometric pressure of 924 millibars (27.30 inches).

While crossing through The Bahamas, the storm struck Eleuthera, New Providence, and Andros, on September 25 and September 26, respectively. Late on September 27, the system weakened to a Category 3 hurricane and re-curved northwestward. At 9 am EDT the next day, the hurricane made landfall near Tavernier, Florida. The storm then entered the Gulf of Mexico and continued weakening, falling to Category 2 intensity late on September 28. While approaching the Gulf Coast of the United States, the hurricane weakened to a Category 1 hurricane. Early on October 1, it made landfall near Panama City Beach, Florida. A few hours later, the hurricane weakened to a tropical storm and then became extratropical over southwestern Georgia shortly after that. The remnants continued northeastward up the East Coast of the United States, until entering Canada and dissipating over Quebec early on October 5.

In The Bahamas, the hurricane brought strong winds and large waves to the archipelago and lasted for three consecutive days over the capital of

Nassau and the island of Andros. To this day, this hurricane was one of the most destructive storms to hit the islands of Andros and New Providence. In the capital city of Nassau, a weather station observed a wind gust of 164 mph. Within the city alone, 456 houses were destroyed, while an additional 640 houses suffered damage. Telegraph service was disrupted during the storm. There were 142 deaths in The Bahamas. Throughout The Bahamas and the Florida Keys, numerous boats and vessels were ruined or damaged. At the latter, strong winds were observed, with a wind gust up to 150 mph in Key Largo, Florida. However, damage there was limited to swamped fishing boats and temporary loss of electricity and communications.

Farther north, heavy rains flooded low-lying areas of Miami. A devastating tornado touched down in Fort Lauderdale and damaged a four-story hotel, a railway office building, and several cottages. In the Florida Panhandle, the storm surge destroyed several wharves and ruined most of the oyster and fishing warehouses and canning plants. Overall, there was approximately $2.36 million in damage and three deaths in Florida; eight others drowned offshore. Although a strong tropical cyclone, the hurricane caused little damage and only three deaths in Florida, a sharp contrast to the Okeechobee Hurricane a year earlier; by comparison, however, the damage was very severe in The Bahamas. In Cuba, the hurricane brought rough seas and dark cloud cover.

The impact of this storm on the islands of Andros and New Providence was tremendous. Had this hurricane continued its west-northwest track, The Bahamas would have been spared, but this dramatic southwest turn caused it to take a direct path over Nassau and then over Andros. Several significant events happened. First, it changed direction and decreased its forward speed, and this was one of the main reasons why it inflicted such great damage over these two islands. This storm dramatically slowed down to about 2 to 3 mph while increasing in strength to a Category 4 hurricane as the center of the cyclone passed over Nassau. The eye of the storm passed over Nassau at 8:30 pm EDT on September 25, but the calm lasted for at least two hours according to local reports, so this hurricane had quite some time pounding and devastating these islands with the strong winds and massive surge of the system. The lowest barometer reading at the time was 936.2 millibars or 27.65 inches at Nassau. This hurricane was a Category 4 storm when it passed over these two islands.

Damages sustained on the major islands of The Bahamas during the Great Bahamas Hurricane of 1929

Nassau

In The Bahamas, the hurricane destroyed the Ministry of Education mansion in Nassau, which was rebuilt shortly after the storm. Offshore, the wreckage of a steamship that sank during the storm was blown up because it was a hazard to shipping. In Florida, the damage from the hurricane knocked out rail service for a week. The United States Coast Guard provided mail service to Key West; an area hit hard by the hurricane. A special session was held by the House of Assembly from October 16-24, 1929, to assess damage and reconstruction needs. The members voted to support a measure authorizing expenditure to provide hurricane relief throughout the islands of The Bahamas.

It was reported that in Nassau, 456 houses were destroyed and 640 were damaged, and this comprised about seventy-three percent of all homes and businesses. Certain sections of the hospital were so severely damaged that they had to be demolished and rebuilt. Long Wharf was destroyed. The roof of the police barracks was blown off, and large sections of the prison roof were blown away. For their safety, 40 prisoners were released. The rebuilding of the prison was considered one of the costliest repairs. Potter's Cay was divided into two sections by the flood waters. There was a significant rise in the cost of food items and building supplies after the storm. After the hurricane, there was also a significant shortage of qualified carpenters throughout the island, and as a result, many of the skilled carpenters were charging exorbitant fees to get the work done. This forced the government to consider enacting new laws to prevent this practice from happening in the future.

The eastern wing of Government House was unroofed on three sides and damaged to the extent that it was not fit for occupancy. His Excellency the Administrator and the Hon. Mrs. Dundas were in grave danger throughout the storm by pieces of falling roof, debris, crumbling ceiling and flying timber when whole sections of Government House blew in. Immediately after the storm, work began to restore Government House to its former glory. Government House is the official residence of the Governor General of The Bahamas. Built on a hill known as Mount Fitzwilliam and completed in 1806, this imposing stuccoed-coral-rock building on Duke Street is the Bahamian archipelago's foremost example of Georgian Colonial architecture. In 1814, Colonel Don Antonio de Alcedo, a Spanish scholar and soldier, wrote admiringly of its effect. The Oriental Herald, in 1825, stated: "The new Government-House, standing on the centre of the ridge that overlooks the town, was built by a sum voted by the House of Assembly from the funds of the Treasury and cost upwards of £20,0000. It is built in the European style of architecture and is universally considered the best building of the kind throughout the West Indies."[92]

The building's original neoclassical aspect, as well as its stone construction, was directly influenced by the arrival of Loyalists from the southern United States in the 1780s. Previously most Bahamian buildings had been built of painted wood. Typically, Bahamian elements, however, include louvred wood shutters and brightly painted exterior, in this case a brilliant shade of conch pink. The primary façade, centred on a pedimented entrance supported by four stout Ionic columns, dates from the 1930s, when the building was remodelled following the Great Bahamas Hurricane of 1929.

Nine persons died in the capital of Nassau, and of the nine persons three died from drowning; the others died of various causes. Among the dead were Patrick Carr, age 34, an unidentified man buried by the police, and another unidentified man drowned in the hurricane. Martha Green, age 45, Nathaniel Dean at Delaporte. Nathaniel Dean drowned near Laboushire while attempting to obtain food from the next village for the people of Gambier, who had run out of supplies. Two additional unidentified bodies' locations unknown were taken to the hospital. An expedition was sent to Athol Island after the storm in the boat *Caroline*, headed by Dr. Cruickshank and Police Officer Lancaster. It was there that they found one death, 30 persons marooned, and several persons injured. Constable Thompson's baby was killed, and his wife's leg was broken while the family was fleeing from their home. Thompson had his wife on his arm and his baby on his back. The house fell at their heels; the baby was knocked from his back and crushed to death. Thompson took the limp body of his baby from under the debris and carried it away for a respectable burial.

---

[92] Wayne Neely, *The Great Bahamas Hurricane of 1929*, (Bloomington, iUniverse Publishing Inc., 2013).

In Nassau, there was destruction everywhere. Gardens, orchards, and fields were devastated and to make matters worse, this was the fifth hurricane in only three years to devastate The Bahamas. Few people throughout Andros and Nassau were unaffected. Crops everywhere were destroyed. Not a bird could be seen immediately after the hurricane. Robert "Robbie" Burnside, who oversaw the public gardens and the entire Bahamas Horticultural Department of the Public Works Department for years, was sent to Jamaica to obtain pairs of suitable wild birds to re-populate the bird life in New Providence.

Telephones were not operable, and telegraphs were also not able to be sent for quite a while after the storm. Also, the Board of Agriculture wrote to Jamaica and Trinidad, requesting a supply of an early maturing crop of vegetables commonly used in The Bahamas. This board also advised persons to plant the kind of vegetables they eat first before planting for sale in the market. Many telephones were so bent out of shape that they had to be replaced, and significant road repairs were required. Only a select few Out-Island settlements had wireless stations, and overseas telephone calls were a long way off in the future. Various governing bodies, such as the Infant Welfare Association, The Bahamas Humane Society, the Wesleyan Methodist Missionary Society and the Daughters of the Empire all organized significant relief for the victims of the storm.

The eastern wall of Fort Montague collapsed, and the canons tumbled down a considerable distance from where they were located. Western Esplanade was devastated after the storm, as several large rock boulders and mounds of sand were washed onto the main thoroughfare. Many of the coastlines throughout the island of New Providence were altered or destroyed, and many of the foreshores looked utterly different than they did before the storm. In many cases, the road itself had been eaten into and torn up, and debris large and small littered the highway. Everywhere along the route, battered and broken houses were to be seen on both sides of the road.

On Village and Fox Hill Roads, there was a trail of devastation as all the homes were destroyed. In some cases, there were still bits of furniture exposed among the debris. The telephone metal poles were also bent at right angles to the ground. Love and Charity Hall, one of the local meeting places, was reduced to rubbles. The Fox Hill fruit trees, which were both the pride and the primary source of living of the neighbourhood, were blown down and the fruits destroyed. On Hog Island (now called Paradise Island), the houses belonging to Mr. Philip Goster and Mr. Davis were swept away by the hurricane. The entire top of Mr. E.V. Solomon's home on East Bay Street was blown off. A stone house on East Street two or three hundred yards east of the Parade partly collapsed except for one room on the upper floor, which had no external wall to it.

Mr. Holmes' house on Bay Street was significantly damaged by water, and the strong winds of the hurricane destroyed the kitchen. The house of Ms. MacDonald, at the corner of East and Shirley Streets, lost part of its roof, including a dormer window that was blown right off. Mr. G.K.K. Brace's house, on the Montague Foreshore, lost its front porch. The new warehouse that was being erected on Charlotte Street for Mr. Damianos had reached the 'skeleton' stage when the storm struck it, and it collapsed on its struts. Mrs. Twynam's home in East Shirley Street had its roof blown off and the walls badly damaged. Two other houses owned and rented by Mrs. Twynam on Mackey Street were unroofed, and in both cases, the walls were severely damaged.

The sponge warehouse belonging to Mr. G. Christolulacis on Bay Street was destroyed. A sponge warehouse on Heathfield Street belonging to Mr. Th. Tiliacos was so severely twisted that it had to be taken down and rebuilt. Several houses on Shirley Slope were badly damaged, as have several of the garages there. Mr. Adams, who oversaw the Bahamas Industrial School, had his house damaged when a large tree fell on the roof. The tenants of Stirrup's cottage, near the Fort Montague Hotel, found themselves surrounded by flood waters and floating in their home during the storm; they eventually got into a boat and drifted into the house of Mr. Henderson Butler. The roof of 'The Hermitage' on the Coast Road several miles east of Nassau was reported to have been blown off. The residence of Mr. George Oliver on the Montague foreshore roof was blown off. The Wesleyan Day School in Grant's Town was considerably damaged. A two-story building owned by Mr. William Dorsett from 'Over-The-Hill' was destroyed. Home Furniture store on Bay Street was severely damaged, and some of the furniture was destroyed; others had to be sold at a reduced price.

The roof of Ebenezer Chapel was blown off. The roof of Trinity Methodist Church also blew off. Several small boats were blown out to sea or was smashed to bits and pieces on to East Bay Street. The roof of St. Ann's Church was blown off and the building destroyed. Two of the 'Jumper Churches' (Brother Eneas and Brother Stanley's churches) in Grant's Town were destroyed; two in the Freetown District were blown down and destroyed. The walls of Wesleyan Church's meeting place were destroyed, and the building itself was left-leaning, and the floodwaters drastically altered the inside. Salem Baptist Church on Parliament Street had its frontage badly torn, and there was a gaping hole on top of the building. For a while after the storm, the services were conducted in the ruins of the church under a torn roof.

The walls and the roof of Zion Baptist Church fell in, and the structure itself was destroyed. After the storm, the congregation of Zion Baptist Church on East and Shirley Streets had to worship for months at Aurora Hall on Charlotte Street. A portion of the roof of St. Matthew's Church was blown off, the walls cracked, and the inside of the church was flooded with rainwater. The roof was blown off in St. Mary's Church on Virginia Street. The Seventh Day Adventists Church on East Shirley Street's roof and building were destroyed. About 300 people were sheltered in Our Lady's Chapel, the Roman Catholic Church in Grant's Town, throughout the storm. Many of them remained there for several weeks after the storm because their homes were destroyed in the strong winds. After the passage of the hurricane, the Sisters of Charity at St. Francis Xavier's Convent visited the poor districts and distributed food and clothing to the needy from their funds.

The roof of Ebenezer Methodist Church on Shirley Street destroyed in the Great Bahamas Hurricane of 1929. The caption on the gate post reads "Every difficulty is somebody's opportunity." (Courtesy of Ronald Lightbourn).

The roof of the store of Messrs. H. and F. Pritchard on Bay Street was destroyed during the hurricane. Mr. L.G. Dupuch's residence on Shirley Street sustained some damage; some of the frontal pillars were blown down, and others were twisted out of shape, and the house suffered some flood damage. Mrs. Augusta Neely's home on Dowdeswell Street was destroyed. The house of Mr. Cleveland H. Reeves, Secretary to the Board of Education, suffered considerable damage. The roof of the right wing was completely torn off, and the eastern side of the building was smashed in. Several windows were shattered, and the windowpanes destroyed, and part of the house was twisted out of shape. St. Hilda's School and the Western Police Station roofs were partly unroofed.

The home of Mrs. Sarah Munnings on Dowdeswell Street lost its roof, and the kitchen and some other parts of the house were destroyed. The house of Mrs. Margaret Rogers on Dowdeswell Street lost part of its roof. The residence of Mr. Thomas S. Smith had its roof blown away. The store of Mr. Logan Dorsett in Deveaux Street was reported to be destroyed, along with part of the stock. A small quantity of liquor also went missing from the store. Mrs. Cedric Farrington's home on East Shirley Street was swept away by the flood waters and destroyed. Mrs. Walter and her entire household had to move out of their house just west of the city of Nassau during the storm. They had to walk to Lucayan Baths, which Mrs. Walter so aptly named "The Ark" because of the significant number of persons seeking refuge in her home during the storm. Schools that were scheduled to be re-opened in September, unfortunately, had to postpone the opening date to the much later period of October 7, 1929. This was because of the damage sustained to most of the school buildings. The remaining ones had to accommodate the homeless residents.

The pig pen and henhouses belonging to Mr. Pyfrom on West Street were destroyed. In several instances, people had to bore holes through the floors of their dwellings to drain the water out of the building. In some cases, it is said that the flood waters were as deep as 18 inches in the living rooms. In a bungalow near the Fort Montague Hotel, the tenants had to take refuge through the utility hole under the roof to escape the floodwaters on the ground floor. The office of the Munson Steamship Line on Bay Street lost its roof. On Dean's Lane, many houses were destroyed. Although the Leper Ward was practically reduced to ruins, the patients who were there were all safely cared for during the hurricane. The same applied to other portions of the hospital, including the lunatic asylum, which was also severely affected structurally. There was a great deal of homelessness in the 'Over-The-Hill' areas of Grant's Town and Bain Town. It is worthy to note that the hurricane destroyed the valuable library at Addington House. The precious picture of King Edward in the House of Assembly was damaged and had to be shipped to England for restoration. In one insurance company alone, the insured losses were estimated at well over £100,000.

The House of Assembly Official Report stated that 64 vessels were wrecked, including ten motor boats, three pilot boats, three ocean-going ships, nine sloops and other boats of various sorts. The mailboat *Princess Montague* ran aground on Tony Rock and was severely damaged. The *SS City of Nassau* replaced *Princess Montague* on its Miami-Nassau routine service. *The Priscilla*, which generally took the Abaco and Eleuthera mail, was washed ashore and wrecked. The *Ollie Forde*, which usually looked after the Andros mail route was destroyed, as was the schooner *Magic*, which had recently been doing the *Ollie Forde's'* work. These losses were significant because at the time the colony depended heavily on maritime commerce. Along the harbour-front, many of the boats were lying on their sides, partially wrecked or just a mass of useless planks. A very large motorboat buffeted by the winds and waves had crossed the Montague foreshore and come to rest in the grounds of the almost completed Fort Montague Beach Hotel.

On Thursday morning, when the water was 6 feet high on West Bay Street, and mountainous boulders were rolling in over the bar, a young girl, Hattie Rolle, a native of Bimini and a passenger onboard the boat *SS Priscilla*, leaped overboard from this vessel into the high seas. While she swam onto the rocks, she held on for dear life. Behind Hattie came Leland Weech, who swam alongside her as they made their way to the shore. They swam to shore to summon assistance for their fellow passengers, who were in great danger. The police station at this point got busy, and a body of men led by Inspector Pemberton attempted time and time again to reach the *SS Priscilla* in a small boat, but on each occasion, the craft was overturned and hurled back on the land. Then young Gordon O'Brien, Bert North, and Nigel Minnis volunteered to swim to the boat to get a life-line tied to the ship. At one moment, they were swallowed up in foam; at another, they were lost to view in the trough of the high waves that were rolling in from the bar; but on each occasion, they reappeared on the crest of the wave. Eventually, they reached their goal, and the most dangerous part of the adventure was over. Connecting a life-line to the ship, they succeeded in pulling the open boat along this line, and in this way, they landed everyone safely on shore. During this process, Hattie lost all her money because it was tied around her neck with a string and when she reached the coast, it was all gone.

There was flooding on the second floor of the Montague Hotel, and it was reported that a piano floated out of the hotel onto the streets and that a boat was found inside the building. Nearby historic Fort Montague was severely damaged when the walls were smashed in, and the cannons were moved quite a distance away. The roof of Mr. Bertram Johnson's house in Dowdeswell Street was completely blown off. All the chickens and poultry farms in Nassau were destroyed. Considerable damage was reported at The Bahamas General Hospital. Practically all the trees in the vicinity of Fort Montague and the hotel there were blown away or stripped of their leaves and branches. The roof of Mrs. Evans' premises on West Street blew off and crashed into another nearby house. A house at the corner of Virginia and West Streets was unroofed and reduced to wreckage. Miss Moseley's house on East Street lost part of its roof, and the upper verandah has practically disappeared. After the hurricane, the government, with approval from the House of Assembly and Senate, built several houses throughout Nassau and Andros to replace the ones that were lost in the storm. Prices for the homes ranged from £40 to £60. They had to pay a down payment for the house, and the remainder had to be paid in monthly installments for four years.

Almost all of the roof of Mr. Roland Cash's house on Union Street was destroyed. The cement shed that formed part of the Administration Building of the Water Supply Department, near the Colonial Hotel, has had its roof destroyed. The walls of the school at Fox Hill were severely cracked and the roof damaged. The Public School on Nassau Street was destroyed. The Eastern Central School sustained some broken windows and some flooding. The Manual Training Shop, which formed part of the Sandilands School at Fox Hill, was blown down. Because of the hurricane, the Magistrate Court was closed for four days. Several persons were stranded on Hog Island during the storm, and some others took refuge in the Government Quarantine Building on Athol Island. Mr. Asa Pritchard, M.H.A.'s, chicken farm was destroyed in the wind from the hurricane. He said that he was not disappointed because soon he would import 2,000 more chickens to replace those ones lost in the storm. A short time before the hurricane, he imported 800 one-day-old chicks from Detroit and raised

500 of them. The cyclone left him with only 90 of that remaining total. He stated that when he went to the chicken farm, he saw many chicken walking around on the farm with no feathers on their bodies because the strong winds from the hurricane blew off all of their feathers.

The destroyed roof of the Munson Steamship Line on Bay Street (building to the right is where the Royal Bank of Canada Main Branch is now located) after the Great Bahamas Hurricane of 1929 (Courtesy of The Charles Whelbell Collection-Bahamas Department of Archives, Nassau, Bahamas).

Significant and catastrophic damage occurred to many of the Bahamian boats and schooners. Carl Brice's powerboat, *Matchbox*, secured for safety in the Fox Hill Creek, was found after the hurricane washed up a quarter mile away, on the high ridge near St Anne's Rectory, which was then east of the Hermitage. Spongers, fishermen, many men who made their living collecting and selling conch and sponges, lost their livelihoods, as well as their boats. The sponge fleet was decimated. Many men with their ships, which were anchored in Nassau Harbour, insisted on staying on board during the hurricane. Their boats were the only property they owned. Many had nothing else at all to call their own, so when the hurricane destroyed their ships, many were left with nothing but the clothes on their back. The fierce wind and sea raced down the Nassau Harbour and swept many boats over the bar, never to be seen again. Captain Fred Smith was hired by the

Bahamas Government to inspect the sponging grounds in the Mud and to report these findings back to the Marine Products Board. Several of the hurricanes of the 1920s severely crippled the local boat-building industry at Abaco and Harbour Island, and they never really regained the momentum and status of the former glory days.

The Tribune was devastated by this storm. "This hurricane was not expected," reported The Tribune on September 28, 1929, on a small one-page sheet produced on a foot press after The Tribune building had been flooded and destroyed. "It is not the one from Puerto Rico," the report continued, "but believed to be of local origin and might have spent itself in The Bahamas. There are seven known deaths on this island, but Grant's Town is under water, and it is unknown if any are drowned over there." Then came the brave words of the 30-year-old editor of The Tribune Etienne Dupuch: "The Tribune has been almost wiped off the map by this hurricane, but we are not discouraged, nor are we downhearted. We have our tools. We have our health and strength, and we still have faith and youth. That's plenty. If everyone who has suffered as badly as we, or even worse, will face the situation with a brave heart and determination to win through, the effect of this calamity may soon be entirely effaced. Today, we are printing a slip on a foot press; so as soon as we get electricity, we will return to normal size."[93] [94]

After this storm and the massive death toll incurred, the British Government decided to put into law a 'Hurricane Warning Act' to establish special hurricane signal flags that would be prominently displayed from the signal staffs on Forts Charlotte and Fincastle. Before this hurricane, signal flags were hoisted at the various forts but only randomly based on the location and strength of the storm. The new regulation required that signal flags be raised high in the air when the barometer fell below a certain point. Besides, the Act also expected that there should be some means by which mariners should become acquainted with any information that was acquired utilizing a telegraph. This was done to prevent the loss of life and property both at sea and on land. Because of this hurricane, all British Imperial Lighthouse Service light stations have issued a set of

---

[93] The Tribune, Saturday, September 28, 1929 pgs. 1&2-'*Courage.*'
[94] The Tribune, Saturday, October 05, 1929 pgs. 1&2-'*Government making estimates of hurricane damage to lay before Legislature*', '*The Bahamas Hurricane Relief Fund 1929*' & '*Here and There.*'

signal flags, which were kept ready once there was an approaching storm to warn incoming or outgoing ships and residents of the impending hurricane.

The official barometer reading at the Bahamas Public Works Building was 27.90 inches, and it occurred at 3 am. The wind speed was estimated at 140 mph when the wind anemometer blew away.

Mayaguana

Andrew White, age 15 years, was taken with a spell of seizure while drawing water from a well in the settlement of Betsy Bay during the storm. He fell into the well and drowned. The body was not recovered until some hours later.

Cat Island

On this island, the storm was not severe, and very light damage to homes was reported. This island experienced gale force winds.

Ragged Island

From this island, it was reported that the public-school house was blown down, but none of the private dwellings were severely impacted.

Eleuthera

Some damage was reported, and North Eleuthera experienced wind speeds between 75 to 100 knots. At Harbour Island, a woman who died during the storm had to be wrapped and strapped to a board for burial because a coffin was not available at the time.

Abaco

There were 19 houses and 12 boats destroyed and many others severely damaged. Among the ships destroyed was the *SS Domira*. It was reported that an American freighter that belonged to the Nelson Line of San Francisco, the *Wisconsin Bridge*, was lost off Abaco when sailing northeast of Hole-In-The-Wall Lighthouse. This lighthouse was also damaged in this storm, and a boat was dispatched from Nassau with materials to repair it.

The most severe damage was inflicted to the massive glass plate in the lantern room. The crew of 34 took to the ship's lifeboats, and sadly they all drowned with one notable exception. The only member of the crew who was saved was the wireless operator who refused to leave the ship when others went because he said it was too risky to battle the storm on the high seas with just a small lifeboat. The hurricane lasted for well over 36 hours, and the highest wind speeds were estimated to be between 75 to 100 mph.

Andros

Andros, which is the largest island in The Bahamas and just some 30 miles west of Nassau, was devastated in this storm. Some said that all 2,300 square miles were inundated with both salt and rainwater from this storm. The Annual Report for the district of Andros for the 1929 fiscal year was submitted to the House of Assembly during a special session commencing on March 18, 1930 and ending July 7, 1930. In this report, it stated that the hurricane destroyed all the crops and most of the fruit trees, livestock, and poultry. The sponge beds also suffered heavily, leaving people worse off than they had been in many years.

Mr. Elgin Forsyth, the Commissioner for the entire island of Andros but stationed at Mangrove Cay, wrote a very detailed report on the impact of this storm on the island of Andros. His report stated that 16 sponging vessels and many unnumbered open boats ranching at Water Cay have all lost their sponges, and many of the ships were destroyed or severely damaged. It also stated that 16 vessels and unnumbered open boats ranching at Water Cay lost all their sponges when their boats were destroyed. The crew of Mr. P.C. Smith's schooner *The Repeat* was lost with some of the crew perishing while they were trying to swim from one of the cays on the southern tip of Andros in Grassy Creek back to the mainland. The significant loss of the sponging vessels in this area had a tremendous impact on the entire Androsian population for many months after the storm.

In Stafford Creek, there were wreckages of many strange boats, including *The Governor Shea* which floated ashore between Blanket Sound and Stafford Creek. The British ship *SS Potomac* was wrecked off Andros, but fortunately, all her crew members were saved but the cargo lost. The *SS Potomac*, owned by the Anglo-American Oil Company, was en-route from Texas to London, transporting a cargo of oil. It ran ashore and split in two on some three miles east-northeast of Mastic Point, Andros. Ten minutes after running aground, her hull was split in two, and her stern swung around in line with the bow. Realizing the danger of an explosion, the chief engineer returned to the engine room. At the risk of great personal danger to himself and the crew, he went into the room and shut off the valves. The men in the stern of the ship employing a rope swung themselves across the bow, which was in a less dangerous position. The men remained on board until Sunday, when the sloop *Memory* took ten of them off and brought them to the mainland. Another sloop came and got an additional fifteen more of the ship, but the captain remained with the boat. As mandated under British laws, the Magistrate conducted an inquiry into the wreck of this British ship to find out if anyone was negligent or culpable.

In Blanket Sound, 13 houses were destroyed, and others damaged. In Staniard Creek, 12 homes were destroyed, and every other house was severely damaged. The recently built bridge called the Staniard Creek Bridge, which was just recently built before the storm at the cost of about £400 was destroyed, and the Fisherman's Wharf was washed away. The storm surge from this hurricane was near 12 to 18 feet, and it swept across the entire western and southern coasts. In Love Hill and Small Hope, five houses were destroyed, while others were severely damaged, and all the vessels there were damaged. In Calabash Bay, the teacher's residence, two society halls, and seven houses were flattened. The roof of the Roman Catholic Church blew off, and there were 22 coffins washed out of the graveyard. In Fresh Creek, six houses were completely flattened and at least ten badly damaged. The seawall and the lighthouse were damaged. The poles of the wireless station blew down, and the building flooded to at least 4 feet deep. Cargill Creek had to be abandoned due to high water because only the hills were above water.

The lowest barometer reading was at Fresh Creek, with a reading of 28.70 inches on September 26th at 7 am. Before it became dark, people were forced to leave their houses and find shelters with neighbours and churches. One of the hurricane shelters was the Wesleyan Mission House, where the Reverend Whitfield took care of the evacuated and distraught residents. During the storm, this building eventually became engulfed in water, so they had to seek refuge elsewhere in the schoolhouse and other private residences in the nearby vicinity. In Behring Point, there were twelve houses flattened, and 15 people reported missing.

In Mangrove Cay, many houses were reportedly destroyed, and the floodwaters were up to 20 feet deep; ten people drowned. In Mangrove

Cay, several fishing sloops were destroyed, among them were *Income, Revive, Trail, Record, Sasin*, and *Glittering.* Any boats that were left in the water were either damaged beyond repair or blown ashore several hundred feet from where they were anchored. Many of the sponging boats were swept into the Pine Barrens. Many of the pine trees were cut down and used as rollers to get the boats back out to the harbour. A young lady was supposed to get married on the weekend of the storm in Mangrove Cay, and she and the bridal family were travelling by boat from Nassau en-route to Mangrove Cay to attend this wedding. A total of 18 persons drowned in this boat when it capsized during the storm.

In South Andros, in the settlement of Rolle Town, there were only three houses left standing and undamaged. During the storm, people had to escape to the hills for refuge from the floodwaters. In Black Point, three houses were left intact out of a total of 27 homes. All the animals, livestock and nearby farms were destroyed. The Public Wharf at Deep Creek was washed away, and boats that were inland during the storm were washed out to sea. These boats held the communities together by providing a way of life for most of the men in the community. It also provided a means of employment for the local fishermen, so this storm, by destroying these boats, severely crippled this aspect of their lives for quite some time after the storm.

The Commissioner for Andros and stationed at Mangrove Cay, Mr. Elgin.W, Forsyth stated; "I regret exceedingly to report that on September 25th, 26th, and 27th, the most extreme destructive hurricane in the history of this district swept the Island. Its extreme duration and sustained violence its without precedent in my experience. The whole place appears as though burned with fire, and fields once full of promise are naked stripped of all vegetation. The situation is the most serious the island has ever had to face." After the storm, the Commissioner went around and gave the residents corn and peas to replant in their farms. Besides, the government also sent assistance to the island in the form of labour, food, clothing, and building supplies.[95]

The schooner *The Repeat* was lost, as the Commissioner's and House of Assembly Reports, indicated, but not with all the crewmembers on board, as these reports suggested. A few of the crew members drowned,

---

[95] Wayne Neely, *The Great Bahamas Hurricane of 1929*, (Bloomington, iUniverse Publishing Inc., 2013).

but the others survived by swimming back to the mainland of Andros. The schooner *The Repeat* broke away from its mooring and drifted out to sea without any persons onboard except for a stubborn dog named 'Busser,' who refused to jump off the ship when he was instructed to do so by his master and the crew members of *The Repeat*. According to all the reports I have seen to this date, they all have all the crew of *The Repeat* being lost at sea. Fortunately, I spoke to two persons that were onboard the schooner during the storm, the late Mr. Illford Forbes and Mr. Daniel Rahming, both of whom lived in South Andros during the storm. Mr. Daniel Rahming and Mr. Illford Forbes have since passed away, but they both insisted that those reports were wrong because both were onboard the vessel *The Repeat*.

Grand Bahama

No significant damage reported, but it experienced severe gale conditions.

Major damage to St. Agnes Church on Blue Hill Road after the Great Bahamas Hurricane of 1929 (Courtesy of the Charles Whelbell Collection-The Bahamas Department of Archives, Nassau, Bahamas).

CHAPTER FIFTEEN

The Great Abaco Hurricane of 1932's Impact on the Islands of The Bahamas

Great devastation in the settlement of Hope Town, Abaco after the Great Abaco Hurricane of 1932 (Courtesy of Carolyn Lowe/Suzanne Russell-Bethel).

On September 6, 1932, the island of Abaco was devastated by a Category 5 hurricane. This hurricane has come to be known as, the Great Abaco Hurricane of 1932. This storm had wind speeds gusting up to 200 mph. When it was over, reports are that 18 people perished, and 300 injured. The Great Abaco Hurricane of 1932 was the first known and well-documented hurricane on record to hit The Bahamas at peak Category 5 intensity. A Category 5 hurricane has sustained winds greater than 156 mph. "Sustained winds" refers to the average wind speed observed over one minute at 10 meters (32 feet) above ground, which is the standard height wind speed is measured at to avoid interference by obstacles and obstructions. Brief gusts in hurricanes are typically up to 50 percent higher than sustained winds. Because a hurricane is (usually) a moving system, the wind field is asymmetric, with the strongest winds on the right side or more specifically the right-front quadrant (in the Northern Hemisphere), relative to the direction of motion in an area where there is positive convergence. The highest winds given in advisories are those from the right side.

The list of Category 5 North Atlantic hurricanes includes 36 tropical cyclones that reached Category 5 strength on the Saffir–Simpson Hurricane Wind Scale within the North Atlantic basin, Caribbean Sea and the Gulf of Mexico. Hurricanes of such intensity are somewhat rare in the North Atlantic basin, occurring only once every three years on average. Only seven times—in 1932, 1933, 1961, 2005, 2007, 2017, and 2019 hurricane seasons—have more than one Category 5 hurricane formed. Only in 2005 have more than two Category 5 hurricanes formed, and only in 2007 and 2016 have more than one made landfall at Category 5 intensity. Between 1924 and 2007, there were only 33 hurricanes that were recorded at Category 5 strength. The years 2016 through 2019 are the longest sequence of consecutive years which all featured at least on Category 5 hurricane each. No Category 5 hurricanes were observed officially before 1924. It can be speculated that earlier storms reached Category 5 strength over open waters, but the strongest winds were not measured. The Bahamas have on record four Category 5 hurricanes to impact this country since 1851, when reliable records were kept and this is tied with the United States as being the top countries being hit by a Category 5 hurricane.

The anemometer, a meteorological recording device used for measuring wind speed and direction, was invented in 1846. However, during major hurricane strikes the instruments were often blown away, unfortunately leaving the hurricane's peak intensity unrecorded. For example, as the Great Beaufort Hurricane of 1879 which devastated North Carolina, the anemometer cups were blown away when indicating 138 mph. Officially, the decade with the most Category 5 hurricanes is 2000–2009, with eight Category 5 hurricanes having occurred: Isabel (2003), Ivan (2004), Emily (2005), Katrina (2005), Rita (2005), Wilma (2005), Dean (2007), and Felix (2007). The previous decades with the most Category 5 hurricanes were the 1930s and 1960s, with six occurring between 1930 and 1939 (before the naming process began).

All Atlantic Category 5 hurricanes have made landfall at some location at hurricane strength. Seventeen of the storms made landfall while at Category 5 intensity; 2007 and 2017 are the only years in which two storms made landfall at this intensity. All North Atlantic Category 5 hurricanes have made landfall at some location at hurricane strength. Most Category 5 hurricanes in the North Atlantic make landfall because of their proximity to land in the USA, Central America, Caribbean and Gulf of Mexico. Many of these systems made landfall shortly after weakening from a Category 5. This weakening can be caused by dry air near land, shallower waters due to shelving, interaction with land, or cooler waters near shore. In southern Florida, the return period for a Category 5 hurricane is roughly once every 50 years. Many of these systems made landfall shortly after weakening from a Category 5. This weakening can be caused by dry air near land, shallower waters due to shelving, interaction with land, or cooler waters near shore. In southern Florida, the return period for a Category 5 hurricane is roughly once every 50 years. In The Bahamas, only four Category 5 hurricanes struck the country at peak Category 5 intensity. It must be noted that Irma in 2017 did become a Category 5 hurricane but not while it was over The Bahamas. The four Category 5 hurricanes impacting The Bahamas were: The Great Abaco Hurricane of 1932, The Great Cuba-Brownsville Hurricane of 1933, Hurricane Andrew in 1992(which was upgraded to a Category 5 hurricane ten years later), and Dorian of 2019.

A reanalysis of weather data is ongoing by researchers who may upgrade, or downgrade other North Atlantic hurricanes currently listed at Categories 4 and 5, using the HURDAT programme. For example, the 1825 Santa Ana Hurricane is suspected to have reached Category 5 strength. Furthermore, paleotempestological research aims to identify past major hurricanes by comparing sedimentary evidence of recent and past hurricane strikes or by looking at coral reefs core samples. For example, a "giant hurricane" significantly more powerful than Hurricane Hattie (Category 5) has been identified in Belizean sediment, having struck the region sometime before 1500.

Great damage and devastation in Green Turtle Cay, Abaco after the Great Abaco Hurricane of 1932 as workers gather amid the ruins looking for survivors, including two girls looking for their father who was later found dead under the rubbles. (Images courtesy of Marysa Malone-Used with permission).

Seven North Atlantic hurricanes—Camille, Allen, Andrew, Isabel, Ivan, Dean, and Felix—reached Category 5 intensity on more than one occasion; that is, by reaching Category 5 intensity, weakening to a Category 4 intensity or lower, and then restrengthening again becoming a Category 5 hurricane again. Such hurricanes have their dates shown together. Camille, Andrew, Dean, and Felix each attained Category 5 status twice during their lifespans. Allen, Isabel, and Ivan reached Category 5 intensity on three separate occasions. However, no North Atlantic hurricane has ever reached Category 5 hurricane intensity more than three times during its lifespan. The recent September 2017 Hurricane Irma holds the record for most time spent as a Category 5.

According to records, two historic churches were destroyed in this 1932 hurricane, and their 3-feet thick walls were reduced to rubble. Records, further, indicate that people had to crawl from house to house to flee to safety during the hurricane. The account of Bluff Point, Abaco was a profoundly compelling event. The settlement disappeared after the passage of the devastating hurricane. On one side of the bluff was deep water which accommodated large vessels; on the other side, there was a cove with marshes and swampland which served as safe harbour for the settlement sloops. This was ideal for the village because the large boats could come in and collect the sponge and trade. Bluff Point was settled by the Swain, Mitchell, Curry, Wilmore, Davis, Simms, Reckley and Williams' families. These families on the coastline were cut off from the rest of Abaco during the great storm and were vulnerable to the deadly storm surge which eventually destroyed the settlement. After this catastrophe and the significant loss of lives and numerous injuries, the colonial government moved these families further inland to what is now known as the settlement of Murphy Town. The government built each family a two-bedroom house and deeded the five-acre tract to each family for a small sum of £2 – £5. The decision back then was a good one and done in the national interest to preserve any future loss of lives or damaged properties, should any future hurricane like this one was ever to strike again.

The minimum central pressures of the more recent systems were measured by reconnaissance aircrafts using dropsondes, or by determining them from satellite imagery using the Dvorak technique. For older storms, pressures are often incomplete. The only readings came from ship reports, land observations, or aircraft reconnaissance. None of these methods can provide constant pressure measurements. Thus, sometimes the only measurement can be from when the hurricane was not a Category 5.

Consequently, the lowest central pressure measurement is sometimes unrealistically high for a Category 5 hurricane. For example, the Great New England Hurricane of 1938 had its lowest recorded central pressure while it was a Category 3 storm. These pressure values do not directly correlate with the maximum sustained winds. This happens because the wind speed of a hurricane depends on both its size and how rapidly the pressure drops as the hurricane's center approaches. Thus, a hurricane in an environment of high ambient pressure will have stronger winds than a storm in an atmosphere of low ambient pressure, even if they have the same central pressures.

The death toll in Abaco after the Great Abaco Hurricane of 1932 was great. This photo shows a man pouring carbolic acid over the decaying corpse to prevent the spread of disease and to lessen the stench, while another man is seen holding his nose because of the stench from the decaying corpses (Courtesy of the Albert Lowe Museum-Used with permission).

Only one Category 5 has been recorded in July, eight in August, twenty in September, four in October, and one in November. There have been no officially recorded June or off-season Category 5 hurricanes. The July and August Category 5s reached their highest intensities in both the Gulf of Mexico and the Caribbean Sea. These are the locations most favourable for tropical cyclone development in those months. It must be noted that September sees the most Category 5 hurricanes. This coincides with the climatological peak of the North Atlantic hurricane season, which occurs on September 10. September Category 5 hurricanes reached their strengths in any of the Gulf of Mexico, Caribbean Sea, and the open Atlantic Ocean. These places are where September tropical cyclones are likely to form. Many of these hurricanes are either Cape Verde-type storms, which develop their strength by having wide and expansive open water; or so-called Bahama Busters, which forms over or just east of The Bahamas primarily by TUTT upper level lows or surface troughs and then go on to rapidly intensify over the warm Loop Current in the Gulf of Mexico. One notable example of this was Hurricane Katrina in 2005.

All five Category 5 hurricanes in October and November reached their intensities in the western Caribbean, a region that North Atlantic hurricanes strongly gravitate toward late in the season. This is due to the climatology of the area, which sometimes has a high-altitude anticyclone that promotes rapid intensification late in the season, as well as warm waters. Initially, there were only three Category 5s discovered in October, but HURDAT reanalysis found out that a hurricane in 1924 also reached that intensity during the month, so four Category 5s developed in October. A Category 5 North Atlantic hurricane is one that is considered by the United States National Hurricane Center (NHC), to have had sustained wind speeds greater than 136 knots (157 mph) on the Saffir–Simpson Hurricane Wind Scale. The NHC considers sustained wind speeds to be those that occur, over one minute at 10 meters (32.8 feet) above ground. These wind speeds are estimated by using a blend of data from a variety of sources, which includes observations from nearby ships, reconnaissance aircrafts, or automatic weather stations and pictures from various satellites.

During the Great Depression, a powerful and deadly hurricane lashed the islands of The Bahamas with devastating force. Its record-setting winds of over 160 mph and over twenty feet storm surge and led to the deaths of 18 persons on the island of Abaco. Abaco is one of the largest islands in The Bahamas and is most frequently affected by storms, mainly because of its large size and geographical location. On average, it gets hit or brushed by a hurricane once every 1.79 years but receives a direct hit once every 3.72 years and is ranked as the sixth (out of a total of 155 cities or islands) on the list of storms affecting cities and islands within this region.[96]

The 1932 North Atlantic was an extremely busy and devastating one for the Caribbean and the Americas. There were many notable and quite destructive hurricanes this year. An early season storm formed during May and skimmed Hispaniola causing minimal damage. Then a powerful hurricane struck the coast of Galveston, Texas finally testing the true worth of a seawall built after the deadly Great Galveston Hurricane of 1900. A Category 1 hurricane hit Alabama, and a late-season Category 4

---

[96] www.hurricanecity.com. Retrieved: 15-07-2017.

hurricane hit Cuba and devastated that island leaving over 3,000 persons' dead. However, the most notable hurricane for The Bahamas was the Great Abaco Hurricane of 1932. This storm was a powerful hurricane which struck The Bahamas with peak winds of more than 160 mph and a barometric pressure of 931 hPa. The island which sustained the most significant damage and the highest death toll was Abaco.

Great devastation in Hope Town, Abaco after the Great Abaco Hurricane of 1932 (Courtesy of Caroyln Lowe/Suzanne Russell-Bethel).

Meteorological History of the Great Abaco Hurricane of 1932

The system was first detected just to the north of the Virgin Islands as a tropical depression late on August 30. The storm moved generally west-northwest, passing to the north of the Greater Antilles and Grand Turk on the night of September 2–3. It reached minimal hurricane intensity as it passed near the Turks and Caicos Islands, and began a period of rapid strengthening shortly thereafter. It became a major hurricane early on September 4 and reached winds of 140 mph, equivalent to those of a Category 4 hurricane, as early as the afternoon. As late as the evening of September 4, however, no winds of hurricane force were reported to the

United States Weather Bureau, the highest wind being 60 mph from a ship 285 miles east of Miami, Florida.

The storm passed just to the east of the main islands and Nassau while continuing to strengthen. A gradual turn to the northwest and north began soon, and late on September 5 the storm peaked at Category 5 status with estimated maximum sustained winds of around 160 mph at that time. Maintaining strength, the storm passed over Great Abaco on September 5 and gradually began to curve northeast away from the mainland United States. It continued northeast while weakening in intensity, delivering sea swells to the northeastern United States and winds of 56 mph to Nantucket as the storm bypassed New England. The storm became extratropical on September 9, crossed south of the Avalon Peninsula, Newfoundland and Labrador, on September 11, and eventually passed near the Snæfellsnes, Iceland, and Jan Mayen Island. It dissipated on September 17.[97]

In the 1930s, the hurricane preparedness technology and tools for tracking hurricanes that are used today were in their infancy, if it had even been conceived in the first place. As such, hurricane preparedness for the 1932 storm was lacking. While there were some tools available for tracking hurricanes in the 1930s, they lacked a certain degree of sophistication, and while they could detect a hurricane in its earlier stages, it was challenging to predict with any degree of accuracy where it might strike or how strong it might be or what direction it was moving to or from. As such, people were only able to put up hurricane shutters and barricades hurricane windows and doors at the last second and hope for the best. Furthermore, this was in a period where mass communications were still in its infancy. Even if they could have, theoretically, been able to predict the exact details of a hurricane, it would have been virtually next to impossible to issue warnings promptly. As such, hurricane preparations on some islands were predictably slim or almost non-existent at all.

Two brick churches were destroyed on Green Turtle Cay, near the island of Abaco mainland, with some of the stone bricks being carried up to a half a mile away. Several vessels were caught in the storm off the coast of Abaco Island. Fortunately, despite some minor hurricane damages, most of the ships survived the ordeal. Sadly, the Great Abaco Hurricane

---

[97] National Hurricane Center; Hurricane Research Division (April 11, 2017). *"Atlantic hurricane best track (HURDAT version 2)"*. United States National Oceanic and Atmospheric Administration. Retrieved: 08-08-2017.

of 1932 occurred well before any national hurricane relief program had been put into place, and while hurricane protection was still a developing concept, hurricane shutters and hurricane windows being relatively new inventions. There was little in the way of government relief for those who had suffered. However, many charitable contributions from many persons and organizations were collected for the Abaco residents affected by the storm. Overall, many residents on most of the Out Islands had to fend for themselves to recover.

The strong winds from the Great Abaco Hurricane of 1932 shifted this house from its foundation into the main road in the settlement of Hope Town, Abaco (Image courtesy of Caroyln Lowe/Suzanne Russell-Bethel).

The entire death toll occurred in The Bahamas, notably on and around Abaco Island; total damage estimates in dollars, however, were not released but it was in the millions of dollars. The storm was very destructive on Abaco Island, where the reported barometric pressure was unofficially below 27.50 inches (931 millibars). On Green Turtle Cay, near Abaco Island was where the greatest devastation occurred. The storm and winds that destroyed two brick churches with winds estimated by one resident to have exceeded 200 mph. Some of the stone blocks from the churches were reportedly carried a half mile away. Newspaper reports and photos helped to establish estimated prevailing winds on Green Turtle Cay possibly exceeded 150 mph during the hurricane.

Green Turtle Cay got its name from the Abaco locals, because of the abundant supply of the green turtles living and nesting in the waters there, which would be caught and sold locally or internationally. For centuries, turtle meat had been a delicacy among Bahamians and foreigners alike. During the 19th century, demand for the shell of the hawksbill and green turtles used to make jewelry, combs, and trinkets, increased substantially. Green Turtle Cay residents like other Bahamians throughout The Bahamas would capture live turtles in nets and keep them in kraals until the time came to ship them to market in Nassau or the U.S. If the voyage was prolonged due to bad weather, many died on the trip. For example, in one instance, an Abaco schooner was taking live turtles to New York when a gentleman came to purchase one, he spotted the lifeless creatures and asked if they were alright. "Certainly," replied a crafty crew member. "Sometimes they sleep like that for weeks at a time." The man picked up a turtle, paid for it and took it home to cook. A Green Turtle Cay resident, Richard Kemp (1825-1908) is credited with the discovery of one of the turtle species, the Lepidochelys kempii. Kemp was the first person to send a specimen of the strange-looking turtle called the Kemp's Ridley Turtle. The origin of the Ridley part is unknown. It is the smallest of all the sea turtles and is among the most stubborn because it is known to fight quite literally to the death, rather than submit to captivity.[98]

After the storm passed over Abaco on September 6th and 7th, several vessels caught in the storm recorded winds of Force 12 (Beaufort Wind Scale) and low barometric pressures; the *S.S. Yankee Arrow* recorded a pressure of 27.65 inches (936 millibars) on the 7th, while the nearby *S.S. Deer Lodge* reported a lower pressure of 27.58 inches (934 millibars). Although storm warnings were posted for the Florida and eastern United States coastlines, the storm's recurvature prevented a landfall, leaving the main effects as heavy coastal swells and high winds. At the storm's closest pass to the country near New England, Nantucket where the highest winds peaked at 56 mph, as the storm remained offshore, although it still packed hurricane-force winds. The storm then passed Newfoundland where it morphed into an extratropical cyclone and passed near Iceland and Jan

---

[98] Diedrick, Amanda, *Those Who Stayed-The tale of the hardy few who built Green Turtle Cay*, (Abaco, Amanda Diedrick Ltd, 2016).

Maven Island where they reported barometric pressures of 29.00 inches or lower.

The story of Bluff Point, Abaco is well known in the annals of Abaco history. Bluff Point was once a thriving sponging and fishing coastal settlement. The settlement disappeared after the passage of the devastating Great Abaco Hurricane of 1932. On one side of the bluff was deep waters, which accommodated large vessels; on the other side, there was a cove with marshes and swamp which served as safe harbour for the settlement schooners and sloops. This was ideal for the village because the large boats could come in and collect the sponges and trade with the locals. Bluff Point was settled by the Swain, Mitchell, Curry, Wilmore, Davis, Simms, Reckley and Williams' families. These families living on the coast were cut off from the rest of Abaco during this great hurricane and were exposed to deadly storm surge which eventually destroyed the settlement.

The colonial government, after this catastrophe, and the significant loss of lives and numerous injuries moved these families further inland away from the coast to what is now known as the settlement of Murphy Town. The government built each family a two-bedroom house and deeded the five-acre tract to each family for a small sum of £2 – £5. The decision back then was a good one and done in the national interest to preserve any future loss of lives or damaged properties, should any future hurricane like this one was ever to strike again.

Damages sustained on the major islands of The Bahamas during the Great Abaco Hurricane of 1932

Nassau

Two conflicting weather reports were received from Washington and Miami regarding the track of the storm. Washington reported the storm on Monday morning to be some 90 miles east-southeast of Nassau, while other weather indications reported that it was well to the northeast of Nassau. Consequently, Monday was an anxious day for most residents, and it was not until the report was received at 10 o'clock that night that the Nassau residents were assured that all the danger from the storm had passed. This proves the supreme value of the Out-Island weather reports. It was not until the Nassau government officials were in possession of news that The

Bight, Cat Island, was feeling the effects of the storm, reporting winds from the northwest, and subsequently, a report of the wind direction from Governor's Harbour confirming this, that some of the experienced citizens and government officials of the island felt reasonably sure that the storm would pass to the north of them.

On Sunday at 6 pm, the three blasts on the sirens situated over New Providence caused considerable alarm. When it was realized that the storm would not pass over New Providence before Monday, many persons went to their evening church services. During Sunday night, gusts of wind reached speeds of 40-45 mph, but the mean wind speed was 30 mph. All the tomato crops on this island were destroyed.

Andros

A report from the Commissioner at Fresh Creek reported that the hurricane passed over that part of the island from 4 pm on Sunday to 3 pm on Monday. No deaths or damages were reported.

Watlings Island

No damage was reported on this island apart from a blown down radio station, which was quickly repaired and put back in service.

Eleuthera

At Governor's Harbour during the peak of the storm, sustained winds were measured at 75 mph from the northwest and then later from the southwest with the peak of the winds occurring between noon and midnight on Monday. Damages were reported to the roads and the tomato crops on the island. A large portion of the stone part of the Government Wharf was demolished, and the foreshore near the wharf was washed away. There was significant damage reported to the island's crops and other plants. The schooner *Forward* rode out the storm on Harbour Island with two anchors, hawsers and one chain holding her down. During the hurricane, she broke away from everything except the mooring chain holding her steady during the storm. Her seams were opened so badly that if the hurricane had hovered over The Bahamas any longer, perhaps she would have been destroyed rather than just being badly damaged.

Grand Bahama

The hurricane passed over this island on September 5th and 6th, destroying a few houses and wrecking several vessels. Many of the crops were destroyed. The Commissioner who was stationed at Sweeting's Cay during the storm reported that several houses were blown down and there was a shortage of food from there to Eight Mile Rock. At Water Cay, the sloop *Regulator* and the schooners *Relief* and *Increase* were destroyed, and considerable damage was done to many of the other remaining boats. The water was said to have risen to a height of 9 feet in Hawksbill Creek on the north side. At West End, there was considerable damage to the citrus crop. The Bahamas Government also dispatched supplies to the districts which suffered significant losses. They were placed in the care of Mr. J.L. Lightbourn, the Auditor and he was also responsible for seeing that the residents of Moore's Island got relief supplies as they also suffered significant damages as well. At Moore's Island, the water rose to a height of 5 feet in some places, causing several houses to float off their foundations. Entire roofs were blown off four houses, and many others were severely damaged. The fields were severely damaged, and several people were slightly injured.

Cat Island

At Cat Island, many telephone lines and poles were blown down but were quickly repaired.

Abaco

The Great Abaco Hurricane of 1932 destroyed this woman's house in Abaco and for a few months after the hurricane had passed, she turned the roof right side up and was forced to live in the roof of her home shown in the background as she related her misfortunes to Mr. Jack Mertland Malone-father of the popular Bahamian folk artist the late Brent Malone (Image courtesy of Marysa Malone-Used with permission).

According to author and Green Turtle Cay native Amanda Diedrick in her compelling book, 'Those Who Stayed-The tale of the hardy few who built Green Turtle Cay' stated that when the strong winds and the torrential rainfall subsided, the residents of Green Turtle Cay were relieved that the worst was behind them. But as they emerged from their battered, flooded shelters, they discovered what misery lay ahead. Six of their own – George Lewis (85), Thomas Roberts (62), Alice Lowe (58), Insley Sawyer (5) and brothers, DeWees and Bert Lowe, (15 and 2, respectively) – had all been killed during the Great Abaco Hurricane of 1932 and many others were severely injured. Water from Settlement Creek had surged across the lowest part of the town and flowed out into the Sea of Abaco, destroying the cemetery and unearthing corpses (Even today, fragments of gravestones remain on the beach that borders the graveyard). The settlement of New Plymouth was unrecognizable. Most homes were either demolished or washed out to sea. The schoolhouse had collapsed, as had the Government Wharf and the New Plymouth Hotel. Four churches, including the 1200-seat Methodist Church, were lost. The top story of the government building had disappeared, leaving only the jail, and stairs that now led nowhere. Nearly every tree had been toppled.

There were no buildings on Green Turtle Cay which were not left unscathed, for example, the two-story building where the Captain Roland Roberts Environmental Center is now located had been hit by another building and shifted it four feet from its foundation. The roof from the church next to John's house was found blocks away in the middle of the settlement. Stone bricks from another church were discovered a half-mile away. Despite being heavily anchored, the mail boat had been dragged seven miles away from its mooring.

The Bahamian Government sent some supplies, and private organizations on other islands collected and forwarded donations, but for the most part, Green Turtle Cay residents were left to fend for themselves. Though they worked tirelessly to put the shattered pieces of their community back together, New Plymouth never fully regained its previous prosperity. Numerous sponging vessels and sponge beds were damaged by the hurricane, and within a few years, a fungus disease wiped out what remained of the industry. The timber mills on the Abaco mainland closed, and the Great Depression of 1929 thwarted a fledgling tourism industry. Many residents left to find work in Nassau or the United States. Most did not return. For those who remained, mere sustenance was a struggle. Residents would go searching all about to find a penny to buy a tuppence worth of lard to make a stew. Sometimes, they would have to fry the oil out of turbot fish livers and make the stew that way. When they didn't have money to buy sugar, they would make a pie with syrup extracted from the sugar cane plant.

Essentially, Green Turtle Cay's history can be divided into two distinct periods – before the Great Abaco Hurricane of 1932 and after this hurricane. In the first week of September 1932, on what was to be the start of the new school year, the first Category 5 hurricane on record descended upon Green Turtle Cay. With only barometers by which to gauge the weather, residents had little warning of the storm and no indication whatsoever of its ferocity. Before long, however, there would be no doubt. For three days, the stalled storm pummeled the cay with full force, trapping residents inside their disintegrating homes where they cowered, praying, in the dark. By the time the storm moved on, much of the town of New Plymouth had been leveled, and six residents were dead.

Especially hard hit was the family of Mr. Basil Lowe. Not only did the family lose their home, but two of their children — their oldest and youngest sons — were killed by debris. Perhaps because of their tender ages, or the unimaginable heartbreak visited upon their family by the loss of two children, the tale of these boys, Dewees and Bert Lowe, appears in many first-hand accounts of the storm. Virtually every family on Green Turtle Cay suffered because of the Great Abaco Hurricane of 1932. Most persons on Green Turtle Cay were left homeless. Many lost their livelihoods. Some lost loved ones. It's hard to imagine, though, that many endured more anguish and devastation than the family of Basil Lowe.[99][100]

There was complete devastation reported on this island. At Green Turtle Cay, it was reported that twelve houses out of a total of eighty were left standing and all the coconut and fruit-bearing trees were blown down. At Green Turtle Cay, initially the winds blew from the north, and then it increased with incredible ferocity until mid-day during the height of the storm. That ominous and practically complete calm followed this as the center passed over, to be followed immediately by strong winds from the south. Over 70 residents found shelter in an old quarry, and at the height of the storm, they were completely surprised when a horse fell on top of them. The heroes of the day were Mr. Murray Atwell and Dr. W. Kendrick, Plymouth Brother, who organized the people in seeking shelter and probably were indirectly the means of saving many lives.

The courage of Mrs. Atwell was superb, for at the height of the storm she went to find food for the little children. Dr. Kendrick had some medical experience and was able to render valuable first aid assistance. His house during the storm was converted into a temporary hospital giving shelter to one hundred injured persons. There were twenty-five persons who suffered broken limbs but were thankfully tended to by Dr. Kendrick at his home. Dr. Kendrick, apart from his medical assistance to the residents of Abaco, organized a united church service after the storm to pray for the storm victims and those who were killed. By the stroke of luck, Dr. Kendrick's electric generator was not destroyed, so he was still able to supply light. Mr. E. H. McKinney oversaw food and building supplies and was also

---

[99] September 7, 1932 - *What Misery Lay Ahead*, Albert Lowe Museum, Green Turtle Cay, Abaco.
[100] September 5, 1932 - *One Family's Heartbreak,* Albert Lowe Museum, Green Turtle Cay, Abaco.

hard at work organizing parties to distribute the hurricane relief aid. The distributions of supplies were put in charge of committees which were appointed by Mr. E.H. McKinney to distribute the goods and clear away the wreckage.

The swiftness and savage fury of the wind and waves were realized by the fact that four churches, the Government Wharf, and the hotel were demolished almost immediately when the storm reached its peak. The wind blew there at an unofficially estimated speed of 200 mph and the terror of those few minutes was added to by a very loud thunderstorm. One hundred dwelling houses were practically damaged or destroyed, and only twelve houses were left standing, along with a few coconut trees. One of the most gruesome sights was the burial ground, where all the tombstones were blown down, and dead bodies were scattered everywhere. Six victims were interred at the local Burial Society grave.

Mr. Arthur Holland, a pilot of a seaplane, was sent out by The Bahamas Government on a fact-finding mission to Abaco following the storm and his report came as a great shock to everyone because of the great devastation on Abaco. After hearing of this great devastation on Abaco, the Acting Colonial Secretary, after consultation, ordered that the *Lady Cordeaux* make a special trip to Abaco with hurricane relief supplies, including food supplies, building materials, blankets and additional tanks of water. When the *Lady Cordeaux* arrived at Hope Town, Cherokee Sound and Marsh Harbour building operations were already in progress; and at the latter place, four sides to a house were already to be seen being built back up again. Among those who boarded the *Lady Cordeaux* at the stricken settlements for the return trip to Nassau were, Mr. and Mrs. F. T. Buel and Mrs. Buel. They were taken on at Green Turtle Cay, Miss Roslyn Roberts, Great Guana Cay, Mr. J. S. Hall, Marsh Harbour, and Mr. R. H. Stratton, Mr. and Mrs. R. C. Johnson, Mrs. C. T. Malone and the Misses Madge and Dorothea Malone, the Rev. Walter Crowe, who were taken on at Hope Town.

Eventually, His Excellency the Administrator and the Hon. Mrs. Bede Clifford with Dr. H.A. Quackenbush would also take a tour, and they left in a seaplane piloted by Captain Arthur Holland to take a survey of the devastated settlements of Abaco. Bluff Point was the first settlement visited by them, and they were stunned to see that the settlement was demolished, forcing Mrs. Bede to remark "There is nothing left" of the settlement. Many of these residents required urgent medical attention and were quickly attended to by Dr. Quackenbush because their wounds were already showing signs of infection. Broken collarbones had to be set, and nail wounds to feet were just some of the injuries he attended to while he was there. Among the injured were Zachary Swain, Napoleon Davis, and Lina Swaine, who because of the nature of their injuries were required to seek medical assistance at the Public Hospital in Nassau. Looking at the damage at Bluff Point, the damage was caused by the storm surge. Every inhabitant in this settlement was left homeless.

Complete and utter devastation in Green Turtle Cay, Abaco after The Great Abaco Hurricane of 1932 (Image courtesy of Marysa Malone-Used with permission).

After visiting Green Turtle Cay, His Excellency remarked "Green Turtle Cay is a sight. They must have had a terrific blow." He noted that the Anglican Church, a solid stone building was reduced to a heap of rubbles. Three persons were so badly hurt that they had to be brought up to Nassau to seek medical attention at the hospital. One man was reported missing, but many believed that he was just buried beneath the rubbles. One witness

Dr. Kendricks told His Excellency of how he saw one government building being blown about 100 yards by the wind and landed on its roof.

In each settlement, His Excellency marveled at the brave and heroic attitude of the people and the way in which they had already started replanting seeds in their farms and rebuilding their houses. Amazingly, His Excellency noticed that in all the settlements, the wooden houses seemed to have withstood the fury of the storm better than the stone buildings which had all collapsed. This was especially noticeable in Hope Town. Three cases of typhoid fever had broken out in Hope Town and Green Turtle Cay after the storm. His Excellency stressed to the people the urgent need to boil all drinking water. He was also of the opinion that it would have been better if the people had stayed in one single sheltered spot before the worst of the storm and not remained in the individual houses. The wisdom of doing this was proven by the group of persons who sought shelter in the quarry at Green Turtle Cay. Those who stayed in their houses were caught like rats in a trap he said.

The members of the Government, Major Hugh M. Bell Director of Publicity, Mr. E.H. McKinney, of the Customs Department, oversaw the distribution of food and building supplies. Miss Webster of The Bahamas General Hospital was responsible for bringing all the necessary medical supplies. She was accompanied by an orderly from the Hospital, press representatives, and about a dozen persons who had relatives in various settlements in Abaco all took the trip to Abaco on the *Lady Cordeaux*. When the team of Government officials travelled to Abaco to render assistance to the people, different works were assigned to various members of the party. Major Lewis was placed in charge of the distribution of clothes which were donated to the centers at Government House and Moseley's Book Store. He was instructed to get in touch with the Commissioner or some responsible person and give the clothes to them for distribution to the needy persons in the community.

The women on the trip were separated into three groups, and each was dispatched to three different hurricane-ravaged settlements. Mrs. Kinneard and Mrs. Brice went to Great Guana Cay, to help the sick people there. Mrs. Millar and Mrs. Mallon went to Bluff Point, and Mrs. Symonette, Mrs. Robertson and Miss Pritchard went to Green Turtle Cay. They took with them milk for the babies, soup for the invalids, but their primary objective was to try and help the people with sanitary conditions, take care of the sick and if necessary, open soup kitchens. Furthermore, a large quantity of provisions and clothing was sent by private individuals and relatives of Abaconians to the distressed people of Abaco. The Hon. Charles Dundas as Chairman of the Agriculture and Marine Products Board issued instructions to see that all available seeds at this office be sent to the hurricane-stricken residents of Abaco.

A Relief Fund in aid of the hurricane victims in Abaco was opened at the Royal Bank of Canada on Bay Street at the request of the Central Government, and many persons contributed to this relief fund. Many churches throughout Nassau held special services to raise funds and made special offerings in the regular services to help the victims of the storm. Furthermore, the Government House was opened to the public as a collection center for relief aid for Abaco, where persons could bring food, clothing and building supplies to ship to Abaco. Various other places also offered this drop off service including, Moseley's Book Store and several other businesses. A benefit show was held at the Nassau Theatre Club where they showed Edward G. Robinson's 'Two Seconds' and the entire proceeds from this show was sent to the victims of the storm in Abaco.

A special meeting of the Daughters of the Empire was held, and a special collection was made to give to the residents of Abaco, and they also held a special luncheon with all the proceeds benefitting the victims in Abaco. A polo match was organized to be played at Fort Charlotte, and all the proceeds from this game were donated to the residents of Abaco. A very enjoyable and well-attended concert was held shortly after the storm at the Victoria Hall in aid of the Hurricane Relief Fund. In attendance at the event were the Governor H.E. Bede Clifford and other high-ranking officials in Government. The Grand Central Café held a special luncheon and dinner, and all the proceeds went to the Abaco victims. His Excellency, the Governor and the Hon. Mrs. Bede Clifford were represented at the dinner. A special dance was held at the Bahama Country Club, and all proceeds were sent directly to the Commissioners at Hope Town and Green Turtle Cay. They were then responsible for distributing the proceeds in small sums to the needy persons. Furthermore, some Miami, Florida residents hired the boat *Ena K.* to bring twenty-one packets of clothing for the hurricane sufferers at Abaco.

The hurricane devastated Bluff Point, which caused persons to move to Moore's Island. As stated earlier, some of the settlers of Bluff Point, Abaco moved to Murphy Town, and the Great Abaco Hurricane of 1932 legacy is preserved in common family names on the island, such as, Davis,

Swain, Curry, Dawkins, and Knowles who all moved there shortly after the hurricane. In settlement of Green Turtle Cay, it was reported to be in a state of complete and utter ruins. Sheets were seen hanging high up on trees as distress signals, and a Red Ensign was seen floating upside-down on a Flagstaff after the storm. The entire population, numbering about 250, was clustered together in large groups and the general atmosphere was one of complete bewilderment. Six persons had been severely injured, and almost everyone had minor injuries. There was no food of any kind in the settlement and as last resort water was obtained from a few small puddles. Every boat had been destroyed, and it was not possible, therefore, to catch any fish. The seas had swept right over the settlement destroying every building and all vegetation. At least six persons were killed and 26 severely injured. Very little food or water could be obtained after the storm.

Dr. W. A. Kendrick, who acted in a medical capacity around the settlements of Abaco, worked night and day untiringly among the injured. Disinfectants were very badly needed to be applied to many of the wounds which occurred because of the injuries sustained during and after the storm. Almost every house had been swept away. At Water Cay, shipping suffered significantly as one schooner, one sloop, and several small crafts were lost. Six homes and all the crops were destroyed at Sales Cay. All the citrus crops were destroyed, but otherwise, there wasn't any other damage reported in this settlement. A report by Mr. J.H. Saunders from Old Place, Abaco, said that 60 families there were left homeless and the following houses were blown down in the various settlements-Blackwood-40, Cornish Town-50, Cedar Harbour-10, Riding Rocks-7, Cherokee Sound-24, and Cooper's Town-40. He also reported a total of 7 deaths, 3 in addition to the four reported by Mr. Salter. During the morning after the hurricane, Mildred Lowe and her family dug throughout the rubble of the New Plymouth Hotel, searching for her parents. Her father, Irwin Lowe, was found alive, though it would be many hours before he could be moved from the pile of rubble on top of him but his wife Alice, he said, had died at about daybreak.

The two-story home of Captain Ronald Roberts had been hit by another building and shifted four feet from its foundation. So complete was the devastation in New Plymouth, Green Turtle Cay, that when these residents such as, Joe Curry emerged, he and others couldn't find his way out of their destroyed homes which littered the streets everywhere. When Joe Curry emerged, he could hardly find his way around the property. His half-brother, Thomas Roberts, and his niece, Insalee Sawyer, had been killed when their house collapsed. Eight days would pass before Roberts' body could be recovered. Though knocked from its stilts, Bessie and John Lowe's house had survived. Others in their family weren't as fortunate, Bessie and Herman Curry's sister, Edith, lost her kitchen building and was blown into the sea never to be seen again. The home of yet another sister, Emmie, was destroyed. The four-bedroom house where Herman and May Curry and their daughters had lived was reduced to a pile of rubble. All that remained was the kitchen roof, which they propped up and lived beneath until a new house could be built. Thomas Roberts, a 60-year old man, was crushed to death beneath the ruins of his three-story house.

At the height of the storm, a woman of colour Alicia Russell-a grandmother at the age of 38 years old living in Green Turtle Cay, was seen dragging herself up a hillside at the back of the settlement to seek shelter in the old stone quarry cut out of the rock. She had in her arms her three-weeks-old grandchild, while the mother, 15-year old Annie Ward followed. Suddenly, they were struck by a large gust of wind and a falling tree, the grandmother suddenly dropped the child, believing it to be dead, she continued her effort to reach the quarry, and stumbling, rested on the stone steps leading up the hill. An hour later she returned to where the baby had landed and amazingly found the baby alive, kicking and screaming but otherwise unharmed.

The pier, 1,400 feet long by 7 feet wide, was swept away. Individuals collected lumber from their ruined houses and took the nails out which were not rusted and re-used again. If a house was 18x24, it was rebuilt to 10x12 or 12x16 as there was not enough lumber to restore it to the same specifications as before. At Great Guana Cay, only four of thirty-five houses were left standing. Fifteen persons had been injured, and one man named James Sands was killed. Mrs. Teresa Sands housed 42 persons during the hurricane, which lasted from midnight on Sunday to 9 pm on Tuesday. The only houses which remained standing were Richard Sands, Melvin Roberts, Thomas Sands, Lawrence Cash, Stanley Weatherford, and Wilfred Albury. The seas swept over this settlement and had taken its toll on the people and the town. Also, boats of all kind, including the mail boat *Priscilla* were blown ashore and destroyed. The *Priscilla* was dragged over seven miles before being blown ashore and wrecked.

All the livestock of all kinds and crops were destroyed, and the wells were contaminated with seawater, and many persons faced starvation after the storm. At Marsh Harbour, extensive damage had been done, and all the crops were destroyed. Thousands of fruit trees of many varieties were destroyed, torn up by the roots, included in this total were 3000 banana trees. The hurricane destroyed the Marsh Harbour Post Office and the school building so the school had to be held in the Methodist Church for quite sometime after the storm until a new school could be rebuilt. The home of Mr. Goodwin Roberts, M.B.E., was severely damaged. According to Mr. Silas Cash, twelve homes were severely damaged, and the water rose over the settlement to a height of over 8 feet. He also said that the storm surge in this settlement was worse than the ones which occurred in the hurricanes of 1926. There were, fortunately, no deaths or injuries in this settlement.

Unfortunately, Hope Town met the same fate. The wireless station was destroyed, and the Methodist Church among other buildings including, the jail and post office were also demolished. All eighty-three homes in Hope Town, except Dr. Dolly's house, were all destroyed. One resident, Captain Holland reported that during the storm, the wind lifted a house out of the settlement, across the harbour, and smashed it on the rocks near the lighthouse, about a quarter of a mile. Ninety persons had to seek shelter in Mrs. Kelly Sand's house during the storm. Again, there was no loss of lives.

Cooper's Town was wiped out, but Cherokee Sound sustained very little damage. Elbow Cay was said to have had a terrific wind velocity estimated by some at 150 mph. It seems as if during the peak winds it was situated directly over the settlement of Elbow Cay. The settlement of Dundas Town began after this disastrous hurricane destroyed Cornish Town, Big Grape Tree, and Old Place. A tin washtub travelled in the hurricane from Hope Town to the eastern end of Marsh Harbour-a distance of seven and a half miles. The strong hurricane winds deprived the roosters of their crowing apparatus. Not a crow was heard in the settlements for several days after the hurricane, and strangely enough, the dogs were also very quiet as well. Commander R. Langdon-Jones, D.S.O., Inspector of Lighthouses, heard from Mr. J. O'Brien, who went to Abaco on the *Lady Cordeaux* reported that the Imperial Lighthouse at Hole-In-The-Wall was undamaged by the hurricane. The lighthouse at Elbow Cay, according to a message received from the ship *Patricia K* received only minor damage.

Mr. and Mrs. Frederick T. Buel, with Mrs. Townsend Buel, Mr. Buel's mother, returned to Nassau from Green Turtle Cay, Abaco on the *Lady Cordeaux* after the storm. The Buels went through a dramatic and unforgettable experience during the storm. Spanish Cay, 30 miles northwest of Green Turtle Cay was before the hurricane a picturesque island of about 300 acres, covered with beautiful shrubs and with an abundance of coconut trees. The Buels bought this Cay quite a while before the storm and built a very charming little home on one of the prettiest spots. Several weeks before the storm they left Nassau, where they had been staying all summer, and headed for Spanish Cay in the motorboat *Tramp*. They had scarcely arrived and moved into their new island home when the hurricane swept down upon them demolishing the house and its contents. Fortunately, the *Tramp* rode out the storm with success, and the Buels left as soon as they safely could for Green Turtle Cay. On the way, they stopped at Cooper's Town, where they rendered valuable first aid to a young coloured boy who suffered a compound fracture of the left leg. After putting the leg in splints, they carried the boy with them to Green Turtle Cay where he was put on board the *Lady Cordeaux* and brought to Nassau. The Abaco boy undoubtedly owed his life to the prompt action of these American visitors.

The following weather observations were made by Mr. David Salter, a resident of Abaco. Marsh Harbour-The height of the storm was at 9 am on Monday. The wind blew from the northeast until 3 pm when it shifted to the southwest and blew until nightfall. The lowest barometer reading was 27.00 inches, and the calm lasted for 15 minutes. Several schools, a teacher's residence, and thirteen houses were destroyed, and most of the remainder of the homes were severely damaged. Fortunately, there were no deaths reported in this settlement, but several boats were destroyed. The various crops and fruit orchards were wiped out, and two Government Wharves were destroyed.

At Hope Town, the peak of the storm occurred at 10 am on Monday. The wind blew from the northeast then shifted to the southeast where it blew the hardest when it was in this direction. The lowest barometer reading was 27.20 inches. In this settlement, there were 83 houses destroyed, 63 severely damaged and 40 slightly damaged. Mr. Russell, Sr., had his house blown down and Mrs. Carey had her dining room destroyed. Two boats were destroyed, but fortunately, there were no deaths reported, but two persons were severely injured. Food supplies were very low, and no medical supplies were available as they were destroyed when the doctor's residence and office were damaged. Little drinking water was available in this settlement as all the wells were contaminated by saltwater. All the public buildings and the radio station were destroyed. The Commissioner's resident and the office were slightly damaged. Both the Anglican and

Methodist churches were destroyed. At Man O' War Cay-11 houses were destroyed and 13 severely damaged.

At Green Turtle Cay, the peak of the storm was at noon on Monday. The wind blew from the northeast and then shifted to the southeast and then to the south. Captain Roberts turned his house into a hospital, and many people were taken there for treatment during and after the storm. All the homes, churches, schools, and Government buildings were destroyed in this settlement. Six persons were killed, and they were, George Lewis, Thomas Roberts, Mrs. Irvin Lowe, Miss Insley Sawyer, Louise Lowe, and Bert Lowe. There were 26 persons badly injured, including limb injuries, head wounds, and bruises of all description were also reported. After the storm, most residents lacked food or good drinking water, and they were in desperate need of medical supplies.

The *M/V Priscilla* reported some damage to the structure of the boat. At Bluff Point, the peak of the storm was at 2 pm on Monday. The winds blew from the north to northwest. The settlement was destroyed with all the boats, churches, school room, and burial grounds were all washed away. The storm surge caused most of the damages sustained. After the storm, no food or water was available in this settlement. Five persons were severely injured when they were sheltering in a house on a wet mat, and the hurricane blew the roof off their house, and this was when they sustained some injuries. At Great Guana Cay, only four homes were left standing, but they all suffered some form of damage, and all the boats were lost. At Cooper's Town, four persons were killed, and only six houses were left standing.

The *Lady Cordeaux* left Green Turtle Cay on Saturday at 1:30 pm and arrived at Marsh Harbour at 7:30 pm. Thousands of fruit trees of many varieties have been destroyed, torn up by the roots. According to Mr. Silas Cash, three thousand and twelve houses were severely damaged. "Water rose over the settlement to a height of 8 feet," Mr. Cash said. "It was worse than the storm surge that swept over the settlement in the hurricanes in 1926. Livestock of all kinds was almost wiped out. At times during the hurricane, the storm clouds appeared to be flying only ten feet above the Earth." Mr. R. S. Stratton, of the Plymouth Brethren, rendered valuable medical aid throughout the storm. The barometer fell to 28.07 inches. At Great Guana Cay, six of the thirty-five houses were left standing, and Mr. James Sands was killed. Mrs. Teresa Sands housed 42 persons during the hurricane, which lasted from midnight on Sunday, to 9 pm on

Tuesday. The owners of houses that were left standing were Richard Sands, Melvin Roberts, Thomas Sands, Lawrence Cash, Stanley Weatherford, and Wilfred Albury.

"Among those who boarded the *Lady Cordeaux* at the stricken settlements were, Mr. and Mrs. F. T. Buel and Mrs. Buel, who were taken on at Green Turtle Cay. Miss Roslyn Roberts, Great Guana Cay, Mr. J. S. Hall, Marsh Harbour, and Mr. R. H. Stratton, Mr. and Mrs. R. C. Johnson, Mrs. C. T. Malone and the Misses Madge and Dorothea Malone, the Rev. Walter Crowe, were taken on at Hope Town. Supplies were placed in charge of select committees, which were appointed to distribute the supplies and committees were also elected to supervise the clearing away of all the wreckage and debris on the island. At Old Place, about 60 families were rendered homeless, and supplies were provided to the residents on a needed basis.

"The sloop *Ethel B*, with Captain Balfour, arrived in Nassau soon after 1 o'clock from Bluff Point, where she left the previous afternoon, with three injured people, Zachary Swain, Napoleon Davis and Swain, and upon their arrival in Nassau, they were immediately taken to the hospital for treatment of their injuries. Dr. Quackenbush attended to these injured persons on Friday. They had been awaiting his return but owing to his delay it was decided that it would be better to bring them as quickly as possible to Nassau."[101]

---

[101] The Nassau Guardian, Monday September 12, 1932. *'Lady Cordeaux' Expected at Dawn Tomorrow: Passengers for Nassau Picked up at Settlements.* Retrieved: 12-12-2016.

CHAPTER SIXTEEN

The 1933 North Atlantic Hurricane Season-The year The Bahamas was Impacted by 4 Hurricanes and 1 Tropical Storm and their Impacts on the Islands of The Bahamas

The 1933 North Atlantic hurricane season was the second most active North Atlantic hurricane season on record, with 20 storms forming in the North Atlantic basin. The 1933 season was the most active of its time, surpassing the previous record-holder of 19 storms in 1887. Fifteen of the season's storms made landfall as tropical cyclones, and another struck land as an extratropical storm. Four hurricanes and one tropical storm hit The Bahamas during the season, and they were, the 1933 Florida–Mexico Hurricane (hurricanes were not officially named during this era, but in most cases, they were unofficially named after the city or country they significantly devastated). The Great Treasure Coast Hurricane, Great Cuba–Brownsville Hurricane which the U.S. Weather Bureau described as one of the most severe in the North Atlantic record books with sustained winds of 160 mph making it a strong Category 5 hurricane on the Saffir-Simpson Hurricane Wind Scale. This hurricane was one of only three Category 5 hurricanes to impact The Bahamas (The Great Abaco Hurricane of 1932 and Hurricane Andrew of 1992 were the other two). There was also the Great Treasure Coast Hurricane of 1933, which also impacted The Bahamas in 1933. For this chapter, I will be concentrating on three hurricanes, The Great Cuba–Brownsville Hurricane (Category 5), The Cuba–Bahamas Hurricane of 1933 (Category 3), and The Great Treasure Coast Hurricane (Category 4).

The season ran through the summer and the first half of fall in 1933; with the significant portion of the activity occurring as early as May and as late as November. A tropical cyclone was active for all but 13 days from June 28 to October 7. The year was surpassed in a total number of tropical cyclones by the 2005 season, which broke the record with 27 named storms and 1 unnamed storm — tropical cyclones that did not approach populated areas or shipping lanes, especially if they were relatively weak and of short duration, may have remained undetected because of the lack of satellite technology. It must be noted that technologies such as radar and satellite monitoring were not available until the mid to late 1940s and 1960s respectively, historical data on tropical cyclones from this period are often not reliable because of this factor. Compensating for the lack of general observation, hurricane researcher Christopher Landsea estimates the season could have produced at least 24 tropical cyclones. Christopher Landsea is an American meteorologist, formerly a research meteorologist with Hurricane Research Division of Atlantic Oceanographic & Meteorological Laboratory at NOAA, and now the Science and Operations Officer at the National Hurricane Center.

Of the 20 storms during the season, 11 attained hurricane statuses, and six of those were major hurricanes, with sustained winds of over 111 mph. Two of the hurricanes reached winds of 160 mph, which is a Category 5 hurricane on the modern Saffir-Simpson Hurricane Wind Scale. The season produced several deadly storms, with eight storms killing more than 20 people. All but 3 of the 20 known storms affected land at some point during their durations. Fifteen of the season's storms made landfall as tropical cyclones, and another struck land as an extratropical storm. The North Atlantic hurricane reanalysis project (HURDAT) found that the storms in 1933 were stronger than initially reported and some of them had to be adjusted to reflect this change and two of the hurricanes hitting The Bahamas were upgraded to Category 4 or 5 status on the Saffir-Simpson Hurricane Wind Scale.

The Florida-Mexico Hurricane of 1933

Meteorological History of the Florida-Mexico Hurricane of 1933

This hurricane lasted from July 24 to August 5 and had a peak wind intensity of 90 mph and the lowest central pressure of 975 millibars (hPa). On July 24, a tropical storm was detected. Located to the southeast of Antigua, it tracked west-northwestward, passing near St. Thomas with winds of up to 60 mph. The storm strengthened and attained hurricane status the next day north of Puerto Rico, and it continued its west-northwest movement. After moving through the northern Bahamas, the hurricane struck near Fort Pierce, Florida, with winds of 85 mph. The hurricane crossed the state and weakened to minimal tropical storm intensity. It turned to the west-southwest and re-strengthened to a hurricane on August 4 off the coast of Texas. It weakened again to tropical storm status and made its final landfall near Brownsville, Texas, on August 5 as a strong tropical storm. The system rapidly dissipated over northern Mexico.

While moving over Saint Christopher, the storm killed six people. Heavy rainfall was reported throughout the Virgin Islands. The hurricane caused the drowning of one person in The Bahamas, and moderate winds produced severe structural damage to the buildings in the archipelago. In Florida, the National Weather Bureau issued storm warnings between Miami to Titusville, while Governor David Sholtz issued a mandatory evacuation for 4,200 residents in vulnerable areas around Lake Okeechobee. Damage in Florida was minimal, limited to minor crops, roofs, and signs. In southern Texas, the hurricane produced moderate damage of $500,000, including disrupted telephone and telegraph lines. The storm produced high tides along the coast of Texas, covering parts of South Padre Island, and heavy rains in northern Mexico caused substantial damage.

On July 27, the cyclone brushed Grand Turk and the Caicos, producing winds visually estimated at 85 mph on the former island, with a fringe pressure reading of 995 MB (29.37 inches). The hurricane gradually bent to the northwest as it followed the arc of the eastern Bahamas. After 11 am EDT on July 28, the Norwegian steamship *Noreg* encountered southeast winds of 70 mph, yet pressures only dipped to 1002 MB (29.58 inches). The storm struck Cat Island, Bahamas, around 2 pm EDT with winds of 80 mph; the next day, the storm made another landfall on the Abaco Islands with the same winds. During this time, the storm turned to the west-northwest, near the east coast of Florida; this was likely due to a robust subtropical ridge in the area. In The Bahamas, sustained winds of 84 mph swept the Abaco Islands early on July 29 but caused only minimal damage there. Other reports indicated more severe damage elsewhere in the islands, including across the Turks and Caicos Islands, and one death occurred from drowning. The American schooner *Adams*, anchored off Grand Turk, was dragged out to sea by the hurricane's waves.

The Great Treasure Coast Hurricane of 1933

Meteorological History of the Great Treasure Coast Hurricane of 1933

This hurricane lasted from August 31 to September 7 and had a peak wind intensity of 140 mph Category 4 hurricane on the Saffir-Simpson Hurricane Wind Scale) and the lowest central pressure of 945 millibars (hPa). A tropical storm was first observed on August 31, 225 miles north-northeast of the island of Antigua. The storm rapidly intensified as it moved quickly to the west-northwest, attaining hurricane status later that day, and major hurricane strength on September 1, while located to the north of Puerto Rico. It continued west northwestward and reached its peak intensity, with maximum sustained winds of 140 mph, on September 2. The hurricane, then at Category 4 intensity on the Saffir-Simpson Hurricane Wind Scale, moved through the NW Bahamas at peak intensity and weakened slightly before making landfall on Jupiter, Florida, with winds of 125 mph on September 4. The system weakened rapidly over Florida to tropical storm status, and after turning to the north, decelerated. The weakening storm slowly moved through Georgia before dissipating near the Georgia/South Carolina border on September 7.

The powerful hurricane moved over or near several islands in The Bahamas. Winds on Spanish Wells and Harbour Island were both estimated at around 140 mph. Winds reached 110 mph at Governor's Harbour, 100 mph on Eleuthera, and 120 mph on the Abaco Islands. The storm was farther away from Nassau, where winds only reached 61 mph. The hurricane damaged a lumber mill on Abaco, washing away a dock. Substantial damage occurred on Harbour Island, including several roofs, the walls of government buildings, and the water system. The hurricane destroyed four churches and 37 houses, leaving 100 people homeless. A 1.5 miles road on Eleuthera was destroyed. Several islands sustained damage to farms, including the total loss of various fruit trees on Russell Island. Despite Category 4 winds on Spanish Wells, only five houses were destroyed, although most of the remaining dwellings lost their roofs. Collectively between North Point, James Cistern, and Gregory Town on Eleuthera, the storm destroyed 55 houses and damaged many others. On Grand Bahama, where 9 to 12 feet storm surge was reported, half of the homes were destroyed, as were 13 boats and two planes, and most docks were wrecked.

The Cuba–Bahamas Hurricane of 1933

Meteorological History of the Cuba–Bahamas Hurricane of 1933

This hurricane lasted from October 1 to October 8 and had a peak wind intensity of 125 mph and the lowest central pressure of 940 millibars (hPa). On October 1, a tropical storm developed off the northeast coast of Nicaragua. It moved slowly northward and gradually intensified, becoming a hurricane on October 3 just west of Jamaica. The hurricane turned to the north-northwest and hit the Cuban province of La Habana with winds of 110 mph on October 4. The hurricane then passed over Havana and turned to the northeast and strengthened, becoming a major hurricane as it moved south of Miami, Florida. The storm reached a peak intensity of 125 mph while moving through The Bahamas on October 6. As the hurricane moved through The Bahamas, it produced winds of 100 mph at Hope Town and 91 mph at Millville, both on the island of Abaco. The storm weakened as it accelerated to the northeast, and it became extratropical on October 8 to the south of Nova Scotia. It paralleled the Nova Scotia coast, turned to the east-southeast, and lost its tropical characteristics on October 9 over the open North Atlantic Ocean.

The Great Cuba-Brownsville Hurricane of 1933

Meteorological History of the Cuba–Brownsville Hurricane of 1933

This hurricane lasted from August 22 to September 5 and had a peak wind intensity of 160 mph and the lowest central pressure of 930 millibars (hPa). The eighth storm of the season was one of two storms in the 1933 North Atlantic hurricane season to reach the intensity of a Category 5 strength on the Saffir-Simpson Hurricane Wind Scale. It formed on August 22 off the west coast of Africa, and for much of its duration, it maintained a west-northwest track. The system intensified into a tropical storm on August 26 and into a hurricane on August 28. Passing north of the Lesser Antilles, the hurricane rapidly intensified as it approached the Turks and Caicos Islands. It reached Category 5 status and its peak winds of 160 mph on August 31. Subsequently, it weakened before striking northern Cuba on September 1 with winds of 120 mph. In Cuba country, the hurricane left about 100,000 people homeless and killed over 70 people. Damage was heaviest near the storm's path, and the strong winds destroyed houses and left areas without power. Damage was estimated at $11 million.

On August 29, the hurricane passed north of the Lesser Antilles as it approached the SE Bahamas. It underwent rapid strengthening: in 24 hours beginning late on August 29, the winds increased from 105 mph to 150 mph. It also became a small storm, as Grand Turk Island reported sustained winds of 156 mph while the hurricane passed slightly to the north on August 30. At 09:30 pm the next day, a ship near Mayaguana reported a barometric pressure of 930 millibars (27.00 inches) and hurricane-force winds. The pressure would ordinarily suggest winds of 152 mph, but because it was not reported in the eye and the storm was smaller than normal, the winds were estimated at 160 mph. The hurricane's winds rank as a Category 5 on the Saffir-Simpson Hurricane Wind Scale, one of two such storms in the 1933 season.

At around 08:00 am EDT on September 1, the hurricane made landfall on northern Cuba near Sagua La Grande, with winds of about 120 mph. The eye moved along the north coast of Cuba, crossing over Matanzas. Shortly after that, the storm exited into the Straits of Florida, and late on September 1, the hurricane passed about 16 miles north of Havana. After entering the Gulf of Mexico, the storm regained strength, and a ship reported a pressure of 948 millibars (28.00 inches) late on September 2; this suggested sustained winds of about 140 mph. The hurricane turned more to the west on September 3, and as it approached southern Texas, it weakened slightly as it decelerated. At midnight on September 5, the hurricane made its final landfall on South Padre Island in south Texas, with winds estimated at 125 mph. It quickly weakened over land as it crossed into northeastern Mexico, and the storm dissipated late on September 5.

Hurricane #18 of 1933

Meteorological History of Hurricane #18 of 1933

This hurricane formed on Octomber 25 and dissipated on November 7. This hurricane had maximum sustained winds of 90 mph making it a Category 1 hurricane on the Saffir-Simpson Hurricane Wind Scale and the lowest barometric pressure of 982 mbar(hPa). After a two-week period of inactivity, a tropical depression was detected in the western Caribbean Sea on October 25. It moved to the east-northeast then curved to the northwest while slowly intensifying. On October 29, it strengthened into a hurricane near Jamaica and reached peak winds of 90 mph before striking the western portion of the island. The hurricane turned to the northeast and weakened. It made landfall on southeastern Cuba as a strong tropical storm on October 31. The weakening storm changed its course to the north-northwest, as it drifted through Cuba and The Bahamas. On November 4, the storm turned once more to the northeast, accelerated, and was absorbed by an approaching cold front on November 7 near Bermuda.

Damages sustained on the major islands of The Bahamas during the hurricane season of 1933 in The Bahamas

Abaco

The Honourable Charles Dundas, the Colonial Secretary, visited Abaco and found the pineapple and citrus crops comparatively moderately damaged. The piers were damaged, and shipments of crops were delayed for about 15 days. At Hope Town, Hurricane #18 passed over Hope Town Abaco at 5 pm on October 5. The lowest barometer reading was 29.06 inches and the highest wind speed recorded was 100 mph. There was no significant damage reported to any of the government properties, and the storm passed just north of Millville, Abaco, where the wind speed was over 90 mph. At Green Turtle Cay, the storm left minor damages to houses with no loss of lives. A significant number of fields and orchards were severely damaged throughout the island. Because of Hurricane #12 on September 3, one of The Bahamas-Cuban Company's lumber mills at Abaco was forced to close to facilitate repairs to the hurricane-ravaged property. The new work on the company's dock was swept away by the storm, and about half of the prior work done to the building was wrecked and most of the equipment destroyed. Most of the stacks and blowpipes were destroyed during the storm.

Eleuthera

The Honourable Charles Dundas, the Colonial Secretary and a team consisting Mr. J.F. Holmes Engineer at Public Works, Mr. W.T. Dalgamo Agricultural Inspector and Mr. F.C. Albury, Secretary to the Agricultural and Marine Products Board, and Captain G.C. Manton, who had a substantial tomato interest in Eleuthera, visited Eleuthera after the storm on a fact-finding mission. They found that people were in bad condition because the loss of their farms which were hard hit by the hurricane. The storm started on Sunday morning when the sea receded about four miles from the shore. This storm left practically dry land where there had been four feet of water, and it came back in a sudden rush, overflowing the whole settlement of Lower Bogue and most of it houses with water. Most of the people at Lower Bogue took refuge in the schoolhouse during the storm, and many homeless families stayed there well after the storm had passed because their homes were destroyed during the storm.

The sloop *Lillian* was destroyed, and the settlement of Upper Bogue reportedly sustained only minor damages. Many people, including Mrs. Bullard, wife of the public-school teacher, narrowly escaped being drowned in the storm surge but one man suffered a broken arm in the process. Many houses were blown down, including the public-school teacher's home, and some houses were struck by lightning and were destroyed. A few people were slightly injured, and one was instantly killed. James Grant, already suffering from internal injuries, received a cut in the side, through which his intestine gushed, he died the following morning. Mrs. Black suffered severe injuries to the head and leg and had to be taken to Nassau for treatment at The Bahamas General Hospital. Thomas Neilly, whose brother George was killed during the storm also arrived for treatment for injuries sustained during the storm. The motor vessel *Ivy S* owned by Mr. M. B. Symonette was destroyed during the hurricane.

At Harbour Island on September 3, the center of the hurricane passed over Harbour Island at 6 am where the barometer read 27.90 inches and sustained winds of 125 mph. Fortunately, no lives were lost, but the damages sustained to houses and property were quite extensive. The Eleuthera's Commissioner's Office and the wireless station were all unroofed, and the southern wall of the Commissioner's Office was blown down. Several houses and churches were unroofed. The government's schoolhouse and water pumping station were all destroyed. The water supply pumping station and machinery were all significantly damaged during the hurricane. The northern half of roof vestry of St. John's Anglican Church was destroyed, and the costs of repairs were estimated at £50 ($6,013 2018 USD). The roof of the Blessed Sacrament Catholic was destroyed, and the Eleuthera Methodist School was destroyed. The jetty west of the Government Dock was also destroyed. The Eleuthera Baptist Church, Friendly Society Hall, and 'Jumper' Church were all destroyed. The private wharf at Mr. A.G. Ely's residence was destroyed.

About 37 dwelling homes were destroyed at Harbour Island, and about 100 people were left homeless. The packing house was destroyed with all the crate material, and the fertilizers inside the building were all destroyed. The damage was most extensive in the Barracks Hill section to the west of the town. At Governor's Harbour they reported maximum sustained winds of 110 mph and a barometer reading of 28.30 inches, but fortunately, there was no loss of lives. There was slight damage to several of the government properties, but extensive damages occurred to the private properties across the island. One and a half miles of road was destroyed at James Cistern, and slight damage was reported to public works in the settlements of Hatchet Bay and Gregory Town. The costs of damage to these settlements were widespread and extensive. At Spanish Wells, there was no loss of lives or injuries, but the damages to the farms were extensive and widespread. All the citrus trees and other fruit bearing trees were destroyed including, the fruit trees at Russell Island. These fruits included were bananas, pears and citrus trees like oranges and grapefruits. Maximum sustained winds at Spanish Wells were reportedly 140 mph making it a strong Category 4 storm on the Saffir-Simpson Hurricane Wind Scale. Given that fact, fortunately, only five houses were destroyed, but a lot of outside toilets were blown away, and practically every watertank in the settlement was unroofed.

The Board of Education School shifted its position and was significantly damaged on the inside of the building, and the roof of the Gospel Hall was severely damaged. At Palmetto Point, the wharf and Bethell's Packing House were all destroyed. There were six boats which were also destroyed in this settlement. At North Point, there were ten houses destroyed and many others significantly damaged. At James Cistern, there were twenty houses destroyed and many others severely damaged. At Gregory Town, there were twenty-five houses destroyed, and many other dwellings were severely damaged including several churches and fishing boats. At Tarpum Bay, Watkins's Packing House and Wharf were severely damaged. At Rock Sound, the wharf was washed away, and many of the crops were damaged. The mailboat *Dorothy S* left Nassau on a special trip to Harbour Island taking relief supplies of food, shingles, nails, and other building materials to the hard-hit residents of Eleuthera. The supplies were distributed to the residents by the Family Island Commissioner Mr. J.A. Hughes.

Berry Island

Several fishing smacks were destroyed and washed up upon the rocks during the storm.

Long Island

The hurricane passed over the island with maximum sustained winds of over 80 mph over the southern settlements. At Clarence Town, the W.T. Station was flooded with water from the hurricane, and the aerials were also blown down putting the station out of commission for a while after the hurricane. Most of the telephone lines were blown down, and throughout the island, there was only light to moderate damage. From Clarence Town to South End, five houses were blown down, and several farms were flooded, and only slight damage was reported to the roads and wharf. The schooner *Mascot* was blown out to sea with eighty heads of livestock aboard but fortunately with no crew members onboard. The schooner *Gold Chaser* with over 20 tons of cargo was lost at the southern end of Long Island. Sadly, one crew member and one passenger were lost with the ship. Most of the crops on the island were destroyed in the hurricane.

Exuma

The government chartered a seaplane from The Bahamas Air Service to search the Exuma Cays for the Ragged Island mail boat schooner *'Saale'* which went missing during the hurricane sailing from Nassau to Ragged

Island. The plane was found, and they rescued the crew of the *Lola Irene* in Farmer's Cay after being stranded by the hurricane. The schooner *Saale* was found a day later with both of its mast broken by the storm, but fortunately, the crew was safe.

Ragged Island

The hurricane destroyed many houses on the island and those that were left standing were simply too unsafe for occupancy. The hurricane also destroyed the salt that was already raked and piled up and ready for shipping, and this resulted in high unemployment throughout the island. The boats, which they depended on for their livelihood, were also wrecked or severely damaged.

Rum Cay

The hurricane passed over this island between 8 pm on September 2, and 1 am on the night of September 3, and the lowest barometer reading was 29.66 inches from 8:30 pm to 10:00pm, and maximum sustained winds were reported at 75 mph. There were no houses on the island damaged, but all the farms reported significant damage and the sea walls were destroyed.

Cat Island

Eight dwelling houses and one society hall were destroyed. However, no vessels were lost, and all persons were safe after the hurricane. Most of the fruit-bearing trees were lost, and all the banana crop was also lost.

Long Cay

Fifteen persons died during the hurricane, and many persons were injured. Several schooners were also destroyed in the storm. There were 18 houses which were blown down, and 21 others were severely damaged. All the government buildings on this island were destroyed. After the hurricane, many residents were near to starvation because there was very little food left on the island. After the storm, 50 bags of provisions from The Bahamas Government were dispatched to Mr. A. L. Symonette J.P. at Matthew Town to be distributed to the residents of Inagua and Long Cay.

Supplies of building materials for Long Cay were dispatched from Nassau on the *MV Alisada*, and it was arranged that they would make a special stop at Ragged Island to land supplies there, but the ship's sail was severely damaged so, the supplies were sent from Nassau to Ragged Island on the sloop *Athletic* instead.

Inagua

The sloop *Lolita* bound from Haiti to Nassau on Thursday, August 31, with a cargo of fruits was wrecked near The Bahamas Government Quarantine Station in Inagua in the heavy winds and the torrential rainfall from the hurricane which passed just north of Inagua. The crew of the wrecked sloop was safe, but the cargo had to be salvaged. This sloop collided with the ship by the name of *Inagua*. Fortunately, the *Inagua* received little damage apart from the shipment of salt which it lost during the accident.

At the request of The Bahamas Government, the mailboat, *MV S.S. Luna* sailed from New York to Matthew Town, Inagua to render assistance after the hurricane. Ordinarily, this ship or one of the Royal Netherlands company ships stopped at Inagua with provisions once every six weeks but because of the storm and a request was made from The Bahamas Government to allow this ship to make a special trip to this island to take hurricane relief supplies. After the storm, 50 bags of provisions were dispatched from the government in Nassau to Mr. A. L. Symonette J.P. at Matthew Town to be distributed among the residents of Inagua and Long Cay. Mr. Symonette offered The Bahamas Government the use of a boat owned by him, on the condition that the government pay the crew wages and the government accepted his offer and used his boat to distribute supplies.

Acklins

In several settlements, every house was destroyed, while throughout the island only two or three of the homes remained undamaged. Fourteen persons were reported drowned, while an additional eight persons were reported missing. The sloop *City Nassau* was damaged beyond repair. The sloop *City Train* owned by Mr. J.P. Darling and several other sloops were destroyed during the storm. Captain Collie's boat secured with a storm anchor in the Reef Harbour was washed onshore fifty feet from the sea. At the settlements of Jamaica Cay, Pleasant Point, Salina Point, and Binnacle Hill every house was blown down and many farm animals drowned, and farms ruined, leaving the inhabitants homeless and out of food. The school and all its materials were destroyed. Mr. H.E. Hudson, the teacher at Binnacle Hill, had to remain in a treetop until daylight because of the high water, after having been badly bruised by a falling house. His boat was destroyed, and he lost everything he owned. Catherine Edwards, an elderly woman, had her knee dislocated, and was brought to Nassau on the sloop *Lillian B* for treatment and due to the shortage of food, this boat ran out of food a day before reaching Nassau.

Crooked Island

There were six houses blown down and destroyed. The schooner *Complete* was blown away and destroyed with all its cargo and live poultry ruined, but fortunately, all the crew members were reported safe.

Mayaguana

Mayaguana was devastated by the hurricane as five persons were injured when winds of gale force tore across the island. Two of the five persons who were hurt were injured by falling houses, and they all suffered severe injuries and had to be taken to Nassau for medical treatment.

Andros

There was no loss of lives, and only minor damages were reported to properties throughout the island, and the fields on the island were flooded. Sadly, five men lost their lives and two sailing vessels *The Iver* and the sloop *The Demirah* were lost trying to sail from Andros to Ragged Island. *The Demirah* owned by Mr. Sam Gordon was lost off Cay Lobos, on a turtle hunting trip on the evening of Wednesday, August 30. The crew slept ashore during the night, and when they went on board the next morning and came back to the shore, they saw that the light station barometer was normal until 2 pm then it started falling rapidly. Later, they returned to the boat to secure it by putting all the anchors down on the sea bottom and then went back to the shore to bunker down for the storm. When they got back to the shore, they watched *The Demirah* begin dragging her anchors until sunset, and they never saw her again. The crew was rescued from the cay by another sailing sloop and was returned to Andros. *The Demirah* frequently visited Cay Lobos to supply the light station with firewood.

Nassau

Just before the impact of Hurricane #18, many small and medium-sized boats were taken to the mangrove swamp at Russell's Swamp on the southern shore of Hog Island opposite Potter's Cay. Many other motorboats were taken to Fox Hill Creek and Old Fort Creek, during the afternoon before the storm struck, while other small sailing boats and dinghies were hauled out of the water and removed to safety on the comparative shelter of side streets and backyards. Just before the storm, Bay Street presented a scene of unusual activity where the stores remained open for well over twelve hours to allow residents to stock up on hurricane supplies for the storm. New Providence sustained hurricane force winds of 100 mph during the hurricane. Trees were uprooted, and many houses had minor damage with a few houses unroofed. There was temporary flooding in several sections of roads in different locations across the island. The storm destroyed most of the telephone cables in the streets of New Providence.

The Pan American Airways barge and float were torn away from their mooring opposite the Eastern Parade and were swept into the Nassau Harbour. The lowest official barometer reading was 29.06 inches, and the highest wind velocity recorded in Nassau was over 100 mph. An iron coffin near the Government Quarantine Station on Athol Island was unearthed during the hurricane. The coffin, buried in the sandy soil which surrounds the old Quarantine Station, was discovered when the sand was blown away, revealing one end of the bullet-shaped casket. The water rose so high that the cellars of the houses and businesses along Bay Street were flooded and, in several homes, the water rose over the lower floors. Pan American Airways placed one of its planes at the disposal of the government free of charge for search and rescue missions and relief aid distributions. The Bahamas Government being very grateful for the gesture thanked Pan Am and used the plane to take government officials and technical experts to the hurricane-ravaged areas of the country to perform damage assessments and distribute aid.

Grand Bahama

After the three storms, the Colonial Secretary dispatched to the island of Grand Bahama Mr. F.H. S. Bowe, a Justice of the Peace to make a post-hurricane survey of the entire island. He found extensive damage was reported at Grand Bahama by Hurricane # 12, which passed over Harbour Island and Eleuthera and near Nassau on Sunday, September 3. The island experienced significant storm damage because half of all the houses were destroyed. There were eleven motorboats, two planes and two sailboats destroyed by the hurricane. Radio towers, schoolhouses, and teacher's residences were all blown down during the storm, and all the docks were swept away. The Church of England building was partly unroofed. The American yacht *Black Jack* with a party of twelve was washed ashore, but fortunately, no one was injured. The surface wind during the peak of the storm was estimated to be about 125 mph, and the storm surge was reported to be between nine to twelve feet above normal sea-level.

The Hurricane of 1936: –A tropical storm was first observed over the southeastern Bahamas on July 27. It tracked to the west-northwest, and made landfall a short distance south of Homestead, Florida, with winds of 65 mph. After crossing the state, it intensified over the eastern Gulf of Mexico and became a hurricane on July 30. The storm continued to strengthen, and on July 31 it hit the western Florida Panhandle near Camp Walton with peak winds of 105 mph. It weakened rapidly over land and dissipated over western Alabama on August 1. This was the first hurricane to impact The Bahamas after the introduction of ZNS 1540 am radio as a hurricane warning station on May 26, 1936. An unusual phenomenon happened in this hurricane, where the water receded out of the harbour leaving only the dry land and the sand exposed in The Bight, Acklins. Many of the residents went out on the newly exposed dry sandy banks and collected a variety of fish and conch to cook, which were left stranded during this event.

CHAPTER SEVENTEEN

The 1941 and 1945 Hurricanes Impacts on the islands of The Bahamas

The 1941 Florida Hurricane: –This hurricane lasted from October 3 to October 12 and had a peak wind intensity of 120 mph and the lowest central pressure reading of 962 millibars (hPa). Tropical Storm #5 was first observed to the north of the Virgin Islands on October 3. The storm generally tracked westward on October 4, strengthening to its peak intensity of 120 mph at 8 am EDT the next day. Now a Category 3 hurricane on the modern-day Saffir-Simpson Hurricane Wind Scale, the storm struck Cat Island, causing significant damage. Nassau sustained very little damage as compared to the islands located in the Central Bahamas. Most of the damages sustained in Nassau were to the wharves, small sloops, large boats, and downed trees and electrical wires provided major obstructions over the major roads across the island. The highest sustained winds at Soldier Road in Nassau was measured at 104 mph before the recording instrument was destroyed. The docks at both the Young's and Colonel Lansing's Estates were all destroyed. Some of the boats destroyed were *The Prince*, and *Zion Mission Boat*.

In Fresh Creek and Nicholl's Town, Andros the hurricane devastated these settlements as all the boats, many houses and outbuildings were destroyed, and there were reported several cases of severe flooding in low-lying areas throughout these two settlements. The sustained winds at Nicholl's Town of 100 miles and the lowest pressure reading was 29.20 inches between 8 pm and 10 pm EDT. Christopher Whyms, aged 53 and Salathiel Johnson 53, drowned while going ashore in a dinghy at Staniard Creek while five others in the boat made it safely ashore. The roof of the

Commissioner's Office was damaged, guttering of the teacher's residence and schoolroom were blown down; while one house and two kitchens were destroyed while many others were severely or slightly damaged. All the farms and fruit-bearing trees were destroyed. All the boats were destroyed, and some were blown up on the rocks and smashed to pieces.[102]

In Cat Island, at least 300 families were left homeless, and a falling house killed Samuel Seymour from the settlement of Old Bight. The highest sustained winds reported during the hurricane at The Bight was 63 mph and the lowest barometer pressure reading was 964.4 mbar or 28.48 inches. A few people were slightly hurt in Port Howe. From Arthur's Town to Port Howe-the damage reported was progressively worse. In some sections, hardly a house was left standing, and all the churches throughout the island were destroyed. One resident stated that in the aftermath of the hurricane it looked as if each settlement was bombed. The sloops, *Valley, Mascot* and *Silver G* were all lost at sea. About half of the houses were destroyed in all the settlements including, all the church buildings and Port Howe schoolhouse. The Commissioner's residence and office were severely damaged, and the wharf was destroyed. All the telephone lines were blown down, and most of the farms on the island were destroyed. The sloop *Valley* foundered near Wemys's Bight, Eleuthera with one-person onboard perishing during the hurricane.[103]

San Salvador suffered more devastation than any other island. The Commissioner for the island of San Salvador Mr. Hallam Ryan reported that very few houses remained standing after the hurricane and the few that remained standing were severely damaged. He stated that more than 120 families were left homeless and all the crops on this island were destroyed. The lowest reported barometric pressure reading was 28.10 inches which occurred at 10:30 am EDT when communications were interrupted when the hurricane destroyed the wireless tower and generator. The Commissioner's Office and residence were severely damaged. When the 1931 census was taken at San Salvador, it had a population of 600 persons and approximately 150 families.[104]

---

[102] The Nassau Tribune, Friday, October 10th, 1941, pg. 1, *'House to Receive Hurricane Messages.'* Retrieved: 22-12-2016.
[103] The Nassau Tribune, Tuesday, October 7th, 1941, pgs. 1 & 6 *'Watlings Island Still Silent, Cat Island Hard Hit.'* Retrieved: 22-12-2016.
[104] The Nassau Tribune, Thursday, October 9th, 1941, pg. 1, *H.E. Views Devastation at Stricken Islands.* Retrieved: 22-12-2016.

After passing Cat Island, the rapidly moving storm soon weakened as its track bent more to the northwest. At 8 pm EDT on October 6, the eye of the storm passed south of Nassau. The waters of Nassau Harbour were lashed into waves increasing in size with the rising tide which was high at about 7:30 pm as the storm reached its peak. The water washed across the abutment and into Bay Street, east and west of the town, bringing with it, debris of all kinds. For five miles eastwards from the city, trees of every description were strewn across the mainroads. Shirley Street was almost impassable in certain places and the streets in and around the town were littered with fallen branches and large trees that had been uprooted. Considerable damage was inflicted to the electrical wires all over the island.

In Nassau, no lives were lost, but significant damage was reported to the wharves, small boats, several houses. The vessels damaged comprised of mostly fishing crafts were in the range of 40 boats, and they extended from the city center to the Montagu Foreshore, and the harbour was littered with damaged ships, and several boats were thrown upon Malcolm's Park, east of the Pan American Airways seaplane base. The largest boat lost in the storm were the yacht *Goodwill II* owned by Mr. Henry Von Berg and the boat *Bitter Sweet* owned by Mr. Ellis Burnside. The sloop *Sarah B* was smashed against Malcolm's Park and was destroyed. Almost every wooden dock from Royal Nassau Sailing Club to the British Colonial Hotel, over two miles, were demolished, including that of the Nassau Yacht Club, Mr. P.M. Lightbourn's Pier and the bathhouse opposite the Pilot House, Mr. W.H.H. Maura's and one at Symonette's Shipyard. Among those severely damaged were at Fort Montague Pier, Captain Christopher Brown's Pier and Captain Harry Knowles Pier. Mr. C.J. Kelley lost a roof, and his residence suffered slight damage. After the hurricane, the Eastern Parade resembled a lake, and the water in the grounds of Fort Montague was nearly two feet deep. The southern verandah of the Colonial Secretary's house on Prospect Ridge was partly blown away. A piece of the roof on the northern side of Mr. Trevor Kelly's home in West Bay Street was blown off and came to rest on the 3rd Court of the Lucayan Tennis Club.

Ten hours later, the small hurricane struck the north end of Elliott Key, Florida, and then made a second landfall within the hour on the mainland at Goulds, near Homestead. Winds at landfall reached 100 mph, and the calm eye was reported over Goulds. After moving across southern Florida, the storm had weakened to a strong tropical storm but then restrengthened as it curved northwestward over the Gulf of Mexico. At about 5 am on October 7, the storm made another landfall along the Florida Panhandle near Carrabelle with winds of 90 mph. Turning toward the north and northeast, it crossed Georgia and South Carolina and entered the Atlantic Ocean on October 8. The storm finally dissipated several days later. Preparations for the storm were extensive; residents boarded up homes and businesses, while evacuations were recommended in some coastal areas.

In The Bahamas, where winds reached 110 mph, the storm killed four persons, 2 in Andros, 1 in Cat Island and one at sea. The city of Nassau was struck particularly hard, though damages sustained elsewhere throughout the country were also severe, with many homes reported destroyed. In Nassau, the maximum wind speed was measured at 104 mph. In Florida, the damage was relatively severe and included the deaths of several people. The high winds brought down trees and power lines, and wind-driven saltwater damaged vegetation well inland across Dade County, though the storm was characterized by unusually light rainfall. Storm surge in the Everglades region flooded local streets, particularly at Everglades City. As the storm progressed northward, the city of Tallahassee suffered widespread power outages and damage to numerous vehicles. Throughout the state, the hurricane inflicted $675,000 (1941 USD) in damages. The cyclone later killed one person in Georgia.

The 1942 Tropical Storm #10: –The Andros Tropical Storm of 1942 or Tropical Storm #10 of 1942. This tropical storm formed on October 13 and dissipated on October 18 of 1942. It had a peak intensity of 50 mph and the lowest pressure reading of 1005 millibars (hPa). A tropical depression developed just offshore modern-day Granma Province in Cuba on October 13, moving ashore within six hours. After emerging into the Atlantic near Gibara early on October 14, the depression turned northward and soon intensified into a tropical storm. During the next 24 hours, the storm moved through the Central Bahamas, striking or passing close to the islands of Exuma, Little San Salvador, and Eleuthera. A barometric pressure reading of 1005 millibars (29.70 inHg) was observed on Eleuthera around 8 am EDT on October 15, which was the lowest known pressure reading in relation to the system. Heavy rainfall was recorded on Eleuthera during the storm and farmers were exceptionally happy because the drought period had been broken and they therefore commenced planting their tomato plants that this island was so famous for growing in great abundance. The storm then turned northeastward and continued to strengthen slowly, peaking with maximum sustained winds of 50 mph on October 16. By late on October 18, the cyclone merged with a cold front while situated about 305 miles southeast of Massachusetts.

On the *Bright Light*, sailing sloop was passenger Bishop Alfred C. Symonette (brother of the famous late Bahamian folk singer George Symonette). His popular songs include, Sponger Money Never Done, Delia Gone, Peas N Rice, Don't Touch Me Tomato, No Lazy Man, The John B. Sails, and See How It Flies. Furthermore, he was the grandfather of present-day Rev. Michael A. Symonette of St. John's Native Baptist Society Church. A.C. Symonette was en-route from Andros to Nassau, him along with others went down with the boat and drowned when they were caught in Tropical Storm #10. Fortunately, two of the crew Mr. Leache Saunders and Mr. Joshua Lewis, who were experienced swimmers, were able to swim ashore during the hurricane.

His death sent a veil of sadness and deep regret over the entire islands of Andros and New Providence because he was a very popular preacher who was loved by all who met him or heard his preaching. On October 15 at 5 pm, the sloop *Bright Light* owned by Mr. George Minnis of Calabash Bay, Andros, on her way to Nassau from Calabash Bay, with twelve passengers on board, capsized and sank in Fresh Creek Channel. Two men reached the shore safely, but unfortunately, ten others were lost. Included in those who perished were Captain Charles Woodside and Bishop Alfred C. Symonette of the St. John's Native Baptist Church in Nassau. A.C. Symonette left Nassau on an inspection tour of the 71 churches throughout the island of Andros. Also included among the dead was Mr. M.J. Poitier, the Public-School Teacher at Calabash Bay, who attended the Commissioner's Conference in Nassau several weeks before the sinking of this boat. Other passengers who were on this ship were Captain Charles Woodside, Mildred Woodside, William (surname unknown), Inez Moxey, Catherine Lewis, Sceva Lewis, Jim Lewis, and Gladys Saunders.[105]

Mr. Symonette, who was 72 years old, was born in Acklins and came to Nassau as a boy. He had taken an active part in the administration of the National Baptist Convention of America and made several trips there in the interests of The Bahamas Mission. He had planned to leave for Nashville, Tennesse in the early part of November to attend the appointment of

---

[105] The Nassau Guardian, Saturday, November 14th, 1942, pg. 2, *'Ten Drowned in Sea Disaster.'* Retrieved: 22-12-2016.

officers of the Baptist Convention in America. Mr. Poiter was born at
Fortune Island, Long Cay in 1917, and in 1934 he won a scholarship to
attend the prestigious Government High School. In 1936 he was appointed
acting School Teacher of Calabash Bay and later held the position of Acting
Headmaster. Mr. T.A. Thompson, Inspector of Schools, described Mr.
Poitier as one of the most promising, passionate and caring teachers. After
this accident at sea, only one body was recovered, and the remaining nine
bodies were never recovered, according to the Andros Island outgoing
Commissioner Elgin Forsyth in his final report. Unfortunately, because
of the extremely rough waters and strong ocean currents, the bodies were
carried out to sea, never to be seen again. The Governor held an official
inquiry into this disaster led by incoming Commissioner Rolle of Nicholl's
Town and eventually ruled it an accident. After the accident, the Governor,
the King of England and Duchess of Winsor sent messages of sympathy to
the family and their relatives.[106]

The 1945 Homestead Hurricane: –This hurricane lasted from
September 12 to September 18 and had a peak wind intensity of 140 mph
(Category 4 hurricane on the Saffir-Simpson Hurricane Wind Scale) and
the lowest central pressure of 949 millibars (hPa). The most powerful
cyclone of the season was first noted as an intensifying hurricane east
of the Leeward Islands early on September 12. It moved west-northwest
gradually, passing north of Puerto Rico as a Category 2 hurricane and
moving through the Turks and Caicos Islands at Category 3 intensity. The
mature storm attained its peak as a Category 4 hurricane with winds of
140 mph after crossing the island of Andros in The Bahamas and soon
began a gradual west-northwest turn. It moved the northern end of Key
Largo ashore at 2:30 pm on August 15, progressing into mainland Florida
near Homestead, and at which point the cyclone became the third strongest
hurricane to hit Miami-Dade County, Florida on record. The system then
curved north throughout the central portions of the state before emerging
offshore and making a second landfall near Savannah, Georgia, with
sustained winds of 70 mph. On the northward track, this took the cyclone
into the South Atlantic States, where it completed extratropical transition
roughly 50 miles east-northeast of Danville, Virginia. The post-tropical

[106] The Nassau Guardian, Friday, November 13th, 1942, pg. 2, *'Nine Drowned in Tragic Sea Accident at Andros-Minister and Teacher Among Those Lost.'* Retrieved: 22-12-2016.

cyclone fluctuated in strength and was last noted east of Newfoundland on September 20.

On Grand Turk Island, up to three-quarters of the structures there were destroyed, and the remainder sustained at least minimal damage. Substantial damage occurred on Long Island, Bahamas as well. Reports suggested that up to 22 people may have been killed across the Turks and Caicos Islands. In Florida, the highest measured wind gust topped 138 mph at Carysfort Reef Light. A total of 1,632 residences were destroyed while an additional 5,372 others received damage, particularly near the landfall point in Homestead. Naval Air Station Richmond suffered catastrophic losses when high winds ignited a fire that engulfed 25 blimps, 366 airplanes, and 150 automobiles across three hangars. Although the station's weather equipment failed, an inspection of the hurricane's damage led to the conclusion that these severe gusts may have reached 150 mph there. Throughout the remainder of the state, communications were severed by downed telephone lines, crops were ruined, thousands of livestock were killed, and four people perished. The overall cost of damage reached $60 million. Farther north across the Carolinas, the hurricane inundated the region affected by heavy precipitation in the days before. The Cape Fear River crested at its highest level on record, flooding large sections of croplands and adjacent homes. In Richmond County, Virginia, broken dams led to significant flash flooding.

In The Bahamas and Turks and Caicos Islands, 22 persons were killed. The hurricane demolished three-quarters of the structures on Grand Turk Island, while the remaining intact buildings were damaged. The cyclone also produced massive damage on Long Island, though losses were not reported in Nassau. Peak gusts were estimated at 40 mph in Nassau. After the storm, the Daily Gleaner initiated a fund to offer aid for residents in the Turks and Caicos Islands. In the aftermath of the storm, more than 1,000 volunteer Red Cross workers were activated in response to the cyclone. A force of 400 German prisoners of wars and 200 Bahamian labourers participated in the cleanup process.

According to the various reports by the respective Out Island Commissioners, the damages sustained to these islands were great. Commissioner of the Long Cay District (comprising of Acklins, Crooked Island and Long Cay), Mr. Harry Malone reported that at Long Cay, the motor vessel, *William Sayle* owned by Mr. R.T. Symonette was sunk and eventually driven ashore during the hurricane, but the crew escaped to the mainland unhurt by the sinking of the ship. A significant amount of damage was reported at Long Cay, but the bananas collected from the boat *Willian Sayle* proved to be a significant advantage and a bountiful harvest to the starving residents because in all the houses the Governor visited while he was there, he noticed large bunches of bananas collected from the ship. On the Governor's journey back to Nassau from Acklins, he took a victim of the storm, Freddie Charlton aged 16, of Mayaguana-the only survivor from the wreck of the sloop *Forest Bird*. He was washed up on a bulk of timber on Acklins Island in a state of complete exhaustion and was suffering from severe shock. He was transported to the Bahamas General Hospital for treatment.[107]

The Long Cay district, which includes Crooked Island and Acklins reported the highest wind speeds. During the hurricane, Long Cay was devastated with sustained wind speeds of 140 mph (Category 4 intensity on the Saffir-Simpson Hurricane Wind Scale) and the lowest barometric pressure reading recorded at Long Cay was 29.48 inches at 2 pm EDT Friday, September 14. Long Cay itself had a population of 101 persons, Crooked Island 1,078 and Acklins 1,744. Many houses in both Acklins and Crooked Island were destroyed during the hurricane; however, there were no damages reported in Inagua. Furthermore, no damages were reported on Ragged Island, Cat Island or Abaco. On Bimini, the seawall was damaged, but otherwise, no damage was reported. In Mayaguana, there were no lives lost and all the farms on the island were destroyed, so they sought assistance from the government. However, the Mayaguana mailboat *River Queen* sunk and was wrecked at Landrail Point, and the sloop *Bahama Eagle* owned by Mr. Bruce Charlton of Mayaguana was wrecked at Long Island, but the crew members were all reported safe.

In the settlement of Clarence Town on the island of Long Island, the maximum sustained wind speeds recorded was 110 mph. The storm severely damaged the Government Wharf and destroyed the Lodge Hall. Also, there was slight damage reported in the settlement of Roses. In the settlement of George Town, Exuma, the Commissioner of this island reported hurricane force winds of over 75 mph and the wireless operator house was destroyed, but no loss of lives was reported. On the island of Andros, the schooner *Captain Roberts* was reportedly sunk in the peak of

---

[107] The Nassau Tribune, Saturday, September 22nd, 1945, pg. 1, *Governor Flies to Stricken Area*. Retrieved: 22-12-2016.

the storm just west of Andros.[108] In New Providence, between sixty and seventy crafts—schooners, motor boats and sailing boats (including the vessels *Paddy Halferty* and the Current Island mailboat), sought shelter on Hog Island (now Paradise Island).[109][110]

The vessel *Captain Roberts* owned by Mr. George Roberts from Harbour Island was wrecked just south of Andros during the hurricane, with a shipment of bananas and melons from Haiti to transport to Miami, Florida. The passengers were rescued by the crew of the motor vessel *Kismet* and then transported by another ship *Jenkin Roberts* to Miami. Of the nine-men crew-Captain John M. Carey, Engineer Alfred Bowe, and seaman Hartley Pinder were all washed overboard and drowned during the hurricane. The six remaining survivors stayed with the boat when it foundered, and they were Mate Vernon Albury, Cook James Fox, Harold Bethel, Asst. Engineer Harry Harding, Gerald Fox, and Seaman Joseph Pratt. After the hurricane, the Governor with an entourage of government officials travelled by Bahamas Airways to the devastated islands of Long Cay, Crooked Island, and Acklins.[111]

On the southern tip of South Andros, Hon. Mr. Basil McKinney, the Member of Parliament representative for the entire island of Andros, reported that the south end of the island was devastated by this hurricane where many houses were destroyed. After the storm, the government dispatched hurricane relief supplies there on the southern tip to ease their hardships caused by the hurricane on the sloop *Malarki*. In the settlement of Fresh Creek, Andros no damage was reported to any of the homes, but the sloop *Camera BA 367* suffered some damage and Captain Hubert McPhee, and three crew members were all reported safe.[112]

---

[108] The Nassau Guardian, Saturday, September 15, 1945, pg. 1, *Three Houses Destroyed at Clarence Town, Long Island*. Retrieved: 22-12-2016.

[109] Governor's Dispatches-Colonial Office Files (CO-23) June-December 1945-*Commissioners' Reports on the Damages Sustained by the hurricane*. Retrieved: 11-12-2016.

[110] The Nassau Tribune, Saturday, September 15, 1945, pg. 1, *Destructive Hurricane Sweeps Through The Bahamas*. Retrieved: 22-12-2016.

[111] The Nassau Guardian, Wednesday, September 19, 1945, pg. 1, *Crew Aboard Doomed Vessel Until Yesterday Morning & His Excellency to Visit Eastern Islands*. Retrieved: 22-12-2016.

[112] The Nassau Tribune, Monday, September 17, 1945, pg. 1, *Small Losses in The Bahamas,* Retrieved: 22-12-2016.

Hurricane Able in 1951: –The 1951 North Atlantic hurricane season was the first hurricane season in which the United States Weather Bureau officially named tropical cyclones. The season officially started on June 15, when the United States Weather Bureau began its daily monitoring for tropical cyclone activity; the season officially ended on November 15. It was the first year since 1937 in which no hurricanes made landfall on the United States; as Hurricane How was the only tropical storm to hit the nation, the season had the least tropical cyclone damage in the United States since the 1939 season. As in the 1950 season, names from the Joint Army/Navy Phonetic Alphabet were used to name storms this season and this continued into the 1952 North Atlantic hurricane season. However, 1952 season was the last year they used the Joint Army/Navy Phonetic Alphabet when they realized that it would cause significant problems in the record books should two major destructive Hurricane Able made landfall in the North Atlantic.

The first hurricane of the season, Able, formed before the official start of the season; before reanalysis in 2015, it was once listed as the earliest major hurricane on record in the North Atlantic basin. It formed on May 16 and executed a counterclockwise loop over The Bahamas; later it brushed the North Carolina coastline. The origins of the first hurricane of the season were from a trough that exited the East Coast of the United States on May 12. A low-pressure area developed on May 14, and two days later it developed into a tropical cyclone about 300 miles south of Bermuda. It formed beneath an upper-level low and initially was not fully tropical. The depression followed the low, initially toward the northwest and later the southwest. Moving over the Gulf Stream, the depression intensified into Tropical Storm Able on May 16. The storm turned to the south, and Hurricane Hunters reported that Able strengthened to hurricane status on May 17 off the coast of Florida.

The outer rainbands of Able produced light rainfall and high seas along the Florida coastline. It later moved through the NW Bahamas early on May 18, where it produced hurricane-force winds of 85 mph. The hurricane then turned to the north, gradually strengthening through May 21. Shortly after that, Able passed about 70 miles east of Cape Hatteras before turning east and reaching its peak of 90 mph early on May 22. Along the coast, the hurricane produced high tides and storm surge but little damage. Able maintained hurricane intensity for two more days before weakening to a tropical storm early on May 24. Able rapidly dissipated that same day, though originally it was assessed as having transitioned into an extratropical cyclone on May 23.

Until 2015, Able was listed as having peak winds of 115 mph and was analyzed to have been the earliest major hurricane on record. Such a storm would be a Category 3 or higher on the Saffir-Simpson Hurricane Wind Scale, a system developed and introduced in the 1970s. Able was also the strongest hurricane outside of the current hurricane season (June 1 through November 30). However, reanalysis by scientists in 2015 determined that Able was in fact, far weaker than listed initially in HURDAT, the official database containing information on storm tracks and intensities in the North Atlantic and Eastern North Pacific regions. It also lost its distinction as the strongest pre-season cyclone on record, the record being held by a Category 2 hurricane in March 1908. The hurricane was one of four North Atlantic hurricanes on record to exist during May, the others occurring in 1889, 1908, and 1970.[113] In The Bahamas, the maximum sustained winds were reported at 90 mph in Abaco near Walkers Cay, an island located 160 miles NE of Miami and 80 mph on the Abaco mainland.[114] A lumber barge ran aground in Grand Bahama approximately 20 miles off Pine Ridge, during the hurricane with 12 men aboard, but several hours later they were found safe. The barge was taking lumber to Jamaica.[115]

---

[113] *"Atlantic hurricane best track (HURDAT version 2)"*. Hurricane Research Division (Database). Miami, FL: National Hurricane Center. April 11, 2017. Retrieved: 03-11-2017.

[114] The Nassau Tribune, *"Hurricane Rakes Walkers Cay"*, May 19, 1951. Pg.1 Retrieved: 05-11-2016.

[115] The Nassau Guardian, *"May Hurricane" & "Lumber Barge Aground at Grand Bahama"*, May 18, 1951. Pg.1. Retrieved: 05-11-2017.

CHAPTER EIGHTEEN

Hurricane Donna's impact on the islands of The Bahamas in 1960

Hurricane Donna was formed in early September and produced heavy thunderstorms and above average rainfall throughout the Central and SE Bahamas. Hurricane Donna was one of the first major hurricanes to affect the SE Bahamas since the major hurricanes of 1926, 1928, 1932, and 1933 hurricane seasons. Donna was first detected in the tropical Atlantic in early September. Donna travelled for some 6000 miles mostly in a west-northwest direction through the extreme Northeastern Antilles, passing some 70 miles due north of Puerto Rico before it entered the SE Bahamas and eventually travelled across Florida.

Meteorological History of Hurricane Donna in 1960

Powerful hurricane Donna roared into the northeast Caribbean at peak intensity on late September 4. It then made its way across Puerto Rico and The Bahamas before swiping southern Florida on September 10, with maximum sustained winds of 135mph with gusts as high as 175 mph. Hurricane Donna was one of the all-time greatest hurricanes to impact The Bahamas. Donna was first detected as a tropical wave moving off the African Coast on August 29. It became a tropical storm over the tropical North Atlantic the next day and a hurricane on September 1. Hurricane Donna followed a general west-northwestward track for the following five days, passing over the northern Leeward Islands and on the September 4 and 5. It became a strong Category 4 hurricane on the Saffir-Simpson Hurricane Wind Scale, and then to the north of Puerto Rico on September 5.

Hurricane Donna turned westward on September 7 and passed through the islands of the SE Bahamas. A northwestward turn on September 9, brought the hurricane to the middle Florida Keys the next day at Category 4 intensity. Hurricane Donna caused a storm surge of up to 15 feet on Inagua in The Bahamas Islands. Also, there was a reported wind gust of up 190 mph at Inagua. At the time, Donna was labeled the 'Killer Hurricane' for damages and destruction it inflicted throughout the Caribbean and North America. This hurricane caused $387 million in damage in the United States and $13 million in the Caribbean. It was responsible for 50 deaths in the United States, and 114 deaths were reported from the Leeward Islands to The Bahamas, including 107 in Puerto Rico caused by mainly by flash flooding from the heavy rains. The public in The Bahamas attributed the low death toll to three factors, first, timely and accurate warnings, second, effective dissemination by the news media and other agencies, and finally, the taking of proper precautions. The accuracy of the warnings was in large part a reflection of the continuous tracking by aircraft reconnaissance and land-based radar, which was probably most complete of any hurricane before it.

Damages sustained on the major islands of The Bahamas during Hurricane Donna in 1960

Workers battening down at Taylor Industries before Hurricane Donna struck The Bahamas (Courtesy of The Tribune).

Hurricane Donna ripped through the islands of the Central and SE Bahamas with torrential rains, storm surge and powerful winds leaving widespread destruction in its' wake. Among the hardest hit islands were Mayaguana, Long Cay, Exuma, Crooked Island, Acklins and Long Island. A Special Committee was appointed by the Governor to oversee hurricane relief and to raise funds for the people affected by the hurricane. After the hurricane, The Bahamas Government dispatched Donald d' Albenas, Senior Representative in the House of Assembly for the Long Island-Ragged Island District. Also, Dr. E.H. Murcott, the Chief Medical Officer of Princess Margaret Hospital, Miss Ann Hopkins, The Bahamas Red Cross Society Director, Capt. Frederick Brown, the Senior Representative in the House of Assembly for Exuma District. Also, other government officials were dispatched to the hurricane-ravaged islands to conduct a preliminary inquiry and access the damage and report back to the government on the state of each island affected by the storm intending to rebuild the affected communities.

Mayaguana

Mayaguana, a 96-square mile island, 350 miles south-east of Nassau, with a population of about 600 persons, received the full brunt of the hurricane during the afternoon of Wednesday, September 7, as Donna progressed westward, gaining in intensity and expanding in size. At Mayaguana, three settlements, Abraham's Bay, Pirates Well and Betsy Bay were devastated with most building reduced to rubbles. Ninety-five percent of Abrahams Bay, ninety-five percent of Pirates Wells, and an estimated fifty percent of Betsy Bay residents were left homeless. The Mayaguana Auxiliary Air Force Base and the missile tracking station was hard hit. Tar and gravel roof covers were almost all blown off, and several buildings destroyed. The school at Abrahams Bay was destroyed because the walls caved in under the strong winds of Hurricane Donna.

The two newly built social halls were also destroyed. Both buildings were solidly constructed of concrete and stone, but after the hurricane, both buildings were reduced to rubbles. Mr. Reggie Charleton and his two daughters spent the entire hurricane in Commissioner M.I. Hepburn's chicken house. Strangely enough, the coop, chickens and the Charletons all survived. "We even collected a couple of eggs!" Mr. Charleton happily reported. Mr. McIntosh laboured two long years to build his house, and sadly Donna took only a few hours to destroy it. The Church at Abrahams Bay was wiped away, but oddly enough, the church's organ was the only thing left standing in the demolished building in perfect working order. There was a small building complete with concrete steps and concrete floor which was picked up and then dropped into a nearby ravine. Patrick Air Force Base in Florida sent two planes to Mayaguana and five other planes to the other affected islands equipped with medical doctors, tents for temporary shelter, food, clothing, and water, to render assistance to the residents affected by the storm.

San Salvador

Damage at San Salvador was reportedly very slight. The roof of the St. John's Baptist Church was blown down but other than that there were no significant damages reported on this island.

Acklins

Acklins suffered considerable damage because about 90% of the houses were wiped out. At Pine Field, 22 homes were destroyed, and 13 others were severely damaged, at Hard Hill, 13 houses were destroyed and 16 others severely damaged, at Anderson Hill, ten houses were destroyed and two others severely damaged. At Snug Corner, 30 homes were damaged, and 12 others were severely damaged, and at Mason's Bay, 18 houses were destroyed and 15 others severely damaged.

Ragged Island

The hurricane struck Ragged Island on September 8, sometime around 2 am and sustained hurricane force winds blew for 16 hours. About a third of the houses located in the settlement of Duncan Town were damaged or destroyed. About 95 percent of the buildings suffered damage to various degrees, but fortunately, there was no loss of lives during the hurricane. Fourteen houses were destroyed, and these included the Commissioner's Office and the Church of God. Many boats were destroyed, and others were blown ashore and severely damaged. Some of these boats included, Captain Hezekiah Moxey's mailboat *Lady Baillieu* and Captain Theodore Wilson boat *Omega*, and others including *Lady Astra* (Capt. Alexis Joffre's boat) and *The Invest* (Captain Henrikas Maycock's boat) along with others were all blown high and dry on the edge of the harbour at Duncan Town. The winds were so strong that even the four anchors holding Captain Hezekiah Moxey's mailboat were no match for the Category 4 hurricane with sustained winds of 140 mph.

The salt ponds which the people were so dependent upon for their livelihood were destroyed because they became completely inundated with water and a year's supply of salt was lost. The windmill operated water system installed in 1957 was severely damaged. Before the windmills were installed, the people drew water from wells located a mile and a half away from the settlement. The yacht *Carol* owned by Dr. C.W. Taylor and captained by Mr. Walters of Miami, Florida left St Thomas in the US Virgin Islands en-route to Florida. Captain Walters accompanied by his wife, and with the yacht's radio not working properly, they did not know of the approaching hurricane, except for what they surmised from the inclement weather. Captain Walters made it to Ragged Island just before Donna struck and made it safely ashore in enough time; however, the yacht *Carol* was blown ashore and suffered significant damage.

Crooked Island and Long Cay

Albert Town, in Long Cay, had several damaged houses.

Long Island

Long Island did not receive the full force of the hurricane; however, the southern and central parts of the island did suffer considerable damage. Many houses were destroyed while many others suffered considerable damage. Most of the farms throughout the island were wiped away by the storm, causing significant hardship to the people who were dependent upon farming for their livelihood. The communications lines were in total disrepair. After the hurricane, the government sent food, clothing, lumber, and medicine to the people of Long Island to ease their pain.

Exuma

Only slight damage was reported throughout the island; however, several persons were reported missing after the storm.

CHAPTER NINETEEN

Hurricane Betsy's impact on the islands of The Bahamas in 1965

Hurricane Betsy was an intense and destructive tropical cyclone that brought widespread damage to areas of The Bahamas, Florida and the central United States Gulf Coast in September 1965. The storm's erratic nature coupled with its intensity and minimized preparation time contributed to making Betsy the first tropical cyclone in the North Atlantic basin to accumulate at least $1 billion in damage. While the storm primarily affected areas of southern Florida and Louisiana, secondary effects were felt in The Bahamas and as far inland in the United States as the Ohio River Valley. Betsy began as a tropical depression north of French Guiana on August 27 and strengthened as it moved in a general northwestwardly direction. After executing a slight anticyclonic loop north of The Bahamas, Betsy proceeded to move through areas of South Florida on September 8, causing extensive crop damage. After emerging into the Gulf of Mexico, the cyclone strengthened and reached its peak intensity equivalent to that of a Category 4 hurricane on September 10 before making its final landfall near Grand Isle, Louisiana shortly after that. Once inland, Betsy was slow to weaken, and persisted for two more days before degenerating into an extratropical storm; these remnants lasted until September 13.

As a developing tropical cyclone, Betsy tracked over the northern Leeward Islands, producing moderate gusts and slight rainfall, though only minimal damage was reported. After tracking over open waters for several days, Betsy had significantly strengthened upon moving through The Bahamas. There, considerable damage occurred, particularly to crops on the archipelago's islands. For the island chain, Betsy was considered the worst hurricane since several tropical cyclones impacted the region in 1929,

1932 and 1933. Widespread power outage and property damage ensued due to the storm's strong winds. Overall, damage on The Bahamas amounted to at least $14 million, and one fatality occurred. From there Betsy tracked westward and made landfall on southern Florida, where it was considered the worst tropical cyclone since a hurricane in 1926.

After Betsy stalled and assumed a southwesterly course towards southern Florida, precautionary measures ceased in the Carolinas but were initiated in Florida and The Bahamas. Mackey Airlines assisted in the evacuation of 227 residents of West End Island to Miami, Fort Lauderdale, and West Palm Beach, Florida, for three flights. Three additional Douglas DC-10 airliners from Mackey Airlines evacuated 240 people, primarily American tourists, from Nassau to Miami. Various commercial flights between the archipelago and Florida were cancelled due to the impending storm.

On September 2, Betsy began to intensify quickly, and after strengthening to a Category 3 hurricane-equivalent – a major hurricane on the modern-day Saffir–Simpson hurricane wind scale – the small storm attained Category 4 intensity and reached an initial peak intensity with winds of 140 mph at 8pm EDT on September 4, while situated well north of the Turks and Caicos. However, on September 5, a blocking ridge of high pressure located over the Eastern United States forced Betsy to make a tight, clockwise loop and track in an unusual southwesterly path, redirecting it towards Florida and The Bahamas. At roughly the same time, the hurricane weakened to Category 2 intensity, though it later restrengthened to Category 3 intensity on September 6. Betsy's atypical southwesterly path brought it directly over several islands in the NW Bahamas, including Great Abaco Island.

Meteorological History of Hurricane Betsy in 1965

Hurricane Betsy in 1965 wrecked or destroyed several boats in Nassau Harbour near Potters' Cay on East Bay Street (Image courtesy of Bob Davies).

On August 23, an area of disturbed weather was spotted in the eastern Atlantic at 7.5°N and 29.5°W. On the morning of August 27, this area morphed into a tropical depression about 350 miles east-southeast of Barbados with a pressure reading of 1007mb (29.74in). Late in the evening, this system became the second tropical storm of the season and was named Betsy with maximum sustained winds of 45 mph and tropical storm force winds extending outward 250 miles from the center. It moved through the Lesser Antilles (no significant damages were reported in these islands) as a tropical storm on a northwest track and a speed of 21 mph. On the afternoon of the 29th Betsy became the second hurricane of the 1965 North Atlantic hurricane season, with maximum sustained winds of 80 mph near the center. It remained a mature hurricane through September 10. This storm never got a category on the Saffir-Simpson Hurricane Wind Scale because this scale was never in use until the 1971 North Atlantic hurricane season.

On August 30 and 31, Hurricane Betsy slowed to a halt, lost intensity and made its first gradual loop about 275 miles north of Puerto Rico. There was a second marked intensification period on September 1 and 2 when the central pressure fell approximately 40mb to 942 mbar (27.82 in.), the lowest recorded pressure reading during the hurricane's life history. This deepening cannot be readily explained because of lack of data. On September 1, a Hurricane Alert was issued for The Bahamas. A Tropical Storm or Hurricane Alert is the first of a three-tier warning system (a Tropical Cyclone Watch and Warning are the other two) that The Bahamas Department of Meteorology issues when a tropical cyclone can impact anywhere in The Bahamas within 60 hours. It's important to note that this Tropical Cyclone Alert warning system is not used anywhere else in the North Atlantic basin.

The Betsy track is an interesting one since pressure (height) rises to the north completely blocked and changed a well-established northward course on two occasions. In both cases, there were reductions in forward speed, just before the near stationary or looping track so that, in this respect, the two significant changes were not entirely unanticipated. On September 3, Hurricane Betsy skirted The Bahamas moving northwest at ten mph, and on September 4, it slowed down to a standstill, and then gradually performed another loop. Betsy was a most unusual storm and was one of the only storms in this region to make two most unusual loops.

Late on September 5, Betsy reached its farthest north location, some 430 miles south of Cape Hatteras, North Carolina. It then began a rather unusual southwestward movement because a large high-pressure system over the Eastern United States prevented any further northward movement. On September 6, Hurricane Betsy was just off Great Abaco Island moving on a southwesterly course at eight mph. Its highest sustained winds of 145 mph in the eyewall near the center, with gale force winds extending outward 300 miles to the north and 150 miles to the south of the center respectively. Residents of The Bahamas were warned of the hurricane on the evening of September 5, and Betsy continued through the NW Bahamas with the eye passing just to the north of Nassau.

At 8pm on the night of the storm, the winds in Nassau were measured at 140 mph and by the following morning it was 150 mph. On September 6, at 8pm the sustained winds recorded at Green Turtle Cay was 125 mph and by 5am the following morning, the winds were measured between 135-150 mph with higher gusts. At Marsh Harbour, the highest sustained winds were recorded between 135-145 mph. The highest sustained winds were measured in Abaco at 150 mph on the evening of the September 6, and hurricane force winds battered Abaco for a grueling 20 hours. After leaving The Bahamas, Betsy moved on a westerly track and passed over the Florida Keys.

Damages sustained on the major islands of The Bahamas during Hurricane Betsy in 1965

During Betsy's initial approach of the Bahamian archipelago on September 2, strong surf and high swells were reported in the Southeastern islands, though no damage was reported. Much of the damage inflicted to The Bahamas caused by Betsy occurred between September 6–8, when the tropical cyclone moved across the NW Bahamas as a Category 3 hurricane. The preceding track was similar to that of another major hurricane called The Great Andros Island Hurricane of 1929, which had also drastically curved southwestward before causing significant damage to the island group. Likewise, Betsy was considered the worst hurricane to strike the region since then. Stalling over The Bahamas for a period of time as it moved through the islands, several locations sustained The Betsy's effects for prolonged periods of time, despite the tropical cyclone's relatively small size. Widespread power outage and communication blackouts ensued, preventing the flow of reports between the NW Bahamas and other outlets as the storm took place. This included NASA communication centers in Cape Kennedy, which had lost contact with downrange missile tracking stations in the archipelago. Over the duration of the hurricane, the lowest pressure measured was 961 mbar (hPa; 28.40 inHg) in Dunmore Town on Harbour Island. However, no wind measurement was recorded alongside the pressure reading due to a resulting power failure.

Passing to the north of Nassau, Betsy caused considerable damage to the capital city and the rest of New Providence Island as the hurricane's eyewall stalled over the area. The last message received by the Miami Weather Bureau office from communication operators in Nassau during the storm was a report of 80 mph winds and rough seas late on September 6. The strong winds downed power lines, trees, and destroyed homes, while the heavy rainfall, having accumulated over several days, flooding city streets. Other streets were littered with coconuts, palm fronds, and other debris blown or felled by the strong winds. Heavy loss of shrubbery was also reported due to the storm's effects. A strong storm surge estimated at 10 feet swept into the Bay Street waterfront shopping district, inundating the renowned shopping area. The local police detachment, which had been holed up within a waterfront barracks, was forced to take refuge in a nearby high school due to the storm surge. Along the coast, 500 American tourists remained stranded in waterfront hotels. Despite the severe effects, only one person died in the Nassau area after his ship was destroyed and capsized in Nassau Harbor; this would be the only fatality associated with Betsy in The Bahamas.

Nassau

Two airplanes damaged by Hurricane Betsy at the old Windsor Airfield, and the one in the foreground was tied to the ground but that was no match for Betsy's strong winds (Courtesy of The Bahamas Department of Archives).

In New Providence, there was one loss of life and damage sustained to businesses and homes were said to be minimal. This was attributed to the fact that the people in New Providence took the warnings seriously, so they took care to batten down their houses and stayed at home. All around the island, there were downed power lines and fallen trees across the major thoroughfares of the island. At the Nassau International Airport, many planes broke away from their holdings and smashed into each other crushing some and damaging others beyond repairs. Sadly, on this island one-person loss his life aboard his ship, which was wrecked in Nassau Harbour during the storm. Compared to the islands of Eleuthera and Abaco, Nassau suffered considerably far less damage, and overall the loss was said to be minimal, resulting in the government diverting most of the resources to Eleuthera and Abaco-the two hardest hit islands.

Abaco

The Premier, the Hon. Sir Roland Symonette, who was vacationing with his family in England, had to interrupt his holiday and flew back home to The Bahamas because of Hurricane Betsy. The Minister Donald D'Albenas, the Minister responsible for Out Island Affairs, John Bethell Minister for Public Works, the Hon. C.W.F. Bethell, the Hon. Joseph Albury Minister for Electricity, the Hon. Foster Clarke Minister for Health and others on the team, took several trips to the affected islands of Eleuthera and Abaco. They went to access the damage and to take with them food supplies, water, and clothing for the people affected by Hurricane Betsy. The Hon. Donald D' Albenas took with him over 500 gallons of water for the people of Hope Town in Abaco alone because they were without drinking water because the saltwater from the storm surge had contaminated the freshwater wells and made them undrinkable. Jamaica, Bermuda, Trinidad, the British Red Cross, the American Red Cross, and Cuba sent offers for help to The Bahamas. Also, the United States Government through the services of the American Red Cross and CARE sent an ample supply of food and clothing to the people of the NW Bahamas affected by this storm. In Green Turtle Cay, a station clocked winds of 151 mph, well into Category 4 intensity on the modern-day Saffir–Simpson Hurricane Wind Scale. Another station in Hope Town measured a peak wind gust of 178 mph.

Bertram Mills and his family were victims of Hurricane Betsy. His son the young Mr. Silbert Mills owner of Bahamas Christian Network (BCN) TV in Abaco is located on the far right. This sad picture shows him standing with his children amid the ruins of his totally demolished home in Abaco (Courtesy of The Tribune).

The entire area of Hope Town, Abaco was covered with sand from the surge which was at least two feet deep. There was extensive damage to Hope Town Harbour Club. A significant number of homes throughout the island were damaged beyond repairs, and many of the docks were either destroyed or badly damaged. Many of the settlements throughout Abaco experienced extensive and widespread flooding of at least two feet in-depth in many areas and many houses were destroyed. Many of the Marsh Harbour homes roofs were blown away, and the teacher's residence was damaged, and half of the roof of the new Masonic Lodge was blown away. The warehouse, which was recently built on the dock, was severely damaged and the old wharf was a scene of utter destruction. Many ships and small dinghies were either destroyed or very severely damaged. Damage to the packing house sheds were extensive and the fertilizer kept inside was destroyed in the storm. The A & A boatyards and the dock were also destroyed.

The propane gas dock and Captain Archer's Dock were reportedly all destroyed during the hurricane. At Sandy Point, a small motorboat was found half a mile inland from where it was anchored. Mr. Talmadge Sawyer of Cherokee Sound was a fisherman for over 45 years, had his livelihood severely impacted when the storm destroyed his boat. Fortunately, he got it repaired but at a hefty price. Mr. Hubert Albury lost his entire crop of bananas and sugar cane to Betsy. In Little Abaco, all the fruit trees and plants were destroyed. Most of the crops in Northern Abaco were wiped out in this storm, and the estimate of the damage was said to be well over several million dollars to the crops alone. Fortunately, there was no loss of lives in Abaco during this storm.

Eleuthera

After cutting his vacation short, the Premier of The Bahamas, the Hon. Sir Roland Symonette and a team from various government ministries took a tour by air to the island of Eleuthera to review the damages caused by Hurricane Betsy. When he got to the settlement of Governor's Harbour, he discovered that the entire island of Eleuthera was devastated by Betsy and had to render temporary housing assistance to over 30 homeless persons immediately. These persons lost most of their homes and were homeless and had to be temporarily housed in the schoolhouse for two days but were moved to the Parish Hall and were taken care of by The Bahamas Red Cross Society under the leadership of Mrs. Pat Brown and Miss McSweeney. Mr. Albenas summed it up best when he stated that, "words can't describe the onslaught of Betsy and what the winds didn't damage, the sea came along and completely damaged and destroyed everything else."

At Tarpum Bay, the sea smashed into the police station and destroyed most of the furnishings, and two large refrigerators were found displaced well over 100 yards away. The Eastern Graveyard was severely damaged, and Barclays Bank was flooded with over two feet of water. Mr. Jack Sweeting's store Eleuthera Supplies Ltd was destroyed with an estimated damage of about £40,000. The raging seas and strong winds also smashed Mr. Richard Rolle's large warehouse open, and most of the contents including the machinery were all swept away at sea. Mr. Lorrain Pyfrom lost his entire warehouse stock and an automobile owned by the Methodist Church was blown from its garage and deposited completely wrecked into the sea, and this added some credence to the strength of the hurricane force winds they experienced.

There was only slight damage to the school, but the dock was destroyed. St. Patrick's Church and manse was in six to eight feet of floodwaters from the hurricane. Many vehicles were severely damaged or crushed by falling debris, trees or the floodwaters of this storm. In James Cistern, most of the road leading to the settlement was washed away, and the main road was rendered impassable. In Spanish Wells, there was widespread destruction, and utter devastation everywhere and the Spanish Wells Fishing Lodge was destroyed. Many of the fishing vessels were destroyed, and the strong winds blew them inland miles away from their original moorings. The Glass Window Bridge suffered considerable damage.

Total losses on this island were estimated at £5 million ($6.3 million 1965 BSD or $51.1 million 2019 USD), and the crops were all destroyed. It was estimated that between at £200,000 (~ $254,000,000), was spent by The Bahamas Government and charitable organizations to repair the damages caused by Hurricane Betsy. Insurance claims alone were estimated at £1.4 million (nearly $4 million).

CHAPTER TWENTY

Hurricane David's Impact on the Islands of The Bahamas in 1979

Meteorological History of Hurricane David in 1979

Hurricane David was an extremely deadly hurricane which caused massive devastation and loss of life in the Dominican Republic in August of 1979. A Cape Verde-type hurricane that reached Category 5 hurricane status on the Saffir-Simpson Hurricane Wind Scale, David was the fourth named tropical cyclone, second hurricane, and first major hurricane of the 1979 North Atlantic hurricane season, traversing through the Leeward Islands, Greater Antilles, and Eastern Seaboard of the United States during late August and early September. David was the first hurricane to affect the Lesser Antilles since Hurricane Inez in 1966. With winds of 175 mph, David remained the only storm of Category 5 intensity to make landfall in the Dominican Republic in the 20th century and the deadliest since the Great Dominican Republic Hurricane of 1930, killing over 2,000 people in its path. Also, the hurricane was the strongest to hit Dominica in the 20th century and was the deadliest Dominican Republic tropical cyclone since a hurricane killed over 200 persons in September of the 1834 season.

On August 25, the US National Hurricane Center reported that a tropical depression had developed within an area of disturbed weather, that was located about 870 miles to the southeast of the Cape Verde Islands. During that day, the depression slowly developed further as it moved westwards, under the influence of the subtropical ridge of high pressure that was located to the north of the system before the next day the NHC reported that the system had become a tropical storm and named it David. Becoming a hurricane on August 27, it moved west-northwestward before entering a period of rapid intensification which brought it to an intensity of 150 mph making it a strong Category 4 hurricane on the Saffir-Simpson Hurricane Wind Scale on August 28. Slight fluctuations in intensity occurred before the hurricane-ravaged the tiny Windward Island of Dominica on the 29th. David continued west-northwest and intensified into a Category 5 hurricane in the northeast Caribbean Sea, reaching peak intensity with maximum sustained winds of 175 mph and a minimum central pressure of 924 millibars (27.29 inches) on August 30.

An upper-level trough pulled David northward into Hispaniola as a Category 5 hurricane on the August 31. The eye passed almost directly over Santo Domingo, capital of the Dominican Republic with over a million people living there at the time. The storm crossed over the island and emerged as a weak hurricane after drenching the islands. After passing the Windward Passage, David struck eastern Cuba as a minimal hurricane on September 1. It weakened to a tropical storm over land but quickly re-strengthened as it again reached open waters. David turned to the northwest along the western edge of the subtropical ridge and re-intensified to a Category 2 hurricane while over The Bahamas, where it caused substantial damage. Despite initial forecasts of a projected landfall in Miami, Florida, the hurricane turned to the north-northwest just before landfall to strike near West Palm Beach, Florida on September 3.

It paralleled the Florida coastline just inland until emerging into the western Atlantic Ocean at New Smyrna Beach, Florida later September 3. David continued to the north-northwest, and made its final landfall just south of Savannah, Georgia as a minimal hurricane on September 5. It turned to the northeast while weakening over land, and became extratropical on the 6th over New York. As an extratropical storm, David continued to the northeast over New England and the Canadian Maritimes. David intensified once more as it crossed the far north Atlantic, clipping northwestern Iceland before moving eastward well north of the Faroe Islands on September 10.

David is believed to have been responsible for 2,068 deaths, making it one of the deadliest hurricanes of the modern era. It caused considerable damage across its path, most of which occurred in the Dominican Republic where the hurricane made landfall as a Category 5 hurricane. While passing through The Bahamas, David brought 70–80 mph winds to the island of Andros as the eye passed over the archipelago. David, though still disorganized, produced heavy rainfall in the country. Strong wind gusts uprooted trees, and overall damage was minimal. The name David was retired following this storm because of its devastation and high death toll and will never be used again for any North Atlantic hurricane. It was replaced with Danny for the 1985 season.

In The Bahamas, the first alert on Hurricane David was issued at noon on Thursday, August 30, while David was just south of Puerto Rico. During this time, the islands of the Turks and Caicos were warned of possible northward recurvature due to a trough in the westerlies just off the coast of the United States. Fortunately, as Hurricane David crossed Hispaniola and eastern Cuba the mountainous terrains on those islands weakened it considerably to a Category one hurricane. On Saturday, it emerged from the mountainous terrain as a weak Category 1 storm near Inagua, the southernmost island. During Saturday night, Sunday and Monday, September 1-3, David moved northwest up the archipelago making a direct passage over the islands of Ragged Island, Andros, and Bimini. Every island felt gale force winds, and gusts to full hurricane force were observed in New Providence, and winds of sustained hurricane force affected Andros and Bimini. During the afternoon of the 2nd, the island of Andros reported winds of 60 to 70 knots shortly before the passage of the eye of David. Heavy rainfall fell on most islands causing widespread flooding, and in one day alone, Long Island reported 9.35 inches, Long Cay 13.04 inches and Bimini 8.16 inches of rainfall.

Citizens on several of the islands were evacuated to public shelters in schoolhouses and churches. Falling trees downed power and communication lines, and damages were inflicted to the roofs, roads, and docks. Considerable damage was inflicted to the agricultural sector, but it was said to be mild in comparison to other countries of the Caribbean. The total cost to The Bahamas was estimated at US $1.74 million (1979 USD, $6.1 million 2017 USD), of which US $1.41 or 81 percent was inflicted to the agriculture sector. Also, a further US $400,000.00 in damage was done to a warehouse, a home and a hotel on New Providence by several tornadoes, which formed on the Monday afternoon of September 3, in the wake of Hurricane David.

Damages sustained on the major islands of The Bahamas during Hurricane David in 1979

Exuma

Exuma is a district of The Bahamas, consisting of over 365 islands, also called cays. The largest of the cays is Great Exuma, which is 37 miles in length and joined to another island, Little Exuma by a small bridge. The capital and largest city in the district is George Town (population 1,437), which was founded in 1793 and located on Great Exuma. The Tropic of Cancer runs across a beach close to the city. The entire island chain is 130 miles long and 72 miles² in area. Great Exuma island has an area of 61-mile² while Little Exuma has an area of 11 miles². Between 2000 and 2018, the population of Exuma more than doubled, reflecting the construction of large and small resort properties and the related direct air traffic to Great Exuma from locations as distant as Toronto, Ontario, Canada. The official population of Exuma in 2010 was 7,314 persons. Damages sustained on this island were slight besides from a few fallen coconuts' trees, fruit and other trees that fell but no loss of lives or severe damages were reported. After the storm, it was said that residents of Little Exuma could not reach Big Exuma due to massive flooding.

Mayaguana

There were no casualties or damage to property because the island only received the side effects of the storm. The 550 residents' population of the island were evacuated to more secure buildings at Betsy Bay and Pirate's Well so, most residents were well secured during the storm.

Crooked Island

There was no loss of life or any significant damage to the properties on the island except for a few fruit crops damaged by the hurricane. All the residents were evacuated to the Colonial Hill Central High School so; these residents were well secured during the storm. This island recorded a total of well over 13.04 inches (the average monthly rainfall for September in Crooked Island is 4.21 inches) during the passage of this storm.

Inagua

There was no loss of lives, injuries or any significant property damage to the 1,200 residents on the island.

Acklins

The island experienced hurricane force winds of 75 mph or a Category 1 hurricane, but there was only slight damage reported to a few trees, but no injuries or loss of lives were reported.

Rum Cay

There were no casualties or damage to property, and this island only received the outer fringes of the storm. However, there were reports of some fallen coconut trees. The 100 residents on the island stayed in their individual homes during the storm so, most residents were well secured during the storm.

Long Island

At Deadman's Cay, the high winds and the flooding damaged many farms and wiped away fruit trees. No one in the settlement of about 250 persons were evacuated. There were no loss of lives or injuries. Most farms on the island suffered significant damage to the crops (especially the banana crop) and livestock mainly in southern parts of the island. After the storm, there was a severe shortage of bananas. At the time, Long Island supplied about 90% of the bananas for the entire country. This resulted in severe economic problems for the Long Island farmers because they depended heavily on the banana crop as their primary source of income. It was reported that in Deadman's Cay alone, about 90% of the bananas were destroyed.

Mr. Alexander Knowles of Deadman's Cay reported to The Tribune Newspaper that he lost about $25,000 to $30,000 worth of bananas alone. Many persons on the southern part of Clarence Town lost a considerable amount of livestock, especially goats and sheep. The torrential rainfall from the hurricane dissolved most of the 1979's yearly solar salt crop at Diamond Crystal's, Long Island's Bahamas facility. Unfortunately, the hurricane struck during the harvesting operation and the heavy rainfall dissolved almost all the unharvested solar salt in the crystallizer ponds. The financial impact of the loss of the harvest was estimated to be approximately $600,000. Long Island reported a total of over 9.35 inches of rainfall from this storm alone.

Andros

There was significant structural damage reported at the Small Hope Bay, facilities in North Andros. There were no reports of fatalities on this island; however, there was substantial and widespread crop damage over the entire island. With winds strengthening from 75 to 90 mph David moved over the southeast Andros at 4 pm on Sunday, September 3, as it moved in a northwest direction at 12 mph. All over the island, there were many downed power lines and trees, and it also destroyed many houses. The roof of the Central Andros School was partially torn off. In South Andros and Mangrove Cay, several farms in low-lying areas were flooded and most of the crops destroyed. The hurricane force winds toppled numerous coconut and banana trees. In Nicholl's Town, there were many downed power lines and fallen trees across the main road thereby, restricting traffic for quite a while after the storm.

Bartad-the farming project in Andros reported minor damage to the structures of the various buildings. However, significant damage was reported to the crops. The scuba-diving fishing resort of Small Hope Bay Lodge near Fresh Creek was destroyed when the storm's massive waves and torrential rainfall battered the lodge until it was destroyed. Fortunately, there were no injuries or deaths as the motel had been evacuated earlier on the Sunday before the hurricane. The hurricane also affected the annual lobster fishing season for many of the fishermen in the Andros district by forcing them to remain at home and to secure their fishing boats. AUTEC (American Underwater Technical Evaluation Center) evacuated over 1000 of their staff at the various bases in Andros to safety in Florida.

After the storm, the Bahamas Red Cross Society shipped 4,000 pounds of food, including sugar, rice, flour and soup and non-food items such as blankets and clothing to alleviate shortages caused by Hurricane David. The airlift was ordered after an evaluation of the hard-hit areas by the Red Cross President Mr. C.B. Moss and Minister of Labour and Home Affairs, Hon. Darrell Rolle and the hurricane evaluation team who visited the island on September 4, on a fact-finding mission. They found downed trees and power lines everywhere, and there were significant damages to roofs of many homes.

Although no injuries were reported at Andros, a considerable amount of damage occurred to the crops, poultry, and livestock. The supplies were landed in Fresh Creek, San Andros, and Kemp's Bay and from there the Red Cross worked in conjunction with the Family Island Commissioners in visiting the settlements and distributing the goods to those who needed them. Some of the affected settlements were Behring Point, Cargill Creek, Fresh Creek, Calabash Bay, Small Hope, Love Hill, Staniard Creek, Blanket Sound, Mastic Point, Kemp's Bay, Nicholl's Town, Morgan's Bluff, Red Bays, Driggs Hill, and The Bluff.

Bimini

The island of Bimini sustained winds of more than more than 110 mph during the peak of the hurricane, leaving great devastation in the wake of the storm. The island famous for its deep-sea sports fishing suffered extensive damage to houses, docks, boats, and trees on the island, but fortunately, there was no loss of life. Some residents took shelter in some government evacuation centers, while others remained at home or moved in with friends and relatives. Bimini which is seven miles long and the widest portion is slightly less than 300 yards and sits on the edge of the ocean about 90 miles from Miami. Hurricane David came down with full force shortly after midnight on Sunday, September 2, with winds of more than 110 mph.

By early Monday morning, the calm center of the eye passed over the island and lasted for about two hours. It ripped trees out of the ground, wrecked houses, destroyed docks and sunk even well-secured boats. Electricity and telephone communications went out on Sunday night and remained out for about two weeks after the storm. Many of the palm trees that lined the famous Bimini Harbour were uprooted. Some boats that did not sink were washed ashore and wrecked beyond repairs. Among the buildings damaged was the famous Bimini Big Game Fishing Lounge which occurred when a large coconut tree fell on it. A huge pine tree fell on the north-east section of Bimini's MIC Public School significantly damaging it. Dorothy Dottin lost her newly constructed house, before the hurricane, her original home was destroyed by fire. The community assisted her, and funds were raised to rebuild a new house. The new house was just about finished when David came along and destroyed it again.

A section of Freddy Weech's Dock was ripped off, that marina catered to charter boat services. The Bimini Hotel Dock was destroyed, and many other docks were also significantly damaged. A hurricane-induced birth was recorded on this island to Miss Faith Dottin who named the baby 'David' after the hurricane. This storm produced a total in one day of over 8.16 inches of rainfall during the passage of Hurricane David (the average monthly rainfall for Bimini is 8.80 inches).

Grand Bahama

Many trees were uprooted along the street, around the hotels and residential areas. Freeport Power and Telephone Company experienced island-wide blackouts and some significant damage to the phone lines. At the Bahama Princess Hotel, bedrooms were without electricity and water as tourists waited for the storm to subside. One big tree near the hotel pool was uprooted by the storm, and small branches were snapped off by the high winds and were lying all over the hotel grounds. The airport was closed for over 24 hours, and flights in and out of Freeport had to be either diverted or cancelled.

Nassau

Several hotels in Nassau suffered significant damage costing thousands of dollars to bring their properties back to some degree of normalcy after Hurricane David. Loew's Paradise Island Hotel sustained the worst damage with cost being estimated between $50,000 and $100,000. Most of the damage was confined to the lighting on the outside tennis courts. The hotel also lost all its beach-side thatched palm huts. Several windows in the main building also became dislodged, and shingles were ripped off the hotel's villas, and the balustrade at the front of the hotel was blown away in the storm. The Nassau Beach Hotel suffered damages estimated between $7,000 and $10,000. At this hotel, several of the windows were broken, and several wooden umbrellas were destroyed. There was some leaking in the building at the Paradise Island Casino, and the hotel roof also suffered some damage. At the Britannia Beach Hotel, only minor damage was reported compared to the other hotels. Paradise Hotel suffered significant damage in the thousands of dollars to both the property and the building itself.

The Ambassador Beach Hotel reported little damage other than a large tree which was blown down near the swimming pool and about six feet of water was reported in the basement. Most of the hotels had to absorb the costs for those guests who were forced to stay over their expected time due to Hurricane David. ZNS television went off the air for about two days after the storm damaged the transmitting tower at South Beach and flooded the equipment room. ZNS Bahamas was also inaudible in some southern islands, where warnings were therefore not heard. All the Ministry of Education schools were delayed in opening for an additional week because many of the schools were severely damaged, flooded and filled with debris from the storm. Uriah McPhee suffered considerable roof damage, but fortunately, it was repaired before the scheduled re-opening of school. Most of the private schools were only delayed opening for three days after the storm.

Power cables were blown down, and roads were blocked by fallen trees in several parts of New Providence. Heavy seas from the storm surge damaged several wooden docks in several parts of the island including, The Nassau Yacht Club. Many sporting activities which were scheduled for the weekend of David, but most were postponed for an additional two weeks. Bahamas Telecommunications work crew had to work overtime for days after the storm to repair damaged cables which left 1,600 subscribers without power in the Soldier Road area. After the storm, about 30,000 persons were out of electricity, and Bahamas Electricity Corporation work crew also had to work overtime to repair the damaged power lines throughout the island. The hurricane also damaged the distribution system and knocked out two gas turbine generators at the Blue Hills power plant. Fallen trees damaged the corporation's distribution system, lines being down and blown fuses in several places. Also, there was water damage to two of the generators at the Blue Hills facility. The loss was extensive, and roughly about half of the island was without electricity for a few days after the storm.

Mr. Charles Gibson's $45,000 home in Lysander and McKinney Drive in Stapledon Gardens was destroyed by a tornado, which was spawned in the remnant spiral rain bands of David. His two boys one five and the other nine were at home watching television but were unharmed during this freak event. Mr. Gibson, an employee of The Bahamas Telecommunications

Corporation, was not at home during the incident but his wife was at home on the outside closing the family's car door when she heard the loud noise. She then heard her two boys screaming her name. When she went to investigate, she could not believe her eyes. She saw the roof falling with only the concrete walls standing with remnants of the completely torn apart roof still perched in a twisted manner on top of the structure.

Mr. Vince Ferguson, a neighbour, said he heard what sounded like a loud explosion. He said he heard this 'varoom' sound and when he looked out he saw this large funnel cloud which had taken off the entire roof of the house. Mr. Ferguson said he could see at least two funnel clouds which touched down to the west of Stapleton Gardens. Another tornado then went on to uproot several pine trees near the Nassau Beach Hotel on the Cable Beach Roadway. Before the tornado hit Mr. Gibson's house, it hit a large warehouse on Carmichael Road owned by Mr. Perry Darville, causing thousands of dollars' worth of damage. After it left Mr. Gibson's house, the tornado sped north to the straw market opposite the Nassau Beach Hotel, destroying most of the stalls and scattering straw work throughout the area. The tornado moved across the street, picked up a small motorbike and hurled it into the air and destroyed it. From there it travelled east to the tennis courts and tore down the fencing. Some of the Hubbard Cottages, just east of the hotel, were also hit by the twister. Before the tornado died out, it went onto destroy several other houses and cottages in the Cable Beach area.

There were no loss of lives on this island, but two persons were injured in several traffic accidents during the storm, and there were 14 hurricane-induced traffic accidents.

A grey steel casket in the Marshall View Cemetery floated to the surface after the storm due to the heavy rainfall. The water in the coffin was removed, and the coffin was resealed and later reburied in the same grave site. Many cars on the day after the storm were stalled along the streets because of several inches of water on the thoroughfares of New Providence. Heavy flooding was reported in many areas of New Providence, including areas such as Bain's Town, Grant's Town, Chippingham, Stapledon Gardens, Soldier Road, Boyd Subdivision, Coconut Grove, Churchill Subdivision and the South Beach-Bamboo Town areas. The worst flooding was reportedly in Bain's Town, where the flood waters caused by heavy rainfall began to seep into many of the wooden homes.

Farmers on New Providence suffered heavy crop and livestock losses. It was the worst livestock losses for them in over 50 years. Most of the losses were sustained on Cowpen Road because all that area was under the flood waters for several days after the storm. Mr. E.J. Rolle's farm on Carmichael Road suffered severe crop damage, especially to his banana crop. Gladstone Farms on Carmichael Road reported massive losses at its poultry farm when the winds blew the roof off a processing plant. It drowned large quantities of the young chickens in the process, while others died from starvation. The heavy rainfall from the hurricane damaged the electrical system at the plants resulting in the non-functioning of the heaters in the coops and feeding systems, causing the birds to literally starve to death.

The Nassau International Airport was closed to all incoming and outgoing flights from 1:30 pm Sunday, when it became clear that Hurricane David, the worst storm to threaten The Bahamas in many years, was headed towards the Northwest and Central Bahamas where it remained closed for well over 24 hours. City Markets, Pantry Pride and Super Value food stores were all opened for an extraordinary day on Sunday and remained open until 1 pm to allow residents to stock up on hurricane supplies. Most of the stores were sold out of candles, lamps, flashlights, kerosene oil and batteries. Also opened on Sunday to supply the public with hurricane supplies were, Kelly's Hardware Store and Maura's, on Shirley Street and Heastie's Lumber Yard on Robinson Road. There was a long line queuing up for hours before those stores were opened to stock up on limited hurricane supplies.

CHAPTER TWENTY-ONE

Hurricane Andrew's Impact on the Islands of The Bahamas in 1992

O n August 19, 1992 a massive shockwave hit The Bahamas, when the 25-year governing Progressive Liberal Party under the leadership of the late Sir Lynden Pindling was soundly defeated by the Free National Movement under the leadership of Rt. Hon. Hubert Ingraham. The country was in a state of shock over the elections results. Sadly, shortly thereafter, a powerful Category 5 hurricane called Andrew hit the islands of the NW Bahamas (mainly North Eleuthera and Chub Cay) and devastated these islands. As a result, the newly elected Prime Minister Ingraham was not able to celebrate or gloat on his party's landslide victory because his first mission was to visit and render assistance to the Bahamian people negatively impacted by the hurricane. His resolve and determination to get the nation through the ravages of Hurricane Andrew were tested and he came through with flying colours according to most Bahamians at that time.

The third-most powerful hurricane to hit the United States in the 20th century, Hurricane Andrew wreaked havoc throughout The Bahamas, Florida, and Louisiana, causing $26.5 billion (1992 USD or $47.1 billion in 2019 dollars) in damage and 43 deaths in the United States. A slow governmental response didn't help, either. Until Hurricane Matthew in 2016, Andrew was one of the costliest hurricanes in Bahamian hurricane history at $250 million. The storm started off slow, but picked up speed quickly. When it hit The Bahamas, Andrew killed 4 people (3 direct and 1 indirect death) and devastated most of the islands in the NW Bahamas. In the aftermath of the hurricane, the stringent Bahamian building codes reduced the amount of damages incurred across most of the islands in The Bahamas, but Florida revised its building codes using the strict Bahamian building codes as a template to ensure residents would be better prepared for future storms.

The storm was also ranked as the costliest hurricane in United States history until being surpassed by Katrina in 2005 and Harvey in 2017. Andrew caused major damage in The Bahamas and Louisiana as well, but the greatest impact was in South Florida, where it produced devastating winds with speeds as high as 165 mph. Passing directly through the town of Homestead, Andrew completely obliterated several blocks of houses, often stripping them of all but their concrete foundations. In the densely populated Miami-Dade County alone, the winds destroyed more than 25,500 houses and damaged more than 101,000 others. The hurricane left 65 people dead along its trail of destruction

Hurricane Andrew was the first major hurricane to affect The Bahamas since Hurricane Betsy in September 1965 and the Great Bahamas Hurricane of 1929. After struggling to develop in the Atlantic, this Category 5 hurricane quickly developed over the Gulf Stream and devastated The Bahamas and South Florida and South-Central Louisiana with strong winds of 165 mph on August 23 to 26. It remains the sixth costliest tropical cyclone in the North Atlantic basin. Hurricane Andrew first inflicted structural damage as it moved through The Bahamas, especially in Cat Cay, pounding the islands with storm surge, hurricane-force winds, and tornadoes. About 800 houses were destroyed in the archipelago, and there was substantial damage to the transport, water, sanitation, agriculture, and fishing sectors.

The hurricane accelerated westward into an area of highly favorable conditions and began to intensify late on August 22 rapidly; in a 24-hour period the atmospheric pressure dropped by 47 millibars (47 hPa; 1.4 inches) to a minimum of 922 millibars (922 hPa; 27.2 inches). On August 23, the storm attained Category 5 status on the Saffir–Simpson Hurricane Wind Scale, reaching peak winds of 175 mph while located a short distance off Eleuthera Island in The Bahamas at 2pm EDT. Despite its intensity, Andrew was a small tropical cyclone, with winds of 35 mph extending out only about 90 miles from the center. After reaching that intensity, the hurricane underwent an eyewall replacement cycle. At 5pm EDT on August 23, Andrew made landfall on Eleuthera with sustained winds of 160 mph. The cyclone weakened further while crossing the Bahama Banks, and at 9pm EDT on August 24, Andrew hit the southern Berry Islands of The Bahamas with sustained winds of 150 mph. As it crossed over the warm waters of the Gulf Stream, the hurricane rapidly re-intensified as the eye decreased in size and its eyewall convection deepened.

Occasionally, there is a hurricane that comes along and changes the course of history of a country and a region so drastically that it will be remembered for generations to come, Hurricane Andrew was that storm. Throughout history, The Bahamas had quite a few memorable hurricanes that made their marks on the region's history like, the Great Nassau Hurricane of 1926, the Great Andros Island Hurricane of 1929, Hurricanes Floyd in 1999, Matthew of 2016, Joaquin of 2015, Betsy of 1965 and Wilma of 2005. This region's hurricane history is no exception, for example, in Belize there was The Unnamed Hurricane of 1931, which occurred from September 5 to 12, 1931. This storm was significant for Belize because it destroyed the then capital of Belize, which was Belize City and killed over 2,500 persons. Because of this storm and Hurricane Hattie in 1961, they decided to change the state capital of Belize from Belize City to Belmopan. This was done because Belize City was on the coast and more susceptible to future hurricanes and it was decided that Belmopan was a more sheltered city and further in from the coast and less prune to future hurricanes.

In 1989, there was Hurricane Hugo which destroyed the island of St. Lucia and other Windward and Leeward Islands and their main agricultural crops of banana and sugarcane. Before 1989, the economy of St. Lucia was almost totally dependent on agriculture as the main revenue earner. After Hurricane Hugo, it forced the government of St. Lucia to change its main dependence from banana and sugarcane to tourism as the main revenue earner and so far, it has worked out tremendously well for that country. In 1988 there was Hurricane Gilbert that was until Hurricane Wilma in 2005, the most intense Category 5 hurricane to ever hit this region.

In 1988, Hurricane Gilbert had the lowest central pressure reading of any hurricane within this region of 888mb, a record that was only recently broken by Hurricane Wilma in 2005. Hurricane Gilbert made a direct hit over the country of Jamaica and destroyed that country's economy and left well over $1.2 Billion in damage mainly to the tourism and agricultural sectors of that country. It also left 45 people dead and well over 500,000 homeless in Jamaica and left about four-fifths of the island's houses damaged or destroyed. According to the Organization of American States, Gilbert losses amounted to 65% of the Gross Domestic Product of Jamaica. Hurricane Gilbert directly and indirectly impacted the island nation of Jamaica to such an extent that it brought their tourism industry to a virtual standstill for almost 2 years. Fortunately, local and international aid brought some stability back to that country.

Then there was Hurricane David in 1979, which left millions of dollars in damage and over 1,200 people dead and over 80,000 homeless in the country of the Dominican Republic. This storm according to most experts set this country's economy back a staggering ten years. This storm also destroyed the island of Dominica where the losses from this hurricane amounted to more than 100% of the Gross Domestic Product. Hurricane Andrew had a similar effect on The Bahamas and the State of Florida in the United States.

Meteorological History of Hurricane Andrew in 1992

Except for several tropical depressions, June, July, and half of August in the 1992 North Atlantic hurricane season was extremely quiet. The last season with a late start had been 1977, with Anita on August 28, in the Gulf of Mexico. But on August 14, satellite imagery indicated a strong tropical wave just off the African coast near the Cape Verde Islands. Satellite imagery and upper-air data on Sunday August 16 indicated that a tropical depression had formed from a tropical wave in the Atlantic, midway between Africa and the Lesser Antilles near 11.6°N and 40.4°W early on August 17. The depression was moving to the west near 21 mph. At 11am on Monday, the depression strengthened and became the first tropical storm of the 1992 hurricane season and was named Andrew with winds of 40 mph. Its position was about 1,175 miles east of the Lesser Antilles. The tropical cyclone continued moving rapidly on a heading that turned from west to west-northwest. The course was in the general direction of the Lesser Antilles. The motion of the weather system was now heading in a west-northwest direction moving at a speed of 25 mph.

This hurricane pulsated with alternating periods of weakening and strengthening but maintained a steady west-northwest track. In fact, on August 20, some meteorologists saw Andrew as dissipating and becoming disorganized because the winds were less than 45 mph and the barometric pressure was that of normal sea-level, leaving the whole system unsteady. For the 30-hour period beginning at 11pm August 19, to 5am August 21, the storm moved on a northwest track near 14 mph. Andrew became better organized and the 11am report of Friday, August 21, suggested that the storm would strengthen to hurricane force within the next 12 to 24 hours. Maximum sustained winds at the time of the report were 60 mph and the storm had shifted to the west-northwest track at 10 mph.

Information gathered from an Air Force Reserve Unit Reconnaissance Aircraft at 5am EDT Saturday, August 22, confirmed that Andrew had reached hurricane intensity. The center of the hurricane was located near latitude 25.8°N and longitude 67.5°W, some 610 miles slightly ENE of Nassau and about 800 miles east of Miami, Florida. The hurricane was moving to the WNW near 10 miles-per-hour with highest sustained winds of 75 mph with a pressure of 29.35 inches. On Saturday, August 22, hurricane warnings were posted for the islands in the NW Bahamas and this warning was maintained until 7am Monday, August 24. Hurricane Andrew continued this basic motion until 11am Sunday, August 23, when it reached Category 4 strength of 135 mph on the Saffir-Simpson Hurricane Wind Scale. Its center was now located near latitude 25.4°N and longitude 75.0°W or about 100 miles to the east of Harbour Island, Eleuthera or 160 miles due east of Nassau.

The track of the hurricane was now set (no more varying) simply west at 16 mph across northern Eleuthera, north of Nassau, thru the Berry Islands, south of Bimini and south of Miami, Florida. Andrew became a Category 1 hurricane, some 625 miles east-northeast of Nassau on Saturday, August 22. At the time, its central pressure was 994 millibars. Hurricane Andrew was interesting because it had what hurricane experts call a 'double eyewall.' This is literally one eye about 8 miles wide inside larger one about 25 miles wide. The strongest winds were in the inner eyewall that surrounds the calm center of the storm. The outer eyewall has weaker winds than the inner wall but stronger winds than those found in the space between the outer and inner eyewalls.

At 5pm EDT on August 23, Andrew made landfall on Eleuthera with winds of 160 mph. The cyclone weakened further while crossing the Great Bahama Banks, and at 9pm on August 24, Andrew hit the southern Berry Islands of The Bahamas with sustained winds of 150 mph. As it crossed over the warm waters of the Gulf Stream, the hurricane rapidly re-intensified as the eye decreased in size and its eyewall convection deepened. Hurricane Andrew brought hurricane-force winds, or maximum sustained wind of over 74 mph, to five districts – North Eleuthera, New Providence, North Andros, Bimini, Berry Islands – as well as three cays. The hurricane also produced tropical storm force winds in seven districts, including Cat

Island, South Abaco, Central Andros, the northern island chain in Exuma, and the three districts on Grand Bahama. The hurricane affected about 2% of the places available for rent in the country, resulting in a significant reduction in tourism. A total of 800 houses were destroyed, leaving 1,700 people homeless. Additionally, five schools were destroyed, and overall the storm left severe damage to the sectors of transport, communications, water, sanitation, agriculture, and fishing.

As Andrew approached and moved through The Bahamas, its central pressure fell steadily, reaching a minimum of 922 millibars (27.23 inches) at about 2pm EDT Sunday August 23, while 60 miles east of Eleuthera. The eye of the hurricane moved over Harbour Island about 5pm that same day, with a central pressure of 935 millibars and wind strength of 150 mph. Hurricane Andrew did not leave The Bahamas without breaking a few wind speed and weather records. One of them was that Hurricane Andrew set a maximum 10-second flight level wind speed of 170 knots, or 196 mph, by the reconnaissance aircraft near northern Eleuthera on August 23. The westward moving system struck the Berry Islands with the same strength but a slight increase in central pressure of 937 millibars. By 9pm August 23, Andrew was in The Bahamas, 180 miles east of Miami. Landfall near Miami was predicted for the early morning hours of August 24.

Between the hours of 4am and 5am Hurricane Andrew struck the Florida coastline just south of Miami with sustained winds of 145 mph and recorded gusts of 164 mph, as reported by the National Hurricane Center in Coral Gables before the main radar at the center was destroyed. However, gusts to 175 mph were later confirmed and other locations were reporting gusts of 160 to 169 mph. Hurricane Andrew crossed the state of Florida with sustained winds of 125 mph and a forward speed of 18 mph, while still moving due west and by now a Category 3 storm with a central pressure of 27.91 inches. The further movement took Hurricane Andrew into the eastern Gulf of Mexico where it attained Category 5. A slight recurving in the Gulf of Mexico steered the hurricane into Louisiana. By 6am on August 25, Hurricane Andrew was 270 miles southeast of New Orleans, Louisiana, moving west-northwest at 17 mph with winds of 140 mph and a barometric pressure of 27.85 inches.

During the evening, the storm slowed down to almost stationary 30 miles southeast of Lafayette, Louisiana. Early on August 26, winds near New Iberia, Louisiana, were reported to be 115 mph with gusts to 160 mph. Landfall occurred between New Iberia and Lafayette, as a Category

3 hurricane. By noon on August 26, Hurricane Andrew was downgraded to tropical storm status for the first time since August 22. The system was in eastern Tennessee by the morning of August 28, the system merged with a cold front, the remains of the Pacific hurricane called Lester. Andrew finally died out in Pennsylvania on August 29.

Hurricane Andrew was reclassified as a Category 5 hurricane with winds estimated to be about 165 mph. The reason for the reclassification was a better mathematical weather models which estimated surface winds based on the data gathered by the Reconnaissance Aircrafts. This improved weather models produced a wind speed higher than previously thought. Hurricane experts agreed and upgraded Andrew from a Category 4 hurricane to a Category 5 hurricane, one of the rare times this has happened where a hurricane was upgraded and reclassified after the hurricane season had officially ended.

Damages sustained on the major islands of The Bahamas during Hurricane Andrew in 1992

Only hours before Hurricane Andrew smashed into South Florida in the United States during late August of 1992, the storm barreled into The Bahamas and ravaged many of the islands in the NW Bahamas leaving The Bahamas with over $250 million worth of damages to these respective islands. While the destruction in The Bahamas does not compare with the devastation in South Florida, the hurricane – the worst to hit these islands in more than 60 years – killed four people and left some 1,700 of the 250,000 residents of the Bahamas homeless. It also wiped out roads, bridges, and resort hotels. However, it must be noted that almost all the significant damage was confined to the northern part of Eleuthera, Harbour Island, Spanish Wells, Cat Cay, Bimini and part of the Berry Islands – that is, to several of the sparsely populated Family Islands. Nassau and Freeport were untouched, except for minor damage from high winds and rain, as were the Abacos, Cat Island, Andros Island, and Exuma and its cays, San Salvador and various other of The Bahamas' 40 inhabited islands.

Prime Minister Rt. Hon. Hubert A. Ingraham, in his speech to the Bahamas Parliament, stated that there was $250 million in damage, with $100 million of it on Cat Cay alone. In a separate, earlier interview Baltron Bethel, The Bahamas Director General of Tourism stated that the physical devastation affected about 2 percent of rooms, cottages, and apartments in The Bahamas. After the hurricane, there was an estimate of a 10 to 20 percent drop in tourism nationwide. To counteract this, the Bahamas Government launched an aggressive tourism advertising campaign designed to assure the public and countries around the globe that 98 percent of the Bahamas was untouched by the hurricane. Still, even though the damage was so limited, The Bahamian economy was affected more than Florida's. This advertising was essential because The Bahamas earns almost 70 percent of its gross domestic product from tourism, and the jobs of 7 out of 10 Bahamians are dependent on the industry.

The restoration and repair of the various properties were quick, but it took years to recover from the loss of wildlife and the uprooting of tens of thousands of trees, plants, and flowers. While most tourists visit The Bahamas to swim, shop and gamble, the loss of some of the islands' natural beauty did hurt the new Bahamian Government's efforts to emphasize tourism for nature lovers and environmentalists. Looking forlornly across eight acres that until pre-Andrew in 1992 which had been graced by stately coconut palm trees, Roger Becht, the owner of the 10-room Runaway Hill Club on Harbour Island, one and a half miles long, lamented three weeks after the hurricane, "With its beautiful beaches and reefs, this island can't help but come back. But for most of us, it just won't have the same look." While the rooms themselves suffered only minor flooding and broken windows, Runaway Hill's landscape and vegetation were all destroyed during the storm.

Several hundred yards down the Pink Sands beach, on 16 landscaped acres that had been a bird sanctuary, the Pink Sands resort is a tangled mess of uprooted palm trees, and rotting vegetation heaped so high that in some places it obscured the windows blown out of the 29 abandoned cottages. But the Pink Sands was an exception; most of the half-dozen other resorts on Harbour Island, which traditionally close from Labour Day to about mid-November, quickly reopened in late November to capitalize on the winter tourism market. For example, the 10-room Ocean View Beach Club, high atop a cliff overlooking the ocean, lost the railing on its deck and sustained other minor damage. Other hotels which reopened in early November were, Ocean View Hotel, the 14-acre beachfront Coral Sands Hotel, the Rock House, a seven-room hotel facing the bay and the 38-room Romora Bay Club.

Andrew also hit and devastated the nearby settlement of Spanish Wells, which after the hurricane, had only one of its two hotels remaining. The northern end of Eleuthera, the narrow, 110-mile long island less than 10 minutes by ferry from Harbour Island and Spanish Wells. The hurricane destroyed the 18-room Current Club Beach Resort and Marina in northern Eleuthera and damaged at least four other hotels and resorts in the area. It caused structural damage to the Club Med Eleuthera's restaurant and water-sports complex, closing the 300-room resort 10 miles from Governor's Harbour Airport. Fortunately, the repairs were completed by November 14, 1992, to capitalizes on the winter tourists. Veering westward, the storm then battered the Berry Islands, Cat Cay, and Bimini. The hurricane destroyed the Chub Cay Club, a hotel and 90-slip marina at the south end of Berry Island. According to Prime Minister Ingraham, Andrew also destroyed the Cat Cay Club and its 110-slip marina on Cat Cay, a three-mile-long luxury hideaway about 50 miles from Florida. Also, on this island, hundreds of palm trees were uprooted or broken in two by the strong winds.

The hurricane damage would have been far worse had Hurricane Andrew significantly damaged Nassau (New Providence) and Freeport (Grand Bahama). On these islands, the storm only briefly interrupted power and telephones, toppled trees, broke windowpanes and flooded roads. Not only are those the most populated cities, but their attractions and gambling casinos lure most of the 3.6 million annual visitors, who in 1991 spent $1.2 billion.

Winds dashing up Bimini Harbour blew off part of the roof at 24-room Brown's Hotel, then continued up the beach where it destroyed the dock and flooded several of the 49 guest rooms at the Bimini Big Game Fishing Club and Hotel, owned by Bacardi. It also smashed windows and downed trees at the 32-slip Blue Water Resort, which host of the annual Hemingway Billfish Tournament in March. The Compleat Angler restaurant and bar and the 12-room hotel in Bimini suffered some flooding and the same power and telephone failure that afflicted most of the Family Islands. But the storm left virtually untouched the ground-floor of the Hemingway Museum, which was filled with old photographs, sketches and other memorabilia of the famous writer, who often held forth in the bar in the 1930s. Up on top of the hill, between the harbour and ocean, the 13-room Anchorage Restaurant and Hotel lost nine coconut trees, a half-dozen windows and much of its vegetation. "I'm 53, and I lived through a lot of storms, but nothing like this," said Ivan Banks Thompson, its longtime bartender. "But everybody pitched in to help, and the storm brought all the people back together who had been divided by the recent election." Mr. Thompson was referring to the bitterly contested election August 19, in which the Free National Movement toppled the Progressive Liberal Party, which had ruled the Bahamas for 25 consecutive years.

According to most insurance estimates, Hurricane Andrew caused more than $250 million worth of damage in The Bahamas alone. A storm surge of 25 feet was reported in the settlement of The Current, and 16 feet in Lower Bogue, Eleuthera. Numerous tornadoes were spawned from thunderstorms associated with Hurricane Andrew. Striated paths in the vegetation and destroyed building structures in the various settlements of Eleuthera evidenced this. Tornadoes also moved across Harbour Island and Spanish Wells. The NW Bahamas suffered considerable damage with one notable exception of Grand Bahama.

In The Bahamas, Andrew produced hurricane-force winds in North Eleuthera, New Providence, North Andros, Bimini, and the Berry Islands. The storm first struck North Eleuthera, where it produced a high storm surge of over 20 feet. At a small fishing settlement in the northwestern portion of the island called Spanish Wells, more than half of the houses were destroyed, and the rest of the buildings sustained minor to significant damage. One person drowned from the storm surge in Lower Bogue, Eleuthera, and two others died in The Bluff. On Current Island, the hurricane destroyed 24 of the 30 houses. Harbour Island, near Eleuthera, reported wind gusts of 138 mph – the strongest gust speed observed in The Bahamas during Andrew's passage. News reports indicated severe damage to 36 houses on Harbour Island.

Hurricane Andrew produced several tornadoes in the area. At the capital city of Nassau, sustained winds reached 92 mph, while gusts up to 115 mph were reported. Only minor damage occurred in Nassau, according to The Bahamas Red Cross, but on the private island of Cat Cay, many expensive homes sustained substantial damage. Additionally, the storm caused severe damage to the various sectors of transport, communications, water, sanitation, agriculture, and fishing. Four deaths in the country were attributed to the hurricane, of which three were direct; the indirect fatality was due to heart failure during the passage of the storm.

The Bimini and Berry Islands District

This district suffered a devastating blow because of Hurricane Andrew, which ripped through the islands and cays on Sunday August 23. Andrew passed through the Berry Islands and made its presence felt on Great Harbour Cay, Bullocks Harbour, Little Harbour and Chub Cay. In addition, the hurricane blazed a path through Cat Cay, Ocean Cay and parts of the Bimini mainland. Damage sustained to the chain of islands were estimated to be in the millions of dollars. One dock was destroyed, and two parks were severely damaged. On South Bimini, the storm caused light damage, including to two hotels on the island. The private island of Cat Cay in the Bimini Islands was severely impacted by the hurricane, with cost estimated at $100 million (1992 USD). Many wealthy homes and the island's marina received substantial damage, with hundreds of trees downed by the strong winds. Later, Hurricane Andrew made its second landfall in the Berry Islands early on August 24 as a Category 4 hurricane on the Saffir-Simpson Hurricane Wind Scale. Damages were substantial and estimated "in the millions of dollars."

North Andros

Although the damage was said to be minimal, the areas hardest hit were the coastal settlements of Lowe Sound, Nicholl's Town, Red Bays, and Pleasant Harbour. The dock in Red Bays was destroyed. Also, the infrastructure on the parks in Morgan's Bluff and Lowe Sound were destroyed.

New Providence

In New Providence, there was a report of only one home on Quakoo Street that was destroyed when bricks from a nearby-unfinished Mason Lodge fell on the roof.

Eleuthera

Along with Bimini and the Berry Islands, the island of Eleuthera (particularly in the north) received the brunt of the hurricane. Homes and other buildings were severely hit.

- The settlements of James Cistern, Gregory Town, Alice Town, and Palmetto Point suffered minor damages. However, the control tower at the airport in Governor's Harbour was destroyed. Coastal main roads were damaged by the high seas, and docks in Palmetto Point, Governor's Harbour, James Cistern, Hatchet Bay and Gregory Town were all extensively damaged. Block walls surrounding cemeteries in Governor's Harbour and James Cistern were destroyed. Minor damage was also reported in The Bluff and Lower Bogue.

- The settlement of Current Island was extensively damaged. On Current Island where there were thirty homes, only six were left standing. In the Current, the Current Club (Hotel, Restaurant, and Bar) and The Bahamas Government Teacher's Residence were destroyed. All remaining homes and buildings received significant damage. The docks were also destroyed.

- On Spanish Wells, the bridge that joined Russell Island to Spanish Wells was destroyed when a fishing boat (broke away from its moorings) crashed into it. Many other fishing boats were lost. Only two homes and a food store were destroyed, while others were damaged.

- On Harbour Island, all the docks were destroyed with only the Government Dock left standing. Most of the cottages and the restaurant for the Pink Sands Hotel were all destroyed. All homes and buildings suffered considerable damage.

Impact on the Wildlife and Plants after Hurricane Andrew

The breeding colonies of White Crown Pigeons in Eleuthera and North Andros, including, colonies at Finley Cay, Schooners Cay, and Joulter Cay between North Andros and the Berry Islands were affected by the hurricane. A 37-year-old corkwood tree in Adelaide, New Providence was blown down.

Deaths

Four deaths were reported, but only three could be directly attributed to Hurricane Andrew. Two persons lost their lives in The Bluff and a third in Lower Bogue, Eleuthera. The death in Lower Bogue was because of drowning in the storm surge. The fourth death resulted from heart failure suffered during the hurricane.[116]

---

[116] Arthur Rolle (October 30, 1992). *Hurricane Andrew in The Bahamas. The Bahamas Department of Meteorology (The Official Bahamas Government Hurricane Report).* Nassau, Bahamas: National Oceanic and Atmospheric Administration, National Weather Service. Pg. 4. Retrieved: 11-11-2006.

CHAPTER TWENTY-TWO

Hurricane Floyd's Impact on the Islands of The Bahamas in 1999

Hurricane Floyd was one of the most destructive and powerful hurricanes to impact The Bahamas in the last century. Floyd was a massive and very intense 'Cape-Verde Type' hurricane, which pounded the islands of the Northwest and Central Bahamas, mainly the islands of Cat Island, San Salvador, Eleuthera, New Providence, Abaco, and Grand Bahama. It reached its peak as a Category 5 hurricane on the Saffir-Simpson Hurricane Wind Scale as it approached The Bahamas. Floyd weakened slightly as it made landfall near Alice Town, Eleuthera around 8 am EDT Tuesday, September 14, 1999, and Cherokee Sound, Abaco about 2 pm the same day. Although there were some fluctuations in its overall intensity, Hurricane Floyd slowly weakened in strength between the September 13 and 14. By the time Floyd made a direct hit on Abaco, during the afternoon of the 14th it had already weakened somewhat from its peak strength, however, it had remained a strong Category 4 hurricane.

Wind analyses from a Reconnaissance Aircraft indicated that sustained winds of about 100 mph occurred in Cat Island and San Salvador, 105 mph in Eleuthera, 63 mph sustained winds with gusts to 78 mph at Nassau International Airport, 115mph in Abaco and 80 mph in Grand Bahama. The eyewall of Hurricane Floyd was 30 miles wide, and during the passage of Hurricane Floyd over The Bahamas, the southwestern portion of the eyewall crossed the islands of Cat Island, San Salvador, Eleuthera, and Abaco. Floyd made landfall near North Eleuthera and again near Cherokee Sound, Abaco. The north and eastern quadrants (the areas of the strongest winds) fortunately remained offshore from The Bahamas over the Atlantic waters throughout the passage of the hurricane.

A dock destroyed on the waterfront from Hurricane Floyd (Courtesy of Mr. Neil Sealey).

Meteorological History of Hurricane Floyd in 1999

At 2 pm EDT, Tuesday, September 7, satellite images depicted the broad center of Tropical Depression #8, approximately 1000 miles east of the Lesser Antilles. The depression was moving toward the west at 14 mph. The following morning at 2 am EDT, Wednesday, September 8, satellite pictures indicated that the tropical depression had strengthened and became the sixth tropical storm for the season and was given the name Floyd. Tropical Storm Floyd strengthened gradually over the next two days with its forward speed moving from a peak of 16 mph to 10 mph, while moving towards the west-northwest for the most part. By 8 am EDT, Friday, September 10, the Reconnaissance Aircraft flew into the storm and confirmed that the hurricane had indeed strengthened to hurricane strength with a central pressure of 989 millibars and maximum sustained winds of 70 knots. The center of the hurricane was then located near latitude 19.1°N and longitude 58.9°W or 780 miles east-southeast of the Turks and Caicos Islands. The hurricane continued moving west-northwest near 12 mph throughout the day.

On Saturday, September 11, Hurricane Floyd further strengthened into a Category 2 storm with maximum sustained winds of about 105 mph while moving west-northwest near ten mph. Early on Sunday, September 12, rising mid to upper-level tropospheric heights to the north of Floyd forced the hurricane to turn west. The westward turn marked the start of significant strengthening. Maximum sustained winds were on the increase at the close of the day, and the central pressure fell about 40 millibars. Floyd reached a Category 3 intensity hurricane at 8 am EDT Monday, September 13, and at 5 pm the same day Floyd further strengthened and became a powerful Category 4 hurricane. At this point, it had maximum sustained winds of 145 mph and located near latitude 23.4°N and longitude 68.2°W or 350 miles east-southeast of San Salvador, 580 miles east-southeast of Nassau and 225 miles northeast of the Turks and Caicos Islands. At this point, a tropical storm warning was issued for the Southeast Bahamas and the Turks and Caicos Islands. A Hurricane Watch was also issued for the Central Bahamas as Hurricane Floyd came within 425 miles east-northeast of Mayaguana at 8 am EDT on the following day.

From 2 am to 2 pm EDT on Monday, September 13, Floyd rapidly strengthened with sustained winds of 155 mph (the upper end of a Category 4 intensity hurricane on the Saffir-Simpson Hurricane Wind Scale). This was due to the warm ocean waters just to the east of The Bahamas, which provided the fuel for growth and strengthening. The hurricane maintained its strength until late on the 13th. While the cyclone was poised to strike the Central Bahamas, it shifted towards the west-northwest and moved some 20 to 30 miles northeast and north of San Salvador around midnight on Tuesday, September 14. It then moved within 25 miles east-northeast and northeast of Orange Creek and Arthur's Town, Cat Island the same day. As Floyd headed towards the west-northwest, it weakened slightly in intensity. On Tuesday morning, September 14, Hurricane Floyd moved west-northwest at 14 mph, on a track parallel to Eleuthera. This track took the eye about 45 to 10 miles, respectively, east of South and Central Eleuthera; with the western eyewall of the hurricane (with winds more than 125 mph) passing over Central and North Eleuthera. The eye of Floyd made landfall near Alice Town, Eleuthera around 8 am EDT. During this time, it passed some 65 miles northeast of New Providence at 11 am EDT New Providence experienced the weaker side of Floyd with winds speeds of 55 to 65 mph with gusts to about 80 mph.

After passing over north Eleuthera and turning towards the northwest, Floyd struck Abaco making landfall around 2 pm EDT during the afternoon hours of Tuesday, September 14, near Cherokee Sound, Abaco. By the time, Floyd hit Abaco it had weakened somewhat from its peak winds, but it was still of Category 4 intensity. The eye of the hurricane moved from the south to the north over Abaco, while pounding the island with maximum sustained winds of 115 mph. It was evident that downdrafts and one or two tornadoes were spawned in the hurricane conditions. As the eye passed over Crossing Rocks, Mastic Point, Woolen Dean Cay, and Cooper's Town Abaco, the winds shifted to the opposite direction, giving winds just as strong. The eye, which was characterized by partly sunny skies with little or no winds, emerged over the waters north of Cedar Harbour, Abaco, at 5 pm EDT, on the same day. During the evening, the hurricane passed 30 miles northeast of eastern Grand Bahama.

The following day, Wednesday, September 15, Floyd at first established a northwest track and then a north-northwest track around 5 am EDT before taking a north-northeast forward track at the close of the day. On Thursday, September 16, Floyd made landfall once again near Wilmington, North Carolina. Maintaining a north-northeast forward motion, Floyd gradually weakened to tropical storm status as it moved along the eastern seaboard of the United States of America. Tropical storm Floyd lost its tropical characteristics on Friday, September 17, and eventually dissipated.

Damages sustained on the major islands of The Bahamas during Hurricane Floyd in 1999

Hurricane Floyd blew through The Bahamas with maximum sustained winds of up to 155 mph, torrential rains and a storm surge of up to 15 feet above normal. The United States Ambassador to The Bahamas, Mr. Arthur Schechter issued a disaster declaration on September 16, 1999, after personally inspecting the damage on Eleuthera and Cat Island during an air reconnaissance flight with the U.S. Coast Guard. On September 16, the Prime Minister of The Bahamas the Rt. Hon. Hubert Ingraham activated CARILEC, an association formed by an agreement between electrical utility departments throughout the Caribbean. Through the activation of CARILEC, 45 technicians and engineers from various countries were deployed to disaster-affected islands to help restore electrical power.

Damage to housing was significant, but not catastrophic. Two deaths were attributed to Hurricane Floyd, one occurred in Grand Bahama and the other occurred in Nassau. In The Bahamas, the first Caribbean country with mandatory building codes, houses built with building codes regulations incurred less severe damage. The most significant losses to housing occurred on Abaco, Moore's Island, and Eleuthera. The banana crop of The Bahamas was destroyed and took over one year to recover. Direct financial losses to farmers and fishermen because of Hurricane Floyd were estimated at $35 million. The Bahamas Government borrowed $21 million to assist in rehabilitating works damaged by Hurricane Floyd. Insurance claims by the local industry for compensation for property damages were in the order of US $250 million. An additional US $150 million (making a total of approximately US $400 million) in claims was estimated for foreign-owned and insured businesses, including touristic and marine sector businesses. Temporary closure resulting from hurricane damage and subsequent repairs affected some 32 hotels, 50% of which were in Abaco. The country also lost revenue from the 13,000 cruise passengers in the week following the hurricane because of disrupted service and visitor arrival at the main airport also fell off during the same week.

Several private ports of calls operated by Norwegian Cruise Lines(NCL) on Great Sturrup Cay, Royal Caribbean Cruise Line(RCCL) on Little Sturrup Cay, Holland American Lines(HAL) on Little San Salvador and Princess Cruise Lines(PCL) on Princess Cays, South Eleuthera, were damaged and services temporarily suspended. The cost of repairs to the beach, landscape, and buildings at the Holland American Lines facility was estimated at US $1.4 million, while the damage to the PCL facilities was US $1 million. Repairs and restoration of electricity by the Bahamas Electricity Corporation were estimated at US $8 million, while revenue lost from billings was US $4 million. Extensive damage to telephone and other forms of communications facilities and equipment (e.g., buildings, radio, and antenna, cellular, fiber and switching equipment) occurred. The Bahamas Telecommunications Corporation's estimate for repair and restoration of services was US $36.23 million.

Two loan programmes were arranged by the government to assist persons who lost their homes and their means of livelihood to the hurricane. The government established, through the Bahamas Development Bank, a loan program with preferential rates of interests to assist small fishermen and business persons who suffered a loss of fishing boats and equipment, or damage to their businesses because of the hurricane. Also, to assist homeowners in the restoration or reconstruction of their homes, damaged or destroyed by Floyd, the government made special arrangements with commercial banks for special mortgage program. The Inter-American Development Bank loan of $21 million to The Bahamas was used to restore bridges, roads, seawalls, dock, and other building projects in the aftermath of the hurricane.

Due to surge effects, freshwater wells fields of The Bahamas Water and Sewage Corporation, along with private wells were inundated and hence contaminated; water supplies were disrupted briefly in Exuma, the Berry Islands, and North Andros and for more extended periods in San Salvador, Cat Island, Eleuthera, and Abaco. The costs of the repairs and restoration of services were due to the contamination of the freshwater lens, which required extensive pumping of saltwater to restore water quality in some areas and other factors. Damage to public roads, seawalls, bridges, and docks was estimated at US $30 million, and beach erosion occurred throughout the island chain. From Florida in the north and Great Inagua Island in the south, the U.S. Coast Guard dispatched patrol boats, a C-130 aircraft and helicopters to survey the northern and eastern islands hardest hit by Floyd and deliver medical supplies and communications gear, including a mobile communications trailer to Nassau.

The American Red Cross donated to The Bahamas Government and The Bahamas Red Cross Society, four satellite phones, plastic sheeting, food items, clothing, medicine, toolkits, hygiene kits, flashlights, bed sheets and tents with a total value of well over $85,000.00. The British Government donated well over $25,000.00 to the Hurricane Floyd relief effort. The Red Cross Societies of Antigua & Barbuda, St. Kitts & Nevis and the Cayman Islands, Canadian Red Cross and Norway Red Cross also donated to the hurricane relief efforts after the storm. USAID/OFDA (Office of U.S Foreign Disaster Assistance) deployed one disaster specialist in advance of the storm. Based on first-hand assessments by the USAID/OFDA team conducted in coordination with the U.S. Embassy, the Bahamian Government, and the international donor community, delivery of potable water, water purification, vector control, and temporary shelter materials were identified as relief priorities. The total USAID/OFDA assistance to Hurricane Floyd amounted to $508,009, and its breakdown was as follows: -

- Ambassadorial Disaster Declaration used to meet immediate roofing needs....$25,000.

- Purchase and transport of 2,500 one-gallon bottles of water to Eleuthera....$15,025.

- Purchase and transport of 140 rolls of plastic sheeting to Abaco.....$68,340.

- Funding to PAHO to meet immediate water and sanitation-related needs....$75,000.

- Funding to U.S. Coast Guard for aerial assessment support....$324,644

Many coastal communities suffered severe flooding and widespread damage. The effects of the extreme winds and huge waves toppled power and telephone lines, severely disrupting electricity and communication services for several days. After the storm, official figures estimated that around 27,000 persons living in the Family Islands were affected and were urgently in need of water, temporary shelter and food after the storm. The worst affected islands were, Abaco, Eleuthera, Grand Bahama, the Berry Islands, Cat Island, San Salvador, and Nassau. More than 1,500 residences were damaged; significant damage occurred to 500, while an additional 200 were destroyed. Roads, seawalls and docks were washed away, and bridges, schools, and health clinics were damaged. Hotels were forced to close on Abaco, Eleuthera, and Cat Island. In New Providence, two hotels were closed for several months to undergo extensive repairs and renovations.

Nassau

Most of the hotels reported only minor damage, including, the Atlantis Resort on Paradise Island, where 2,000 tourists weathered the storm. However, the British Colonial Hilton suffered significant roof and structural damage to one wing. There were two deaths reported, and one death occurred when Mr. Bobby Tinker swam from a flooded car and drowned in Freetown, Grand Bahama. Another death occurred when a lady was electrocuted after the power was restored to her home after the storm in the capital of Nassau. She tried to open her refrigerator and was electrocuted while clinging to the refrigerator door.

Nassau and Paradise Island experienced 70-80 mph winds with higher gusts and generally fared 'better' being some distance away from the center on the weaker side of the storm. There were a significant number of downed trees, significant landscaping destroyed, several small private docks were destroyed, and there were many boats damaged, but overall, Nassau experienced very little property damage and no significant injuries. A few homes, offices and hotels did report many windows had been blown out. Some private homes have experienced minor structural damage such as, carport roofs that were blown down. The historic wooden structure called Balcony House did collapse but fortunately with no injuries. Several small marinas and private docks were damaged because of the storm surge, and some small boats were beached or sunk in Nassau Harbour.

Forty-one shelters were operated on Nassau by The Bahamas Red Cross Society. New Providence sustained significantly less damage than on the Family Islands. Many trees were blown down, and utility services were disrupted, and some ripped roofs off homes throughout Nassau. Trees blocked the main highway linking the eastern and central parts of New Providence, and two barges were washed ashore one on the Western Esplanade near Cocktails and Dreams nightclub, and workers had to shovel three feet of sand from the inside of the bar. Public work crews were dispatched throughout the island to clear roads and restore services. Some houses sustained roof damage, and several homes along the coastline were affected by the floods. There were reports of flooding up to 3 feet high in some areas. Several people, including one who fell off a roof, were treated at the hospital for severe to minor injuries sustained before and after the storm.

Abaco

On Wednesday, September 29, a team of five county firefighters from West Palm Beach were dispatched to the island of Abaco to help with the rebuilding relief efforts on this island. The storm left well over 2,000 people homeless on the island of Abaco alone, and approximately 10% of the island's homes were destroyed, and 40% were severely damaged. There were approximately 400 houses (home to about 2,000 people) severely damaged or destroyed in the Mud Town area. The Mud Town is a settlement of Haitian immigrants who live in poor substandard housing situated in low-lying areas. The northern and southern extremes of Abaco sustained substantial damage where certain residential areas were uninhabitable for quite sometime after the hurricane.

Bahamian Parliamentarian, Mr. Robert Sweeting estimated that the damage in Abaco alone was in the range of over $750 million. At Elbow Cay, it left extensive flooding, numerous holes in roofs, many signs were strewn in the streets, and widespread beach and marsh erosion and many boats were tossed onto the shore. The Conch Inn and Abaco Inn were hit hard by the storm and were completely wiped out, and in some areas, there was no evidence that houses were ever there. In Hope Town, which sits on the ocean's edge, some houses were destroyed and looked as if they had been blown up. Further south in the settlement of Crossing Rocks, several homes were submerged under water for quite a while after the storm. Both airports at Treasure Cay and Marsh Harbour were submerged under water after the hurricane passage and were remained closed due to the standing water, debris, damage and associated destruction for a few days after the storm had passed.

Florida Yacht and Marine Industries of Florida purchased about $15,000 in building materials and paid for a freight charter from Florida to Abaco and Eleuthera to be donated to the residents of these two islands severely impacted by the hurricane. The shipping company G & G facilitated the shipping of over 800,000 lbs. of much needed donated goods from South Florida to Abaco free of charge. Virtually all import duties and tariffs on hurricane relief materials were temporarily waived at three of the major islands hard-hit by the hurricane by order of the then Prime Minister Rt. Hon. Hubert Ingraham.

Settlements on the northern end of Abaco (Fox Town, Coopers Town, Crown Haven, Fire Road, and other nearby settlements) suffered catastrophic damage with most, if not all the homes were destroyed. Virtually no housing for the homeless was made available to house these residents severely impacted by the hurricane. This was because most of the homes were destroyed. Fox Town and the other northern settlements reported storm surge of over 20 feet. Many said that it was almost a miracle, that no one died or had a significant injury due to the severity of the storm. In Fox Town, several persons in a shelter left the church during the eye of Floyd and ran to another shelter because the roof was severely damaged during the storm. To their surprise, after the storm when they returned to the church, the church roof was gone. Bluff House, due to its elevation and unprotected position above the sea of Abaco, was especially hard-hit. Parts of New Plymouth in the low-lying areas as well as the residential areas bordering the waterfront of Abaco were also damaged by storm surge and the strong hurricane force winds. Approximately, 75% of the homes in the settlement of Moore's Island were rendered uninhabitable or destroyed.

The New Plymouth's perimeter road (including the newly completed stretch along Settlement Creek) were wiped out in several sections of the road. In Marsh Harbour, many large buildings were destroyed, and much of the settlement suffered considerable flooding after the storm. Sandy Point, Cherokee Sound, Little Harbour as well as Coopers Town suffered significant damage. The connecting road between Marsh Harbour (south central Abaco) and Treasure Cay was rendered impassable after the storm. Very limited water was available in many of the settlements due to saltwater intrusion of the wells and soil. Also, this failed the mainland's primary pumping station which was also damaged during the storm. Green Turtle Cay reported sustained winds of over 140 mph, while Marsh Harbour reported sustained winds of 150 mph. Marsh Harbour suffered most of its damage along the waterfront which was more developed and more vulnerable to water and wind damage.

Most of the docks in Marsh Harbour were destroyed. An unoccupied houseboat broke loose from its mooring at Admiral's Yacht Haven and was smashed to pieces on the nearby shoreline. There were many boats which suffered significant damage including, *Mark Kim* which sank, *Phoebus* suffered substantial hull damage to the starboard side, *Justice Bonjour*, *Bethsheeba*, *Elegante* and others also sustained considerable damage during the storm. A large fig tree was toppled down and pulled down power lines in the process, causing the main transmission pole to snap beside Royal Bank of Canada in Marsh Harbour. The Pizza Hut restaurant building was destroyed and the shopping center where A&K Liquors was located suffered severe damage. The Spin Maker Restaurant had about eight windows blown in during the storm and damaging the kitchen and destroying the entire carpet in the process. Little Abaco reported storm surge of over 23 feet and the surge at Government Dock was estimated to be between 15 to 20 feet.

Many boats were washed ashore along the northern Abaco coastline, especially in Little Abaco. A forty-foot fishing boat was washed ashore onto the road on the causeway separating Little Abaco from Abaco. The Earl Russell family in Green Turtle Cay was forced to move to the second floor of their Black Sound-Green Turtle home after the first floor was inundated with water. The strong winds of the storm unroofed several houses in Green Turtle Cay. Many of the docks on the out-lying cays were destroyed, and many of the boats without secure moorings were washed onto the western shores of these cays. Significant flooding occurred in the low-lying offshore areas, with significant tree and foliage loss observed throughout the north-central Abaco. The most severe beach erosion occurred in south Abaco and Elbow Cay, notably at White Sound. Virtually all the homes in Sandy Point experienced significant flooding. On Elbow Cay, one of a series of small cays off the northwestern side of Abaco had an entire area that was wiped away by the ocean, and the houses across the road were directly on or hanging over the ocean. A new inlet was reportedly formed creating two islands in the place of one. Most of the severe damage appeared to the White Sound area of Elbow Cay.

The entire citrus harvest for Abaco, from an estimated 3,000 acres, was lost for the 1999 season. The government had to provide significant relief and assistance to farmers and fishermen by restoring lost income, re-establishing farm businesses and replacing fishing equipment. Abaco Big Bird poultry farm, which provided The Bahamas with 12% of the Bahamian chicken production, suffered only minimal loss. Most of the schools in Abaco were delayed opening for about three weeks. The area just to the south of the Abaco Inn through to (but not including) "Third Sunrise" has been wiped out and all the houses along this stretch were destroyed and replaced by a 'flat white beach.'

In some cases, there was no evidence that a house was ever there. Kiki Graetz almost drowned from the storm surge of the hurricane. Fortunately, she held onto a pole or piling in her home and pulled herself to safety while the water was gushing through the house. John Williams's car was engulfed in sand from the storm. The Tillberg house roof collapsed, and the storm destroyed the home, but Mr. and Mrs. Tillberg survived by leaving the house and escaping to a shelter during the eye of the storm.

On October 13, the Prime Minister Rt. Hon. Hubert Ingraham delivered an 84-page report in an emergency session of the House of Assembly on the impact of Hurricane Floyd on The Bahamas. He reported that the National Disaster Relief Fund grew from $140,000 before Floyd to well over $3 million, a sum that he said would go a long way in restoring the islands after the hurricane's widespread devastation. Total claims for hurricane damages exceeded $400 million, and claims payments were in the region of $240 million. He also reported that 1,700 residences suffered significant damage on Abaco, including 347 that were extensively damaged and 170 of them were destroyed. There were 35 houses which were destroyed on Moores Island, 30(including resorts) on Elbow Cay, 27 in Cooper's Town, 10 in Fox Town and 18 in Crossing Rocks. The Prime Minister noted that Crossing Rocks might have to be relocated. He also stated that hurricane clips worked well and that the painting white of asphalt shingles, as practiced in Spanish Wells, led to a dramatic reduction in shingle damage. He concluded by saying that all future homes will be built subject to greater scrutiny to ensure that the building codes of The Bahamas are strictly adhered to and that all homes should be insured for hurricane damage. The Government ordered $1 million worth of construction materials to be used mainly for the construction of homes for the aged, the indigent and welfare recipients.

Grand Bahama

One death was reported on the island of Grand Bahama. Freeport International Airport remained closed a few days after the storm due to heavy flooding. On the western end of Grand Bahama, some areas were flooded, and stranded residents had to be rescued in boats. Hurricane Floyd reduced the stand of established citrus trees from 1,500 acres to 150 acres. Chicken production in Grand Bahama, which accounts for 30 percent of the national output, was lost. There was a significant loss of other livestock, including pigs, goats, and sheep. The agricultural land areas of Grand Bahama also suffered significant inundation of soil by the intrusion of saltwater. This resulted in the setback of planting of new fruit trees and the vast array of vegetable crops for several months.

Eleuthera

Valentine's Marina and Resort was destroyed, and at least ten rooms were destroyed in the storm. On Northern Eleuthera, the winds were reported to be over 110 mph. About 25% of the houses in Eleuthera with a total population of about 10,500 persons sustained some roof damage, but less than 1% could be considered completely destroyed. Crops and all the mail-boat docks suffered significant damage. Many homes were left without roofs, and half of the cemetery was washed away. The old terminal building at the Rock Sound Airport and the Rock Sound Primary School were severely damaged. The dock and customs warehouse at The Bluff were significantly damaged, and the dock at Jean's Bay was destroyed.

All the farms in Eleuthera were severely damaged. Docks and roadways on the western side of Harbour Island were severely damaged, and beaches on the eastern side of the island were severely eroded. The Spanish Wells fishing fleet was significantly damaged, many of these fishing vessels were breached, while others were sunk in the harbour. It was estimated that 25% of the houses on Eleuthera sustained some damage because of the storm. Based on recommendations of disaster response specialists in Nassau, USAID/OFDA provided a C-130 aircraft to fly 2,500 one gallon bottles of water to Eleuthera on September 18th and 19th. The island, which is typically supplied with potable water by boat, however, storm surge associated with Hurricane Floyd severely impacted port facilities on Eleuthera, temporarily preventing delivery of water by sea. The United States Coast Guard delivered approximately 7,000 gallons of locally donated bottled water to Eleuthera from Nassau. The water bottles, collected by a local radio station, were shipped by the United States Coast Guard C-130 aircraft.

San Salvador

The eye of hurricane Floyd passed just north of San Salvador at approximately 11:30 pm EDT on the evening of September 14, placing the island well within the hurricane force winds. Most of the structural building failure occurred on the west coast of the island and was created by the storm surge. Damage totals were quite high in San Salvador, while, many of the communications infrastructures were taken out along with the main roadways and substantial damage to housing. This island was severely hit and sustained significant structural damage to many properties and its two major hotels. No injuries were reported, but power and telecommunications systems remained down for quite sometime after the storm.

Three major tourist facilities existed on San Salvador, the Gerace Research Center (formally the Bahamian Field Station (BFS)), Club Med Columbus Isle resort, and the Riding Rock Inn. The Gerace Research Center is a converted U.S. Navy base serving as a research/tourism facility for university faculty and students, and ecotourists. The Gerace Research Center specializes in ecotourism or tourism that is based upon the observation and research of the island's natural systems such as coral reefs, caves, and iguana colonies. Approximately, 1500 visitors stay at the Gerace

Research Center each year. The Club Med Columbus Isle Resort is a full-service resort offering entertainment facilities along with island excursions of scuba diving. Club Med arranged flights out of The Bahamas for 380 guests who rode out the storm at its San Salvador resort and another 350 in Paradise Island and both resorts had to close temporarily after the storm to allow for repairs to the two properties. Club Med sustained some damage to the roof of their property, damage to the chain link fencing surrounding the tennis courts and vegetation was buried by sand and washed over the stern during the hurricane.

San Salvador's Riding Rock Inn, one of the four biggest employers on the island, sustained substantial damage to the roof, the bar and restaurant building and cabin damage due to fallen trees. The severity of the damage was due to the Inn's location along a westward-facing beach. Storm surge along this beach eroded the foundation of the restaurant and bar building, hotel building, and several cabins. Beyond the foundation damage, the porch attached to the restaurant and bar lost its roof and supports, making it unstable and unusable. Part of the roof of the restaurant and bar was removed during the hurricane; extensive water damage was evident, including standing water in the building. Extensive water damage was also evident in the guestrooms. A tree fell along the beach, crushing two cabins. It was estimated that 100% of the buildings on Riding Rock Inn grounds experienced significant damage. The local museum sustained some roof damage. The water supply facilities at the Gerace Research Center were also damaged, creating diminished capacity for eco-tourism and the island residents, also exterior damage to the dormitory building where windows were blown out in the center of the building and the interiors of the rooms were severely damaged from fallen debris.

There was also damage to Queen's Highway, and Fernandez Bay, so the highway was reduced to one lane and damage was done to the Town Square and straw market at Cockburn Town where it was covered by debris, and waves created significant structural damage to the square buildings and structures. The beaches on San Salvador suffered substantial beach erosion. The most common erosion of the beaches and the adjoining coast was the transport of sand above the berm, burying the vegetation adjacent to the beach. Due to the removal of debris at or above the beach berm and the transport of sand inland beyond the berm, and the beaches were also widened in many locations.

Cat Island

Cat Island with its total population of around 1,700 persons suffered significant damage that was heavy in many of the settlements with communications being taken out along with the main roads and substantial damage to housing. In Cat Island, two medical centers lost their roofs, and 2 ½ miles of coastal roads were washed away. In response to US's Ambassador Schechter's disaster declaration on September 16, USAID/OFDA provided $25,000 to the US Embassy in Nassau to meet immediate, disaster-related needs. The funds were used to pay for materials and bought replace lost roofs of two health clinics on Cat Island.

CHAPTER TWENTY-THREE

Hurricane Michelle's Impact on the Islands of The Bahamas in 2001

H urricane Michelle was the fifth costliest tropical cyclone in Cuban history and strongest of the 2001 North Atlantic hurricane season. The thirteenth named storm and the seventh hurricane that year, Michelle developed from a tropical wave that had traversed into the western Caribbean Sea on October 29; the wave had initially moved off the coast of Africa 13 days prior. In its early developmental stages, the depression meandered over Nicaragua, later paralleling the Mosquito Coast before intensifying into tropical storm intensity on November 1; Michelle was upgraded to hurricane strength the following day. Shortly after, rapid intensification ensued within favorable conditions, with the storm's central barometric pressure dropping 51 millibars (hPa; 1.51 inches) in 29 hours. After a slight fluctuation in strength, Michelle reached its peak intensity as a Category 4 hurricane with winds of 140 mph and a minimum pressure of 933 millibars (hPa; 27.55 inches). At roughly the same time, the hurricane began to accelerate northeastward; this brought the intense storm to a Cuban landfall within the Bay of Pigs later that day. Crossing over the island, Michelle was weakened significantly and was only a Category 1 hurricane upon reentry into the Atlantic Ocean. The hurricane then transitioned into an extratropical cyclone over The Bahamas on November 5, before being absorbed by a cold front the following day.

Meteorological history of Hurricane Michelle in 2001

On Monday, October 29 at 4 pm EST, Tropical Depression #15 developed near the coast of Nicaragua, or 40 miles south-southwest of

Puerto Cabezas Nicaragua, where it remained virtually stationary until 4 am EST, Wednesday, October 31. Maximum sustained winds were about 35 mph near the center, with a central pressure of 1005 millibars. At 10 am EST Wednesday, October 31, the depression began to move slowly towards the north at about six mph, with no change in strength. At about 4 am EST, Thursday, November 01, the central pressure dropped to 997 millibars, with a corresponding increase in the winds to 60 mph, resulting in the formation of the 14th tropical storm for the season-it was given the name Michelle.

Michelle then shifted more towards the north-northwest with a forward speed near five mph. While moving at a slower forward speed of about three mph, tropical Storm Michelle slowly intensified to hurricane strength at around 7 am EST, Friday, November 02, with maximum sustained winds of 75 mph and a central pressure of 980 millibars. On Saturday, November 03, at about 10 am EST, the somewhat erratic Michelle rapidly intensified, and became a dangerous Category 4 hurricane on the Saffir-Simpson Hurricane Wind Scale with sustained winds of 135 mph, nearing the end of the day. Hurricane Michelle slowly picked up forward speed with a shifted track towards the north-northeast. At this point, residents in the Northwest and Central Bahamas were urged to monitor the progress of Hurricane Michelle closely and be prepared to take quick action. Hurricane Michelle's forward speed accelerated to 13 mph at about 1 pm EST Sunday, November 04. Later, at about 7 pm Michelle began to lose strength, while over Cuba, as her maximum sustained winds decreased to 125 mph. By 10 pm EST, Hurricane Michelle's winds weakened to 110 mph, and this weakening trend continued.

At 1 am EST, Monday, November 05, while on the northern shores of Central Cuba, and about 175 miles southwest of Red Bays, Andros, the leading edge of the tropical storm force winds associated with a weaker Hurricane Michelle began to pound the island of Andros. About an hour later the first effects on New Providence began. By 7 am, the eye was over the island of Andros with maximum sustained winds around 85 mph with higher gusts in heavy showers and continuous rain. Later during the morning hours while on a northeast track the eye moved over the island of New Providence between 9 am, and 10 am EST moving rapidly towards the northeast at ten mph. The passage of the eye over the island caused some persons to believe that the hurricane had passed but a second battering began just before 11 am with winds shifting northwest to north and increasing from 16 mph to 46 mph sustained with peak winds up to 103 mph.

At about 4 pm EST, the eye moved toward the east-northeast, and the forward speed increased further to 21 mph. By 10 pm EST, all warnings were dropped as Hurricane Michelle raced towards the east-northeast. On Tuesday 06th November, while near latitude 29.0°N and longitude 65.3°W, Hurricane Michelle weakened to a minimal hurricane with sustained winds of only 75 mph. Michelle began to lose its tropical characteristics and rapidly moved on the same east-northeast track at a maximum forward speed of 35 mph. All tropical cyclone watches, warnings, and alerts were subsequently dropped.

Damages sustained on the major islands of The Bahamas during Hurricane Michelle in 2001

Storm surge heights of about 8 feet were measured in the southern district of New Providence near the South Beach pool. Additional measurements were also recorded near Coral Harbour, where heights reached approximately 12 feet. Many of the islands suffered moderate to severe coastal flooding. The impact of the storm was also evident by the washouts of roads in New Providence, Andros, Eleuthera, Cat Island, Exuma, and Abaco. In some areas, the hurricane ripped roofs of several wooden houses and tore down many traffic lights. The radio station More 94.9 fm transmission tower was snapped in half by the winds, and several other stations were placed out of commission because of the storm.

After the storm, the Minister of Transport, Aviation and Local Government, Mr. C.A. Smith, Mr. Ronald Bosfield-Deputy Speaker and MP for the area, Parliamentary Secretaries Mr. Zhivargo Laing and Mr. David Wallace and a team of technical officials from various government ministries made a special trip to Central and South Andros to inspect the damages caused by this storm. When they got there, they found that there was extensive flooding, two houses were blown down, and others suffered structural damage especially to roofs. There were downed electrical and telephone lines, busted water pipes, and noticeable coastal erosion. Minister Smith said he was pleasantly surprised at the extent of the damages because he thought the damages would have been significantly greater than the team had seen. He commended Androsians for their preparedness, which he attributed to the strict building codes and adequate hurricane preparations made before the storm. It was estimated that the local insurance companies alone paid out well over $100 million in total claims. On the island of Andros, the Small Hope Lodge was closed for repairs due to hurricane Michelle from November 5-19 and was re-opened on the 19th, but the dock needed additional time for repairs.

CHAPTER TWENTY-FOUR

Hurricanes Frances and Jeanne's Impacts on Islands of The Bahamas in 2004

The main road near the caves on the western end of New Providence was severely damaged by Hurricane Frances storm surge in 2004 (Courtesy of Neil Sealey).

The Bahamas on average gets brushed or hit by a hurricane once every three years and gets hit by a major hurricane once every 12 years. There are three Bahamian islands ranked in the top 10 effects from tropical systems of all cities, islands, and countries in the

North Atlantic basin - Andros, Abaco, and Grand Bahama. It must be noted that 2004 was a busy year for hurricanes impacting The Bahamas (notably the island of Grand Bahama), as both Hurricanes Frances and Jeanne made their presences felt in a big way. Their presence was so significant, that well over 14 years later and the government of The Bahamas is still dealing with the negative repercussions from these two hurricanes.

Hurricane Frances was the sixth named storm, the fourth hurricane, and the third major hurricane, of the 2004 North Atlantic hurricane season. The system crossed the open Atlantic in mid to late August, moving to the north of the Lesser Antilles while strengthening. Its outer bands struck Puerto Rico and the British Virgin Islands while passing north of the Caribbean Sea. The storm's maximum sustained wind peaked at 145 mph, achieving Category 4 on the Saffir-Simpson Hurricane Wind Scale. As the system's forward motion slowed, the eye passed over San Salvador Island and very close to Cat Island in The Bahamas. Frances was the first hurricane to impact the entire Bahamian archipelago since 1928 and almost destroyed the agricultural economy there. Hurricane Frances was the first hurricane to affect The Bahamas since Hurricanes Michelle in 2001 and Floyd in 1999. Hurricane Frances was an extremely large hurricane which because of its size it affected all the islands of The Bahamas.

Hurricane Jeanne was the deadliest hurricane in the 2004 North Atlantic hurricane season. It was the tenth named storm, the seventh hurricane, and the fifth major hurricane of the season, as well as the third hurricane and fourth named storm of the season to make landfall in Florida. After wreaking havoc on Hispaniola, Jeanne struggled to reorganize, eventually strengthening and performing a complete loop over the open Atlantic. It headed westwards, intensifying into a Category 3 hurricane on the Saffir-Simpson Hurricane Wind Scale and passing over the islands of Great Abaco and Grand Bahama in The Bahamas on September 25. Jeanne made landfall later in the day in Florida just 2 miles from where Frances had struck a mere three weeks earlier. Building on the rainfall of Frances and Ivan, Jeanne brought near-record flood levels as far north as West Virginia and New Jersey before its remnants turned east into the open Atlantic. Jeanne is blamed for at least 3,006 deaths in Haiti with about 2,800 in Gonaïves alone, which was nearly washed away by floods and mudslides. The storm also caused seven deaths in Puerto Rico, 18 in the Dominican Republic and at least 4 in Florida, bringing the total number of deaths to at least 3,025; Jeanne is the 12th deadliest North Atlantic hurricane ever. Final property damage in the United States was $6.8 billion.

Meteorological history of Hurricane Frances in 2004

At 11 pm Tuesday, August 24, satellite images indicated that a tropical depression had formed from a strong tropical wave in the Eastern Atlantic, some 870 miles west-southwest of the Cape Verde Islands. Its movement was to the west at 17 mph with maximum sustained winds near 30 mph. On Wednesday, August 25, about 1,400 miles east of the Lesser Antilles, the depression was upgraded to tropical storm status and was given the name Frances with maximum sustained winds of 40 mph. At 5 pm on Thursday, August 26, Hurricane Frances rapidly strengthened to become the fourth hurricane of the 2004 hurricane season. Maximum sustained winds were near 80 mph and was about 1005 miles east of the Lesser Antilles. On Friday, August 27, Hurricane Frances strengthened rapidly into a strong Category 3 hurricane on the Saffir-Simpson Hurricane Wind Scale with maximum sustained winds near 115 mph and moving towards the northwest near ten mph.

At 11 pm on Saturday, August 28, Frances strengthened to a Category 4 hurricane with maximum sustained winds near 135 mph. Frances's intensity fluctuated over the next few days reaching a peak value of 145 mph with a central pressure of 937 millibars on September 2 at 2 am. During this time, it was centered at latitude 22.7°N and Longitude 72.5°W or some 35 miles northeast of Mayaguana. It was with that wind force that Frances passed directly over the island of San Salvador and very near to Cat Island. Until 8 am September 3, Hurricane Frances moved at an average speed of 13 mph in a west to west-northwest direction. It was at this point that the hurricane moved over the island of Eleuthera in the vicinity of the settlement of James Cistern. Later, in the day the hurricane underwent a weakening process as it passed in the vicinity of Abaco and directly over Grand Bahama. Before moving over Grand Bahama, Hurricane Frances weakened from a Category 3 hurricane to a Category 2 hurricane with a further decrease in the forward speed of approximately five mph. At 3 am Hurricane Frances left The Bahamas, and the large eye of Frances finally moved inland over Florida.

Hurricane Jeanne in The Bahamas

Meteorological History of Hurricane Jeanne in 2004

Tropical Depression #11 formed from tropical wave located 70 miles east-southeast of Guadeloupe in the evening of September 13 and was upgraded to Tropical Storm Jeanne the next day. Jeanne passed south of the U.S. Virgin Islands on September 15 and made landfall near Yabucoa, Puerto Rico later the same day. After crossing Puerto Rico, it reached hurricane strength on September 16 near the eastern tip of the Dominican Republic on the island of Hispaniola but fell back to tropical storm strength later that day as it moved inland across the Dominican Republic. Jeanne continued to move slowly over the Dominican Republic on September 17 before finally leaving the island late that afternoon. By that time, Jeanne had weakened to another stage to tropical depression strength.

On September 18, while the system was being tracked near Great Inagua and Haiti, a new center formed well to the north-east and the previous circulation dissipated. The new center strengthened again, becoming a hurricane on September 20. Jeanne continued to meander for several days (making a complete loop in the process) before beginning a steady westward motion toward The Bahamas and Florida. Jeanne continued strengthening as it headed west, passing over Great Abaco in The Bahamas on the morning of September 25. Shortly after that, it reached Category 3 status. It maintained this intensity as it passed Grand Bahama during the remainder of the day. At 11:50 pm EDT September 25, Jeanne made landfall on Hutchinson Island, just east of Stuart, Florida and Port Saint Lucie, Florida, at Category 3 strength. Jeanne's track continued to follow within 20 miles of that of Frances until it reached Pasco County, Florida. It then swung more rapidly to the north, and the center remained over land all the way to the Georgia state line. It became extratropical over Virginia on September 28, and the remnant returned to sea off the New Jersey coast the next day.

Damages sustained on the major islands of The Bahamas during the Hurricanes Frances and Jeanne in 2004

The Bahamas Electricity Corporation workers repairing damaged electrical wires in Nassau after Hurricane Frances (Courtesy of Neil Sealey).

In total, 6,682 houses suffered damage during the two hurricanes. Of that amount, 4,100 suffered minor damage but are usable, while 1,851 suffered significant damage more than $10,000 per house but are usable. Some 671 houses (in a value of over $110,000 per house) were destroyed while some 2,000 homes might fall into the category of significant repairs and rebuilds. The severity of the winds and sea surges resulted in the worst damages being inflicted to the housing sector, where the damage assessment exceeded $99 million. It is extremely difficult to place an exact value to the total amount of damages, both public and private, which incurred because of the passage of Hurricane Frances; however, estimates range from $125 million to $250 million.

In response to Hurricane Frances and Hurricane Jeanne, USAID/ OFDA provided a total of nearly $445,000 in emergency assistance to The Bahamas. This amount included $100,000 offered to the U.S. Embassy in Nassau to support local air transport and distribution of emergency relief supplies, as well as $50,000 to The Bahamas Red Cross for emergency relief activities on the islands of Abaco and Grand Bahama. Also, USAID/ OFDA dispatched six airlifts of emergency relief supplies to The Bahamas, carrying 4,000 blankets, 4,464 hygiene kits, 4,800 water containers, 400 rolls of plastic sheeting, 12 water bladders, and one high capacity water purification unit. The value of airlifted items plus transport totaled nearly $3,000, 000.00. The Office of U.S. Foreign Disaster Assistance (OFDA) is an organizational unit within the United States Agency for International Development (USAID) that is charged by the President of the United States with directing and coordinating international United States government disaster assistance.

In Grand Bahama, not only there was a storm surge of some 12-15 feet in some places, but also seawater affected both the northern and southern shores and, in some cases, converged to worsen the flooding. Officially, there were two deaths which were directly attributed to Hurricane Frances throughout The Bahamas. One man was found floating face-down on the western end of Grand Bahama. It is believed that the man had been trying to swim to safety. The old airport building in Grand Bahama was destroyed, but the new building survived well. Our Lucaya Westin property had some 1000 rooms damaged by the storm. Xanadu in Freeport also lost its roof and was severely damaged.

Hurricane Jeanne caused significant damage on the islands of Grand Bahama and Abaco. Almost all of the affected areas impacted by Hurricane Jeanne were the same areas that were impacted by Hurricane Frances. Jeanne severely damaged many of the homes that were weakened by Frances. In Eight Mile Rock, the largest community on Grand Bahama, over 75% of the homes suffered severe structural damage, with roofs were partially or entirely torn off. All the shelters in Eight Mile Rock sustained significant structural damage and severe flooding. The eastern portion of the island was cut off by the storm surge, and reports indicated considerable flooding of homes, particularly along the coastline.

The Bahamian Trade and Industry Minister, Hon. Leslie Miller threatened to revoke the licenses of any businesses found engaging in price gouging. He said his agency had been inundated with calls from people complaining businesses were hiking prices for plywood, flashlights, batteries, and water. "We will shut you down," Miller warned at a news conference. "It is against the law to jack up prices in times of a national crisis…. We will not hesitate in fining them the $5,000 and a year in jail if they chose to take advantage of our people in their time of need."[117]

Because of its size, wind velocity and its coordinates that generally took the storm on a northeasterly track over The Bahamas, hurricane Frances had an impact on almost every island in The Bahamas. Only the islands of Inagua, Ragged Island, and Long Cay, in the southeastern Bahamas, were spared the direct impact of the hurricane and sustained little damage. With regards to the remainder of The Bahamas, the scale of the damage varied in range and intensity and some instances, there was significant devastation while in others the damage was not as extensive.

Hurricane Jeanne impacted the northern Bahamas including, Abaco, Andros, Berry Islands, Bimini, Eleuthera, Exuma, Grand Bahama, and New Providence on September 25-26. The storm surge, heavy rains and hurricane force winds caused wind damage, and flooding as Hurricane Jeanne moved across the islands of The Bahamas. Several areas were evacuated, and thousands weathered the storm in shelters. In Grand Bahama, officials continued to ask residents living on the western part of the island to evacuate and move into the shelters before the hurricane arrived to join the 1,100 persons who rode out the storm there. Some heeded the warnings, but others refused to listen. As a result, many of those who stayed had to be rescued during the storm from the high flood waters which inundated their homes. At least six people on Grand Bahama sustained significant injuries during the storm, from a toddler who had her face cut by a piece of flying glass to a man who hurt himself trying to cut down a tree in his yard, said Sharon Williams, the Island Administrator of Rand Memorial Hospital.

Beginning on Sunday, September 5, several assessment teams led by the Prime Minister Rt. Hon. Perry G. Christie and a team of Cabinet Ministers and technical assessment teams began an assessment of damages to the various Family Islands. The assessment team first visited the southeastern islands travelled with water and other emergency supplies of food items which could be transported by aircraft. On Monday, September 06, the assessment team visits continued when the Prime Minister and teams of Ministers travelled to Grand Bahama, Abaco, and the Berry Islands.

---

[117] Wayne Neely, *The Major Hurricanes to Affect The Bahamas-Personal Recollections of the Greatest Hurricanes to Affect The Bahamas*, Author House Publication, Indianapolis, USA, 2006

By Friday, September 10, one week after the passage of the hurricane, assessment teams had visited all the areas struck by the hurricane, including Rum Cay, Ragged Island, and Exuma. Members of Parliament, including members of the Opposition, travelled on all assessment visits and were fully integrated into each of the visits, as were several leaders of churches. Ministry of Social Services and Community Development, the Hon. Melanie Griffin announced that a Hurricane Relief Desk had been set up in the Department of Social Services to assist qualified old age pensioners, persons with disabilities and other persons with limited income who were incurring undue hardship due to the aftermath of Hurricane Frances and Jeanne.

Nassau

There were trees down blocking Dumping Ground Corner and across many streets throughout Nassau. A roof caved in at a hurricane shelter at Bethsheda United Missionary Baptist Church, but no injuries were reported. The occupants were moved to Calvary Deliverance Shelter. The ships *Mia Dean* and *Nay Dean* (sister ships) run aground at Rose Island and two elderly persons aboard *Mia Dean* were assisted by the Defence Force Harbour Patrol. Trees blocked the corner west of Harbour Bay Center. Many trees and poles were blown down in the Montague and Fox Hill areas.

The estimated damages sustained on the island of New Providence as completed by the Ministry of Works and Utilities, listed the magnitude of damages as follows:

Transportation/Infrastructure	$3,000,000
Schools	$10,000,000
Clinics (Public Facilities)	$1,000,000
Government buildings/agencies	$1,000,000
Private houses	$4,000,000
Total	$19,000,000

The Japanese Government made a significant contribution to The Bahamas hurricane relief effort with the donation of relief supplies, equipment, and goods totaling more than $60,000. The shipment, which was flown into The Bahamas under the auspices of Japan International Cooperation Agency included tents, generators, blankets, plastic sheeting, and goods. Kerzner International Development Limited donated $1 million to the National Disaster Relief Fund. An 18-year-old boy Kenrad Delaney was electrocuted as he tried to fill a generator with diesel fuel. Police feared another man in his 80s was likely killed when his house collapsed near the western tip of Grand Bahama, but he survived; police said they found him at a neighbour's home. The man was hospitalized with internal injuries. Also, several people were injured when a roof collapsed in a clinic in South Abaco Island; about 30 miles west of Grand Bahama, the victims were airlifted to Nassau for treatment at the PMH Hospital. One man was arrested as he attempted to steal appliances while another broke into a gas station and was arrested.

Sections of the island remained without power for a few days. Prime Minister Perry Christie made a brief tour around Nassau to find damaged buildings, flooded streets, and debris everywhere. Prime Minister Perry Christie designated the islands of Grand Bahama and Abaco disaster areas which allowed them to receive assistance from the government and declared a state of emergency. Immediately following the passage of Hurricane Frances, work teams from relevant government agencies, including the Ministry of Works, the Department of Environmental Health Services, the Royal Bahamas Defence and Police Forces were all deployed to clear roadways and other public areas of fallen trees and debris. The utility corporations were immediately engaged in the restoration of electricity, water supply, and telephone services on the island of New Providence. The Nassau International Airport, which was closed during the hurricane, but was opened by late Saturday afternoon for international flights and by Sunday morning for domestic flights to destinations in The Bahamas that allowed airplanes to land.

San Salvador

Caught in the slow-moving storm for more than 30 hours on Thursday and Friday, 15-20% of the homes were damaged, and the two schools were severely damaged. Five families were rendered homeless, while another 100-persons reported significant damage to their homes. There was considerable damage to two government schools and other government buildings, and localized flooding was reported throughout the island.

Approximately, 80% of Club Med's roof was moderately damaged, and there was estimated $60,000 damage at the field station. The Gerace Research Center sustained massive losses, and several windows and doors were blown away. Damage was observed along the road adjacent to north Pigeon Creek, indicating that the storm surge had travelled to the headwaters of the Creek. The storm deposited large rocks onto the main road. Ocean House received massive storm surge damage with up to 3 feet of sand accumulated inside the house as well as large beach rocks.

A survey of structures in Cockburn Town indicated that about 20% of the buildings had substantial damage, 65% light damage, and 12% with no real cost. The Riding Rock Inn and Marina received minimal damage, mostly loss of shingles and some breaching of sea walls. The San Salvador Airport's new security structure received substantial damage during the storm, but the remaining buildings at the airport received very light damage. Wendy's Snack Shop across the road from the airport experienced a complete failure. Several semi-truck trailers parked near the airport were blown over onto their side.

A survey of structures between Club Med and Rocky Point, including Victoria Hill settlement, indicated 6% of structures received substantial damage, 79% receiving light damage, 15% receiving no damage, and no complete structural failure. Of all the settlements on San Salvador, United Estates received the most significant damage where seven structures experienced complete failure during Frances. Approximately, 30% of the structures in the settlement received massive roof damage, about 60% received light damage, and 5% had no damage. The San Salvador Primary School received extensive roof damage on the backside of the building. The books and other materials in the building were also damaged, and the San Salvador High School received substantial damage to the roof on the lower structure.

The estimated damages sustained on the island of San Salvador as completed by the Ministry of Works and Utilities, listed the magnitude of damages as follows:

Transportation/Infrastructure	$2,500,000
Schools	$3,000,000
Private Houses	$3,000,000
Total	$8,500,000

Mayaguana

In total, 68 persons were evacuated to hurricane shelters, and significant damage to roofs and power lines were reported throughout the island, and a storm surge of 15 feet caused considerable damage to the port.

Grand Bahama

In Freeport, Grand Bahama, Queen's Cove was underwater, and personnel had to be taken to higher ground. Persons were also advised to evacuate from the flood-prone the low-lying areas. The airport was flooded with over six feet of water; 500 persons were evacuated from the Hawksbill area, adding to the 1,200 persons who occupied the shelters. There was a massive evacuation effort from low-lying areas. There was considerable roof damage in certain areas, and electrical and telephone services came to a halt due to damaged or destroyed electrical infrastructures. In West End, a rescue effort was conducted at Holmes Rock and West End due to flooding. Electrical and telephone poles were blown down throughout the island resulting in major blackouts and no phone services for several weeks after the storm. The roof was blown off from the barracks at Hanna Hill, and the area of Fishing Hole was flooded. Residents of Queens Cove-as well as weather personnel and the Freeport Airport had to be evacuated.

The estimated damages sustained on the island of Grand Bahama as completed by the Ministry of Works and Utilities, listed the magnitude of damages as follows:

Transportation/Infrastructure	$3,000,000
Schools	$5,000,000
Clinics (public facilities)	$1,000,000
Government buildings/agencies	$3,000,000
Private Houses	$50,000,000
Grand Bahama Airport (privately owned)	$12,000,000
Total	$74,000,000

Long Island

The strong winds of Hurricane Frances tore the roof off a high school, and residents also experienced some flooding and a four feet storm surge.

The estimated damages sustained on the island of Long Island as completed by the Ministry of Works and Utilities, listed the magnitude of damages as follows:

Transportation/Infrastructure	$750,000
Private Houses	$500,000
Total	$1,250,000

The Berry Islands

This island experienced sustained winds of 70-80 mph, a storm surge of 8-10 feet and most of the homes damaged from Hurricane Frances sustained additional damages from Hurricane Jeanne. There was severe flooding in low-lying areas and significant erosion to the causeway and some damage to the local schools.

The estimated damages sustained on the Berry Islands as completed by the Ministry of Works and Utilities, listed the magnitude of damages as follows:

Transportation/Infrastructure	$350,000
Schools	$100,000
Clinics (Public facilities)	$150,000
Government Buildings	$400,000
Private Houses	$600,000
Total	$1,600,000

Eleuthera

North Eleuthera was affected by sustained winds of more than 100 mph, and experienced widespread environmental damage and impassable roads downed power lines and extensive flooding and beach erosion.

Phillip Bethel Shopping Center received significant damage and had its roof blown off. Lawrence Griffin Esso Service Station's gas pumps and roof were blown away. The police station at Governor's Harbour was under several feet of water and was evacuated. During the storm, some 300 persons had to be evacuated to various shelters. The roof at Green Castle and Rock Sound Schools sustained some damage. In North Eleuthera, there was significant flooding, and Jane Bay Dock was underwater because of the floodwaters, making it impassable for residents to travel to the mainland for quite some time after the storm's passage. Queen's Highway was flooded, and North Eleuthera residents could not gain access to South Eleuthera.

The estimated damages sustained on the island of Eleuthera as completed by the Ministry of Works and Utilities, listed the magnitude of damages as follows:

Transportation/Infrastructure	$2,000,000
Schools	$2,000,000
Clinics (Public facilities)	$2,000,000
Government buildings/agencies	$1,000,000
Private Houses	$500,000
Total	$7,500,000

Abaco

There was massive flooding, and the storm surge was over 8 feet. At Sandy Point, significant water damage resulted in the destruction of 6-10 houses, while another 7-10 homes suffered severe damage in Hurricane Jeanne alone. There was no loss of lives on this island, but a part of the roof used as the Emergency Operations Center collapsed, causing minor injuries to the occupants. In Sandy Point, there was flooding and property damage to roofs, and some roofs were blown off in the Crossing Rocks area. There were also several persons injured after the Cooper's Town Clinic roof collapsed. The injured were airlifted to the Princess Margaret Hospital in the capital city of Nassau that Sunday with the assistance of the United States Coast Guard. There was also significant damage in the Treasure Cay area.

The estimated damages sustained on the island of Abaco as completed by the Ministry of Works and Utilities, listed the magnitude of damages as follows:

Transportation/Infrastructure	$1,500,000
Schools	$2,000,000
Clinics (Public facilities)	$500,000
Private Houses	$1,500,000
Total	$5,500,000

Cat Island

The hurricane-force winds tore the roof of a church, and there was severe flooding in the northern part of the island, and several homes had minor roof damage. Coastal erosion and debris made the roads impassable.

The estimated damages sustained on the island of Cat Island as completed by the Ministry of Works and Utilities, listed the magnitude of damages as follows:

Transportation/Infrastructure	$1,500,000
Schools	$500,000
Clinics (Public facilities)	$100,000
Private Houses	$500,000
Total	$2,600,000

Andros

The estimated damages sustained on the island of Andros as completed by the Ministry of Works and Utilities, listed the magnitude of damages as follows:

Transportation/Infrastructure	$250,000
Schools	$50,000
Government Buildings	$350,000

Private Houses	$500,000
Total	$1,150,000

Acklins

There was significant damage to a marine docking facility and other coastal erosion caused by the battering waves and storm surge. Many utility poles were blown down in Chester's Bay.

The estimated damages sustained on the island of Acklins as completed by the Ministry of Works and Utilities, listed the magnitude of damages as follows:

Transportation/Infrastructure	$750,000
Private Houses	$100,000
Total	$850,000

Rum Cay

The estimated damages sustained on the island of Rum Cay as completed by the Ministry of Works and Utilities, listed the magnitude of damages as follows: -

Transportation/Infrastructure	$100,000
Schools	$100,000
Private Houses	$25,000
Total	$225,000

The total country estimate in damages: $125 million.

The full extent of damage to private homes and public infrastructure may well be in the region of $200 million. In addition to this, the agricultural sector has sustained an estimated $45 million in losses.

CHAPTER TWENTY-FIVE

Hurricane Wilma's Impact on the Islands of The Bahamas in 2005

In the most recent and reliable records, most tropical cyclones which attained a pressure of 900 hPa (millibars) (26.56 inches) or less occurred in the Western North Pacific Ocean. The strongest tropical cyclones recorded worldwide, as measured by minimum central pressure, was super Typhoon Tip also known in the Philippines as Typhoon Warling. This storm reached a pressure of 870 hPa (25.69 inches) on October 12, 1979, which was also the most intense tropical cyclone ever recorded. The most intense storm in the North Atlantic by lowest central pressure was Hurricane Wilma. The strongest storm by 1-minute sustained winds was Hurricane Allen in 1980. The most intense storm in the Eastern Pacific Ocean by both sustained winds and central pressure was Hurricane Patricia. Its sustained winds of 215 mph are also the highest on record globally.

<u>Below are some of the worldwide cyclone records set by North Atlantic storms</u>

- Costliest tropical cyclone: Hurricane Harvey – 2017 – US$198.63 billion in damages.

- Fastest seafloor current produced by a tropical cyclone: Hurricane Ivan – 2004 – 5 mph.

- Highest confirmed wave produced by a tropical cyclone: Hurricane Luis – 1995 – 98 feet.

- Highest forward speed of a tropical cyclone: New England hurricane – 1938 – 70 mph.

- Longest time a tropical cyclone has continuously had sustained winds of at least 185 mph: Hurricane Irma – 2017 – 37 hours.

- Most tornadoes spawned by a tropical cyclone: Hurricane Ivan – 2004 – 120 confirmed tornadoes.

- Smallest tropical cyclone on record: Tropical Storm Marco – 2008 – gale force winds extended 11.5 miles from storm center (previous record: Cyclone Tracy 1974 – 30 miles).

- **Smallest tropical cyclone eye on record: Hurricane Wilma – 2005 – diameter 2.3 miles. Longest duration as a Category 5 hurricane.**

- **Most intense North Atlantic Hurricane on record-Hurricane Wilma of 2005 with a sea-level pressure of 882 mb.**

Meteorological History of Hurricane Wilma in 2005

Wilma formed from a large area of disturbed weather that stretched across much of the Caribbean Sea during the second week of October. A surface low-pressure gradually became more defined and better organized as it approached Jamaica, and a tropical depression developed about 215 miles southeast of Grand Cayman on October 15. The tropical cyclone moved erratically southward for two days while slowly strengthening into a tropical storm. Wilma became a hurricane and began a west-northwestward movement on October 18. Hurricane Wilma was the twenty-first named storm, twelfth hurricane, and sixth major hurricane of the record-breaking 2005 North Atlantic hurricane season. It was also the third Category 5 hurricane of the season, beating the records set by the 1960 and 1961 hurricane seasons. At its peak, it was and remains the most intense tropical cyclone ever recorded in the North Atlantic basin. It was also the tenth most intense tropical cyclone globally, with the lowest atmospheric pressure ever recorded in the western hemisphere of 882 millibars (26.05 inches) at sea-level, exceeding the record previously held by Hurricane Gilbert of 888 millibars in 1988.

Wilma was the third Category 5 hurricane to develop in October, the other two being Mitch of 1998 and Hurricane Hattie of 1961. It was the second 21st storm in any season and formed nearly a month earlier than the only previous 21st storm (in 1933). Wilma was also the fastest intensification hurricane from a tropical depression to a Category 5 hurricane (1-minute sustained surface winds) in just 54 hours. Hurricane Wilma went from 35 mph to 170 mph from 8 pm October 17 to 2 am EDT October 19. Wilma was also the fastest intensification hurricane from a tropical storm to a Category 5 hurricane within just 24 hours. It went from 70 mph to 170 mph from 2 am EDT October 18 to 2 am EDT October 19. It also had the maximum pressure drop in 12 hours of 83 millibars and 975 millibars (28.80 inches) to 892 millibars (26.30 inches) – from 2 pm EDT October 18 to 2 am EDT October 19. Wilma had the maximum pressure drop in 24 hours of 97 millibars. Wilma went from 979 millibars (28.90 inches) to 882 millibars (26.00 inches) from 8 am EDT October 18 to 8 am EDT October 19.

Residents gather amid the rubbles after Hurricane Wilma to collect valuables and personal items (Courtesy of Kevin Ewing).

Wilma made several landfalls, with the most destructive effects felt in the Yucatan Peninsula of Mexico, Cuba, and the U.S. state of Florida. At least 47 deaths have been attributed to this hurricane, and insured damage is estimated at between US$8-12 billion (about $6-9 billion in the US) and total cost was estimated to be in the $15-20 billion range, which would rank Wilma among the top costliest hurricanes ever recorded in the North Atlantic basin. It reached tropical storm strength at 5 am EDT October 17, making it the first storm ever to use the 'W' name since alphabet naming began in 1950, and tying the record for the most storms in a season with 1933. Moving slowly over warm waters with little wind shear, it strengthened steadily and became a hurricane on October 18. This made it the 12th hurricane of the season, tying the record set in 1969. Hurricane Wilma began to intensify rapidly during the late afternoon on October 18 around 4 pm EDT. Over 10 hours, a Hurricane Hunter aircraft measured a 78-millibars pressure drop.

In 24 hours from 8 am EDT October 18 to the following morning, the pressure fell by an incredible and record-breaking 90 millibars. Its minimum central pressure dropped to an estimated 882 millibars, and in this same 24-hour period, Wilma strengthened from a strong tropical storm with 70 mph winds to a powerful Category 5 hurricane with sustained 175 mph winds. In comparison, Hurricane Gilbert of 1988-the previous record holder for the lowest North Atlantic pressure-recorded a 78-millibars pressure drop in 24 hours. This was a record for the North Atlantic basin until Wilma in 2005 and is the second most rapid deepening phases ever undergone by a tropical cyclone anywhere on Earth. The previous record holder was Super Typhoon Forrest in 1983. With Hurricane Wilma, 2005 became the first year on record to have three Category 5 storms in the North Atlantic basin (the other two being Hurricane Katrina and Hurricane Rita).

During its intensification on October 19, the eye's diameter shrank to as small as 1.5 to 2.0 nautical miles-one of the smallest eyes ever seen in a tropical cyclone. Quickly thereafter, Wilma set the record for the lowest pressure ever recorded in a North Atlantic hurricane when its central pressure dropped to 884 millibars (26.10 inches) at 8 am EDT on October 19, then further dropped again to 882 millibars (26.04 inches) three hours later before rising slowly in the afternoon (while still retaining its status as a Category 5 hurricane). Also, at 11 pm EDT October 20, Wilma's pressure dropped again to 894 millibars-as the storm weakened slightly to a Category 4 with winds of 155 mph. Wilma was the first hurricane ever in the North Atlantic basin to have a central pressure below 900 millibars (26.58 inches) while at Category 4 intensity (in fact, only two other recorded North Atlantic hurricanes have ever had lower pressures even at this point).

The most intense North Atlantic Hurricanes

Rank	Hurricane	Year	Minimum Central Pressure
1	**Wilma**	**2005**	**882 millibars (hPa)**
2	Gilbert	1988	888 millibars (hPa)
3	Great Labour Day	1935	892 millibars (hPa)
4	Rita	2005	895 millibars (hPa)
5	Allen	1980	899 millibars (hPa)
6	Camille	1969	900 millibars (hPa)
7	Katrina	2005	902 millibars (hPa)
8	Mitch	1998	905 millibars (hPa)
9	Dean	2007	905 millibars (hPa)
10	Maria	2017	908 millibars (hPa)
11	Irma	2017	914 millibars (hPa)

The most intense North Atlantic Hurricanes (Courtesy of The Weather Channel, Wikipedia, NOAA-NHC, HURDAT).

At the time, Wilma was the most intense hurricane (i.e., a tropical cyclone in the North Atlantic, Central Pacific or Eastern Pacific) ever recorded; however, there have been many more intense typhoons in the Pacific. For example, Super Typhoon Tip is still the most intense tropical cyclone on record at 870 millibars (25.69 inches). On October 20, Wilma weakened slightly and turned northwestward toward the Northern Yucatan Peninsula. On October 21, Hurricane Wilma made landfall on Mexico's Yucatan Peninsula as a powerful Category 4 hurricane, with sustained winds more than 150 mph. The hurricane's eye first passed over the island of Cozumel and then made an official landfall near Playa del Carmen in the state of Quinta Roo around midnight on October 22 with winds near 140 mph.

Portions of the island of Cozumel experienced the calm eye of Wilma for several hours with some blue skies and sunshine visible at times. The eye slowly drifted northward, with the center passing just to the west of Cancun, Quintana Roo. Some portions of the Yucatan Peninsula experienced hurricane force winds for well over 24 hours. The hurricane began accelerating in the early morning hours of October 23, exiting the NE tip of the Yucatan Peninsula and entering the Gulf of Mexico as a Category 2 storm. Hurricane Wilma's southeast eyewall passed the greater Key West area in the lower Florida Keys in the early morning hours of October 24. After the hurricane, there was a 10-feet storm surge from the Gulf of Mexico that completely inundated a large portion of the Lower Keys. Most of the streets in and near Key West were flooded with at least 3 feet of saltwater, destroying tens of thousands of vehicles. Many houses as well were inundated by the rising sea water. Despite significant wind shear in the Gulf, Hurricane Wilma regained some strength before making a third landfall just north of Everglades City, Florida, near Cape Romano, at 6:30 am EDT October 24 as a Category 3 hurricane.

The re-intensification of Hurricane Wilma was due to its interactions with the Gulf Loop Current. At landfall, Wilma had sustained winds of 125 mph. Over the Florida Peninsula, Wilma weakened slightly to a Category 2 hurricane, and exited Florida and entered the Atlantic at that strength about six hours later. Unexpectedly, Wilma regained strength over the Gulf Stream and once again became Category 3 hurricane 85 miles north of The Bahamas and regained all the strength it lost within 12 hours. Even though Wilma never made landfall in The Bahamas, its impact in the extreme northwestern islands was still significant. However, on October 25, the storm gradually began weakening and became extratropical later that afternoon south of Halifax, Nova Scotia in Canada while still at hurricane strength and affecting a large area of land and water with stormy conditions. Considering the great damages over many countries, only 48 deaths have been attributed to Wilma, 1 in Jamaica, 1 in The Bahamas, 12 in Haiti, 8 in Mexico and left some 300,000 persons homeless, 4 in Cuba and left some 638,879 homeless, 22 in Florida. Wilma caused extensive damage in northeastern Yucatan (including Cancun and Cozumel), Southern Florida and The Bahamas. The hurricane also produced major flooding over Western Cuba.

Damages sustained on the major islands of The Bahamas during the passage of Hurricane Wilma in 2005

Due to past experiences from Hurricanes Wilma, Frances, and Jeanne, where some persons refused to move from areas declared as unsafe and vulnerable to storm surge during the storm, several new laws were proposed to be enacted to prevent this from occurring again in the future. The Bahamas Government under the leadership of Prime Minister, Rt. Hon. Perry Christie proposed to put into effect some laws that would declare some parts of The Bahamas vulnerable areas and empower the Royal Bahamas Police Force and Royal Bahamas Defense Force to forcefully remove reluctant persons when ordered to do so by order of the Prime Minister. Mr. Christie stated that, under these new laws, areas like Hawksbill, Queen's Cove, West End, Hepburn Town, and Hanna Hill in Grand Bahama and other areas around The Bahamas that are prone to flooding, prone to being inundated with sea surge coming in and destroying everything in its' wake.

Mr. Christie further specified that these areas could be declared 'vulnerable areas' once they've gotten sound expert advice from NEMA (National Emergency Management Agency) and meteorological officials and environmental engineers to that effect. He continued by saying that once it is perceived and declared that a disaster can take place, and warnings go out, then the full force of the law will be brought to bear on that area. Mr. Christie said the legislation would contain provisions which would allow the public to contest the designation of an area as vulnerable. These laws should also be established for the National Emergency Management Agency (NEMA) to be considered as a statutory body.

The Government of The Bahamas was concerned that Hurricane Wilma caused widespread devastation to residential and commercial properties and, therefore, took urgent action on many fronts to mitigate the hardships and damage caused by the hurricane. One of these measures was to assist homeowners in rapidly overcoming the disruption to their lives caused by the losses suffered to their homes and to support the business sector of the economy in returning to full normal operations as quickly as possible. For these purposes, a program of government guaranteed loans was made available under the Emergency Relief Guarantee Fund Act, 1999, and the regulations made under the Act. Under this Act persons over the age of 18 could borrow funding to repair or replace occupied residential property, furnishings and appliances damaged or destroyed by the hurricane or to replace or repair businesses damaged by it including rental accommodations, fishing boats, engines, farm buildings, farm equipment, citrus or fruit trees, vegetable crops, livestock, restaurant, processing plants and other commercial enterprises.

In response to the damage caused by Hurricane Wilma, the U.S. Agency for International Development (USAID) provided $50,000 to The Bahamas National Emergency Management Agency (NEMA) for the local purchase and distribution of emergency relief supplies and an additional $9,000 for locally contracted helicopter assessments of the affected areas. Kerzner International Development Limited donated two containers full of furniture to NEMA on Monday, October 17, 2005. A group of workers off-loaded the furniture comprised of colourful lounge chairs, sofas, drapery and lamps and they and handed over to NEMA. Hotels throughout the northern Bahamas estimated as much as a 10% fall-off in tourism business due to Hurricane Wilma.

After the storm, a group of agencies and charity organizations moved into the devastated areas throughout Grand Bahama to deliver water, food, and hope to many stranded, hopeless, and homeless Grand Bahamians. With most of the homes along Bay Shore Road in Eight Mile Rock destroyed by Hurricane Wilma, International Rescue, along with Island Helicopters, Million Air, and the New Providence Community Church collaborated to bring aid to those residents in need quickly. The group, along with Our Lucaya Hotel, the Rotary Club of Grand Bahama and the FNM began distributing food into the devastated communities.

Nassau

The PLP political party re-activated their Hurricane Relief Committee under the Chairmanship of Mr. George Smith to help the residents of the affected islands with rebuilding supplies, labour and food items. New Providence suffered no significant damage and reported sustained winds of only 35 knots with gusts to up to 46 knots. Most of the major hotels reported significant cancellations because of the storm, but most of them were back to their normal capacity within two to three days after the storm. Senators from both political parties came together in a bipartisan way to bring to the public's attention, the plight of children affected by Hurricane Wilma. By requesting from the public donations of food, water, clothing, toys, canned goods; medicine to bring to the Senate and the Senators would then ship the goods to the affected victims of Hurricane Wilma.

Abaco

Treasure Cay reported significant flooding with over three to four feet of standing water. Some residents had to relocate to hurricane shelters because their homes were destroyed or engulfed in floodwaters. In Grand Cay, there were ten homes destroyed including the Government Clinic.

Berry Island

Only minor damage was reported on this island. The storm slightly damaged the causeway between Bullocks Harbour and Great Harbour Cay.

Andros

North Andros suffered only slight damage to trees, buildings, and farms. Farmer, Mr. Leonard Newton reported some minor loss to his farm. Most of the fruit orchards on North Andros feared well, so shipment of grapefruits and oranges were only delayed for about two weeks.

Bimini

Bimini suffered significant damage with the roof of several homes blown away. There were also numerous trees and power lines that were blown down. The beaches around the island also suffered significant beach erosion. A 20-room hotel was severely damaged by the hurricane, of the 20 rooms, ten were wiped away, and ten were left unaffected, resulting in 30 people becoming unemployed.

Grand Bahama

Grand Bahama experienced sustained winds of 96 mph and peak gusts of 119 mph as Hurricane Wilma moved some 80 miles north of the island. In the outlying areas, roofs were blown off, and the strong winds flattened homes. The storm surge swept away buildings and roads and unearthed coffins at public cemeteries in various settlements along the bay side. The passage of Hurricane Wilma, the third major storm to hit the country in the space of two years, has left over 500 students of several Grand Bahama primary schools displaced. The students attending the Martin

Town and West End primary schools had to be temporarily relocated until these school buildings were repaired as they were rendered unusable and required immediate repairs before these schools could be reoccupied. Both school buildings suffered significant damage from Hurricanes Frances and Jeanne in 2004, and again they suffered more damage from Hurricane Wilma in 2005. The repair work resulted in these primary schools having to be relocated to buildings in Freeport. Meanwhile, the schools at Eight Mile Rock, Lewis Yard and Holmes' Rock suffered minor damage.

It was estimated that some 200 homes were destroyed leaving well over 1,500 persons homeless. About 400 residents of Pinder's Point were rescued from the rising flood waters and taken to shelters in Freeport. There were 67 buildings in the settlements from Mack Town to Bootle Bay that were destroyed and 30 considered uninhabitable. The entire stretch of small shops and businesses at Sunset Village along Jones Town, Eight Mile Rock, were completely wiped out. Homes were flooded, cemeteries along the coastline were unearthed, and in some cases, entire communities such as the whole of the Haitian community in Bevan's Town was wiped out by the storm. The hurricane damaged public infrastructures, including schools, roads, health clinics, and electrical systems. The southwest portion of Grand Bahama experienced powerful winds and storm surges that caused significant damage and destruction to residential areas on the island. In Eight Mile Rock, approximately 180 residents were rescued during the storm by fire service officers and volunteers and taken to the Eight Mile Rock High School Gym.

The storm became what many Grand Bahama residents described as the most devastating hurricane the island has ever seen in over 50 years and even more destructive than Hurricane Frances and Jeanne in 2004. It left well over 1,500 persons homeless, and hundreds more went without power for well over two weeks after the storm had passed. Some Grand Bahamians had to scramble up into their attics to escape the storm surge of well over 15 feet. Small, remote fishing villages of the western end of Grand Bahama like, Eight Mile Rock sustained the most substantial damage. Most residents in these communities said they experienced a storm surge of over 12 feet high and swept away more than a hundred homes and killed a one-year-old child Matario Pintard, of Hanna Hill, Eight Mile Rock, who was washed away in the storm surge. While 21-year-old Ms. Crystal Pintard the mother was attempting to flee to safety, the storm surge which was as high as the roof of her home engulfed her and the rest of the family members in this residence and swept her 12-month-old son Matario Pintard away. The boy's body was eventually found several hours later about a mile away from home.

Approximately 5 miles west of Eight Mile Rock, Wilma's toll was perhaps less grim, but significant damage still occurred none the less. Several caskets and bodies were unearthed at several cemeteries, including one in Eight Mile Rock. Paradise Cove, a resort that draws snorkelers and scuba divers with its nearby clear waters and large coral outcrop called Deadman's Reef, was rearranged by the storm. The massive storm surge caused significant damage to the nearby coral outcrop called Deadman's Reef where the powerful sea swells broke off large chunks of the reef and destroyed colonies of sea fan coral. Wilma's storm surge lifted three of the resort's five bungalows from their cement footings and placed them 100 yards inland, dropping them in the middle of the access road leading to the resort. The swells also damaged two other buildings and covered what remained with 4 feet of sand. Settlements in the eastern portion of the island, McClean's Town, Pelican Point, Sweeting's Cay, Smith's Point, Mather Town, High Rock, and Bevan's Town, suffered only minimal damage. The Bahamas Telecommunications Company communications grid suffered only minor loss. The storm also uprooted approximately ten coffins on the beachside of Eight Mile Rock Cemetery.

In the communities of Pinder's Point, Hepburn Town, Bootle Bay and others in the western district of Grand Bahama, blocks of neighbourhoods were destroyed. After the storm, the Prime Minister Rt. Hon. Perry Christie and his entourage of Cabinet Members and other Members of Parliament from both the Opposition and the Government, religious leaders, technical experts, and others toured the storm-ravaged areas of Grand Bahama. Mr. Christie expressed shock and sadness over the enormous damage caused in some regions of Grand Bahama. He was deeply moved by the utter devastation he saw at Pinder's Point, where many homes were wiped out by a powerful storm surge. As Mr. Christie made his way through the affected areas, storm victims in Pinder's Point, Eight Mile Rock, and West End were busy searching among the ruins to salvage clothing, food, mattresses, and furniture from mountains of debris. He estimated that the government would have to spend some $24 million to rebuild the storm-ravaged areas of Grand Bahama.

Hurricane Wilma tore the roof of this Grand Bahama church (Courtesy of Kevin Ewing).

There were many horror stories about the storm from people mainly in the settlement of Eight Mile Rock, 10 miles northwest of Freeport, where Wilma's damage was most extensive. Several young men said they had to swim over trees and debris in their yards to rescue their family members from the storm's brutal waves. One Eight Mile Rock resident, Yale Tynes, told The Nassau Guardian newspaper that he and his father had a brush with death when the ocean engulfed their home. "The first surge came and pushed our truck right through our front door. We started to run but the second surge came about three feet higher and broke the door down," he said. "Then the door hit my father, and I had to swim over to get him because the surge was taking him back into the yard. He was disoriented after the door hit him, but I was able to get him." Stephanie Ellis of Williams Town told a horror story of her brother pulling her into his house to save her from the strong storm surge. "One minute we (she and her three children) were in the house and the next minute the sea was racing at us, and it came up about three feet high. So, we all jumped in our car and before we could get far, the car stalled out," she said. "The car door would not open so we had to jump out of the window and the water caught us up to our chin at that point. We had to swim over to my brother's house." She continued, "He pulled my children through the bedroom window, but it was hard for me to get through. Fighting and trying to get through the window, I got cut under my feet, and I got bruises on my body. It was frightening."

Progressive Liberal Party Senator Caleb Outten reported in The Nassau Guardian that he and his team had to rescue 57 persons in Hanna Hill and Pinedale areas. There was also widespread devastation in Mac Town, Pinder's Point, Lewis Yard, Hunters, Hanna Hill, and Bartlett Hill areas. In the aftermath of Hurricane Wilma, nearly 300 displaced Grand Bahamians from the southern settlements were assigned temporary housing at the Royal Oasis Resort. A 75-room wing at the Country Club was occupied by 280 adults and children who lost their homes during the storm from various settlements between Mack Town and West End. The Prime Minister Rt. Hon. Perry Christie negotiated with Lehman Brothers for the use of the resort property to house those left homeless by the storm. After the storm, The Bahamas Red Cross Society donated $15,000 worth of food to Grand Bahamians in need. Eight Mile Rock police station was relocated to the fire station in the same compound. Police said the move was made because the extensive damage to the station caused by Hurricane Wilma, rendering it unusable.

The Preliminary Damage Assessment for Grand Bahama after Hurricane Wilma was as follows (Information courtesy of The Bahamas Information Service/Bahamas Government):

EIGHT MILE ROCK
Location: Hunters
Estimated Cost for Rebuild: $1,110,00.00

Location: Mack Town
Estimated Cost for rebuild: $111,003.00

Location: Pinder's Point
Estimated Cost for rebuild: $555,120.00

Location: Lewis Yard
Estimated Cost for rebuild: $1,110,180.00

Location: Andros Town
Estimated Cost for rebuild: $185,055.00

Location: Bartlett Hill
Estimated Cost for rebuild: $740,240.00

Location: Hanna Hill
Estimated Cost for rebuild: $185,085.00

Location: HarbourWest
Estimated Cost for rebuild: $370,140.00

Location: Hepburn Town
Estimated Cost for rebuild: $925,375.00

WEST END
Location: West End
Estimated Cost for rebuild: $37,032.00

Location: Deadman's Reef
Estimated Cost for rebuild: $185,130.00

Location: Holmes Rock
Estimated Cost for rebuild: $37,027.00

Location: Jones Town
Estimated Cost for rebuild: $185,085.00

Location: Martin Town
Estimated Cost for rebuild: $185,090.00

Location: Seagrape
Estimated Cost for rebuild: $185,120.00

EAST END
Estimated Cost for rebuild: $296,256.00

FREEPORT (LUCAYA)
Location: Williams Town

Estimated Cost for rebuild: $37,040.00

Hurricanes Katrina, Noel, Irene and Sandy's Impacts on the Islands of The Bahamas in 2005, 2007, 2011 and 2012

Hurricane Katrina in 2005

Hurricane Katrina formed as Tropical Depression Twelve over the central/southeastern Bahamas on August 23, 2005, as the result of an interaction between a tropical wave and the remnants of Tropical Depression Ten. The storm caused significant flooding over The Bahamas, notably Long Island. The storm strengthened into Tropical Storm Katrina on the morning of August 24. The tropical storm moved towards Florida and became a hurricane only two hours before making landfall between Hallandale Beach and Aventura on the morning of August 25. The storm weakened over land, but it regained hurricane status about one hour after entering the Gulf of Mexico, and it continued strengthening over open waters. After very briefly weakening again to a tropical storm, Katrina emerged into the Gulf of Mexico on August 26 and began to rapidly intensify. The storm strengthened into a Category 5 hurricane over the warm waters of the Gulf of Mexico but weakened before making its second landfall as a Category 3 hurricane on August 29, over southeast Louisiana and Mississippi. As Katrina made landfall, its front right quadrant, which held the strongest winds, slammed into Gulfport, Mississippi, devastating it.

Hurricane Katrina was "the single most catastrophic natural disaster in U.S. history," according to the Federal Emergency Management Agency. At first, the Category 3 Katrina seemed like it was losing its power as it drifted over the Gulf. But it picked up speed south of Louisiana and became a Category 5 hurricane. On August 28, government officials ordered all New Orleans residents to evacuate the city. The city's levees broke, and soon 80 percent of the city was underwater. Katrina cost more than 1,836 lives and over $108 billion. It displaced about 400,000 people to cities across the U.S., and many never returned to New Orleans.

The second costliest North Atlantic hurricane and one of the strongest hurricanes in history, Hurricane Katrina was the infamous storm of the 2005 North Atlantic hurricane season. Over 90% of the Mississippi beachfront towns were flooded, storm waters pushed boats and casino barges onto buildings in coastal areas. Cars and houses were severely damaged by flowing debris. Floodwaters of Hurricane Katrina reached as far inland as 6 to 8 miles. New Orleans was one of the worst sufferers in the storm where 80% of the city and neighbouring areas were flooded, all modes of communication were lost, and levee and floodwater failure drowned many persons.

<u>Hurricane Noel in 2007</u>

There was severe flooding in Exuma after Hurricane Noel passage in 2007. Hurricane Noel dumped record amounts of rainfall of 29.43 inches (747.5 mm) at a station in Long Island alone.

Hurricane Noel was the fourteenth named storm and sixth hurricane of the 2007 North Atlantic hurricane season. Noel formed on October 27 from the interaction between a tropical wave and an upper-level low in the north-central Caribbean. It strengthened to winds of 60 mph before making landfall on western Haiti and the north coast of eastern Cuba. It turned northward, and on November 1 it attained hurricane status. The hurricane accelerated northeastward after crossing The Bahamas, and on November 2 it became an extratropical cyclone. The storm caused at least 163 direct deaths along its path, primarily in Hispaniola, due to flooding and mudslides. It was the deadliest North Atlantic hurricane of the 2007 season.

Tropical Storm Noel dropped heavy rainfall across portions of The Bahamas, reaching a record total of 15 inches (380 mm) at one station and 29.43 inches (747.5 mm) at a station in Long Island. Sustained winds were around 40 mph throughout the central and northwestern regions of the island chain. Extensive flooding was reported, especially on Abaco Island, forcing the evacuation of over 700 people. Long Island was hit the worst, where flood waters reportedly reached 5 feet deep. Residents of the island deemed the damage "devastating," reporting that flood waters were the highest in 60 years. In some locations, houses were under several feet of water, while roads throughout The Bahamas suffered damage. The Deadman's Cay Airport was also flooded, and on the island of Exuma, six of the nine schools received extensive damage. About 16,000 people were affected by the floods, including 10,000 on Long Island. The Nassau International Airport was closed due to the storm, and most cruise ships failed to arrive on schedule. One fatality occurred when a man on the island of Exuma abandoned a stalled truck and was subsequently swept away by flood waters into a nearby pond. When Prime Minister Rt. Hon. Hubert Ingraham visited the hard-hit areas to assess the damage; he stated that it would be possible for Public Works to "be able to get some pumps in to pump some of the water out." However, he also noted that "In some areas that will be very difficult because you have ponds on both sides of the road."

The total amount of record rainfall for The Bahamas after various hurricanes

Rank	Rainfall in mm	Rainfall in inches	Storm Name	Island/Location	Year
1	747.5	29.43	Noel	Long Island	2007
2	436.6	17.19	Flora	Duncan Town	1963
3	390.1	15.36	Inez	Nassau International Airport	1966
4	337.1	13.27	Fox	Nassau International Airport	1952
5	321.1	12.64	Michelle	Nassau International Airport	2001
6	309.4	12.18	Erin	Church Grove, Crooked Island	1995
7	260.0	9.88	Fay	Freeport	2008
8	236.7	9.32	Floyd	Little Harbour, Abaco	1999
9	216.4	8.52	Cleo	West End, Grand Bahama	1964

The total amount of record rainfall for The Bahamas after some of the various hurricanes (Courtesy of The Bahamas Department of Meteorology).

Hurricane Irene in 2011

Meteorological History of Hurricane Irene in 2011

Prime Minister Rt. Hon. Hubert Ingraham accompanied by North Eleuthera MP and House Speaker Hon. Alvin Smith and local government officials view damage to a dock in Eleuthera (BIS Photo/Kristaan Ingraham).

Hurricane Irene was a large and destructive tropical cyclone, which affected much of the Caribbean and East Coast of the United States during late August 2011. Irene is ranked as one of the top ten costliest hurricanes in United States history. The ninth named storm, first hurricane, and first major hurricane of the 2011 Atlantic hurricane season, Irene originated from a well-defined Atlantic tropical wave that began showing signs of organization east of the Lesser Antilles. Due to development of atmospheric convection and a closed center of circulation, the system was designated as Tropical Storm Irene on August 20, 2011. After intensifying, Irene made landfall in St. Croix as a strong tropical storm later that day. Early on August 21, the storm made a second landfall in Puerto Rico. While crossing the island, Irene strengthened into a Category 1 hurricane. The storm paralleled offshore of Hispaniola, continuing to slowly intensify in the process. Shortly before making four landfalls in The Bahamas, Irene peaked as a 120 mph Category 3 hurricane.

Costliest U.S. North Atlantic Hurricanes

Rank	Hurricane	Year	Damage
1	Harvey	2017	$198.63 billion
2	Katrina	2005	$108 billion
3	Maria	2017	$103.45 billion
4	Sandy	2012	$71.4 billion
5	Irma	2017	$66.7 billion
6	Ike	2008	$29.5 billion
7	Andrew	1992	$26.5 billion
8	Wilma	2005	$21 billion
9	Ivan	2004	$18.8 billion
10	**Irene**	**2011**	**$15.6 billion**
11	Charley	2004	$15.1 billion
12	Matthew	2016	$15.09 billion
13	Rita	2005	$12 billion

Costliest U.S. North Atlantic hurricanes (Courtesy of NOAA-NHC/ HURDAT/Wikipedia).

After that, the storm slowly leveled off in intensity as it struck The Bahamas and then curved northward after passing east of Grand Bahama. Continuing to weaken, Irene was downgraded to a Category 1 hurricane before making landfall on the Outer Banks of North Carolina on August 27, becoming the first hurricane to make landfall in the United States since Hurricane Ike in 2008. Early on the following day, the storm re-emerged into the Atlantic from southeastern Virginia. Although Irene remained a hurricane over water, it weakened to a tropical storm while making yet another landfall in the Little Egg Inlet in southeastern New Jersey on August 27. A few hours later, Irene made its ninth and final landfall in Brooklyn, New York City. Early on August 29, Irene transitioned into an extratropical cyclone hitting Vermont after remaining inland as a tropical cyclone for less than 12 hours.

Trees blocked the main road on Shirley Street after the passage of Hurricane Irene in 2011 (Courtesy of Neil Sealey).

Throughout its path, Irene caused widespread destruction and at least 56 deaths. Damage estimates throughout the United States are estimated near $15.6 billion, which made it one of the top ten costliest hurricanes in United States history, only behind Hurricane Andrew of 1992, Hurricane Ivan of 2004, Hurricanes Wilma and Katrina of 2005, Hurricane Ike of 2008, Hurricane Sandy in 2012, and Hurricanes Harvey, Irma and Maria in 2017. Also, monetary losses in the Caribbean and Canada were $830 million and $130 million respectively for a total of nearly $16.6 billion in damage.

In the islands of the Turks and Caicos, on August 24, Irene passed over the British Overseas Territory of Turks and Caicos Islands at Category 1 strength. The hurricane produced high winds that blew off roofs and downed power lines throughout the islands. In Cockburn Town, residences reported a loss of power and light poles were toppled. Many homes on Grand Turk Island also reported a loss of electricity during Irene's passage, although structural damage in the area was very light but only confined to specific sections of the islands. The strongest of the rains and gusts occurred in Providenciales, where light wind damage was reported to roofs and resorts. The Grand Turk cruise port also sustained some minor damage from the storm, but operations resumed three days after impact.

Hurricane Irene's impacts by individual countries

Country/Region	Deaths	Damage (USD)
The Bahamas	0	$40 million
Canada	1	$130 million
Dominican Republic	4	$30 million
Haiti	3	$260 million
United States	49	~$15.6 billion
Puerto Rico	1	$500 million
Other islands	0	Unknown
Total	56	~$16.56 billion

Hurricane Irene's impacts by individual countries (Courtesy of Wikipedia, NHC & Wunderground).

In The Bahamas, Hurricane Irene trekked right through The Bahamas, with its eye making landfall on several of the islands. A peak wind gust of about 140 mph was recorded at the height of the storm, and localized heavy rains of up to 13 inches (330 mm) fell in the area. The extreme winds damaged at least 40 homes on Mayaguana Island, and dozens of homes on Acklins were destroyed. On the latter island, the hurricane reportedly wiped out 90 percent of the settlement at Lovely Bay. Similar winds tore off the roof and shattered the windows out of a high school, where wind gusts as high as 99 mph were reported. Also, a local church on the island partially collapsed due to the storm. The worst of the destruction occurred in Cat Island, characterized by widespread shattered glass and devastated houses. In all, the storm caused "millions of dollars" worth in structural damage and significant property damage on the island, and left many homeless. Across New Providence and Grand Bahama, only limited impact occurred as Irene remained well offshore; businesses operations were scheduled to return to normal shortly after the storm. Nationwide, the damage was estimated at $40 million. Despite the overall extensive structural damage inflicted, there were no reports of fatalities on the islands in the wake of the disaster.

Hurricane Sandy in 2012

Meteorological History of Hurricane Sandy of 2012

Hurricane Sandy roared through the Caribbean before making its way up the East Coast and eventually to New Jersey and New York City in October 2012. The storm was so strong that some parts of lower Manhattan were submerged under 13 feet of water. More than 650,000 New England homes were damaged, and 117 people were killed. Sandy caused $65 billion in damage, making it the third-costliest hurricane in U.S. history. Hurricane Sandy was the strongest hurricane of the 2012 hurricane season. The storm made landfall in Cuba in 2012 as a Category 3 hurricane. Two hundred thirty-three people were killed across eight countries under the influence of the Hurricane Sandy, and huge damage to property occurred. About 70% of the citizens of Jamaica were left without power. In Haiti, flooding killed 54 individuals and left 200,000 homeless and without access to food resources. Two people died in the Dominican Republic, and one person was swept away in the floodwaters in Puerto Rico.

Two lives were lost in the hurricane in The Bahamas, Mr. Norbert Yonker, drowned in his home in Grand Bahama after he was ordered to leave by the police but refused. Another was a 66-year-old Deltec Bank executive, Mr. Timothy Fraser Smith who lost his life when he tried to secure and fix a hurricane shutter which had come loose in the hurricane and was blown of the second floor of his house in Lyford Cay in the capital of New Providence by a strong gust of wind. Canada also experienced loss of lives and property damage. Hurricane Sandy affected 24 US States, flooded streets, subway lines, and tunnels in various cities. Power outages and road blockages in many places were also associated with Hurricane Sandy.

Hurricane Sandy left a trail of destruction across The Bahamas in late October, ripping off roofs, toppling trees, damaging infrastructure and claiming two lives. The Caribbean Catastrophe Risk Insurance Facility (CCRIF) estimated $20 million in losses to the government. When Sandy finally made landfall, it had strengthened into a Category 2 hurricane, with sustained winds of at least 100 mph. Schools and businesses remained closed for two days impacting the major islands during this time. Several islands lost telecommunications service and water supply for several days. Severe flooding and structural damage were reported throughout Eleuthera and Grand Bahama, particularly Queen's Cove. The Nassau Port sustained significant damage, and some private dwellings and businesses across the country were also significantly impacted. The hurricane damaged 20 to 30 homes in New Plymouth, South Abaco after the structures were flooded by waters as high as five feet. Widespread crop damage was reported in Long Island. After the storm, the Prime Minister Rt. Hon. Perry Christie signed exigency orders that allowed residents impacted by the hurricane to bring in certain goods duty free.[118]

---

[118] The Nassau Guardian, *Hurricane Lashes Bahamas*, December 31, 2012. Retrieved: 15-05-2017.

CHAPTER TWENTY-SEVEN

Hurricanes Joaquin, Alex and Matthew's Impacts on the Islands of The Bahamas in 2015 and 2016

Hurricane Joaquin in 2015

Hurricane Joaquin was a powerful tropical cyclone that devastated several districts of The Bahamas and caused damage in the Turks and Caicos Islands, parts of the Greater Antilles, and Bermuda. It was also the strongest North Atlantic hurricane of non-tropical origin in the satellite era. The tenth named storm, third hurricane, and second major hurricane of the 2015 Atlantic hurricane season, Joaquin evolved from a non-tropical low to become a tropical depression on September 28, well southwest of Bermuda. Tempered by unfavorable wind shear, the depression drifted southwestward. After becoming a tropical storm, the next day, Joaquin underwent rapid intensification, reaching hurricane status on September 30 and Category 4 major hurricane strength on October 1. Meandering over the SE Bahamas, Joaquin's eye passed near or over several islands. On October 3, the hurricane weakened somewhat and accelerated to the northeast. Abrupt re-intensification ensued later that day, and Joaquin acquired sustained winds of 155 mph, just short of Category 5 strength.

Hurricane warnings were hoisted across most of The Bahamas as the hurricane threatened the country. Battering the nation's southern islands for over two days, Joaquin caused extensive devastation, most notably on Acklins, Crooked Island, Long Island, Rum Cay, and San Salvador Island. Severe storm surge inundated many communities, trapping hundreds of people in their homes; flooding persisted for days after the hurricane's departure. Prolonged, intense winds brought down trees and power lines, and unroofed houses throughout the affected region. As airstrips were submerged and heavily damaged, relief workers were limited in their ability to quickly help residents affected by Joaquin, one of the strongest storms on record to impact the nation. Offshore, the American cargo ship *El Faro* and her 33 members were lost to the hurricane. After the passage of Hurricane Joaquin, BTC, a local telecommunications company, discovered 59 cell sites offline negatively impacting 59 communities in the Central and SE Bahamas.

Coastal flooding also impacted the nearby Turks and Caicos, washing out roadways, compromising seawalls, and damaging homes. Strong winds and heavy rainfall caused some property damage in eastern Cuba. One fisherman died when heavy seas capsized a small boat along the coast of Haiti. Storm tides resulted in severe flooding in several departments of Haiti, forcing families from their homes and destroying crops. The weakening hurricane passed just west of Bermuda on October 4, attended by strong winds that cut power to 15,000 electric subscribers but caused only minor damage otherwise. After passing near Bermuda, Joaquin curved northeastward and accelerated, weakening further and becoming extratropical as it entered colder waters.

Collectively, Joaquin killed 34 people and caused $200 million USD in damages. With all 34 deaths attributed to the storm occurring at sea, Joaquin has the highest offshore death toll for any North Atlantic hurricane since the Escuminac Hurricane in 1959, which killed 35 people in the Northumberland Strait.

Although Joaquin never directly affected the United States, another large storm system over the southeastern states drew tremendous moisture from the hurricane, resulting in catastrophic flooding in South Carolina. Hurricane Joaquin was a powerful Category 4 tropical cyclone that devastated several islands of The Bahamas and caused damage in the Turks and Caicos Islands, parts of the Greater Antilles, and Bermuda. The tenth named storm, third hurricane, and second major hurricane of the 2015 North Atlantic hurricane season, Joaquin evolved from a non-tropical low to become a tropical depression on September 28, well southwest of Bermuda. Hindered by unfavorable atmospheric wind shear, the depression drifted southwestward. After becoming a tropical storm, the next day Joaquin underwent rapid intensification, reaching hurricane status on September 30 and Category 3 hurricane on the Saffir-Simpson Hurricane Wind Scale on October 1. Meandering over the southeastern

Bahamas, Joaquin's eye passed near or over several islands for a few days. On October 3, the hurricane weakened somewhat and accelerated to the northeast. Abrupt re-intensification ensued later that day, and Joaquin acquired sustained winds of 155 mph; this made it the strongest North Atlantic hurricane since 2010's Igor.

Meteorological History of Hurricane Joaquin in 2015

On September 25, 2015, the US National Hurricane Center (NHC) began monitoring an upper-level low, accompanied by a surface trough, several hundred miles south-southwest of Bermuda for possible tropical cyclogenesis. The system gradually consolidated as it drifted north-northwest, acquiring a closed surface low late on September 26. Convective showers and thunderstorms steadily increased on September 27, and at 11 pm EDT on September 28 the NHC assessed the system to have become a tropical depression, situated roughly 405 miles southwest of Bermuda. Although the depression featured a well-defined low, strong wind shear displaced convection and exposed the circulation. A ridge to the north was forecast to steer the system slowly northwest into a region of higher shear; meteorologists at the NHC initially depicted the system dissipating within 96 hours based on modeling depictions. Convection developed and persisted closer to the circulation center throughout September 28, and early on September 29, Dvorak satellite classifications indicated the system became a tropical storm. Accordingly, it was assigned the name Joaquin, becoming the tenth named storm of the season.[119]

Strengthening of the mid-level ridge prompted a sudden shift in Joaquin's trajectory to the southwest, directing it towards The Bahamas. Forecasters at the NHC noted considerable uncertainty in the future of Joaquin, with forecast models depicting a wide range of possibilities. Throughout September 29 the storm steadily intensified as its circulation became embedded within deep convection and upper-level outflow became increasingly prominent. High sea surface temperatures and decreasing shear aided strengthening, and early on September 30 the storm achieved hurricane status. Rapid intensification ensued after that, with an eye

---

[119] John P. Cangialosi (September 29, 2015). *Tropical Storm Joaquin Discussion Number 5* (Report). Miami, Florida: National Hurricane Center. Retrieved: 10-05-2017.

developing within a symmetric central dense overcast. Data from an aircraft reconnaissance indicated that Joaquin reached Category 3 status on the Saffir–Simpson Hurricane Wind Scale by 11 pm EDT on October 1. Around 8 am EDT the eye of Joaquin passed over Samana Cay, Bahamas, with winds of 130 mph, making it a Category 4 hurricane. Around this same time, its eye contracted from 41 to 27 miles in diameter, representing significant intensification. During this time Joaquin was located just 15 miles northwest of Crooked Island. The storm's central pressure bottomed out at 931 millibars (hPa; 27.49 inches) around 8 pm EDT on October 2.[120]

As the high-pressure ridge, previously steering Joaquin southwest began retreating north, the hurricane's movement slowed and shifted west, and later north, early on October 2. An eyewall replacement cycle—a process whereby a second, larger eye develops while the inner eye collapses—began that morning; its eye became increasingly ill-defined in satellite imagery. Slight weakening took place accordingly, and the hurricane passed over Rum Cay, and San Salvador Island around 12 pm EDT and 3 pm EDT as a strong Category 3 hurricane with winds of 125 mph; a pressure near 944 millibars (hPa; 27.88 inches) was observed on the island of San Salvador. An amplifying trough over the southeastern United States enhanced southwesterly flow over Joaquin on October 3 and prompted the hurricane to accelerate northeast away from The Bahamas. Throughout the day the storm's eye became increasingly defined, and re-intensification ensued. A reconnaissance aircraft found a considerably stronger system that afternoon; based on flight-level winds of 166 mph. It is estimated that Joaquin attained surface winds of 155 mph—a high-end Category 4 hurricane—by 12 pm EDT. This made Joaquin the strongest North Atlantic hurricane of non-tropical origin in the satellite era.[121]

Shortly after peaking, the hurricane's overall structure began to deteriorate, signaling a weakening trend. On October 4, the storm curved towards the north-northeast between a large low-pressure system to its west and a mid-level ridge to its east. As deep convection over its core continued to wane, Joaquin passed about 70 miles west-northwest of Bermuda near 8

---

[120] Daniel P. Brown; Stacy R. Stewart (October 2, 2015). *Hurricane Joaquin Advisory Number 16A* (Report). Miami, Florida: National Hurricane Center. Retrieved: 10-05-2017.

[121] Richard J. Pasch (October 7, 2015). *Post-Tropical Cyclone Joaquin Advisory Number 42 (Advisory)*. Miami, Florida: National Hurricane Center. Retrieved: 10-05-2017.

pm EDT on October 5, with winds of 85 mph. The weakening trend slowed that day as the storm's satellite presentation improved slightly, marked by brief reappearances of a distinct eye feature. Joaquin gradually turned northeastward around the periphery of the weak ridge, and subsequently accelerated toward the east-northeast as it entered the prevailing westerlies.

The system-maintained hurricane intensity until 11 am EDT on October 7, by which point strengthening, wind shear, and an increasingly colder environment began to take their negative toll on the system. The cloud pattern became lopsided as colder, drier air infiltrated the circulation, forming the first stages of a frontal structure. With its extratropical transition well underway, Joaquin lost its identity as a tropical cyclone at 11 pm EDT on October 8, about 850 miles southeast of Cape Race, Newfoundland. During the next several days, Joaquin's extratropical remnant continued heading eastward across the Atlantic, before reaching Portugal on October 10. During the next five days, Joaquin's remnant slowly moved southward along the coast of Portugal, until the system was absorbed by another frontal system to the east of Spain, on October 15.

Damages Sustained on the Major Islands of The Bahamas during Hurricane Joaquin in 2015

Hurricane warnings were hoisted across most of The Bahamas as the hurricane threatened the country. Battering the nation's southern islands for over two days, Joaquin caused extensive devastation, most notably on Acklins, Crooked Island, Cat Island, Long Island, Rum Cay, and San Salvador Island. Severe storm surge inundated many communities, trapping hundreds of people in their homes; flooding persisted for days after the hurricane's departure. Prolonged, intense winds brought down trees and power lines and unroofed houses throughout the affected region. As airstrips were submerged in floodwaters and heavily damaged, relief workers were limited in their ability to help affected residents quickly. Joaquin was one of the strongest storms on record to affect the nation, and the strongest to hit this island nation since Category 5 Hurricane Andrew in 1992.[122]

---

[122] Ian Livingston (October 2, 2015). *Hurricane Joaquin among the strongest storms on record in the Bahamas*. Capital Weather Gang. The Washington Post. Retrieved: 04-10-2015.

On September 29, 2015, at 8:10 pm, the ship *SS El Faro* left Jacksonville, Florida for San Juan, Puerto Rico, carrying a cargo of 391 shipping containers, about 294 trailers and cars, and a crew of 33 people—28 Americans and 5 Poles. The ship's master, Captain Michael Davidson, charted a course that, took the vessel a reasonably safe distance away from the hurricane. At the time of departure, Hurricane Joaquin was still a tropical storm, but meteorologists at the National Hurricane Center forecast that it would likely become a hurricane by the morning of October 1, on a southwest trajectory toward The Bahamas. The vessel's charted course took it within 175 nautical miles of the storm, where seas more than 10 feet were likely.

The management and owners could have vetoed the captain's sail plan into the area of a predicted hurricane but chose not to and opted for the ship to continue. The company said there was no incentive for Davidson to maintain the ship's schedule, but that the schedule also appeared to be a safe one. At least one of the deck officers voiced concern prior to sailing, and wrote in an email to friends and family, "there is a hurricane out here, and we are heading straight into it." In the end, all 33 personnel onboard died when the ship encountered the hurricane just east of Crooked Island in The Bahamas.

Coastal flooding also impacted the nearby Turks and Caicos, washing out roadways, compromising seawalls, and damaging homes. Strong winds and heavy rainfall caused some property damage in eastern Cuba. One fisherman died when heavy seas capsized a small boat along the coast of Haiti. Storm tides resulted in severe flooding in several of Haiti's departments, forcing families from their homes and destroying crops. The weakening hurricane passed just west of Bermuda on October 4, attended by strong winds that cut power to 15,000 electric subscribers. Damage on Bermuda was minor. Although Joaquin steered clear of the mainland United States, another large storm system over the southeastern states drew tremendous moisture from the hurricane, resulting in catastrophic flooding in South Carolina.

Large swells ahead of the storm's arrival in The Bahamas washed out the main road on San Salvador Island. Widespread power outages affected several islands as the hurricane closed in. Reports of flooding and people in need of assistance were received from Acklins, Crooked Island, Rum Cay, San Salvador Exuma, and Long Island. Prolonged power and communication failures overwhelmed the nation's southeastern islands, leaving several islands effectively isolated in the immediate aftermath of Joaquin. The hurricane took all 59 of The Bahamas Telecommunications Company's cell sites in the central and southeastern Bahamas offline negatively impacting these islands, most of them returned to service within two weeks. By October 21, The Bahamas Electricity Corporation had remedied about 80% of its power outages, aided by crews from New Providence and the Caribbean Association of Electric Utilities group. Early aerial surveys revealed that Acklins, Rum Cay, Crooked Island, and San Salvador Island were devastated.

A view of the significant structural and roof damage to this Landrail Point-Seven Day Adventist Church and the adjacent pastor's residence after Hurricane Joaquin hit Crooked Island in The Bahamas (Courtesy of Wayne Neely).

Throughout the archipelago, flooding from the hurricane trapped over 500 residents. Floodwaters up to 5 feet deep submerged at least 70% of nearby Crooked Island, where the storm left widespread structural damage. The hurricane "destroyed" a Bahamas Electricity Corporation power plant, where two large diesel tanks were shifted off their bases, allowing more than 10,000 gallons of fuel to leak into the ground. In the days following the storm, about 100 evacuees—including 46 from Crooked Island—were flown to New Providence, where several of them sought medical attention. On Long Island and Crooked Island, septic tank seepage contaminated residential wells, leaving residents without clean drinking water. Both areas still had extensive standing water on October 7. Acklins endured severe flooding, with many homes inundated and numerous calls for rescue; the island's sea barrier was breached by 9:00 a.m. local time. Some residents reported the entire island to be under water. A bridge in Lovely Bay was destroyed.[123]

Long Island was subject to an immense 18 feet storm surge that flooded homes with up to 12 feet of water. Southern areas of the island suffered considerable devastation; the surge washed out coastal roadways and drove numerous fishing boats ashore. The Member of Parliament for Long Island, Loretta Butler-Turner, estimated that 75% of all fishing vessels there were destroyed. This, combined with heavy losses to farms and crops, threatened the livelihoods of many residents. About 20 individuals required rescue on Long Island, while some hurricane shelters became compromised by water entrance. The bodies of dead animals were seen floating in the water. Strong winds unroofed dozens of homes, and many structures were fully destroyed. Northern parts of the island fared better in comparison. The winds and flooding took a large toll on native vegetation, even well inland.[124] In an amazing spirit of community organization, many former residents from Long Island and presently living in the capital of Nassau organized many clothing, food and other charity drives as well to assist the storm-ravaged island. This was also very true for other storm ravaged islands like Acklins and Crooked Island as well.

Several weeks after the storm, The Bahamas national disaster agency NEMA officials estimated that 836 residences had been destroyed, including 413 on Long Island, 227 on San Salvador, 123 on Acklins, 50 on Crooked Island, and 23 on Rum Cay. The storm's effects were considered comparable to the destruction wrought by Hurricane Andrew in 1992, which struck the northwestern Bahamas as a Category 5. Initial claims of numerous casualties throughout the island chain proved unsubstantiated, and although one man died during the storm on Long Island, his death was unrelated to the hurricane.[125] In the aftermath of the hurricane, one person was reported missing on Ragged Island, which escaped with relatively minor effects. Initially, Prime Minister of The Bahamas, Rt. Hon. Perry

---

[123] Sean Breslin (October 1, 2015), *Hurricane Joaquin's Bahamas Impacts: More Than 500 Residents Trapped in Their Homes, Excessive Power Outages*. The Weather Channel. Associated Press. Retrieved: 02-10-2015.

[124] Sancheska Brown (October 15, 2015), *Fishing and Farming Industries Are 'Completely Devastated.'* The Tribune. Retrieved: 16-10-2015.

[125] Krishna Virgil (October 22, 2015), *Hurricane Wiped Out 836 Homes*. The Tribune. Retrieved: 26-10-2015.

Christie, estimated that damages from Joaquin would exceed $60 million, but he increased this damage total to over $100 million while addressing a climate change conference for world leaders in Paris, France, on December 1, 2015.[126] Then in 2016 following the final assessments report done by the Inter-American Development Bank in conjunction with the Economic Commission for Latin America and the Caribbean (ECLAC), the Pan American Health Organization, stated that Hurricane Joaquin severely damaged islands in the southeast, central, and northwest Bahamas on its path from 30 September to 2 October, 2015. In November 2015 the members of The Bahamas Government assessment team visited the five most severely affected islands of hurricane Joaquin: Acklins, Crooked Island, Long Island, Rum Cay, and San Salvador. The estimated total damage to the affected islands was $104,788,224.[127]

On April 25, 2016, it was announced by the World Meteorological Organization that the name Joaquin was retired due to the severe damage in The Bahamas and sinking of the *SS El Faro*. It will be replaced with Julian for the 2021 North Atlantic hurricane season.

Hurricane Alex in 2016: –Hurricane Alex was the first North Atlantic hurricane in January since the Alice in the 1954/1955 seasons and the first to form in the month of January since 1938. Alex originated as an extratropical cyclone near The Bahamas on January 7, 2016. The system initially travelled northeast, passing Bermuda on January 8 before turning southeast. It subsequently deepened and acquired hurricane-force winds by January 10. Slight weakening took place thereafter, and the system eventually turned east and northeast as it acquired tropical characteristics. On January 13, it developed into a subtropical cyclone well south of the Azores, becoming the first tropical or subtropical system during January in the North Atlantic since an unnamed storm in 1978.

The National Hurricane Center in Miami categorized it as a subtropical storm on Wednesday, January 16, Alex took on a surprisingly healthy structure, with a symmetric core of showers and thunderstorms around its clearly defined eye. According to Bob Henson and Dr. Jeff Masters of the private weather company Weather Underground in the United States,

---

[126] Neil Hartnell (December 2, 2015), *Joaquin Damages Grow to $100 million*. The Tribune. Retrieved: 02-12-2015.

[127] *Economic Commission for Latin America and the Caribbean (ECLAC), the Pan American Health Organization, Bahamas National Emergency Management Agency-Hurricane Joaquin Assessment Report 2015.* Retrieved: 16-02-2018.

"sea-surface temperatures beneath Alex are only around 20-22°C (68-72°F). Although these are up to 1°C above average for this time of year, they are far cooler than usually required for tropical cyclone development. However, upper-level temperatures near Alex were unusually cold for the latitude, which means that instability–driven by the contrast between warm, moist lower levels and cold, drier upper levels–is higher than it would otherwise be. That instability allowed showers and thunderstorms to blossom and consolidate, strengthening the warm core that makes Alex a hurricane as opposed to an extratropical or subtropical storm."[128]

As it turned north-northeast, Alex transitioned into a full-fledged tropical cyclone on January 14 and became a hurricane. The storm peaked as a Category 1 on the Saffir–Simpson Hurricane Wind Scale with maximum sustained winds of 85 mph and a barometric pressure of 981 millibars (hPa; 28.97 inches). After weakening slightly, Alex made landfall on Terceira Island as a tropical storm the next day. Simultaneously, Alex began transitioning back into an extratropical cyclone; it completed this cycle hour after moving away from the Azores. The system ultimately merged with another extratropical cyclone over the Labrador Sea on January 17.

In records going back to 1851, only two hurricanes are known to have existed in the North Atlantic during the month of January: an unnamed tropical storm that became Hurricane #1 on January 4, 1938, and Hurricane Alice, which maintained hurricane strength from December 31, 1954, to January 4, 1955. Alice topped out at 80 mph, so Alex is officially the strongest January hurricane on record in the North Atlantic. Much like Alice, another tropical cyclone called Tropical Storm Zeta of the very active 2005/06 hurricane seasons–formed in December and extended into January, and a tropical storm was recorded in early January 1951. There was also a subtropical storm in January 1978.[129]

The hurricane prompted the issuance of hurricane and tropical storm warnings for the Azores and the closure of schools and businesses. Alex ultimately brought gusty winds and heavy rain to the archipelago, causing generally minor damage. One person died from a heart attack when the

---

[128] Jeff Masters (January 13, 2016). *Unprecedented: Simultaneous January Named Storms in the Atlantic and Central Pacific.* Weather Underground. Retrieved: 15-01-2016. Henson, Bob. *Astounding Alex Hits the Azores: January's First Atlantic Landfall in 61 Years.* Weather Underground. Retrieved: 16-01-2016.

[129] Neely, Wayne, *The very unusual Subtropical Storm Alex/Hurricane Alex,* The Nassau Guardian, January 15, 2016. Retrieved: 16-01-2016.

inclement weather prevented a helicopter from transporting them to a hospital. The World Meteorological Organization reuses storm names every six years for both the North Atlantic and eastern Pacific basins. The nation hardest hit by a storm can request its name be removed because the storm was so deadly or costly that future use of the name would be insensitive or cause confusion among persons in the region. The removal also avoids confusion caused by a future storm having the same name. North Atlantic storm names can be either French, Dutch, Spanish or English, reflecting the languages of the various countries in the region that they can hit.

Hurricane Matthew in 2016

Hurricane Matthew was a very powerful, devastating, long-lived and deadly hurricane which became the first Category 5 North Atlantic hurricane since Hurricane Felix in 2007. The thirteenth named storm, fifth hurricane and second major hurricane of the active 2016 North Atlantic hurricane season, Matthew caused widespread destruction and catastrophic loss of life during its journey across the Western Atlantic, including parts of Haiti, Cuba, Dominican Republic, The Bahamas, the southeastern United States, and the Canadian Maritimes. After Matthew dissipated its death toll was great, at least 522 to over 1,381 estimated deaths have been credited to the storm, including 473 to 1,332 in Haiti, 1 in Colombia, 4 in the Dominican Republic, 1 in Saint Vincent and the Grenadines and 43 in the United States, making it the deadliest North Atlantic hurricane since Stan in 2005, which killed more than 1,600 in Central America and Mexico.

In assessments done by the Inter-American Development Bank in conjunction with the Economic Commission for Latin America and the Caribbean (ECLAC), the Pan American Health Organization. Hurricane Matthew in 2016 cost The Bahamas more than three times as much did as Hurricane Joaquin did in 2015. The total was approximately $438.6 million. Damage accounted for 62.5 percent of the total, followed by losses and additional costs with 25.3 percent and 12.3 percent, respectively. From the sectoral point of view, the social sector absorbed 52.1 percent of the costs, followed by the productive sectors, 26.1 percent.[130] It was costlier than all

---

[130] *Economic Commission for Latin America and the Caribbean (ECLAC), the Pan American Health Organization, Bahamas National Emergency Management Agency-Hurricane Matthew Assessment Report 2017.* Retrieved: 16-02-2018.

the other prior storms because it struck the two top cities in The Bahamas of Nassau and Freeport with Category 4 intensity winds.

Hurricane Matthew was a very large, strong and destructive hurricane which impacted several islands in the Caribbean and the countries of Venezuela and Columbia on northern parts of the South American coast. It then skirted the southeastern most seaboard states in the United States. It was one of the weaker Category 5 (wind speeds of 157 mph or greater on the Saffir-Simpson Hurricane Wind Scale) hurricanes to strike the North Atlantic within the last 10 to 15 years. In fact, it was the first Category 5 hurricane (Matthew had sustained winds of 160 mph) since Hurricanes Dean (175 mph) and Felix (175 mph) of 2007. Matthew set several records during its long and destructive journey. Matthew intensified into a Category 5 hurricane at a latitude of 13.4°N, breaking the record set by Hurricane Ivan in 2004, which had reached that intensity at a latitude of 13.7 °N. Matthew also maintained at least Category 4 status for the longest duration on record for the month of October, doing so for roughly 5 days.

A KFC sign blown down and destroyed by Hurricane Matthew and is supported by utility lines on Carmichael Road in Nassau, Bahamas (Courtesy of Wayne Neely).

Meteorological History of Hurricane Matthew

Members of The Bahamas Red Cross Society and NEMA preparing to fill a trailer with water for shipment to the hurricane damaged islands of The Bahamas (Information Courtesy of Lindsay Thompson/NEMA).

Originating from a tropical wave that emerged off the African coast on September 22, Matthew developed into a tropical storm just east of the Lesser Antilles on September 28. It became a hurricane north of Venezuela and Colombia on September 29, before undergoing explosive intensification, ultimately reaching Category 5 intensity on October 1 at just 13.4°N latitude – the lowest latitude ever recorded for a storm of this intensity in the Atlantic basin, breaking a record set by Hurricane Ivan in 2004. Matthew weakened slightly and fluctuated in intensity while making a northward turn toward the Greater Antilles, remaining a strong Category 4 hurricane as it made its first landfall over Haiti's Tiburon Peninsula early on October 4, and then a second one in Cuba later that day. Matthew weakened somewhat but re-intensified as it tracked northwest, making landfall in the northern Bahamas. The storm then paralleled the coast of the southeastern United States over the next 36 hours, gradually weakening while remaining just offshore before making its fourth and final landfall over the Cape Romain National Wildlife Refuge near Myrtle Beach, South Carolina as a Category 1 hurricane on the morning of October 8. Matthew re-emerged into the Atlantic shortly afterward, eventually completing its transition into an extratropical cyclone as it turned away from Cape Hatteras, North Carolina on October 9.

Around 11am EDT on October 8, the hurricane made landfall at Cape Romain National Wildlife Refuge, near McClellanville, South Carolina, with winds of 85 mph and a central pressure of 963 millibars (28.4 inches), which made it the strongest to strike the United States in terms of pressure since Hurricane Isaac in 2012, and the first hurricane to make landfall north of Florida in October since Hurricane Hazel in 1954. Convection became displaced from the center as Matthew moved away from land due to increasing wind shear, with NHC declaring the system an extratropical cyclone about 200 miles east of Cape Hatteras, North Carolina, on October 9. The remnants persisted for another day before they were absorbed by a cold front.

Damages sustained on the major islands of The Bahamas during Hurricane Matthew in 2016

Prime Minister Rt. Hon. Perry Christie and North Andros resident Mrs. Reckley share a few words as he toured the North Andros community to view devastation after Hurricane Matthew (Image courtesy of Lindsay Thompson/NEMA).

Widespread effects were felt from Matthew across its destructive path; however, the most significant impacts were felt in Haiti, with US$1.9 billion in damage and 546 deaths. The combination of flooding and high winds disrupted telecommunications and destroyed extensive swaths of land; around 80% of Jérémie sustained significant damage. Four people were killed in Cuba due to a bridge collapse, and total losses in the country amounted to US$2.58 billion, most of which occurred in the Guantánamo Province. major hurricane, Matthew spread damage across several islands, compounding relief efforts from Hurricane Joaquin which had pounded similar areas just the previous year.

Grand Bahama was hit directly, where most homes sustained damage in the settlements of Eight Mile Rock and Holmes Rock. Preparations began in earnest across the southeastern United States as Matthew approached, with several states declaring states of emergencies for either entire states or coastal counties; widespread evacuations were ordered for extensive areas of the coast because of predicted high wind speeds and flooding, especially in the Jacksonville Metropolitan Area. In Florida, over 1 million lost power as the storm passed to the east, with 478,000 losing power in Georgia and South Carolina. While damage was primarily confined to the coast in the Florida and Georgia, torrential rains spread inland in the Carolinas and Virginia, causing widespread flooding.

Matthew inflicted widespread destruction and catastrophic loss of life during its journey across the Western Atlantic, including parts of Haiti, Cuba, Dominican Republic, The Bahamas, the southeastern United States, and the Canadian Maritimes. At least 1,655+ estimated deaths have been attributed to the storm, including about 1000 to 1600 in Haiti, 1 in Colombia, 4 in the Dominican Republic, 1 in Saint Vincent and the Grenadines and 43 in the United States, making it the deadliest North Atlantic hurricane since Stan in 2005, which killed more than 1,600 in Central America and Mexico. The death toll in some countries within the region like Jamaica, the Dominican Republic, the Leeward Islands and The Bahamas was relatively low due to well executed warnings and timely evacuations. Prime Minister and Minister of Finance, the Rt. Hon Perry Christie and Minister for the Environment and Housing the Hon. Kenred Dorsett viewed an example of the damage caused by Hurricane Matthew in a Misty Gardens residence, during a recent visit of the southern New Providence community.

Long lines at the few gas stations throughout the capital of New Providence left open after the passage of Hurricane Matthew in 2016 (Courtesy of Neil Sealey).

With the storm causing damages estimated more than US $8.1 billion, it was also the costliest North Atlantic hurricane since Hurricane Sandy in 2012. It was the fourteenth tropical cyclone, thirteenth named storm, fifth hurricane and second major hurricane of the very busy 2016 North Atlantic hurricane season. Matthew was a very active storm which impacted many countries within the Caribbean including, Grenada, St. Vincent, St. Lucia, Dominica, Aruba, Bonaire, Curaçao, Cuba, Haiti, the Dominican Republic, Jamaica, The Bahamas and Cuba. It also impacted Colombia and Venezuela on the South American continent and the southeastern United States on the North American continent.

On September 29, the circulation of Matthew became exposed from the convection due to an increase in wind shear in the upper atmosphere attacking the system. Even with that circumstances, the winds continued to increase. Both the Hurricane Hunters and a Special Sensor Microwave Imager/Sounder (SSMIS) satellite pass revealed an eye feature had developed by early morning of September 30. Close to Matthew's peak intensity, a rare phenomenon known as 'lightning sprites' were observed above the storm in Puerto Rico. Despite the northwesterly wind shear, Matthew began to undergo a period of explosive intensification, doubling its wind speed from 80 mph to 160 mph over a period of 24 hours. Hence, Matthew intensified from a Category 1 hurricane on the Saffir-Simpson Hurricane Wind Scale to a Category 5 hurricane in just 24 hours. Matthew became a Category 5 hurricane at 13.3 degrees north, surpassing Hurricane Ivan as the southernmost hurricane of this intensity on record in the North Atlantic basin.

Heavy rains and strong winds battered the Lesser Antilles as Matthew entered the Caribbean Sea as a strong tropical storm. The winds caused significant and widespread power outages and damaged crops, particularly in St. Lucia where it destroyed 85% of the banana crop, while flooding and landslides caused by the rainfall damaged many homes and roads. The storm's unusually low latitude resulted in widespread flash flooding on the Guajira Peninsula, which saw its first heavy rain event in three years. Extensive preparations took place in Cuba, Jamaica, and Hispaniola as the strong hurricane approached, including the opening of numerous shelters and the evacuation of roughly 1 million people in Cuba. Although Jamaica avoided significant impacts, Haiti on-the-other-hand, experienced major impacts, including more than US$1 billion in damage and at least 1,000 deaths. The bad combination of flooding particularly flash flooding and high winds interrupted and crippled telecommunications and destroyed extensive areas of land; around 80% of Jérémie sustained significant damage. Heavy rainfall spread eastward across the Dominican Republic, where only four persons were killed. Effects in Cuba were most severe along the coast, where storm surge caused extensive damage in Guantánamo Province.

The RUBIS Gas Station on East Bay Street in Nassau, Bahamas roof gave way to the strong 140 mph winds of Hurricane Matthew of 2016 (Courtesy of Wayne Neely).

Passing through The Bahamas as a major hurricane, Matthew inflicted severe damage across several islands, particularly Grand Bahama, where an estimated 95% of homes sustained damage in the settlements of Eight Mile Rock and Holmes Rock. The capital city of Nassau and the northern section of Andros were totally devastated, due to substantial flooding, fallen trees everywhere, numerous downed utility lines, significant crop failure mainly in North Andros-the agricultural belt of The Bahamas. In the settlement of Lowe Sound in North Andros, most of the homes suffered from severe flooding and most of them were destroyed either by the strong winds or the floodwaters. Power outages in some hurricane ravaged areas lasted for over two weeks before the electricity was restored. The Prime Minister Perry Christie in a speech given in the Bahamian Parliament, estimated that to bring The Bahamas back to a state of normalcy, it would cost well over $600 million. This makes this storm the costliest hurricane in Bahamian history and eclipsing the previous record holder Hurricane Andrew in 1992 with $250 million in damage.

Preparations began in earnest across the southeastern United States as Matthew approached, with several states declaring a state of emergency for either entire states or coastal counties; widespread evacuations were ordered for extensive areas along the coast. In Florida, over 1 million lost power as the storm passed to the east, with 478,000 losing power in Georgia and South Carolina. While damage was primarily confined to the coast in the Florida and Georgia, torrential rains spread inland in the Carolinas and Virginia, causing widespread flooding. At around 11:00 a.m. EDT on October 8, Matthew made landfall at Cape Romain National Wildlife Refuge, near McClellanville, South Carolina as a Category 1 hurricane with winds of 75 mph. This made Matthew the first hurricane to make landfall in the United States north of Florida in the month of October since Hurricane Hazel in 1954. As it moved away from the coast, Matthew began to undergo a period of extratropical transition, with most of the convection becoming displaced to the north, and the hurricane became post-tropical on October 9 while situated to the east of the Outer Banks of North Carolina. The remnants persisted for another day before dissipating on October 10 as it merged with another low over Atlantic Canada.

Nassau

Matthew, which pounded the more lightly populated SE Bahamas starting Wednesday night as a Category 3 hurricane, strengthened by one category as it churned on a northwestern route over the warm waters of the archipelago on Thursday morning. By the time the storm's center hit the nation's most populous island, New Providence, just before midday, winds had escalated to 140 mph. It was the first major hurricane to strike Nassau and New Providence, home to the bulk of The Bahamas' population of 375,000, since 1929. "We got hit very, very hard," said Bishop Walter Hanchell, a Baptist minister in one of Nassau's impoverished communities, as Matthew charged across the city early Thursday afternoon. "People are stuck in their homes, trees are down, roofs are down." Storm surge in Faith Gardens in southern New Providence forced residents from their homes during the hurricane. "At one point there wasn't anything, just a lot of breeze," 15-year-old resident Ebony Thompson said. "Then suddenly, the water went from nothing to over two feet of water."

The gas company-RUBIS Bahamas said that they had to launch an extensive cleanup effort after at least two of the company's service stations in New Providence sustained substantial damages. The roof of the company's garage on East Bay Street collapsed and one in Carmichael Road, New Providence reportedly lost its entire roof. A family in Pinewood Gardens had to be evacuated after the roof of their home caved in. The family was able to make it out to safety on their own. The Department of Meteorology in Nassau had to be evacuated to from the old Nassau Airport Terminal after a window storm shutter came loose and the window was shattered by strong winds, however, no one was injured. Smith's Hotel also had to be evacuated after its roof was blown off, and Riu Palace on Paradise Island sustained extensive exterior damage with part of the facade ripped off, exposing rooms. Evacuation orders were issued just before the storm in Grand Bahamas for residents in West End, outlying settlements along the southern coast and in East Grand Bahama. Princess Margaret Hospital in Nassau said only senior citizens with medical emergencies were to be brought to the Accident and Emergency department during the storm.

The Bahamas National Trust (BNT) Retreat Gardens lost many palms and large trees. Palms that could have been saved were pulled up and propped. Those that couldn't be saved were replaced in preparation for the upcoming Wine and Art Festival in November of 2016. The buildings, except for minor roof damage to the dining room, were unscathed. In Eleuthera, the Leon Levy Preserve was spared the brunt of Matthew and was left relatively intact. A BNT representative, Mr. Henry Nixon reported all was well in Inagua with the park infrastructure and that the flamingos were back and feeding on the lake. The boardwalk and observation pavilion at Bonefish Pond suffered some damage but the BNT was able to salvage it and get it back in operation. At least one piling under the pavilion was replaced. The Primeval Forest had no damage to the buildings, but some of the safety railings were damaged. Thankfully, their majestic, signature mahogany tree survived the onslaught of Matthew. Andros reported no damage to the pavilions at the Blue Holes National Park. Park Warden Henry Haley was just able to reach the Exuma Cays Land and Sea Park on Saturday, October 8th, and reported no major structural damage.

There were no reported deaths on New Providence, The Bahamas' most populated island, after Hurricane Matthew passed over it with 140 mph winds. The storm damaged many roofs on homes throughout the island, including Maxwell Johnson's. He had lived in the home in Nassau for over five years, but says the roof is more than 20 years old and was no match for Hurricane Matthew's 140 mph winds. After the hurricane, Prime Minister Perry Christie took an aerial survey of the other islands that make up the archipelago. Government leaders reported trouble with the water system in Andros. Teams flew from the capital to that island to assess and fix the problem. There were long lines at the few restaurants and gas stations open the day after the hurricane passed.

Following the aftermath of Hurricane Matthew, Sandals Resorts International announced that the re-opening of Sandals Royal Bahamian was postponed until October 25th. The hotel in Nassau was scheduled to open on October 14th, but damage from the hurricane has added extra work and time to that scheduled reopening date. Sandals Emerald Bay in Exuma was also damaged and remained closed until December 15th. After an initial assessment, the decision was made to close the hotel until December 15th, to carry out the extensive repairs. Customers who have booked stays during the closure of the two hotels had 12 months to travel to the same resort at no extra cost. If travelers wanted to change their hotel, they could at no extra cost if they stay at a resort before December 20, 2016. Sandals covered the flight fees or penalties for any booking changes made before October 31, 2016. The Sandals Foundation donated $150,000 to aid medical care, shelter and clean-up efforts in Haiti and The Bahamas.

The Bishop of several West Indies islands hit by Hurricane Matthew has spoken of how the diocese "fared relatively well". But Bishop Laish Boyd said that several church and school buildings were damaged and said that "the struggle is real." In a pastoral letter read in churches in the diocese of The Bahamas and the Turks and Caicos Islands after the hurricane, Bishop Boyd said that "God is mightier than Hurricane Matthew and all of the damage and displacement caused. Whatever the damage and disruption that Matthew has wrought, God can and will do ten times that amount in healing, recovery and restoration." Listing some of the more serious damage to churches and schools, he said that the roof of Bishop Michael School was damaged over its auditorium and classrooms; and a covered walkway collapsed. Several churches on the island of New Providence suffered damage; including the church of the Holy Spirit, which lost its bus; St Agnes' Church, which had damage to several windows and roof damage leading to leaking; and St Gregory's Church, which lost its steeple.

The same fate befell the Church of the Good Shepherd at Pinder's Point on Grand Bahama. Another Grand Bahama church, St Mary Magdalene at the island's West End, was deluged by an eight-inch sea surge, which flooded the church. The hurricane hit the church on the evening of Thursday October 6. By Sunday October 9, parishioners had cleaned and prepared the church in time for the weekly mass. The worst-hit church in the diocese was St Stephen's at Eight Mile Rock, also on the island of Grand Bahama. The rectory lost two areas of its roof and there were many shingles off the church building. Bishop Boyd reports that there was "much water" inside both the church and the rectory. "This is a serious blow that will take time to recover from," Bishop Boyd said in his letter to congregations in the diocese. "As your bishop, I encourage you to read 1 Corinthians 15:58, 'be steadfast, immovable, always excelling in the work of the Lord, because you know that in the Lord your labour is not in vain,' and then I ask you to be steadfast. "God is bigger than Hurricane Matthew. As we survey the devastation that Matthew brought, remember that God can do ten times that in healing, recovery and restoration. Believe me."[131]

---

[131] www.anglicannews.org/hurricane-matthew-effects-on-bahamas-schools-and-church/Nov. *4th 2016*. Retrieved: 20-12-2016.

Grand Bahama

On Thursday, October 6, Category 4 Hurricane Matthew hit the island of Grand Bahama with maximum sustained winds of 140mph and higher gusts. At 5 am Matthew was 198 miles southeast of West End, Grand Bahama. At 11am it was 133 miles southeast of West End, Grand Bahama. Tropical force winds were felt by 12 noon. Due to the predicted storm surge of 10 - 15 feet residents were urged to seek higher ground or move to their closest hurricane shelter. The eye of the storm remained to the west of Grand Bahama Island as it made its way northward to Florida. Everyone was hunkered down as winds increased and night fell. Close to 11 pm Thursday, when the eye was between the Florida coast and the island, pleas for help went out via social media and WhatsApp for rescues in two areas. One was Castaways Resort where a woman and her four children, who were seeking shelter there, had their window blown out and were hiding in the bathroom. They were rescued and were moved to the lobby. The hotel soon after had part of the roof blow off. Grand Bahama was one of the hardest hit islands. All the parks on Grand Bahama all suffered vegetative damage and the mangrove boardwalk at the Lucayan National Park needed to be repaired.

Although forecasters told those in Grand Bahama to expect hurricane conditions to be the worst of the storm between 4 pm and 9 pm, those conditions went further into the night. Other pleas were from Hunters and Lewis Yard as water levels rose. Grand Bahama emergency services took calls but were unable to deploy help to any areas of the island due to the severe weather conditions and the dark. Thankfully everyone who needed rescue were taken care of, and there will no doubt be many stories yet to come out as communications get back in order. Those Grand Bahama residents tuning in via social media waited with bated breath. The first sigh of relief was by way of a statement before midnight by MP for East Grand Bahama, Peter Turnquest who provided a much-needed update: "Despite reports of major damage that will negatively impact the lives of many Bahamians for months and possibly years to come, thank God there has been no loss of life reports. God is indeed good. Let's keep it that way folks as the recovery efforts begin. This is a dangerous phase and many persons are injured as they begin removing debris and making repairs. Please be careful and wait until the all clear is given before venturing far from home. Be careful with power tools and look for other hazards as you move about. Continue to be vigilant family. Finally, thank you to all the hard-working men and women of the Royal Bahamas Police Force and Defense Force who risked their lives rescuing people and saving lives. Also, thanks to Tammi and the good folks at NEMA, the news reporters that kept us informed, the weather forecasters and all people of good will who volunteered their assistance where needed."[132]

On Friday morning, October 7th, Grand Bahama woke up to a new reality. They had already suffered the horrors of the night. The sounds of the battering wind - and for some the destruction of those 140 mph winds, as windows crashed through, and roofs lifted off. Everyone was grateful that they made it through alive. The first scramble for those that were safe, was to assess damage of homes there were in or left; and to check in on loved ones. On the farthest southeastern tip of Grand Bahama, things did appear the worst at Lewis Yard, Hawksbill and Pinder's Point through photos making their way to social media. An all clear for the entire Bahamas was issued around 9:30 am Friday, October 7th by The Bahamas Department of Meteorology and NEMA.

Approximately 95% of the buildings in the Eight Mile Rock and Holmes Rock areas in Grand Bahama received significant damage from Hurricane Matthew on Thursday night and Friday morning, Brenda Colebrooke, the island administrator for West Grand Bahama, said that, portions of the homes were blown out and roofs were completely blown off shortly before 9am on Friday as authorities began making initial assessments of the damage the Category 4 storm caused in Grand Bahama. There were, however, no reports of lives lost. "We had some very, very high winds," Ms. Colebrooke said. "We think we caught 140 mph conditions in the west. We had people still stuck in the west end area, reaching out for help. Right now, we're trying to clear roads to make them passable. Our team has not reported back yet though." A senior police officer on Grand Bahama told The Tribune earlier on Friday morning that more than 72 homes reported experiencing significant roof damage from Matthew although that did not include the western area of the island.

"It was horrendous," Harvey Roberts, the island administrator for East Grand Bahama, said of the hurricane. He said he received calls

---

[132] http://www.thebahamasweekly.com/publish/grand-bahama-Bahamas/Hurricane_Matthew_aftermath_photos_of_Grand_Bahama. Retrieved: 12-12-2016.

from residents to be rescued all throughout Thursday night, but could not do anything about it. "We couldn't go out and risk our lives," he said. Mr. Roberts was in Acklins last year during Hurricane Joaquin, which devastated the island. "I thought I would not experience anything like that in my lifetime again, but this was even worse," he said. "The winds were tremendous." When he spoke to The Tribune shortly after 8.30am, Mr. Roberts was riding alongside the island's top police officer to begin assessments. He was at the Grand Bahama airport, which received minimal damage though "debris was everywhere."[133]

The storm prompted a change in itineraries for several cruise ships bound for The Bahamas, according to Cruise Critic. While most cruise lines got back to normal itineraries a few days after the passage of Hurricane Matthew, the storm affected some ports in The Bahamas, most notably Freeport on the archipelago's Grand Bahama island. Freeport sustained serious damage from Matthew, which hit Grand Bahama as a Category 4 storm. Several weeks after the passage of the hurricane, some schools were still not in session, also, power was still in the process of being restored with some officials saying it could take several additional weeks, due to in part to no power and limited water resources, prompting Betty Bethel, Director of Tourism for Grand Bahama to declare that leisure travel is not being encouraged at that time.

Norwegian Sky canceled its October 11 stop and instead called at Key West. Carnival canceled its October 21 call on Freeport and replaced it with an overnight in Nassau. Other ships that were scheduled to visit Freeport in the next two weeks included after the hurricane were Norwegian Sky, as well as Carnival Elation, Carnival Victory and Bahamas Paradise Cruise Line's Grand Celebration. "Hurricane Matthew's impact on Grand Bahama was significant and it will take some time to complete the necessary repairs to the local infrastructure," Carnival noted in a statement. "Until Freeport is ready for us to resume our calls, we are making some short-term changes to various ship itineraries. "We will return to Freeport as soon as possible not only to resume our regularly scheduled itineraries but also because we know how important our calls will be in helping the people of Grand Bahama to support their tourism recovery efforts." Freeport remained closed to cruise ships until late October to mid-November. On its October

---

[133] http://www.tribune242.com/news/2016/oct/07/grand-bahama-suffers-significant-damage-matthew. Retrieved: 12-12-2016.

10 sailing, Norwegian Sky substituted Freeport with a stop in Key West. The line also has replaced Freeport with Nassau on Norwegian Sky's October 13 departure and Key West on its October 17 departure. Bahamas Paradise Cruise Line's Grand Celebration, which sails short cruises to/ from Palm Beach and Grand Bahama island, has replaced Freeport with the Bahamian island of Bimini.

On March 26, 2017, it was announced by the World Meteorological Organization that the name Matthew was retired due to the extensive damage and loss of life it caused along its track, particularly in The Bahamas, Haiti, Cuba, and the United States, and will never be used to name a North Atlantic hurricane again. It will be replaced with Martin for the 2022 North Atlantic hurricane season.

CHAPTER TWENTY-EIGHT

Hurricanes Arlene, Irma, and Dorian's Impacts on the Islands of The Bahamas in 2017 & 2019

The season was hyperactive, featuring both the highest total accumulated cyclone energy (ACE) and the highest number of major hurricanes since 2005. It had the greatest number of consecutive hurricanes in the satellite era, with Franklin through Ophelia all reaching winds of at least 75 mph. In addition, it was a very destructive season and is the costliest hurricane on record, with a preliminary total of over $317 billion (USD) in damages, nearly all of which was due to three of the major hurricanes of the season — Harvey, Irma, and Maria. This season was also one of only six years on record to feature multiple Category 5 hurricanes. Irma's landfalls on multiple Caribbean islands and Maria's landfall on Dominica made 2017 the second season on record (after 2007) to feature two hurricanes making landfall at Category 5 intensity. In addition, Irma was the strongest hurricane ever recorded to form in the Atlantic Ocean outside of the Gulf of Mexico and the Caribbean Sea. 2017 was the only season on record in which three hurricanes each had an ACE of over 40: Irma, Jose, and Maria.

The season officially began on June 1 and ended on November 30. These dates historically describe the period of a year when most tropical cyclones form in the North Atlantic basin and are adopted by the convention. However, as shown by Tropical Storm Arlene in April, the formation of tropical cyclones is possible at other times of that year. Arlene also marked 2017 the third consecutive year to feature a pre-season storm. In mid-June, Tropical Storm Bret struck the island of Trinidad, which is only rarely struck by tropical cyclones due to its low latitude. A few days later, Tropical

Storm Cindy struck the state of Louisiana. In late August, Hurricane Harvey became the first major hurricane to make landfall in the United States since Wilma in 2005, while also setting the record for the costliest tropical cyclone on record, as well as the most rainfall dropped by a tropical cyclone in the US.

In early September, Hurricane Irma, a Cape Verde-type hurricane, became the first Category 5 hurricane to impact the northern Leeward Islands on record, as well as equaling the strongest hurricane ever to make landfall in the North Atlantic basin—the Great Labour Day Hurricane of 1935. With Hurricane Maria striking Puerto Rico as a top-end Category 4, the season was the first on record to feature three North Atlantic hurricanes making landfall anywhere in the United States or one of its territories at Category 4 intensity or stronger. The season also featured the fastest tropical cyclone ever recorded in the Gulf of Mexico (Nate). This was the first season to have three hurricanes make landfall in the mainland United States (Harvey, Irma, and Nate) since 2008, and the first season to feature four hurricanes making landfall in the overall United States (Harvey, Irma, Maria, and Nate) since 2005. The season also featured Ophelia, the easternmost major hurricane in the North Atlantic basin on record.

The 2017 North Atlantic hurricane season ended on November 30th, but if you've even glanced at the headlines in the summer and fall of 2017, you would already know that 2017 storms have already left an indelible mark on the region. Consider the following stretch, which began in late August and early September: First there was Harvey, which dumped three or more feet of rain over Houston, causing 75 deaths. Then Irma leveled some of the Caribbean's Leeward Islands and slashed up through Florida, killing 14 people in the Florida Keys alone and some 134 overall. If that wasn't bad enough, Maria later hit Dominica, Anguilla, Puerto Rico, and The Bahamas, which even to this day, are all still struggling to recover. In addition to the loss of lives, the damage left in the wake of these hurricanes added up to hundreds of billions of dollars. For many Bahamians, Hurricane Matthew's impact in 2016, Hurricane Joaquin's impact in 2015 and Irenes's Impact in 2017 were some of the worst hurricanes' seasons since Hurricanes Frances, Jeanne in 2004 and Hurricane Wilma of 2005 when they devastated The Bahamas.

At first or even second glance, the 2017's hurricane season seems like it was among the worst. But was it really? If so, why? And how does climate change fit in? September 2017 was truly unique in the annals of the North Atlantic hurricane history. That month, not just one but three unusually long-lived, strong hurricanes—Irma, Maria, and Jose—formed near the central Atlantic's Cape Verde archipelago and moved northwards. Scientists track a statistic called hurricane days, which a hurricane accrues for every day it lives. If three hurricanes coexist on the same day, they rack up three days. In this respect, September was the worst month in recorded history. It had more named storm days, more hurricane days, and more days with a Category 3 or higher hurricane than ever before. Hurricane watchers also track a figure called accumulated cyclone energy (ACE), which is like the total kinetic energy of every storm this season put together. In the North Atlantic, that total wind energy was more than twice the average measured between 1981 and 2010. The 2017 season also broke a lucky streak for the continental USA, which hadn't been hit by a major hurricane (Category 3 or higher) since 2005.

But even after all of that, the remarkable September 2017 won't even take the overall crown as the previous year's storms were some of the worst-ever year, it was a top-ten year, because there have been other years in the past that were more active. While that qualifies the 2017 hurricane season, it does not take away from it. These storms in 2017 did grow big and strong. We won't know how exactly that happened until scientists have performed careful, quantitative analyses. But broadly speaking, two major factors are to blame. First, the Northern Atlantic hosted swaths of warm water, revving up the engine that fuels hurricanes. The 2017 hurricane season was heightened by warmer-than-usual water. In the key month of September, the tropical Atlantic was the third warmest it has ever been, said Phil Klotzbach a research scientist at Colorado State University, where he noted that the only warmer years were the infamous 2005, which produced four separate Category 5 hurricanes, and 2010, which was also a very active and intense hurricane year.

Second, the other major factor behind this unusual season was that, in 2017, the wind patterns that normally quench hurricanes didn't appear, thanks to La Niña-like conditions. This can be a major weakness since the tops and bottoms of hurricanes are exposed to other winds unrelated to the hurricane that blows at different speeds and in different directions. This effect, called 'vertical wind shear', can kick the bottom out of a hurricane's central engine, transforming it into an unsteady Jenga tower. It blocks storms from ever reaching their full potential. As a result, in 2017 vertical wind shear in the tropical Atlantic was weak. Blame it on conditions related to La Niña, the atmospheric phenomenon that's the cooler counterpart to El Niño, which occurs when the Pacific Ocean warms. La Niña, though centered on the Pacific, also helps hurricanes form in greater quantities and intensities in the North Atlantic.[134]

Although 2017 wasn't an official La Niña year, it was at least similar enough to cause a long chain of consequences. The Pacific was cooler than usual, and that shifted rainfall patterns which in turn changed atmospheric currents over the North Atlantic—which in turn lessened the difference between winds close to the surface and winds higher up. That gave hurricanes a more stable atmosphere in which to form, allowing them to power up and maintain that power over a longer period. On top of this, the La Niña conditions also cooled the upper atmosphere above the North Atlantic, further boosting the temperature gap between the warm ocean and the cold atmosphere. These factors primed the pump for an active season. But there's another potential reason why 2017 hurricane season was so intense, and that's climate change but that's a debate for another time.

The low risk to hurricanes forming in the North Atlantic is due to an increase in westerly winds at most levels of the atmosphere across North America. These winds tend to steer any potential tropical systems away from the Atlantic Seaboard and the central and western Gulf of Mexico's coast. Meanwhile, compensating stiff easterly winds farther south in the tropics work toward disrupting the development of storms in the Caribbean Sea and the south-central Atlantic. August and September brought great devastation due to hurricanes Harvey, Irma, and Maria striking heavily populated areas. However, these storms struck when conditions were conducive for supporting tropical cyclones as these hurricane seasons were at or approaching their climatological peak.

Ocean temperatures were like bath water and winds aloft were light during late August and September. While hurricanes have formed and even struck The Bahamas during November, the odds of such an occurrence is very low on average. Even though the North Atlantic hurricane season officially lasts until the end of November, the weather pattern, statistics and the daily hurricane forecast strongly suggest that the possibility of significant hurricane hitting The Bahamas mainland during this time is extremely small for the rest of the season, because the peak of the hurricane

[134] http://www.pbs.org/wgbh/nova/next/earth/2017-hurricane-season-explainer/ Why Was This Year's Hurricane Season So Intense? Retrieved: 02-11-2017.

season is on September 10 and shortly after that, the chance of a hurricane forming is minimal at best.

Tropical Storm Arlene in 2017: –The 2017 North Atlantic hurricane season was an above average one in the annual formation of tropical cyclones in the Northern Hemisphere. The season officially began on June 1, 2017 and ended on November 30, 2017. These dates historically describe the time-period each year when most tropical cyclones form in the North Atlantic basin and are adopted by the World Meteorological Organization international agreement. However, as shown by the exceptionally rare Tropical Storm Arlene, which was only the second named storm on record to form in April, the formation of tropical cyclones is possible at any time of the year. In fact, there has been a tropical cyclone in every month of the year in the North Atlantic. Tropical Storm Arlene is just the second storm on record to form in April, and the only other tropical storm to form during the month was Ana in 2003. Tropical storms in April are extremely rare and in fact, Arlene is only the second one observed in this month, since the satellite era began in the early 1960s. Before that time, such storms were practically impossible to detect. Arlene is also the farthest north a tropical storm has formed in the Atlantic so early in the season.

Tropical Storm Arlene gained some strength that Thursday, April 21st. At 5 am EDT, Arlene's maximum sustained winds were at 50 mph, with higher gusts. Tropical-storm-force winds extended outward up to 230 miles from the center, according to the National Hurricane Center. The storm moved west rapidly, at 31 mph, and this general motion continued until that late Friday. During which time, Arlene was located about 1,135 miles west-northwest of the Azores. While Arlene didn't pose a threat to The Bahamas, the storm generated quite a few large northerly to northeasterly ocean swells along the shores of The Bahamas during its short lifespan, creating high surf conditions and dangerous rip currents along the northern and eastern shores of The Bahamas.

Hurricane Irma of 2017–Hurricane Irma was an extremely powerful Cape Verde hurricane that caused widespread destruction across its path in September 2017. Irma was the first Category 5 hurricane to strike the Leeward Islands on record, followed by Maria two weeks later. The ninth named storm, fourth hurricane, second major hurricane, and first Category 5 hurricane of the 2017 season, Irma caused widespread and catastrophic damage throughout its long lifetime, particularly in the northeastern Caribbean and the Florida Keys. It was also the most intense hurricane to strike the continental United States since Katrina in 2005, the first major hurricane to make landfall in the state of Florida since Wilma in the same year, and the first Category 4 hurricane to strike the state since Charley in 2004. The word 'Irmageddon' was coined soon after the hurricane to describe the damage caused by the hurricane. Hurricane Irma was the top Google searched term in the US and globally in 2017.

Hurricane Irma destroyed this school room on the island of Ragged Island (Courtesy of NEMA).

Irma developed from a tropical wave near the Cape Verde Islands on August 30. Favorable conditions allowed Irma to rapidly intensify into a Category 3 hurricane on the Saffir–Simpson Hurricane Wind Scale by late on August 31. However, the storm's intensity fluctuated between Categories 2 and 3 for the next several days, due to a series of eyewall replacement cycles. On September 4, Irma resumed intensifying, becoming a Category 5 hurricane by early on the next day. Early on September 6, Irma peaked with 1-minute sustained winds of 180 mph and a minimum pressure of 914 hPa (27.0 inHg). Irma was the second-most intense tropical cyclone worldwide in 2017 in terms of barometric pressure, and the strongest worldwide in 2017 in terms of wind speed.

The most intense landfalling hurricanes in the Contiguous United States

(Intensity is measured solely by central pressure)

Rank:	Hurricane:	Season:	Landfall Pressure:
1	Great Labour Day	1935	892 millibars (hPa)
2	Camille	1969	900 millibars (hPa)
3	Katrina	2005	920 millibars (hPa)
4	Andrew	1992	922 millibars (hPa)
5	Great Indianola	1886	925 millibars (hPa)
6	Great Florida Keys	1919	927 millibars (hPa)
7	Great Okeechobee	1928	929 millibars (hPa)
7	**Irma**	**2017**	**929 millibars (hPa)**
9	Great Miami	1926	930 millibars (hPa)
9	Donna	1960	930 millibars (hPa)

The most intense landfalling hurricanes in the Contiguous United States (Courtesy of the National Hurricane Center-HURDAT-Hurricane Research Division/Wikipedia).

Another eyewall replacement cycle caused Irma to weaken back to a Category 4 hurricane, but the storm re-attained Category 5 status before making landfall in Cuba. Although Irma briefly weakened to a Category 2 storm while making landfall on Cuba, the system re-intensified to Category 4 status as it crossed the warm waters of the Straits of Florida, before making landfall on Cudjoe Key on September 10. Irma then weakened to Category 3 status, prior to another landfall in Florida on Marco Island later that day. The system degraded into a remnant low over Alabama and ultimately dissipated on September 13 over Missouri.

Prior to the storm's arrival over Ragged Island most residents and government officials were evacuated for their own safety and to this day many have not returned to that island. In the Bahamas, the eye of the storm passed over Duncan Town, the major settlement of the Ragged Islands chain, on September 8. It also passed "almost directly over" Inagua and South Acklins, according to The Bahamas Department of Meteorology. Damages were largely concentrated to the islands in the SE Bahamas starting the morning of September 8. On Mayaguana and Great Inagua, downed power lines knocked out communications. On Great Inagua, 70% of homes sustained roof damage, and the island's school lost its roof entirely. The Morton Salt Company's signature sea salt production facility, one of the major employers in the country and the main employer on the island of Iguana, experienced millions of dollars in damages. The Acklins settlement of Salina Point was cut off from the rest of the island by flooding, while Crooked Island had widespread roof damage. In the NW Bahamas, the worst property damage came on September 10 as the outer bands of the system produced tornadic activity on Grand Bahama and Bimini. Damage and losses across The Bahamas amounted to $135 million. While Irma was making landfall in Florida and The Bahamas, the ocean was drawn away from some western shorelines of the Bahamas and South Florida leaving the beaches exposed on dry land due to strong easterly winds and low barometric pressure in a process called negative storm surge.

By the afternoon of September 9, Bahamas Power and Light Company (BPL) had dispatched crews across the archipelago to repair infrastructure damage. The southernmost islands, which were most severely affected by Irma's eye, remained largely inaccessible for days. Assessments showed that 15% of the national telecommunications network had been affected, with at least one tower destroyed. The worst devastation occurred on Ragged Island, over which Irma's eye had directly passed. After days of the National Emergency Management Agency (NEMA) not being able to physically reach the island, officials were finally able to inspect it; they promptly declared it uninhabitable. Prime Minister Hubert Minnis said that it was the worst disaster area he or his officials had ever seen, and that all remaining residents would need to leave, potentially permanently. Business leaders and other officials called for a new long-term development model to shift the population away from such sparsely-settled islands. On Grand Bahama and Bimini, where tornadoes associated with Irma touched down on September 10, more than 100 people were left displaced. Infrastructure damage included docks, parks, and the power system.

Irma set multiple records for intensity, especially at easterly longitudes, time spent at such intensity, and its intensity at landfall. When Irma reached Category 5 intensity with winds of 175 mph at 11:45 UTC on September 5 at 57.7°W, it became the easternmost North Atlantic hurricane of this strength on record, surpassing Hurricane David of 1979. By 00:15 UTC on September 6, Irma reached peak intensity with 180 mph winds and a minimum central pressure of 914 mbar (914 hPa; 27.0 inHg). This ties it with Hurricane Mitch of 1998 and Hurricane Rita of 2005 as the sixth-strongest North Atlantic hurricane by wind speed. Only five other North Atlantic hurricanes have been recorded with wind speeds higher than Irma: Hurricane Allen of 1980, which had maximum sustained winds of 190 mph, and the Great Labour Day Hurricane of 1935, Hurricane Gilbert of 1988, Hurricane Wilma of 2005, and Hurricane Dorian of 2019, all of which had peak winds of 185 mph. At the time, Irma was also the strongest hurricane ever recorded in the Atlantic Ocean outside the Caribbean Sea and Gulf of Mexico; later surpassed by Hurricane Dorian, and was the strongest North Atlantic hurricane since Wilma in terms of maximum sustained winds, and the most intense in terms of pressure since Dean in 2007.

Something very unusual happened with Hurricane Irma in 2017, and that is, it drained away the water and exposed the beaches on Long Island in The Bahamas (also

two other Bahamian islands of Acklins and Exuma reported similar events) during Hurricane Irma's passage. The water receded and disappeared for several hours in a phenomenon known as 'negative surge', the storm absorbed the seawater. The last time this happened in The Bahamas was Hurricane #5 of 1936, which had a similar track as Irma as it passed through The Bahamas.

Furthermore, Irma achieved one of the longest durations of Category 5 strength winds, and the third-highest accumulated cyclone energy (ACE) index for a tropical cyclone in the North Atlantic basin, with a value of 64.9 units. Only the 1899 San Ciriaco hurricane and Hurricane Ivan in 2004 achieved higher values. ACE is a measure used by the National Oceanic Atmospheric Administration (NOAA) to express the activity of individual tropical cyclones and entire tropical cyclone seasons, primarily North Atlantic hurricane seasons. It uses an estimated value of energy used by a tropical system over its lifetime and it is calculated every six-hour period. The ACE of a season is derived by finding the value of the ACEs for each storm and t takes into account the number, strength, and duration of all the tropical storms in the season.

On September 6, Irma made landfall on the islands of Barbuda, Saint Martin, and Virgin Gorda at peak strength. This ties Irma with cyclones Monica of 2006 and Winston of 2016, and typhoons Zeb of 1998, Megi of 2010, and Yutu of 2018 as the sixth-strongest tropical cyclone to make landfall globally – in terms of sustained winds – trailing only Typhoon Haiyan of 2013 and Typhoon Meranti of 2016, which bore winds of 190 mph at landfall, and the Great Labour Day Hurricane of 1935, Typhoon Joan of 1959, and Hurricane Dorian of 2019, which bore winds of 185 mph at landfall. Irma is second to the Great Labour Day Hurricane of 1935 and Hurricane Dorian of 2019 as the strongest landfalling cyclone on record in the North Atlantic basin and is the first hurricane to make landfall anywhere in the North Atlantic at Category 5 status since Felix in 2007. Irma is the first recorded Category 5 hurricane to affect the northern Leeward Islands and was one of the worst storms to hit the region on record, along with Hurricane Donna in 1960 and Hurricane Luis in 1995. In addition, Irma is only the second hurricane on record to make landfall in Cuba at Category 5 intensity, with the other being a hurricane in 1924. Furthermore, when Irma made landfall on the islands of Barbuda, Saint Martin, Virgin Gorda, and Cuba as a Category 5 hurricane, it became one of only two recorded North Atlantic storms to make landfall in multiple nations at this strength; the other was Hurricane Andrew in 1992, which struck both Eleuthera and the United States as a Category 5 hurricane.

The Prime Minister of The Bahamas-Dr. Hon. Hubert Minnis inspects a damaged school in Ragged Island (Courtesy of NEMA).

On April 11, 2018, at the 40th session of the Region IV hurricane committee, the World Meteorological Organization retired the name Irma from its rotating naming lists, due to the extensive amount of damage and loss of life it caused in the northeastern Caribbean, The Bahamas, and the United States, particularly in Florida, and it will never again be used for another North Atlantic hurricane. It will be replaced with Idalia for the 2023 North Atlantic hurricane season.

Hurricane Dorian of 2019–Every once in a long while a country is hit by a major storm that impacts that nation in such a unique and significant way that it will be remembered for generations to come for the great devastation it created in its' wake-Hurricane Dorian was definitely that storm. Category 5 Hurricane Dorian was the most powerful tropical cyclone on record to strike The Bahamas and is regarded as the worst natural disaster in the country's modern history. Furthermore, it is regarded as the second strongest hurricane in terms of sustained winds to affect the

North Atlantic region. It attained cataclysm status when it barreled into two islands of the NW Bahamas-Abaco and Grand Bahama.

These oil storage tanks at the Equinor South Riding Point in East End, Grand Bahama were compromised and leaked 5 million gallons of oil into the environment during Hurricane Dorian (Courtesy of Cleveland Duncombe).

Category 5 hurricanes are extremely rare in the North Atlantic with one occurring on average only once every three years. Since 1851 when reliable hurricane records have been kept, only 36 of these storms have occurred. The Bahamas is one of the most popular areas to be struck by Category 5 hurricanes in the North Atlantic. Since 1851, The Bahamas was struck by 4 Category 5 hurricanes at that intensity and they were the Great Abaco Hurricane of 1932, the Cuba-Brownsville Hurricane of 1933, Hurricane Andrew of 1992 and Dorian of 2019. This ties the record with the United States as the most active countries struck by Category 5 hurricanes in the North Atlantic region. When looking at Category 5 hurricanes or any other category hurricanes for that matter, we tend to look at atmospheric pressure, wind speed, duration of the storm, cost of damages, and fatalities and it is fair to say that Hurricane Dorian ranks very high in all of those categories.

Residents of 'The Mud' in Marsh Harbour, Abaco gather amid the rubbles to salvage what they could after Hurricane Dorian.

Dorian was the fourth named storm, second hurricane, and the first major hurricane of the 2019 North Atlantic hurricane season. Dorian struck the Abaco Islands on September 1 with maximum sustained winds of 185 mph and gusting to 210 mph, tying the record with the Great Labour Day Hurricane of 1935 for the highest sustained winds of a North Atlantic hurricane ever recorded at landfall. Dorian went on to strike Grand Bahama at a similar intensity, stalling just north of the island with unrelenting winds for at least 24 hours. The last hurricane on record to do this in The Bahamas other than Dorian was the Great Andros Island Hurricane in 1929 which remained nearly stationary (2-3 mph) over Nassau and Andros in 1929 for three consecutive days. The resultant damage from Dorian to these two islands was catastrophic; most structures were flattened or swept to sea, and at least 70,000 people were left homeless. After its ravaged The Bahamas, Dorian proceeded along the coasts of the Southeastern United States and Atlantic Canada, leaving behind considerable damage and economic losses in those regions.

Team Rubicon disaster response and storm cleanup crew from Canada working on the inside of St. John The Baptist Anglican/Episcopal Church in Marsh Harbour, Abaco. During Hurricane Dorian this church was engulfed in over 5 feet of water.

Dorian developed from a tropical wave on August 24 over the Central Atlantic. The storm moved through the Lesser Antilles and became a hurricane north of the Greater Antilles on August 28. Dorian proceeded to undergo rapid intensification over the following days to reach its peak as a Category 5 hurricane with one-minute sustained winds of 185 mph and a minimum central pressure of 910 millibars (26.87 inHg) by September 1. It made landfall in The Bahamas in Elbow Cay, just east of Abaco Island, and again on Grand Bahama several hours later, where it remained nearly stationary for the next day or so. After weakening considerably, Dorian began moving northwestward on September 3, parallel to the east coast of Florida. Dwindling in strength, the hurricane turned to the northeast the next day and made landfall on Cape Hatteras at Category 1 intensity on September 6. It transitioned into an extratropical cyclone before striking first Nova Scotia and then Newfoundland with hurricane-force winds on September 8. It finally dissipated near Greenland on September 10.

The inside view of the destroyed terminal at Freeport International Airport in Grand Bahama (Courtesy of Cleveland Duncombe).

The effects of Hurricane Dorian in The Bahamas were widespread and devastating for the two major impact areas of Grand Bahama and Abaco in the NW Bahamas. On September 1, 2019, Abaco experienced hurricane conditions and a few hours later, destructive conditions arrived, with Hurricane Dorian making landfall as a Category 5 hurricane at 12:40 PM EST, becoming the strongest hurricane in modern records to strike the NW Bahamas. Around 12:30 PM, Category 5 winds arrived at The Bahamas with the eyewall passing over Abaco. Gusts of over 200 mph also occurred. Devastating storm surge of up to 23 feet swept away many buildings and submerged a large part of the affected areas. Both Abaco and Grand Bahama received "catastrophic damage", and over half of the homes in Abaco had been damaged. Both Freeport and Abaco airports (Treasure

Cay and Marsh Harbour- Leonard M. Thompson International Airport) were underwater and the building structures were almost destroyed. There was significant flooding on streets and beaches, damage to trees and with some home's roofs ripped off entirely.

In Marsh Harbour, the damages inflicted by Dorian were massive and widespread. Marsh Harbour was unrecognizable with electrical wires and the majority of the downed poles lay across many streets for over a month and BPL's powerstation was badly damaged in this storm. The bakeries, gas stations, and other businesses that were once bustling with people and activity are now missing walls, windows, doors, and roofs. Many of these buildings are no longer standing. The Dove Plaza building was destroyed. The Aldergate Methodist Church, St. John The Baptist Anglican Church, the Great Abaco Inn, Auskell Medical Center were all destroyed in Marsh Harbour. The St. Andrew's Methodist Church in Dundas Town was also destroyed. In Treasure Cay, 95% to 98% of the homes and businesses were destroyed or rendered unlivable and not fit for occupancy. Many of these areas had severe looting challenges because most residents left the island, but eventually, the officers from the Royal Bahamas Police Force were able to bring that problem under control.

Most of the schools on the island were either destroyed or significantly damaged, causing a delay in the school term reopening. In most cases, the students had to be accommodated by transferring them to the New Providence schools to finish the school term there. Most of the surrounding Abaco cays like, Green Turtle Cay and Man-O-War Cay were almost completely wiped out with most of the homes and businesses destroyed. Many Abaco residents shortly after the storm had to move to the United States or other islands, with most of them coming to the capital city of Nassau in search of living accommodations and employment. Many of them had to stay in several of the temporary shelters provided by the government for weeks after the storm or stay with family members. Most of the utility poles were blown down during Dorian preventing any kind of communications, and the electricity, cable, and running water were virtually non-existent for months after the storm. As a result, private portable generators had to be used for the generation of electricity.

Great Devastation in The Mud Haitian community after Dorian flattened every building structure with its powerful 185 mph winds.

In Freeport, the runway of Freeport International Airport was flooded after the storm. This prevented relief workers and hurricane relief supplies from being delivered to the residents in desperate need of assistance on a timely basis. But the buildings that surrounded the landing strip had been ripped open. The control tower remained upright, but the attached office building was stripped to its skeleton. After the storm, the airstrip was being operated by U.S. Navy personnel who were orchestrating the traffic from the tarmac via radios for a few days after the hurricane. In East End, most of the homes were either destroyed or entirely flooded by the storm surge. Many of these residents lost everything they had, including their cars and homes, and had to start all over again trying to get their lives back to some degree of normalcy. The Rand Memorial Hospital was severely damaged, and in some cases, the charity group Samaritan's Purse, field hospital headed by Franklin Graham, had to fill this void temporarily. The Equinor South Riding Point oil storage facility on East End, Grand Bahama was compromised during the storm resulting in the spillage of over 5 million gallons of oil into the surrounding environment. The University of The Bahamas campus in Grand Bahama suffered severe flood damage, which washed out the ground floor of both buildings. The University President Dr. Rodney Smith indicated that the institution doesn't plan to reopen UB's Northern campus at its current location but at a site that is less prone to flooding.

Three weeks after Hurricane Dorian, the pastors of various church dominations around The Bahamas gathered at Bahamas Faith Ministries for a prayer and praise meeting for the grieving families, emotional healing and for God's Divine protection.

Sunken and overturned boats and hurricane damaged homes in this harbour located in Treasure Cay, Abaco.

Up to time of publication, the official death toll in The Bahamas was 65 persons and hundreds still declared missing. On Thursday, September 12, over 1,300 people were declared missing or unaccounted for in The Bahamas, a number which plummeted from 2,500 over the previous two weeks. By September 20, the death toll in The Bahamas rose to 51 direct and one indirect. On September 26, the number of people missing in The Bahamas dropped to 600, while the official death toll rose to 56, by October 4, it went to 61 persons declared dead, and by October 17, it climbed to 65 persons. The United Nations projected that as of Saturday, September 7, at least 70,000 people were left homeless on Grand Bahama and the Abaco Islands.

The destroyed homes in 'The Mud' district, an area in Marsh Harbour, Abaco where migrant workers reside in sub-standard houses.

The International Federation of Red Cross and Red Crescent Societies (IFRC) reported that as many as 13,000 homes were damaged or destroyed on Abaco Island. Extensive flooding is also believed to have caused water wells to be contaminated with seawater, creating an urgent need for clean water. Property damage alone in the country were estimated at $7 billion, which is expected to make it by far the costliest storm in Bahamian history, eclipsing the previous record holder Hurricane Matthew in 2016 which had an estimated value of over $600 million.

An aerial view of the flood damaged vehicles caused by Hurricane Dorian in Freeport, Grand Bahama.

With sustained winds of 185 mph, Dorian is the strongest hurricane on record to strike The Bahamas since records began in 1851. Dorian is tied with the Great Labour Day Hurricane of 1935 for the highest sustained winds at landfall in a North Atlantic hurricane; by the same metric, it is also the strongest North Atlantic hurricane since Hurricane Wilma in 2005. In terms of barometric pressure, it was the fifth hurricane with the lowest pressure upon landfall. Dorian is one of only two Category 5 hurricanes to make landfall on the Abaco Islands, the other having occurred in 1932 called the Great Abaco Hurricane of 1932 and Dorian is the only such storm on record to have impacted Grand Bahama. Furthermore, Dorian attained the highest sustained winds in a North Atlantic hurricane recorded at latitude (26.6°N), and was the strongest hurricane detected outside the main development region (MDR), surpassing Hurricane Irma to become the most intense tropical cyclone ever recorded in the open Atlantic Ocean. Dorian also tracked the least distance in a 24-hour period recorded for a North Atlantic major hurricane since Hurricane Betsy in 1965. The storm also impacted a single land area as a Category 5 hurricane for the longest duration recorded in the North Atlantic basin, with portions of Dorian's eyewall striking Great Abaco Island and Grand Bahama with Category 5 winds for about 22 hours.

CHAPTER TWENTY-NINE

Personal Recollections of Past Bahamian Hurricanes

While writing my first book, 'The Great Bahamas Hurricane of 1929', I was interviewing an elderly lady in the presence of her daughter. She gave me a riveting and detailed account of her experience with this hurricane as if this storm had only recently occurred, and her recollection was just remarkable. She was one of the persons who cried as she related the experience, she had with the Great Bahamas Hurricane of 1929.

As I was finished with the interview, her daughter pulled me inside the kitchen, out of earshot of her mom. She then said that she didn't know what I did to her mother because if she asked her mother what she ate that morning or what she wore the previous day she wouldn't be able to say. However, she was able to recall her experiences with this storm in such great details that it amazed and baffled even her. I merely smiled and told her that was one of the reasons I needed to write that book, because of the enormous impact that this storm and many other storms had on the residents of The Bahamas at the time. Well, major hurricanes have such significant impacts on people's lives that most persons who experienced these storms will have that experience etched in their memories for the rest of their lives. My goal is to retrieve that information from a select few persons and present it to you, the reader. My journey was a very noble one and here are my results from this journey.

Personal Recollections of The Great Bahamas Hurricane of 1866's Impact on Various Islands of The Bahamas

This account describes the great impact this hurricane had on the city of Nassau and on the island of Eleuthera: -

The 1866 Hurricane in The Bahamas-
Nassau Half Destroyed

A terrible hurricane commenced in The Bahamas on September 30 and lasted for two days. Almost half of the town of Nassau was destroyed by the storm. Houses were blown down, roofs carried away, and trees uprooted. Trinity Methodist Church was demolished, the Government House lost part of its roof, and the roof of the Marine Hospital was entirely blown off. Vessels were driven ashore and smashed to pieces, and wharves were demolished. The neighbouring islands suffered in the same degree, and many vessels were lost or damaged. The hurricane was the severest one which was experienced since 1813. The Nassau Guardian of the October 3 reported that the hurricane commenced on Sunday night, September 30 at 8 pm, blowing all night from the north. On Monday morning, the barometer readings starting to drop suddenly, a good indicator that the hurricane was well on its way to moving over The Bahamas, and later the hurricane force winds became even stronger.

A part of the town of Nassau was destroyed. Trinity Methodist Church was destroyed. The Government House suffered considerably and lost a great part of the roofing. The entire roofing of the Military Hospital was blown away. From the Arsenal, West Bay Street, to the Eastward, no one could pass, because of the obstruction in the way caused by the ruins of houses, boats, fragments of vessels and of the wharves. The Arsenal Wharf was destroyed. Many of the houses and stores were blown away by the hurricane, including the beef and fish markets. The personal files of the property were destroyed.

The gunboat *Nimble* was blown up on the bank in front of the Arsenal, notwithstanding the great efforts of her commander and officers. She does not appear to have suffered any major damage, so it is expected that she will be back on the waters doing her normal duties in a short time period.

The Canal Company's steamer *Relief* was blown hard and fast near the tower of the lighthouse, and the steamer *General Clinch* was smashed to pieces near the public abutment. The only vessel that rode out the hurricane was the *Minnie Gordon*, even though her spars and rigging were blown down. Most of the older person stated that this was one of the worse hurricanes to impact The Bahamas since a similar one in 1813. The most doleful accounts were being received daily of the effects of the hurricane in the adjacent islands. The St. John's Church, and thirty-six houses on Harbour Island, were destroyed, and the establishments in the settlements of Spanish Wells, Current, Governor's Harbour, and Eleuthera were swept away; Green Turtle Cay, Hope Town, and North Harbour were in a state of ruins after the hurricane. A correspondent at Great Harbour Cay reported that the hurricane ruined all the estates, destroyed the cisterns of water, public schools, and that the poorer classes were exposed to starvation. The schooners *Victory* and *President*, and the bark *Ticker* of New York, were lost here.

Rev. John Davey's account of the Great Bahamas Hurricane of 1866

This account was taken from 'The History of Religion in The Bahamas' series by Author and Historian Jim Lawlor in The Nassau Tribune dated Thursday, December 10th & 17th, 2009: -

The Baptist Magazine of 1866 contains a letter from Rev John Davey as follows: -

The arrival of the Rev John Davey enables us to furnish our readers with more of the effects of the Great Bahamas Hurricane of 1866 on the Mission property in Nassau. Through the good providence of God, Mr. Davey and his family reached their destination in safety, but not without experiencing very severe weather along the way. Under the date of November 17, he writes: -

"Our voyage across the Atlantic was a long and dangerous one, and we were detained in New York for a month, which was a great disappointment both to ourselves and the people.

The *Corsica* reached the bar of Nassau early on the morning of November 7 but found that the passengers would not be landing in boats the usual way because of the heavy seas that were running. She gave signals respecting passengers and freight and then proceeded in the direction of Cochrane's anchorage, in the hope that schooners would soon be dispatched to us, however, no schooner came alongside us until the following morning.

Though the people were looking and waiting for us all day, and there was great uncertainty as to the time the schooner would arrive the following day, yet when we got to the landing site about noon, we found the shore lined with the members of the church, waiting to welcome us.

Their congratulations were very hearty, and two or three days after we arrived, we were fully employed in receiving visitors. But, though it was pleasant to see the people, it was distressing to hear their accounts of the desolating hurricane with which the colony had been visited.

I asked them in what light it was generally regarded, and some said as a judgment from God. One aged African woman said to me, "Massa, God has punished we this year, nothing left to pick a copper," referring to the destruction of the crops."

The Mission property has sustained considerable damage because of the hurricane. The portico of our large chapel, which was put up last year, was blown down, stripping away the cornice and the gutter, and thus laying the chapel open to the rams. The chapel gates were blown down and broken, and a great quantity of glass destroyed in the chapel. The roofs of the Mission-House and outbuildings were so damaged that they must be shingled immediately.

But the saddest part of the story remains to be told. Bethel, the original Baptist Chapel in The Bahamas, in which Mr. Burton laid the foundation of this Mission after he was driven from Morant Bay, Jamaica (called 'Morant Bay Rebellion') was level with the ground. This is a great grief to the poor people, especially the aged, who have worshipped in it so many years. It is very desirable that it should be rebuilt as speedily as possible, as the bulk of the members live about that chapel. But they cannot possibly rebuild themselves in their present distressed circumstances, and therefore, I hope, that when the news of this great calamity reaches England, the friends of the Mission will kindly help us to repair our damaged chapel and rebuild those that have been blown down. The Episcopalians and Wesleyans have suffered as badly as us, and therefore, we cannot look to them for help, who need all the means they have got to rebuild their own places of worship.

The hurricane was very severe upon other islands, but I believe that the two principal chapels of our society, beyond New Providence, sustained very little damage. There was not much damage done to the properties in

Inagua, and even though there were many private properties destroyed at Turk's Island, fortunately, the places of worship sustained very little damage. Many of the Out-Island chapels were destroyed, but the buildings themselves were not very costly buildings to rebuild, I think they may soon be rebuilt.

From the Nassau Guardian we take the following description of the tempest: -

"A fresh breeze blew on Sunday evening last, and those who walked on the Esplanade or elsewhere, congratulated themselves on the favorable change in the weather; but to those used to observe the weather, appearances decidedly bespoke a 'blow.' The winds rapidly increased during the night, and at about 7 o'clock on Monday morning, it had become a regular gale, accompanied with rain. The bar of the harbour appeared as a ridge of foam, and the harbour itself, formed by the long, low rocky land "Hog Island" though it kept off the main sea, yet left all exposed to the violence of the wind, which kept steadily increasing. The rough seas were breaking in rapid succession upon the line of wharves along Bay Street, the abutment of the Barrack-Square, the Esplanade, and rocky shore to the west, sending dense wreaths of spray over everything. The rumor soon reported that much damage occurred among the shipping. Small boats, lumber, various gear, and fragments began to bestrew the Ordnance Wharf, etc.…and on Bay Street, the scene was excitingly sad, most of the spacious stores and warehouses (on the north side next to the harbour), principally with roofs of corrugated iron or other metals, were unroofed. Immense sheets of metal were whirled along in the wind and torn up like sheets of paper, and the whole thoroughfare was covered with portions of shipping and houses.

The passage was not only difficult in the extreme, but the few people who had seen it were not prepared for a storm of this magnitude. They were about being frequently brought to a stand-still by the corner of a street and obliged to cling to lampposts or pillars of the piazzas until a partial lull in the wind, which enabled them to make a run forward to go on afresh. The public market and wharf exhibited a scene of wild excitement, many vessels jammed together against the abutment-fishermen and boatmen shouting to the crews of the vessels, who, like those on shore were equally unable to save their property-the larger vessels rolling against the smaller, and smashing them to fragments, and in their turn were broken up against the stone wall of the wharf. The other streets began to show the effects of the storm-parts of the verandahs, window shutters, and branches of trees, and occasionally a whole tree was blown down.

About 1:30 pm or 2 pm, it was impossible to remain abroad; it was dangerous to take shelter under walls or houses, and totally impossible to remain standing when exposed to the presence of the wind, which shook every building. The sensation within doors was like the vibrations of a railway car attached to an express train. The noise of the wind, combining with the sound of the waves, kept up a loud bellowing roar, varied with thunder-like gusts, and were succeeded by a crashing sound which indicated destruction of some kind or other.

Green seas were now breaking upon the wharves of the town and government property, sending their spray over the tops of the houses, and together with the heavy falling of rain and hail. This made the air as obscure as the thickest fog, which, as it is now and again cleared partially for a few moments, shows some further damage, houses being dismantled in all directions, and the fragments, intermingled with branches of trees, swept along at an alarming pace. The trees that remained standing were being rapidly stripped of their leaves. Every house was in a state of commotion, the wind and rain penetrated everywhere, doing every kind of damage, and causing indescribable inconvenience. A lull in the storm occurred about 7:30 pm or 8 pm, which fortunately enabled those who had some shelter remaining, to offer a share of it to their less fortunate neighbours. About 9 o'clock it sprung up again in a south-easterly direction, but with far less violence, and altogether subsided by daybreak. By the next morning, the whole scene was indeed a desolation, the most familiar objects were scarce to be recognized; some gone entirely. Distressing accounts of the effects of the hurricane on the Out Islands are being received.

We learned with sorrow that St. John's Church and thirty-eight houses at Harbour Island were destroyed and that the settlements of Spanish Wells, the Current, Governor's Harbour, and other parts of Eleuthera were nearly swept away. At Abaco, the wrath of the hurricane was awful. Our correspondent at Great Harbour, in a letter dated the 4th instant says, "I am sorry to inform you that we had a severe hurricane on October 1. It ruined all the plantations, making the water in the tanks unfit for human consumption due to saltwater intrusion into the soil and the wells. It blew down all the kitchens, several dwelling-houses, the public schoolhouse, the assistant keeper's dwelling, belonging to the Elbow Cay Lighthouse, and causing a significant more damage than I can mention. The poorer classes were relying on their plantations for food, however all them were destroyed, and I expect they will starve."

As we look back in history after the Great Bahamas Hurricane of 1866, once again as so many times in the past, the faithful residents rebuilt their lives, homes, and community with the assistance of many other generous people. And nature reached out her healing hands as the flora and fauna slowly regenerated to bring back the enchantment and beauty of The Bahamas.

United States Consul Mr. Kirkpatrick's account of the Great Bahamas Hurricane of 1866

On Monday, November 12, the United States Consul Mr. Kirkpatrick stationed at Nassau reported on some of the damages sustained in The Bahamas by the Great Bahamas Hurricane of 1866, concentrating mainly on American interests in shipping to the State Department in Washington. Below is his detailed account of this storm: -

The Late Hurricane of 1866

Its Terrible Effects of The Bahamas Islands-Report from the United States Consul at Nassau

Washington, Monday, November 12, 1866

United States Consul Kirkpatrick, at Nassau, in a letter dated October 10, to the State Department, says: "I have the honour to inform you since my dispatch No. 170 was forwarded, via Havana, that I am able to give you more correctly the losses to shipping in this vicinity and to those who have arrived here. There are a great many of whom nothing will be known. The British schooner *Elite,* from Teneriffe and bound for Nassau, was totally wrecked at Andros Island; all hands-on board were saved. The British bark, *Sickle, Friend*, from New York en-route to Havana, Cuba with a shipment of general cargo, was totally wrecked at Eleuthera on September 30 but fortunately, all hands-on board were saved.

The British brig *Active*, Willingate, the ship's Master, from St. John and bound for Matanzas, with a shipment of lumber, arrived at Nassau in distress, with the loss of topmasts and part of deck load lost. The United States steamship *Tahoma*, Mr. Gibson, the ship's Commander, from Pensacola, was in distress during the hurricane with a shipment of coal but eventually proceeded on her voyage after being impacted by the hurricane. The American brig *John Hastings*, of New-York, was last seen on the October 5, abandoned. The foremast and the mainmast-head were all gone, the sails shredded in ribbons and the boat on the deck was found turned upside down. The American schooner *Sath Rich* originated out of New York, and Mr. Bantroff was the ship's Master. While the ship was located at Nassau, it broke away from her anchorage at East Harbour and was blown out to sea on September 30. It eventually arrived in Nassau on the October 8, with the loss of ship's anchors, chains and the mainmast. The American bark *John Curtis*, of Brunswick, Maine, reached the harbour badly damaged (she was from Havana and bound for Turks' Island,) with the loss of the mast, rudder-head, and other material damage. She was brought in by a wrecker, who assisted in getting her off from being stranded at Southwest Bay. The American bark *Anna M. Palmer*, from New York and bound for Turk's Island, arrived in Nassau on the October 13. She encountered the hurricane and it destroyed the ship's mainmast along with other material damages.

A French bark was wrecked and destroyed at Great Stirrup Cay. All hands-on board were lost. Five bodies were picked up nearly naked. An American bark of Searsport, Me., Mr. J.B. Nichols the ship's Master, was brought here by wreckers on October 14. She was originally coming from Wilmington, N.C., en-route to Havana, Cuba with a shipment of lumber; the ship's masts were destroyed in the hurricane along with other damages to the ship. The American ship *John N. Cushing*, from Newburyport, Mr. W.W. Swap was the ship's Master, and it was en-route from Boston to New-Orleans, with a general cargo. It arrived in New Providence on the October 9, with mainmast destroyed and fore topmast wrung off and other damages were also reported. Mr. Charles M. Hoit, the ship's 2nd Mate, was washed overboard and drowned on the October 3. The British barque *Lupeil*, of London, Gibbus, the ship's Master, was en-route from Pensacola, Florida en-route to Liverpool, England ran aground and initially leaking badly and was then wrecked on October 2, at Turtle Rocks, but fortunately the entire crew were saved.

The brig *Rival* of New-York, Mr. J.R. Monish the ship's Master, was totally wrecked and abandoned at Moore's Island. This ship was en-route from New-York to Galveston, Texas with a general cargo, some of the shipment was partly salvaged and brought to Nassau. The ship was wrecked on the October 2. Fortunately, the crew and officers were saved and transported to Nassau. They were comprised of, Mr. J.R. Monish, the ship's Master; Mr. W.W. Delano and Mr. Roderick Dhin, the ship's Mates, and Mr. Alfred S. Polk, Mr. Geo.T.Warren alias Mason, Mr. Joseph Allen, Mr. Dennis Canna, Mr. Arch Addergreen, and Mr. Neilsou, the ship's Seamen.

The American bark *S. Willis Rich*, of Stockton, Me., Mr. J. L. Panno, the ship's Master, was en-route from Boston to Matanzas, with a shipment of ice and general cargo. It was totally wrecked on Gordo Aburo on the October 2. Part of the wrecked cargo along with the officers and crew were brought to Nassau. The American brig *William Henry*, Mr. W.M. Burnard, the ship's Master, en-route from Portland to Havana, Cuba with a shipment of lumber and shooks, was totally wrecked on the morning of October 2, at Gordo Cay, Abaco. After the hurricane hit Abaco, three of the crew were washed overboard and drowned and they were: Mr. William Baker and Mr. William Jones, of Buffalo, New York, and Mr. James Brown, of Brooklyn, New York. The other officers and the remainder of the crew were brought to Nassau with a small portion of their personal effects. The officers and crew arriving in Nassau were as follows: Mr. William Burnard, the ship's Master, Mr. Thomas R. Ray, and Mr. Charles Bishop, the ship's Mates, and Mr. Peter Derlem and Mr. Charles Johnson, the ship's Seamen.

The British brig *Grace Worthington*, Mr. Dessant the ship's Master, was travelling from New York en-route to Belize and Honduras and was towed to Nassau by Bahamian wreckers on October 12, partially dismasted and the loss of the ship's rudder. The American brig *John R. Plater*, of Norwich, Conn., and Mr. James W. Yales was the ship's Master, this ship was en-route from New York for Havana, Cuba with a general cargo and was totally wrecked at Eleuthera, on October 1. A portion of her cargo, with the officers and crew, were saved and brought to Nassau. The officers and crew were as follows: Mr. Jas. W. Yates, the ship's Master, Mr. Albert R. Douglas, and Mr. Michael J. Nicholson were the ship's Mates; Mr. John S. Bradley, Mr. R.M. Fowles, Mr. Chas. McPherson, Mr. Henry White, and Mr. Patrick Moore were the ship's Seamen.

The old American brig *Baltic*, Mr. John Maddocks was the ship's Master of New York. The ship was en-route from New York to Galveston, Texas with a general cargo, and encountered the hurricane at Eleuthera and was totally wrecked on October 1. A small part of her cargo was lost, with the entire officers and crew who were also lost with the ship. They were as follows: Mr. John Maddocks, the ship's Master, Mr. Francis R. Maddocks, and Mr. Robert C. Wooster, the ship's Mates, and Mr. Gilbert Sinclair, Mr. W.M. Boyd, Mr. John Morrison, Mr. Manfred A. Dyer, and Mr. John S. Ferris, were the ship's Seamen.

The American schooner *Swam*, Mr. G.W. Mitchell of Baltimore, was the ship's Master, and was wrecked at Fortuna Island. The officers and crew arrived at Nassau on October 14. She was wrecked on the September 30. Her officers and crew were as follows: Mr. Geo. W. Mitchell, the ship's Master, Mr. John D. Boyer, the ship's Mate; Mr. Jas. H. Perry, Mr. Geo Johnson, Mr. Geo Vithul and Mr. John Brown, were the ship's Seamen. The British brig *Chile*, Mr. Whitehead was the ship's Master. The ship was en-route from Nassau to Havana with a shipment of coal, was totally wrecked at Andros Island on October 1. The ship *American Eagle*, of Boston, turned over between Cat Island and San Salvador. There were many dead bodies picked up on the shores of these two islands. She was loaded with a shipment of fine brandy and wine and was brought to Nassau as a derelict ship. It is reported that 100 dead bodies floated on shore, which by looking at the bodies seems to indicate that she was from a European port and had migrant passengers on board. The owners of her cargo, notably the Americans' interest was advised to immediately put in their claims to the proceeds of the cargo, however, they will be subject to salvage and expenses of the court here.

The American brig *Joseph Baker* was abandoned and lost at Matthew Town, Inagua. The American brig *Julio*, with the ship's Master being Mr. Bartlett, of Bangor, Maine was destroyed. The ship *Nevassa* from Philadelphia was lost near Lantern Head, Inagua. The crew of this ship was saved except for two men, who drowned. The ship's materials were salvaged and sold at Inagua. The British schooner *Laura*, of Annapolis, Maryland and Mr. N. S. Bismark was the ship's Master, Bray, the ship's Mate, was en-route from Bangor, Maine to Port Au Prince, Haiti with a supply of lumber, was dismasted and drifted on a reef at Harbour Island and was destroyed. Her officers and crew arrived at Nassau, and were as follows: Mr. Jonathan Bray, the ship's Master; Mr. Harvey Watson and Mr. W.M. Welch, were the ship's Mates, and Mr. Chas. M. Tripp, Mr. John Franis, Mr. James Donald and Mr. Patrick Farley, were the ship's Seamen. A French bark temporarily damaged in the storm was towed into Mayaguana and then towed into Matthew Town, Inagua, loaded with a shipment of logwood. A three-mast schooner was reportedly wrecked at

Grand Bahama and the ship's cargo was salvaged and transported to Green Turtle Cay, Abaco.

A large center-board schooner was totally wrecked on Crossing Rock, Abaco. All hands were drowned; no name or nationality ascertained. Part of a clinometer-box marked "P.L. De Morey, New York," was picked up near the wreck, which may lead to her identity. She was loaded with coconuts, which were pitched.

A large vessel, whose name was ascertained to be *The Race*, her port and nation unknown, was loaded with a shipment of lumber, and was overturned at Berry Island; all persons onboard drowned. The schooner *Advance*, formerly of Baltimore, was leased by the Bahama Guano Company and was sunk and destroyed with the entire crew perishing onboard with the ship during the hurricane. Ten of her original crew on board at the time of the disaster originated from Baltimore in the United States. The American schooner *Union,* of Harrington, reported in my last letter was driven ashore but will probably be afloat in a few days, as well as the British war-ship *Nimble*. This comprised of all that has been ascertained up to this date, but I fear there are many not yet known. The crews of these ships now here will be forwarded to the United States at once.

In October of 1981, 'The Journal of The Bahamas Historical Society', published in its magazine an excellent report on the Great Bahamas Hurricane of 1866 as researched and written by Bahamian historian, author, anthropologist and University of The Bahamas lecturer Mrs. Nicolette Bethel. She was the Director of Culture in The Bahamas and is now a full-time lecturer in Social Sciences at the University of The Bahamas. She blogs at Blogworld and tweets at @nicobet. Below is an excerpt of that report: -

The Great Bahamas Hurricane of 1866 by Nicolette Bethel

The Bahamas in 1866:

First settled over two hundred years before, the colony of The Bahamas had progressed little by 1850, and then in fits and starts rather than continuously. In 1866, it was working its way out of a depression which followed the prosperous years of the American Civil War. Blockade running, the act of slipping into the Union guarded ports of the South to supply the Confederate States with manufactured goods they needed, brought quick, easy money into the country. But the era, though great, was also short-lived, and in 1865, three years after the beginning of the blockade running, the industry closed when the Confederation was defeated by the North. The colony suffered a sudden economic collapse.... The Bahamas was not prepared for a disaster which would stir up the sea and flood the land, which would sink ships, wreck mansions and sweep away flimsy shacks of the Valley. Nevertheless, the colony was visited by one. For in October 1866, a hurricane the likes of which had never been seen by Bahamians living then swept the archipelago.

The Hurricane of 1866:

The hurricane later to be known as the "Great Bahama Hurricane" left St. Thomas, the Virgin Islands, on the morning of September 28, 1866. By the early hours of September 30, it was affecting The Bahamas; Mayaguana recorded gale force winds coming from the north-east. By eight o'clock that morning the hurricane had progressed as far as Matthew Town, Inagua, and a "light wind" was reported at Fortune Island (now Long Cay), just northwest of Crooked Island. San Salvador (then Watlings Island) received the fringe winds of the cyclone at three in the afternoon, and by eight o'clock in the evening of Sunday, September 30, Long Island was being struck.

It was at that time that the first evidence of the storm was felt in Nassau. The day had passed as usual; the people had attended evening church services, spending the hours after on their verandahs socializing. The air was still; "all was calm and tranquil...there was, however, a peculiar reddish hue in the heavens...and an unusual warmth in the atmosphere." At eight o'clock, "a northerly breeze sprung up, which grew stronger throughout the night and the barometer fell from 30.16 inches on the day of the 30th to 29.80 inches at 11:00 am the following morning. The hurricane remained over Nassau for the rest of the day, the eye passed over the town in the early evening. There was a lull then for as long as an hour and a half; then the wind "sprung up from the opposite quarter and continued to blow violently till 2:00 am (on October 2) when it gradually subsided." The barometric pressure, taken during the lull, was as low as 27.70 inches and was recorded about half an hour before the winds began to blow again.

Seas of tidal wave proportions swamped the harbour, disregarding the islands which normally acted as a buffer against storms…The hurricane moved away from New Providence quickly; by the morning of October 3, it had left Bahamian waters, entering the mid-Atlantic where presumably it dissipated. As there are no records of the hurricane had hit any of the eastern states of the USA, it is reasonable to assume that the storm simply died upon reaching cooler waters.

Effects of The Hurricane:

Nassau suffered in the sunshine which followed the storm. No level of society had been left unscathed; the houses on the ridge, affected worst by the gales, lost roofs, and those still standing stood askew. Trees felled by the winds had caused much damage, crashing into houses and across streets. Along the harbourside, the warehouses which were the shelters of the unemployed were for the most part demolished. The low-lying valley, covered in swamp water had overflowed and covered the land, and the water became stagnant, and was an ideal breeding place for bacteria and flies. The few houses which had survived the hurricane stood like towers above the debris, and the fruit and vegetables which were the sole means of survival for the people of the valley lay strewn across the lanes and valleys of the settlement. In total 601 houses were destroyed, and at least that number damaged; one thousand people were estimated to have been made homeless by the hurricane.

On the Out Islands; the results were much the same as those of New Providence. At Harbour Island, then the largest Out Island settlement, the year's vegetable crop was ruined; "hardly a house" was left undamaged. Upon appeal to the capital for assistance, the settlement was denied it; all the money possible was to be spent in rebuilding Nassau. At Rum Cay, the entire salt harvest was reclaimed by the ocean and every house was flattened.

If the damage done on land was extensive, the damage at sea was even worse. In Nassau Harbour, sheltered from most blows by its barrier islands "of more than 200 vessels…only one remained intact." Harbour Island lost every one of its boats to the hurricane and other settlements on other islands suffered the same fate….Wrecks were plentiful, and the income from the industry at the end of the year totaled £108,000, having increased 375% from £28,000 the year before.

Although the hurricane caused much damage, it left as a legacy an industry which would help lift the colony out of the depression of the following years. In 1870, wrecking was to bring over £150,000 into the colony, to send The Bahamas on its way up to prosperity again.

This account below was reported by the Resident Justice of Andros to the Colonial Secretary located in Nassau. This account was taken from the August 26th, 1899 issue of the Nassau Guardian Newspaper. Since our last publication, the following official information has been furnished to The Bahamas Government by the Resident Justice at Andros Island with reference to the late hurricane: -

"August 17th-Arrived at Nicholl's Town this afternoon. What a sad and distressing sight it presented from the sea? Looked as if it had been scorched by fire. On landing, I found that with a few exceptions, all the houses had been leveled by the mighty force of the hurricane, and the poor people without food, except that of coconuts. I at once distributed some food finishing up the next morning."

"Nicholl's Town is in a dreadful state, I cannot see, unless aid is rendered how the people will be able to subsist for the next two or three months, they are in a dreadful plight, no food, no home. Some of the people crawl under the roofs of their houses which lie on the ground and find shelter from the wind and rain.

"August 18th-I distributed food to about 175 or more starving people at Nicholl's Town and about fifteen ship-wrecked spongers from Red Bays. A total number of barrels of provisions distributed at Nicholl's Town-12.

"From information received I understand that there was very little of the storm at Williams Cays but the loss of life and damage to property at Red Bays (the ranching place of spongers) are something terrible. I intended to take in Williams Cay but after hearing there was no hurricane there, I thought it advisable to change my route and proceed to Bimini via Orange Cays.

"August 19th-I arrived at Orange Cays, had a search, found nothing, came onboard, and proceeded for Bimini. August 20, arrived at Bimini just before dark, too late to find out anything. August 21, I had a meeting this morning of the leading gentlemen of the town, they informed me that there was no immediate want at Bimini, but they would need aid very soon, owing to all their crops being destroyed by the hurricane. The schooner *President of this town* turned up just as I was leaving. She scudded from

Beach Cay up over the Bahama Banks, out over Gingerbread Ground and eventually brought up at Grand Bahama.

"August 22nd-I arrived at 8 Mile Rock this morning had a walk of about four miles around the settlements. Destruction and distress reign supreme. Mr. Adderley, R.J., informed me that my arriving with food was a "God-send" and that the people would appreciate it very much. I landed the balance of provisions, eleven barrels in all, and gave instructions to the Resident Justice. I might mention that this coast (Grand Bahama) is settled for several miles, three houses here, five there and so, therefore, I was able to superintend the distribution of food personally. Great destitution prevails at Grand Bahama, many of the people are homeless. The Resident Justice alone having four families at his house. The fury of the hurricane was not so great at Grand Bahama apparently as at Andros. Bay Street all along the settlements are filled with debris, cast there from the bed of the ocean. The best way of locomotion is along the sea rocks."

This account of the aftereffects of the storm was written by Mr. E.Y.V. Sutton who was dispatched by the Central Government in Nassau to take relief supplies to the residents of Andros and to give a complete report on the damages sustained on the island. This was taken from the Nassau Guardian Newspaper on Friday, September 02, 1899: -

"I left Nassau for Andros Island, on the morning of the 17th, arriving at Nicholl's Town the next day at daybreak. At this place, I met Mr. W.T. Cleare, who was distributing supplies to the people. I immediately made a personal inspection of the settlement and found that the inhabitants were in a destitute condition, many of the houses had been blown down, rendering numbers homeless, and I gathered from the people, that the small supply of provisions at the settlement had been badly damaged. The crops owing to the severity of the weather, are destroyed, orange, grapefruit, and coconut trees were blown down and stripped of fruit and foliage. The fields of corn and potatoes, etc. have been so badly damaged that it will take months for them to recover. Potatoes are rotting in the fields. Stranded on the beach was a schooner owned by Mr. H.G. Albury. Many homes were damaged or destroyed. Three Government buildings have suffered. The jail roof has fallen in, part of the roof of the schoolhouse has lifted, and the teacher's residence destroyed.

"After consultation with Mr. Cleare, who was relieving the immediate wants of the people, I decided to proceed at once to the Red Bays settlement and call again at Nicholl's Town on my way back, which I did, and with the assistance of Mr. McGregor, the Public-School Teacher, I distributed one barrel of flour and two barrels of grits. Having been informed that the people at Conch Sound were in a very bad shape, I handed over to Mr. Gostick two barrels of flour, he is having kindly undertaken to give them to the superintend for distribution of it to the people at that place. I should have gone to Conch Sound, and would have personally relieved the people, but hearing that the people at Red Bays were in a much worse condition, I thought it advisable to accept the services of Mr. Gostick, and proceed at once to Red Bay Cays, at which place I arrived on Sunday morning, and landed immediately.

"Frederick McQueen having informed me that he knew where several dead bodies were lying unburied, after a considerable amount of persuasion, I induced James Uling one of the crews of my vessel, and McQueen to go with me, and Messers, Johnson and Pritchard again accompanying me. I went down to the beach and found on the Red Bay shore, three bodies and at Crab Cay one body. The first body we found had been buried but had been dug up by land crabs. We again buried it. The next body we discovered was so wedged under the roots of the mangroves that it was impossible for us to get at it, so I caused it to be freely sprinkled with carbolic acid. The third body was found a short distance away under the roots of a tree, which we buried. The fourth body was found lying on the shore, at Crab Cay, this we also buried.

"I was unable to obtain the names of these people, except for the body found in the *Alicia* which was supplied to be the remains of one Elijah Pinder. The great loss of life at this place, which from information I received, I estimate to be between 100 and 150, (I enclose a list of names given me by men of the different vessels who are supposed to have been drowned) was caused by the sudden uprising of the sea, like a tidal wave which arose when the wind shifted to the southwest after a sudden calm. The man has taken advantage of the calm to go to the small cays to gather some of the dead bodies.

"Judging from the smell, which is most noticeable, I am of the opinion that there are yet remaining unburied a number of bodies through the creeks in the vicinity of Red Bays settlement, but not being able to obtain any reliable information as to the state of the people at the other places that I had visited after leaving Red Bays and having done what I could for the living at this place, I decided that the living at other places had prior claim to my attention, and I was, therefore, unable to make a more thorough search for dead bodies.

The houses and crops at these places were also destroyed by the sea at this time and two women and one man I am informed were drowned while swimming in the pineyard.

This sudden uprising of the sea, in my opinion, was undoubtedly caused by the shifting of the wind to the southwest which drove the sea with tremendous force upon a very low-lying coast, and it was at this time that most of the damage was done. The houses at these settlements are very nearly all damaged or destroyed. The people are living under the roofs of the houses that have been blown down. The crops are all destroyed, and as I have already said in respect to Nicholl's Town, some time must elapse before the people can derive any benefits from their fields. I regret to add while reporting on this settlement that everything that can possibly be removed from the vessels is being stolen. I might state as a most glaring instance, the cutting into the bottom of a new sloop to get at her cargo of sponge, and the chopping away of the brass rudder braces.

Having done all in my power to relieve the distress of the people of this place, I left on Monday for Nicholl's Town and issued provisions as before stated. On the way to Nicholl's Town, I called in at Lowe Sound and found the people in great distress, twenty-three houses having been blown down, and four damaged and the people in great want of food. I, therefore, landed two barrels of flour and one barrel of grits for distribution. I was informed by Charles Sherman and others that they had buried eight bodies that had been washed up. I sailed from Nicholl's Town on Wednesday 23, for Mastic Point. I landed at Mr. Chamberlain's Wharf and walked from there to the settlement, about a mile in distance. On the way, I inspected and made a list of the houses that had been damaged and blown down during the storm. The information gathered from this settlement was given me by Mr. Bernice Albury, the Public-School-Teacher, and was on par with what I had received with regards to the destruction of property, etc., at the other places. I supplied him with three barrels of flour and three barrels of grits, for distribution to the people of the two districts in this settlement. At this place, quite many vessels were capsized but there was no loss of life. The place had been flooded by the sea during the NE wind. The crops at this place are also destroyed.

Leaving Mastic Point on Thursday morning, I arrived at Staniard Creek at 10 am on the same day, where I met Mr. K.G. Malcolm, who was distributing provisions. The people at this place were in a most destitute condition. The damage done by the storm in every situation, had appeared to me, was much greater than at any of the other places that I had visited. The sea had flooded the entire settlement, houses were blown away completely, trees uprooted and blown across houses, some of the occupants of which narrowly escaped with their lives. I immediately landed the remaining six barrels of provisions that I had with me and handed them over to Mr. Malcolm who undertook to supply them to the people. All the crops at this place were destroyed but there was no loss of life.

I left Staniard Creek with the intention of reporting myself to the Resident Justice, who I heard was at Fresh Creek. Upon my arrival there I found he had gone to Mangrove Cay. From this place I walked to Calabash Bay; neither of those places appeared to have suffered very much from the storm. Some houses had been blown down, several vessels had been capsized, but there had been no loss of life...."

Here's an account of some person's preparation for the Great Bahamas Hurricane of 1899 as reported by the Nassau Guardian Newspaper, August 14, 1899: -

"We feel assured that our subscribers and patrons will understand that the issue of the Guardian on Saturday was prevented by the circumstances attending the hurricane and will, therefore, excuse this our first departure from the regular day of publication since the Hurricane of 1883. Destruction of houses, vessels, fruits, and many lives feared to be lost. The weather on Thursday night indicated that a storm was approaching, yet the barometers did not cause any immediate alarm until early on Friday morning when the regulation warning signals were hoisted at the light station at Hog Island, and at the signal staffs at Forts Charlotte and Fincastle, and a little later the customary flags for a falling barometer were displayed on the Imperial Lighthouse Tender Richmond. The winds came in squalls during the previous night and at times was very strong and on Friday morning, the rain continued at short intervals with winds of considerable force from the northeast.

The mercury kept falling during the day, and shortly before noon, a cable was recorded from Washington stating that the wind and readings of the barometer indicated that the hurricane center was approaching Nassau. This information was soon put in circulation and special attention was given to the mooring of the vessels in the harbour, the small craft having already been removed to the eastward anchoring ground. Precautions were also taken on board the steamer *Cocoa* which had been alongside of R.H. Sawyer & Co.'s Wharf discharging cargo; she steamed into the stream and her heavy anchors were put down. The occupiers of houses also saw to the fastenings of their dwellings, and everybody became deeply interested in the storm which was correctly believed to be slowly moving towards us. The glass continued to fall and at sunset, there was a difference of five tenths in the reading of the glass between morning and evening. After sunset, the squalls came in faster and faster and the winds also increased in strength all the time, until the rain became incessant and the wind howled. The mercury went down more rapidly as the night advanced but at two o'clock on Saturday morning it became steady and showed signs on rising. During the night, the wind shifted more easterly going to the east and then southeast from which direction it was blowing at daylight. It continued to blow furiously during the day, and it was not until the afternoon that it began to moderate; the cyclone lasted about eight hours.

When morning arrived, the light revealed the damages that had occurred from the storm in the night. Among the first serious losses observed by us was the destruction of a new building recently erected by Mr. G.B. Adderley to the west of the Sponge Exchange which was completely leveled to the ground. It had been constructed of a wooden frame and enclosed with corrugated iron and being near the waterside and very much exposed was blown over from the foundation. The covering of the J.S. Johnson Company's Wharf fell in and a portion of the wharf to the east was carried away. Numerous sheds in front of the stores on Bay Street and other streets were blown down and some business signs destroyed. House properties in the city sustained as far as we are aware comparatively little damage, but in the suburbs, the humble dwellings of the poor suffered considerably more damage. Small houses here and there were to be seen in a state of complete collapse and many outbuildings were also blown down. The number of houses destroyed was estimated to be forty. The Colonial Hotel was not in the least shaken by the effects of the storm. A force was engaged in watching the temporary cloth frames that are set in the windows through which the water found access to the building and which will probably inflict damage to the new plastering. The building otherwise is intact. The walls of the building during erection at the Hotel Royal Victoria fell to some extent."

This account of the storm was written by an unnamed person living at Clarence Town, Long Island on August 12, 1899, just after the storm.

This was taken from the Nassau Guardian Newspaper on Wednesday, September 30, 1899: -

Sir,

Sweet is the breath of morn, writes Milton, and after all is passed over, on this morning with a clear azure sky on which begins to forget the anxiety and terror experienced on the 10th of this month.

For some time, you could hear the weather-wise mariners saying "I don't like the looks of the weather! Here we are in the month of August with the wind blowing from the Northeast and so cool indoors, but hot outside."

Well at 6 pm on the 10th things began to bear a suspicious aspect, wind E by N, and a drizzly rain. The barometer began to fall very gradually, but by 10 o'clock the sky was overcast and looked gloomy and the wind increases much. The sloop *Lucy Ann* had dragged ashore high on the beach, and the waves were running high on the shore. The next few minutes the schooner beached, and the wind now in small gusts tells us without referring to the barometer that the hurricane was on us. A fall of nearly 3/10ths of an inch in the barometer confirmed it, and hammers could be heard everywhere. As the wind hauled eastwardly and inclined southward, I was satisfied that the center of the cyclone was to the south of us. Yet it blew terribly. This kept up with continual rain until 4 am on the 11th when we began to realize that its force was much lessened, and all appearances of better times coming. The weather remained unsettled until about 8 pm on the 11th, when fair weather has begun to dawn on us again, which continued to improve up to this time.

It was severe but not to be compared with the hurricanes of '66 and '83, yet it has done some damage on shore. Five houses have been blown down or so much damaged as to cause them to be untenantable, and 9 others are seriously damaged, but can be lived in fair weather. As most of our homes are of thatched roofs, all suffered from being flooded with rain, and the tanks are nearly filled with water. None of the government buildings suffered from the storm, and the vessels ashore are slightly damaged. The *Lucy Ann* suffered nothing to speak of, and *The Brave* had a few sheets of metal rubbed off, and her rubber displaced, and spindles bent or broken. The schooner *Addie* is expected but not heard from; the *Hattie H. Roberts* also; all we can hear of her, or supposed to be of her, is that early on Thursday morning a large schooner was seen passing

Burrow's Harbour. If it is her, I fear she has had it bad. The lower portion of the land on the northern districts are under water, and large trees have been thrown across the roads to make them impassable, which prevents us hearing from Deadman's Cay until the debris is removed. The local Board of Works has the work in hand, and labourers are employed to clear away. Not one accident has occurred to any person to my knowledge, nor one animal injured so far as heard from. Should any further news come in from the north it will come to you.

The Loss of the Schooner Addie-The Tale of the Captain

"On Wednesday the 9th, at 5 pm we were anchored in Hog Cay Cut; the weather looked queer and we thought we would lay there until tomorrow which we did when we set sailed for home (Long Island) on the morning of the 10th, our barometer reading was 30.10 inches. Between 10-11am with moderate weather before, we now find it changing, a high sea running and squalls passing in gusts of wind, and although the barometer was the same, we thought it advisable to turn back to the cut. We got safely again into the cut at 1:30 pm. Between 12 midnight and 1 am on the 11th the barometer fell to 29.95 inches and the schooner commenced dragging. We took to anchor and were forced in a strong gale to scud down the Exuma shore.

With the barometer falling rapidly and the gale increasing, we thought of beaching the schooner, but it was so dark we could not see where to put her, so we kept on scudding at the mercy of the wind and sea. Presently, we brought up on a bar near a projecting point of the land and lay there from 4 pm on the land until 4 am the following morning. The tide was running so strongly around this point that it prevented us from getting ashore at the next point to fasten a hawser to a projecting rock to keep us there. The wind now shifting to the SE blew us off the bar. I then noticed the barometer was 29.40 inches. We brought up again on the next point of land to leeward where she lay until 6 am when the wind shifted to the SW. We took to the boat to save our lives, loading her with those who could not swim. Three of the crew with the mate volunteered for the safe landing to swim, holding on the gunwale of the boat which we sculled ashore to the land that was overflowed with the extra high tide. Our boat got under the lee of some mangroves which we held to until 2 pm.

The weather moderating, we made for the mainland which we found to be the Pond at Exuma, and we went to the house of Mr. Knowles, Mr. Brice's overseer, who took us in and sheltered us. On the next day, we went to the schooner to save what cargo we could and did so to the extent of 22 barrels, some goods, 2 boxes of tobacco, 2 tins of kerosene, 1/2 barrel of beef, 1 tin of Lard, a few other articles, some clothing of the passengers and crew. I went to Rolle Town engaged the schooner *Dial* put in the freight and passengers with the crew and some of the schooner's materials and arrived here yesterday afternoon. The people of the place acted very unchristianly like. They got almost deliriously drunk with the liquor they stole from our cargo and acted in such a way that upon rising the schooner to inspect her bottom we were afraid to go under her fearing that they would let up and crush us. They seem to think that this vessel and her cargo was a Godsend to them and barrels could be found all through the bushes broken open and their contents taken away. The old clothing of the crew lying on deck was taken away before our eyes although we sanctioned them not to take them. Everything they could lay their hands on they took and converted to their own use. I regret that such things could occur to distressed vessels in our islands especially. The port planks of the schooner are broken but she can be repaired and floated although she is 200 feet from the sea over a ridge of sand.

Captain William Bethel of the schooner *Excel* left for Nassau to be repaired, reported to me while at Exuma it was wrecked and that he was in the schooner *Raven* on which he was a passenger; that *Raven* was lost at Soldier's Cay, no loss of life but everything else with the vessel and also that a sponger with eleven hands on board had been lost at Rocky Point and only five saved. The schooner *Celeste* on which I freighted some cargo in Nassau, to the extent of 32 barrels and other things was last heard of on Tuesday afternoon when she landed some passengers at the settlement of Cottage on Exuma and then left there for the North End of this island. I have not heard anything further of her yet, nor have I heard of the *Hattie Darling* which sailed from Nassau on Wednesday the 9th. I have heard from others of several losses, but I cannot say they are authentic enough to speak of."

The Great Bahamas Hurricane of 1929

Message from the King of England

The following message from His Majesty, King George V was addressed to the Governor and the people of The Bahamas, which was received from the Secretary of State for the colony: -

September 30, 1929.

"His Majesty, King George V, is deeply concerned at the news that the colony has once more been ravaged by a hurricane. His Majesty anxiously awaits further tidings and desires, through you, to assure all sufferers of his personal sympathy."

The following reply was dispatched from Nassau to the Secretary of State for the colony: -

"On behalf of the colony, I desire humbly to thank His Majesty for his gracious message of sympathy. Further reports confirm that New Providence and Andros have been the central points of devastation, but in both islands, the casualties have been remarkably few. The main distress is occasioned by the destruction of the houses and the wreck of local craft. The public services are restored, and normal life is practically resumed. The population is facing disaster with fortitude and calm, and the situation is well in hand."

The following remarks were made by Charles Dundas, Governor of The Bahamas, with regards to the hurricane: -

"I desire to express my deepest sympathy with all of those who have suffered in any way in this terrible disaster, more particularly with those who have suffered bodily injury and who count relatives among the victims of the storm. This disaster is extremely disappointing because up until now the prospects were singularly encouraging, and inevitably there will be a severe setback to the efforts of all those who have earnestly endeavored to promote the prosperity of the colony. Nevertheless, it is vital that we should not be downhearted. The greater the calamity, the more need there is for courage and perseverance. I am speaking to a people injured to disasters and of a country in which there is manifestly no place for the faint-hearted ones. I decline to despair despite the frustration of so much that we had hoped and striven for, and I sincerely believe that in this respect I shall have with me the stout hearts of the Bahamians. Going around the town on Friday, it was to me most heartening to witness much cheerful courage displayed amid ruin and devastation. With staunchness and faith in ourselves, we shall set ourselves to repair the damage and prove to the world that Bahamians are undaunted."

Charles Dundas,
Government House
September 28, 1929.

The loss of the schooners Venture, Forward, and Iona

"At 9 o'clock that morning, the crew were all huddled in the cabin. One man, Reuben Albury, had his head above the companion-way, keeping an eye on things. There came a violent squall. The *Forward* leaped and snapped the anchor chain. Mr. Albury shouted to the crew "Make for the deck – the chain is gone!" The *Forward* sheared around, the wind and sea caught her broadside and rolled her over like a piece of cork. She drove her masts into the sandy bottom, snapped them and a piece caught the mate on the head – and for a few seconds, he was seen floating face down, being carried away by the sea.

The *Forward* had a crew of eight. When she flipped over, Mr. Reuben Albury was able to get a hold of the fore-boom which was floating, but still tied to the vessel. He looked about to discover to his dismay that he was the only man left with the wreck. For four hours he held on to that boom – a feat of endurance which is beyond understanding. Holding to the loose end of that boom, Mr. Albury was taken from the surface to the bottom with every trough, and back to the surface with which to cover himself. Two men onshore, native Androsians, themselves castaways, I would think, saw that solitary man sitting out there. They got off a dinghy and rescued him – which was a brave thing to do. For as you know, the second half of a hurricane hits like a thunderbolt – no gradual build up as is the case with the first part – and not knowing when it will strike.

To Reuben Albury's surprise, two other men of the *Forward's* crew were safely ashore. They had made it by going along with one of the vessel's swamped dinghies. Alternately, they held on to it when it was on the surface and swam when the "suck" took it to the bottom. And that too was an epic tale of survival...But they endured two miles of this before getting to the solid ground. The two had shed their clothes and were stark naked and they and Mr. Albury huddled together under an upturned dinghy for the remainder of the hurricane.

What of the two schooners? Unlike the *Forward*, they had started to drag their anchors during the night. After daylight, the *Venture* broke her two hawsers and began to pull the hurricane anchor along at a rapid clip so much so that she began to veer severely-sometime getting nearly broadside to the sea. Several times she came close to rolling over and it was decided to cut away the masts. This was a wise decision and after it was done, she steadied wonderfully. The anchor finally took hold and held until one of the flues was sheared off. Then, of course, the *Venture* was carried along at great speed. You can imagine the astonishment of the crew when they saw the tops of pine trees passing by. It was then they realized that the water had risen greatly and covered the land in that area to some depth. They finally ended up against some stout pine trees about a foot or so in trunk diameter and to these they tied the vessel.

An interesting observation is that at the time of the commencement of the calm; the crew of any vessel had no idea what had happened to the other two schooners.

On board the *Venture*, tied up there to the pine trees the men surmised that perhaps the *Forward* and *Iona* had washed in over the land as they had done. With the object of attracting them if they were close by, they discharged shotguns at regular intervals. And lo and behold, before the second half of the hurricane descended, the crew of the *Iona* came along in their small boats, sculling and rowing through the pine trees. This *Iona* was the one which had left Nassau when the hurricane was reported, to be on the way. Her story was much the same as that of the *Venture*, with one notable exception; her crew had failed to cut the masts. As a result, she capsized – but by then she was overland. And she did not turn bottom up as the *Forward* had done, but lay straight out on the side, with the masts on the surface of the water.

The men were able to get into the boats and when the *Iona* came to rest against the pine trees – she provided a little shelter for them. And there they stayed until they heard the gunshot from the *Venture*. Apart from the mate, who might have been killed by the main boom, four of the *Forward's* crew were drowned. Three survived to go to sea again. Mr. Reuben Albury who clung so desperately to live on that restless fore boom was gouged up something terrible to see. He had to be taken home on a stretcher, and it was six weeks before he could walk again. No lives were lost on the other two schooners, which carried nine men each. But most likely they would have all drowned had the Venture not cut her masts. A few weeks later, the *Forward* was turned the right way up, patched up and repaired and sailed again; and lived to a ripe old age.

When the water receded, the *Venture* was seen to be about four miles inland and the Iona about two miles. As incredible as it may sound, both vessels were retrieved from the pine barrens and they also sailed again. About fifty Androsians using large rollers and blocks and tackle performed the Herculean task. The *Venture*, which had to be dragged four miles, foot by laborious foot, wore through her keel after a mile or so. And the launching had to be suspended until a new keel was put in. This wore through too, and yet another keel had to be put in probably the only vessel in history to wear out two keels on dry land."

Special Session of the House of Assembly- The Administrator's Charles Dundas Speech on the Great Bahamas Hurricane of 1929

In accordance with his Proclamation calling the General Assembly together for a special session, His Excellency the Administrator, the Hon. Charles Dundas, O.B.E., met with both Houses of the Legislature in the Council Chambers on Wednesday night and opened the session with a speech.

His Excellency, who was attended by his A.D.C., Captain Lancaster, M.C, was met at the entrance to the Council Chamber by His Honour, the Acting Chief Justice, (Mr. G.H.F. Cannon) the Hon. Acting Colonial Secretary (Mr. C.P. Bethel, I.S.O., the Hon. Receiver General (Mr. N. Stafford Solomon), and the Hon. Acting Director of Medical Services (Dr. W.J. Woodman) and the Commandant of Police (Mr. C.J. Whelbell), who accompanied him to the Council Chamber. The members of the Legislature Council present were the Hon. W. Miller, I.S.O., the Hon. P.

W. D. Armbrister, O.B.E. the Hon. Nigel B. Burnside, I.S.O.., the Hon. C.O. Anderson, and the Hon. Ronald Young.

The attendance of the Speaker and members of the House of Assembly, having been commanded by a message delivered by the A.D.C., the House, led by the Speaker preceded by the Sergeant-at-Arms bearing the Mace, arrived at the Bar of the Council Chamber, and His Excellency delivered the following speech: -

"Mr. President and Honourable Gentlemen of the Legislative Council. Mr. Speaker and Gentlemen of the Honourable House of Assembly."

"I deeply deplore the catastrophe which has obligated me to summon you to a Special Session. That my first formal meeting with you should be occasioned by an emergency so distressing is a matter of sincere regret to me. Prior to the recent hurricane, I had reason to believe that if the colony was spared from the adversity of the nature we have now sustained, her prospects were the brightest. It was also my earnest hope that the fourth century of The Bahamas as a British colony would usher in an era of stable prosperity, that instead the anniversary for which preparation had been made with joy and pride should perforce be commemorated in the shadow of misfortune and privation is a circumstance that adds poignancy to our sorrow.

With havoc still painfully in evidence on all sides, one cannot be unmindful of the suffering and material loss caused to all sections of the community, and it is idle to gloss over the temporary check the colony has sustained. But though I am keenly alive to these facts and in no way, wish to minimize their consequences, and while it is due to you that I should make a full statement of the situation, I deprecate any inclination to harp on the disaster still less to magnify its discouraging aspects. It is rather my desire to divert attention from what has happened and give prominence to the constructive task now to be faced.

The praiseworthy spirit manifested by all sections of the community inspires me with confidence in the ability of the colony to retrieve the situation, and if the work of reconstruction is undertaken with energy and with resolve to avert a far as possible the repetition of destruction on the same scale. I believe that the sore trial the colony has experienced may be not devoid of its compensations. Every recurrence of the hurricane devastation serves to demonstrate the need for sound construction, and that lesson be it said applies not only to works but to the whole economic structure of the colony. I am indeed tempted to say that given this teaching of nature is taken to heart and acted upon, God may yet come to evil.

The disaster has aroused widespread commiseration. His Majesty the King has with his customary solicitude graciously expressed his anxiety and has commanded me to convey his sympathy to all those who have suffered. Numerous messages of condolence have reached me, notably from our sister colonies of the western hemisphere. Offers of emergency aid came from the United States, and a generous donation from abroad enabled me to open a hurricane fund which will, I trust, afford relief to those most affected.

I am happy to say that on most of the Out Islands, the storm was either not felt at all or was so moderate as to cause no damage. In the case of a few islands, the effect was, in fact, beneficial in that the only result of the disturbance was much-needed rainfall. The destructive range of the hurricane embraced the islands: Eleuthera, Harbour Island, and Spanish Wells, Abaco and Andros, but serious damage is reported only in Andros, I have still no reliable data as to the loss of life and property on Andros, but I fear that it has been heavy and that the sponging industry must be severely affected by the destruction of boats and damage to the sponge beds. In a lesser degree, Abaco has suffered; twelve boats and nineteen houses are reported wrecked and damaged.

It is, however, probable that wherever the storm attained hurricane velocity, standing crops were destroyed. It is not too late to repair this damage, the people have been encouraged to replant and have responded well, and steps have been taken to ensure an ample seed supply, some of which has already been issued. But it is to be feared that until fresh crops can be harvested, food shortage will prevail on some of the Out Islands, necessitating moderate rationing in return for labour. It is an unfortunate coincidence that certain islands, as for instance Long Island and Long Cay, though not affected by the storm are suffering from food shortage due to prolonged drought. Now that rain has fallen, I hope that with the expenditure of monies already provided under the ordinary votes, distress in this area will be sufficiently alleviated.

I regard it as the supreme importance that there should be no undue suspension of the progress made in respect to agricultural production. I am unable to subscribe to the view that the frequency of hurricanes rules out the possibility of prosperous peasant cultivation, rather does it seem to me that because of the greater hazards to other occupations arising from the same cause it is the more necessary to look to agriculture as a basic industry of the colony. I have therefore endeavored to stimulate the cultivators to renewed effort, and their response to such encouragement is most gratifying.

I need not enter details of the havoc caused in New Providence; suffice it to say that 456 houses were demolished and 640 damaged in varying degree. By singular good fortune, the loss of life and other casualties have been comparatively slight, the number of fatalities being seven, of which two were from drowning, while of serious injuries only twenty-two were reported. The ultimate loss of shipping cannot be stated with accuracy since it remains to be seen how many of the sixty-four vessels of all types wrecked out of Nassau Harbour can be salvaged. Reports received immediately after the hurricane indicated the total loss of ten motorboats, three pilot boats, three ocean-going motor vessels, nine sloops, and two lighters - twelve other motor vessels were doubtfully recoverable. The remainder, twenty-five craft of various sorts, were damaged and stranded. This is a heavy toll entailing a substantial loss, not only to the owners but to the colony which so greatly depends on its marine transport facilities.

The lighting and telephone systems have been extensively damaged, and although everything has been done to repair the damage, there must be some lapse of time before these services can be completely restored. It is gratifying to note that the water supply has been barely interrupted and that the damage done to both the water and sewage works has been negligible an indication, I presume, of sound construction. The fact that from the point of view of navigation the Nassau Harbour has not been affected by the terrific seas that raged first from the one quarter and then from the other and that the wharf and shed have suffered only negligible injury prove that these works can withstand a maximum of strain. Most of the dilapidations of the shed roof were in evidence before the hurricane.

In other directions, however, the damage to public property has been most extensive. The arterial road of the island has been wholly or partly demolished over considerable stretches and has been seriously damaged in several sections.

This account was taken from the Monthly Weather Review of September 28, 1929, and it discusses the loss of life and property in Nassau after the Great Bahamas Hurricane of 1929: -

The severest hurricane struck Nassau from the west at 1:30 pm, Wednesday (September 25), followed by a 24-hour gale from the west in the early stages of the storm. The water rose very high, flooding roads and carrying away seawalls and houses. After seven hours, the winds blew from the west and southwest as the center passed over Nassau. The lull lasted for over four hours. It resumed at midnight, blowing harder than before from the southeast and east. Major damage occurred. It continued all Thursday (26th), and the barometer reading at the height of the storm was 27.64 inches, but the storm abated on Friday (27th). Still, the strong winds kept blowing. Damage to private property was enormous. Few houses escaped, many unroofed, especially in the coloured quarter. Stores, churches, and shipping were affected very severely. The mailboat *Princess Montague* was blown out of the harbour and stranded on Tony Rock. The passengers and crew were safely rescued from the boat. The mail vessel Ena K was found safe in the harbour. Many lives were lost and casualties numerous, however, it is impossible to estimate yet. No news from the Out Islands, but it is feared that they suffered severely.

This account of the Great Abaco Hurricane of 1932 was written the Nassau Guardian Newspaper as told to this newspaper by a boat Captain Mr. Holland as he arrived at Abaco to render assistance to the people of Abaco just after the storm. This account was taken from the Nassau Guardian Newspaper on Saturday, September 10, 1932.

Captain Holland's Story

In an interview with a Nassau Guardian reporter Captain Holland told the following story:

"We were heading for Green Turtle Cay, but as we neared Bluff Point, 15 miles this side of our destination, we saw that the settlement was in a state of ruins. Sheets were hanging high up on trees as distress signals and a Red Ensin could be seen floating upside-down on a flagstaff. The entire population, numbering about 250, was clustered together in large groups and the general atmosphere was one of complete bewilderment. Six persons had been badly injured and almost everyone had minor injuries. There was no food of any kind in the settlement and as a last resort water was obtained from small puddles. Every boat had been destroyed and it was not possible, therefore, to catch any fish. The seas had swept right over the settlement

556

destroying every building and all vegetation. We then continued to Green Turtle Cay where we discovered it equally bad. Six persons had been killed and 26 badly injured. Very little food or water was to be had. Mr. W. A. Kendrick, who acts in a medical capacity around the settlements of Abaco, worked untiringly night and day among the injured. Disinfectants were very badly needed. Almost every house had been swept away.

At Great Guana Cay, ten miles below, only four houses were left standing. Fifteen persons had been injured and one killed. The seas swept over this settlement also and had taken its toll on the people and the town. At Marsh Harbour, extensive damage had been done and all the crops were destroyed. There were fortunately no deaths or injuries in this settlement. Hope Town met the same fate. The wireless station was destroyed and the church among other buildings were demolished. Again, there was no loss of lives. Cooper's Town was wiped out, but Cherokee Sound sustained little damage. Elbow Cay was said to have had a terrific wind velocity estimated by some at 150 mph. It seems that the very height of the storm raged over this part." Captain Holland concluded.

Mr. Andrew McKinney

During the Great Nassau Hurricane of 1926, there was a man by the name of Mr. P.C. Cavill who was a former long-distance swimmer. He was the first person to swim the English Channel in record time. He unofficially broke the record but when he got to the coast of England, the weather was so unsettled, and the seas were so rough that he had to be taken on the shore without ever touching land, a requirement that was needed to have the record be made official. Mr. Cavill lived in Australia with his family before migrating to The Bahamas. In Australia, his family had a large swimming pool in their yard. On a regular basis, they had several children come over to play and to use the pool. As boys, they would compete while swimming in the pool but Mr. P.C. Cavill always swam faster than the other boys. His family kept wondering how was it that he was able to swim much faster than the others getting from one end of the pool to the next. Upon further investigation, then they noticed that when he swam, he would swim with his legs going up and down and rather than from side to side as it was common to do in those days.

Over time, he and his family perfected this move and it became patented and known worldwide as the 'Australian Crawl' and today it is now referred to as, 'the American' or 'Australian Crawl.' Today, this method is used in international swimming competitions throughout the world. This unique way of swimming came in quite handy in 1926. Mr. Cavill lived on an island near the Southern Bight in Andros. During the Great Nassau Hurricane of 1926, this island became inundated with flood waters from the storm. As a result, he had to swim across the creek to get to dry land and before that he was forced to climb to the top of a pine tree for three days until the flood waters subsided. He was indeed lucky because 9 other persons drowned in this storm trying the same fate of trying to swim across the same creek to get to the mainland.

Sir Clifford Darling

The former Governor General of The Bahamas Sir Clifford Darling was four years old at the time the Great Nassau Hurricane of 1926 hit The Bahamas and remembers this storm very well. I was living in the settlement of Chester's on the island of Acklins. At the time, there were no weather reports or weather office to warn us or anybody about an approaching storm. The Family Island Commissioner of Acklins had a barometer, and whenever he saw the pressure reading starting to drop significantly, he would go about informing the residents throughout the settlements to take the necessary precautions for an approaching storm. This was a difficult task because sometimes it was difficult to distinguish the pressure drop between a severe weather event such as a thunderstorm or a hurricane passing over the island. Fortunately, in Nassau, some of the residents knew when a storm was approaching the island from a man by the name of Mr. Cambridge, who would go and put a hurricane flag on top of the hill on Fort Fincastle to warn the residents of this approaching storm.

When the Nassau Hurricane of 1926 hit the island of Acklins, my uncles were busy working on the island of San Salvador in the wreckage and salvaging industry, meanwhile, my father was working in Florida, picking fruits and vegetables. In Acklins, several ships were wrecked with various supplies during the storm with a significant number of valuable goods such as candy, ropes, flour, rice, lumber, sugar, and the locals made good use of these shipwrecked goods in their homes and gave others away to persons in other settlements. When the residents of my settlement in Chester's found out that this hurricane was approaching Acklins, we immediately started making our way from our various homes to get to higher ground on the hills. Unfortunately, the hurricane arrived before we were able to reach our destination, so we were forced to ride out the storm in the open wilderness. I was so afraid as a little boy by the heavy rainfall and the loud and powerful winds of the storm and my brother noticed this and so he took me and placed me in a canvas bag with just my head hanging out of the bag as we made our way to the hills. My other brother took my little sister and placed her in a similar bag and placed her on his back also with only her head hanging out of the bag. After the storm subsided a bit, we went to my cousin's house which was the only one left standing where we rode out the remainder of the storm.

When we got back home after the hurricane had passed, we found out that the storm blew the roof off our house. My brother turned the roof right side up and then cut a hole in the roof. We were forced to live in that roof for about 2 to 3 weeks until my father was able to come home from working on the farms in Florida to build them a new house. Unfortunately, four of my uncles drowned in this storm when they left San Salvador to return to Acklins in a sailing boat, but they were caught in the storm. After this hurricane, Acklins became a hurricane-ravaged barren wasteland, because there was total devastation everywhere as far as the eyes could see. The hurricane demolished almost all the homes on the island and sunk every ship at sea, and the death toll was unbearably high. Several sloops were caught travelling from Acklins to Nassau but were forced to stop in Long Island or the Exuma Cays to seek shelter from the storm. The journey from Acklins to Nassau by boat often took quite a long time and sometimes as much as a month by sailboat depending on the prevailing weather and wind conditions.

Mrs. Viola Collie

I was 10 years old at the time and recalled experiencing the Great Nassau Hurricane of 1926 living on the coast in the settlement of Mason's Bay, Acklins. During this era, we had no knowledge that a hurricane was travelling other than when the weather showed up and destroyed our homes. Unfortunately, we had no radios or barometers to give us any kind of advanced warnings of an approaching hurricane. When we began to feel the initial effects of the hurricane, my grandfather Moses Kemp and my auntie came to ride out the storm in our house because they felt our house was much sturdier than their respective homes and felt they stood a better chance of surviving the storm in that house which was also relatively new. During the storm, the roof of the house blew off and landed over 300 feet away and suddenly the water came rushing into our house. At this point, my sister Wilda had some large boulders fell on top of her and several of the boulders had her feet trapped for quite a while before my grandfather was able to free her feet.

The surge of the storm was at least 20 feet high and we had to swim to get out of the way of the flood waters. Unfortunately, two of my sisters were not so lucky because they drowned in the storm surge. My two sisters who died were, Melvern who was 3 years old and Julia, who was 3 months old. As a matter of fact, Julia was supposed to be christened on the same day the hurricane struck and was already dressed in her new christening clothes and she was washed away out of my aunt's hands. My grandfather later found her body drifting in the floodwaters and took my sister's dead lifeless body and wrapped her up in this dress and he held onto her and stayed with the body until the morning after the storm had passed. My baby sister was later buried in the same Christening clothes because all the other clothes we had were washed away by the storm.

After the hurricane, there was widespread devastation and many deaths throughout the island of Acklins, especially in the low-lying areas and the areas that were near to the sea. There were so many dead bodies lying around that they had to bury them in mass graves rather than individually. In fact, during the storm, many bodies were washed out to sea never to be seen again to be given a proper burial. I can recall our neighbour Mr. Ferguson, had just recently returned to Acklins a day before the storm struck Acklins from Florida working on the farms there picking fruits and vegetables. Sadly, he lost both his wife and his son in this storm. On his return, he had just bought a new roll of cloth fabric from Florida to sew some new dresses and pants for his wife and son. The strong winds from the hurricane blew away the entire roll of cloth and scattered it all throughout their yard. Their deaths affected him so much that he would often go by their graves and cry for hours for years after the storm.

After the storm, my family and I had to live in one of our neighbour's house for months until our new house was rebuilt. Furthermore, my father who was in Florida at the time of the hurricane working on the farms picking fruits and vegetables came home and built us a new house at the same location where the previous one was destroyed. Today, the ruins of that old house next to our new house are still there. I will always remember the Great Nassau Hurricane of 1926 for as long as I live, and to ensure that the memory of this storm will never be forgotten. I made sure and related the experiences with this hurricane to my children and I asked them to pass on this story to future generations of their children.

Mr. Conrad Knowles

The late Mr. Knowles, the former chairman of the Bahamas Licensing Authority Board stated that he encountered the Great Nassau Hurricane of 1926 living in the settlement of Braddox's, Long Island. This is a small settlement located between McKann's and Thompson's Bay. My father's home was located near the sea about 300 yards on the water's edge. My father was named Timothy Knowles and my mother was Rebecca Knowles. He was a boat captain who took farm produce and sea produce from Long Island to be sold in the markets in Nassau. In return to Long Island, he took back with him groceries and other manufactured goods. This hurricane had a traumatic effect on my life. Back then, we lived in an era when we lacked the ability to know when a hurricane was approaching Long Island, nor did we track these storms due to lack of advanced technology like satellites and radars or even radios. We did have the local knowledge of looking at the clouds and weather patterns but even with those knowledge, we still lacked the ability to know with definite certainty that we will be impacted by a storm or what intensity it will be when it struck Long Island.

Whenever a hurricane was approaching, my father and others had a 'six sense' so to speak by watching the waters and looking at the clouds which would move much faster than normal. Furthermore, they knew that the storm was approaching by the roaring of the waters coming into their respective yards near the water. Just before the onset of this hurricane, the water started to come into the house and my father immediately grabbed and placed me on the partition while him and my mother gathered some clothing and foodstuff he felt they would need after they evacuated the house and sought shelter elsewhere. When the first set of waves from the storm surge crashed against the house and realizing the urgency to leave the house immediately, my father grabbed me and placed me on his shoulders as we all left. At this point, I became very afraid and held onto my father's neck very tightly so as not to fall off. As I was looking back at the house as we were leaving, I saw the roof of the house being blown off, the house being engulfed with water and the waters starting to break the walls apart.

My father then took me, my mom, my two sisters Chalotilda and Ida and my brother George on the top of a hill in the bushes to shelter from the storm. We said they stayed there exposed to the torrents of the heavy rainfall and strong winds all evening and all night until the following morning. The next morning, we went to the public-school house in McKann's where the families of that settlement had gathered after the hurricane destroyed their homes. We made that schoolhouse our home for about three months after the storm because my dad had to rebuild his home from scratch. However, my father never rebuilt his home at the original location but at a new location in the settlement of McKann's because of the bad memories associated with that storm. This newly built home is still standing in that settlement even though it has weathered many storms after the Great Nassau Hurricane of 1926.

A significant number of persons drowned on the island and the storm destroyed all the farms and most of the homes on Long Island. For example, one of them I vividly remembered was a lady by the name of Mrs. Bowe from the settlement of Thompson's Bay. She was swept away by the storm surge and her house was destroyed. She was found dead the next day with her hair wrapped around the trunk of a tree. During the storm, the water went out of the bay exposing the sand and many fish were caught surprised on dry land. We survived on by eating some of these fish and the remainder we threw away because there were so many it was impossible for us to eat all of them. Several animals like sheep and goats were also killed in this storm.

In 1926, most of the Long Island residents of were either subsistence farmers, fishermen or sponger men. After this storm, all these occupations were hampered in one way or the other. The late Sir Albert Miller, former Chairman of Bahamas Port Authority and I are two cousins (he and I are two sisters' children) and his mother who is my aunt had reason to come to Nassau to seek emergency medical attention at the hospital in Nassau. They were caught in the same hurricane and had to seek refuge on one of the cays in the Exumas and miraculously they all survived on that cay during this very intense hurricane. I admonish people not to take hurricane warnings lightly because in my era of growing up on the Family Islands we didn't have that luxury so they should appreciate the warnings of today.

Mr. Floyd Lowe

I was twelve when the most destructive hurricane in living memory hit Green Turtle Cay. Three of my brothers had gone fishing at Carters Cay, about 40 miles north of Green Turtle Cay, and should have been back in three days. The only sign of an approaching hurricane we had then was a drop in the barometer. When this happened, we were worried about my brothers. The hurricane struck on Monday, September 5, 1932, and lasted for three days. The people of New Plymouth tried to ride the storm out in their houses, but the water rose and flooded the town and forced them to evacuate to higher ground. The wind was so fierce that it destroyed every church and most of the houses.

Several persons lost their lives in the hurricane of 1932. My eldest brother Basil lost two sons, one sixteen and the other two. The sixteen-year-old died of a broken neck while carrying the two-year-old to a safer place after their house blew down. The doctor determined that the two-year-old died from exposure in the arms of his dead brother. I can also remember a sixty-five-year-old man and a six-year-old child being killed in the storm. The good news was that my brothers had ridden out the hurricane in Carters Cay and returned home safely."

H.E. Arthur D. Hanna

The former Governor General and Deputy Prime Minister of The Bahamas said that the 1929 Hurricane was a very powerful storm and that many persons died in this storm. I experienced several storms while growing up as a boy in The Bight on the island of Acklins. Among them was a powerful hurricane in 1936, where I saw the water going out of the harbour, leaving all the boats stranded and laying on the sand. By midday, a few hours later, the water came rushing back onto the land. Growing up on Acklins, we were not as fortunate as the people of today to get advanced storm warnings, with all the sophisticated weather equipment that the meteorologists use nowadays.

To make matters worse, no one on Acklins had a radio to give them any advanced warnings. During my childhood years, we had three ways in which to determine when a hurricane was travelling or approaching Acklins. The first was the use of a barometer, and all seamen had a trusty barometer on their ships, and they would never leave the shore without it. They would watch the barometer at sea, and if there was a steep drop in pressure, these seamen would immediately make their way back to shore and prepare for a hurricane.

Second, they knew a storm was approaching Acklins was by watching the movement and types of clouds ahead of the hurricane. Most residents didn't know the names of the clouds, but they certainly knew the types of clouds associated with a hurricane. Finally, they knew a storm was approaching Acklins was by watching the behavior of seagulls and other seabirds. Just before the onset of a hurricane, these birds always flew in from out at sea in large flocks and made their way onto the mainland in search of a safe resting area. Armed with this information, we would start the process of battening down our houses. Strangely enough, after the storm passage over the island, the birds would make their way back out to sea, unharmed.

Mr. Rupert Roberts Jr.

Mr. Roberts, the President of Super Value Food Stores, recalled that his Father Mr. Rupert Roberts Sr. and his mother Mrs. Miriam Roberts often spoke vividly about these terrible and powerful storms in 1926, while he was growing up as a boy in the settlement of Marsh Harbour, Abaco. In 1926 my father lived on the coast in Marsh Harbour in a house with rolling pins. During the Great Nassau Hurricane of 1926, as my father was preparing for the storm, he placed my young Aunt Winifred on the bed and in his excitement in preparing for this storm; he took a heavy suitcase filled with clothes and threw it on top of my Aunt Winifred by accident while she was lying on the bed. Fortunately, she was not injured but had quite a story to tell her friends and family members for years to follow the storm had passed.

When the storm was over, my father tried to open the door but to his amazement, it was stuck and was not able to get out, so he tried to open one of the windows in the house but again to surprise it was also stuck and was not able to open it either. To get out of the house, he had to break down the back door. His initial assessment after observing pine trees everywhere was that the Pine Barrens had come out to them in the settlement. However, the entire house had moved and travelled all the way into the Pine Barrens quite a distance from where we were initially located in Marsh Harbour. The noise from the storm was so loud that none of us in the house realized that the house had moved off its rolling pins quite some distance from where we were initially located. My Aunt Winifred distinctly remembered that when my dad took us to the back steps of the house to get out, the water from the storm was so deep that it was up to his neck. After the storm, a search party was assembled and went looking for us, fearing the worse for us, but fortunately, we were all okay. Coming out of the Pine Barrens, we saw that many of the pine trees were broken off by the house during its movement into the Pine Barrens. I recalled that in the settlement of Marsh Harbour, August Van Ryn's baby girl Pearl Eleanor Van Ryn died when she was washed out of his arms by the storm surge.

Mr. Chester Thompson

At the time of the Great Nassau Hurricane of 1926, my mother, Lena was seven months pregnant and patiently awaiting my birth. My parents lived in a one-story cottage in the up-a-long area of Hope Town, Abaco, on a gentle hill overlooking other houses to the north. My father Maurice, a sea captain, had just returned from a voyage to Cuba. Three older brothers of six, four and two, Hartis, Leonard and Roscoe, always underfoot and hungry, kept my mother quite busy. They were housebound by intermittent showers from low scudding clouds, driven by increasing winds from the northeast. Earlier, my father had spotted two frigate birds (or often called the "hurricane bird" by many of the Family Island residents) flying near the ground-a sure sign that there was an approaching hurricane he said. He reminded my mother of an ancient mariners' portent "Frigatebirds fly low it's going to blow." The barometer was falling, and he was thankful that his ship, the *Alma R.*, had been secured into the harbour and was safely at a hurricane mooring. Muffled sounds of hammering were heard as the neighbours battened down their houses.

My mother sat awkwardly in a rocking chair, cradling her swollen stomach, frightened by increasing gusts of winds. Darkness came quickly. Kerosene lanterns were lit, and the boys tucked themselves into makeshift beds, on the floor. "I don't feel right" moaned my mother "I believe the baby's coming." My father was worried. Aunt Louisa, the midwife, lived at the far end of the village, its narrow streets now made dangerous by wind-driven coconuts, tree branches, and other debris. The house creaked in every joint as blasts of wind, like the judgment of the Lord, battered the house.

A single lantern dimly lighted the room. My father crouched near my mother whispering encouragement but aware that their lives were in danger. The boys, who lay just beside them, whimpered and clung to each other. Suddenly there was an almighty crash from the attic. A wind-blown object had shattered the dormer window, and wind came shrieking down the stairs. My parents fell to the floor, their bodies protecting the boys. Flurries of rain and salt spray swept in from the ocean and water poured down from the attic, drenching the floor. "The roof will go soon," shouted my father, "I'll take you to Ben Russell's house." "No, no," screamed my mother. "Take the boys first." My father crept and hugged the ground for fear of being blown away, wriggled under some sea grape branches, with my brothers held onto him—clinging onto him like terrified monkeys. Occasional gusts pinned them to the ground. Sheets of salty rain, driven horizontally, drenched them to the skin. Aided by frequent lightning flashes, my father made his way to the lee side of Ben Russell's house. Banging on the door, he thrust the boys into Ben Russell's arms and shouted, "I'm going for Lena, the baby's coming."

When I was eighteen, my mother told me, what happened back then. The edges of her memory were blurred by time, and she was hesitant to relate the physical details of birth to a teenage son. With the boys on the way to safety, she felt a great relief, which turned to terror as the house moved on its foundations and a portion of the roof blew away. Her labour pains were increasing in frequency. She remembered my father's wet body and his strength as they tried to reach Ben Russell's house. Halfway there they sheltered under the low spreading branches of a giant sea grape tree where they found Ben Russell on his way to help. During the storm and under that sea grape tree I was born. The two men carried my mother and baby to Ben Russell's house. There Ceva Russell and her sister took charge. Faced with the ageless drama of birth they forgot their fear of the hurricane. Calmly and competently, they made my mother comfortable and brought the baby to her. Overcome with emotion; my mother burst into tears. She told me years later: "You were a scrawny, tiny thing and I thought you wouldn't live. But you were whimpering and waving your matchstick arms and leg around. Mr. Russell weighed you on his fish scale, and you were only three pounds."

As the eye of the hurricane passed directly over Elbow Cay, its savagery gave way to an unearthly calm. There was feverish activity in both assessing the damage and reinforcing doors and windows on what had been the lee side. It was known that, when the eye passed through, the wind would blow from the opposite direction. In about an hour the wind increased, with violent gusts and driving rain. As dawn came reluctantly, the hurricane was raging at its former force. Squalls came sweeping over at shorter intervals. The crashing of wind-blown debris punctuated the wind's eerie shrieking. The women became hysterical and prayed to God for help. Mr. Russell's father started singing 'We Shall Meet in the Sweet By and By' but was told to be quiet.

Suddenly, there was a splintering crash from the roof as if the sky and the earth had come together. Water poured in torrents into the living room sending everyone scurrying to the bedroom. When there was a lull, Mr. Russell, clinging to the ground, made his way to the adjoining house. He returned to say that the roof was undamaged, and we would be welcomed there. My father wrapped me in flannel, pushed my feet first into a quart measure and ran crouching through the storm, dodging around piles of wreckage. My mother followed, assisted by Mr. Russell. A dry place was found for her to lie down with her baby. "You were hungry," she told me, "and you've never lost your appetite." During the morning the wind moderated to a strong gale, and by afternoon the danger had passed.

Like animals hesitantly leaving their lairs, people emerged dazed and disoriented from their damaged houses. The devastation was so widespread that women cried, and men were speechless. Litters of broken timbers and uprooted trees covered the village street. Many houses had disappeared. My father told me years later "It was a miracle of cooperation. Families without homes were given temporary housing by the more fortunate. Everyone, even children, helped in re-building." We returned to our house where an old sail was used to make a temporary cover for the hole in the roof. To my mother's relief, the kitchen building was undamaged, and the daily routine of cooking for four boys could continue. With the help of his crew, all repairs were completed before my father left on the next voyage.

Mr. August Van Ryn

There were several severe hurricanes in 1926. The first one was in July which greatly affected the city of Nassau and surrounding places. It also struck some of the vessels engaged in the sponging and fishing trades. Some of the men saved earlier that year were lost in that July storm. The next violent storm struck the United States, especially between Miami and West Palm Beach and it did a lot of damage. And the third one that affected us so hit the island of Abaco, where we lived; especially the town of Marsh Harbour, accompanied by a fearful tidal wave which did nearly all the damage. We must tell you a little of our experience in connection with the storm.

We had had beautiful weather in October, as usual in those islands. The night before everything broke loose it was a lovely, balmy evening. We had some friends staying with us, and as we looked at the beautiful full moon and felt the gentle ocean breeze, we said to each other, "There will certainly be no hurricane tonight." For the report had come somehow that a hurricane was on its way to us. So, we went to bed but were awakened around midnight by the roaring of the wind, when the violence began to smash the town. The velocity of the wind increased till it blew close to 200 miles an hour, as we learned later. Our house stood firm (I had built it myself and knew it was solid and well-founded as were near all the homes in the town). Those folks were accustomed to hurricanes, and as the gale increased that night it drove the heavy rain through the roof, and it soaked through the upstairs floor and into the rooms downstairs, and I spent part of the night trying to dry things out a little. But the house stood.

Then, about 7 o'clock in the morning there fell a complete calm. It was an eerie sensation-this perfect calm seconds after the raging winds. So, I said to my father-in-law, who had lived in the islands all his life, "What does this sudden calm mean?" And he said, "It means that we are in the exact center-the eye of the hurricane. The storm is moving ahead at the rate of 15 miles per hour or so, and in a short time the winds will come again, and they will come from the opposite direction." Then I said to him, "Well, if the gale comes again it will come from the ocean this time (for until then it had been blowing from the land side); won't it bring the sea along with it?" "Oh no," he replied.

"We have never seen a tidal wave, but he (and we too that day) saw and felt one that morning. Our house stood very close to the water-not to the ocean itself, but to inland waters with direct access to the ocean in the distance some five miles away. It is from there-from the Atlantic-that the storm surge came and drove its furious course in till it reached our town. There was about half an hour of this curious calm, and then the sea drove in-at first a solid wall of water about six feet high. It smashed against our house; drove in the front door and windows and broke away an addition to the house I had recently built. Now the water stood about two or three feet high in our living room. It was too deep for us with our small children to remain there; so, we stood together on the stairs that led to the second floor. There we were with our four little children, not knowing what to do; but we could and did pray. Our oldest girl was then seven years old, the next one, a boy, about four and one half, then a little girl two and a half, and the baby, about five months old. I had grabbed the baby out of the arms of a young lady who was staying with us at the time, while the other three children stood between us. And then, in a few minutes more the storm surge rolled in. We could hear its fearful roar before we could see it; it was a solid wall of water rising about twenty feet high. When my wife and I saw it bearing down on us and our home, we kissed each other, and I said to her, "Goodbye darling, we'll see each other in the glory."

"That's all we expected at that moment; it did not seem possible that any one of us could escape death. The storm surge struck the house and smashed it to smithereens. I went through the glass window on the stairway by which we stood, for my left leg had great big cuts on it. The next thing I knew I came to my senses lying on a piece of wreckage. I had been knocked unconscious and had lost our dear baby. When I came to, I saw my wife in the raging waters further inland, with the three small children clinging to her and her to them. My wife held onto the wreckage of houses and boats that had floated all around. Praise God; they were all still alive and unhurt. So, I dropped off the side of a house. I was lying on and let the sea, driven by the violent winds, carry me down her way till after a while we managed to be together.

"Then, between us, we sheltered the children as best as we could. It is amazing how easy children take things in their stride. So long as we were with them, they did not panic in the least. It later struck me as quite a lesson of how we should trust in our heavenly Father. I prayed aloud, while we were banged around, that it might please, God to spare us and we thanked Him for the wonderful way He kept us till then. I prayed it might be His will to bring us safely through this ordeal. I had hardly done so when a roof of a house washed by us. The rafters of the second floor were bare and visible, so I hoisted the children one by one and made them lie flat on those rafters, keeping them out of the way of the junk flying about. Since there was less danger of drowning now, we all felt a little safer. And so, our oldest girl, our seven-year-old, Lorraine, spoke up and said, "Daddy, pray again, the Lord heard us that time." A little while after Elliot, the almost five-year-old one, while we were still in real danger, said, "Daddy, where are you going to put the house next time?" Kids don't get discouraged very quickly.

When we got under the roof of this broken up house, I noticed how badly my upper left leg was cut; it was bleeding profusely; it was likely due to the heavy bleeding that I had lost consciousness at first. So, my wife tore off her underskirt and tied it as tightly as possible above the wound to try and stop the loss of blood, later it took 38 stitches to close the cuts. After a while, the strong gale drove the wreckage we clung onto the dry land, and the roof settled down at a steep angle against the hillside and other wreckage.

While we were caught and jammed underneath this wreckage, unable to get out, the tidal wave kept rising, and we had to move from the lower end of the roof all the way to the higher end to keep our heads and the children's above the water. Eventually, the water rose so high that we had to lift the heads of the youngsters right against the roof of the place and it began to look as if the water would drown us right there. And then, at the extreme moment, there was a terrific crash, and the upstairs of my father-in-law's house crashed on to the roof we were under, with my wife's mother in it. This broke our roof and enabled us to crawl on the top of it. Then we could see why the water had risen and had made us move to the upper end. Had we remained at the lower end where we first sat, we would have been crushed to death. As for the house above us, it crumbled along with the roof we were taking shelter under during the storm. With amazement and joy, we realized that very morning our God had twice saved us from death. The first from the sea, and now on the land. Oh! How we praised His glorious Name-then and ever afterward.

There was not even a bruise on the bodies of our dear children, but my wife and I were covered with them from head to toe. We had kept the children between us to save them from harm. We are not saying this in pride, but in humble gratitude to God. After a while, as is well known, those storm surges go back where they came from in a strong undertow, and so did this one. It carried every bit of our property with it; we never saw the smallest piece of it again. I built the house, spent many weeks remodeling it and enlarging it, and the whole thing went in fifteen seconds.

A good deal of the town was destroyed in the storm and storm surge. The houses close to the shore were all smashed, and those further back were damaged, or some drifted away, carried away by the sea. There were not many lives lost; just two or three, I believe. The reason for this was that many felt that their homes might not stand the force of the winds, so they had left them and had gone further back into the hills; while others found shelter in the strongly built schoolhouse which stood some distance in from the shore. So, we were thankful for not much loss of life, but there was a great deal of property loss.

We later on learned to our great joy that, while there were quite a number of sailing vessels broken up, as well as a very large three-masted sailing vessel which was driven high up on the rocks by the waves, our boat-*The Evangel* was the only vessel which came through it all without any damage; most of the others were injured or driven on the rocks. The anchors of our yacht held it secure which was indeed another great mercy from our God; we could also use it immediately to get needed help, food, supplies, etc.

As I said before, the Lord gave us four dear children before the hurricane; we lost our little baby-Pearl Eleanor in the storm-who has gone ahead of us, and we believe we shall see her again in the glory by and by. That left us three children and then, about a year later God gave us another boy, Carroll, in place of the one who had left us for brighter scenes. So now we again have four children-two boys and two girls. We built another house with the materials which the government provided to those who had been stricken by the storm.

Cleo Deveaux Dean

Mrs. Dean, who now lives in the settlement of Kemp's Bay, South Andros, said that she was a child at the time the Great Andros Hurricane of 1929. I can recall quite a number of details about this storm. What made this storm so dangerous was the fact that it lasted for three days and three nights. This country never had a storm like that before and has never had a storm of this magnitude since. For that, I can thank God that we never saw a storm like this again because this country can't take another storm of this magnitude again. The community of South Andros and Mangrove Cay had quite a number of boats went down in this storm. One of the boats that went down in this storm was a boat called *'The Electric'*, which went down in the vicinity of Cay Lobos and was never heard from again. My auntie's son and several other crew members went down with this boat in this storm. Some of the crew members I can recall were George Johnson and a man by the name of Alfred; the others I can't remember. The Lighthouse Keepers on Cay Lobos reported that they saw when the storm carried the boat out to sea in the east but were helpless to rescue them.

I can also recall that my father had a dinghy boat which was called *'The AC'*, and it was named after my youngest sister. After the hurricane left Andros, there was water everywhere (up to 20 feet in some instances), and my dad had to use the boat to rescue people out of their homes and take them to dry land. The Catholic Church came to Andros in the late 1920's, and at the time they held church services in the home of a man by the name of John Rolle, here in Kemp's Bay. Unfortunately, this hurricane destroyed his house, so they had to move into Mrs. Ellen Forbes' home to have church services for several months after the storm.

When the storm initially started to really blow hard, there was like a loud noise like a train, and it was then that I kept shouting repeatedly, "Lord, I am in your care!" The water came and flooded the entire community, and my father's house was totally flooded up to its roof. After this storm, the western and eastern shores of Andros were joined because of the great amount of water that was on the land. The winds were so strong that a large grape tree fell between our house and the well. In the settlement there was only one road, which was called the Bay Road. After the storm, the elders in the settlement had to find another route to our homes because the hurricane had eroded and washed away the original road. The Commissioner for the island of Andros was a man by the name of Mr. Elgin Forsyth, who was stationed in Mangrove Cay. After the storm, he came over to South Andros and gave many of the residents' food, clothing and seeds to replant on their farms. After the storm, many of the residents in South Andros were near starvation because the storm destroyed everything they had, including their farms and livestock, which they greatly depended upon for survival.

Most residents had to start life all over again because nothing was left after the storm. I can distinctly recall that during the lull of the storm, me and many of the neighborhood kids became very curious about the storm and ventured outside to look at the storm damage. One of the things we saw during the storm was a coconut tree falling on top of a man's house by the name of Mr. Thomas, destroying it. Also, another coconut tree fell on the neighbor's John Forbes' house. The vessel *'The Pretoria'* went down in this storm, and all of the persons on board drowned, with the exception of the captain and two crew members. They survived by clinging onto a hog, which was being taken to Andros by the captain to start a pig farm. In addition to the three vessels Blind Blake sang about in his popular tune *'Run Come See Jerusalem'*, there were two other vessels which went down in this storm, and they were *'The Bright Eyes'* and *'The Andros.'*

Francita Rolle

I can recall living in the settlement of The Bluff, South Andros, during the 1929 Hurricane. During the hurricane, I stayed with my family in a cave called 'Lumbo Hole.' We stayed in this sheltered cave for 3 to 4 days with about 100 other persons. This group comprised mostly of women and children because most of the men were out at sea on a sponging trip in the area of the Mud and the southern tip of South Andros. In this cave along with me were my mother Sarah Rolle, my sister Elizabeth Rolle, Token Lewis, Verna Stubbs, Dick Solomon, Simeon Davis, Florence Rolle and her Family, Kita Johnson and many more persons. Simeon Davis, who was the pastor of Friendship Native Baptist Church in the Bluff, held church services in the cave for the three to four days we stayed in this cave. Throughout the storm, we sang spiritual hymns and prayed and asked God for His divine protection. For three days, we cooked in this cave and were able to grind corn and eat corn grits. When we got out of the cave, we were surprised to find out that most of the houses in the settlement were destroyed and there were floodwaters everywhere. There was so much water on the land that the two seas of the western and eastern shores of Andros were joined. After the storm, Commissioner Elgin Forsyth came and gave many of the residents food, clothing and seeds to replant their farms because all of their crops were destroyed by the hurricane.

My father, Prince *'Par-Warthy'* Rolle, told me how he was able to survive in this storm by clinging onto a dog by the name of *'Speak Your Mind.'* The storm blew the schooner *'The Repeat'* out to sea, and my father along with others were forced to swim back to the mainland. He said initially the dog kept swimming around him while they were swimming into the land. He became very tired, and he then grabbed the dog by its tail. He held onto the dog's back and held onto that dog for his dear life because he realized that if he ever let that dog go, he would surely drown. The dog swam him into the shore. When he got to the shore, the dog caught a crab, and he ate the body of the crab and gave the back of the crab to the dog, and that was how they were able to survive. My uncle Lewis drowned trying to swim to the shore. Furthermore, a man by the name of Simeon Davis, who had a son named Josh Davis, also drowned in this storm. Two other men named James Smith and Sam Black also drowned trying to swim from one cay to the next during this storm. There were also 2 men from the settlement of Smith's Hill who drowned in this storm, and if my memory serves me correct, a lady named Missy also died in the storm.

Before the storm, my father and other crew members were onboard the schooner *'The Repeat'*, playing checkers, cooking, eating dumpling soup and pancakes. However, unknown to them the barometer indicator got stuck while they were in the vicinity of Grassy Creek in South Andros. Unfortunately, they were unable to get a precise or accurate reading after this occurred, and so they had to try and get back to the mainland when they realized a storm was travelling. It was doing this time that some of the men drowned when they tried to swim from Beach Cay to the Andros mainland. Fortunately, the surviving crew members were able to survive when they swam back to the shore. They came ashore at a lady name Arfee's, who lived in the settlement of Hawk's Nest. She cooked a hot meal for them and gave them some clothing to wear because they were starving and naked. Their clothing went out to sea on *'The Repeat'* during the storm. In fact, Arfee gave my dad a dress to wear because that was all she had, and he gladly took the dress and was happy to put it on because he had nothing to wear.

Ruben Green

In 1929, most people in Andros simply referred to this deadly storm as the '*1929 Gale.*' I was 11 years old at the time when this storm hit Andros. I recalled a boat by the name of the '*The Repeat*', which went down in this storm. This boat was owned by Hardy McKinney, and they were on a sponging trip in the area of the southern tip of Andros. The storm caught them by surprise on this sponging trip because their barometer, which they had on their boat, somehow was broken so it was not able to provide the crew with an accurate reading. Because the storm caught them by surprise, they were forced to swim from Beach Cay back to the Andros mainland. While they were swimming back to the land, a number of the men drowned. After the weather subsided, a search team was organized and went back up to the Grassy Creek and Beach Cay areas to look for the dead bodies. They found their bodies scattered several hundred feet inland at Grassy Creek. They brought the bodies back to the Andros mainland and put them all in a large dinghy boat and buried them in that boat in a mass grave in St Andrew's Cemetery.

What was usual about this incident I recalled was that after the hurricane, the top mass of '*The Repeat*' drifted all the way down to the settlement of McKinney Hill, directly in the front of the boat's Captain Hardy McKinney's house. After the storm, there was devastation everywhere, and most of the roofs of the houses were blown off. Most of the roofs were made of straw, so they simply had to go out and gather new straw and replaced the old ones with the new ones. This hurricane destroyed most of the farms, so to survive everyone had to go out and pick up coconuts that the hurricane had blown off the trees. One thing that I will always remember was the fact that all the trees were wiped out. All the leaves were blown off the remaining trees, and the entire settlement looked as if it had been burned by fire. In fact, during the storm I saw the top of a coconut tree flying through the air like a bird.

There were several ways that residents of Andros knew a hurricane was travelling. The first was by the Family Island Commissioner and the police who went about informing residents that a storm was approaching the island and that they should make preparations for a storm. Another way was by watching the rising sea-level; most persons could look at this rising sea level before the storm and saw that a storm was travelling. Another way they could tell a storm was approaching was by watching the clouds and their movements. Finally, most experienced navigators could look at the sea bottom and tell if there was a storm travelling. Once we realized that a hurricane was approaching the Andros mainland, we would go out and immediately tie the house down with a strong rope and batten down the house.

I can recall that in the Settlement of Red Bays, North Andros, several persons died in the storm when they were washed away from their homes and boats, never to be seen again. As a memorial to the ones who had died in this storm, they erected three large crosses at the entrance of the settlement. This was the worst storm to ever hit this country, and I hope that there will never be another storm like this one ever again.

Jerry Gibson

(Mr. Gibson is my grandfather, and I can vividly recall growing up in South Andros how he and my grandmother, the late Joanna Gibson, frequently talked about this storm and its significant impact on the island of Andros). At the time of this storm, I was living in the Bluff, South Andros. During the storm, God kept us safe in the midst of a tremendous disaster. This was a very powerful storm. It was a rare storm and was one of the only times I could recall where the two seas on the western and eastern shores of Andros met because of massive amounts of water that the hurricane dumped over Andros. This storm lasted for three long, grueling days. Many areas were flooded with some four feet of water for several days after the storm. Our family home was blown down, and we were forced to seek shelter in a neighbor's house to weather the remainder of the storm. When the eye passed over South Andros, the men went into the farms to salvage as many crops as they could. I can remember my father returning in waist-high water with cassava, corn and sweet potatoes in his bag. But others were caught in the storm and drowned before they could get back to the safety of their homes. The family's hogs and dogs were kept in the house with us during the storm, and afterwards my father wouldn't let anyone go out because the water was everywhere. Somehow, curiosity got the better part of us because we sneaked out to look at the damage, which was shocking. My grandfather was the first person to tell me the story about the courageous act of the dog 'Speak Your Mind,' which we will hear about later.

Florence Stubbs-Rolle

Mrs. Rolle still lives in the Bluff, South Andros. This was a powerful and massive storm, and I can recall this storm as if it was yesterday. When my family and others heard that this storm was approaching Andros, we went and hid in a cave at the back of our yard called Lumbo Hole. There were more than 30 people with us in the cave, and we brought all of our belongings in the cave with us out of the fear that they would be destroyed in the hurricane. I recalled securing the family's corn mill in the cave. Most of the men from the settlement were not present, as they were busy on a sponging trip to an area called Bulla Hill, at the extreme southern end of the island. This storm was so large that it made that the two seas on the western and eastern shores of Andros meet inland, and many persons drowned as a result. Among the names I remembered were Bulla Lewis and Sam Black. When my family and other persons came out of Lumbo Hole after three days, there were floodwaters everywhere. All of the cassava and potatoes were destroyed. We made molasses syrup from the destroyed sugar cane and used it to sweeten tea and bread. Despite the difficulties, I consider this time of my life as the 'good ole days.'

Dan Rahming

I can distinctly remember the Great Hurricane of 1929. During the storm, I along with other spongers went up to Grassy Creek for a sponging trip. The sponging trip started while we were sailing on the schooner 'The Repeat', which was captained by Mr. Hardy McKinney from the settlement of The Bluff, South Andros. I could tell that a hurricane was approaching by the use of the ship's barometer when the pressure started rapidly falling and the hand indicator was pointing to a hurricane on the dial. We also sensed that a storm was approaching because the seas were beginning to get very rough. It was at this time that the captain told us that it was time to head back to the shore. We went into Grassy Creek and anchored the schooner 'The Repeat' in the harbour at Grassy Creek. We then took the sponges off the schooner and the dinghy boats and put them in the kraals. While we were at Grassy Creek, the schooner 'The Repeat' drifted out of the harbour, breaking away from the anchor holding her and going out to sea with the dinghy boats in tow. So, after this unfortunate turn of events we decided to swim to the nearest cay called Beach Cay to get back to the mainland. Several of the men drowned in this attempt to get back home, including a man named James Smith. I only survived because I was with a strong swimmer named Ditmus Dames, who the locals affectionally referred to as 'Ba-Did.' After the storm, vessels that were not damaged were able to rescue us from Beach Cay. When we got to our settlement of the Bluff, we were surprised to find out that many of the houses were destroyed and the entire settlement was flooded. To make matters worse, the two seas on the western and eastern sides of the island had joined together during the storm.

Illford Forbes

I lived in the settlement of High Rock, South Andros, and was a sponge fisherman on the schooner *'The Repeat.'* I can recall trying to take shelter from the approaching storm at Grassy Creek, on the southern tip of South Andros. However, we couldn't get the vessel as far into the creek as we would have liked, so we put five anchors down on the sea bottom to hold her steady. We left the vessel empty except for a dog by the name of Busser. Unfortunately, the vessel broke away from its mooring and drifted out to sea. At this point, I called for Busser to jump off the boat, but the dog refused and was lost with the vessel. I can also recall a dog named *Speak Your Mind*, who was on the vessel (this dog was a true hero, but his exploits would have gone unreported had I not decided to write this book). *Speak Your Mind* belonged to a man named Berse, who perished in the storm. At Grassy Creek, a man named Prince Rolle (the locals called him Warthy or Papa Warthy) suggested that we swim to Beach Cay, which was closer to the mainland. At the time, *Speak Your Mind* was with me, Elon, Jim, Dan and Travis Taylor. Not all of us made it to Beach Cay, including a man named Josh Smith, who became exhausted and drowned right in front of us. Warthy then yelled out, "Oh my God, he drown now!" At this point, I was swimming with Herman Rolle, Preston Smith, and Jim Smith. Jim told the group he couldn't make it any further, and he also drowned in the front of us. I can further recall his last words were, "For God so loved the world that He gave His only begotten Son, that whosoever believeth in Him shall not perish but have everlasting life!" This scripture was taken from John 3:16, and then he sank and drowned. Nick Rolle also gave up and drowned, along with two other men named Lewis and Phillips. Also swimming were Falcom and Urm Taylor, and Urm swam with his clothes on top of his head. Although some men were swimming together, no one was strong enough to rescue anyone else in the heavy seas. Rip currents were also very strong.

Warthy was able to hang onto *Speak Your Mind*, who swam with him on his back to shore. When Warthy and *Speak Your Mind* got to the shore, the dog once again came to his rescue by going into the bushes and catching a land crab, which they both ate raw. Warthy said it was the best tasting crab he had ever ate, and had it not been for *Speak Your Mind*, he would have surely died.

I can further recall that either the stern or bow of the schooner somehow found its way all the way back to the Bluff, at McKinney Hill to be exact (where it was built). The top mast of the schooner turned up at Long Road, in High Rock, and the hull was found on Bel-Tongue Bank. *The Catherine*, another vessel lost in the storm, was found at Money Rock, in The Bluff. Both vessels were lost at Grassy Creek, some 30 miles away from where they were later found.

Mrs. Wendy Bethel

After the Great Abaco Hurricane of 1932, my grandfather Thomas Horace Roberts was responsible for pouring carbolic acid over the corpses on Green Turtle Cay to prevent the spreading of Cholera. During the hurricane, it is my understanding that 6 people died in Green Turtle Cay, including George Lewis who was 85, Thomas Roberts who would have been my great-great-grandfather and he was 62. He was the one who was found under the walls of his collapsed home. There was also Alice Lowe who was 58 and she died under the collapsed part of the hotel, there were the brothers Dewees and Bert Lowe who were 15 and 2 years old respectively. They were found on the street behind building where the Commissioner's Residence was located. There was Insley Sawyer and she was 5 years old when she died during the storm. In Green Turtle Cay, the injury count was great. My grandparents on my mother's side were Hubert and Miriam Lowe and their daughter was named Agnes who is also my mom.

My grandfather Hubert injured himself when he stepped on a opened corned beef can limiting his mobility during the hurricane. He literally filleted the heel of his foot, so he was in a lot of pain and was not able to walk on that foot. The forefathers of Green Turtle Cay knew when a storm was travelling by using a barometer instrument. Whenever there was a storm approaching the island, they would look at the barometer for a low atmospheric pressure reading on the instrument and if there was this steep drop in pressure, they would prepare for the approaching storm. At this point, they would race to secure their homes and the men of the community would move their boats into safe harbour or on dry land.

My grandparents Hubert and Miriam along with my mom Agnes rode out the storm in their home. Unfortunately, when the weather started to deteriorate, they tried to move because their home was just being blown to pieces and everything was collapsing around them, so they desperately tried to escape the wreckage. They tried to get to the New Plymouth Inn a short distance away, however my grandfather was a hindrance and was not much help to my grandmother because his foot was severely hurt limiting his mobility. As a result, he was of no help to my grandmother and he was unable to walk and had to literally crawl on the ground to escape the strong winds and torrential rainfall. My grandmother held onto my mother who was a 4-year-old scared little child at the time. The winds were so strong they blew my mother's hands away from my grandmother and the winds blew my mom under the staircase of building next door to the New Plymouth Inn. She then waited for the winds to subside before she decided to move from her precarious position. Eventually, my mother made it to the New Plymouth Inn without my mom fearing she had died so off course she was very upset and crying when she entered the building and everybody inside was crying too and they too were thinking that my mother had died in the storm. Sometime later when the winds subsided, my mom crawled across to the New Plymouth Inn that she saw her mom go into and she knocked on the door and they let her in and everyone were so happy that she was still alive and safe.

The story of my daddy's side was just as compelling and my grandfather who was Thomas Horace Roberts and his wife Lola Roberts also suffered greatly during the storm. My great grandfather's house collapsed around them and Thomas Roberts was found under the walls of the collapsed house after the hurricane. My dad's older sister said that she heard grandpa Thomas Roberts groaning during the storm but assumed it was just the loud winds blowing rather than him screaming for help. They eventually found him crushed to death under the rubbles. My father during the storm had his home destroyed so him and his wife and my father had to move from one location to another for lodging. My father was blown out of his mother's arms and he landed headfirst on a short picket fence and had the picket fence lodged between his two eyes leaving a big scar on his face for the rest of his life.

Mrs. Lurey Curry Albury

In describing her experience during the Great Abaco Hurricane of 1932, Lurey Curry Albury remembered Dewees and Bert Lowe:

Uncle Charlie's eldest brother's children, the eldest son and the youngest son, they were like Belle and me. I was carrying Belle, and Dewees had his youngest brother on his hip, trying to get to Mr. Kendrick's house. They think a piece of lumber must have come from Mr. Stanley Sawyer's house when that broke up, and it hit Dewees in his head. Both he and the youngest brother were dead after the hurricane. They found them down on that road, dead. When the wind and rain subsided, the residents of Green Turtle Cay were relieved that the worst was behind us. But as we emerged from our battered, flooded shelters, we discovered what misery lay ahead. Six of our own – George Lewis (85), Thomas Roberts (62), Alice Lowe (58), Insley Sawyer (5) and brothers, DeWees and Bert Lowe, (15 and 2, respectively) – had been fatally wounded. Countless others were injured.

Water from Settlement Creek had surged across the lowest part of town and out into the sea of Abaco, destroying the cemetery and unearthing corpses. Even today, fragments of gravestones remain on the beach that borders the graveyard. When the storm was over, the aftermath was just as overwhelming. After the hurricane, we were literally walking on house roofs. Clothes were blown everywhere – even hanging in the trees. The settlement of New Plymouth was unrecognizable. Most of the homes were either demolished or washed out to sea. The schoolhouse had collapsed, as had the government wharf and the New Plymouth Hotel. Four churches, including the 1200-seat Methodist church, were lost. The top story of the government building had disappeared, leaving only the jail, and stairs that now led nowhere. Nearly every tree on the island had been toppled.

The two-story building where the Captain Roland Roberts Environmental Center is now located had been hit by another building and shifted four feet from its foundation. The roof from the church was found blocks away in the middle of the settlement. Stone bricks from another church were discovered a half-mile away. The Bahamian Government sent some supplies, and private organizations on other islands collected and forwarded donations, but for the most part, Green Turtle Cay residents were left to fend for themselves. Even though we worked tirelessly to pull the shattered pieces of our community back together, New Plymouth never fully regained its previous prosperity. The hurricane damaged numerous sponging vessels and sponge beds and within a few years, disease wiped out what remained of the industry. The timber mills on the Abaco mainland closed, and the Great Depression of 1929 thwarted a fledgling tourism industry. Many residents left to find work in Nassau or the United States. Most did not return.

Bishop Michael C. Symonette

The 1942 storm was a storm which I will never forget because it claimed the life of my grandfather Bishop Alfred C. Symonette. I was a young boy when this tragedy occurred. They were travelling en-route from Fresh Creek, Andros to Nassau. They were travelling on the *Bright Light* sailing sloop and he along with nine others went down with the boat and drowned when they were caught in Tropical Storm #10. Fortunately, two of the crew Mr. Leache Saunders and Mr. Joshua Lewis, who were experienced swimmers, were able to swim ashore during the hurricane. His death sent a veil of sadness and deep regret over the entire islands of Andros and New Providence because he was a very popular preacher who was loved by all who met him or heard his preaching.

On October 15 at 5 pm, the sloop *Bright Light* owned by Mr. George Minnis of Calabash Bay, Andros, on her way to Nassau from Calabash Bay, with twelve passengers on board, capsized and sank in the Fresh Creek Channel. Two men reached the shore safely, but unfortunately, ten others were lost. Included in those lost were, the Bishop Alfred C. Symonette of the St. John's Native Baptist Church in Nassau, who left Nassau on an inspection tour of the 71 churches throughout the island of Andros. Mr. M.J. Poitier, Public School Teacher at Calabash Bay, who attended the Commissioner's Conference in Nassau several weeks prior to the sinking of this boat. Other passengers who were on this ship who died were, Captain Charles Woodside and his wife Mildred Woodside,

William (surname unknown), Inez Moxey, Catherine Lewis, Sceva Lewis, Jim Lewis, and Gladys Saunders. My grandfather was 72 years old and was born in Acklins and came to Nassau as a boy. He had taken an active part in the administration of the National Baptist Convention of America and made several trips there in the interests of The Bahamas Mission. He had planned to leave Nassau for Nashville, Tennesse in the early part of November to attend the appointment of officers of the Baptist Convention in America but died before this journey began.

Mrs. Crystal Pintard

I will always remember Hurricane Wilma because I lost my son during this hurricane. Words can't describe great the impact that this hurricane had on my life. I was staying in my house in the settlement of Hanna Hill in Grand Bahama with my three children and my uncle. During the peak of the storm, the water just started rushing into the house and breaking down the building walls and washing them away. I then took two of my kids to my uncle for safe keeping and then made my way back for the other one. For a while, I was then trapped by the door, which kept me from getting to the other side of the house to join them. At this point, the water had already risen to over 6 feet inside the house and forced me to swim to get my other child who was still in the house. Then there was a scream coming from my next child in the other room, and I then went there to investigate the reasoning for her scream. I then went to where the children were located and my uncle who also nearby came there at the same time and asked my daughter where my baby was? She then pointed to the door and said that the baby was washed away in the flood waters. My uncle then called me and asked me to help him look for the baby. We searched frantically everywhere in and outside of the house, but we never found my baby Matario until several hours later that day, and by this time the baby was already dead.

Mr. Glen Bartlett

Unfortunately, I had the agony of experiencing all three hurricanes (Frances and Jeanne in 2004 and Wilma in 2005) on Grand Bahama, but the worse of them was Wilma. Wilma was a bad girl that wreaked havoc on Grand Bahama. I lived in the settlement of Hepburn Town in Grand Bahama about one thousand feet away from the water. During the hurricane, I went upstairs with my headset on listening to the Darold Miller Radio Show on ZNS 1540AM. During the storm, I had three of my kids and four of my nieces and nephews staying with me. My son came running to me, very much afraid and excited and said, "Daddy! Daddy! Water! Water!" At this point, I didn't pay any attention to him because during the other two previous Hurricanes Frances and Jeanne; I also had some water that came into my house, but not a significant amount. However, when I went to look, to my surprise, I saw my house was engulfed in water, and the water was swirling around like a whirlpool inside my house.

My first reaction was to say, "Oh My God!" When I went to the front door, I became engulfed in over 5 feet of water. At that point, my concerns centered on the safety of my children who were in the house. I quickly rushed to move my car out of the water and move it into the road, and I then noticed my sister's car floating away in the storm. Suddenly, the bottom portion of my house started collapsing in the front of me, and everything in the house began drifting away. I started swimming in the water towards the house and kept thinking that my kids will surely die from this storm. During this time, the winds and the rain were stinging my face like missiles of sand grains pelting my face. Fortunately, my brother-in-law also sensing the immediate danger from the storm had already moved the children into his house and placed them in the kitchen sink because the water was also engulfing his home. My thoughts then centered on the people who had experienced the Tsunami in Southeast Asia in December 2004. It was only then that I understood what insurmountable odds they had to go through to survive.

I then went to the top floor of my house and to my surprise, I saw the water crashing into the bottom of my house and saw these huge swells coming off the ocean and towards my house. I became terrified and very concerned for my children. At this time, my thoughts ran back to Hurricane Frances where I had to rescue some persons out of the roof their houses, and as a bizarre twist of fate, I had to be rescued in Hurricane Wilma. My mother-in-law lived right next to me, and when she turned her back and looked back at her house, she saw her home float away in the flood waters. I must say that the people of Grand Bahama are a very strong and resilient set of people. We thanked God for sparing our lives during these hurricanes and we will start all over again with the help of the Almighty

God because you can certainly replace property, but you can replace a human life. We here in Grand Bahama and the rest of The Bahamas had no lives lost, so we do have something to be thankful to God for after the passage of this hurricane.

Adrian Farrington

Abaco resident, 38-year-old Adrian Farrington carried his 5-year-old son Adrian Farrington Jr., on his back as the father treaded raging floodwater on Abaco Island, where refuge was vanishing under a storm surge. Schools disappeared. Businesses floated away. And Farrington's home, like many others, was no longer a viable place to ride out Hurricane Dorian. Adrian Farrington's 5 year old son was killed, and he was severely injured in Hurricane Dorian. Farrington, along with his wife and their two children, moved from house to house in Abaco during the storm, hoping for a reprieve. Blood flowed from the father's leg wound. Then he spotted a roof he could swim toward. He sat down Adrian Farrington Jr. for a moment. The child, nicknamed A.J., wailed for his father. "I keep telling him, 'Don't cry. Close your month. Don't cry. Keep breathing. Don't cry. Close your mouth,'" Farrington said. Then, the father said, the unthinkable happened: a powerful gust of wind sent his son tumbling across the roof and into the murky waters, where he watched him disappear amid floating debris, while screaming "Daddy help me!" He then watched in dismay as his son was being engulfed by the massive storm surges from Category 5 Hurricane Dorian that covered most of Abaco during the peak of the storm.

As soon as the surge took his son, Farrington pushed through debris and rushed to the other side of the roof, where his son had vanished into the murky waters. He frantically dove underwater and reached in with his hands, hoping to feel his skin or clothes, but sadly he could not locate his son. "I didn't find anything, so I come back up to catch a breath of fresh air and once again dove back down. I held my breath and frantically search underwater for him," he said. "All this time, people carried my wife to safety and they kept calling me, but I didn't want to go because I didn't want to leave without my son." After a weary search that yielded no signs of the boy, he reluctantly moved to higher ground.

He lamented that he had lost all hope of ever finding him alive but hope that he can retrieve his body and give him a proper burial. At the time of the storm, the water was very high, and he was forced to take his son up on the roof of a house. During this time, while struggling to get a steady footing on the roof, a strong gust of wind blew and dragged his son across the roof back into the massive storm surge on the next side. The grieving father stated that he did everything in his power to save his son, but the sad reality was that he couldn't save him, and he will live with that regret for the rest of his life. "I know it isn't my fault that he is gone, but I did everything in my power to save him", he stated. After the storm swept his son off the roof, he spent the next 11 hours trying to stay afloat and keeping his head above water. He stated that even to this day, he is still traumatized about this event because lives were lost right in front of his eyes, and this causes him to lose sleep sometimes. Farrington stated that he plans to move to Cat Island to be with his sister, and it is unlikely he will ever return to Abaco.

Citha Cilien

Citha Cilien lived with her mother in the Haitian shanty town settlement of Pigeon Peas during Dorian's wrath. She stated that the two of them were in a church shelter, and they, along with five others, left to go to Pigeon Peas to secure their valuables because they felt reasonably confident that it was safe to do that. They misjudged the strength of the hurricane, thinking it was a weaker storm, and its strength was exaggerated, and that was a regret that she would have to live with for the rest of her life she indicated. Sadly, she lost her mother, 63-year-old Elvitha Charles, during Hurricane Dorian when a piece of plywood struck her in her head and killed her instantly. Mrs. Cilien stated that her mom's last words were "forgiveness, forgiveness," which she shouted in Creole before the plywood flew towards her. Mrs. Cilien said her 25-year-old brother when he saw this; he immediately dropped their two-year-old nephew and began to cry when his mother fell into the floodwaters. "I had to grab hold of my nephew's hand and put him over my shoulder and at the same time tie my mother's body to something sturdy so that she won't drift or get wash away in the floodwaters." "My cousin died in a similar fashion when a piece of plywood came flying through the air and took his head completely off his body."

Her loss didn't end there. Her husband was with her for a while but went back to the Pigeon Peas settlement to retrieve his father but was killed when the roof of an unfinished church he used to seek safe refuge in collapsed on top of him. Unfortunately, two other persons, her cousin, and godfather also died in that unfinished church. Her aunt died near the Chances webshop in Marsh Harbour, and her uncle's body was found in a bush near a Catholic Church.

Erick Auguste

Throughout the island of Abaco, Bahamians spoke of "Erick the barber," the man whose outstretched left arm was sliced off by a sheet of plywood while he clung to his elderly mother in Hurricane Dorian's surging waters, sending his limb and his mom out to sea. On an island with no cell phone reception, ravaged by the most powerful cyclone in the nation's recorded history, word of Erick the barber and his mangled arm and his dead mom spread like folklore, with each man telling a different version. In the end, the story of Erick the barber, Erick Auguste, is the story of tragedy and resiliency, a storm's savagery, and how family and strangers came together as a group to save one man's life. Erick Auguste, a Bahamian citizen, born to a Haitian mother and Bahamian father was airlifted to South Florida after he was injured as a result of Hurricane's Dorian's destruction said he lost his home, his arm and his mother in a matter of minutes.

Erick Auguste faces a long and challenging road ahead of him to recovery as he remained a patient at Jackson Memorial Hospital, shortly after the passage of Hurricane Dorian. "I thank God that I saved the most that I could. I couldn't save my mom," he said. Fighting through pain, agony, regrets, and loss, Auguste described the day when he said, Dorian, the Category 5 monster storm, took everything. "I don't have anything. There is nothing left," he said. Auguste stated that he was with his family on September 1 when the hurricane quickly moved in and unleashed catastrophic wind and rain. "When I look over, I have glass in my house, and I look at the water, and the waves came, and the water was about five feet high," he said as he pointed to his chest. Aware that he was the only family member who could swim, so prevent them from drowning, Auguste began pulling his two small children, wife, sister, and mother to safety. "I gripped onto the tree tightly while trying to make a chain with each outstretched hand gripping the other,'" he said. "I was like, 'Nobody leaves,' and I was like, 'I don't care, whatever happens, do not let go of me.'"

When he reached for his elderly mother, Auguste said, he lost most of his left arm while attempting to grab her, and he was forced to watch the raging storm surge sweep her away. "This is when this piece of plywood flew off and cut the arm off when I'm lifting up so high," he said. "By the time I'm looking, my eyes were open, and I saw her, and she was just smiling at me." Heartbroken and in disbelief, Auguste said he spent the next 14 hours in excruciating pain, with no medication, all while he continued to search for help. He stated that it was like someone took a dull knife and just kept cutting his hand.

When first responders arrived, they rushed Auguste to a nearby hospital. He was later sent to Jackson Memorial Hospital, where he underwent multiple surgeries on his arm. In a twist of irony, as he begins his long road to recovery, Auguste said he'd make the same decision again if it meant saving his mother's life. "It was for Mom. It was for Mom. If I had to do it again, I'd do it again," he said. Auguste's wife, sister, and children were staying with family members in South Florida while he received medical treatment at Jackson Memorial Hospital in Miami.

On Sunday night, September 1, Auguste, his sister, Yorline, his wife, Elsie, his mother, Matinise Elysee, his son, Erin, and his daughter, Chloe, waited in the TV room of his house on the east side of the house on Hummingbird Way, no more than 800 feet from the raging sea. The children slept, and his mother, a Seventh Day Adventist, prayed in every corner of the room. "We call her our prayer warrior," he said. "She gets up at 4 a.m., prays. All-day, she prays. Kisses me, goodnight prays." Auguste realized the storm would be a worthy adversary when a new gust blew off the plywood, he had nailed outside a sliding glass door. The door flew open, and his wife turned to him and said, "Baby, we have to leave," he recalled. It was too late to flee. The storm was raging. It wasn't long — 30 minutes, Auguste supposes — before the roof shingles peeled off and waters surged into his house from the ceiling, the doors, the windows. Auguste grabbed his 2-year-old daughter, Chloe, and pressed her body against his chest as waves reached his neck. His sister, Yorline, held onto 8-year-old Erin. The family clutched one another, forming a chain that worked its way outside. They sought refuge, but there was no standing home insight. The water kept rising higher and higher.

Auguste is 5-feet, 11-inches tall, but his wife, mother, and sister all are 5-foot-3. If the waves reached his neck, he thought, his family behind him must be underwater. He turned around to check and saw his mother struggling as swells washed over her. He held Chloe in his right arm and extended his left to his mother, a woman in her 70s. Matinise Elysee was visiting from Haiti when the storm hit. At that moment, Auguste said, he thought about how he had begged his mother to return to Haiti before the storm. "She told me, 'If you fight, I fight with you guys,'" Auguste said. Auguste had just clasped Elysee's hand when the plywood flew past. It hacked his arm off just above the elbow so quickly that he didn't immediately feel pain, he said. He watched helplessly as the ocean took his mother and his severed arm. He swears he saw his mother smiling as she was swept away. Her body has not been recovered.

Yorline Auguste, a 20-year-old college student, saw it all. With her right arm wrapped around a tree — a Caribbean pine or maybe a Coconut palm, she thought — her left hand gripped her nephew's upper arm. As the surging ocean water slammed into her, she faced the hardest decision of her life: Let go of her nephew, who would surely be swept to sea, or help her brother, who no longer could hold back the waves with just one arm. "I thought we were all going to die anyway," she said. She held onto Erin, but sadly her brother floated away.

Auguste wrapped a loose palm frond around his right index finger, hoping to latch onto anything. It didn't hold up against the storm surge but did nudge him into downed pines that formed a sort of dam and held him in place near a stop sign on Hummingbird Way, just yards from his home. He guesses he sat there for an hour before the water started to recede. The winds were still raging and brisk, and the rain was still pouring. He heard his wife scream his name. He called out, "I'm here, I'm here, and I'm near Uncle Lou's house." Uncle Lou — that's what he called his neighbour two houses down. An ex-policeman named Steven and another neighbour — who the family doesn't know, even now — swam out to help survivors. The two men found Auguste and carried him to his van, where his wife, children, and sister hid.

Knowing Auguste needed immediate medical attention — better help than the wet T-shirt they'd pressed against his stub — they decided to drive to the Treasure Cay Fire Station a mile away. But the wind lashed the van so hard that it only moved what felt like inch-by-inch, the family said. A trip that once took a minute took 30. They made it to the fire station — or what was left of it. Hurricane Dorian had peeled the roof off and sliced a fire truck in half. There was an intact ambulance. The paramedic inside, though, insisted he couldn't get the family to a shelter because he had to check on his children. The ex-policeman, Steven, offered to drive the ambulance. "He was a stranger, who out of the kindness of his heart left his wife behind to help us," Yorline Auguste said. "A hero."

Things seemed promising. They had found harbour in a sturdy emergency vehicle, and the storm appeared to be slowing down. They didn't know at that moment that they were entering the eye of the Category 5 hurricane, the calm center surrounded by the hurricane's most powerful winds in the eyewall an area in the storm where the most intense thunderstorms are found. They had weathered the gale's western wall, but its eastern wall was coming for them.

The doors of the ambulance had swung open during the storm, and the emergency supplies inside were swept to sea. Still, Auguste's wife, children, sister, and the hero ex-policeman piled into the ambulance and inched toward the government complex in Marsh Harbour, a settlement located about 15 miles away. By then, the clearly defined storm's eye had shifted, offering relief to the settlements on the island's northern end, and the eastern wall began to pummel Treasure Cay. The ambulance lost traction and slipped into the waters. They had to park on a low-lying street, where waters still surged, but winds were less likely to topple the vehicle. Fourteen hours. That's how long the six Bahamians waited inside a bruised ambulance for the slow-moving cyclone to creep, at one mph, past their tropical paradise called Abaco. They had a half-full gallon jug of water and nothing else.

"I don't know how, but by the Grace of God, I watched that gallon of water empty and refilled," Auguste said from his Miami hospital bed. "God literally filled my cup." In reality, as Auguste drifted in and out of consciousness, Yorline Auguste periodically stepped outside the ambulance and filled the jug with rainwater, she said Tuesday in Treasure Cay. Baby Chloe, at one point, begged her mother for water, Yorline recalled. "No, it's for daddy," Elsie Auguste said to the toddler. Chloe didn't ask twice. "We were severely dehydrated in that ambulance," Auguste said he then heard two voices in his head: one who told him that he would die, and another which told him he would be used "as a vessel to touch hearts." Yorline Auguste said. "But Erick needed as much water as he lost blood." Elsie and Erin, the 8-year-old, took turns holding Erick Auguste's remaining hand until the storm dwindled and drifted away.

His rescue mission to save his life was nothing short of a miracle. With the help of countless Abaco residents who used chainsaws and axes to hack at the pines that blocked the road, the ambulance made its way to the government center on Monday, more than 30 hours after the storm first struck. A Coast Guard chopper airlifted Auguste to Nassau, where doctors decided he needed special attention and surgery he could get only in Miami. He, his wife and kids left behind Erick's siblings and a pile of debris that was once their precious home and made their first-ever trip to America. In Treasure Cay, a couple of locals, Yorline Auguste said, found Erick the barber's arm under a pickup truck near his house while searching for their passports in the rubble.

They call him 'Erick the barber' because he gave the best haircuts from his Treasure Cay home. Cutting hair is Auguste's side gig. He's a full-time electrician at Baker's Bay, the wealthy coastal community on Great Guana's Cay, a tiny island off the coast of Treasure Cay, and a 30-minute ferry ride away. After the hurricane, Treasure Cay became a wasteland where indistinguishable heaps of debris sit in place of most high-end homes and resorts. Auguste stated that he cried only once when he relayed his saga. It was when he spoke about the Abaco residents who risked their lives to clear the two-lane highway, the only road from Treasure Cay to Marsh Harbour, to get him out. Certainly, God was on his side that day, he claimed. "God, I may not be able to lift my left hand to raise you up," he cried. "But I give my word; I'll raise my right." "I want to speak for God just as I promised him the night of my ordeal," he said. "I want to do that and spend time with my family."

Terrence Keogh's two accounts of the Great Abaco Hurricane of 1932

While I was writing my second book called 'The Major Hurricanes to Affect The Bahamas' this Terrence Keogh's account of 'The Great Abaco Hurricane of 1932' was brought to my attention by Patricia Beardsley Roker. It is such a compelling account of this great hurricane that I decided to include it in this book. I hope that you find it just as fascinating as I did when I first read it. This account describes the great impact this hurricane had on the island of Abaco as experienced by Terrence Keogh:

"On the morning of Wednesday, August 31, 1932, I noticed that the signal station at Nassau was flying advisory storm warnings, indicating that the center of the storm was expected to pass close by the island of Nassau. I had arranged to take passage on the following day for Abaco Island, in the diesel mail boat *Priscilla*. At ten o'clock the following morning-Saturday, September 3, the *Priscilla* came to anchor at Green Turtle Cay. At the time the people made their living by sponging, fishing, and growing fruits on a small scale. The day of my arrival, which was Saturday, September 3, I spent almost entirely with Basil Lowe, a fine fellow who used to be in the shark-fishing business. We sat around all day and talked the business over from one end to the other in detail, as I was thinking of going into it.

"The weather in the meantime was beautiful with not the slightest sign of an approaching hurricane. As a matter of fact, I had forgotten all about it, and I guess everybody else had too. I spent that night in the Court House, where the resident Commissioner had kindly arranged for me to sleep while I was in Green Turtle Cay. The next morning, Sunday, September 4, I did not get up till very late. During the afternoon, I took a long walk along the sandy shore of the Cay with three boys of the town. One of them was Basil Lowe's son, a fine strapping young fellow of sixteen. Little did I think that the following day I should be picking up his dead body with the dead body of his baby brother clutched tightly in his arms. The fateful day of Monday, September 5, dawned with the hurricane obviously only a few hours off. At daylight, when I turned out, it was blowing a heavy gale of wind with a steady downpour of rain.

"By ten o' clock that morning it was blowing such a violent gale, and the rain was pouring in such a deluge that it was impossible to do anything more outside. With four or five other men I went to a store kept by Mr. Willis Bethel and there sat talking and waiting to see what was going to happen next. Mr. Bethel had a barometer, and when I looked at it, I am sure that my heart missed several beats. I have spent practically my entire life at sea, which means continuously watching barometers in all parts of the world and under all kinds of weather conditions; but I had certainly never seen anything like this before. It then read 28.82 inches, which is disconcerting enough in this part of the world, but what was worse, I could see it going down all the time. I tried to time it but found that my watch had stopped and was full of water. When the barometer reached 28.00 inches, I thought it would surely stop, but instead, it started going faster. The last time I can remember noticing it, it read 27.50 inches. I had never even heard of a barometer being this low.

"The wind had by now reached what I judged to be hurricane force and seemed to be getting worse every moment. The squalls came sweeping over at shorter intervals and would strike with a terrific blast of wind and driving stream of water like a fire hose. Shingles, fence palings, and almost every other kind of article imaginable were by this time flying. It was beginning to look serious. The building which I was in would not hold together for much longer, and Mr. Bethel decided to abandon it altogether and take refuge in his dwelling with his family. I abandoned it too, with the idea of going back to the Court House, which I considered the most substantial building in the settlement. But when I got outside, I realized just how hard it was blowing. To stand upright was almost impossible, but I managed to get down the main street by crouching over and pulling myself along the sides of buildings, fences, or anything that happened to be within reach. The buildings were still standing all right although there were plenty of boards and pieces of lumber flying about the area.

"Right in the center of the town there was a store kept by a woman named Mrs. Roberts, and I stopped in there on my way by as I noticed the door on the lee side was open. Inside the store at the time I found Mrs. Roberts, her daughter, one old man almost sixty years old, and a little girl of about five or six. They all appeared very frightened and were naturally anxious to have news of what was happening on the outside and how other people were making out. The water got so deep on the floor that I ripped up a plank in the lowest part to let it run out underneath. I was in the store, and I should say, at a guess, for about fifteen minutes before the whole strength of the hurricane struck. It came with one terrific blast of wind and water, like a judgment of the Lord, sweeping everything before it. The building creaked in every joint, and the sides bulged like rubber balloons. The women immediately became hysterical and after a few moments threw themselves upon their knees and prayed. Never in my life have I felt so utterly helpless and insignificant. There was nothing that anybody could do.

"Any estimate that I make of the velocity of the wind is only the wildest guess. I do know that the weather observatory at Hope Town, twenty-five miles away, registered a speed of one hundred and sixty miles an hour before the place blew down. This was several hours before the real hurricane struck. When the onslaught hit, my first impulse was to run outside as it was perfectly obvious that the building was not going to stand it. I went to the door and stood there looking out, trying all the time to remain cool and keep my senses, which was nearly impossible with the hurricane howling outside and the women hysterically screaming inside.

"Never have I seen such frightful destruction. The crash of the buildings being smashed to pieces could be heard even above the roaring of the wind and rain. Directly across the street there stood a big three-story stone house in which fourteen people were gathered to ride out the storm. As I stood there watching, the first few blasts ripped all the shingle off the roof and sent them off to the leeward side like a shower of leaves. An instant later the entire building collapsed, some of the heavy stones being carried off with the wind, but most of them crashing down among the wreckage of floors and partitions that remained. I had not seen anybody leave the house and thought that they had surely been killed. If they had not been killed, they were probably trapped in the wreckage, but even so, I was utterly powerless to give them any help. To leave the shelter of the house and go out in the storm now seemed like sure death. There were roofs, whole sides of homes, boats, and all kinds of wreckage hurling through the air and crashing right and left into other buildings.

"It is impossible for me to describe the terrible havoc, as anything I say is inadequate. At about this time a man suddenly appeared, apparently from nowhere, crawling up to the house on his hands and knees as best he could, his head streaming with blood. I dragged him to the door and tried to find out where he had come from, but he did not seem to know himself. He said that he had been in two different houses that had gone down and had been struck on the head by something. He had quite a bad cut just over his ear which I bound up as well as I could with a handkerchief. After this, he just sat on the floor moaning and praying. His nerve was gone entirely, but I could not make out if he was just scared or if he had been hurt. He certainly did not improve the morale of the women, who by this time were screaming and carrying on most frightfully.

"The next people to come in for shelter were a young fellow about my age with his wife and a little boy who had been in the big stone house that I had seen demolished. They had had an awful time. As the building was collapsing the man had thrown his wife, with the baby in her arms, out clear of the wreckage, and then jumped after himself. They seemed to think that the other people had been killed instantly. Since then they had been buffeted about the storm, desperately fighting to get in under shelter. How that fellow managed to drag his wife and child over piles of wreckage and protect them from the fury of the hurricane will always be a mystery to me. They were cut, bruised and completely exhausted. Their nerves were also completely gone, and they immediately joined the others in weeping and praying.

"During all this time the hurricane had been raging unabated-getting worse if this were possible. I had been watching the building which was creaking very loudly and very close to being blown away. At this point, I had just about decided that it was time to leave, as it would most certainly not hold together much longer. The sides were bulging out, and the roof seemed about to lift off any minute. The fastenings had started in all joints, and the ends of the rafters had come away from the plates about six inches. I broke up the prayer meeting and suggested that we all go out and fight our way to the nearest house that was standing, and which could be reached by crawling over the ruins of two other houses. As I was talking there came one terrific gust of wind accompanied by a ripping and tearing noise, and then the whole building just took off from its foundation like an airplane. All hands were sent sprawling on the floor, and the things on the shelves came piling down on us. It was an awful moment. The whole building, with us in it, was flying, and it seemed to me then as though it would never come to Earth. It finally landed with a splintering crash that broke in the floor in several places.

"This was enough for me. I decided to leave without any further loss of time and try to find shelter in some other house that would have more regard for laws of gravitation. I sang out to the others that I was going, and I tried to persuade Mrs. Roberts and her daughter to come with me. However, by this time they were in such a state of combined hysterics and devotion that they had not even got up off the floor. I started out the door, which was on the lee side of the building, and immediately was picked up, off my feet by a puff of wind, blown bodily in the air across the street, and crashed through a picket fence on the other side, which for some reason was still there. I was then blown and bumped over a pile of wreckage that had once been a house until I finally got a firm grip with both hands on an old piece of a floor joist. I hung on to this for dear life, trying to collect my thoughts, while the deluge poured down on my back, and the wind roared by with such force that it sometimes took all my strength to keep from being torn away. It was hard for me to see anything in the driving rain; in fact. It was altogether impossible even to open my eyes if I was facing it.

"The howling of the hurricane and the general noise and confusion of the destruction going on around me, combined with the constant danger of having my brains knocked out by something flying in mid-air, made it very difficult even to think. From the position I was in, I could see only two houses left standing. The rest of the town was simply a tangled mass of wreckage and ruins. There was certainly no point in remaining where I was, lying flat on my stomach, completely exposed to the weather and everything else. I began to make my way towards the nearest house, which I should say, was about two hundred yards off. Getting there was an awful job. I did it on my hands and knees, sometimes crawling and sometimes literally dragging myself along against the wind. In the particularly heavy squalls, I had to stop all progress and stretch flat on the ground, hanging on to whatever was near with all my strength to keep from being blown away. I had one very close call. The whole gable end of a house suddenly appeared from nowhere, driving through the air and coming right at me. I did not have time to do anything but throw myself flat on my stomach, and when I looked up again, it had passed clear over me and was disappearing to leeward, gaining altitude all the time.

"I finally managed to work my way round to the leeward side of the house that I was heading for and went in through an open door. Everything inside was crazy. There were five or six men and women and two little children, all in a state of hysterics. The house was shaking and vibrating so that you could hardly stand up, and the water was pouring down through the ceiling in a perfect deluge. As soon as I got inside one of the men told me that he was afraid the house would collapse at any moment and that they were all about to leave it. Before he had finished talking, there was a noise like an explosion, and the roof and part of the second story were torn off. Next, the windward wall blew in, and the ceiling above started to come down on top of us. All hands piled pell-mell through the door, out into the hurricane. As I went, I grabbed one of the children, a little girl about six or seven, who had got separated from her family. The confusion and chaos outside had by this time reached a point impossible to describe. I had no idea what the others intended doing, but I immediately started struggling along, with the child under my arm, toward a house that was still standing nearby.

"The rest of the people, or rather those of them that I could see, struck out in the opposite direction. They looked like ants as they crawled along the ground, desperately clutching at pieces of wreckage and cowering behind ruins of buildings. It was a fearful moment, and I will confess that I was having difficulty in thinking clearly myself. The child simply clung to me, with her two arms around my waist, whimpering and crying. I looked back once and saw the remains of the house we had just left being smashed to matchwood by the fury of the wind. The next moment a whole dinghy boat came flying out of space through the air and landed with a terrific crash a few feet from us. My face was cut and bleeding badly in several places from the sand and gravel driven horizontally before the wind, and I was having great difficulty in protecting the child from it. After going a little way, I noticed a flight of stone steps built up from the ground and leading apparently to nowhere, but just rising into space. There was a section of a roof wedged in behind them, and several other pieces of wreckage lying strewn about which gave evidence that a house had once stood there. I got around to leeward of the steps and crouched behind them to rest for a few moments before continuing my way. The first thing I noticed was a pair of legs protruding from under the roof. I pulled on them and dragged out the body of a rather old man, cold and quite dead.

"After I had finally reached the house for which I was aiming I had quite a job to get in, as all the windows and doors were boarded up and nailed shut. The door on the lee side was fastened from within, and it was only after I had started to batter it down with a piece of the rafter that the people realized somebody was trying to get in. This house was a large two-story stone building that had formerly been used as a store. It had been unoccupied for some time, but when the hurricane struck, several families took refuge there, as it was a most substantial building. When I arrived, there were about fifty people all told inside, men, women, and children. Never have I seen a more frightened, helpless, and thoroughly miserable gathering of human beings. The windows were all boarded up, and it was as black as night inside. The water was pouring down in streams from the floor above, and everybody was soaked to the hide. The women and children lay huddled together on the floor, their teeth chattering with the cold, praying hysterically to the Lord for mercy. The roaring and howling of the hurricane outside made it almost impossible to think, and to talk it was necessary to shout at the top of your lungs.

"Although the storm was now at its very height, the house showed no signs of giving way. I was afraid that if anything struck it, it would come down very quickly and, therefore, started at once to plan a course of action in case we should have to leave it. I stood at the door on the lee side and from there could see only one house standing-and that had half the roof gone. This house, I was told, belonged to Dr. Kendricks, the local doctor, and was obviously the place to go next if we had to move. The darkness came quickly and with it, to my great relief, came a decided change for the better in the weather. The wind in the space of a few moments went right down to nothing, but a stiff breeze and the rain stopped altogether. The general opinion of the rest of the men seemed to be that this was the end of the hurricane, but I did not think so. I was afraid that it was just a temporary calm while the center passed over us. As soon as it moderated, all hands went to work at something.

"The most critical need was something to eat for the women and children, as most of them had had nothing to eat for the entire day. Three men went to the remains of Mrs. Roberts' store to search around for some food and some lanterns and oil. Two other men went to work on the building, battering up windows on the top floor which had blown open, reinforcing doors, and a hundred other much-needed repairs. I tried to get them to nail up the doors and windows on the south side, which so far had been to leeward, in case the wind came from that direction, but they did not think this was necessary. I would have done it myself, but we had only one piece of iron for a hammer, practically no nails, and only what lumber we could rip off partitions inside. Their failure to do it nearly cost the lives of everybody in the building an hour or so later.

"In the meantime, I went to Dr. Kendricks' house to see how many were there, and to try to find out what the barometer was doing. I found Dr. Kendricks' house in much the same condition as the one I had just left. There were about one hundred people crowded into it, many of them quite badly hurt. The women and children lay huddled together in the darkness crying and praying. I tried to raise their spirits and comfort them, but there was practically nothing that I could do. Never in my life have I been so totally unable to cope with a situation. Nobody had any idea of how many people had been killed, and the darkness and confusion of the night it was certainly impossible to find out. Dr. Kendricks appeared to be the only man who was keeping his head. He went about his work of giving first aid to the injured in the calm, businesslike manner, although he had himself suffered as much loss of property as anybody. I found Mrs. Roberts here, unconscious, with a fractured skull. Dr. Kendricks had brought her in himself. Kendricks' barometer stood at 27.60 inches and showed no signs of rising. This convinced me that the hurricane was only half over and that the calm which now prevailed would soon be broken by the wind coming howling from out of the south.

"I had no sooner got back inside the stone house than the wind came again, this time from the southward, in violent squalls, accompanied by the usual downpour of driving rain. There were several more people in the building now, who had taken advantage of the lull to crawl from under the ruins of their homes to this shelter. By this time the known deaths amounted to seven, with about two hundred still unaccounted for. I now began to feel a pain in my right side which was caused, I found out a week later, by one of my ribs being broken. This had probably happened when I was blown through the picket fence but had not noticed it until now.

"The hurricane was now raging outside with the same violence and destruction but from the opposite direction. Right away we found ourselves in an awful position because the windows and doors on the south side of the building had not been boarded up. Because of the shift of the wind, this was now the windward side. The very first squalls had smashed the sash right out the window frames and torn the doors off their hinges. The water was pouring in, and there was a steady barrage of sand, rocks and small pieces of wreckage. All hands had to move to the leeward side, which meant almost sure death if the building collapsed. It would not have been possible to get out as all these doors and windows were fastened on the outside. I was afraid that the wind, by getting inside the building, would lift the roof off or blow the walls right out. Already the wooden partitions inside were beginning to buckle badly. Something had to be done and done quickly. I went outside with two men to help me, and after an awful battle, lasting nearly an hour; we managed to get the openings boarded up. It was a surprising thing to me how a lot of these men appeared to lose their nerve. Many of them just simply gave up and joined the women in prayer, rather than make any effort to help themselves.

"The moaning of the injured, together with the weeping and screaming of the women, made a most frightful experience that could be heard even above the storm. One old man started singing hymns at the top of his lungs and was immediately joined by everyone else. This would have been very nice except that he chose for his opening number "We will meet in the Sweet By and By." It was the last straw for me, and I could not help suggesting that he sing something a little more cheerful. It was about midnight when I noticed that the wind had started to moderate slightly. The rain continued just as hard, but the gusts were considerably lighter than they had been. Somebody came up from Dr. Kendricks' house with the welcome news that the barometer had started rising rapidly. This was very reassuring and convinced me that the worst of the hurricane was now over. For the remainder of the night the weather continued to improve steadily until by daylight the wind had moderated to a strong gale, and the rain, though still pouring down, was nothing like what it had been. As soon as the danger was obviously past the people, all began to brighten up. Somebody during the lull had managed to get a kerosene stove out of Mrs. Roberts' store, so I turned to and made strong tea for all hands. We also had a couple of boxes of soda biscuits. After this, the women and children lay down on the floor and through sheer exhaustion were soon fast asleep. I had dried out my pipe and tobacco over the stove.

"After drinking six cups of boiled black tea, munching a couple of handfuls of biscuits, and smoking three pipes of strong tobacco, I was once again ready for anything. I thought that dawn would never come. People kept coming in with reports from different parts of the town, and the list of the dead and injured was mounting steadily. The most pressing thing for the immediate present was the condition of the people who were still living but trapped under the ruins of their houses unable to get out. This was the first job to be tackled. Every man who was physically able turned to, but it was a slow, hard job to get these poor people out, as the gale of wind and pouring rain made it very difficult to work.

"With the first signs of daylight, I started for Basil Lowe's house to see how he and his family had come through. Nothing appeared to be left standing, and the streets were piled so high with wreckage that it was impossible to follow them. Where Basil Lowe's house had stood the day before was a litter of broken timbers. In the middle of the mess, I came across the body of his eldest son, a fine boy of sixteen, lying face downward on the ground, cold and stone dead. I rolled him over and found that his neck had been broken. With a death grip, he still held in his arms the body of his baby brother, also cold and dead. I carried them both out to an open space and laid them on the ground side by side, then covered them with loose boards, weighted down with stones so that they would not blow away. As I was doing this Basil, himself appeared. It was the most harrowing moment of my life, and there was little that I could say to him at the time. He had had a frightful experience during the hurricane and was in an unconscious condition. When his house collapsed, he, his wife, six children, and his mother-in-law all had to run for their lives. His wife had fallen through the floor and was unconscious, which meant that he had to carry her in his arms after dragging her out. He had seen his two children killed, by the gable end of the building, as they ran through the door. In some way or other he had managed to get the rest of them into a nearby-house but had only been there a short while before this also collapsed.

"I returned to the stone house, in which there were now about one hundred additional people who had come in from different parts of the town, all in the same state of exhaustion and hysteric. It was now so full that it was almost impossible to get in through the door. By this time everybody in the settlement had been accounted for, and the death toll amounted to eighteen, with twenty-five badly injured. We held a kind of council of war to talk over our position and see what was to be done next. Obviously, the dead had to be buried, but this was practically impossible until the weather cleared up. It was still blowing too hard to walk around without holding on to something, and the rain was pouring down in a steady torrent. Luckily, there had been quite a quantity of food salvaged from the ruins of the various stores. Some people had managed-how, the Lord only knows-to unearth some clothing, blankets, and quilts that were still dry, and these were immediately distributed amongst the women and children. The women got busy brewing gallons of strong tea and baking Johnny cakes. Somebody collected several dead chickens from among the ruins, and we soon had steaming hot soup, which I thought at the time, was the best thing I ever tasted.

"Very discouraging reports came back of how people in other communities had feared in the storm. Their houses were all built in one district at the eastern end of the town and had all been destroyed with the very first blasts of the hurricane. The people had run out and, not knowing where to turn, had very sensibly taken to the open country. At the very height of the storm, men, women, and children, about eighty of them altogether, had desperately crawled, dragged, and fought their way up the side of a high hill, and had taken refuge in a stone quarry at the top. The quarry was a huge round pit about three hundred feet in diameter and sixty feet deep, which afforded shelter from the wind but not from the cold and wet. They had all huddled together at the bottom on the windward side, while the hurricane went thundering by overhead. The poor people of colour in the quarry, nearly blue with the cold, had been in this godforsaken hole, completely exposed to the weather with nothing to eat, for over twenty-four hours. I had brought a few tins of beef along with me, which I quickly divided up among the women, and then dispatched somebody back to town for more. They were all so terrified and exhausted that I had difficulty in persuading anybody to venture up out of the pit. I noticed a dead horse lying at the bottom of the quarry and was wondering how in the world it had got there. They told me that they had no idea where it had come from, but at the height of the storm it had suddenly appeared flying through the air and had dropped about sixty feet to where it now lay.

"One Negro preacher said that he had thought it was the dove coming down upon the Apostles but could not exactly see the smile. He apparently considered it as an omen and immediately launched out into a long sermon, much to the edification of his audience, about the Ark full of animals landing on "Mount Arral" after forty days of the flood. He managed to work into it something about the waters of the Red Sea being opened, then rambled on about Saint Simon fishing in the Lake of Galilee; in fact, he used every part of the Scripture that had anything to do with water. I thought it was most appropriate as both he and his congregation looked more than half drowned. I spent the afternoon in the quarry, trying to keep out of the rain by crouching under a shelf of rock, getting colder, wetter, and more miserable every minute. Toward evening the wind seemed to moderate considerably, and I returned to the town in search of a more comfortable place. There was not much comfort to be found. But at least the hurricane was over."

A Hurricane-Terrence Keogh's Description

Interviewed for the second time in New York, Mr. Terrence Keogh gives the following entertaining description of his adventures in The Bahamas during the Great Abaco Hurricane of 1932. This account was taken from the Nassau Guardian, December 31, 1932. Below is the excerpt of his report of the storm:

Terrence Keogh, one of the last of a long line of Irish adventurers and filibusters, was in New York recently for the first time in four years, visiting his aunt, Mrs. Nicholas Biddle, at 530 East Sixty-Sixth Street. Although he has never led a revolution, as did his great-great uncle, Robert Emmet who was hanged for it with the gallant Lord Edward Fitzgerald and others of his United Irishmen in 1803 and although he has never been in the public eye as anything more than a minor member of scientific expeditions, he has his legend. A trip to The Bahamas, alone in an open boat that ended in a hurricane and the salvaging of an island community has recently added to it.

From Cowes, where he goes after the trans-Atlantic races he delights in, to the dives of Shanghai that knew him when he passed years with the Roosevelt Lines, the exploits of the son of the "lame judge," the late Martin J. Keogh, Justice of the New York Supreme Court, have created excitements. Last winter he was in America again, and by spring he was in America again, and by spring he was finding a family life dull. To escape it he sold all his worldly possessions and brought a one-volume edition of Shakespeare, a large supply of provisions and The Snug, a twenty-foot sloop which he modestly describes as "rather a small boat." On May 14, he set off alone in it from Woods Hole, on Cape Cod, for Kingston, Jamaica.

Finds Weather Unreliable

Sitting in Mrs. Biddle's pleasant dining room over coffee and a glass, after an excellent luncheon, he seemed an inconspicuous, ruddy sort of person until he began to tell his story. He had made the southern trip often enough and expected fair weather after the first day or so. He was disappointed.

"I had vile weather all the way down," he said; "southerly that meant tacking constantly and six bad storms. It was cold the first day or so, but after I crossed the Gulf Stream, it was all right."

He described how he treated the storms, which he called "little dangerous in a boat as small as that." He would take all sail off, lash the tiller, put out a sea anchor and retired to his cabin with his pipe and Shakespeare until the wind had gone down enough to make sailing sensible again.

"One of them lasted for three days and nights," he said, "and one of them fooled me. Of course, the only really difficult thing in such a small boat is staying on it. Sometimes that's something of a problem. About 200 miles south of Bermuda, when I was twenty-five days out of Woods Hole, a bad blow came up. Nothing would have happened, except that the calm center passed right over us, and therefore, the wind change. Supplies were getting low, so I wanted to run before it. I went up to set the mainsail, and while I was at it, I slipped, tripped on something, and went over.

Fortunately, I had hold of a rope. In those circumstances, you hang on hard, and I was able to pull myself in."

The rest of the trip to Kingston was he said, uneventful. He ran into the worst storm he has ever seen at sea, and only saved himself from being blown onto the seashore of a small island by stripping all sail and hiking The Snug over a bar into a harbour. The storm had passed, and he sailed to Nassau for supplies and was stayed there for ten days.

Arrived at Kingston on August 18, he found himself penniless and raised much-needed funds by selling The Snug. Between parties in Nassau he had interested himself in the shark fisheries, and, after a "dull week at Kingston," he returned to Nassau and there went to Abaco Island, one of the larger ones in The Bahamas. On Sunday, September 4, he was ensconced in the courthouse at Green Turtle Cay, a settlement of 500 whites on an islet off Abaco. They lived by sponge fishing, shark fishing, turtling, and he was getting to know them, and finding out more about shark fishing quietly in their midst.

"That Sunday night we had our first warning," he said. "Of course, before I left Nassau, there had been storm warnings from Washington of a hurricane brewing by Turk's Island, but that was so far away no one paid it any attention. On Sunday night the whole eastern sky was pitch black. On Monday morning, there was a good gale and rain in squalls. At noon, I decided we were going to have real trouble, so I started for the general store to get some kerosene so that I could lock myself in the courthouse, which was a stone building, and read until it was over. By that time, it was so bad you could barely walk, and shingles and bits of porches were getting kind of active. I got to the store, and ten minutes later it started."

There were five others in the building with him, two men and three women, and their immediate reaction were to throw themselves face down on the floor and pray.

Sees Stone House Crumple

"I looked out," he went on, "and the first thing I saw was a big stone house across the street, that I knew had fourteen people in it, go down before my eyes. It went in like a spokeless umbrella. I tried to go out to rescue some of them, but I could barely hold on to the side of the store. You can't describe a hurricane. The wind is simply an incredible force, and the rain strikes you so hard that it left my back black and blue and skinned my face as you'd skin an animal. So, I went back into the store."

"That didn't do much good, since the minute I got into it, it took off like an airplane and sailed for what seemed like an hour, about a hundred feet, to land on some rocks with the floorboards bursting like an explosion and people and provisions flying in every direction. After that, I concluded there might be a healthier place, so I said goodbye."

He crawled out on his hands and knees, with his head well down, trying to find another place. "Getting about was quite a business, but it was just possible that way." He said. "I passed two or three corpses and any amount of wreckage. I looked up once and saw two boats flying along overhead. I reached a house, where there were a man, his wife, and two children, and as soon as I got there, the roof took off. The man had a broken leg, so the woman grabbed one child and I the other, and we started again, with the man crawling after. We were out fifteen minutes that time, but we finally got to a stone house which seemed to be standing up well. It had thirty people in it, all with hysterics, not one of them knowing what members of his or her family were alive."

At 9 pm the wind went down slightly, but it was useless to try to do anything in the dark. Tuesday dawned, with wind and rain still strong, but the rescue work began. Every house on the island was down except the stone house in which Keogh had taken refuge. Three persons had been blown off the island. The wind had lifted the tombstones in the churchyard and deposited them on the beach. A horse had been dropped over a cliff "like a seagull." An iron washtub was found seven miles away on another island, and three houses had been taken across the channel to Abaco. Eighteen persons had been killed, and most of the livestock was buried in the ruins. The velocity of the wind as registered Monday morning was 160 miles an hour.

"In point of fact," he said, bringing the attention back to the quiet dining room by pausing for a moment to light the pipe that had accompanied Shakespeare, "the island was a complete, absolute wreck. That was the worst part of it. Everyone was hurt somehow, I had a rib broken, but we all turned to dig out the ruins, with people finding relatives or not finding them as the case might be. There was one old man he had been in the first house I saw go down, whose wife had had her arm cut off in the falling house. He was near her; she was almost in his arms. She died six hours later, and he was there next to her for forty-eight hours. He was made when we got him out."

Rescue Work Gets Under Way

The next day the sun came out. Provisions were getting low, and only two of the cisterns that contained the island's water supply were standing. He helped launch a motorboat, which had been carried some hundred feet inland, and he and its owner started for Nassau to get help.

"When I got back to Green Turtle Cay," he continued, "things were still in terrible shape. If a thing like that had happened in New York, it would have been about like Jehovah smiting Sodom, but their things weren't so close together. Still, typhoid and cholera had appeared, and the island's doctor, Kendrick, was doing an unbelievably good job. I had offered my services, so I put myself in unofficial charge of Green Turtle Cay. We organized camps, and some of the people found a kind of shelter under the roofs that were lying about across the island. We collected as much household goods as we could and started to build again out of the wreckage. Many of the timbers were still useable, so we were able to rebuild a smaller house. The main concern, however, was to the overall health of the residents."

After two months of it, he had done all he could and set out for Nassau again in the schooner.

"We had quite a trip," he said. "I was captain, of course. My crew consisted of two beldames, neither able to do more than cook, which they did on the deck, an epileptic, a lunatic and a leper. The last was by far the most useful man on the boat. The lunatic was an old man who thought he was an admiral. He spent most of his time forward, a bottle held to his eye like a glass."

At last, he sailed for the United States, but not before making friends with Nassau's plentiful population of rum runners. He expected to land at Miami on Election Day. He did so but was immediately utilized by a detachment of his new friends to help capture a steamer with some of their property aboard from hijackers. He succeeded, left it for a pilot boat beyond the twelve-mile limit and arrived in Jacksonville in sneakers, and old yachting cap and a few odds and ends of clothing, with $2 in his pocket. Funds were supplied to him, and he set off for Boston by bus.

"Things always seem to happen to me," he said as he closed his tale. "A woman in the bus proceeded to have a baby several miles from nowhere, and I had to act as assistant midwife."

This account of the Great Abaco Hurricane of 1932 was written by the Nassau Guardian Newspaper as told to them by an Anglican Bishop as he arrived in Abaco to render assistance to the people of Abaco just after the storm. This account was taken from the Nassau Guardian Newspaper on Saturday, September 17, 1932.

The Bishop's visit to Abaco-Altar in ruins but the church intact

"I left Nassau at 2 am on Wednesday in the *Malola* for Green Turtle Cay. The weather was very rough at first, and there were heavy squalls of rain."

"I arrived at Green Turtle Cay about 5 pm and was met at the dock by the Catechist and the principal people of the place. I then proceeded to go around the settlement. Enough has already been said of the absolute ruin to the place. The church, a solid building, built of quarried stone, is destroyed, the stonework having fallen inwards. I noticed that in the middle of all the ruin the altar is standing uninjured and has still one candlestick with the candle in place while the chalice and paten which were in the church when it collapsed are quite undamaged."

"The Rectory, a well built two-story wooden house, was lifted completely off its pins and set gently down again about 12 feet back where it stands as a building. I was able to walk upstairs, and one of the windows which is glazed had only one small pane broken. The school too is quite destroyed."

"I then walked around the settlement calling on the sick and bereaved, and just as it was growing dark, I gathered the people around me by the new graves in the churchyard and held a short service."

"I then went back to the motorboat and early next morning said a Mass for the people in one of the rooms of the Rectory as I had brought all requisites for the service with me and gave Communion. I then saw some more sick folks but had to hurry on board as the *Malola* was ready to leave for Nassau."

"It is to be realized that many people have lost all they once had. They have no houses or clothes or crockery or cooking utensils, and many have no shoes. Gifts in kind would be very acceptable."

"It was a great disappointment to be unable to visit Blackwood Point situated on the mainland six miles to the west of Green Turtle Cay. There they are in a very bad way indeed and are short of everything. All I could do was to leave behind the 200 pounds of grits I brought with me and to ask that they might be sent over from Green Turtle Cay. This they gladly promised to do. I brought the grits for the people of Green Turtle Cay, but they suggested that Blackwood Point was in even a worse condition than they were. This seemed to me, an appealing instance of outstanding generosity. All of the people appreciated my visit whether belonging to the Church of England or not."

"The impossibility of visiting Blackwood Point affected the Bishop very much as there is a very faithful band of church people. The instance demonstrates the necessity of the Bishop having his own yacht. Subscriptions towards a new one have already been received towards the cost which is estimated to be about £1500 and Mr. Cox of Messers Cox, and Stevens has consented to prepare the plane free of cost. The boat will be an auxiliary motorboat."

Mr. Alexander Reckley, Schoolmaster at Bluff Point, gave the Nassau Guardian Newspaper a most graphic description of the Great Abaco Hurricane of 1932 as he experienced the peak and the after-effects of the storm. This account was taken from the Nassau Guardian Newspaper on Saturday, September 10, 1932.

Schoolmaster at Bluff Point Records Pitiful Story

As early as 2 o'clock on the morning of Monday, September 5, Mr. Reckley and his wife and four children were up and dressed watching the weather, their two-story wooden house being securely battened up, except for one small aperture. Twelve hours later, between 2 and 3 in the afternoon the storm was at its worst, the wind blowing from the north. When they saw the weather increasing, they said their prayers. "Then," said Mr. Reckley, "We waited to see what the Lord would do." Just then they heard ominous creaks in the timbers of the house. "Then the Spirit led me, my wife and four children to the nearest neighbouring shelter." This was an outside-kitchen, 8x10. "Every house on Bluff Point," he continued, "Was almost down. Then the wind fell off, there were ten minutes of calm, and the wind blew fierce from the south. Just after dark, every house was down."

In the kitchen where a fire was kept burning until the storm abated in the early hours of Thursday morning, round about 100 people collected, attracted by the glow and warmth. Here they passed the time singing hymns and praying. "The Lord heard us and kept the roof on, though it nearly came off." Already the people lived on young canes, which are sour, and rotten and bruised pears. All the chickens were drowned, except two roosters which found shelter in the kitchen. Mr. Reckley, who came in the Ethel B on Monday is wearing his only suit of clothes left, the jacket of which he found in a pond. He hopes to take back with him tonight food and clothes for the people."

The loss of the ship HMS Valerian

Late in the summer of 1926, two hurricanes (The Great Nassau Hurricane and The Great Miami Hurricane) brought considerable damage to the British Colony of The Bahamas. The Governor of The Bahamas, Sir Harry Cordeaux sent an urgent appeal to the King of England George V, requesting his assistance in providing a British warship to take him and a few Government representatives to the various islands which were greatly devastated by these two storms. Also, to bring much-needed hurricane relief supplies such as building materials, freshwater, food and clothing to the starving residents. As the naval headquarters for the British West Indies, the HMS Dockyard at Ireland Island dispatched a sloop, a minor vessel from its fleet to render what aid it could to The Bahamas. A duty which, today, would fall on the West Indies Guard Ship, a frigate that the Navy rotates through deployments to protect the British West Indian Waters, and that with the HMS Dockyard long closed, only stops in Bermuda on its way to and from its deployment). The ship sent to the aid of The Bahamas was the *HMS Valerian*. An Arabis type of the Flower Class built during the Great War, she was under the command of Commander W.A. Usher, with a full complement of 115 men.

On October 18, having rendered what assistance it could, it then left Nassau to return to her base in Bermuda. Due to a shortage of coal in The Bahamas, the boat began the voyage with little more than what it needed to complete the 1,100-mile journey. This left the ship relatively light in the water with a detrimental effect on its stability. A day after she began her voyage, the *HMS Valerian* received reports from the US weather service that a tropical storm was forming to the south of Puerto Rico. This storm initially moved north and seemed to be no threat to the ship, but unfortunately, it soon began curving to the northeast to follow the *HMS Valerian* home route. Since the weather reports indicated that the "eye" would pass some 300 miles north of the island, Commander Usher never really gave it much thought. Besides, no major hurricane had hit Bermuda in October for well over 100 years - a dangerous precedent on which to rely on because it meant that Bermuda was well overdue for a major hurricane to hit this island. Despite the late date, the storm quickly grew far more powerful than the weather forecasters had predicted. The *HMS Valerian*, unaware of the actual strength or speed of the wind still raced for home, not wanting to be caught at sea in a precarious condition and lacking the coal to fight the weather for long if she were ever to encounter this storm at sea. She very nearly made it.

By 8 am on the morning of the 28 October she radioed the Bermuda Dockyard to say that she was situated about eight miles from Gibbs Hill Lighthouse, to the southwest of Bermuda. At that time, Commander Usher would report, there was no sign of the approach of a massive storm inhibiting the ship from making it safely into port at Bermuda. Even though the wind howled about them and waves came with tremendous force over on her deck; still, he anticipated no difficulty making Timlin's Narrows-the channel, located a handful of miles to the east of Bermuda, which provided the sole access through the Isles' enclosing reefs. Commander Usher anticipated no difficulty in entering the Narrows, having done so many times before under similar conditions. Inside the reefs, the vessel would be well protected from the worst the sea had to offer. But this was not to be because; this would be his last report from this ship.

Only when the few survivors were plucked from the waters near Bermuda and only by the following day would the extent of this tragedy be known, because the *HMS Valerian* was finally succumbing to the powerful winds and rough seas of the storm. At 10:00 am the following day, 19 men were picked from the waters surrounding Bermuda by the cruiser *HMS Capetown* which rode the storm out safely at sea. The *HMS Capetown* had begun a search for the *HMS Valerian* the previous day but had been called away by the SOS of the steamer the *SS Eastway*, which also reported being in a desperate plight with her bunkers awash. While the *HMS Valerian* went down less than five miles from the safety of the Royal Naval Base in Bermuda, another ship called the *SS Eastway* sunk near Bermuda in the same storm, taking 22 crew members with her. The dead persons from the *HMS Valerian* numbered four officers and 84 men. A commemorative plaque for those who lost their lives first hung in the Dockyard RN Chapel in Bermuda but was moved and is now held at Commissioner's House at the Bermuda Maritime Museum. This storm would become one of the most powerful hurricanes in Bermuda's history.

A survivor of the *HMS Valerian,* one of only 19, would recall the events of that day on the front page of The Royal Gazette and Colonist Daily. But the circumstances surrounding the loss of the *SS Eastway,* and the rescue were never published until much later. As a survivor would later testify before a court-martial, he said: "Indeed, at that time, I felt assured of reaching harbour in safety as there was no immediate indication of a violent storm, also there was a complete absence of swells that sometimes denotes the approach of a storm." However, this was no ordinary storm and a half-hour later the weather changed so drastically that Commander Usher himself realized he could no longer proceed through the Narrows. He turned the ship around and headed straight into the storm. Gale force winds were lashing the boat at more than 100 mph with a driving rain and flying spray obliterating everything from view.

By noon the center of the storm was reached, and the clearing came, but with-it mountainous seas that seemed to approach the ship from all sides, shooting the vessel onto a crest and dragging it down into the trough until it appeared, she would snap in two. Once the center of the storm had passed over, the winds picked up from the northwest and again tossed the ship from crest to trough as if it were no more than a bath toy. At 1 pm a series of squalls struck the boat on the port side with such force that it was thrown on its' beam ends and heeled 70 degrees over to starboard in a stomach-churning movement. It was at this moment that the mainmast and wireless equipment were carried away in the storm and preventing the possibility of sending out another SOS to Bermuda or any other passing ships. Above the howling winds, Commander Usher heard the engines stop, and word reached him that the *HMS Valerian* had run aground. Before he could catch his breath, the enormous vessel keeled over about 60 degrees and started going down fast. Word spread "all-hands-on-deck" and with only enough time to cut away one raft, the crew had less than one minute to abandon ship before the ocean claimed the *HMS Valerian.*

Hanging onto the bridge, Commander Usher was swept away by waves, bumped his head and finally came up alongside a raft to which he and 28 of his men clung. In his account before the court later, Commander Usher recalled the events that followed: "Unfortunately, the bottom of the raft got kicked out and this entailed much greater effort in holding on. The experience of clinging to this raft for 21 hours, with only a problematical chance of being picked up was indeed trying enough for the hardest. Luckily, the water was warm, but the northwest winds felt bitterly cold to those parts which were exposed. Sunset came, and as it grew dark, we looked for Gibbs Hill Light, or some other light, as we had no idea of our position, but nothing was seen, not even the glare. The 12 hours of night, with waves breaking over us, was an experience never to be forgotten and many gave up during that time. They got slowly exhausted and filled up with water and then slipped away. The raft was slowly losing its buoyancy, and as everyone wanted, as far as possible, to sit on the edge, it capsized about every 20 minutes, which was exhausting; we all swallowed water in the process and the effort of climbing back again. Twelve held out until the end when *HMS Capetown* was most thankfully sighted at about 10 am the following day." By the time the *HMS Capetown* picked up the survivors, the buoyancy of the raft was such that it would not have supported anyone for another hour. The *HMS Capetown*, which had ridden the storm out safely at sea, had begun a search for the *HMS Valerian* the previous day but had been called away by the SOS of the steamer, the *SS Eastway*, which was about 70 miles south of Bermuda and in serious trouble.

During a formal investigation in the United Kingdom in April of the following year, it was revealed that the *Eastway* was overloaded by 141-tons when she left Virginia. This decision cost the crew their lives, and the registered manager, Watkin James Williams, was found "blame-worthy" and guilty and ordered to pay £1,000 towards the costs of the inquiry. On the other hand, a court-martial on the survivors of *HMS Valerian* was conducted, but later this court acquitted all the survivors of the *HMS Valerian* of all blame. They examined 15 or 16 witnesses, including ten of those who were saved from the shipwreck, others being technical witnesses. While it was described as a court-martial, it was an inquiry. A court-martial was held because it was, pursuant to the practice of the British Naval Laws in such cases, to inquire into the cause of the wreck, loss, and destruction of the *HMS Valerian*.[135]

[135] http://www.geocities.ws/gpvillain/news3novpg1.html. Retrieved: 14-11-2009. The Royal Gazette, November 3, 1926. Pg.1. Wind and Weather Swept Valerian to Doom-Court Martial Acquit Survivors of Negligence. Retrieved: 15-11-2009.

CONCLUSION

This thoroughly researched history considers these intense Bahamian hurricanes and their aftermaths, offering an exploration of important historical weather events that have been neglected in previous studies. Through unique historical photographs of actual damages, this book shows the widespread devastation left in the wake of these great storms. Drawing upon many various newspaper accounts, personal recollections, ship reports, and Family Island Commissioners' reports from throughout The Bahamas, this book provides a fascinating glimpse of these hurricanes and the great devastation they caused on the islands of The Bahamas.

For example, recently the effects of Hurricanes Frances, Jeanne and Wilma in The Bahamas in 2004 and 2005 were generally unexpected and primarily concentrated on the island of Grand Bahama. While passing the archipelago, these hurricanes produced hurricane-force winds and powerful storm surge, flooding the coastal areas of Grand Bahama and other islands in the NW Bahamas and destroying hundreds of buildings. For example, in Frances, about 75% of the island chain lost power for a few hours during the storm and remained off until the electrical and telephone infrastructures were restored to the island several weeks later. One person, which was an 18-year-old man Kenrad Delaney died when he was electrocuted trying to get his portable generator started in New Providence.

Damage occurred to downed trees and wooden homes. Between 13 and 17 percent of the non-native Australian pines on San Salvador Island experienced damage, primarily from snapping, though some browning from salt spray was noted. Several feet of water flooded the Freeport International Airport. In The Bahamas, insurers and reinsurers estimated industry insured losses from Frances at about $300 million (2004 USD). All cool-season vegetable plantings and the entire banana crop were lost during Frances. The pineapple crop was significantly impacted by wind damage in Eleuthera, while the whole fruit crop was lost for similar reasons. The corn crop on Long Island and Cat Island was lost entirely. Significant poultry losses were also experienced. Shelters were set up at the churches and schools on Abaco Islands, Eleuthera, Grand Bahama. At least 700 people went to a shelter in Abaco Islands alone.

For Wilma, damage totaled about $100 million (2005 USD), almost entirely on the western half of the island of Grand Bahama. Central Grand Bahama, including the Freeport area, reported minor to moderate damage, while the eastern end received little to no damage. Storm surge from the hurricane killed one child, the only casualty 1-year-old Matario Pintard directly related to Wilma in the archipelago. Elsewhere in The Bahamas, moderate damage occurred on Abaco and Bimini, while islands further to the south reported minimal wind damage. Significant damage was reported in the coastal areas of Grand Bahama Island, with widespread destruction of roofs and vehicles, along with downed poles and trees. Power and telephone services were disrupted throughout the island. A total of 400 structures sustained damage, of which about 200 commercial buildings were severely damaged and recommended by engineers not to be repaired. Among the destroyed buildings was a police station on the western end and several buildings in Freeport. More than 500 automobiles were flooded, including five police cars. The storm surge also raised 54 corpses in five graveyards on the island. Several resorts were closed for an extended period, further depressing the island's economy of tourism's sector, all on the western portion of the island.

Damage was also heavy on the island of Bimini, where heavy rainfall and powerful storm surge damaged homes, trees, and utility poles. On the island, the hurricane severely damaged a hotel and eight waterfront homes. On Abaco, eight houses and a government clinic were destroyed. The storm surge destroyed a government dock and caused flooding and beach erosion near the coast. New Providence and the Berry Islands also reported minor wind damage from Wilma, primarily to downed trees and power lines. Throughout The Bahamas, Wilma damaged public infrastructures such as schools, roads, health clinics, and electrical systems.

The devastating effects of hurricanes Joaquin, Matthew, Irma, and Dorian which hit The Bahamas in early September and October of 2015, 2016, 2017, and 2019 respectively, caused substantial damage to the economy of The Bahamas. According to preliminary assessments by NEMA and former Bahamian Prime Minister Rt. Hon. Perry Christie and current Prime Minister Rt. Hon. Hubert Minnis, direct and indirect losses from three of these natural disasters have reached more than US$900 million (excluding Hurricane Dorian in 2019) in The Bahamas, notably the islands of Acklins, Crooked Island, Ragged Island, Long Island, Inagua, Grand Bahama, Andros, and New Providence. The Rt. Hon. Hubert Minnis stated that Hurricane Dorian alone will perhaps run into the billions of dollars when the final damage total will be calculated for The Bahamas. The worst human and socio-economic losses occurred in the least developed islands of the SE Bahamas and the nation's capital of Nassau and the second and third most developed islands of Grand Bahama and Abaco. The Bahamas, an ecologically fragile archipelago whose most significant part of the territory is its patrimonial sea, suffered the quadruple assault of hurricanes Joaquin, Matthew, Irma, and Dorian. Many of the residents of the SE Bahamas had to be evacuated before the onset of Hurricane Irma in 2017 for their own safety. In Dorian, many migrants were evuacated from areas in Abaco, notably The Mud and Pigeon Pea shanty towns but sadly many choose to stay at those locations and many of them paid with their lives when these substandard homes were destroyed by Dorian's 185 mph winds.

As stated before, their combined effects caused by direct and indirect damages and economic losses worth more than $900 million (USD), that is, more than 10% of the previous year's current Gross Domestic Product (GDP). This has meant that an economy expected to grow almost 3% thanks to rising tourist activity and new investments in this activity and its free trade zone saw its economic activity fall to at least 1.7% in 2017. Even though the final assessment of Hurricane Dorian is still being carried out, one should expect this storm to exceed many of these records inflicted by previous hurricanes impacting The Bahamas. While the damages inflicted to businesses, homes and infrastructures were serious, productive sectors were the most affected. Because of this, the country will need international cooperation in the coming months and possibly years and has applied to the Inter-American Development Bank (IDB) emergency facility. For over 30 years, The Bahamas has developed an integrated methodology for evaluating the socio-economic and environmental impacts of disasters caused by extreme natural events notably hurricanes. Because it uses actual procedures to assess the damages and losses, this has become a standard instrument for the current and future governments of The Bahamas, proving to be an essential part of any strategy for the country's recovery, beyond the initial emergency phase.

From June 1 through November 30 each year, The Bahamas comes under the threat from the ferocious winds and floodwaters of the hurricanes that form in the North Atlantic Basin. Every year during this period (commonly called hurricane season), hurricanes threaten the islands of The Bahamas. In other parts of the world, the same types of storms are called typhoons or cyclones. Hurricanes wreak havoc when they make landfall, and they can kill thousands of people and cause billions of dollars of property damage when they hit densely populated areas. Hurricanes are severe tropical cyclones, which, though not nearly so frequent as mid-latitude cyclones, receive a great deal of attention from laypeople and scientists alike, mainly because of their impressive intensity and strength and their great destructive powers.

Abundant, even torrential rainfall and winds of high speeds (from 75 to 150 mph or more) characterize hurricanes. Though these storms developed over the warm oceanic waters and often can spend their entire lives there at times their tracks do take them over islands and coastal lands. The results can be devastating, destruction of property and sometimes death. It is not just the rains and winds; however, that can produce such damage to people and their surroundings, for accompanying the hurricane are unusually high seas, called the storm surge, which can flood entire coastal communities. It would seem clear that people should avoid living in low coastal areas that are subjected to hurricanes.

There are many reasons for studying hurricanes, one of the objectives is to observe and explain the physical world-the world of nature. In meteorology, it is the phenomena occurring in the atmosphere that is to be explained and understood with the aim or objective of trying to lessen the consequences for us here on this Earth. To understand the complicated nature of our environment, it is required that we go in-depth into the study of hurricanes. This is done with a goal to fully understand the various elements of hurricanes with a hope and desire to become more aware of the processes and forces that produce and shape them. However, with increased understanding of the structure and dynamics of hurricanes, and improved methods of forecasting them, we can expect the adjustment of human activities to take better advantage of favorable aspects and avoid the unfavorable aspects of our atmospheric environment when it comes to hurricanes. Many factors can affect the conditions that give rise to devastating hurricanes and among the most important are the heating of the Earth by the sun and the differences in atmospheric pressure.

Low atmospheric pressure usually means stormy weather, such as found at the center of a hurricane. Although causes of extreme weather such as hurricanes are often well understood and studied, it is still impossible to predict the weather with a pinpoint degree of accuracy more than a few days ahead. This is because the weather is a very complex system that even small incremental changes in the Earth's heating system can affect how the weather develops and behaves daily. Hurricanes are one of the most dangerous and unpredictable of all the natural forces at work on our planet. Thanks to weather satellites, reconnaissance aircraft, and radars, scientists can track hurricanes and try to predict where and when they might make landfall. Earth's chaotic atmosphere can and often strikes at random with little or no warnings, and the result is devastating consequences and these hurricanes that hit The Bahamas over the years and centuries proved this certainly beyond a shadow of a doubt.

The Bahamas on average gets brushed or hit by a hurricane once every three years and gets hit by a major hurricane once every 12 years. There are three Bahamian islands ranked in the top 10 effects from tropical systems of all cities, islands, and countries in the North Atlantic basin - Andros, Abaco, and Grand Bahama. The Bahamas geographic location persuades us to be more aware of the past hurricanes since history guarantees that they will come again with the same or greater fury that in the past. We can identify patterns and commonalities between storms just as human history helps us learn from our society's disasters and hopefully with this knowledge we can better prepare and adapt to the next big hurricane.

SOURCES

❖ _Reports from the House of Assembly of The Bahamas_ commencing, September 17, 1866 to January 11, 1867.

❖ _Reports from the House of Assembly of The Bahamas_ commencing, September 19, 1883 to January 10, 1883.

❖ _Reports from the House of Assembly of The Bahamas_ commencing, August 20, 1899 to March 10, 1900.

❖ _Reports from the House of Assembly of The Bahamas_ commencing, May 19, 1908 to January 17, 1909.

❖ _Reports from the House of Assembly of The Bahamas_ commencing, March 18, 1930 to July 07, 1930.

❖ _Reports from the House of Assembly of The Bahamas Special Session_ commencing October 16, 1929 to October 24, 1929.

❖ _Reports from the House of Assembly of The Bahamas Special Session_ commencing October 13, 1999.

❖ _García-Herrera, Ricardo; Gimeno, Luis; Ribera, Pedro; Hernández, Emiliano (2005), "New records of Atlantic hurricanes from Spanish documentary sources", Journal of Geophysical Research._

❖ _The Great Andros Hurricane_ by Pierce S. Rosenberg/RCA/AUTEC Environmental Science Section.

❖ _Rt. Hon. Hubert Ingraham, Prime Minister. October, 1999. Communications on the Reconstruction Effort Following Hurricane Floyd._

❖ _Prime Minister Hon. Perry G. Christie Address to Parliament on The Impact of Hurricanes Frances and Jeanne on The Bahamas._

❖ _Wilma's Wrath-The Aftermath & Recovery Plans_-Special Hurricane Issue Volume 8, No. 1, by Bahamas Information Service.

❖ _"HURRICANE!" A Familiarization Booklet by NOAA, April 1993._

❖ _National Weather Service, Weather Forecast Office, Miami Florida, Memorial Web Page for the 1928 Okeechobee Hurricane._

❖ _The Great Andros Island Hurricane of 1929_ by. Pierce S. Rosenberg/ RCA/AUTEC Environmental Science Section.

❖ *"HURRICANE!" A Familiarization Booklet by NOAA, April, 1993.*

❖ *National Weather Service, Weather Forecast Office, Miami Florida, Memorial Web Page for the 1928 Okeechobee Hurricane.*

❖ *The Dept. of Meteorology Climatological Section, Official Hurricane Reports on Various Hurricanes* by Arthur Rolle, Basil Dean, Jeffery Simmons, Kenneth Lightbourne, Neville Woodside, Trevor Basden, Nicklo Small et al….Nassau, Bahamas.

❖ *The Illustrated London News, November, 24th 1866 pg.505 'The Hurricane At Nassau, New Providence.'*

❖ *The Bahamas Journal of Science Vol. 6 No.1 Historic Weather at Nassau-*Ronald V. Shaklee, Media Publishing Ltd.

❖ *The Bahamas Journal of Science Vol. 5 No.1 Historical Hurricane Impacts on The Bahamas, Part I: 1500-1749* Ronald V. Shaklee, Media Publishing Ltd.

❖ *The Bahamas Journal of Science Vol. 5 No.2 Historical Hurricane Impacts on The Bahamas, Part II: 1750-1799* Ronald V. Shaklee, Media Publishing Ltd.

❖ *The Bahamas Journal of Science Vol. 8 No.1 Historical Hurricane Impacts on The Bahamas: Floyd on San Salvador & Early Nineteenth Century Hurricanes 1800-1850 Ronald* V. Shaklee, Media Publishing Ltd.

❖ *Harper's Weekly-A Journal of Civilization Vol. X-No. 516, Saturday 17, 1866 'Hurricane in The Bahamas.'*

❖ *Harper's Monthly Magazine-'Hurricane in The Bahamas' by Terrance Keogh,*

❖ *Bahamas Gazette 1784-1875. John Wells, editor. Nassau, Bahamas.*

❖ *Florida Historical Society: The Florida Historical Quarterly volume 65 issue 3.*

❖ *The Nassau Guardian, Colonial Summary December 17, 1853.*

❖ *The Tribune, Saturday, July 31, 1926 pgs. 1,2 & 3 'Out Islands Devastated.'*

❖ *The Tribune, Wednesday, August 04, 1926 pgs. 1 & 2 'Hurricane Relief Movements.'*

❖ *The Tribune, Wednesday, August 11, 1926 pgs. 1,2 &3 'Hurricane Damage.'*

❖ *The Tribune, Saturday, August 14, 1926 pg. 1 'Relief.'*

❖ *The Tribune, Wednesday, September 19, 1928 pgs. 1 & 2 'Extraordinary Hurricane Hits Bahamas.'*

- Chris Landsea, et al. (2011). *"Documentation of Atlantic Tropical Cyclones Changes in HURDAT: 1928 Hurricane Season"*. NHC-Hurricane Research Division.
- *Votes of the House of Assembly-1917-1930-*The Department of Archives-Nassau, Bahamas.
- *The Sponging Industry Booklet-Department of Archives Exhibition February 18-24, 1974. Pgs. 1-31.*
- Wxeltv-Heritage, Episode 10: *Hurricane of 1928.*
- *A Columbus Casebook-A Supplement to "Where Columbus Found the New World" National Geographic Magazine, November 1986.*
- *Annual Colonial Reports (CO-23-Governor's Dispatches) for The Bahamas, 1917-1929-*The Bahamas Department of Archives-Nassau, Bahamas.
- *Censuses of the Bahama Islands, 1891, 1901, 1911, 1921. Department of Archives-Nassau, Bahamas.*
- *"Hurricanes and the Shaping of Caribbean Societies,"* Florida Historical Quarterly, 83:4 (2005), pgs. 381-409.
- *Miami Daily News, Monday, September 24, 1928, Miami Public Library.*
- *Miami Daily News, Monday, September 25, 1928, Miami Public Library.*
- *Miami Herald, Monday, October 1, 1928, University of Miami, Fla. Otto G. Richter Library.*
- *The Palm Beach Post,* September 13, 1928.
- *The Palm Beach Post,* September 20, 1928.
- *The Tribune,* Wednesday, September 19, 1928 pgs. 1 & 2 'Extraordinary Hurricane Hits The Bahamas.'
- National Weather Service, *Weather Forecast Office, Miami Florida, Memorial Web Page for the 1928 Okeechobee Hurricane.*
- *The Florida Historical Quarterly,* January 1987. Published by the Florida Historical Society.
- Mitchell, Charles L., *"The West Indian Hurricane of September 10-20, 1928."* Monthly Weather Review Vol. 56, No. 9. Weather Bureau. 1928. Pgs. 347-350.
- Saunders, Gail, *The Social History of The Bahamas 1890-1953*, A thesis presented to the University of Waterloo in fulfillment of the thesis requirement for the degree of Doctor of Philosophy in History, 1985.

❖ *The Governor's Dispatches-CO-23 January-December 1929.*

❖ *Votes of the House of Assembly-1929 & 1930-Bahamas Department of Archives.*

❖ *The Nassau Guardian*, Saturday, November 23, 1844 Vol. 1-*'Log of the Rio.'*

❖ *The Nassau Guardian*, September 13 & 4, 1882, *The Hurricane,* pg. 1.

❖ *The Nassau Guardian*, *Destructive Cyclone.* September 8, 1883, pg.1

❖ *The Nassau Guardian*, September 20, 1919 *The Hurricane*, pg. 2.

❖ *The Nassau Guardian, Saturday, September 28, 1929 pg. 1-'The Hurricane,' 'Hurricane Briefs' & 'Message from the Administrator.'*

❖ *The Nassau Guardian, Wednesday, October 02, 1929 pgs. 1,2&3-'The Hurricane,' 'Message from the King,' & 'Hurricane Briefs.'*

❖ *The Nassau Guardian, Saturday, October 05, 1929 pg. 1-'Hurricane Relief,' 'Trail of the Storm' & 'Hurricane Briefs.'*

❖ *The Nassau Guardian, Saturday, October 19, 1929 pg. 1-'Special Session-The Administrator's Speech.'*

❖ *The Tribune, Saturday, September 28, 1929 pgs. 1&2-'Courage.'*

❖ *The Tribune, Saturday, October 05, 1929 pgs. 1&2-'Government making estimates of hurricane damage to lay before Legislature', 'The Bahamas Hurricane Relief Fund 1929' & 'Here and There.'*

❖ *The Tribune, Wednesday, October 09, 1929 pg. 1-'Here and There,' & 'Captain and crew saved from Storm-Driven "Wisconsin Bridge."'*

❖ *The Tribune, Saturday, October 01, 1929 pg. 1-'Here and There,' & 'Hurricane Reconstruction.'*

❖ *The Tribune, Wednesday, October 02, 1929 pg. 1-'All traces of hurricane damage are being quickly effaced by cheerful workers.'*

❖ *The Tribune, Saturday, October 19, 1929 pg. 1-'Here and There,' & 'It can be done is the verdict of Asa Pritchard, M.H.A.'*

❖ *The Tribune, Saturday, October 26, 1929 pg. 1-'Here and There,' & 'Hurricane Relief.'*

❖ *The Tribune,* Saturday, September 28, 1929 pg. 3. *'Here and There.'*

❖ *The Nassau Guardian,* Wednesday, October 2, 1929 pg. 1 *'The Hurricane.'*

❖ *The Nassau Guardian,* October 09, 1929 pg. 3 *'Trial of the Storm.'*

❖ *The Nassau Guardian,* November, 06, 1929 pg.3. *'Andros and the Acting Colonial Secretary's Visit.'*

❖ *The Governor's Dispatches-CO-23 January-December 1933.*

- *The Tribune,* Thursday, August 31, 1933 pg. 1. *'Storm is approaching Nassau'* & *'Sloop 'Lolita' wrecked at Inagua today.'*
- *The Tribune,* Friday, September 01, 1933 pg. 1. *'Nassau escapes storm damage-Another Hurricane Reported.'*
- *The Tribune,* Saturday, September 02, 1933 pg. 1. *'Out Island Hurricane Losses-Seven person reported Dead.'*
- *The Tribune,* Monday, September 04, 1933 pg. 1. *'Hurricane Damage Out Islands.'*
- *The Tribune,* Tuesday, September 05, 1933 pg. 1. *'Hurricane caused extensive damage at Grand Bahama.'*
- *The Tribune,* Wednesday, September 06, 1933 pg. 1. *Relief for storm affected Out Islands.'*
- *The Tribune,* Friday, September 08, 1933 pg. 1. *'Long Cay District Deaths Total 15'* & *'Mail M.V. "IVY S" is a total loss.'*
- *The Tribune,* Saturday, September 09, 1933 pg. 1. *'Mayaguana Hard Hit By Recent Storm.'*
- *The Tribune,* Monday, September 11, 1933 pg. 1. *'Five more lost in recent Hurricane.'*
- *The Tribune,* Tuesday, September 12, 1933 pg. 1. *'Extensive Storm Damage at Grand Bahama.'*
- *The Tribune,* Wednesday, September 13th 1933 pg. 3. *'Hurricane News from Acklins Island District.'*
- *The Tribune,* Thursday, September 14, 1933 pg. 1. *'Officials Leave to Inspect Storm Damage.'*
- *The Tribune,* Monday, September 25, 1933 pg. 1. *'Seeks Assistance for Harbour Island Hurricane Sufferers.'*
- *The Tribune,* Friday, October 06, 1933 pg. 1. *'Hurricane passed over Hope Town.'*
- *The Tribune,* Tuesday, October 7, 1941, pgs. 1 & 6 *'Watlings Island Still Silent, Cat Island Hard Hit.'*
- *Governor's Dispatches-Colonial Office Files (CO-23) September-December 1941-1965, Commissioners' Reports on the damages on various Out Islands.*
- The Tribune, Thursday, October 9, 1941, pg. 1, *'H.E. Views Devastation at Stricken Islands.'*
- The Nassau Guardian, Friday, November 13, 1942, pg. 2, *'Nine Drowned In Tragic Sea Accident at Andros-Minister and Teacher Among Those Lost.'*

❖ The Nassau Guardian, Saturday, November 14, 1942, pg. 2, 'Ten Drowned in Sea Disaster.'

❖ *The Tribune, Friday, September 09, 1960 pgs. 1 & 3 'Eastern Islands Hard Hit-Nassau Escapes The Fury.'*

❖ *The Tribune, Saturday, September 10, 1960 pg. 1 'Seven are missing as Donna pulls out-Houses, Ships, and Crops Damaged.'*

❖ *The Tribune, Monday, September 12, 1960 pgs., 1, 3, 4 & 5 'Ragged Island Salt Industry Washed Out.'*

❖ *The Tribune, Wednesday, September 14, 1960 pg. 1 'Crops in Southern Andros Demolished.'*

❖ *The Nassau Guardian, Monday, September 12, 1960 pgs. 1,2,8,9 & 14 'Widespread Damage on Mayaguana.'*

❖ *The Nassau Guardian, Tuesday, September 13, 1960 pgs. 1 & 9 'Peter Bethell again flies on storm damage mission.'*

❖ *The Tribune, Wednesday, September 8, 1965 pgs. 1,2,3 & 8 'Cabinet Reports on Damage.'*

❖ *The Tribune, Thursday, September 9, 1965 pgs. 1,2,3 & 11 'Damages of Hurricane Betsy.'*

❖ *The Tribune, Saturday, September 11, 1965 pgs. 1,2,3, 9 &11 'Parts of Eleuthera Are 'Truly Disaster Area.''*

❖ *The Tribune, September 15, 1965 pg. 1 'Statement By Cabinet On Hurricane Relief.'*

❖ *The Tribune Monday, September 03, 1979 pgs. 1 &3 'David No Goliath.'*

❖ *The Tribune Tuesday, September 04, 1979 pgs. 1 &7 'The day David dropped in'& 'TORNADO-Twister crosses island.'*

❖ *The Tribune Monday, September 05, 1979 pg. 1 'Bimini assesses David damage.'*

❖ *The Tribune Monday, September 09, 1979 pg. 1 'Banana shortage feared.'*

❖ *The Tribune Thursday, September 13, 1979 pg. 1 'Salt Crop Ruined.'*

❖ *The Tribune Friday, September 14, 1979 pg. 1 'Red Cross Aids Andros.'*

❖ *The Nassau Guardian, September, 04, 1979 pgs. 1 & 3 'Hurricane affects island utilities.'*

❖ *The Nassau Guardian, September 04, 1979 pgs. 1 &3 'David's rains cause widespread flooding' & 'Hurricane committee coordinating all relief efforts.'*

❖ *The Nassau Guardian, September 05, 1979 pgs. 1 & 3 '30,000 without electricity; over 1,600 telephones out.'*

❖ *The Nassau Guardian,* September 06, 1979 pg. 1 'Red Cross sends emergency supplies to Central Andros.'

❖ *The Bahama Journal,* Saturday, September 05, 1992 pg. 1 'Hurricane Relief Committee.'

❖ *The Bahama Journal,* Saturday, May 15, 1993 pg. 1 'Hurricane Relief Center Reopens.'

❖ *The Nassau Guardian,* Tuesday, August 25, 1992 pgs. 1,2 &3 'Andrew cuts a path through island', 'Storm leaves devastation' & 'PM tours ravaged island areas.'

❖ *The Nassau Guardian,* Friday, August 28, 1992 pgs. 1,2,3 & 13 'United States gives $25,000 in hurricane relief funds.'

❖ *The Nassau Guardian,* Monday, October 05, 1992 pg. 1 'Hurricane Andrew and me.'

❖ *The Tribune,* Tuesday, August 23, 1992 pgs. 1 & 12 'Woman tells hurricane horror story.'

❖ *The Tribune,* Wednesday, August 24, 1992 pgs. 1,2,3 & 11 'Spanish Wells Lucky.'

❖ *The Tribune,* Thursday, August 25, 1992 pgs. 1, 2, 3 & 11 'Hurricane also affected nature, Trust president says' & 'Harbour Island visitor gives first-hand account of storm.'

❖ *The Tribune,* Thursday, September 03, 1992 pg. 1,2,3 & 11 'Hurricane damages courts in Family Islands' & 'Hurricane Relief pours in.'

❖ *The Tribune,* Wednesday, December 23, 1992 pg. 1 'Natural disasters abounded in 1992.'

❖ *The Tribune,* Friday, October 28, 2005 pg. 13 'Storm leaves a trail of destruction.'

❖ *The Tribune,* Tuesday, November 01, 2005 pg. 1 &10 'Forced evacuation laws considered.'

❖ *The Tribune,* Wednesday, November 02, 2005 pg. 7 'Hurricane Wilma victims settle in to life at Royal Oasis Resort.'

❖ *The Bahama Journal,* Wednesday, October 26, 2005 pg. 1 '100 houses destroyed' & 'Grand Bahamians "shocked" by storm's impact.'

❖ *The Bahama Journal,* Thursday, October 27, 2005 pg. A2 'Displaced Grand Bahamians coping with life after Wilma.'

❖ *The Illustrated London News,* November 24, 1866 pg. 505 'The Hurricane At Nassau, New Providence.'

❖ *Harper's Weekly-A Journal of Civilization Vol. X-No 516,* Saturday, 17th 1866 Hurricane in The Bahamas.'

❖ *The Official Report of Governor Rawson on the impact of the Great Bahamas Hurricane of 1866 on the various islands of The Bahamas. Governor's Dispatches Files-CO23* (The Bahamas Department of Archives), Nassau, Bahamas.

❖ *Bahamas Gazette 1784-1815*. John Wells, editor. Nassau, Bahamas.

❖ *Miami Daily News*, Monday, September 24, 1928, Miami Public Library.

❖ *Miami Daily News*, Monday, September 25, 1928, Miami Public Library.

❖ *Miami Herald*, Monday, October 1, 1928, University of Miami, Fla. Otto G. Richter Library.

❖ *RAIV Hurricane Committee*, March, 1980 'Hurricane David in The Bahamas, 1 to 3 September, 1979.'

❖ *Florida Historical Society: The Florida Historical Quarterly volume 65 issue 3*

❖ *U.S. Department of Commerce*, Sept. 15th 1965, 'Hurricane Betsy-Preliminary Report with Advisories and Bulletins Issued.'

❖ Ahrens, D. *Meteorology Today, An Introduction to Weather, Climate, and The Environment*, (USA, Brooks/Cole Publishing, 2000).

❖ Albury, Paul, *The Story of The Bahamas*, (Oxford, Macmillan Publishers Ltd., 1975).

❖ Allaby, M. *DK Guide to Weather-A Photographic Journey Through The Skies,* (London, Dorling Kindersley Ltd., 2000).

❖ Barratt, P. *Bahamas Saga-The Epic Story of the Bahama Islands,* (USA, Author House Publishers, 2004).

❖ Burroughs, Crowder, Robertson, et al. *The Nature Company Guides to Weather*, (Singapore, Time-Life Publishing Inc., 1996).

❖ Butler, K. *The History of Boat Builders from 1800-2000*, Unpublished

❖ Butler, E. *Natural Disasters*, (Australia, Heinemann Educational Books Ltd., 1980).

❖ Challoner, J. *Hurricane and Tornado,* (Great Britain, Dorling Kindersley. 2000).

❖ Clarke, P., Smith, A. *Usborne Spotter's Guide to Weather*, (England, Usborne Publishing Ltd., 2001).

❖ Colledge, J. J.; Warlow, Ben, *Ships of the Royal Navy: The Complete Record of all Fighting Ships of the Royal Navy* (Rev. ed.). London: (Chatham Publishing, (2006) [1969]).

❖ Craton, M. *A History of The Bahamas Vol. 3*, (Canada, San Salvador Press., 1986).

❖ Diedrick, Amanda, *Those Who Stayed-The tale of the hardy few who built Green Turtle Cay*, (Abaco, Amanda Diedrick Ltd., 2016).

❖ Douglas.S.M., *Hurricane,* (USA, Rinehart and Company Inc., 1958).

❖ Drye, W., *For Sale-American Paradise-How Our Nation Was Sold an Impossible Dream in Florida* (USA, Rowman & Littlefield, 2016).

❖ Duedall, I., Williams, J., *Florida Hurricanes and Tropical Storms 1871-2001,* (USA, University Press of Florida., 2002).

❖ Field, R., *A Summary and True Discourse of Sir Frances Drake's West Indian Voyage*, (USA, Richard Field, 2018).

❖ Goyco Garcia, *Tales of the Gods: How the Caribbean Sea was born,* (Puerto Rico, Xlibris Corporation, 2016).

❖ J.D. Jarrell, Max Mayfield, Edward Rappaport, & Chris Landsea *NOAA Technical Memorandum NWS TPC-1 The Deadliest, Costliest, and Most Intense United States Hurricanes from 1900 to 2000 (And Other Frequently Requested Hurricane Facts).*

❖ Kahl, J. *National Audubon Society First Field Guide To Weather,* (Hong Kong, Scholastic Inc., 1998).

❖ Kindersley, D., *Eyewitness Weather,* (London, Dorling Kindersley Ltd., 2002).

❖ Lauber, P. *Hurricanes: Earth's Mightiest Storms*, (Singapore, Scholastic Press., 1996).

❖ Lawlor Anne & Jim, *The Harbour Island Story*, (Oxford, Macmillan Publishers Ltd., 2008).

❖ Lawlor, Jim, *Paul Albury: A Man and His Writings*, (Nassau, Media Publishing Ltd., 2013).

❖ Lightbourn, R. & Moss, V, *Reminiscing, Memories of Old Nassau,* (Nassau, Media Publishing Ltd., 2001).

❖ Lightbourn, R. *Reminiscing II, Photographs of Old Nassau,* (Nassau, Ronald Lightbourn Publishing, 2005).

❖ Lyons, A.W. *The Handy Science Weather Answer Book,* (Detroit, Visible Ink Press., 1997).

❖ MacPherson, J. *Caribbean Lands-A Geography of The West Indies, 2nd Edition,* (London, Longmans, Green and Co Ltd., 1967).

❖ Millas C.J., *Hurricanes of The Caribbean and Adjacent Regions 1492-1800,* (Miami, Florida, Edward Brothers Inc/Academy of the Arts and Sciences of the Americas, 1968).

❖ Moore, J. *Pelican Guide To The Bahamas*, (USA, Pelican Publishing Company., 1999).

❖ Neely, Wayne, *The Major Hurricanes to Affect The Bahamas-Personal Recollections of Some of the Greatest Hurricanes to Affect The Bahamas*, (Bloomington, Authorhouse Publishing Inc., 2006).

❖ Neely, Wayne, *Rediscovering Hurricanes-The Major Hurricanes of the North Atlantic*, (Bloomington, Authorhouse Publishing Inc., 2007).

❖ Neely, Wayne, *The Great Bahamian Hurricanes of 1926-The Story of Three of the Greatest Hurricanes to Ever Affect The Bahamas*, (Bloomington, iUniverse Publishing Inc., 2009).

❖ Neely, Wayne, *The Great Bahamas Hurricane of 1866-The Story of One of the Greatest and Deadliest Hurricanes to Ever Impact The Bahamas*, (Bloomington, iUniverse Publishing Inc., 2011).

❖ Neely, Wayne, *The Great Bahamian Hurricanes of 1899 and 1932: The Story of Two of the Greatest and Deadliest Hurricanes to Impact The Bahamas*, (Bloomington, iUniverse Publishing Inc., 2012).

❖ Neely, Wayne, *The Great Hurricane of 1780: The Story of the Greatest and Deadliest Hurricane of the Caribbean and the Americas*, (Bloomington, iUniverse Publishing Inc., 2012).

❖ Neely, Wayne, *The Great Bahamas Hurricane of 1929: The Story of the Greatest Bahamian Hurricane of the Twentieth Century*, (Bloomington, iUniverse Publishing Inc., 2013).

❖ Neely, Wayne, *The Great Okeechobee Hurricane of 1928: The Story of the Second Deadliest Hurricane in American History and the Deadliest Hurricane in Bahamian History*, (Bloomington, iUniverse Publishing Inc., 2014).

❖ O'Neil A. *It's a new era' of hurricanes-Experts: String of intense storms is part of normal cycle*, (CNN-September 23, 2005).

❖ P.J. Webster, G.J. Holland, J.A. Curry and H.R. Chang, *Journal Science-Changes in Tropical Cyclone Number, Duration, and Intensity in a Global Warming Environment,* (Vol. 309 no. 5742 pgs. 1844-1846).

❖ Pearce, A.E., Smith G.C. *The Hutchinson World Weather Guide,* (Great Britain, Helicon Publishing Ltd., 1998).

❖ Redfield; W.C., *On Three Several Hurricanes of The Atlantic and their Relations to the Northers of Mexico and Central America*, (New Haven, 1846).

❖ Reynolds, R., *Philip's Guide To Weather*, (London, Octopus Publishing Group Ltd., 2000).

❖ Rose, S. *El Nino and La Nina*, (USA, Simon Spotlight., 1998).
❖ Saunders, G. & Craton, M. Gail Saunders & Michael Craton, *Islanders in the Stream-A History of the Bahamian People Vol.1*, (University of Georgia Press, USA, 1998).
❖ Saunders, G. & Craton, M. Gail Saunders & Michael Craton, *Islanders in the Stream-A History of the Bahamian People Vol.2*, (University of Georgia Press, USA, 1998).
❖ Siepel, K. *Conquistador Voices-Christopher Columbus & Hernán Cortés*, (New York, Spruce Tree Press., 2015).
❖ Stevens K.W. *The Change in The Weather: People, Weather, and the Science of Climate*, (New York, Random House Inc., 1999).
❖ Swartz, S. Sea of Storms-The History of Hurricanes in the Greater Caribbean from Columbus to Katrina, (USA, Princeton University Press, 2015).
❖ www.nhc.noaa.gov
❖ www.aoml.noaa.gov
❖ www.deadlystorms.com
❖ www.snapshotsofthepast.com
❖ www.pewclimate.org
❖ www.stormcarib.com
❖ www.weather.com
❖ www.wunderground.com
❖ www.floridamemory.com
❖ www.palmbeachpost.com
❖ www.wikipedia.org
❖ www.publicaffairs.noaa.gov
❖ www.nationalgeographic.com
❖ www.usaid.gov
❖ www.caribbeannetnews.com
❖ www.oii.net
❖ www.cidi.org
❖ Numerous persons throughout The Bahamas who gave me their first-hand recollections of these past hurricanes.

ACKNOWLEDGMENT

To acknowledge everyone who contributed in some way or the other in this book project would fill another book but so in summary here are the persons I wish to thank in no defined order: -

My Father and Mother Lofton and Francita Neely and my sisters and brothers

My Grandparents Mrs. Joanna and Jerry Gibson & Benjamin and Elizabeth Neely

Ms. Inger Simms

Mr. Rupert Roberts Jr.

Mr. Andrew McKinney

Mr. Wendall Jones

Mrs. Oxygen Qhcuiyang-China Meteorological Office

The late Mr. William Holowesko

The Hon. Gleny's Hanna-Martin

His Excellency the Hon. A.D. Hanna

Mr. Murrio Ducille

Sir. Charles Carter

Mr. Eddie Carter

Mr. Dwight Strachan

Mrs. Jasmine Brown

Mr. Darold Miller

Mrs. Betty Thompson-Moss

Mrs. Cara Brennen

Ms. Shenique Miller

Mr. Juan & Paige McCartney

Mrs. Shavaughn Moss

Ms. Faith McDonald

The late Sir Clifford Darling

Mr. Joshua Taylor and family

Mr. Ronald V. Shaklee

The Staff and Management of Super-Value/Quality Market Food Stores
Mrs. Stephanie Hanna and the Staff & Management of J.S. Johnson Insurance Company
Mr. Dwayne Swaby and the Staff & Management of Sunshine Insurance Company
Mr. Kevin Hudson and the Staff & Management of Bahamas First Insurance Company
Mr. Ray Duncombe and the Staff & Management of Bobcat Bahamas
Mr. Byron Lowe and the Staff & Management of Insurance Management Company
Mrs. Shelley Moree and the Staff & Management of Royal Star Insurance Company
Mr. Philip Smith and the Staff & Management of d'Albenas Agency Company
The late Mr. Daniel Rahming Sr.
The late Mr. Illford Forbes
The late Mrs. Viola Collie
Mrs. Crystal Pintard
Mr. Kevin Ewing
Mrs. Nicolette Bethel
Mr. Michael and Phillip Stubbs
Mr. Neil Sealey
Ms. Sherrine Thompson
Mrs. Lulamae Gray
Mrs. Queenie Butler
Mrs. Karen Dorsett
The late Dr. Myles Munroe
Dr. Timothy Barrett
Dr. Kevin Moss
Mrs. Carole Balla
Mr. Jack and Karen Andrews
Mr. Jim and Anne Lawlor
Mrs. Margaret Jeffers
The late Mr. Charles Whelbell
The late Rev. Theo and Blooming Neely and family
Mr. Coleman and Diana Andrews and family
Staff and Management of The Nassau Guardian newspaper
Staff and Management of Media Enterprises

Staff and Management of The Tribune Newspaper
Staff of IslandFM Radio Station
Staff and Management of Cable Bahamas-Our News
Staff of The Broadcasting Corporation of The Bahamas (ZNS)
Staff of The Bahamas Department of Archives
Staff of The Caribbean Meteorological Institute
Staff of NOAA and National Hurricane Center in Miami

The good people of The Bahamas who opened their doors, hearts and minds to assist me with this project and provided me with overwhelming research materials, and many others too numerous to mention who gave me their recollections of these memorable and devastating hurricanes that affected The Bahamas.

Contact Information: -

Mr. Wayne Neely
P.O. Box EE-16637
Nassau, Bahamas
E-Mail: wayneneely@hotmail.com
        or wayneneely@yahoo.com

Main Office
34 Collins Ave.
P.O. Box N-8337
Nassau, Bahamas
Phone: 242-322-2341
Fax: 242-323-3720
E-Mail: info@jsjohnson.com
Website: www.jsjohnson.com

Branch Office
Thompson Blvd
P.O. Box N-8337
Nassau, Bahamas
Phone: 242-676-6300
Fax: 242-325-3979
E-Mail: info@jsjohnson.com
Website: www.jsjohnson.com

Branch Office
Soldier Road
P.O. Box N-8337
Nassau, Bahamas
Phone: 242-676-6301
Fax: 242-394-5376
E-Mail: info@jsjohnson.com
Website: www.jsjohnson.com

Sunshine House
East Shirley Street
P.O. Box N-3180
Nassau, Bahamas
Phone: 242-502-6500
Fax: 242-394-3101
E-Mail: info@sunshine-insurance.com
Website: www.sunshine-insurance.com

Branch Office
Sunshine Plaza, Blue Hill Road
Nassau, Bahamas
Phone: 242-322-3511
Fax: 242-322-3518
E-Mail: info@sunshine-insurance.com
Website: www.sunshine-insurance.com

University Drive Branch Office
Sunshine Plaza, Thompson Blvd/University Drive
Nassau, Bahamas
Phone: 242-502-6500
Fax: 242-394-3101
E-Mail: info@sunshine-insurance.com
Website: www.sunshine-insurance.com

BAHAMAS FIRST

FIRST IN INSURANCE. TODAY. TOMORROW.

32 Collins Avenue
P.O. Box SS-6238
Nassau, Bahamas
Telephone: 242-302-3900
Fax: 242-302-3901
Email: info@bahamasfirst.com
Website: www.bahamasfirst.com

Royal Star House
John F. Kennedy Drive
P.O. Box N-4391
Nassau, Bahamas
Tel: (242) 328-7888 / 677-2221
Fax: (242) 325-3151
Website: www.rsabahamas.com

Crawford St. Oakes Field
P.O. Box N-8170
Nassau, Bahamas
Tel: 242-323-5171 or 242-323-5171
Fax: 242-322-6969

Your Bahamian Supermarkets

SUPER VALUE

&

QUALITY SUPERMARKETS

Golden Gates Shopping Center Branch #5/Executive Offices
P.O. Box N-3039
Nassau, Bahamas
Phone: 242-361-5220-4
Fax: 242-361-5583
E-Mail: svfsltd@batelnet.bs

Branch Store #1-East Street
P.O. Box N-3039
Nassau, Bahamas
Phone: 242-325-5844/325-5917
Fax: 242-356-6295
E-Mail: svfsltd@batelnet.bs

Branch Store #2-Blue Hill Road
P.O. Box N-3039
Nassau, Bahamas
Phone: 242-323-5402/323-5489
Fax: 242-356-4872
E-Mail: svfsltd@batelnet.bs

Your Bahamian Supermarkets

SUPER VALUE & QUALITY SUPERMARKETS

Branch Store #3-Nassau & Meadow Street
P.O. Box N-3039
Nassau, Bahamas
Phone: 242-323-4861/323-4862
Fax: 242-326-4874
E-Mail: svfsltd@batelnet.bs

Branch Store #6-Prince Charles Drive
P.O. Box N-3039
Nassau, Bahamas
Phone: 242-393-0116/393-5229/393-6266
Fax: 242-394-6526
E-Mail: svfsltd@batelnet.bs

Branch Store #7-Mackey Street (Top of the Hill)
P.O. Box N-3039
Nassau, Bahamas
Phone: 242-393-4533/393-4534
Fax: 242-394-2991
E-Mail: svfsltd@batelnet.bs

Branch Store #8-Wulf Road & Montrose Avenue
P.O. Box N-3039
Nassau, Bahamas
Phone: 242-325-5903/325-7794
Fax: 242-325-37794
E-Mail: svfsltd@batelnet.bs

Branch Store #9-Robinson Road & East Street
P.O. Box N-3039
Nassau, Bahamas
Phone: 242-325-4564/325-4492
Fax: 242-326-4886
E-Mail: svfsltd@batelnet.bs

Branch Store #10-Cable Beach Shopping Center
P.O. Box N-3039
Nassau, Bahamas
Phone: 242-327-8879
Fax: 242-327-3494
E-Mail: svfsltd@batelnet.bs

Branch Store #11-Winton Shopping Center
P.O. Box N-3039

Nassau, Bahamas
Phone: 242-324-2186/324-2172
Fax: 242-364-6492
E-Mail: svfsltd@batelnet.bs

Quality Supermarkets Store #13-Sea Grape Shopping Center
P.O. Box N-3039
Nassau, Bahamas
Phone: 242-324-0946
Fax: 242-364-0709
E-Mail: svfsltd@batelnet.bs

Quality Supermarkets Store #12-South Beach Shopping Center
P.O. Box N-3039
Nassau, Bahamas
Phone: 242-392-1058 or 392-1113
Fax: 242-364-0709
E-Mail: svfsltd@batelnet.bs

Quality Supermarkets Store #4-Cable Beach
P.O. Box N-3039

Insurance Management Nassau Office
Rosetta Street East
P.O. Box SS-6283
Nassau, Bahamas
Phone: 242-394-5555
Fax: 242-323-6520
E-Mail: info.nassau@imbbah.com

Insurance Management Grand Bahama Office
1 Pioneers Way
P.O. Box F-42451
Freeport, Bahamas
Phone: 242-350-3500
Fax: 242-350-3510
E-Mail: info.freeport@imbbah.com

Insurance Management Abaco Office
Queen Elizabeth Drive
P.O. Box AB-20666
Abaco, Bahamas
Phone: 242-367-4204
Fax: 242-367-4206
E-Mail: info.abaco@imbbah.com

Insurance Management Eleuthera Office
Queens Highway
P.O. Box EL-25190
Eleuthera, Bahamas
Phone: 242-332-3211
Fax: 242-332-2863
E-Mail: info.eleuthera@imbbah.com

Insurance Management Exuma Office
Queens Highway
Exuma, Bahamas
Phone: 242-336-2304
Fax: 242-336-23050
E-Mail: info.exuma@imbbah.com

ABOUT THE BOOK

A hurricane begins over Africa and then moves innocently enough into the Northern Atlantic Ocean, in waters so warm that it clocks in warmer than 26.5°C or 80°F down to a depth of 150 feet. Add in a warm breeze that passes over the top of the water and begins to transform it into water vapour. That vapour rises into the air, carried by tropical winds. A tropical disturbance occurs when that water vapour condenses into a cyclical cloud. From there, a complicated and dynamic process of heating and cooling forces these clouds and the wind carrying them to induce or spawn thunderstorms and fierce winds. If the conditions are just right, that simple patch of warm ocean water can hit land as the most powerful storm on Earth, a hurricane.

Even though hurricanes can only form in select areas of the planet, The Bahamas is ideally located directly in the path of these storms. These massive tropical cyclones have been ravaging The Bahamas since the Lucayan Indians blessed these islands with their presence. Now for the very first time, these greatest and deadliest Bahamian hurricanes have been presented and documented in book-form. Such named storms include, Hurricanes Andrew, Floyd, Donna, David, Matthew, Betsy, Frances, Jeanne and Wilma. While other unnamed storms include, The Great Nassau Hurricane of 1926, The Great Abaco Hurricane of 1932, The Great Bahamas Hurricane of 1866, The Great Okeechobee Hurricane of 1928, and The Great Andros Island Hurricane of 1929. The Bahamas hurricane season, which lasts from June to the end of November, has seen plenty of catastrophic storms throughout history. Here's a look at some of the greatest, deadliest, and most horrific storms that have hit The Bahamas over the past 5 centuries.

ABOUT THE AUTHOR

Wayne Neely is an international speaker, best-selling author, lecturer on hurricanes, educator, and meteorologist. Traveling extensively throughout the region and the world, Wayne addresses critical issues affecting all aspects of hurricanes, especially Bahamian Hurricanes which is one of his central areas of expertise. The central themes of his books are always on hurricanes in general and the impact of hurricanes on all aspects of mankind's ever-expanding society. He's a meteorologist in Nassau, Bahamas and has been there for well over 29 years. He has a great passion for writing and does it in his spare time when he is not working at his main job as a Weather Forecaster at the Department of Meteorology.

Wayne Neely is a certified Meteorologist working at the Department of Meteorology in Nassau, Bahamas-prior to that he majored in Geography, History and Environmental Science at the University of The Bahamas (UB) in Nassau. He then attended the Caribbean Meteorological Institute in Barbados where he majored and specialized in weather forecasting. His love for hurricanes and the weather came about while growing up on the island of Andros where he listened quite regularly to his parents, grandparents and other older residents within the community talking about a major hurricane which occurred in 1929 and devastated the Bahamas. That piqued his interest in hurricanes and got him started on writing his first book called 'The Great Bahamas Hurricane of 1929.' He has written 13 best-selling books on hurricanes and are used as textbooks in many universities and colleges around the region and world-wide (as far away as Japan, USA, Canada, The Caribbean, China, Pakistan and Australia). He then went onto write 13 best-selling books on hurricanes.

Over the years, Wayne has written or contributed to several articles on hurricanes and other severe weather events for some of the major local and international newspapers and magazines, including National Geographic, Weather-Wise Magazine, Weather Brains, Hurricane-City, The New York Times, Time, Newsweek, People, Huffingpost, The Washington Post, and the American Meteorological Society. He speaks quite regularly to schools, colleges, universities and frequently does radio and television interviews both locally and abroad about the history and impact of Bahamian, American and Caribbean hurricanes and hurricanes in general. He has been a hurricane advisor for both "Jeopardy" and "Who Wants to be a Millionaire" on several occasions. Locally he speaks to many schools, UB, and private organizations like the Rotary Club. He contributed to and was featured in the very popular PBS/NOVA Documentary called *"Killer Hurricanes"*.